SUPERMAN

· THE MANY WOR

KRYPTON

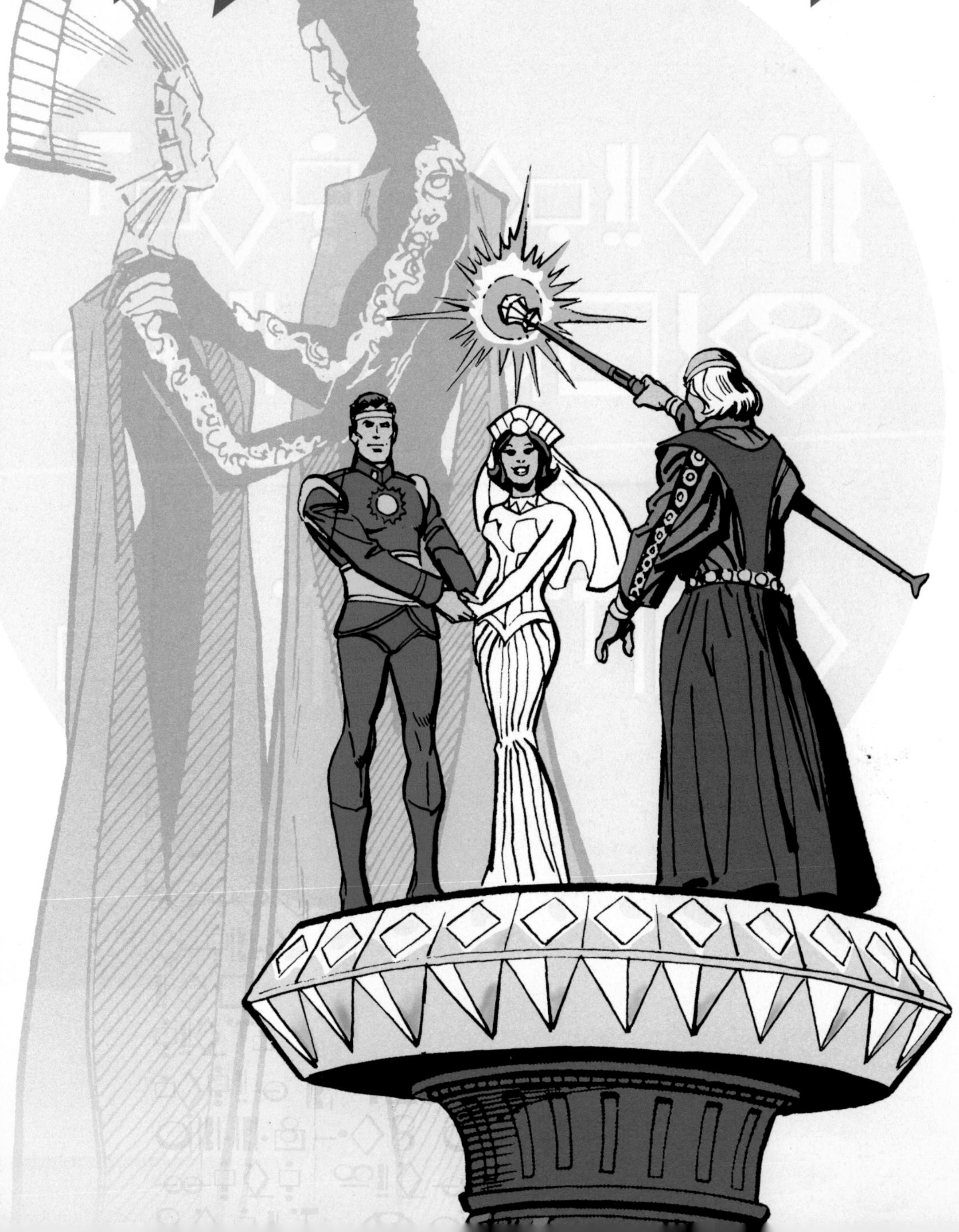

SUPERMAN

THE MANY WORLDS OF KRYPTON

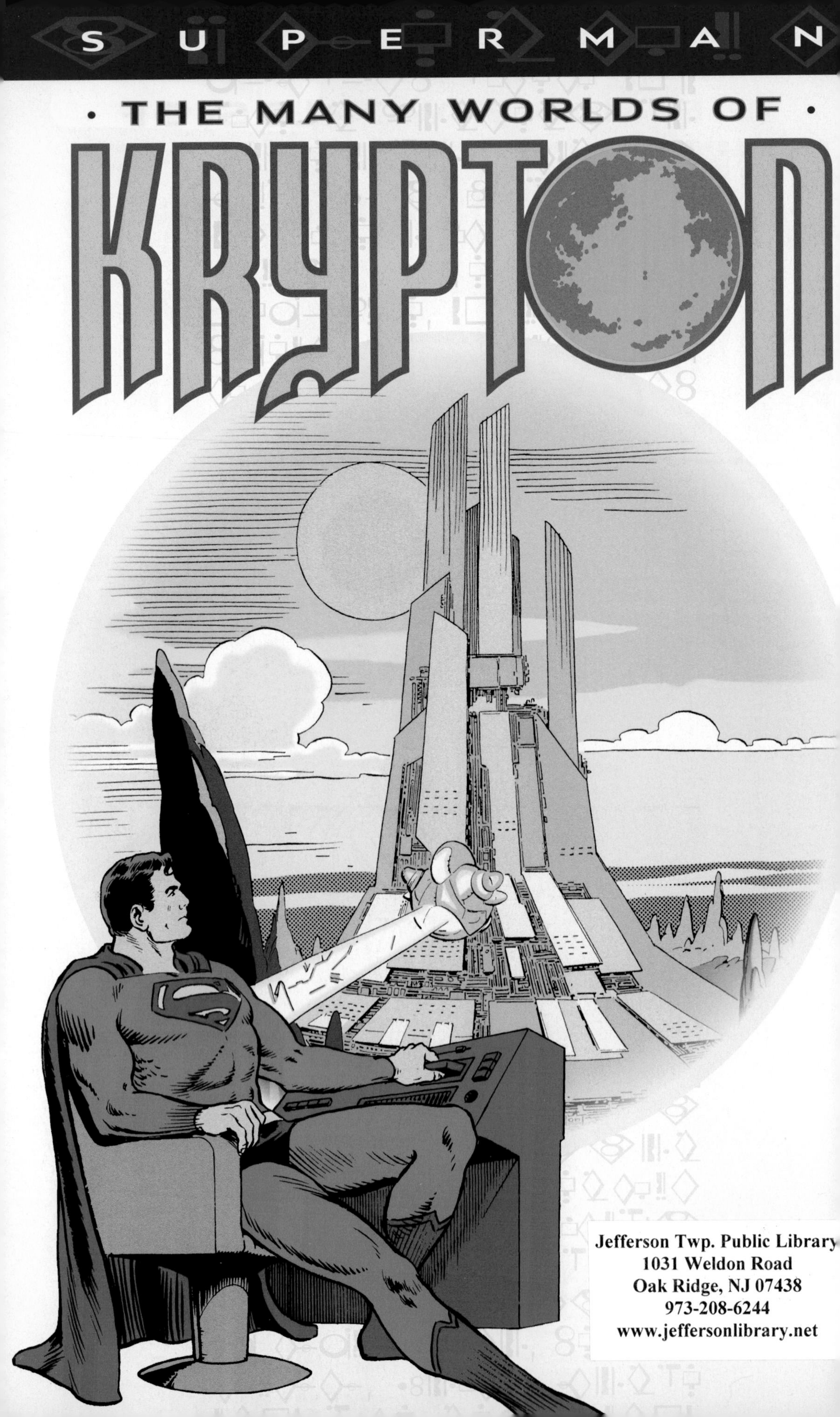

PAUL KUPPERBERG
JOHN BYRNE
E. NELSON BRIDWELL
DENNY O'NEIL
CARY BATES
MARV WOLFMAN
ELLIOT S. MAGGIN
WRITERS

HOWARD CHAYKIN MIKE MIGNOLA
RICK BRYANT MURPHY ANDERSON
FRANK CHIARAMONTE DICK GIORDANO
GRAY MORROW MICHAEL KALUTA
DAVE COCKRUM DICK DILLIN
JOE GIELLA MARSHALL ROGERS
FRANK SPRINGER CARLOS GARZÓN
ARTISTS

ADRIENNE ROY
JERRY SERPE PETRA SCOTESE
COLORISTS

BEN ODA
SHELLY LEFERMAN
JOHN WORKMAN
LETTERERS

ROSS ANDRU,
DICK GIORDANO
& WES HARTMAN
COLLECTION COVER ARTISTS

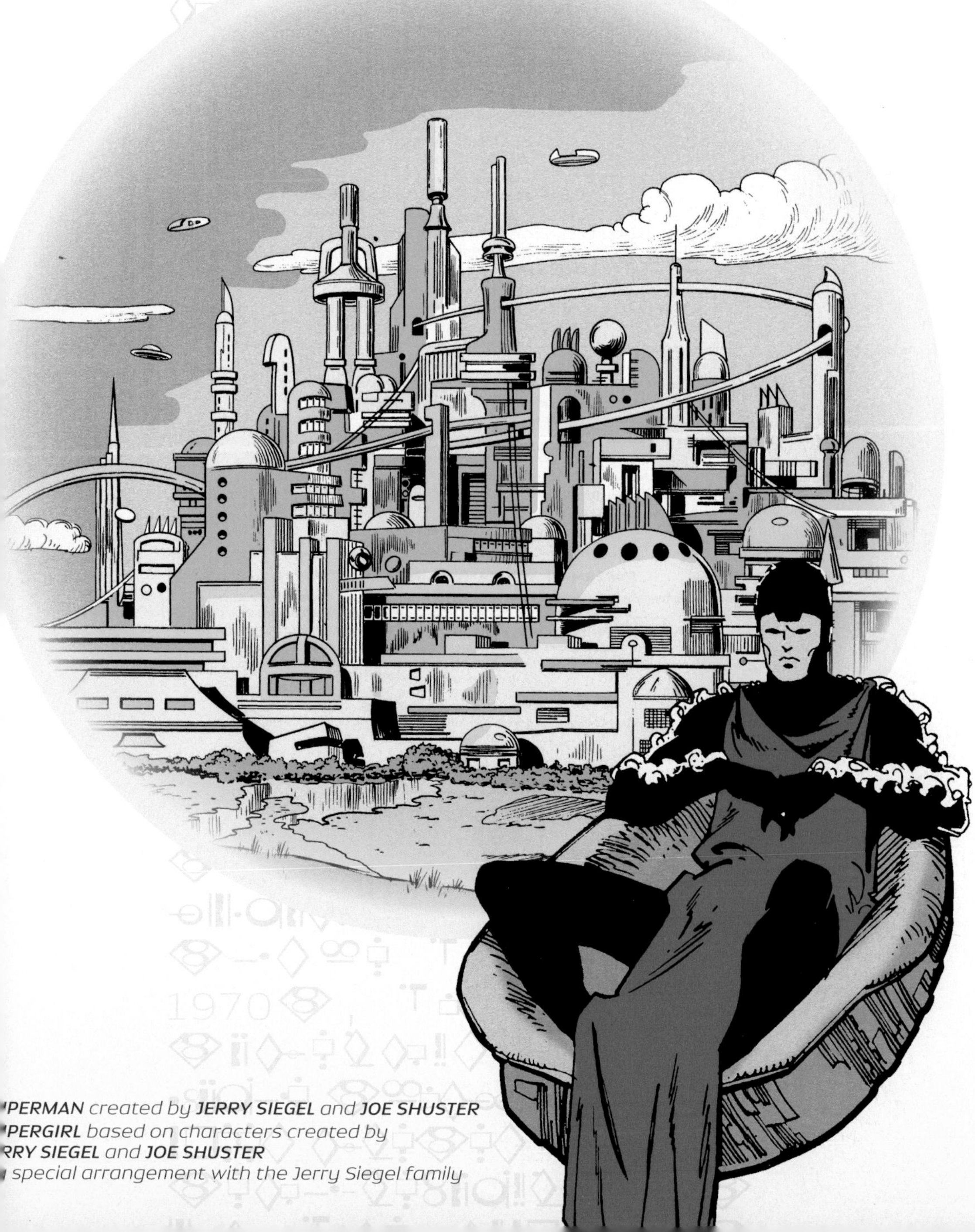

E. NELSON BRIDWELL MIKE CARLIN
JULIUS SCHWARTZ DENNY O'NEIL Editors – Original Series
JEB WOODARD Group Editor – Collected Editions
ALEX GALER Editor – Collected Edition
STEVE COOK Design Director - Books
CURTIS KING JR. Publication Design

BOB HARRAS Senior VP – Editor-in-Chief, DC Comics
PAT McCALLUM Executive Editor, DC Comics

DIANE NELSON President
DAN DiDIO Publisher
JIM LEE Publisher
GEOFF JOHNS President & Chief Creative Officer
AMIT DESAI Executive VP – Business & Marketing Strategy, Direct to Consumer & Global Franchise Management
SAM ADES Senior VP & General Manager, Digital Services
BOBBIE CHASE VP & Executive Editor, Young Reader & Talent Development
MARK CHIARELLO Senior VP – Art, Design & Collected Editions
JOHN CUNNINGHAM Senior VP – Sales & Trade Marketing
ANNE DePIES Senior VP – Business Strategy, Finance & Administration
DON FALLETTI VP – Manufacturing Operations
LAWRENCE GANEM VP – Editorial Administration & Talent Relations
ALISON GILL Senior VP – Manufacturing & Operations
HANK KANALZ Senior VP – Editorial Strategy & Administration
JAY KOGAN VP – Legal Affairs
JACK MAHAN VP – Business Affairs
NICK J. NAPOLITANO VP – Manufacturing Administration
EDDIE SCANNELL VP – Consumer Marketing
COURTNEY SIMMONS Senior VP – Publicity & Communications
JIM (SKI) SOKOLOWSKI VP – Comic Book Specialty Sales & Trade Marketing
NANCY SPEARS VP – Mass, Book, Digital Sales & Trade Marketing
MICHELE R. WELLS VP – Content Strategy

Color reconstruction by Digikore Inc. and Michael Kelleher

SUPERMAN: THE MANY WORLDS OF KRYPTON

Published by DC Comics. Compilation and all new material Copyright © 2018 DC Comics. All Rights Reserved. Originally published in single magazine form in SUPERMAN (vol. 1) 233, 236, 238, 240, 248, 257, 266, SUPERMAN FAMILY 182, WORLD OF KRYPTON (vol. 1) 1-3, THE WORLD OF KRYPTON (vol. 2) 1-4, SUPERMAN: THE WORLD OF KRYPTON. Copyright © 1970, 1971, 1972, 1973, 1976, 1977, 1979, 1987, 2008 DC Comics. All Rights Reserved. All characters, their distinctive likenesses and related elements featured in this publication are trademarks of DC Comics. The stories, characters and incidents featured in this publication are entirely fictional. DC Comics does not read or accept unsolicited submissions of ideas, stories or artwork.

DC Comics, 2900 West Alameda Ave., Burbank, CA 91505
Printed by LSC Communications, Kendallville, IN, USA. 1/26/18. First Printing.
ISBN: 978-1-4012-7889-2

Library of Congress Cataloging-in-Publication Data is available.

TABLE OF CONTENTS

THE WORLD (OF KRYPTON) ACCORDING TO PAUL (KUPPERBERG)

Whenever I'm asked about Krypton, the first question I ask is "Which Krypton?"

There have been a lot of them over the years, one for practically every artist who ever drew Superman. The default image of Krypton for me will always be that of Wayne Boring, the lead artist on Superman for most of the 1950s, the decade in which Krypton received a lot of play in the developing Superman mythology.

Boring's art had a distinctive and, even for its time, dated look, a very old-school, 1930s pulp illustration sensibility. His people were stiff and posed; his Earth-bound cities heavy, buildings looking like they were carved from great slabs of granite that could withstand Superman lifting them by their corners to move out of harm's way. His Krypton, on the other hand, was sleek and delicate, boasting gleaming, graceful minarets towering over spotless streets filled with streamlined art deco vehicles.

To me, Boring's art represents the very essence of Krypton, that world of super-men that spawned my favorite comic book character.

But that's just me.

As I mentioned, every artist brought his own interpretation to the page, particularly Curt Swan, Boring's 1960s successor as lead Superman artist. And that's not to forget the contributions of Al Plastino, George Papp, John Forte and the rest. And after 1978, film designer John Barry's Krypton in *Superman: The Movie* added yet another version to the popular imagination. As did John Byrne's 1986 MAN OF STEEL miniseries.

I've even had the opportunity to put my two cents into the ongoing development of Krypton. In fact, my very first assignment for DC Comics in 1975 was writing a ten-page "World of Krypton" story for SUPERMAN FAMILY.

I was following in some big footsteps with my little ten-pager, as the stories in this volume illustrate. Since the early 1970s, then-new Superman editor Julie Schwartz had been presenting the semi-regular tales of "The Fabulous World of Krypton: Untold Stories of Superman's Native Planet" as a backup feature in SUPERMAN. Julie packed "The Fabulous World of Krypton" stories with such luminaries as Dennis O'Neil, Dick Giordano, Cary Bates, Gray Morrow, Gil Kane, Michael Kaluta, Marv Wolfman, Martin Pasko, Dave Cockrum, Dick Dillin and many others. Each short, six or eight pages long, took on some aspect of Kryptonian history or culture from the very beginning, as in "A Name Is Born" (SUPERMAN #238, June 1972) with the meeting of the aliens Kryp and Tonn (thank goodness for the future of the universe that two genetically compatible humanoid aliens of the opposite sex just happened to get stranded together on this uninhabited paradise of a planet) to the very end, "The Greatest Green Lantern of All"

(SUPERMAN #257, October 1972), in which we learn that Green Lantern Tomar-Re used his power ring to keep Krypton from exploding long enough for Jor-El to finish his rocket and send Kal-El, whose destiny the Guardians of the Universe had sensed, to safety. In between, other stories told ecological or political parables, such as "The Doomsayer" (SUPERMAN #236, April 1971) and "...And Not A Drop To Drink" (SUPERMAN #367, January 1982) or set up small tales that brought Kryptonian history into line with other events in the DC Universe, like "The Last 'Scoop' on Krypton" (SUPERMAN #375, September 1982). The latter was a specialty of E. Nelson Bridwell, Julie Schwartz's assistant editor and DC's reigning king of continuity. Nelson liked nothing better than taking a whole heap of events, bits of business and facts from stories and tying them all together into a nice, neat package. Nelson's knowledge of DC history and continuity—not to mention the Bible and the works of Shakespeare, but that's neither here nor there— was encyclopedic, and he wanted everything to go with everything else.

That first story of mine, "The Stranger," was notable mostly for being some of the earliest DC work of the late Marshall Rogers (Marshall and I would "team up" for one more story, also Krypton-related, in the Nightwing and Flamebird feature—the superhero duo of the bottle city of Kandor—I wrote for subsequent issues of SUPERMAN FAMILY). My real immersion in the world of Krypton—and the world of Nelson Bridwell—came about two years later when I was asked to script a three-issue run of SHOWCASE, a try-out comic that showcased (get it?!) features to determine if a feature sold well enough to warrant a title of its own. In its day, SHOWCASE had introduced such features as the Flash, Challengers of the Unknown, the Atom, Green Lantern, Adam Strange and others, running for 93 issues, from 1956 to 1970, before being revived in 1977 for eleven more issues. I wrote the revival's first three-issue story arc ("The New Doom Patrol"), followed by a co-writing credit on the epic 100th issue, and then, beginning with SHOWCASE #105, I wrote the next three-issue arc, showcasing "The World of Krypton."

Unfortunately, the SHOWCASE revival was cut short with #104.

Fortunately, this happened in 1978, the year of *Superman: The Movie*.

Because of legal entanglements over the screenplay written by Mario Puzo, DC could not publish any comics based on the film...but there was nothing stopping them from putting out Superman products based on their own versions of the character. And with that in mind, the Powers-That-Were turned to my leftover and nowhere-to-be-published issues of "World of Krypton," the life story of Superman's father (played in the movie by superstar Marlon Brando) all written and drawn (pencilled by Howard Chaykin and inked by

Murphy Anderson on #1-2 and Frank Chiaramonte on #3), ready and waiting to go.

And that, boys and girls, is how WORLD OF KRYPTON became the very first comic book miniseries.

"My" Krypton was straight out of the stories of the 1950s and 1960s, complete with the fun and goofy elements like the Crystal Mountains, the Flame Forest and, at Nelson's insistence, such Superman kin as sadistic cousin Kru-El. (Really.) It had all of Nelson's trademark editorial touches, including his adding obscure references, such as Kryptonian words and expressions, to the dialogue that required the addition of footnotes to explain them. But that miniseries, which was kept in print for many years as a black-and-white paperback compilation published by Tor Books, became, for the time being, the accepted version of Krypton.

That, I've been told over the years, many readers considered to be their definitive version as well, just as Wayne Boring's was mine.

In 1986, John Byrne was handed the task of revitalizing Superman, revamping the character from square one. John opened the landmark MAN OF STEEL miniseries with Krypton's last moments, offering readers of the new Superman a tantalizing glimpse of a Krypton quite different from what they were used to seeing. His interpretation was a mix of old-school comic book science fiction and the frozen wasteland it was portrayed as in *Superman: The Movie*, taking the cold, sterile Kryptonian environment and extrapolating from that architectural sensibility that a people living in such an environment would themselves be cold and emotionless.

That glimpse brought demands for a deeper look, leading to the *second* WORLD OF KRYPTON miniseries (1987), scripted by Byrne, with art by Mike Mignola, Rick Bryant and Carlos Garzon. In it, we learn how the deep emotions aroused over human rights for clones once led Krypton to the brink of civil war and a nuclear blast that destroyed Kandor, causing Kryptonians to turn away from emotion and embrace cold, hard logic to avoid a repetition of that great tragedy. And yet, it is ultimately an act of love and personal sacrifice that saves the life of Kal-El, destined to be Krypton's greatest legacy.

And to readers of that miniseries, the Byrne/Mignola vision *was* Krypton.

So, what's yours?

But before you answer, check out the stories in this volume. One of them may contain a vision of Krypton that you never considered before.

—**Paul Kupperberg**

Introduction originally published for
SUPERMAN: THE WORLD OF KRYPTON in 2008

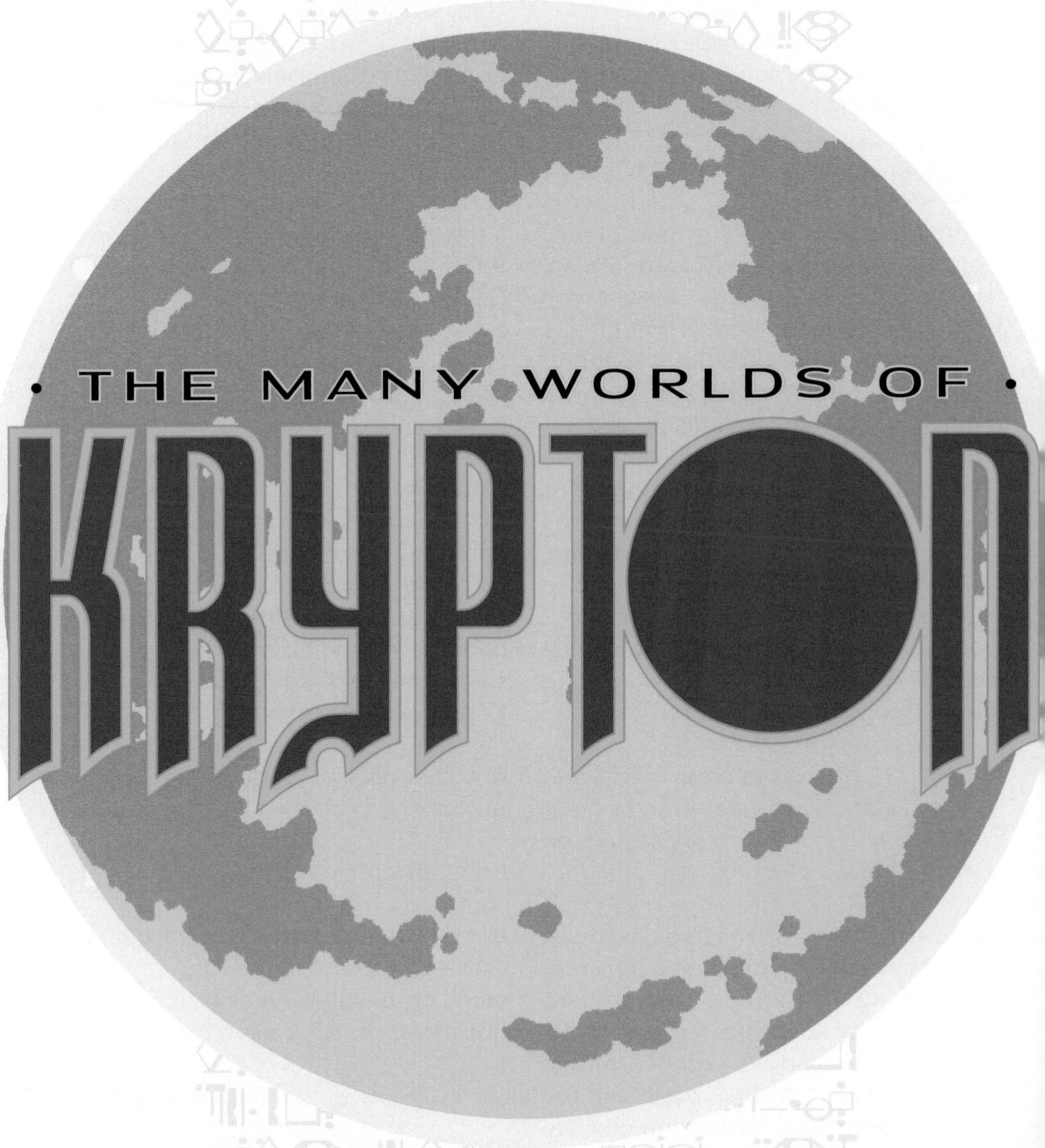

• THE MANY WORLDS OF •
KRYPTON

CHAPTER ONE
THE FABULOUS WORLD OF KRYPTON

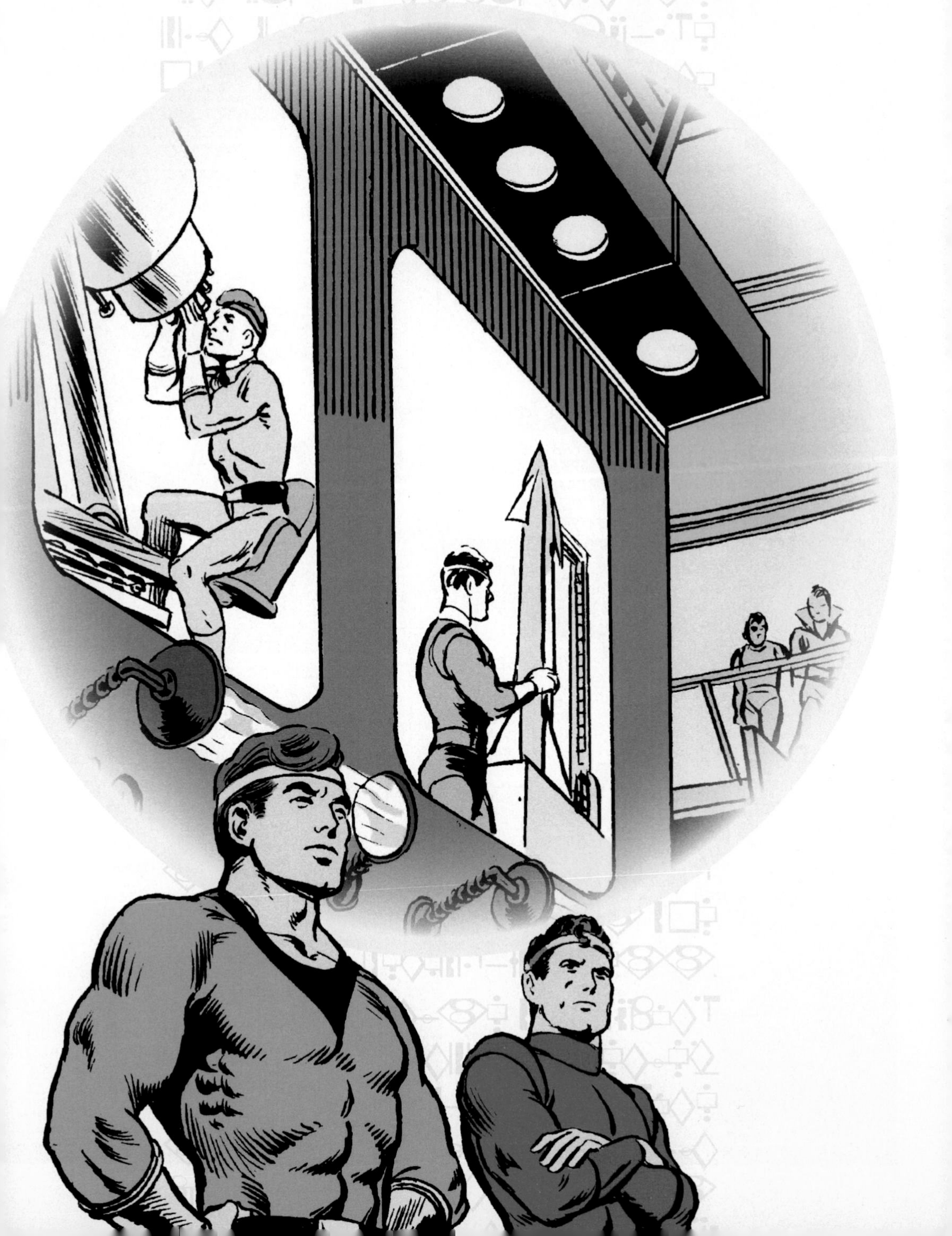

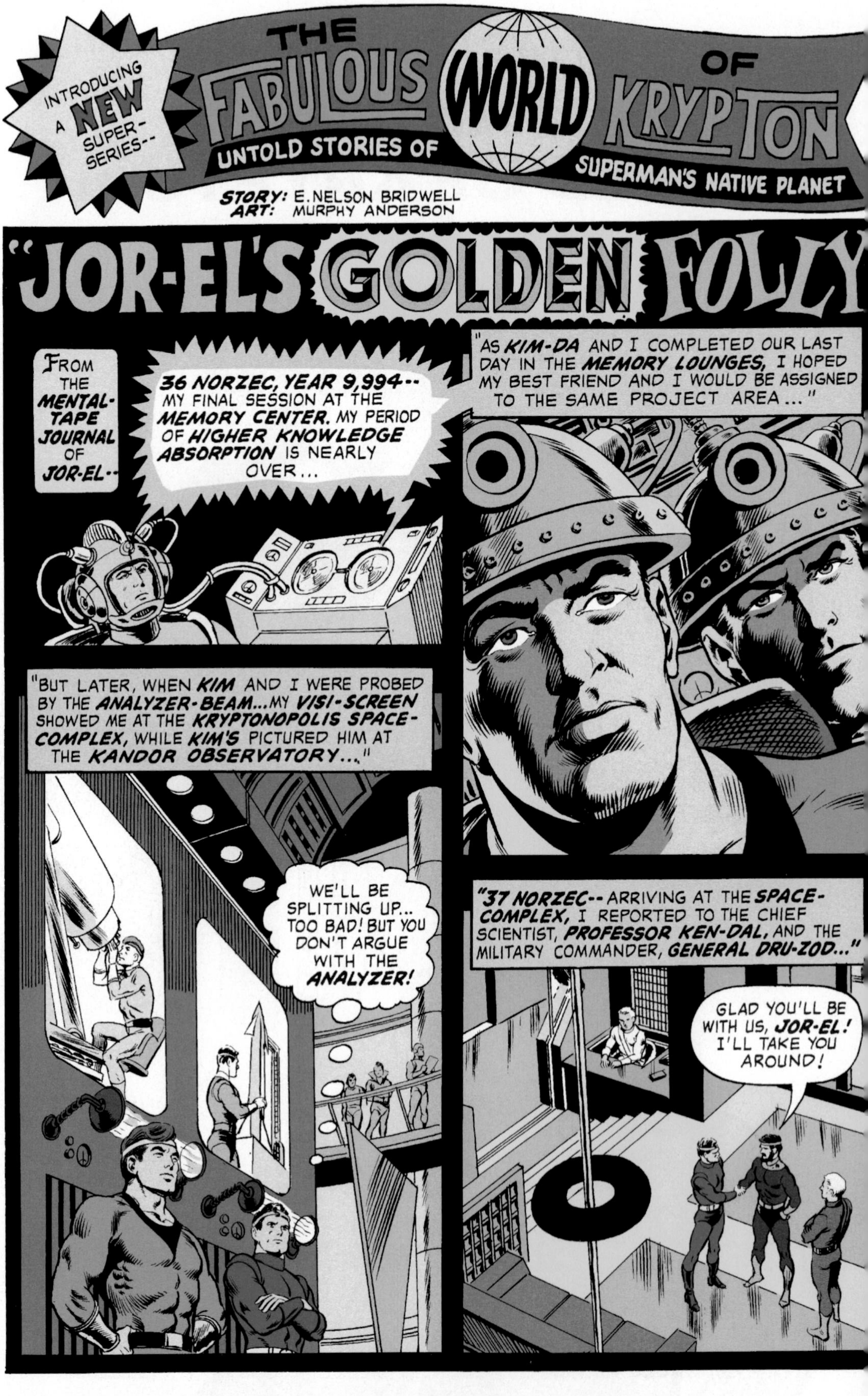
INTRODUCING A NEW SUPER-SERIES--
THE FABULOUS WORLD OF KRYPTON
UNTOLD STORIES OF SUPERMAN'S NATIVE PLANET
STORY: E. NELSON BRIDWELL
ART: MURPHY ANDERSON
"JOR-EL'S GOLDEN FOLLY
FROM THE MENTAL-TAPE JOURNAL OF JOR-EL--
36 NORZEC, YEAR 9,994-- MY FINAL SESSION AT THE MEMORY CENTER. MY PERIOD OF HIGHER KNOWLEDGE ABSORPTION IS NEARLY OVER...
"AS KIM-DA AND I COMPLETED OUR LAST DAY IN THE MEMORY LOUNGES, I HOPED MY BEST FRIEND AND I WOULD BE ASSIGNED TO THE SAME PROJECT AREA..."
"BUT LATER, WHEN KIM AND I WERE PROBED BY THE ANALYZER-BEAM...MY VISI-SCREEN SHOWED ME AT THE KRYPTONOPOLIS SPACE-COMPLEX, WHILE KIM'S PICTURED HIM AT THE KANDOR OBSERVATORY..."
WE'LL BE SPLITTING UP... TOO BAD! BUT YOU DON'T ARGUE WITH THE ANALYZER!
"37 NORZEC-- ARRIVING AT THE SPACE-COMPLEX, I REPORTED TO THE CHIEF SCIENTIST, PROFESSOR KEN-DAL, AND THE MILITARY COMMANDER, GENERAL DRU-ZOD..."
GLAD YOU'LL BE WITH US, JOR-EL! I'LL TAKE YOU AROUND!

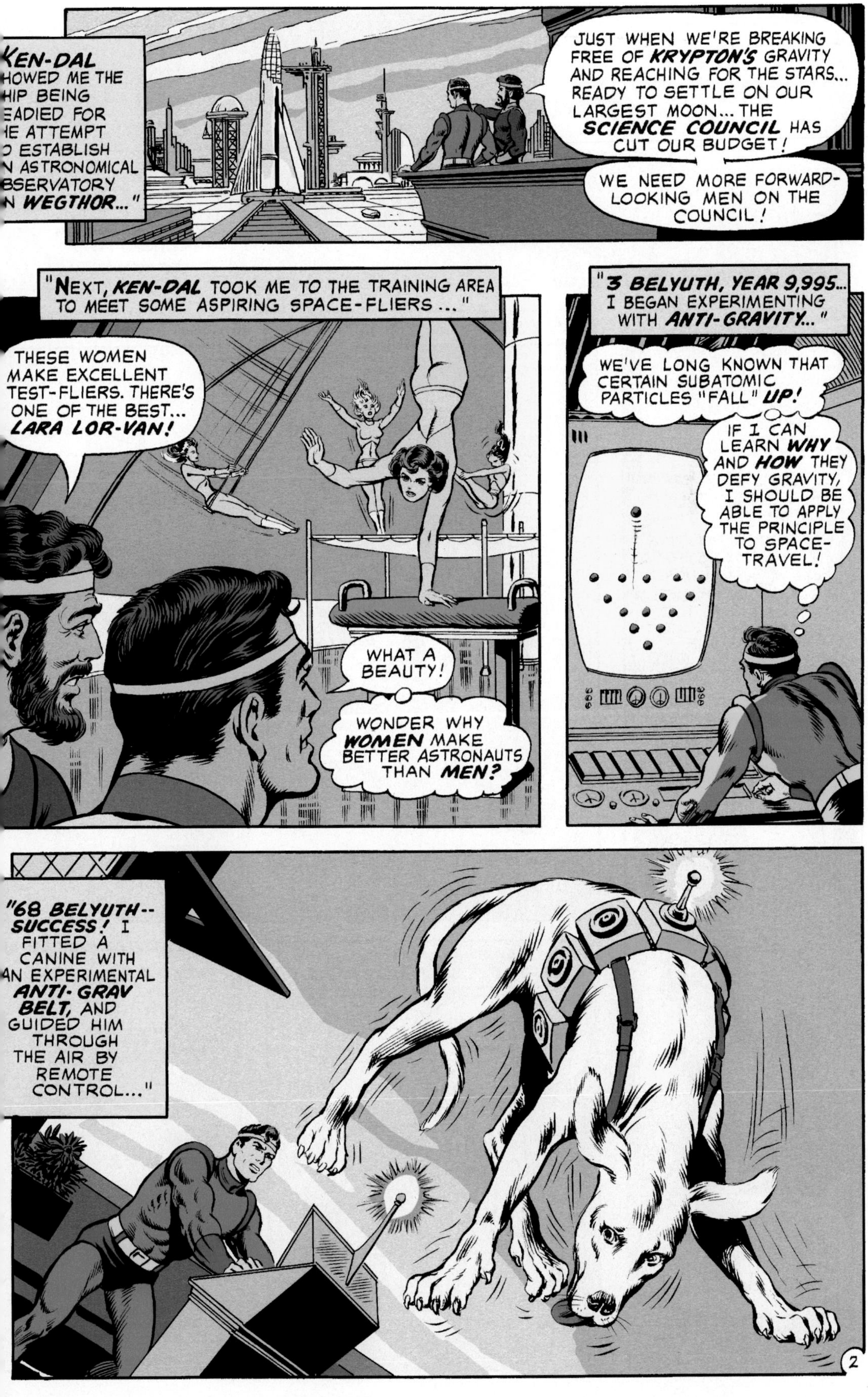

KEN-DAL HOWED ME THE HIP BEING EADIED FOR HE ATTEMPT O ESTABLISH N ASTRONOMICAL BSERVATORY N WEGTHOR..."
JUST WHEN WE'RE BREAKING FREE OF KRYPTON'S GRAVITY AND REACHING FOR THE STARS... READY TO SETTLE ON OUR LARGEST MOON... THE SCIENCE COUNCIL HAS CUT OUR BUDGET!
WE NEED MORE FORWARD-LOOKING MEN ON THE COUNCIL!
"NEXT, KEN-DAL TOOK ME TO THE TRAINING AREA TO MEET SOME ASPIRING SPACE-FLIERS..."
THESE WOMEN MAKE EXCELLENT TEST-FLIERS. THERE'S ONE OF THE BEST... LARA LOR-VAN!
WHAT A BEAUTY!
WONDER WHY WOMEN MAKE BETTER ASTRONAUTS THAN MEN?
"3 BELYUTH, YEAR 9,995... I BEGAN EXPERIMENTING WITH ANTI-GRAVITY..."
WE'VE LONG KNOWN THAT CERTAIN SUBATOMIC PARTICLES "FALL" UP!
IF I CAN LEARN WHY AND HOW THEY DEFY GRAVITY, I SHOULD BE ABLE TO APPLY THE PRINCIPLE TO SPACE-TRAVEL!
"68 BELYUTH--SUCCESS! I FITTED A CANINE WITH AN EXPERIMENTAL ANTI-GRAV BELT, AND GUIDED HIM THROUGH THE AIR BY REMOTE CONTROL..."
2

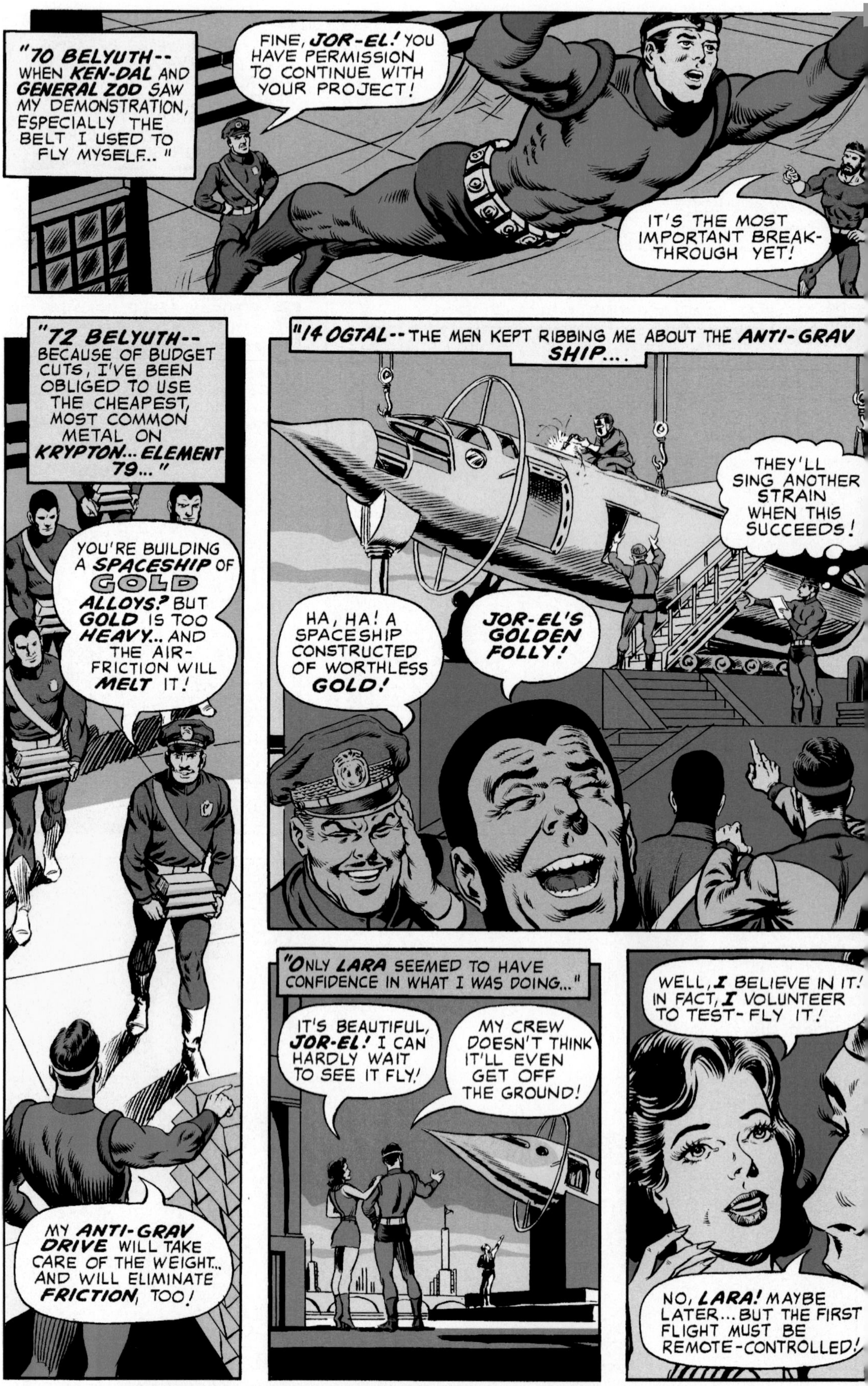
"70 BELYUTH-- WHEN KEN-DAL AND GENERAL ZOD SAW MY DEMONSTRATION, ESPECIALLY THE BELT I USED TO FLY MYSELF..."
FINE, JOR-EL! YOU HAVE PERMISSION TO CONTINUE WITH YOUR PROJECT!
IT'S THE MOST IMPORTANT BREAK-THROUGH YET!
"72 BELYUTH-- BECAUSE OF BUDGET CUTS, I'VE BEEN OBLIGED TO USE THE CHEAPEST, MOST COMMON METAL ON KRYPTON... ELEMENT 79..."
YOU'RE BUILDING A SPACESHIP OF GOLD ALLOYS? BUT GOLD IS TOO HEAVY... AND THE AIR-FRICTION WILL MELT IT!
MY ANTI-GRAV DRIVE WILL TAKE CARE OF THE WEIGHT... AND WILL ELIMINATE FRICTION, TOO!
"14 OGTAL-- THE MEN KEPT RIBBING ME ABOUT THE ANTI-GRAV SHIP....
THEY'LL SING ANOTHER STRAIN WHEN THIS SUCCEEDS!
HA, HA! A SPACESHIP CONSTRUCTED OF WORTHLESS GOLD!
JOR-EL'S GOLDEN FOLLY!
"ONLY LARA SEEMED TO HAVE CONFIDENCE IN WHAT I WAS DOING..."
IT'S BEAUTIFUL, JOR-EL! I CAN HARDLY WAIT TO SEE IT FLY!
MY CREW DOESN'T THINK IT'LL EVEN GET OFF THE GROUND!
WELL, I BELIEVE IN IT! IN FACT, I VOLUNTEER TO TEST-FLY IT!
NO, LARA! MAYBE LATER... BUT THE FIRST FLIGHT MUST BE REMOTE-CONTROLLED!

30 OGTAL-- THE OFFICIALS, INCLUDING *FAL-THU* AND *WAZ-EM,* OF THE *SCIENCE COUNCIL,* GATHERED FOR THE "BIG TEST..."

WATCH... YOU'LL BE CONVINCED THAT THE ROAD TO THE STARS WILL BE BY *ANTI-GRAV!*

NONSENSE! THIS WHOLE SPACE PROGRAM IS A BIG BLUNDER-- A COLOSSAL WASTE OF MONEY!

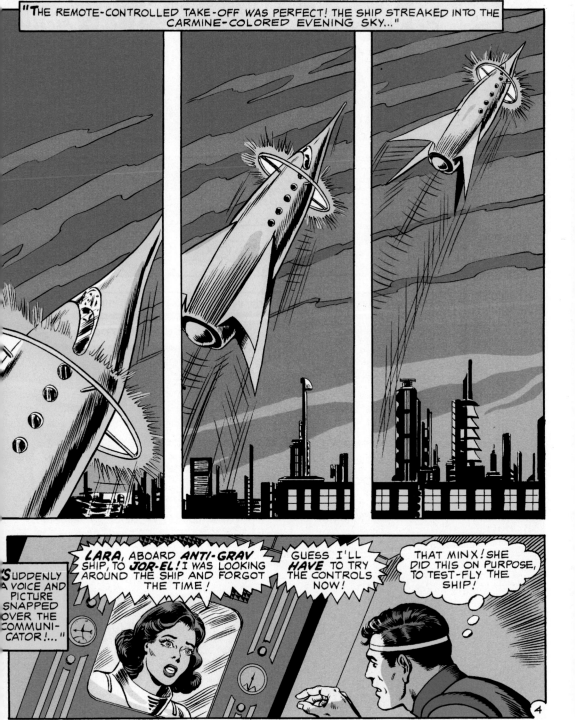

"THE REMOTE-CONTROLLED TAKE-OFF WAS PERFECT! THE SHIP STREAKED INTO THE CARMINE-COLORED EVENING SKY..."

"SUDDENLY A VOICE AND PICTURE SNAPPED OVER THE COMMUNI-CATOR!..."

LARA, ABOARD *ANTI-GRAV* SHIP, TO *JOR-EL!* I WAS LOOKING AROUND THE SHIP AND FORGOT THE TIME!

GUESS I'LL *HAVE* TO TRY THE CONTROLS NOW!

THAT MINX! SHE DID THIS ON PURPOSE, TO TEST-FLY THE SHIP!

4

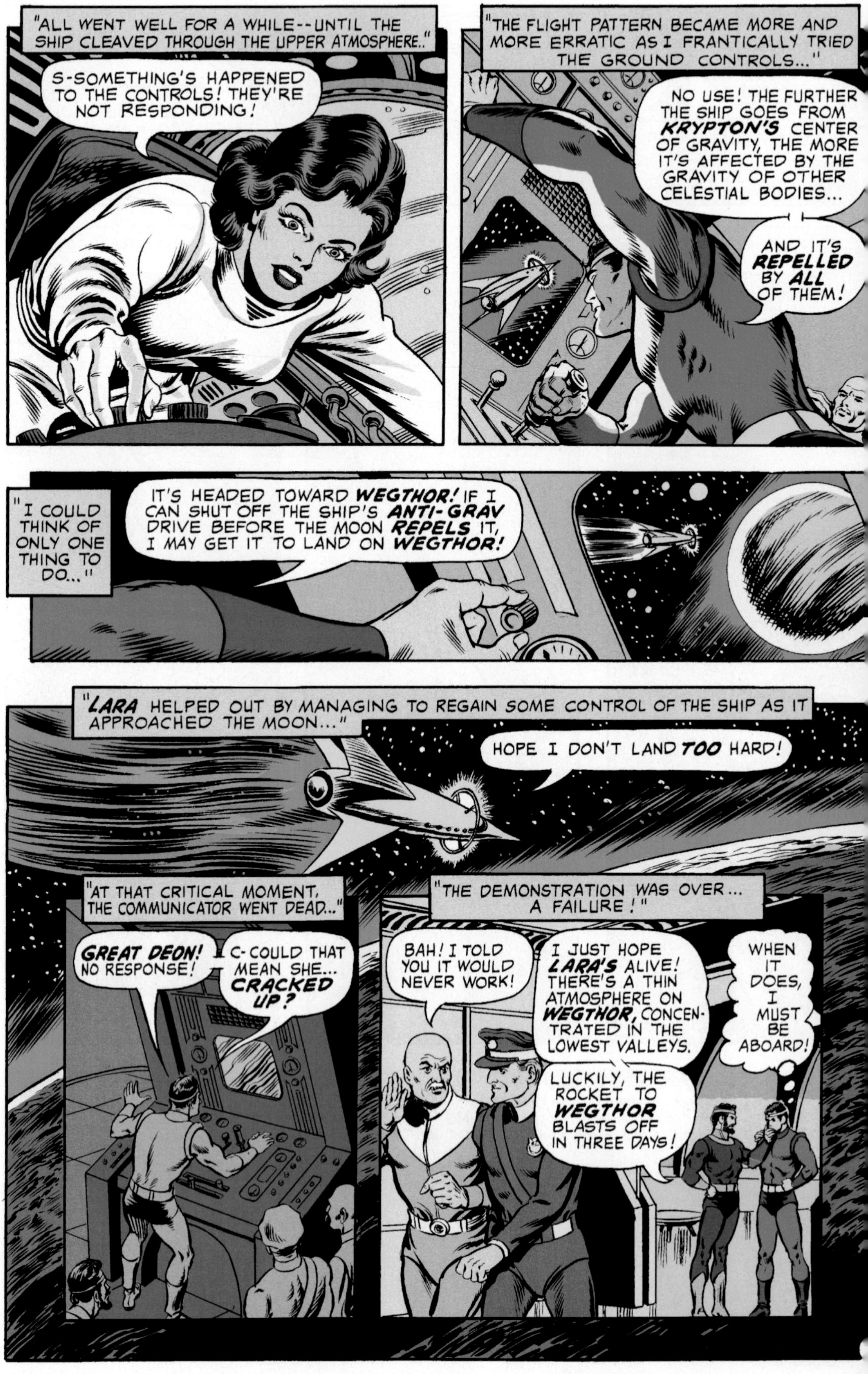
"ALL WENT WELL FOR A WHILE--UNTIL THE SHIP CLEAVED THROUGH THE UPPER ATMOSPHERE."
S-SOMETHING'S HAPPENED TO THE CONTROLS! THEY'RE NOT RESPONDING!
"THE FLIGHT PATTERN BECAME MORE AND MORE ERRATIC AS I FRANTICALLY TRIED THE GROUND CONTROLS..."
NO USE! THE FURTHER THE SHIP GOES FROM KRYPTON'S CENTER OF GRAVITY, THE MORE IT'S AFFECTED BY THE GRAVITY OF OTHER CELESTIAL BODIES...
AND IT'S REPELLED BY ALL OF THEM!
"I COULD THINK OF ONLY ONE THING TO DO..."
IT'S HEADED TOWARD WEGTHOR! IF I CAN SHUT OFF THE SHIP'S ANTI-GRAV DRIVE BEFORE THE MOON REPELS IT, I MAY GET IT TO LAND ON WEGTHOR!
"LARA HELPED OUT BY MANAGING TO REGAIN SOME CONTROL OF THE SHIP AS IT APPROACHED THE MOON..."
HOPE I DON'T LAND TOO HARD!
"AT THAT CRITICAL MOMENT, THE COMMUNICATOR WENT DEAD..."
GREAT DEON! NO RESPONSE!
C-COULD THAT MEAN SHE... CRACKED UP?
"THE DEMONSTRATION WAS OVER... A FAILURE!"
BAH! I TOLD YOU IT WOULD NEVER WORK!
I JUST HOPE LARA'S ALIVE! THERE'S A THIN ATMOSPHERE ON WEGTHOR, CONCEN-TRATED IN THE LOWEST VALLEYS.
LUCKILY, THE ROCKET TO WEGTHOR BLASTS OFF IN THREE DAYS!
WHEN IT DOES, I MUST BE ABOARD!

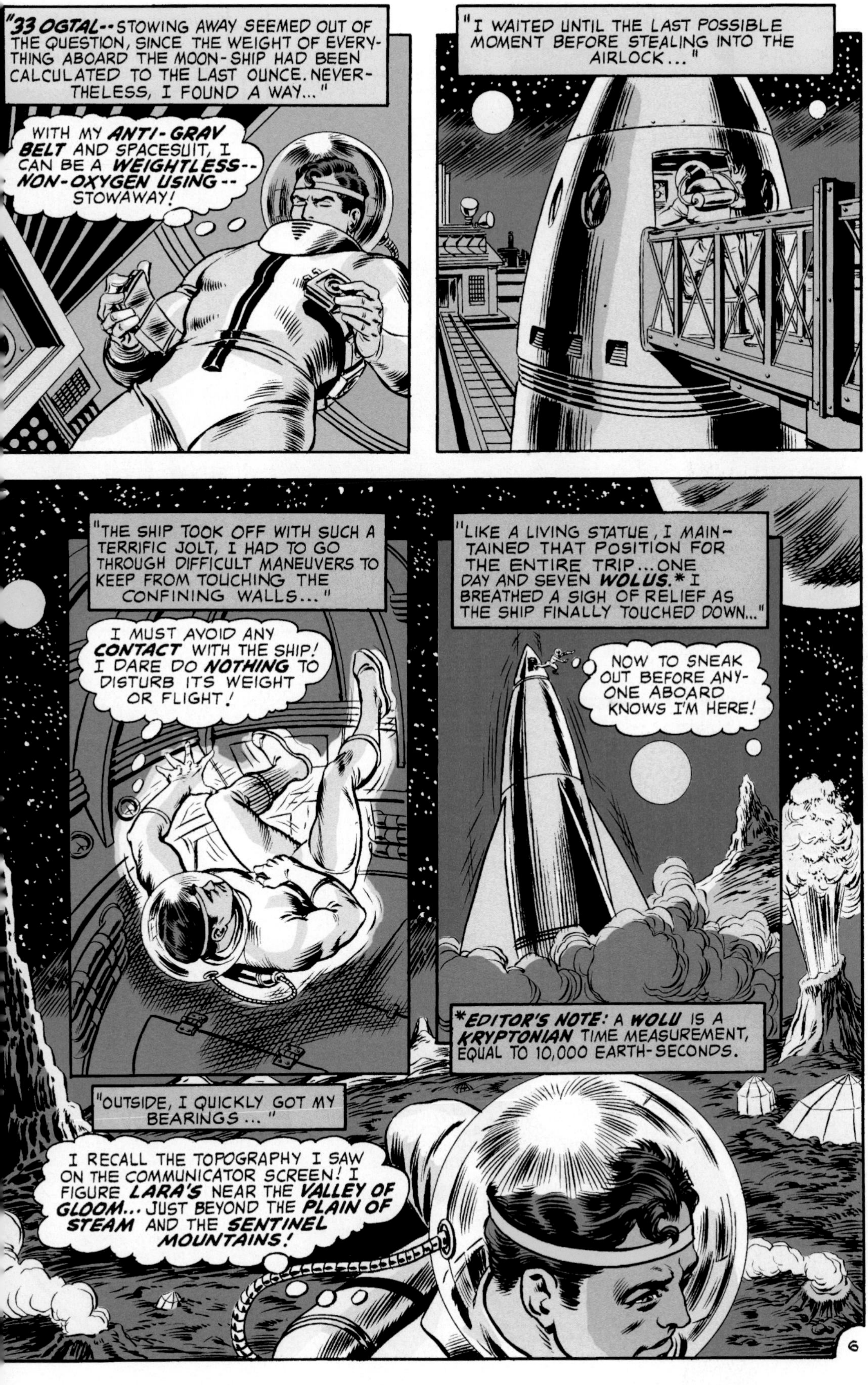
"33 OGTAL-- STOWING AWAY SEEMED OUT OF THE QUESTION, SINCE THE WEIGHT OF EVERYTHING ABOARD THE MOON-SHIP HAD BEEN CALCULATED TO THE LAST OUNCE. NEVERTHELESS, I FOUND A WAY..."
WITH MY ANTI-GRAV BELT AND SPACESUIT, I CAN BE A WEIGHTLESS-- NON-OXYGEN USING-- STOWAWAY!
"I WAITED UNTIL THE LAST POSSIBLE MOMENT BEFORE STEALING INTO THE AIRLOCK..."
"THE SHIP TOOK OFF WITH SUCH A TERRIFIC JOLT, I HAD TO GO THROUGH DIFFICULT MANEUVERS TO KEEP FROM TOUCHING THE CONFINING WALLS..."
I MUST AVOID ANY CONTACT WITH THE SHIP! I DARE DO NOTHING TO DISTURB ITS WEIGHT OR FLIGHT!
"LIKE A LIVING STATUE, I MAINTAINED THAT POSITION FOR THE ENTIRE TRIP...ONE DAY AND SEVEN WOLUS.* I BREATHED A SIGH OF RELIEF AS THE SHIP FINALLY TOUCHED DOWN..."
NOW TO SNEAK OUT BEFORE ANYONE ABOARD KNOWS I'M HERE!
*EDITOR'S NOTE: A WOLU IS A KRYPTONIAN TIME MEASUREMENT, EQUAL TO 10,000 EARTH-SECONDS.
"OUTSIDE, I QUICKLY GOT MY BEARINGS..."
I RECALL THE TOPOGRAPHY I SAW ON THE COMMUNICATOR SCREEN! I FIGURE LARA'S NEAR THE VALLEY OF GLOOM... JUST BEYOND THE PLAIN OF STEAM AND THE SENTINEL MOUNTAINS!
6

"THE PLAIN WAS ROUGH ENOUGH. I NEVER KNEW WHEN ONE OF THE STEAMING-HOT GEYSERS WOULD ERUPT NEAR ME. BUT I DIDN'T NEED TO USE MY ANTI-GRAV BELT TO DODGE THEM..."
IN THIS MOON'S WEAK GRAVITY, I'M ALMOST A SUPERMAN--MAKING FANTASTIC LEAPS!
"WHEN I CAME TO THE MOUNTAINS, I COULDN'T RESIST JUMPING OVER THE TALLEST PEAK..."
"AT LAST I REACHED THE SHIP! IT HAD NOT MADE IT TO THE VALLEY... AND ITS ATMOSPHERE. THERE WAS NOTHING BUT A LIFELESS HULK..."
NO SIGN OF LARA! AT LEAST THAT LEAVES SOME HOPE SHE GOT AWAY...
"HEART POUNDING, I RACED ON TO THE VALLEY OF GLOOM, A DEEP CLEFT IN THE GROUND WHERE LIGHT SELDOM REACHES! THERE, I SAW A LIGHT... LARA IN A FLUORESCENT SPACESUIT!"
"WITH SPECTACULAR LEAPS, I BOUNDED TO HER SIDE... GRABBED HER IN MY ARMS..."
I TOOK THIS SPARE SUIT ALONG, AND WORE IT TO REACH THE VALLEY!
MY DISCOVERY MAY HAVE BEEN A FAILURE, LARA... BUT IT DID HAVE ONE SUCCESS--BRINGING US TOGETHER!
THUS JOR-EL AND LARA MET AND FELL IN LOVE, LITTLE GUESSING WHAT FATE HAD IN STORE FOR THEM, FOR KRYPTON, AND FOR THE SON THEY WOULD SOMEDAY HAVE--KAL-EL... TO BE KNOWN ON EARTH AS
SUPERMAN.

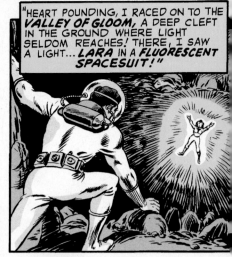

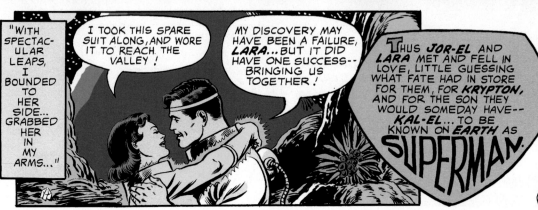

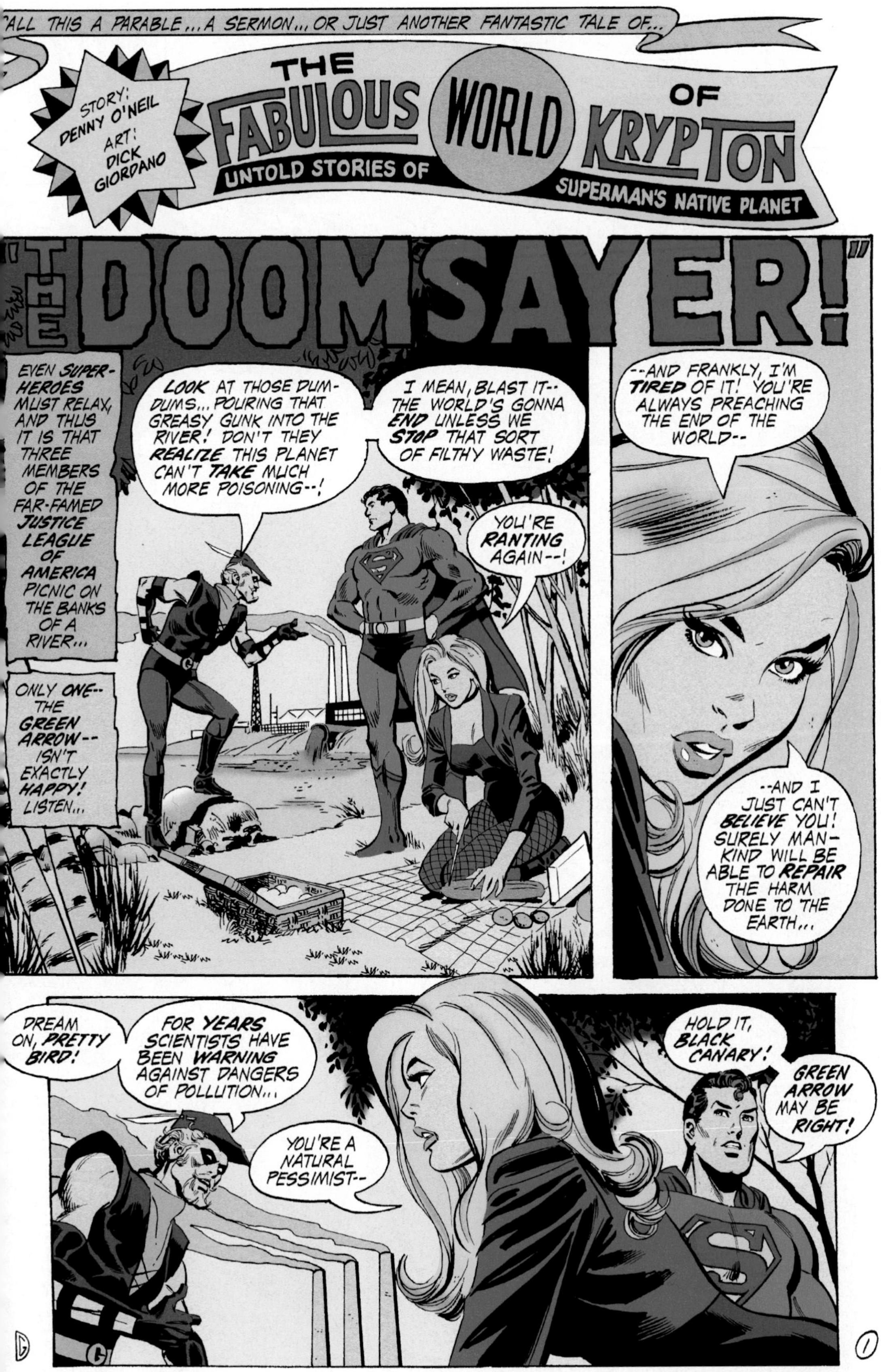
CALL THIS A PARABLE... A SERMON... OR JUST ANOTHER FANTASTIC TALE OF...
THE FABULOUS WORLD OF KRYPTON
UNTOLD STORIES OF SUPERMAN'S NATIVE PLANET
STORY: DENNY O'NEIL
ART: DICK GIORDANO
"THE DOOMSAYER!"
EVEN SUPER-HEROES MUST RELAX, AND THUS IT IS THAT THREE MEMBERS OF THE FAR-FAMED JUSTICE LEAGUE OF AMERICA PICNIC ON THE BANKS OF A RIVER...
ONLY ONE-- THE GREEN ARROW-- ISN'T EXACTLY HAPPY! LISTEN...
LOOK AT THOSE DUM-DUMS... POURING THAT GREASY GUNK INTO THE RIVER! DON'T THEY REALIZE THIS PLANET CAN'T TAKE MUCH MORE POISONING--!
I MEAN, BLAST IT-- THE WORLD'S GONNA END UNLESS WE STOP THAT SORT OF FILTHY WASTE!
YOU'RE RANTING AGAIN--!
--AND FRANKLY, I'M TIRED OF IT! YOU'RE ALWAYS PREACHING THE END OF THE WORLD--
--AND I JUST CAN'T BELIEVE YOU! SURELY MAN-KIND WILL BE ABLE TO REPAIR THE HARM DONE TO THE EARTH...
DREAM ON, PRETTY BIRD!
FOR YEARS SCIENTISTS HAVE BEEN WARNING AGAINST DANGERS OF POLLUTION...
YOU'RE A NATURAL PESSIMIST--
HOLD IT, BLACK CANARY!
GREEN ARROW MAY BE RIGHT!
1

LISTEN... THIS IS A STORY I FIND VERY *PAINFUL*... BUT MAYBE THERE'S A LESSON TO BE LEARNED FROM IT!

IT BEGAN MANY YEARS AGO, ON MY HOME WORLD-- *KRYPTON*...

"...IN A CITY CALLED *SURRUS*, ON A SOUTHERN CONTINENT! AN *ODD* CITY... FOR THERE GREW THE STRANGE FLOWERS THAT GAVE THE SETTLEMENT ITS NAME..."

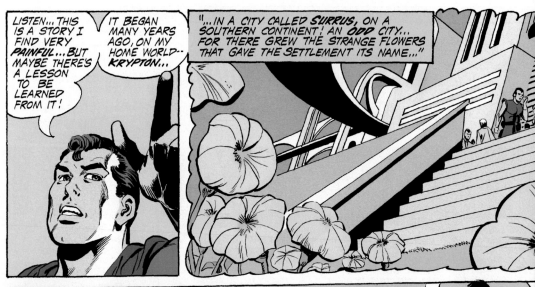

"...THE *SURRUS* BLOSSOMS! THESE PLANTS COULD *SING*... MADE THE MOST BEAUTIFUL MUSIC ANYONE HAD EVER HEARD! THE LIVING WAS EASY, AND THE CITIZENS SPENT MOST OF THEIR WAKING HOURS SIMPLY... *LISTENING*--"

"ONE MAN, HOWEVER, *DIDN'T* LISTEN... HE WAS *DOCTOR MO-DE*--A RENOWNED SCIENTIST! HE LIVED WITH HIS WIFE IN A LABORATORY HE'D BUILT HIMSELF..."

YOU SEEM *TROUBLED*, DEAR!

INDEED I *AM*! MY CALCULATIONS ARE *UNMISTAKABLE*...

GREAT TENSIONS ARE BUILDING IN THE CORE OF *KRYPTON*,'--

TENSIONS WHIC[H] COULD END IN *EXPLOSION* THA[T] WILL DESTROY EVERYTHING.

I ESTIMATE WE HAVE LESS THAN *TWENTY YEARS* TO CORRECT THE SITUATION!

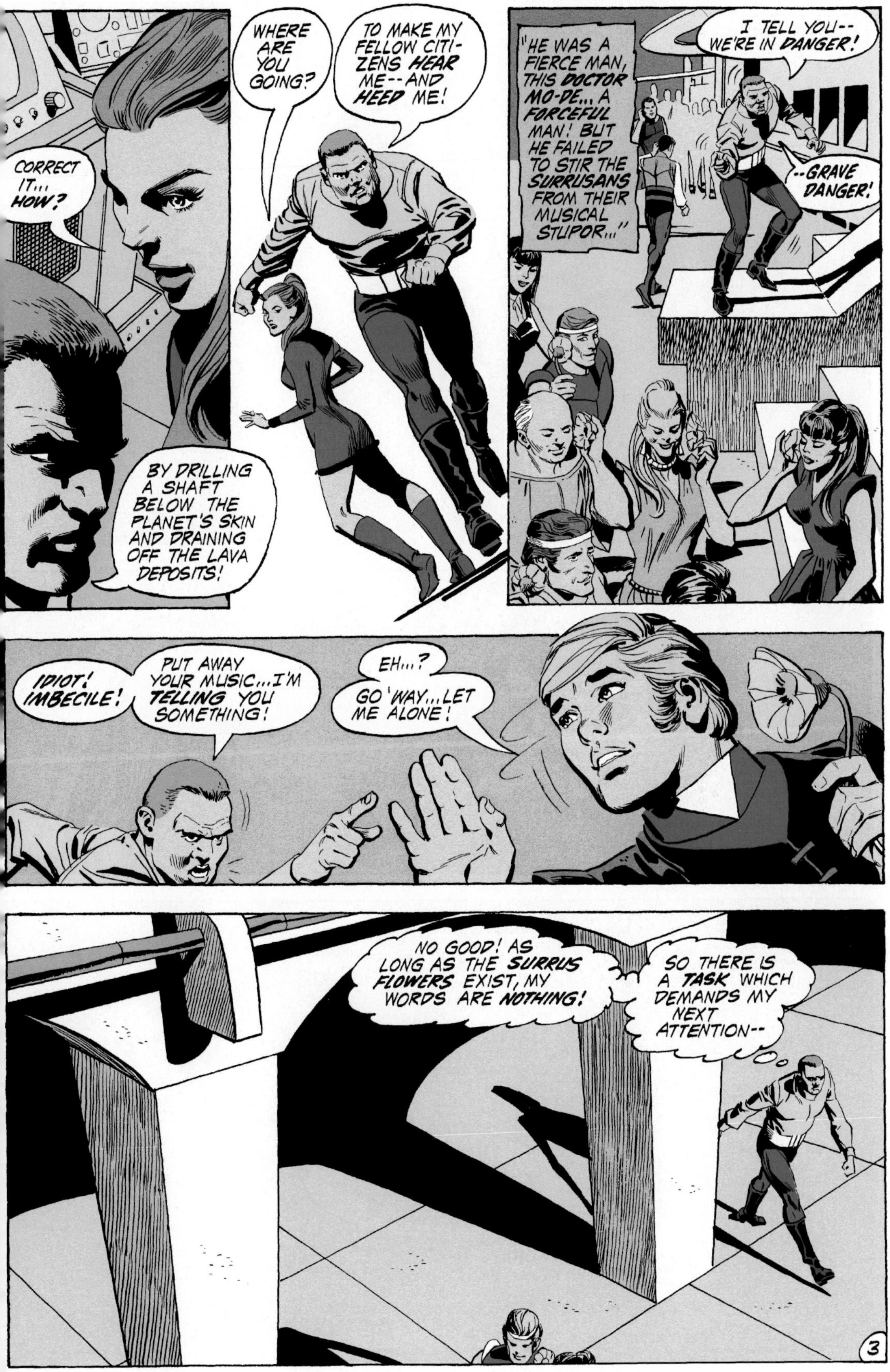

CORRECT IT... HOW?
BY DRILLING A SHAFT BELOW THE PLANET'S SKIN AND DRAINING OFF THE LAVA DEPOSITS!
WHERE ARE YOU GOING?
TO MAKE MY FELLOW CITIZENS HEAR ME--AND HEED ME!
"HE WAS A FIERCE MAN, THIS DOCTOR MO-DE... A FORCEFUL MAN! BUT HE FAILED TO STIR THE SURRUSANS FROM THEIR MUSICAL STUPOR..."
I TELL YOU--WE'RE IN DANGER!
--GRAVE DANGER!
IDIOT! IMBECILE!
PUT AWAY YOUR MUSIC...I'M TELLING YOU SOMETHING!
EH...?
GO 'WAY...LET ME ALONE!
NO GOOD! AS LONG AS THE SURRUS FLOWERS EXIST, MY WORDS ARE NOTHING!
SO THERE IS A TASK WHICH DEMANDS MY NEXT ATTENTION--
3

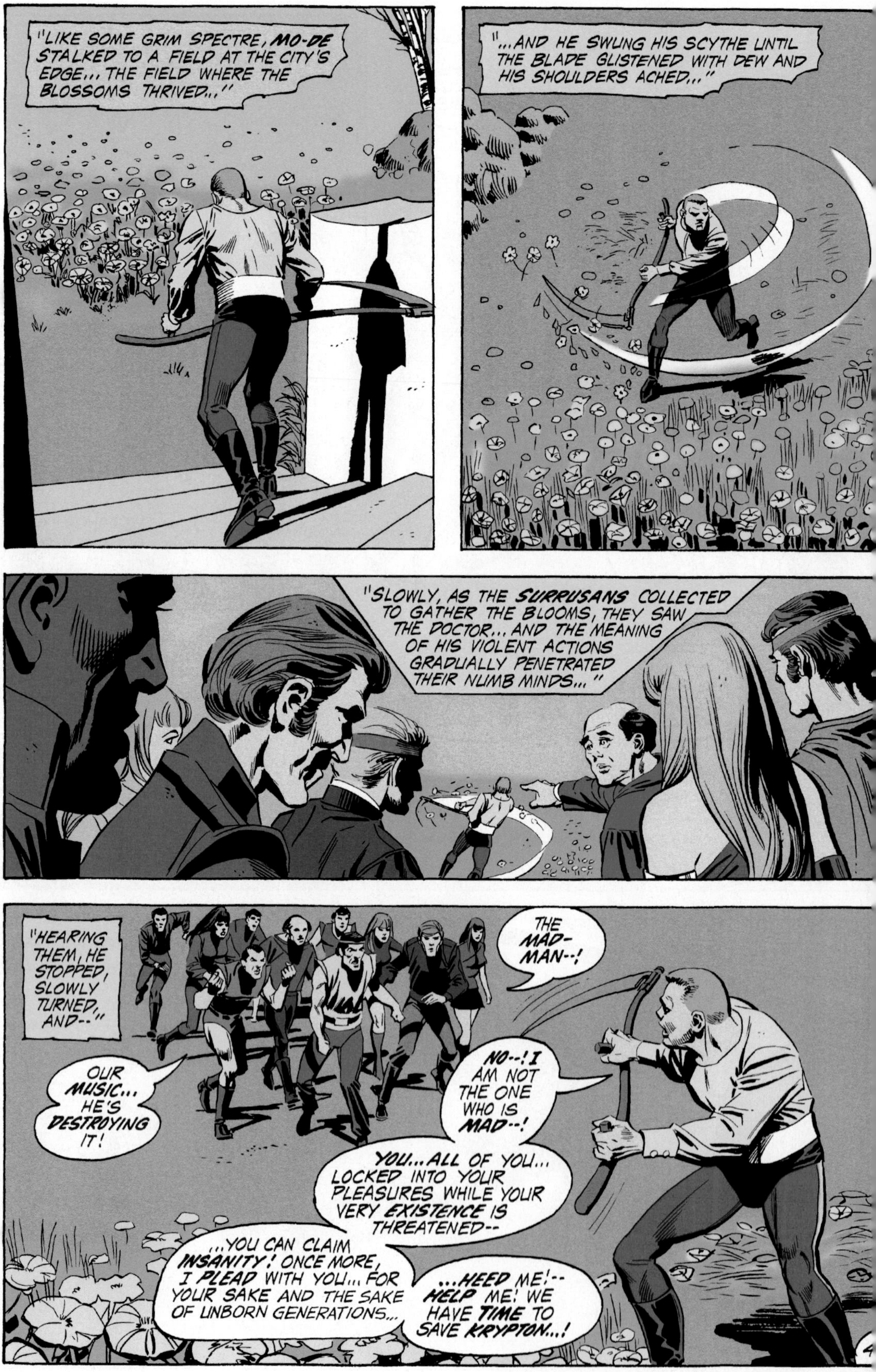
"LIKE SOME GRIM SPECTRE, MO-DE STALKED TO A FIELD AT THE CITY'S EDGE... THE FIELD WHERE THE BLOSSOMS THRIVED..."
"...AND HE SWUNG HIS SCYTHE UNTIL THE BLADE GLISTENED WITH DEW AND HIS SHOULDERS ACHED..."
"SLOWLY, AS THE SURRUSANS COLLECTED TO GATHER THE BLOOMS, THEY SAW THE DOCTOR... AND THE MEANING OF HIS VIOLENT ACTIONS GRADUALLY PENETRATED THEIR NUMB MINDS..."
"HEARING THEM, HE STOPPED, SLOWLY TURNED, AND--"
OUR MUSIC... HE'S DESTROYING IT!
THE MAD-MAN--!
NO--! I AM NOT THE ONE WHO IS MAD--!
YOU...ALL OF YOU... LOCKED INTO YOUR PLEASURES WHILE YOUR VERY EXISTENCE IS THREATENED--
...YOU CAN CLAIM INSANITY! ONCE MORE, I PLEAD WITH YOU... FOR YOUR SAKE AND THE SAKE OF UNBORN GENERATIONS...
...HEED ME!-- HELP ME! WE HAVE TIME TO SAVE KRYPTON...!

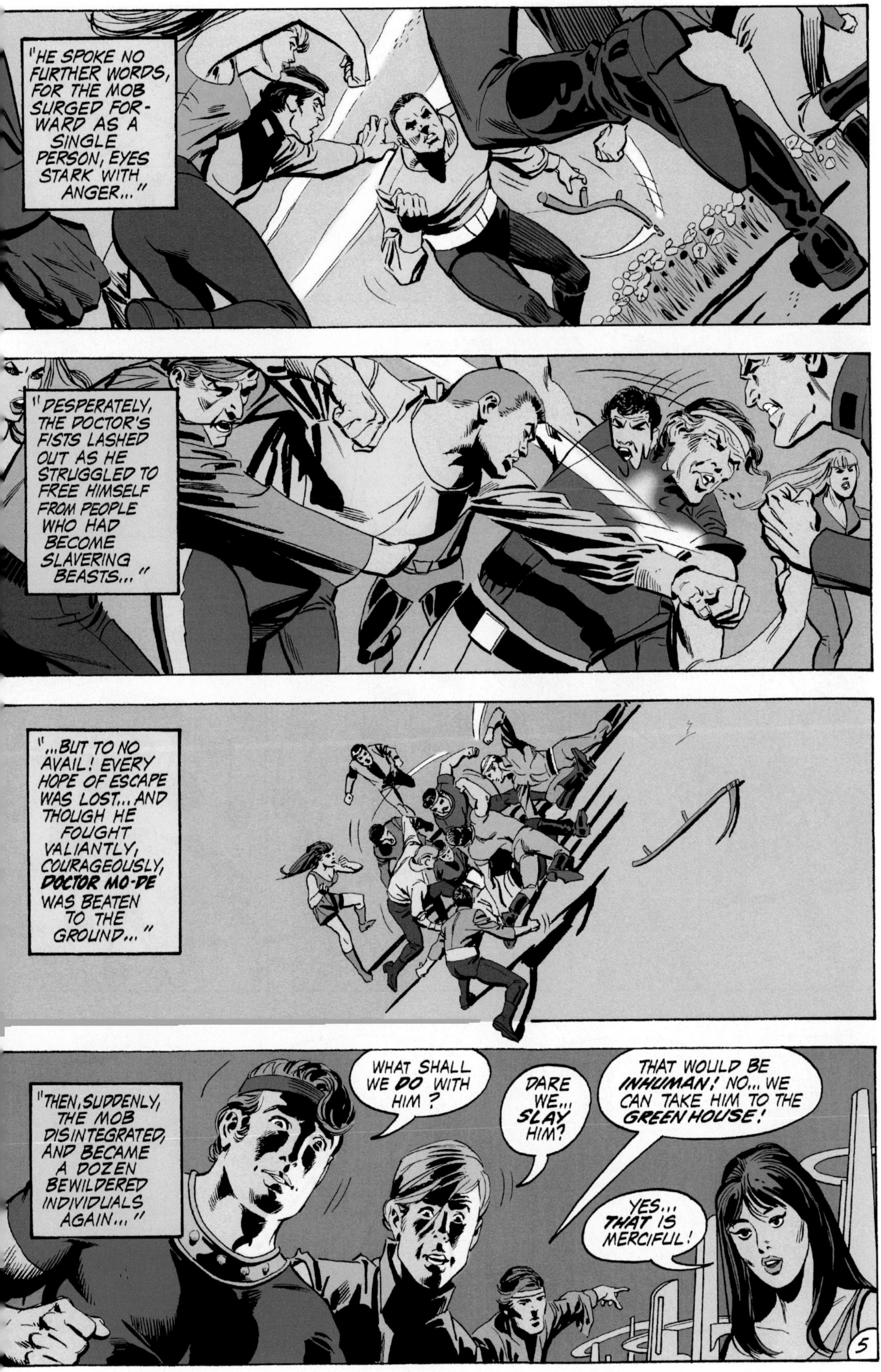
"HE SPOKE NO FURTHER WORDS, FOR THE MOB SURGED FORWARD AS A SINGLE PERSON, EYES STARK WITH ANGER..."
"DESPERATELY, THE DOCTOR'S FISTS LASHED OUT AS HE STRUGGLED TO FREE HIMSELF FROM PEOPLE WHO HAD BECOME SLAVERING BEASTS..."
"...BUT TO NO AVAIL! EVERY HOPE OF ESCAPE WAS LOST... AND THOUGH HE FOUGHT VALIANTLY, COURAGEOUSLY, **DOCTOR MO-DE** WAS BEATEN TO THE GROUND..."
"THEN, SUDDENLY, THE MOB DISINTEGRATED, AND BECAME A DOZEN BEWILDERED INDIVIDUALS AGAIN..."
WHAT SHALL WE **DO** WITH HIM ?
DARE WE... **SLAY** HIM?
THAT WOULD BE **INHUMAN!** NO... WE CAN TAKE HIM TO THE **GREEN HOUSE!**
YES... **THAT** IS MERCIFUL!
5

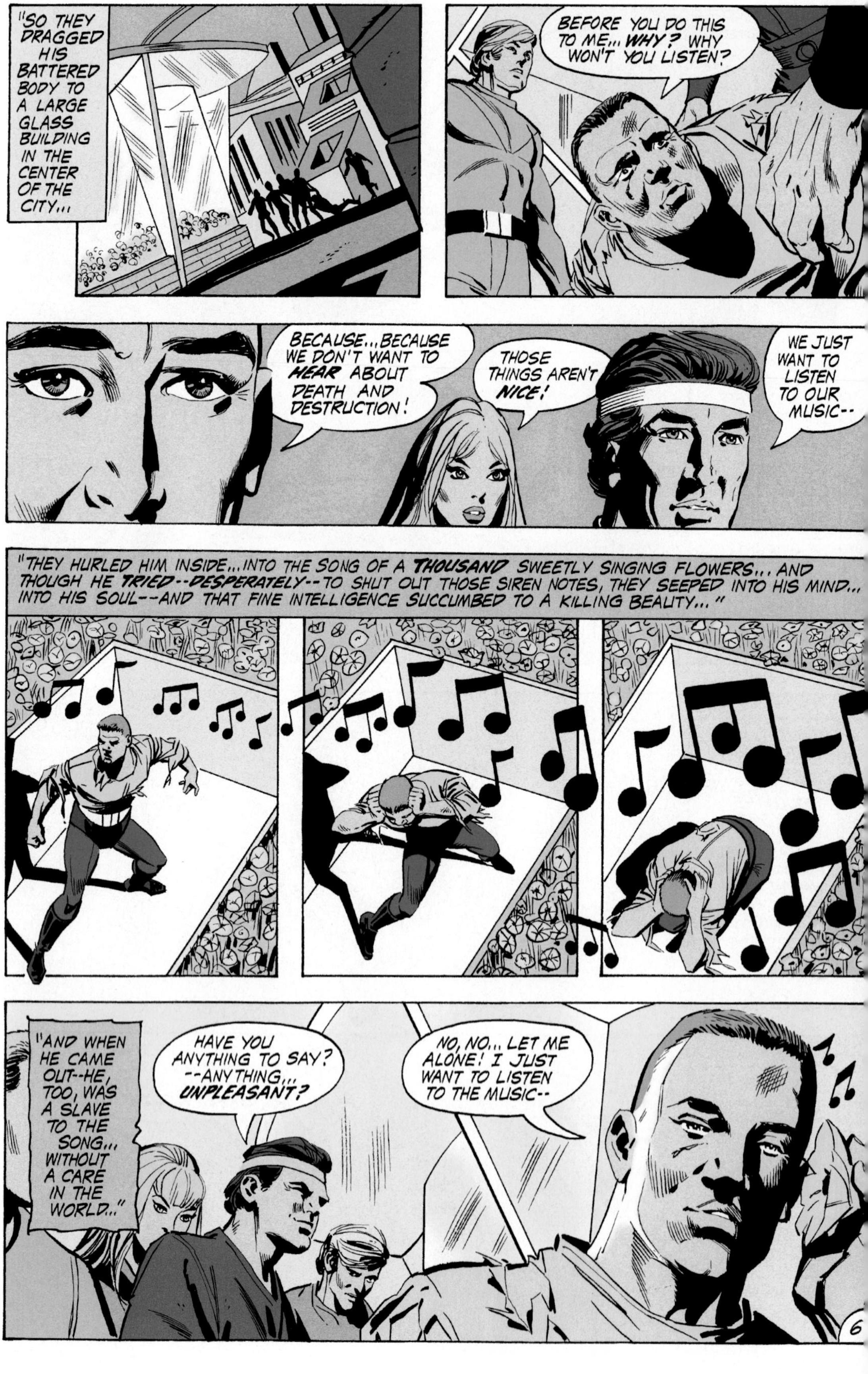
"SO THEY DRAGGED HIS BATTERED BODY TO A LARGE GLASS BUILDING IN THE CENTER OF THE CITY...
BEFORE YOU DO THIS TO ME... WHY? WHY WON'T YOU LISTEN?
BECAUSE...BECAUSE WE DON'T WANT TO HEAR ABOUT DEATH AND DESTRUCTION!
THOSE THINGS AREN'T NICE!
WE JUST WANT TO LISTEN TO OUR MUSIC--
"THEY HURLED HIM INSIDE...INTO THE SONG OF A THOUSAND SWEETLY SINGING FLOWERS... AND THOUGH HE TRIED--DESPERATELY--TO SHUT OUT THOSE SIREN NOTES, THEY SEEPED INTO HIS MIND... INTO HIS SOUL--AND THAT FINE INTELLIGENCE SUCCUMBED TO A KILLING BEAUTY..."
"AND WHEN HE CAME OUT--HE, TOO, WAS A SLAVE TO THE SONG... WITHOUT A CARE IN THE WORLD.."
HAVE YOU ANYTHING TO SAY? --ANYTHING... UNPLEASANT?
NO, NO... LET ME ALONE! I JUST WANT TO LISTEN TO THE MUSIC--
6

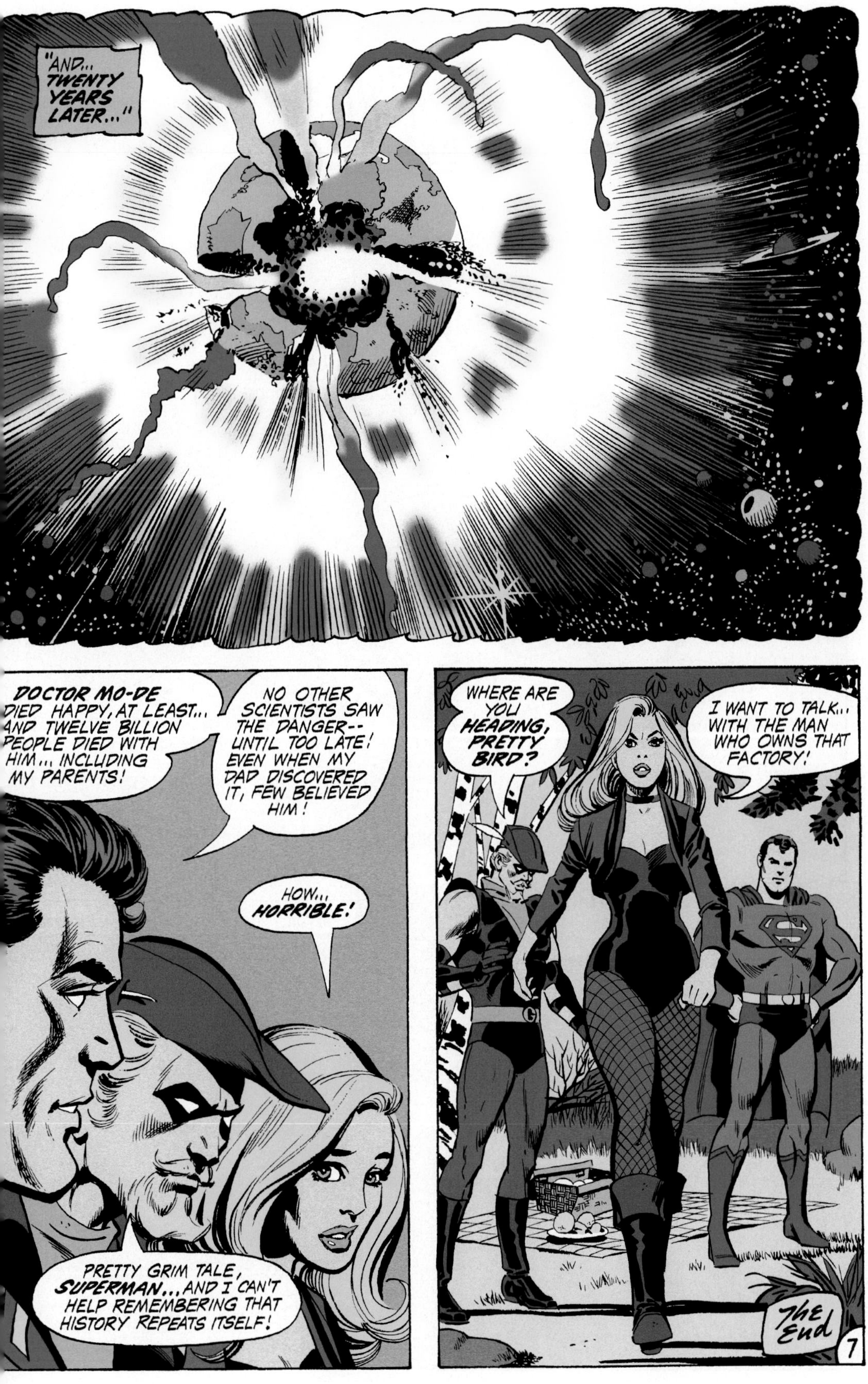
"AND... TWENTY YEARS LATER..."
DOCTOR MO-DE DIED HAPPY, AT LEAST... AND TWELVE BILLION PEOPLE DIED WITH HIM... INCLUDING MY PARENTS!
NO OTHER SCIENTISTS SAW THE DANGER-- UNTIL TOO LATE! EVEN WHEN MY DAD DISCOVERED IT, FEW BELIEVED HIM!
HOW... HORRIBLE!
PRETTY GRIM TALE, SUPERMAN... AND I CAN'T HELP REMEMBERING THAT HISTORY REPEATS ITSELF!
WHERE ARE YOU HEADING, PRETTY BIRD?
I WANT TO TALK... WITH THE MAN WHO OWNS THAT FACTORY!
The End
7

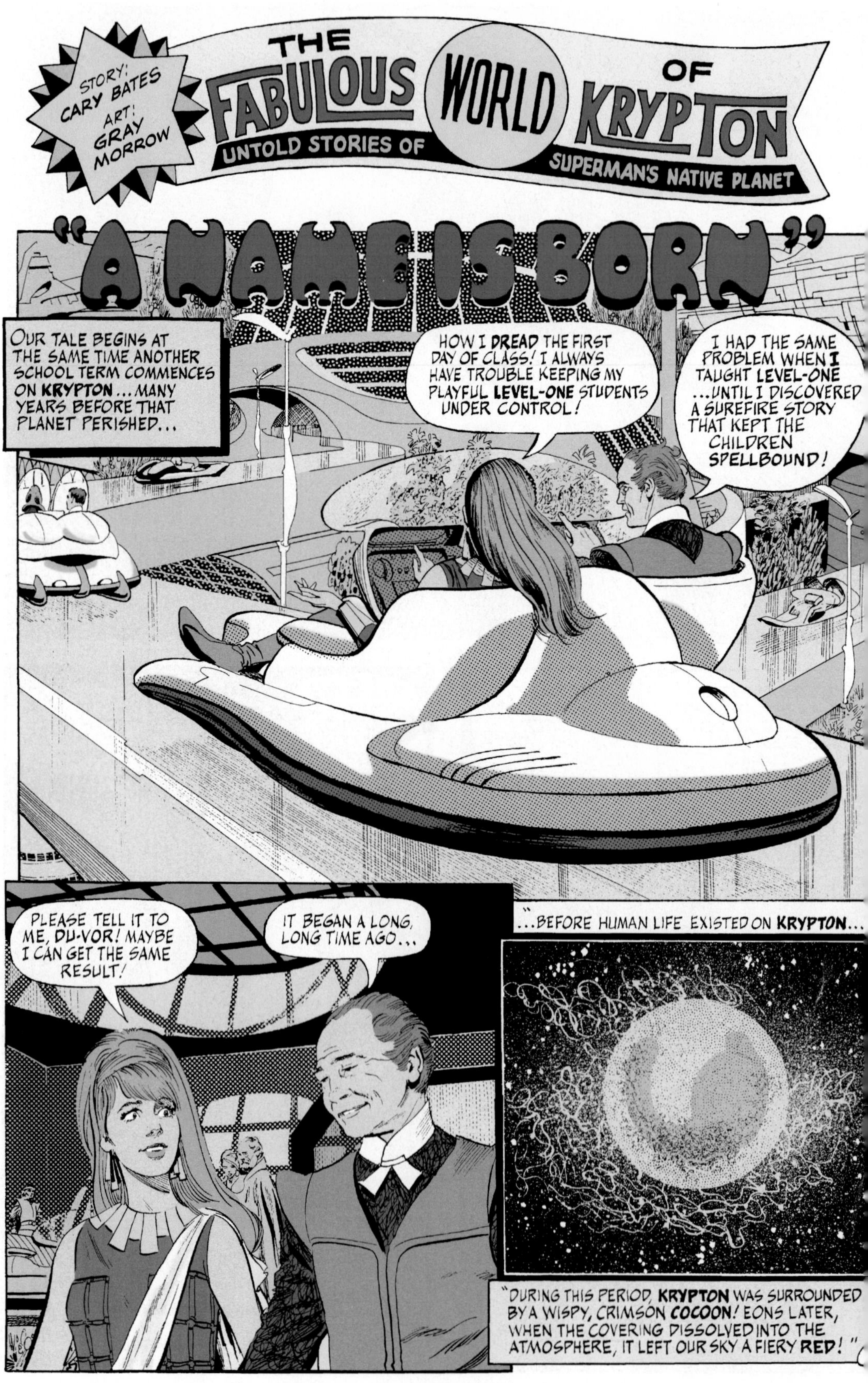
STORY: CARY BATES
ART: GRAY MORROW
THE FABULOUS WORLD OF KRYPTON
UNTOLD STORIES OF SUPERMAN'S NATIVE PLANET
"A NAME IS BORN"
OUR TALE BEGINS AT THE SAME TIME ANOTHER SCHOOL TERM COMMENCES ON KRYPTON... MANY YEARS BEFORE THAT PLANET PERISHED...
HOW I DREAD THE FIRST DAY OF CLASS! I ALWAYS HAVE TROUBLE KEEPING MY PLAYFUL LEVEL-ONE STUDENTS UNDER CONTROL!
I HAD THE SAME PROBLEM WHEN I TAUGHT LEVEL-ONE ...UNTIL I DISCOVERED A SUREFIRE STORY THAT KEPT THE CHILDREN SPELLBOUND!
PLEASE TELL IT TO ME, DU-VOR! MAYBE I CAN GET THE SAME RESULT!
IT BEGAN A LONG, LONG TIME AGO...
"...BEFORE HUMAN LIFE EXISTED ON KRYPTON...
"DURING THIS PERIOD, KRYPTON WAS SURROUNDED BY A WISPY, CRIMSON COCOON! EONS LATER, WHEN THE COVERING DISSOLVED INTO THE ATMOSPHERE, IT LEFT OUR SKY A FIERY RED!"

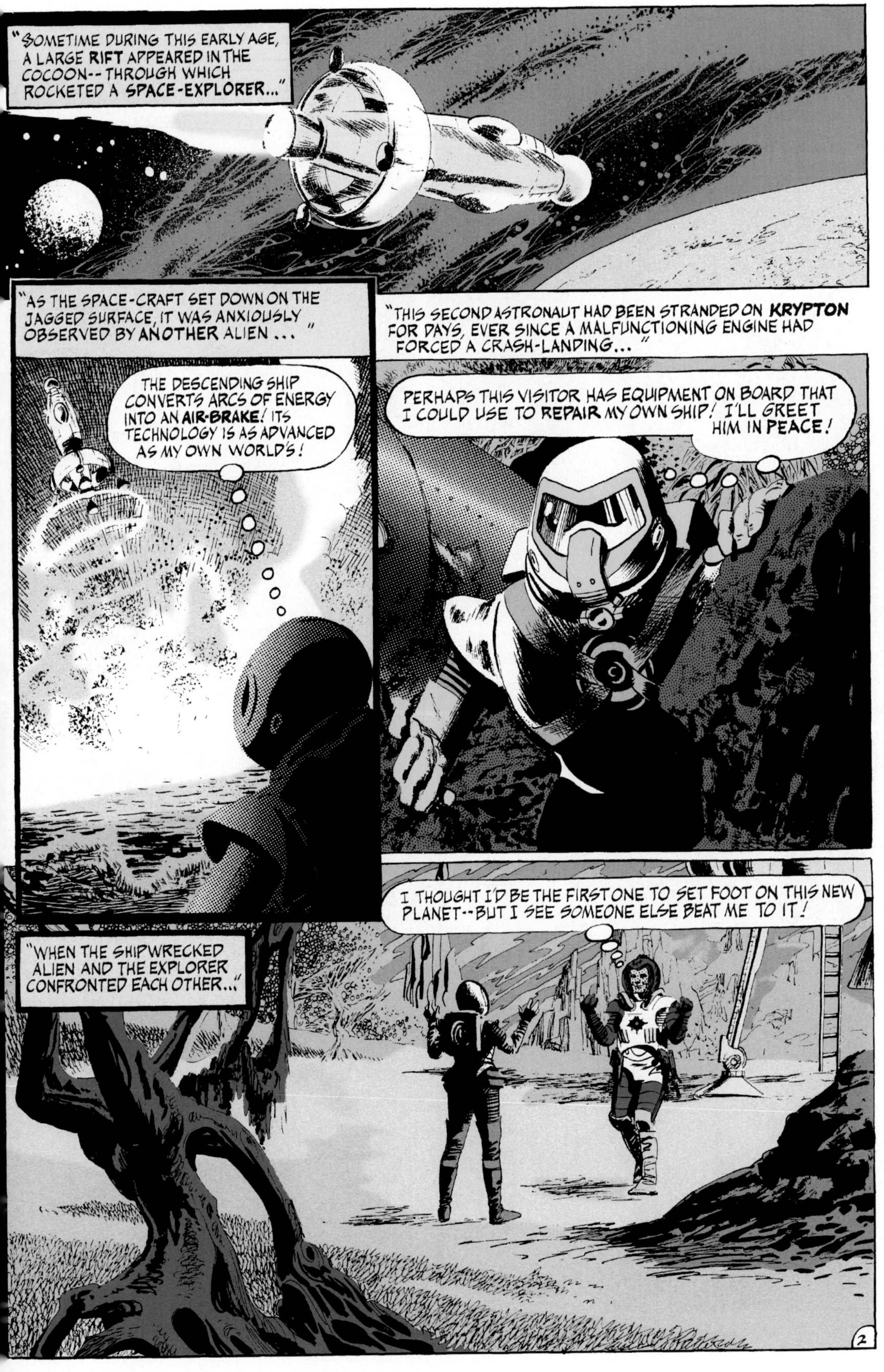
"SOMETIME DURING THIS EARLY AGE, A LARGE RIFT APPEARED IN THE COCOON--THROUGH WHICH ROCKETED A SPACE-EXPLORER..."
"AS THE SPACE-CRAFT SET DOWN ON THE JAGGED SURFACE, IT WAS ANXIOUSLY OBSERVED BY ANOTHER ALIEN ..."
THE DESCENDING SHIP CONVERTS ARCS OF ENERGY INTO AN AIR-BRAKE! ITS TECHNOLOGY IS AS ADVANCED AS MY OWN WORLD'S!
"THIS SECOND ASTRONAUT HAD BEEN STRANDED ON KRYPTON FOR DAYS, EVER SINCE A MALFUNCTIONING ENGINE HAD FORCED A CRASH-LANDING..."
PERHAPS THIS VISITOR HAS EQUIPMENT ON BOARD THAT I COULD USE TO REPAIR MY OWN SHIP! I'LL GREET HIM IN PEACE!
"WHEN THE SHIPWRECKED ALIEN AND THE EXPLORER CONFRONTED EACH OTHER..."
I THOUGHT I'D BE THE FIRST ONE TO SET FOOT ON THIS NEW PLANET--BUT I SEE SOMEONE ELSE BEAT ME TO IT!
2

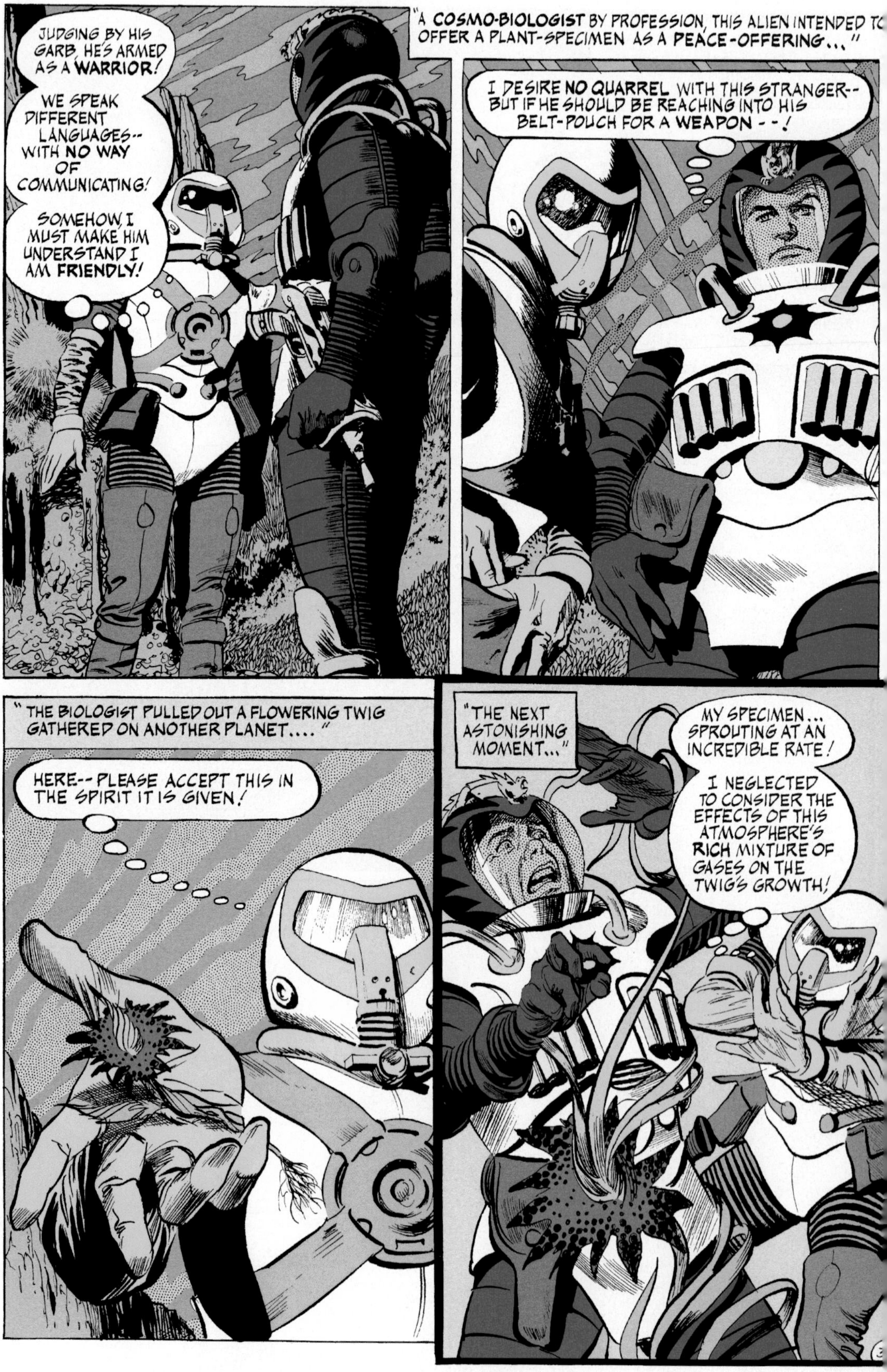
JUDGING BY HIS GARB, HE'S ARMED AS A **WARRIOR**!
WE SPEAK DIFFERENT LANGUAGES-- WITH **NO WAY** OF COMMUNICATING!
SOMEHOW, I MUST MAKE HIM UNDERSTAND I AM **FRIENDLY**!
"A **COSMO-BIOLOGIST** BY PROFESSION, THIS ALIEN INTENDED TO OFFER A PLANT-SPECIMEN AS A **PEACE-OFFERING**..."
I DESIRE **NO QUARREL** WITH THIS STRANGER-- BUT IF HE SHOULD BE REACHING INTO HIS BELT-POUCH FOR A **WEAPON** - -!
"THE BIOLOGIST PULLED OUT A FLOWERING TWIG GATHERED ON ANOTHER PLANET...."
HERE-- PLEASE ACCEPT THIS IN THE SPIRIT IT IS GIVEN!
"THE NEXT ASTONISHING MOMENT..."
MY SPECIMEN... SPROUTING AT AN INCREDIBLE RATE!
I NEGLECTED TO CONSIDER THE EFFECTS OF THIS ATMOSPHERE'S **RICH** MIXTURE OF GASES ON THE TWIG'S GROWTH!

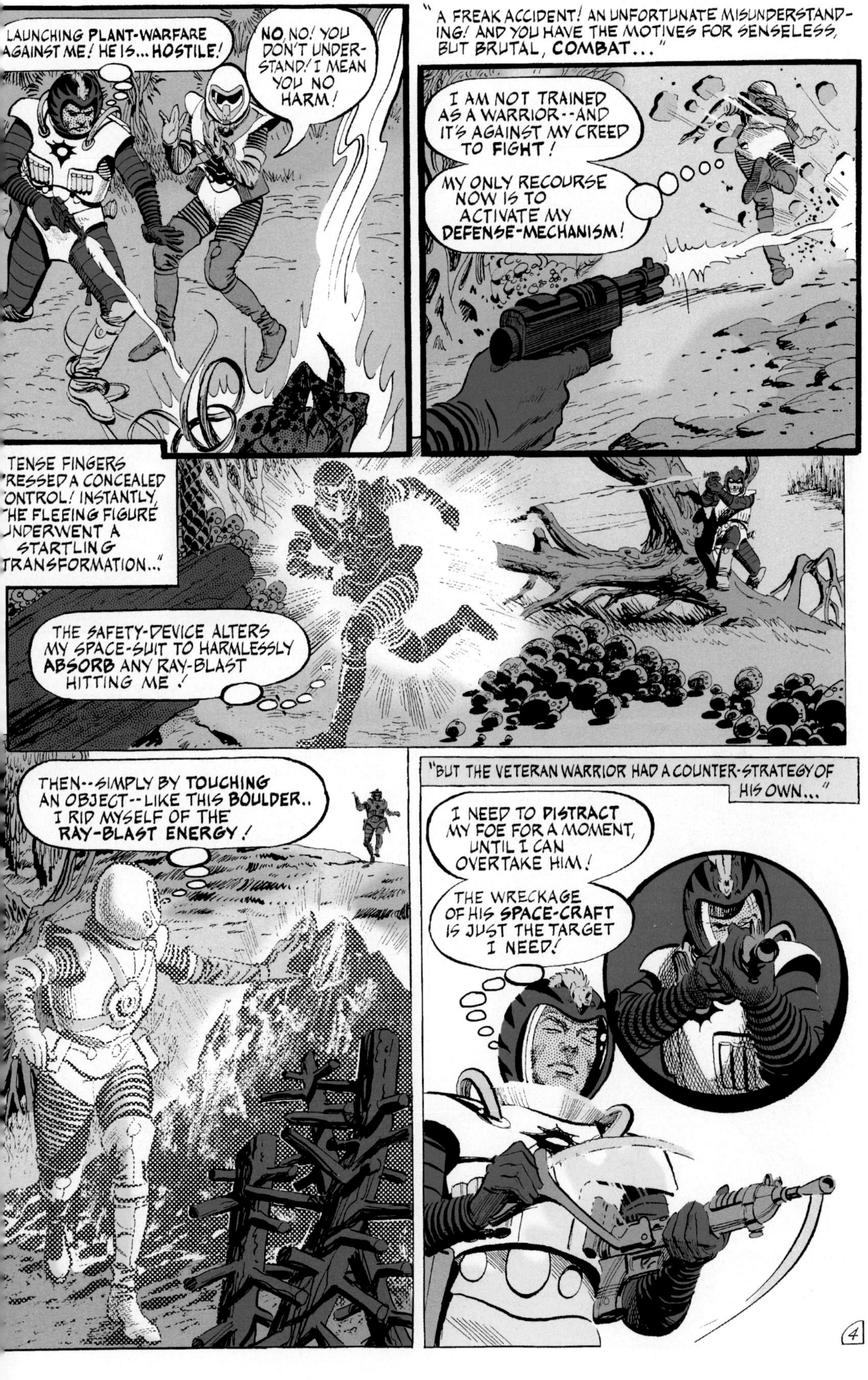
LAUNCHING PLANT-WARFARE AGAINST ME! HE IS... HOSTILE!
NO, NO! YOU DON'T UNDERSTAND! I MEAN YOU NO HARM!
"A FREAK ACCIDENT! AN UNFORTUNATE MISUNDERSTANDING! AND YOU HAVE THE MOTIVES FOR SENSELESS, BUT BRUTAL, COMBAT..."
I AM NOT TRAINED AS A WARRIOR--AND IT'S AGAINST MY CREED TO FIGHT!
MY ONLY RECOURSE NOW IS TO ACTIVATE MY DEFENSE-MECHANISM!
TENSE FINGERS PRESSED A CONCEALED CONTROL! INSTANTLY, THE FLEEING FIGURE UNDERWENT A STARTLING TRANSFORMATION..."
THE SAFETY-DEVICE ALTERS MY SPACE-SUIT TO HARMLESSLY ABSORB ANY RAY-BLAST HITTING ME!
THEN--SIMPLY BY TOUCHING AN OBJECT--LIKE THIS BOULDER.. I RID MYSELF OF THE RAY-BLAST ENERGY!
"BUT THE VETERAN WARRIOR HAD A COUNTER-STRATEGY OF HIS OWN..."
I NEED TO DISTRACT MY FOE FOR A MOMENT, UNTIL I CAN OVERTAKE HIM!
THE WRECKAGE OF HIS SPACE-CRAFT IS JUST THE TARGET I NEED!
4

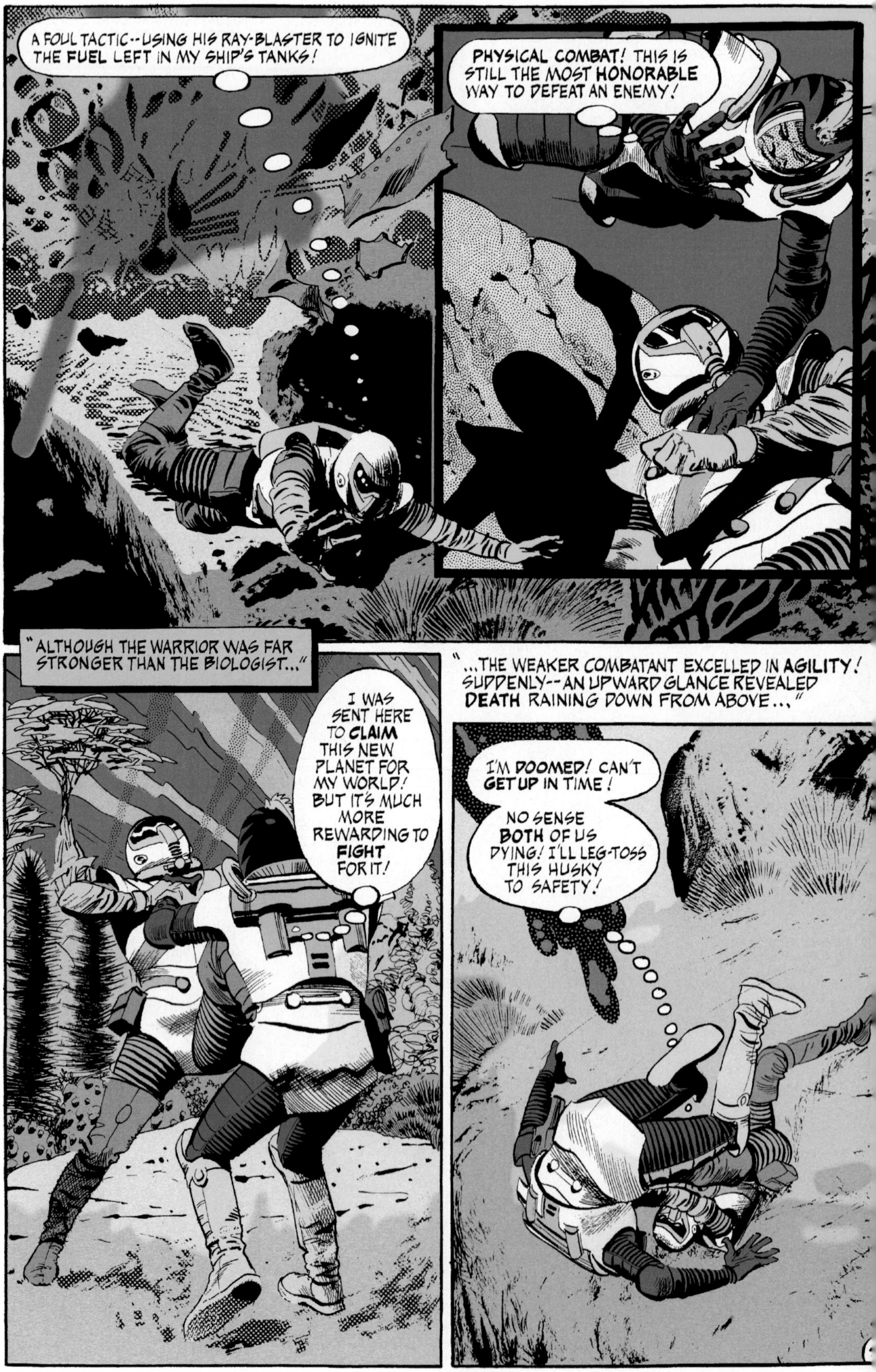
A FOUL TACTIC--USING HIS RAY-BLASTER TO IGNITE THE FUEL LEFT IN MY SHIP'S TANKS!
PHYSICAL COMBAT! THIS IS STILL THE MOST HONORABLE WAY TO DEFEAT AN ENEMY!
"ALTHOUGH THE WARRIOR WAS FAR STRONGER THAN THE BIOLOGIST..."
I WAS SENT HERE TO CLAIM THIS NEW PLANET FOR MY WORLD! BUT IT'S MUCH MORE REWARDING TO FIGHT FOR IT!
"...THE WEAKER COMBATANT EXCELLED IN AGILITY! SUDDENLY--AN UPWARD GLANCE REVEALED DEATH RAINING DOWN FROM ABOVE..."
I'M DOOMED! CAN'T GET UP IN TIME!
NO SENSE BOTH OF US DYING! I'LL LEG-TOSS THIS HUSKY TO SAFETY!

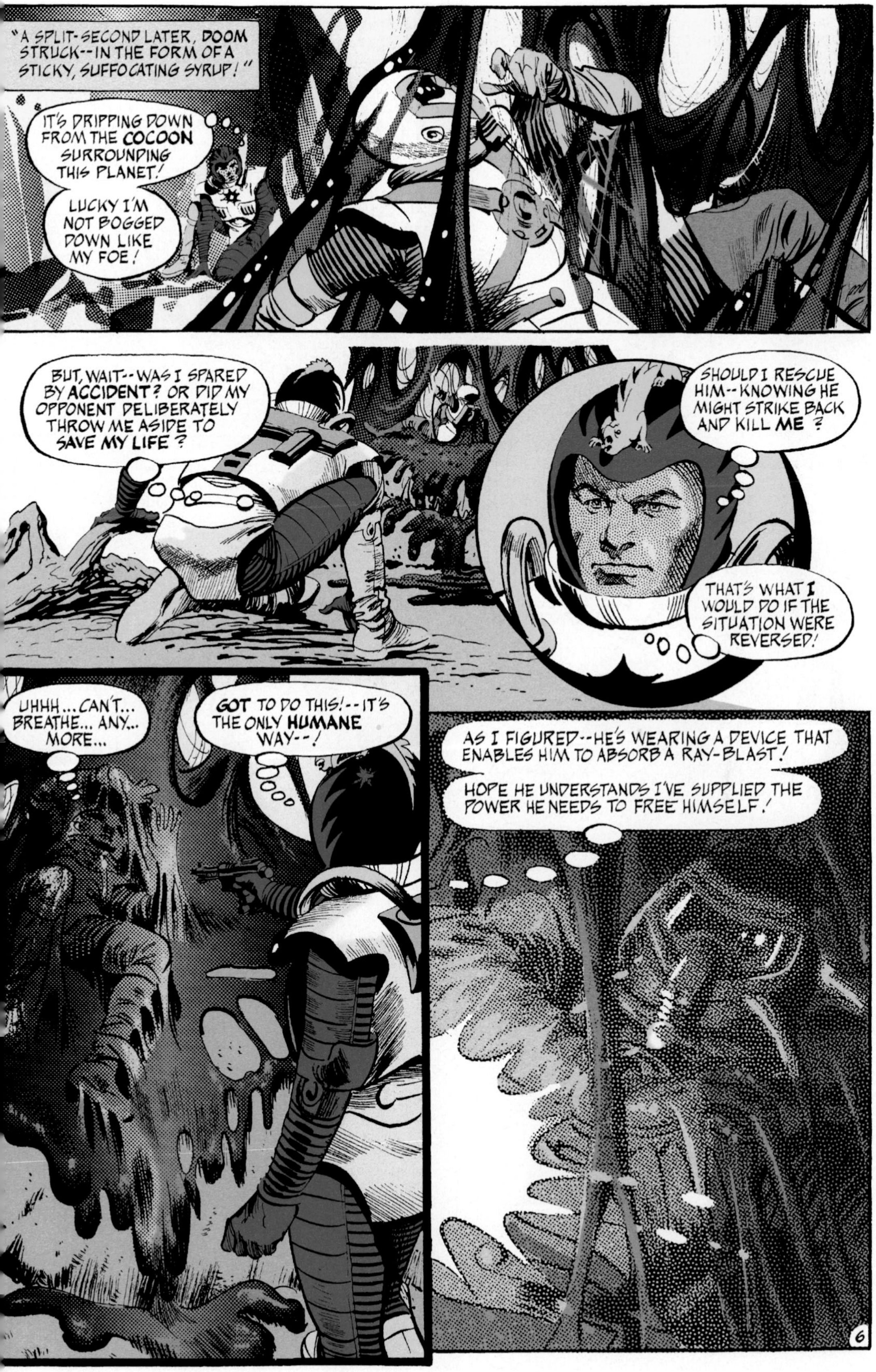
"A SPLIT-SECOND LATER, DOOM STRUCK--IN THE FORM OF A STICKY, SUFFOCATING SYRUP!"
IT'S DRIPPING DOWN FROM THE COCOON SURROUNDING THIS PLANET!
LUCKY I'M NOT BOGGED DOWN LIKE MY FOE!
BUT, WAIT--WAS I SPARED BY ACCIDENT? OR DID MY OPPONENT DELIBERATELY THROW ME ASIDE TO SAVE MY LIFE?
SHOULD I RESCUE HIM--KNOWING HE MIGHT STRIKE BACK AND KILL ME?
THAT'S WHAT I WOULD DO IF THE SITUATION WERE REVERSED!
UHHH... CAN'T... BREATHE... ANY... MORE...
GOT TO DO THIS!--IT'S THE ONLY HUMANE WAY--!
AS I FIGURED--HE'S WEARING A DEVICE THAT ENABLES HIM TO ABSORB A RAY-BLAST!
HOPE HE UNDERSTANDS I'VE SUPPLIED THE POWER HE NEEDS TO FREE HIMSELF!
6

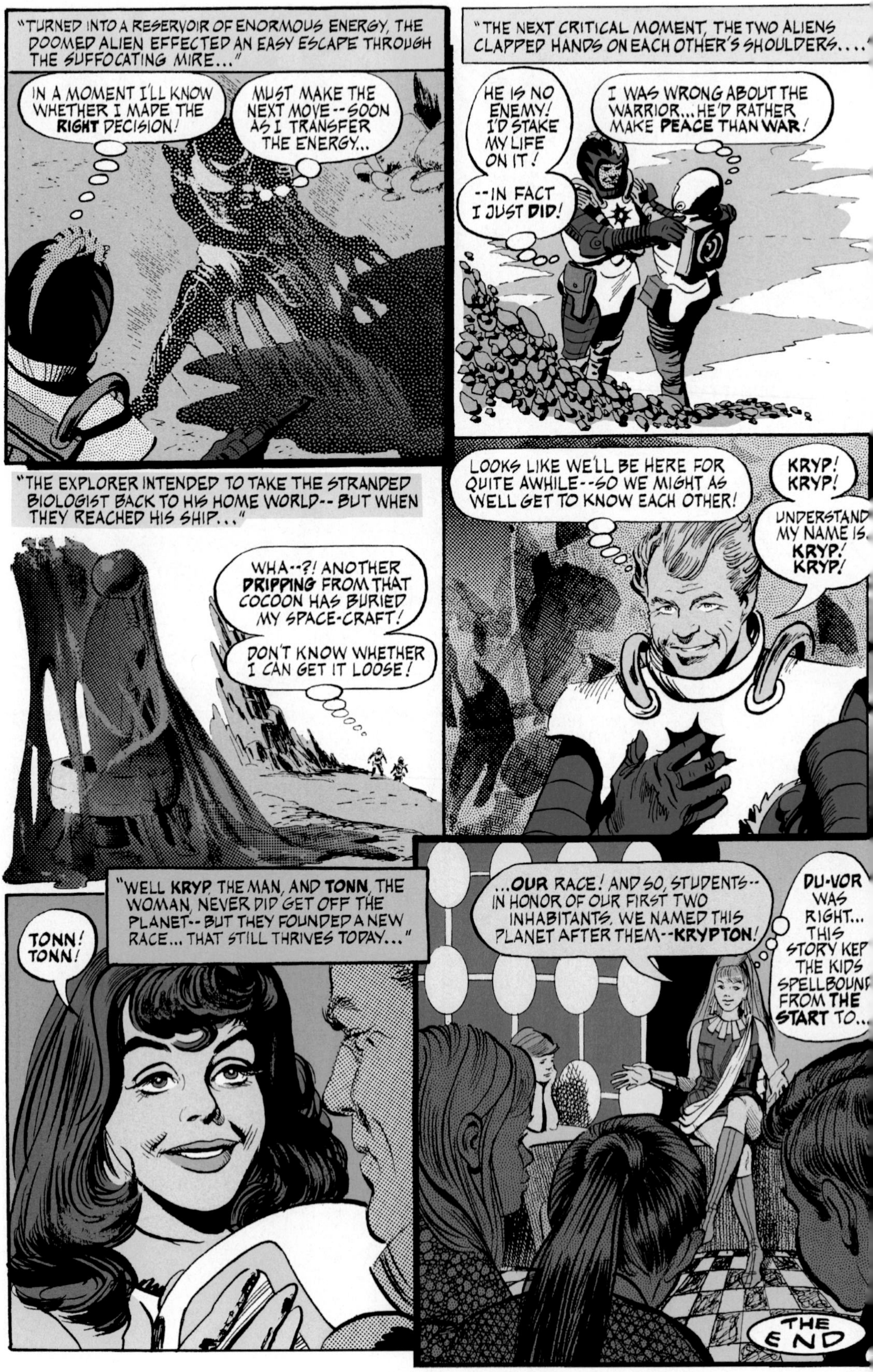
"TURNED INTO A RESERVOIR OF ENORMOUS ENERGY, THE DOOMED ALIEN EFFECTED AN EASY ESCAPE THROUGH THE SUFFOCATING MIRE..."
IN A MOMENT I'LL KNOW WHETHER I MADE THE RIGHT DECISION!
MUST MAKE THE NEXT MOVE--SOON AS I TRANSFER THE ENERGY...
"THE NEXT CRITICAL MOMENT, THE TWO ALIENS CLAPPED HANDS ON EACH OTHER'S SHOULDERS...."
HE IS NO ENEMY! I'D STAKE MY LIFE ON IT!
--IN FACT I JUST DID!
I WAS WRONG ABOUT THE WARRIOR...HE'D RATHER MAKE PEACE THAN WAR!
"THE EXPLORER INTENDED TO TAKE THE STRANDED BIOLOGIST BACK TO HIS HOME WORLD-- BUT WHEN THEY REACHED HIS SHIP..."
WHA--?! ANOTHER DRIPPING FROM THAT COCOON HAS BURIED MY SPACE-CRAFT!
DON'T KNOW WHETHER I CAN GET IT LOOSE!
LOOKS LIKE WE'LL BE HERE FOR QUITE AWHILE--SO WE MIGHT AS WELL GET TO KNOW EACH OTHER!
KRYP! KRYP!
UNDERSTAND MY NAME IS KRYP! KRYP!
TONN! TONN!
"WELL KRYP, THE MAN, AND TONN, THE WOMAN, NEVER DID GET OFF THE PLANET-- BUT THEY FOUNDED A NEW RACE... THAT STILL THRIVES TODAY..."
...OUR RACE! AND SO, STUDENTS-- IN HONOR OF OUR FIRST TWO INHABITANTS, WE NAMED THIS PLANET AFTER THEM--KRYPTON!
DU-VOR WAS RIGHT... THIS STORY KEP THE KIDS SPELLBOUN FROM THE START TO...
THE END

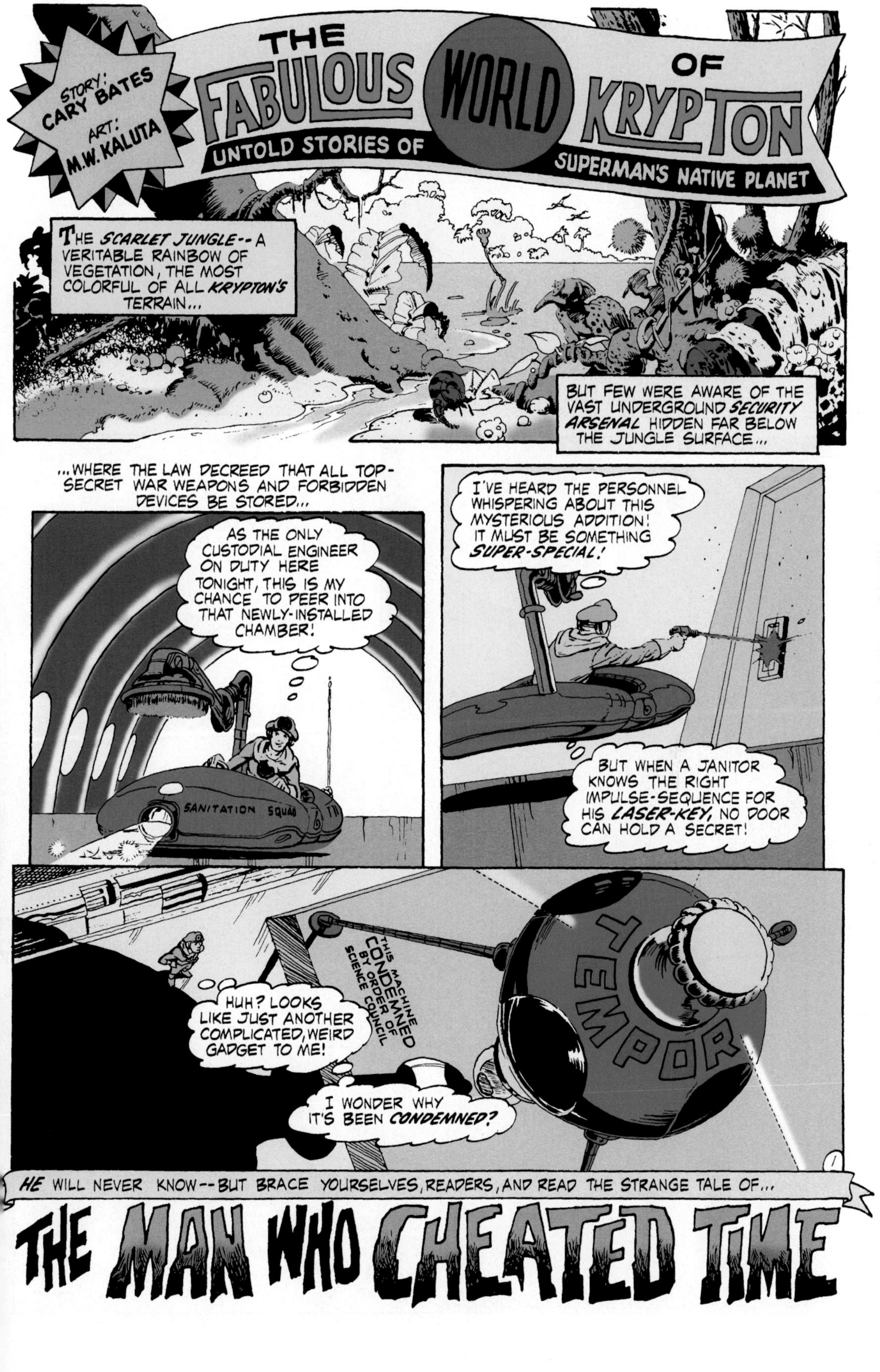
THE FABULOUS WORLD OF KRYPTON
UNTOLD STORIES OF SUPERMAN'S NATIVE PLANET
STORY: CARY BATES
ART: M.W. KALUTA
THE SCARLET JUNGLE-- A VERITABLE RAINBOW OF VEGETATION, THE MOST COLORFUL OF ALL KRYPTON'S TERRAIN...
BUT FEW WERE AWARE OF THE VAST UNDERGROUND SECURITY ARSENAL HIDDEN FAR BELOW THE JUNGLE SURFACE...
...WHERE THE LAW DECREED THAT ALL TOP-SECRET WAR WEAPONS AND FORBIDDEN DEVICES BE STORED...
AS THE ONLY CUSTODIAL ENGINEER ON DUTY HERE TONIGHT, THIS IS MY CHANCE TO PEER INTO THAT NEWLY-INSTALLED CHAMBER!
SANITATION SQUAD
I'VE HEARD THE PERSONNEL WHISPERING ABOUT THIS MYSTERIOUS ADDITION! IT MUST BE SOMETHING SUPER-SPECIAL!
BUT WHEN A JANITOR KNOWS THE RIGHT IMPULSE-SEQUENCE FOR HIS LASER-KEY, NO DOOR CAN HOLD A SECRET!
THIS MACHINE CONDEMNED BY ORDER OF SCIENCE COUNCIL
TEMPOR
HUH? LOOKS LIKE JUST ANOTHER COMPLICATED, WEIRD GADGET TO ME!
I WONDER WHY IT'S BEEN CONDEMNED?
1
HE WILL NEVER KNOW--BUT BRACE YOURSELVES, READERS, AND READ THE STRANGE TALE OF...
THE MAN WHO CHEATED TIME

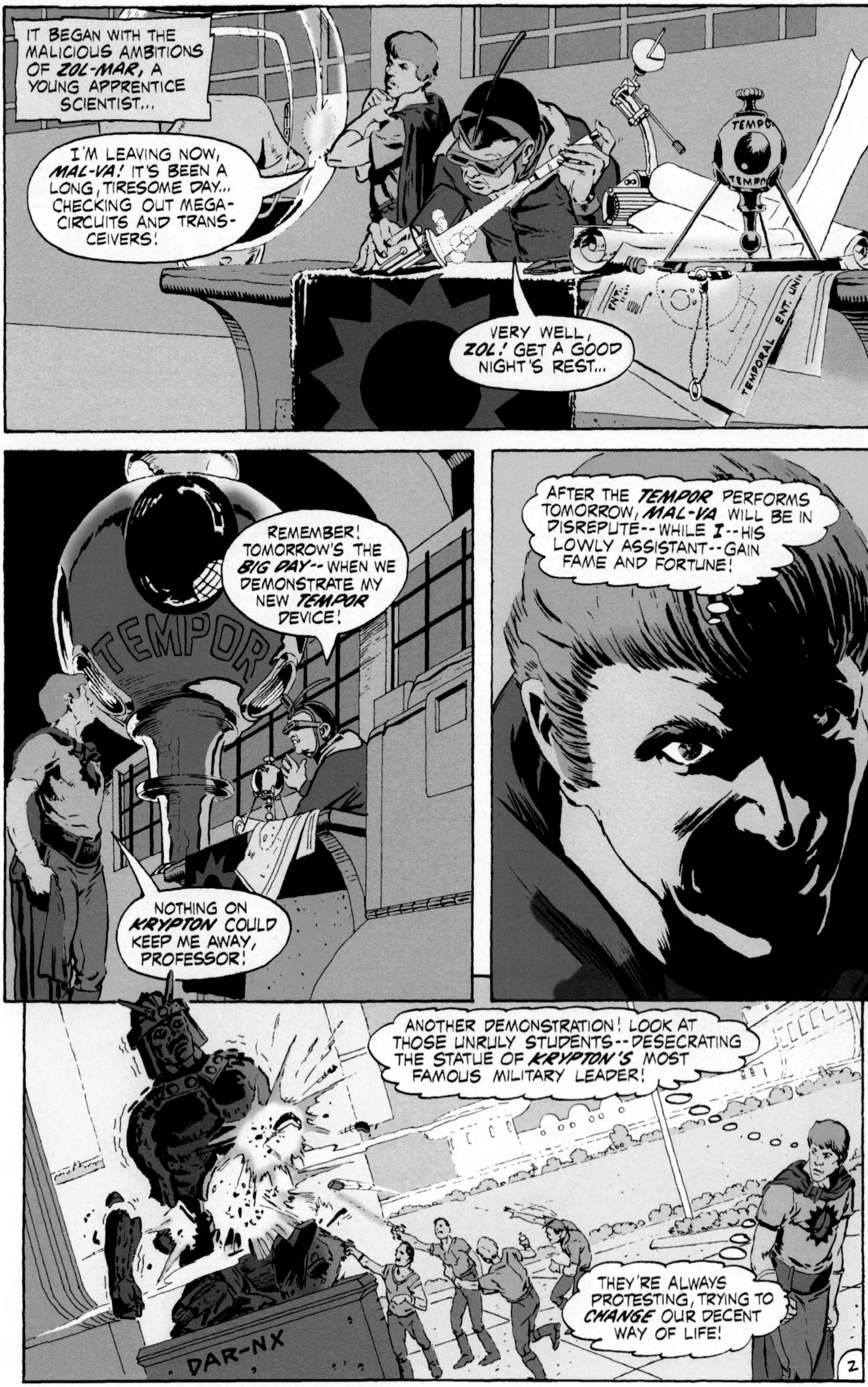
IT BEGAN WITH THE MALICIOUS AMBITIONS OF ZOL-MAR, A YOUNG APPRENTICE SCIENTIST...
I'M LEAVING NOW, MAL-VA! IT'S BEEN A LONG, TIRESOME DAY... CHECKING OUT MEGA-CIRCUITS AND TRANS-CEIVERS!
TEMPOR
VERY WELL, ZOL! GET A GOOD NIGHT'S REST...
TEMPORAL ENT. UNI
REMEMBER! TOMORROW'S THE BIG DAY-- WHEN WE DEMONSTRATE MY NEW TEMPOR DEVICE!
TEMPOR
NOTHING ON KRYPTON COULD KEEP ME AWAY, PROFESSOR!
AFTER THE TEMPOR PERFORMS TOMORROW, MAL-VA WILL BE IN DISREPUTE--WHILE I--HIS LOWLY ASSISTANT--GAIN FAME AND FORTUNE!
ANOTHER DEMONSTRATION! LOOK AT THOSE UNRULY STUDENTS--DESECRATING THE STATUE OF KRYPTON'S MOST FAMOUS MILITARY LEADER!
DAR-NX
THEY'RE ALWAYS PROTESTING, TRYING TO CHANGE OUR DECENT WAY OF LIFE!
2

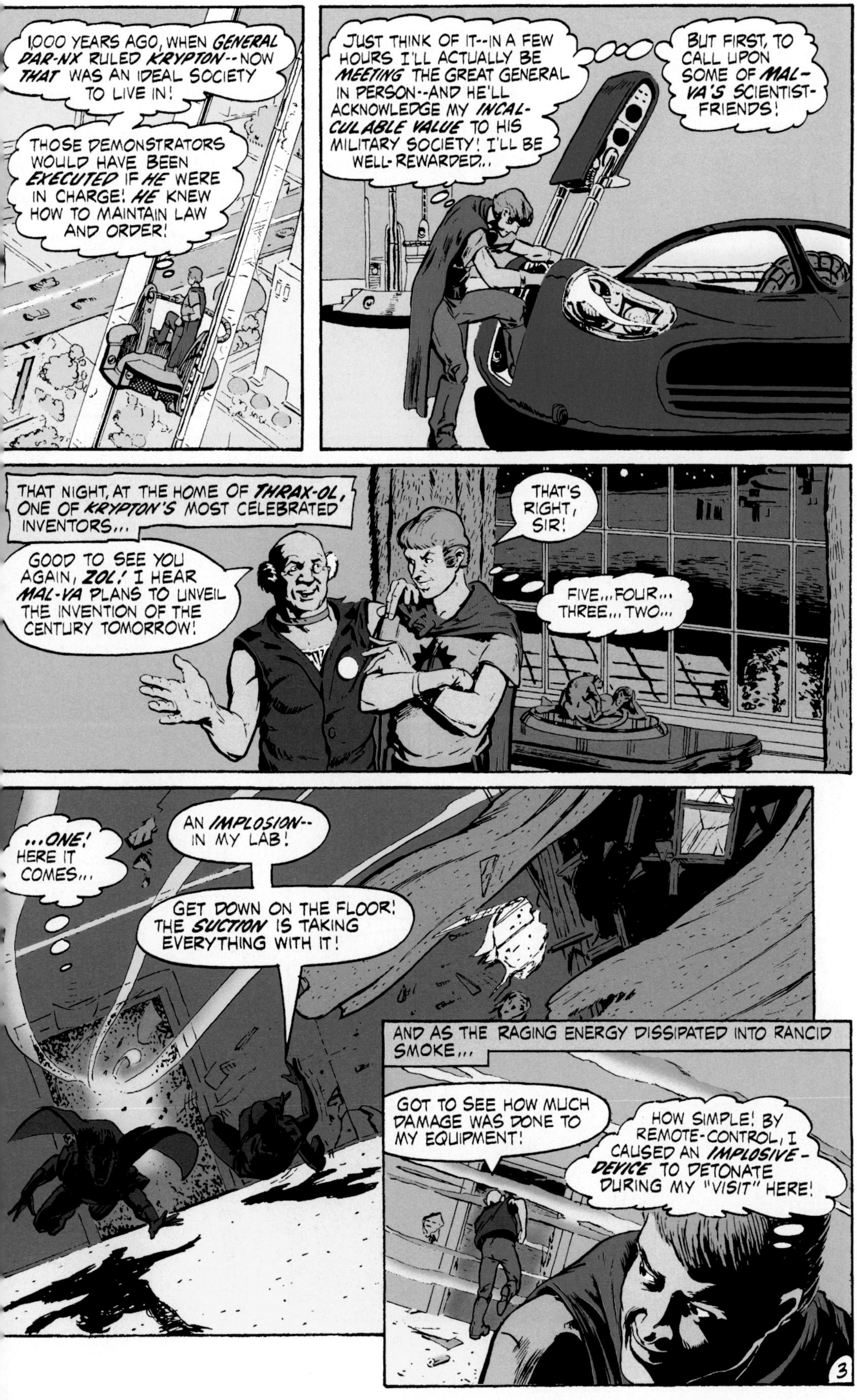

1,000 YEARS AGO, WHEN GENERAL DAR-NX RULED KRYPTON--NOW THAT WAS AN IDEAL SOCIETY TO LIVE IN!
THOSE DEMONSTRATORS WOULD HAVE BEEN EXECUTED IF HE WERE IN CHARGE! HE KNEW HOW TO MAINTAIN LAW AND ORDER!
JUST THINK OF IT--IN A FEW HOURS I'LL ACTUALLY BE MEETING THE GREAT GENERAL IN PERSON--AND HE'LL ACKNOWLEDGE MY INCALCULABLE VALUE TO HIS MILITARY SOCIETY! I'LL BE WELL-REWARDED...
BUT FIRST, TO CALL UPON SOME OF MAL-VA'S SCIENTIST-FRIENDS!
THAT NIGHT, AT THE HOME OF THRAX-OL, ONE OF KRYPTON'S MOST CELEBRATED INVENTORS...
GOOD TO SEE YOU AGAIN, ZOL! I HEAR MAL-VA PLANS TO UNVEIL THE INVENTION OF THE CENTURY TOMORROW!
THAT'S RIGHT, SIR!
FIVE...FOUR... THREE...TWO...
...ONE! HERE IT COMES...
AN IMPLOSION--IN MY LAB!
GET DOWN ON THE FLOOR! THE SUCTION IS TAKING EVERYTHING WITH IT!
AND AS THE RAGING ENERGY DISSIPATED INTO RANCID SMOKE...
GOT TO SEE HOW MUCH DAMAGE WAS DONE TO MY EQUIPMENT!
HOW SIMPLE! BY REMOTE-CONTROL, I CAUSED AN IMPLOSIVE-DEVICE TO DETONATE DURING MY "VISIT" HERE!
3

IT'S THE *DIVERSION* I NEED TO STEAL HIS *ILLUSICON*--A THEFT *THRAX-OL* WON'T EVEN KNOW HAS OCCURRED...

ILLUSICON PROTOTYPE

...UNTIL TOO LATE!

WITH THIS INVENTION IT'S POSSIBLE TO ALTER THE APPEARANCE OF ANY SOLID OBJECT BY PURE THOUGHT!

I'M TRANSFORMING THIS PIECE OF POTTERY INTO A *PSEUDO-IMAGE* OF THE *ILLUSICON!*

WHEN *THRAX-OL* DISCOVERS THE SWITCH, I'LL BE *FAR GONE!*

THEN, AT THE LABORATORY OF *KRYPTON'S* FOREMOST METEOROLOGIST...

OF COURSE YOU CAN BORROW MY MINIATURE *WEATHER-REGULATOR*, *MAL-VA!* IT'S THE LEAST I CAN DO FOR ALL THE SCIENTIFIC HELP YOU'VE GIVEN ME!

BUT SURPRISINGLY, IN THE DARKNESS OUTSIDE...

IT WORKED TO PERFECTION! I SIMPLY USED THE *ILLUSICON* TO MAKE MYSELF LOOK LIKE PROFESSOR *MAL-VA!*

ONE MORE STOP... AND I'LL BE READY FOR THE MOST WONDERFUL DAY OF MY LIFE!

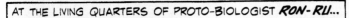

AT THE LIVING QUARTERS OF PROTO-BIOLOGIST *RON-RU...*

...I'D BETTER TUNE OUT NOW... MY *DOOR-BLINKER* IS FLASHING!

UNTIL LATER, RON!

MAL-VA! WHAT A SURPRISE!

GREETINGS, *RON!* MAY I COME IN? I HAVE A SPECIAL FAVOR TO ASK OF YOU!

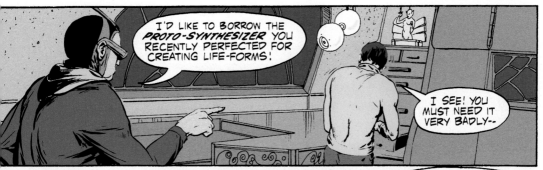

I'D LIKE TO BORROW THE *PROTO-SYNTHESIZER* YOU RECENTLY PERFECTED FOR CREATING LIFE-FORMS!

I SEE! YOU MUST NEED IT VERY BADLY--

--WHOEVER YOU ARE! YOU *CAN'T* BE *MAL-VA*-- BECAUSE I WAS TALKING TO HIM ON THE *VISI-PHONE* WHEN YOU WERE AT MY DOOR!

I'M TURNING YOU OVER TO THE *SECURITY POLICE!*

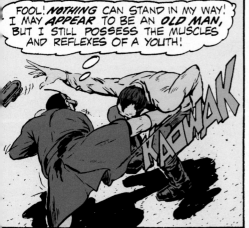

FOOL! *NOTHING* CAN STAND IN MY WAY! I MAY *APPEAR* TO BE AN *OLD MAN,* BUT I STILL POSSESS THE MUSCLES AND REFLEXES OF A YOUTH!

KA-WAK

THEN, TO KEEP HIS DECEPTION A SECRET...

NO! DON'T KILL-- UNNGH!

YOU LEAVE ME NO CHOICE!

ZZZZZ

I'VE GOT AN IMPORTANT TRIP TO TAKE TOMORROW!

ATER...

WITH THIS *PROTO-SYNTHESIZER,* I'LL BE ABLE TO CREATE ANY SPECIES OF LIFE! WITH THE *WEATHER-REGULATOR,* I CAN CONTROL THE CLIMATE! WITH THE *ILLUSICON,* I CAN MAKE DUPLICATES OF ANY OBJECT!

1000 YEARS AGO THESE INVENTIONS WERE *UNDREAMED* OF! BACK IN *DAR-NX'S* TIME I'LL BE ACCLAIMED A SCIENTIFIC WIZARD! I'LL BE THE GENERAL'S RIGHT-HAND MAN!

THIS IS MY *LAST NIGHT* AS AN INSIGNIFICANT NOBODY!

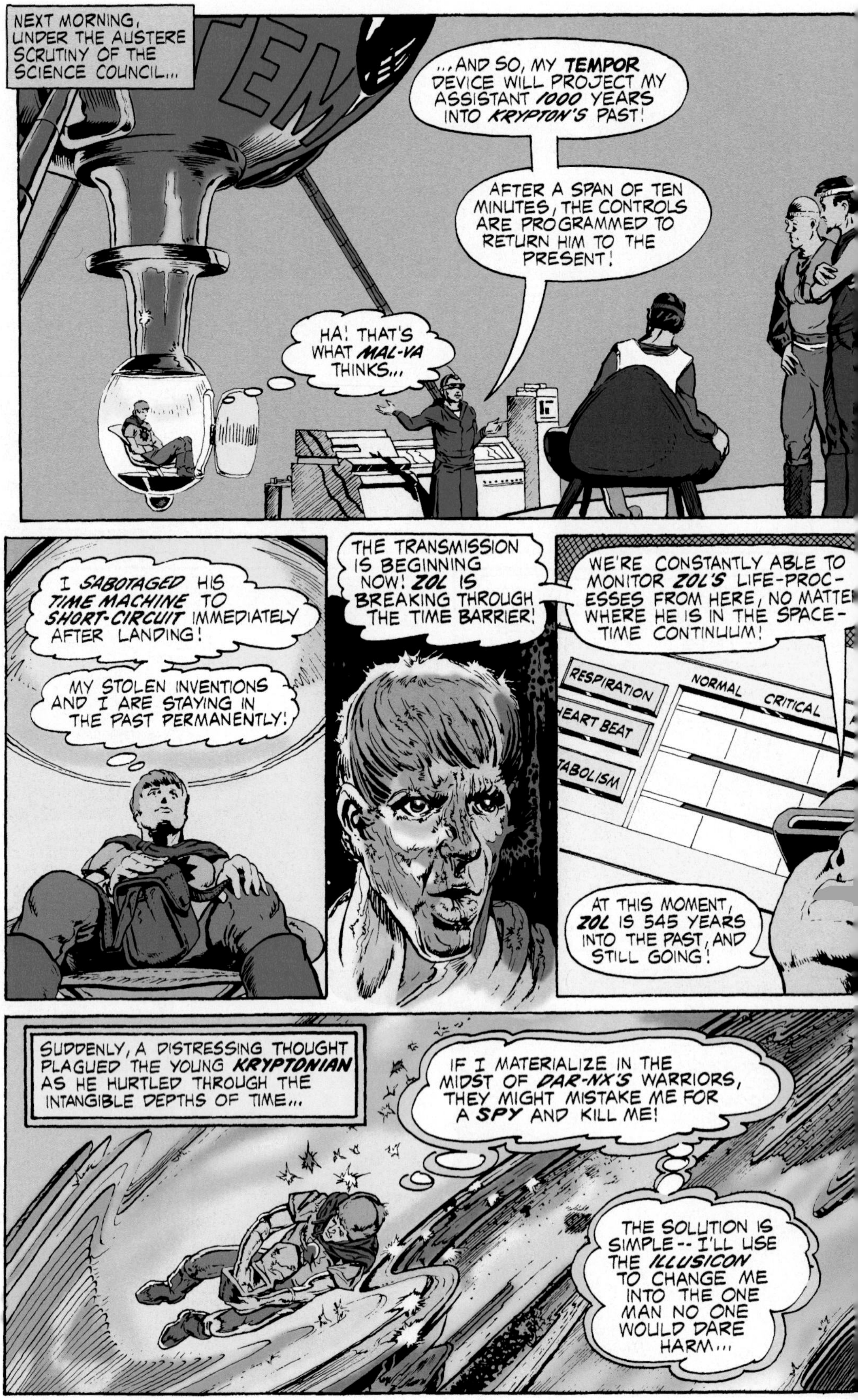
NEXT MORNING, UNDER THE AUSTERE SCRUTINY OF THE SCIENCE COUNCIL...
...AND SO, MY TEMPOR DEVICE WILL PROJECT MY ASSISTANT 1000 YEARS INTO KRYPTON'S PAST!
AFTER A SPAN OF TEN MINUTES, THE CONTROLS ARE PROGRAMMED TO RETURN HIM TO THE PRESENT!
HA! THAT'S WHAT MAL-VA THINKS...
I SABOTAGED HIS TIME MACHINE TO SHORT-CIRCUIT IMMEDIATELY AFTER LANDING!
MY STOLEN INVENTIONS AND I ARE STAYING IN THE PAST PERMANENTLY!
THE TRANSMISSION IS BEGINNING NOW! ZOL IS BREAKING THROUGH THE TIME BARRIER!
WE'RE CONSTANTLY ABLE TO MONITOR ZOL'S LIFE-PROCESSES FROM HERE, NO MATTE WHERE HE IS IN THE SPACE-TIME CONTINUUM!
RESPIRATION
NORMAL
CRITICAL
EART BEAT
TABOLISM
AT THIS MOMENT, ZOL IS 545 YEARS INTO THE PAST, AND STILL GOING!
SUDDENLY, A DISTRESSING THOUGHT PLAGUED THE YOUNG KRYPTONIAN AS HE HURTLED THROUGH THE INTANGIBLE DEPTHS OF TIME...
IF I MATERIALIZE IN THE MIDST OF DAR-NX'S WARRIORS, THEY MIGHT MISTAKE ME FOR A SPY AND KILL ME!
THE SOLUTION IS SIMPLE -- I'LL USE THE ILLUSICON TO CHANGE ME INTO THE ONE MAN NO ONE WOULD DARE HARM...

GENERAL DAR-NX himself! I'll have nothing to worry about when my time-trip ends!

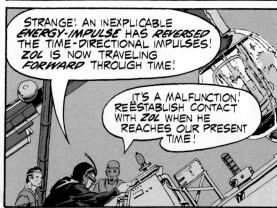

HOWEVER, AT THE SPLIT-SECOND *ZOL* FIRED THE *ILLUSICON*...

STRANGE! AN INEXPLICABLE ENERGY-IMPULSE HAS REVERSED THE TIME-DIRECTIONAL IMPULSES! ZOL IS NOW TRAVELING FORWARD THROUGH TIME!

IT'S A MALFUNCTION! REËSTABLISH CONTACT WITH ZOL WHEN HE REACHES OUR PRESENT TIME!

AS THE CRUCIAL SECONDS TICKED BY...

SOMETHING'S WRONG! I CAN'T BRING ZOL BACK!

HE'S ALREADY PASSED US BY... GONE 2 YEARS INTO THE FUTURE!

MOMENTS LATER, THE TIME MACHINE SMOKED AND FIZZLED--ONLY THE *LIFE-MONITORS* STILL OPERATED, REVEALING A GRIM FATE...

FATAL

YOUR MACHINE IS FAULTY, MAL-VA! THE READINGS SHOW THAT ZOL IS DEAD-- 5 YEARS FROM NOW IN KRYPTON'S FUTURE!

YOUR INVENTION IS HEREBY CONDEMNED! IT IS OUR DECISION THAT HENCEFORTH ALL TIME-TRAVEL EXPERIMENTATION BE FORBIDDEN!

NOT THE *SCIENCE COUNCIL*-- NOT *MAL-VA*-- NOR ANYONE ELSE SUSPECTED THE HORRIBLE TRUTH... THAT 5 YEARS IN THE FUTURE, WHEN "ZOL" MATERIALIZED...

THERE WAS *NO* PLANET TO LAND ON! *KRYPTON* HAD EXPLODED ONE DAY BEFORE HIS JOURNEY ENDED!

The End

7

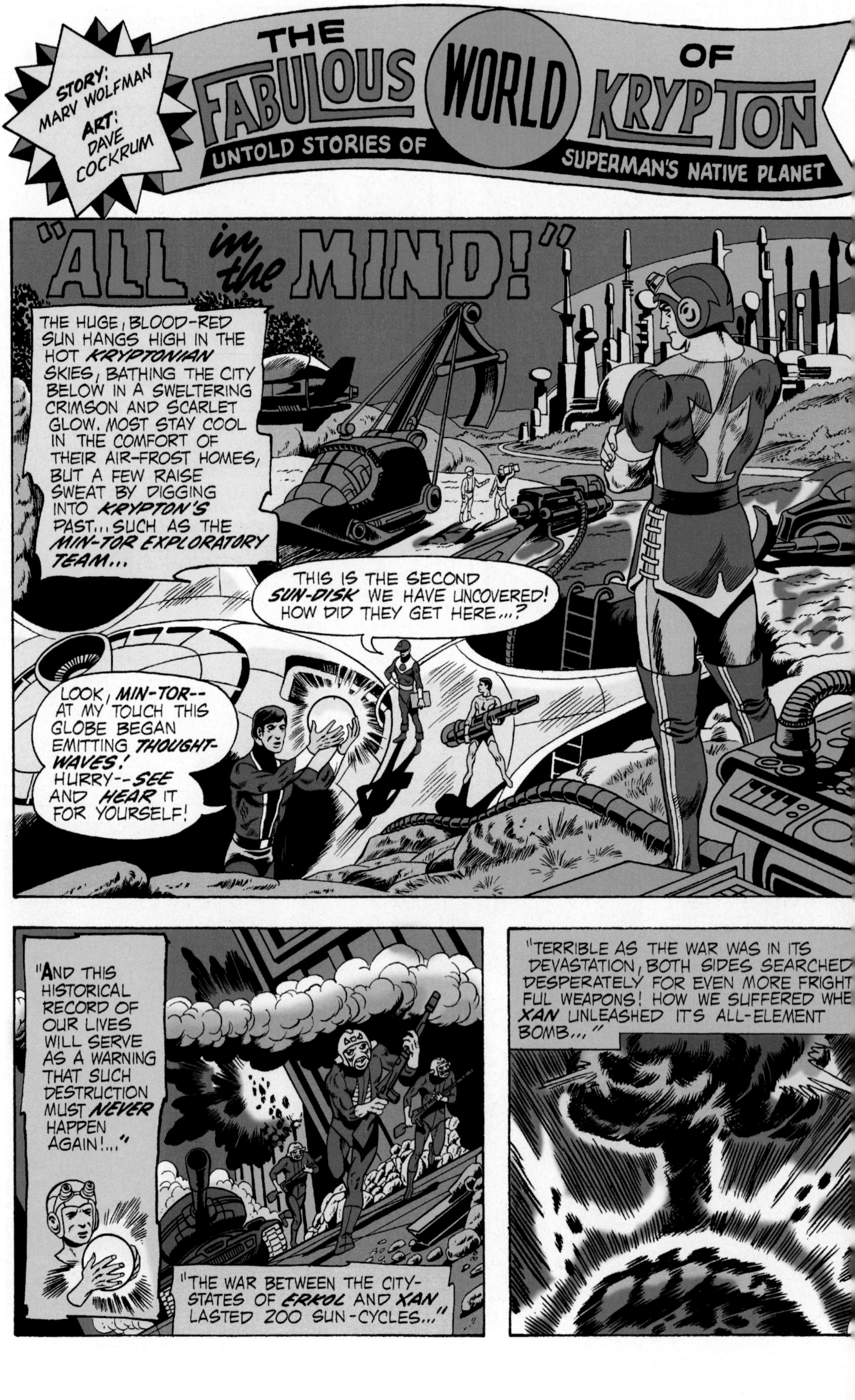
STORY: MARV WOLFMAN
ART: DAVE COCKRUM
THE FABULOUS WORLD OF KRYPTON
UNTOLD STORIES OF SUPERMAN'S NATIVE PLANET
"ALL in the MIND!"
THE HUGE, BLOOD-RED SUN HANGS HIGH IN THE HOT KRYPTONIAN SKIES, BATHING THE CITY BELOW IN A SWELTERING CRIMSON AND SCARLET GLOW. MOST STAY COOL IN THE COMFORT OF THEIR AIR-FROST HOMES, BUT A FEW RAISE SWEAT BY DIGGING INTO KRYPTON'S PAST...SUCH AS THE MIN-TOR EXPLORATORY TEAM...
THIS IS THE SECOND SUN-DISK WE HAVE UNCOVERED! HOW DID THEY GET HERE...?
LOOK, MIN-TOR-- AT MY TOUCH THIS GLOBE BEGAN EMITTING THOUGHT-WAVES! HURRY--SEE AND HEAR IT FOR YOURSELF!
"AND THIS HISTORICAL RECORD OF OUR LIVES WILL SERVE AS A WARNING THAT SUCH DESTRUCTION MUST NEVER HAPPEN AGAIN!..."
"THE WAR BETWEEN THE CITY-STATES OF ERKOL AND XAN LASTED 200 SUN-CYCLES..."
"TERRIBLE AS THE WAR WAS IN ITS DEVASTATION, BOTH SIDES SEARCHED DESPERATELY FOR EVEN MORE FRIGHTFUL WEAPONS! HOW WE SUFFERED WHEN XAN UNLEASHED IT'S ALL-ELEMENT BOMB...,"

BOTH SIDES HAVING GROWN WEARY, THE WAR EVENTUALLY STOPPED...NO AGREEMENT SIGNED, NO TRUCE DECLARED! SHORTLY THEREAFTER, THE HORRIBLE AFTER-EFFECTS IN *ERKOL* BECAME APPARENT..."

OBSERVE, *LAN-NU*-- OUR SON HAS NO *THUMBS!* HE WILL HAVE GREAT DIFFICULTY GRASPING OR HOLDING OBJECTS...

...AND HIS HEAD...*ENLARGED* AND DEFORMED... LIKE *ALL* BABIES CONCEIVED DURING THE *DAY OF THE BOMB!*

"AND IN DUE TIME, THE DESPAIRING PARENTS APPEALED TO THE *COUNCIL OF ELDERS...*"

LOOK AT THEM! OUR OFFSPRING! *LARGE* HEADS...AND *SMALL* BRAINS!

THEY SAY NOTHING... UNDERSTAND NOTHING!

IS THE FUTURE OF *ERKOL* TO BE PLACED IN THEIR DEFORMED HANDS?

NO--IT CANNOT BE!

SOONER OR LATER, OUR WAR WITH *XAN* WILL BE *RENEWED!* BUT WE WILL NEED MIGHTY WARRIORS, NOT *MINDLESS CREATURES!*

WHY...THEY CANNOT EVEN *HOLD* A WEAPON, LET ALONE *FIRE* ONE!

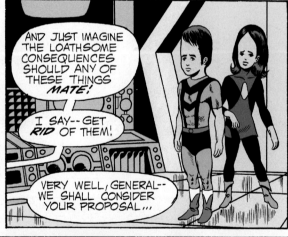

AND JUST IMAGINE THE LOATHSOME CONSEQUENCES SHOULD ANY OF THESE THINGS *MATE!*

I SAY-- GET *RID* OF THEM!

VERY WELL, GENERAL-- WE SHALL CONSIDER YOUR PROPOSAL...

"AT FIRST THERE WAS SOME PUBLIC RESISTANCE, BUT IT COLLAPSED WITH THE IMMINENT RESUMPTION OF THE WAR..."

THE COUNCIL HAS ISSUED ITS PROCLAMATION! *LET THE ROUND UP BEGIN!*

SURRENDER TO THE GOVERNMENT-- NOW!

41

"THERE WAS HATRED EVERYWHERE IN *ERKOL.* THE CHILDREN, SO NAIVE AND INNOCENT, WERE HERDED INTO STOCKADES..."

"THE COLDNESS OF THE NIGHT HUGGED THE FRIGHTENED PRISONERS IN A BLANKET OF SHIVERING MAGENTA, MOVING THEM ON TO THE MORNING OF THEIR EXILE..."

MOVE ON! AFTER TODAY WE'LL BE RID OF YOU FOREVER...*THANK RAO!*

"THE SUN-DISKS SPREAD THEIR HUNGRY FINGERS TOWARD THE SUN, GRASPING THE SOLAR POWER TO MOVE THEM ONWARDS -- OVER THE *DANDAHU OCEAN*...PAST THE *SCARLET JUNGLE* AND *FIRE-FALLS,* UNTIL THEY FINALLY CAME TO REST NEAR THE GOLDEN SEA OF *EIU...*"

"SLOWLY, FEARFULLY, THE YOUNGSTERS PUSHED THEIR 'MIS-SHAPEN' HEADS OUT INTO THEIR NEW WORLD..."

JAN-AR--WHERE ARE WE?

I DO NOT KNOW, *SALA,* BUT IT IS NOTHING LIKE THE WAR-TORN LAND OF OUR BIRTH!

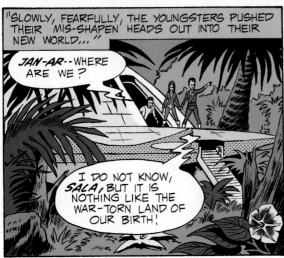

"UNKNOWN TO THE ELDERS, THE CHILDREN *WERE* ABLE TO COMMUNICATE...BUT TELE-PATHICALLY AND ONLY WITH EACH OTHER..."

HOW *BEAUTIFUL* IT IS, *JAN-AR*...GREEN PLANTS AS FAR AS THE EYE CAN SEE!

AND THE AIR, SO FRESH... THE SKY SO CLEAR...

YOU DRINK IN THE BEAUTY, *SALA*... WHILE *I* THINK ABOUT HOW TO SURVIVE HERE!

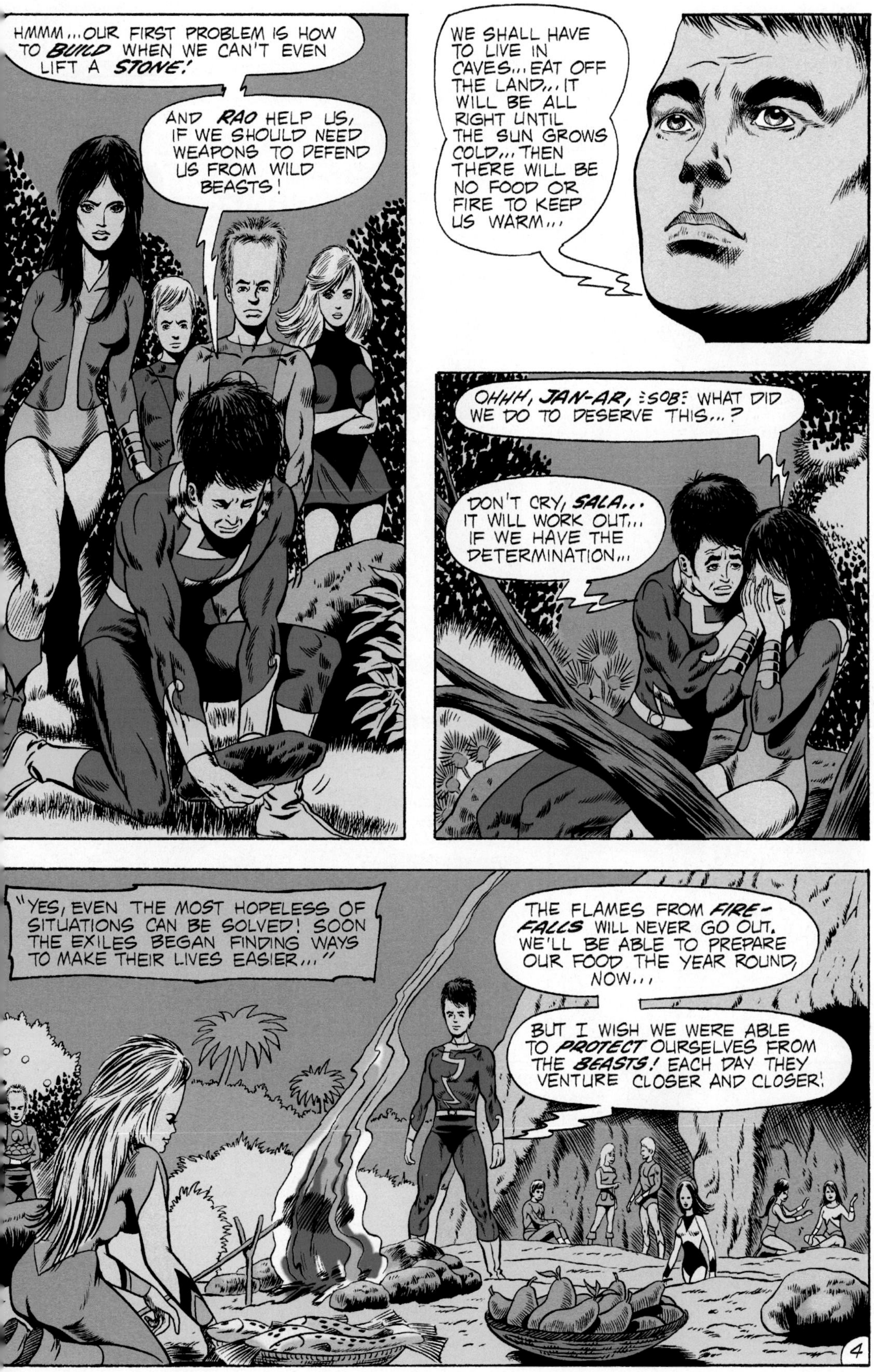
HMMM...OUR FIRST PROBLEM IS HOW TO BUILD WHEN WE CAN'T EVEN LIFT A STONE!
AND RAO HELP US, IF WE SHOULD NEED WEAPONS TO DEFEND US FROM WILD BEASTS!
WE SHALL HAVE TO LIVE IN CAVES... EAT OFF THE LAND... IT WILL BE ALL RIGHT UNTIL THE SUN GROWS COLD... THEN THERE WILL BE NO FOOD OR FIRE TO KEEP US WARM...
OHHH, JAN-AR, :SOB: WHAT DID WE DO TO DESERVE THIS...?
DON'T CRY, SALA... IT WILL WORK OUT... IF WE HAVE THE DETERMINATION...
"YES, EVEN THE MOST HOPELESS OF SITUATIONS CAN BE SOLVED! SOON THE EXILES BEGAN FINDING WAYS TO MAKE THEIR LIVES EASIER..."
THE FLAMES FROM FIRE-FALLS WILL NEVER GO OUT. WE'LL BE ABLE TO PREPARE OUR FOOD THE YEAR ROUND, NOW...
BUT I WISH WE WERE ABLE TO PROTECT OURSELVES FROM THE BEASTS! EACH DAY THEY VENTURE CLOSER AND CLOSER!
4

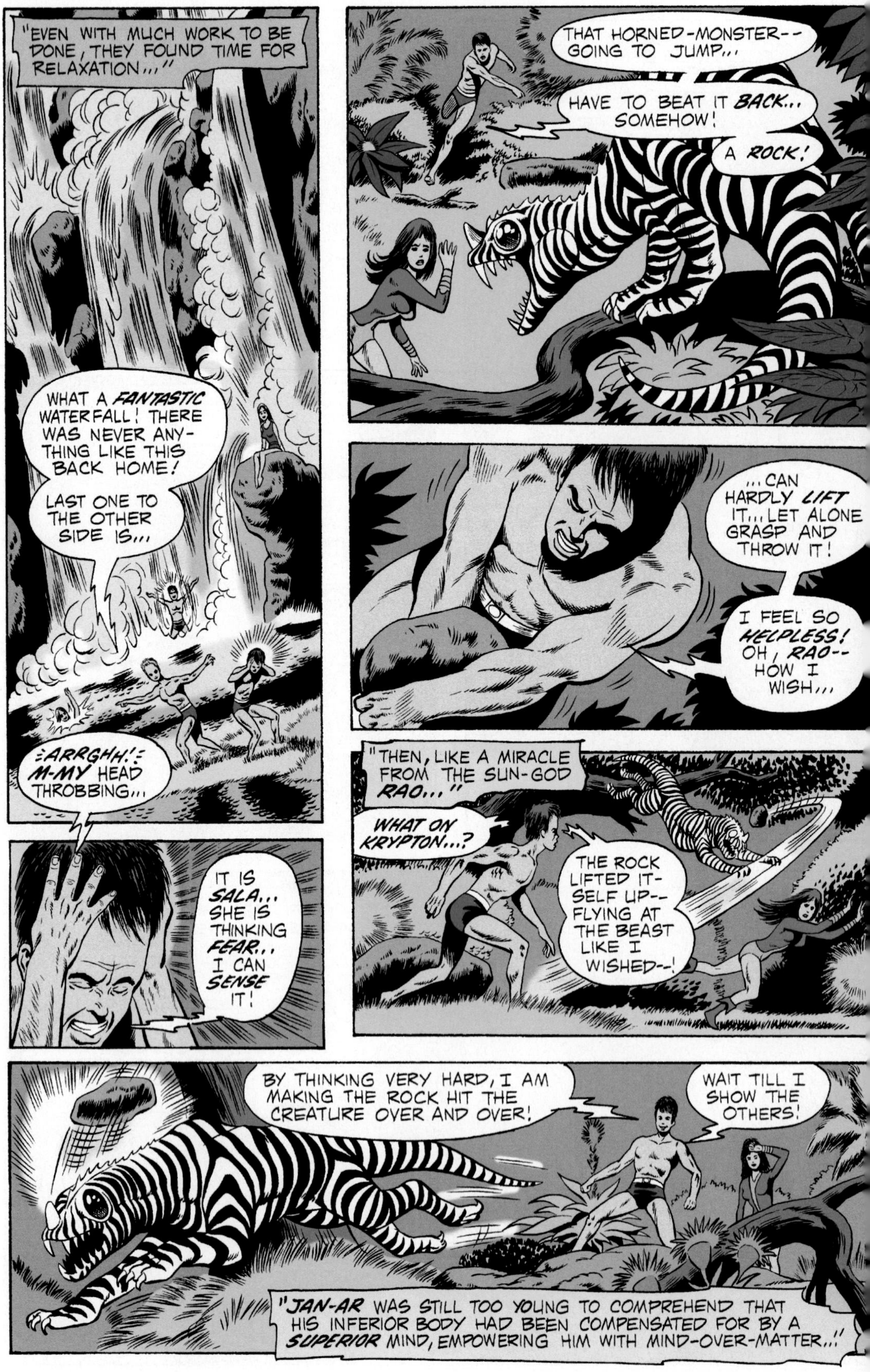

"EVEN WITH MUCH WORK TO BE DONE, THEY FOUND TIME FOR RELAXATION..."
WHAT A *FANTASTIC* WATERFALL! THERE WAS NEVER ANYTHING LIKE THIS BACK HOME!
LAST ONE TO THE OTHER SIDE IS...
ARRGHH! M-MY HEAD THROBBING...
THAT HORNED-MONSTER--GOING TO JUMP...
HAVE TO BEAT IT *BACK*... SOMEHOW!
A *ROCK!*
IT IS *SALA*... SHE IS THINKING *FEAR*... I CAN *SENSE* IT!
...CAN HARDLY *LIFT* IT... LET ALONE GRASP AND THROW IT!
I FEEL SO *HELPLESS!* OH, *RAO*--HOW I WISH...
"THEN, LIKE A MIRACLE FROM THE SUN-GOD *RAO*..."
WHAT ON KRYPTON...?
THE ROCK LIFTED ITSELF UP--FLYING AT THE BEAST LIKE I WISHED--!
BY THINKING VERY HARD, I AM MAKING THE ROCK HIT THE CREATURE OVER AND OVER!
WAIT TILL I SHOW THE OTHERS!
"*JAN-AR* WAS STILL TOO YOUNG TO COMPREHEND THAT HIS INFERIOR BODY HAD BEEN COMPENSATED FOR BY A *SUPERIOR* MIND, EMPOWERING HIM WITH MIND-OVER-MATTER...!"

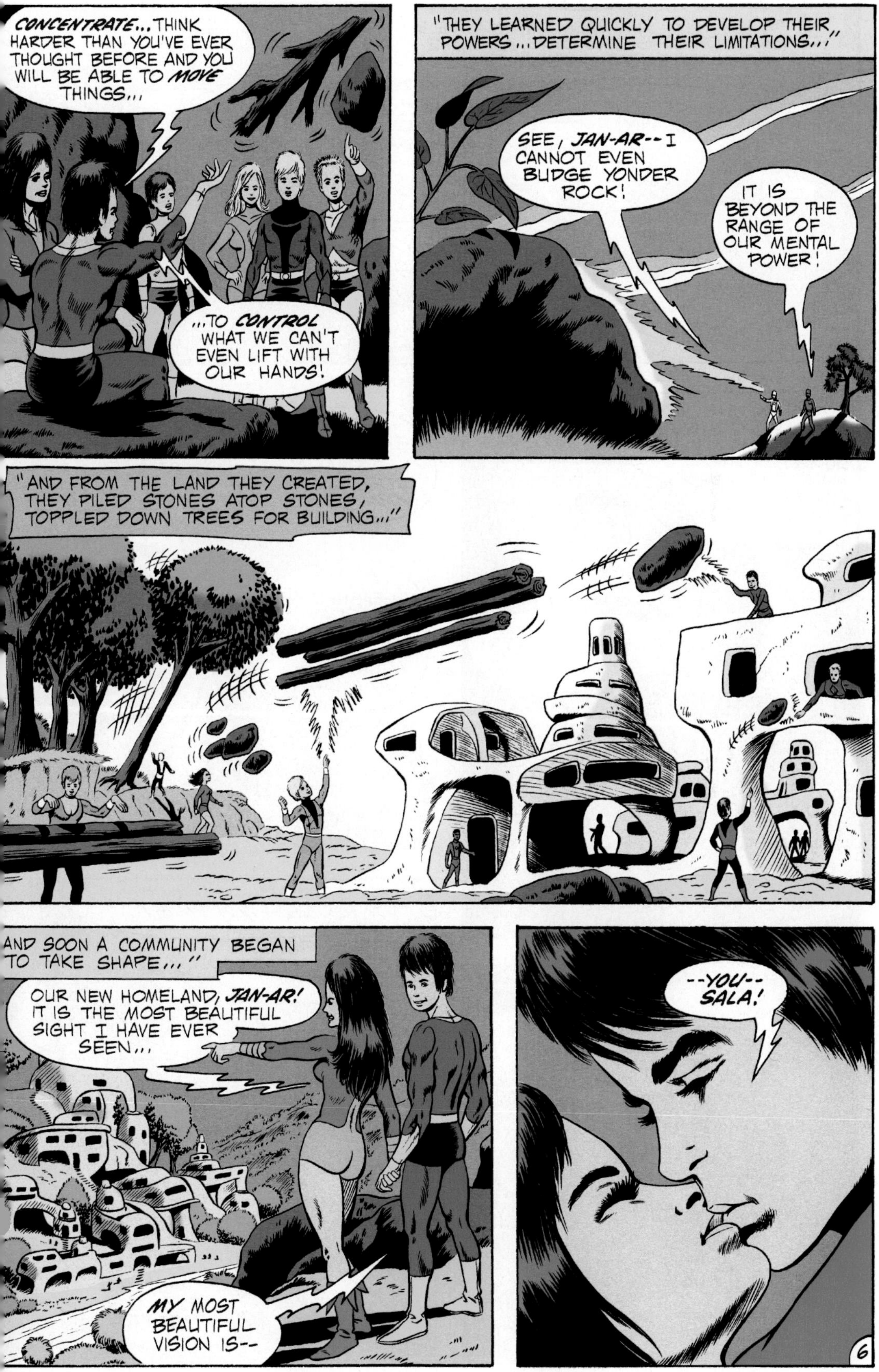
CONCENTRATE... THINK HARDER THAN YOU'VE EVER THOUGHT BEFORE AND YOU WILL BE ABLE TO MOVE THINGS...
...TO CONTROL WHAT WE CAN'T EVEN LIFT WITH OUR HANDS!
"THEY LEARNED QUICKLY TO DEVELOP THEIR POWERS...DETERMINE THEIR LIMITATIONS..."
SEE, JAN-AR--I CANNOT EVEN BUDGE YONDER ROCK!
IT IS BEYOND THE RANGE OF OUR MENTAL POWER!
"AND FROM THE LAND THEY CREATED, THEY PILED STONES ATOP STONES, TOPPLED DOWN TREES FOR BUILDING..."
AND SOON A COMMUNITY BEGAN TO TAKE SHAPE..."
OUR NEW HOMELAND, JAN-AR! IT IS THE MOST BEAUTIFUL SIGHT I HAVE EVER SEEN...
MY MOST BEAUTIFUL VISION IS--
--YOU--SALA!
6

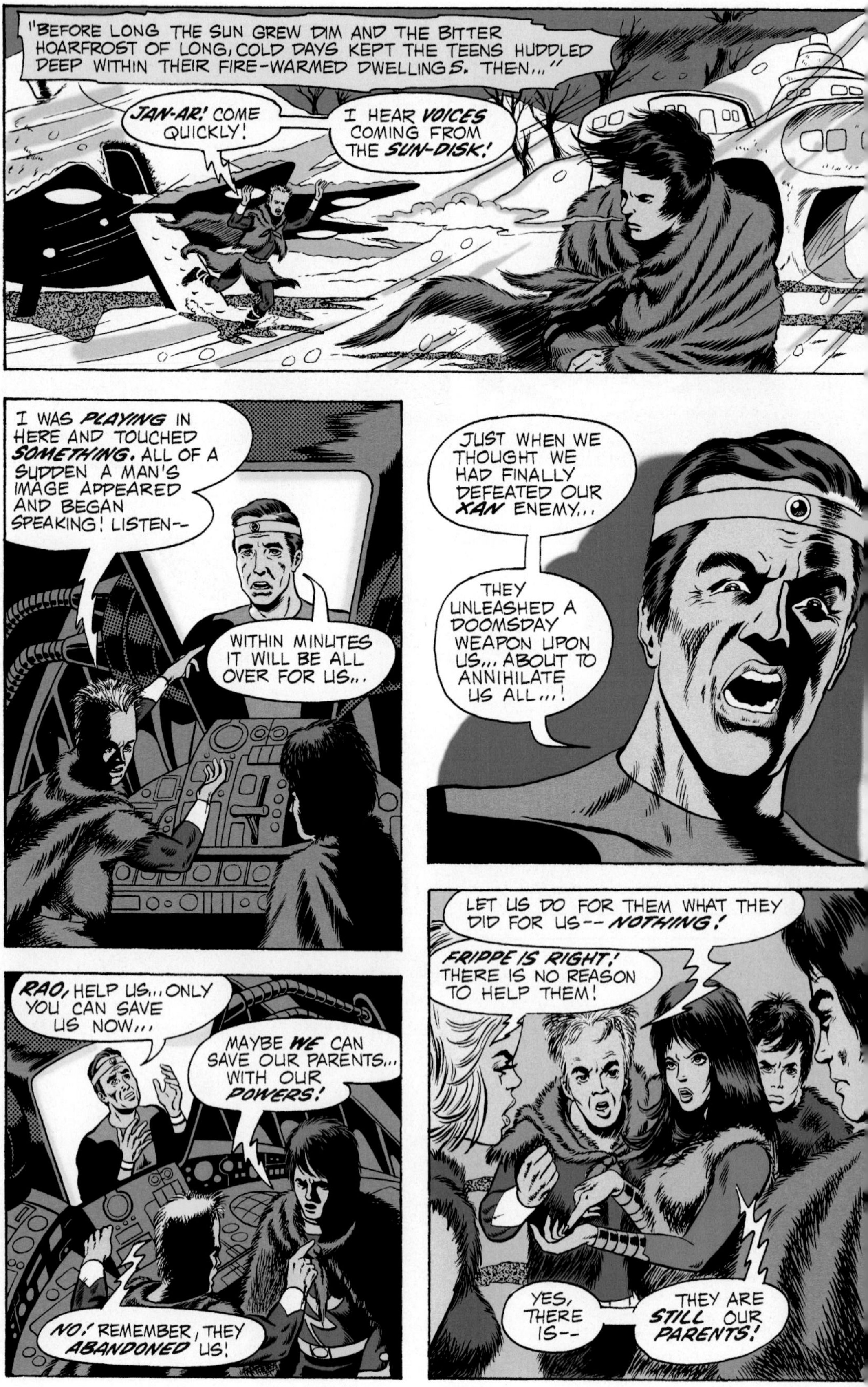

"BEFORE LONG THE SUN GREW DIM AND THE BITTER HOARFROST OF LONG, COLD DAYS KEPT THE TEENS HUDDLED DEEP WITHIN THEIR FIRE-WARMED DWELLINGS. THEN..."
JAN-AR! COME QUICKLY!
I HEAR VOICES COMING FROM THE SUN-DISK!
I WAS PLAYING IN HERE AND TOUCHED SOMETHING. ALL OF A SUDDEN A MAN'S IMAGE APPEARED AND BEGAN SPEAKING! LISTEN--
WITHIN MINUTES IT WILL BE ALL OVER FOR US...
JUST WHEN WE THOUGHT WE HAD FINALLY DEFEATED OUR XAN ENEMY...
THEY UNLEASHED A DOOMSDAY WEAPON UPON US... ABOUT TO ANNIHILATE US ALL...!
RAO, HELP US... ONLY YOU CAN SAVE US NOW...
MAYBE WE CAN SAVE OUR PARENTS... WITH OUR POWERS!
NO! REMEMBER, THEY ABANDONED US!
LET US DO FOR THEM WHAT THEY DID FOR US-- NOTHING!
FRIPPE IS RIGHT! THERE IS NO REASON TO HELP THEM!
YES, THERE IS--
THEY ARE STILL OUR PARENTS!

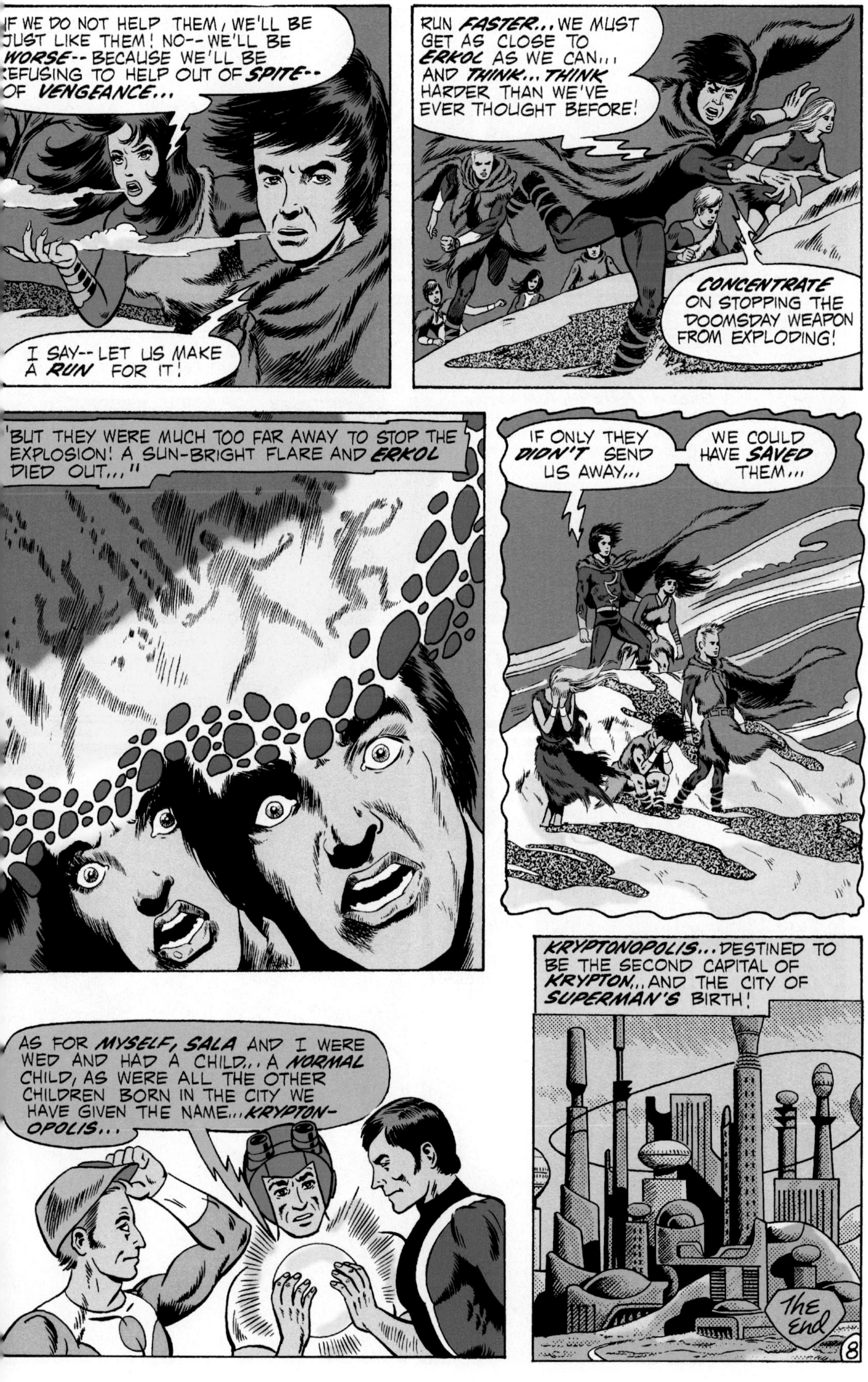
IF WE DO NOT HELP THEM, WE'LL BE JUST LIKE THEM! NO-- WE'LL BE WORSE-- BECAUSE WE'LL BE REFUSING TO HELP OUT OF SPITE-- OF VENGEANCE...
I SAY-- LET US MAKE A RUN FOR IT!
RUN FASTER... WE MUST GET AS CLOSE TO ERKOL AS WE CAN... AND THINK... THINK HARDER THAN WE'VE EVER THOUGHT BEFORE!
CONCENTRATE ON STOPPING THE DOOMSDAY WEAPON FROM EXPLODING!
"BUT THEY WERE MUCH TOO FAR AWAY TO STOP THE EXPLOSION! A SUN-BRIGHT FLARE AND ERKOL DIED OUT..."
IF ONLY THEY DIDN'T SEND US AWAY...
WE COULD HAVE SAVED THEM...
AS FOR MYSELF, SALA AND I WERE WED AND HAD A CHILD... A NORMAL CHILD, AS WERE ALL THE OTHER CHILDREN BORN IN THE CITY WE HAVE GIVEN THE NAME... KRYPTON-OPOLIS...
KRYPTONOPOLIS... DESTINED TO BE THE SECOND CAPITAL OF KRYPTON... AND THE CITY OF SUPERMAN'S BIRTH!
THE END
8

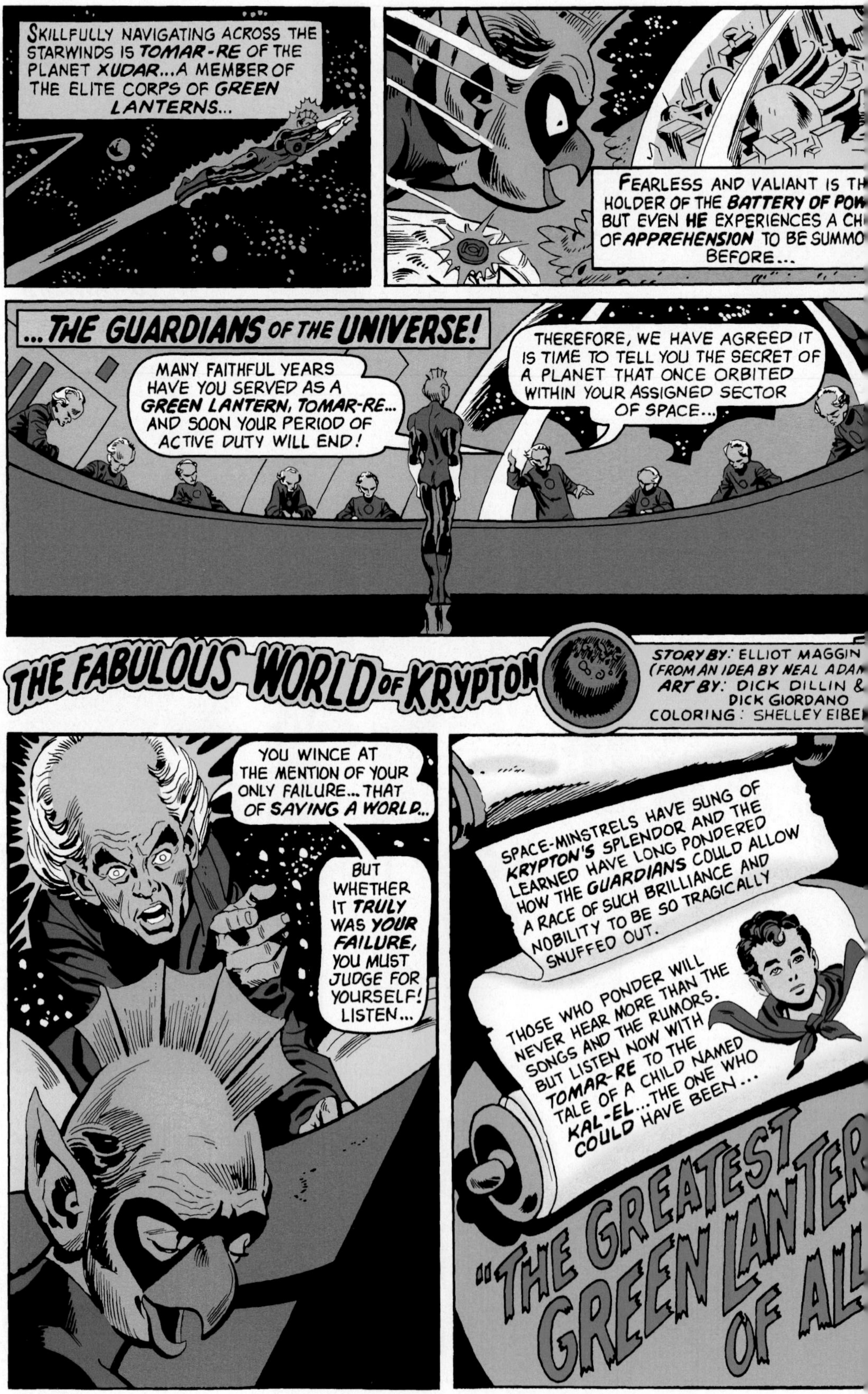
SKILLFULLY NAVIGATING ACROSS THE STARWINDS IS TOMAR-RE OF THE PLANET XUDAR...A MEMBER OF THE ELITE CORPS OF GREEN LANTERNS...
FEARLESS AND VALIANT IS TH HOLDER OF THE BATTERY OF POW BUT EVEN HE EXPERIENCES A CH OF APPREHENSION TO BE SUMMO BEFORE...
...THE GUARDIANS OF THE UNIVERSE!
MANY FAITHFUL YEARS HAVE YOU SERVED AS A GREEN LANTERN, TOMAR-RE... AND SOON YOUR PERIOD OF ACTIVE DUTY WILL END!
THEREFORE, WE HAVE AGREED IT IS TIME TO TELL YOU THE SECRET OF A PLANET THAT ONCE ORBITED WITHIN YOUR ASSIGNED SECTOR OF SPACE...
THE FABULOUS WORLD OF KRYPTON
STORY BY: ELLIOT MAGGIN
(FROM AN IDEA BY NEAL ADA
ART BY: DICK DILLIN &
DICK GIORDANO
COLORING: SHELLEY EIBE
YOU WINCE AT THE MENTION OF YOUR ONLY FAILURE... THAT OF SAVING A WORLD...
BUT WHETHER IT TRULY WAS YOUR FAILURE, YOU MUST JUDGE FOR YOURSELF! LISTEN...
SPACE-MINSTRELS HAVE SUNG OF KRYPTON'S SPLENDOR AND THE LEARNED HAVE LONG PONDERED HOW THE GUARDIANS COULD ALLOW A RACE OF SUCH BRILLIANCE AND NOBILITY TO BE SO TRAGICALLY SNUFFED OUT.
THOSE WHO PONDER WILL NEVER HEAR MORE THAN THE SONGS AND THE RUMORS. BUT LISTEN NOW WITH TOMAR-RE TO THE TALE OF A CHILD NAMED KAL-EL...THE ONE WHO COULD HAVE BEEN...
"THE GREATEST GREEN LANTER OF AL

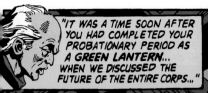

"IT WAS A TIME SOON AFTER YOU HAD COMPLETED YOUR PROBATIONARY PERIOD AS A GREEN LANTERN... WHEN WE DISCUSSED THE FUTURE OF THE ENTIRE CORPS..."

AS WE ARE IN ACCORD THAT OUR EONS-OLD EXPERIMENT OF THE GREEN LANTERN CORPS HAS BEEN COMPLETELY SUCCESSFUL--

--I MOVE TO MAKE THE CORPS INDEPENDENT OF THE GUARDIANS!

THOUGH NO CURRENT BATTERY-HOLDER HAS THE QUALITIES NECESSARY TO LEAD AND PERPETUATE SUCH AN INDEPENDENT FORCE--

--THERE SOON MAY BE SUCH AN INDIVIDUAL...

...HERE-- ON THE PLANET KRYPTON!

A SCIENTIST KNOWN AS JOR-EL HAS RECENTLY FORMED A MARRIAGE-BOND WITH A YOUNG ASTRONAUT NAMED LARA...

THE MERGING OF THEIR GENETIC BACKGROUNDS WOULD PRODUCE OFFSPRING OF AN INCOMPARABLE NATURE.

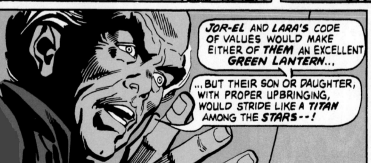

JOR-EL AND LARA'S CODE OF VALUES WOULD MAKE EITHER OF THEM AN EXCELLENT GREEN LANTERN...

...BUT THEIR SON OR DAUGHTER, WITH PROPER UPBRINGING, WOULD STRIDE LIKE A TITAN AMONG THE STARS--!

THIS WAS STRONG LANGUAGE FROM A GUARDIAN... STRONG YET TRUE...

②

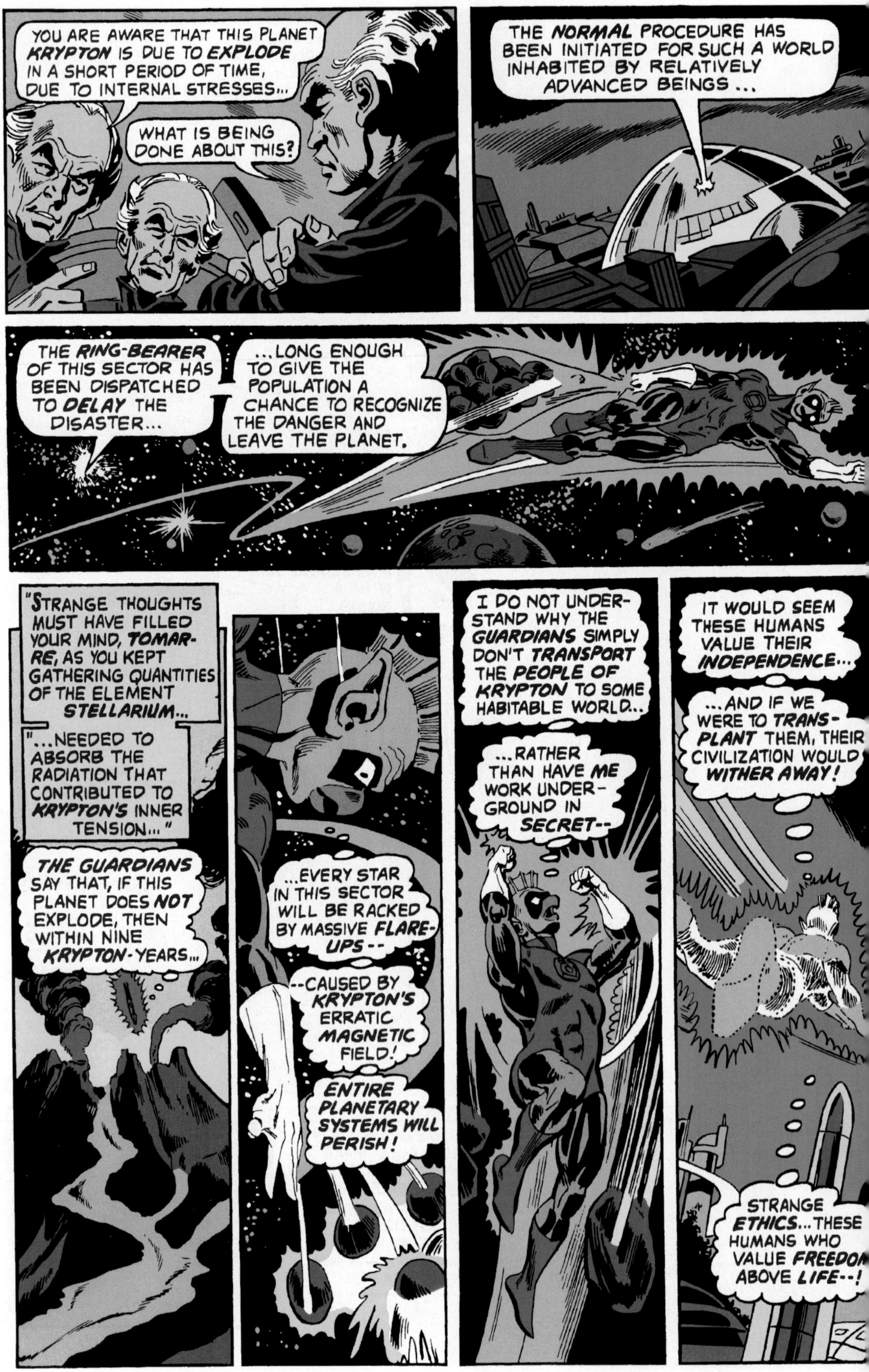
YOU ARE AWARE THAT THIS PLANET KRYPTON IS DUE TO EXPLODE IN A SHORT PERIOD OF TIME, DUE TO INTERNAL STRESSES...
WHAT IS BEING DONE ABOUT THIS?
THE NORMAL PROCEDURE HAS BEEN INITIATED FOR SUCH A WORLD INHABITED BY RELATIVELY ADVANCED BEINGS ...
THE RING-BEARER OF THIS SECTOR HAS BEEN DISPATCHED TO DELAY THE DISASTER...
...LONG ENOUGH TO GIVE THE POPULATION A CHANCE TO RECOGNIZE THE DANGER AND LEAVE THE PLANET.
"STRANGE THOUGHTS MUST HAVE FILLED YOUR MIND, TOMAR-RE, AS YOU KEPT GATHERING QUANTITIES OF THE ELEMENT STELLARIUM...
"...NEEDED TO ABSORB THE RADIATION THAT CONTRIBUTED TO KRYPTON'S INNER TENSION..."
THE GUARDIANS SAY THAT, IF THIS PLANET DOES NOT EXPLODE, THEN WITHIN NINE KRYPTON-YEARS...
...EVERY STAR IN THIS SECTOR WILL BE RACKED BY MASSIVE FLARE-UPS--
--CAUSED BY KRYPTON'S ERRATIC MAGNETIC FIELD!
ENTIRE PLANETARY SYSTEMS WILL PERISH!
I DO NOT UNDERSTAND WHY THE GUARDIANS SIMPLY DON'T TRANSPORT THE PEOPLE OF KRYPTON TO SOME HABITABLE WORLD...
...RATHER THAN HAVE ME WORK UNDERGROUND IN SECRET--
IT WOULD SEEM THESE HUMANS VALUE THEIR INDEPENDENCE...
...AND IF WE WERE TO TRANSPLANT THEM, THEIR CIVILIZATION WOULD WITHER AWAY!
STRANGE ETHICS...THESE HUMANS WHO VALUE FREEDOM ABOVE LIFE--!

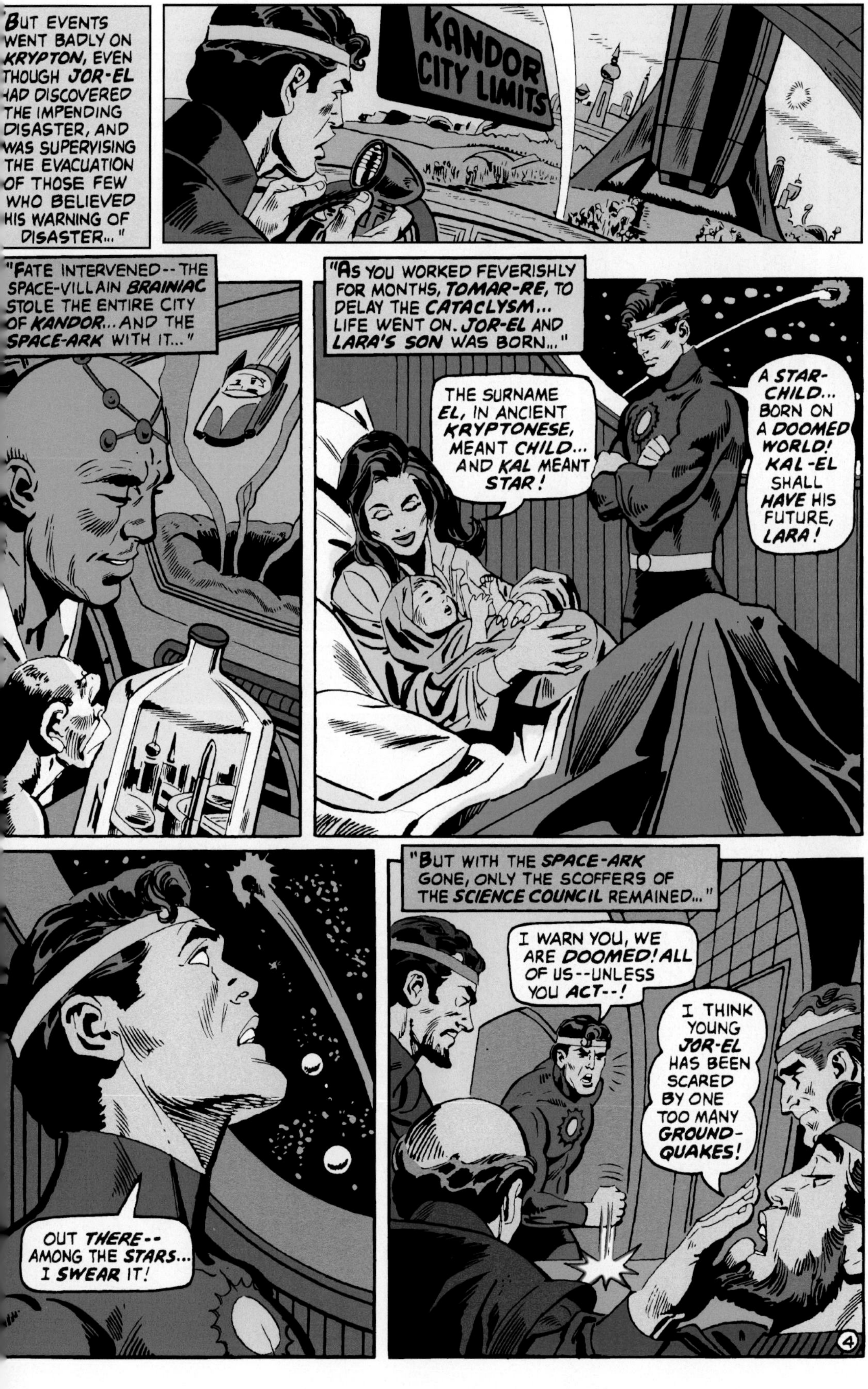
"BUT EVENTS WENT BADLY ON KRYPTON, EVEN THOUGH JOR-EL HAD DISCOVERED THE IMPENDING DISASTER, AND WAS SUPERVISING THE EVACUATION OF THOSE FEW WHO BELIEVED HIS WARNING OF DISASTER..."
KANDOR CITY LIMITS
"FATE INTERVENED -- THE SPACE-VILLAIN BRAINIAC STOLE THE ENTIRE CITY OF KANDOR... AND THE SPACE-ARK WITH IT..."
"AS YOU WORKED FEVERISHLY FOR MONTHS, TOMAR-RE, TO DELAY THE CATACLYSM... LIFE WENT ON. JOR-EL AND LARA'S SON WAS BORN..."
THE SURNAME EL, IN ANCIENT KRYPTONESE, MEANT CHILD... AND KAL MEANT STAR!
A STAR-CHILD... BORN ON A DOOMED WORLD! KAL-EL SHALL HAVE HIS FUTURE, LARA!
OUT THERE -- AMONG THE STARS... I SWEAR IT!
"BUT WITH THE SPACE-ARK GONE, ONLY THE SCOFFERS OF THE SCIENCE COUNCIL REMAINED..."
I WARN YOU, WE ARE DOOMED! ALL OF US -- UNLESS YOU ACT--!
I THINK YOUNG JOR-EL HAS BEEN SCARED BY ONE TOO MANY GROUND-QUAKES!
4

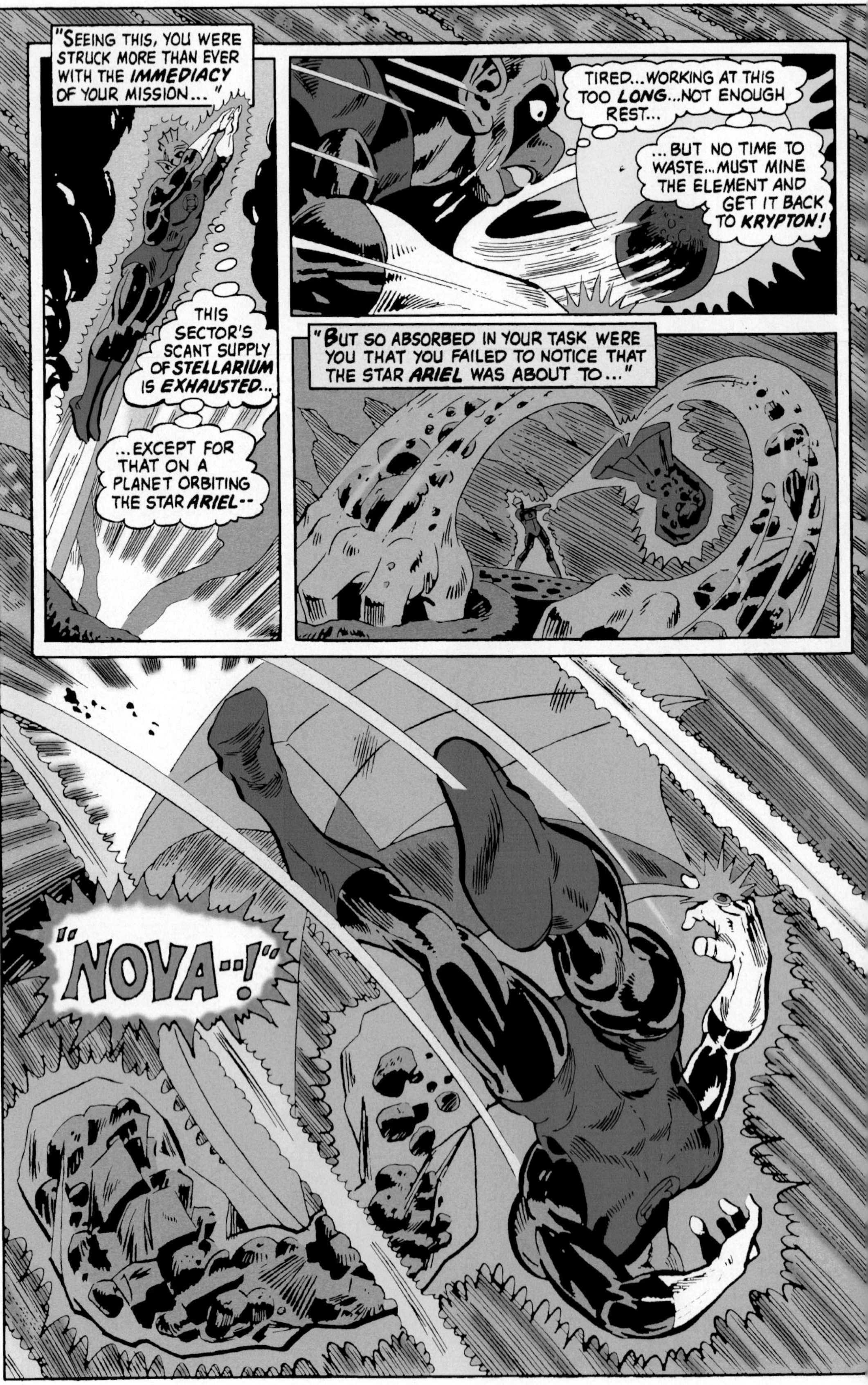
"SEEING THIS, YOU WERE STRUCK MORE THAN EVER WITH THE IMMEDIACY OF YOUR MISSION..."
THIS SECTOR'S SCANT SUPPLY OF STELLARIUM IS EXHAUSTED...
...EXCEPT FOR THAT ON A PLANET ORBITING THE STAR ARIEL--
TIRED...WORKING AT THIS TOO LONG...NOT ENOUGH REST...
...BUT NO TIME TO WASTE...MUST MINE THE ELEMENT AND GET IT BACK TO KRYPTON!
"BUT SO ABSORBED IN YOUR TASK WERE YOU THAT YOU FAILED TO NOTICE THAT THE STAR ARIEL WAS ABOUT TO..."
"NOVA--!"

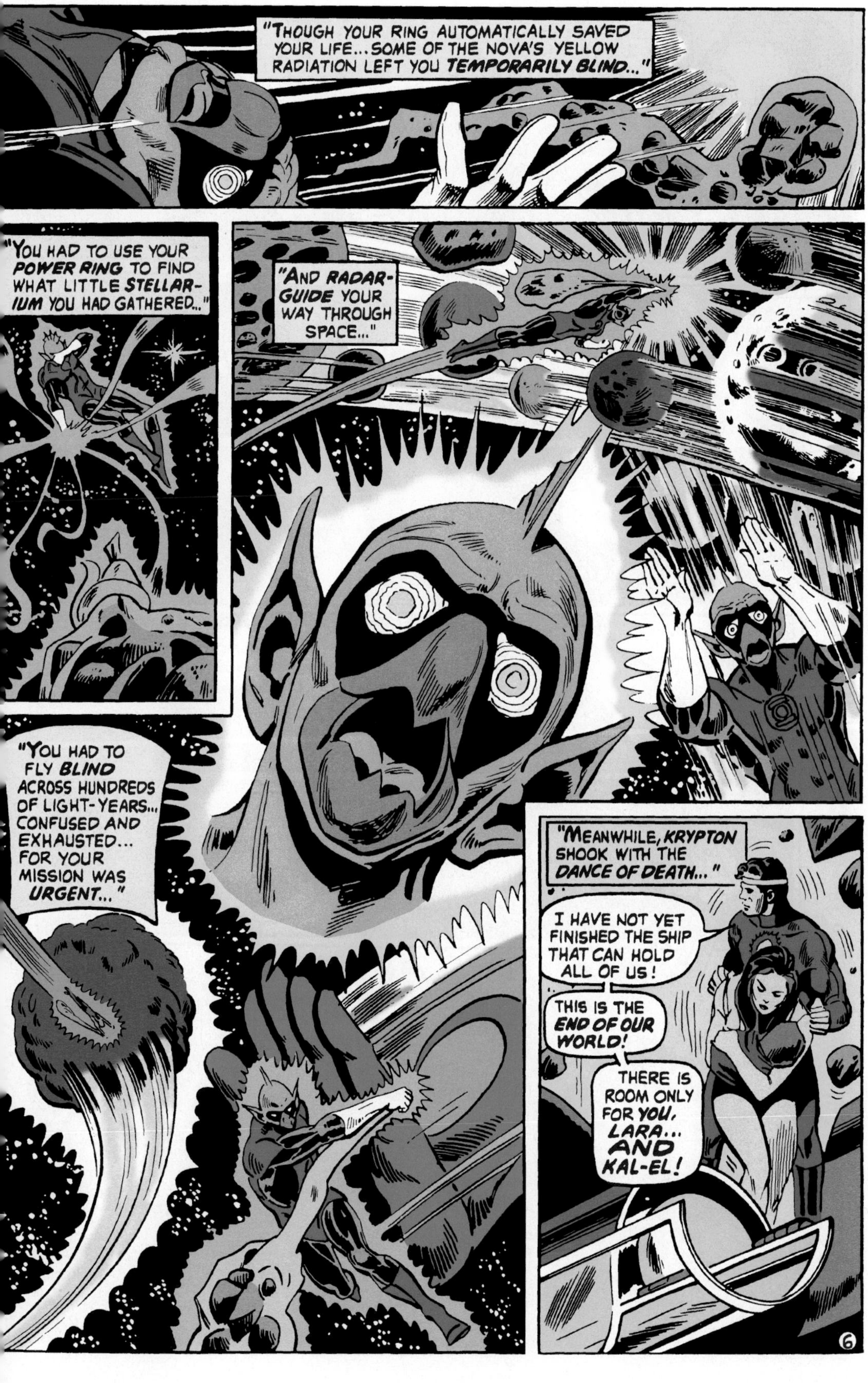
"THOUGH YOUR RING AUTOMATICALLY SAVED YOUR LIFE... SOME OF THE NOVA'S YELLOW RADIATION LEFT YOU TEMPORARILY BLIND..."
"YOU HAD TO USE YOUR POWER RING TO FIND WHAT LITTLE STELLARIUM YOU HAD GATHERED..."
"AND RADAR-GUIDE YOUR WAY THROUGH SPACE..."
"YOU HAD TO FLY BLIND ACROSS HUNDREDS OF LIGHT-YEARS... CONFUSED AND EXHAUSTED... FOR YOUR MISSION WAS URGENT..."
"MEANWHILE, KRYPTON SHOOK WITH THE DANCE OF DEATH..."
I HAVE NOT YET FINISHED THE SHIP THAT CAN HOLD ALL OF US!
THIS IS THE END OF OUR WORLD!
THERE IS ROOM ONLY FOR YOU, LARA... AND KAL-EL!
6

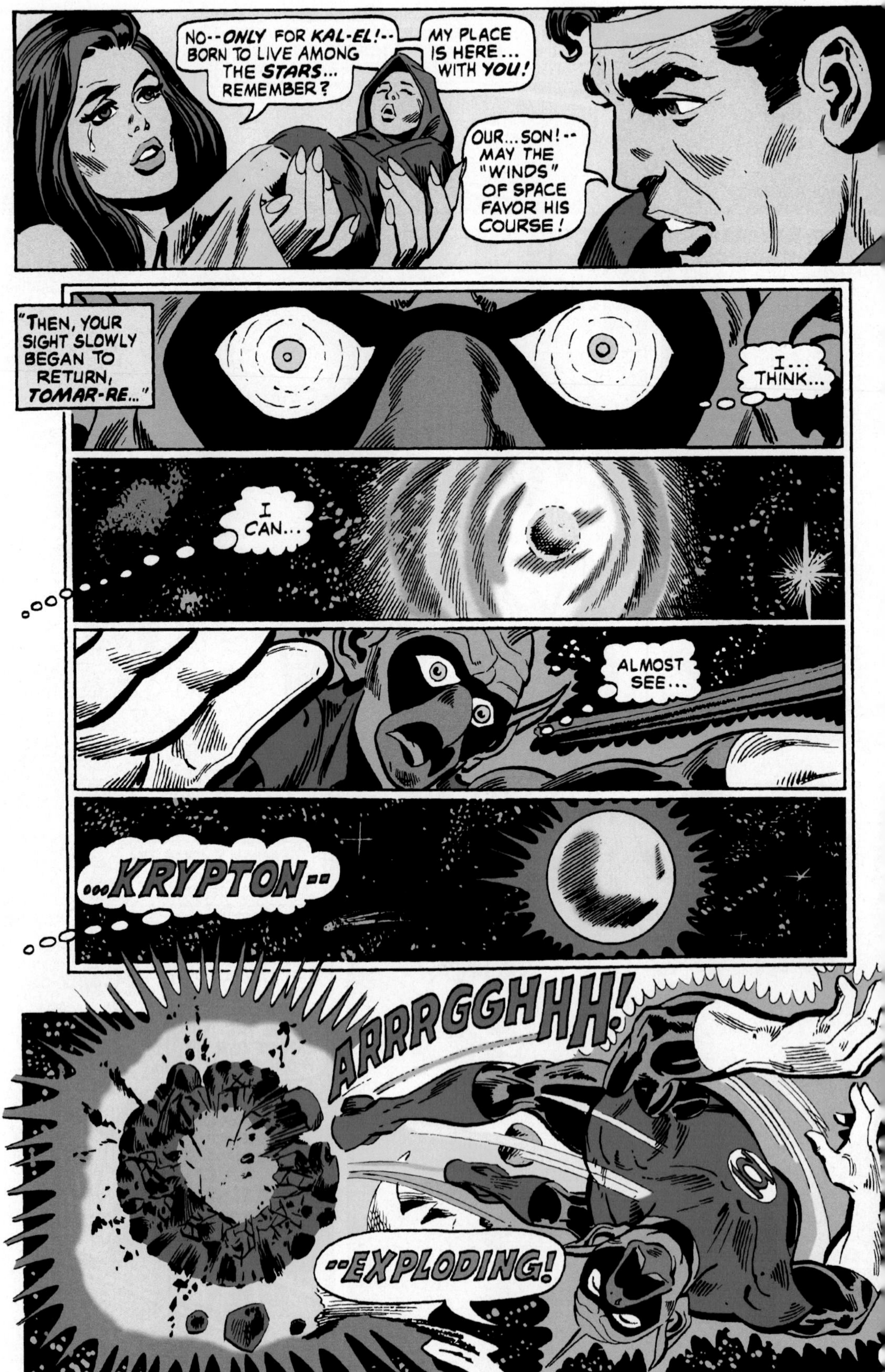
NO--ONLY FOR KAL-EL!-- BORN TO LIVE AMONG THE STARS... REMEMBER?
MY PLACE IS HERE... WITH YOU!
OUR... SON!-- MAY THE "WINDS" OF SPACE FAVOR HIS COURSE!
"THEN, YOUR SIGHT SLOWLY BEGAN TO RETURN, TOMAR-RE..."
I... THINK...
I CAN...
ALMOST SEE...
...KRYPTON--
ARRRGGHHH!
--EXPLODING!

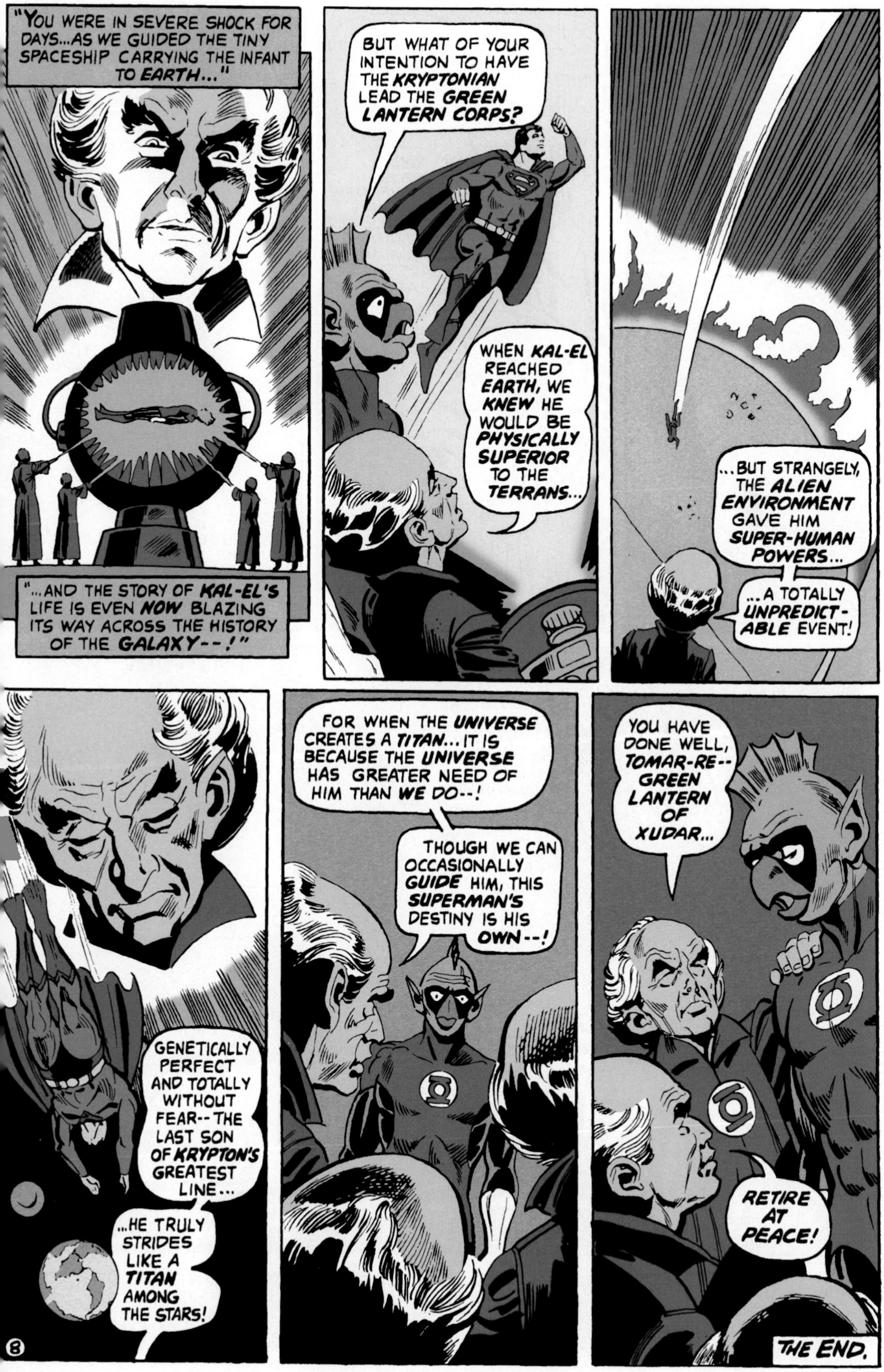
"YOU WERE IN SEVERE SHOCK FOR DAYS...AS WE GUIDED THE TINY SPACESHIP CARRYING THE INFANT TO EARTH..."
"...AND THE STORY OF KAL-EL'S LIFE IS EVEN NOW BLAZING ITS WAY ACROSS THE HISTORY OF THE GALAXY--!"
BUT WHAT OF YOUR INTENTION TO HAVE THE KRYPTONIAN LEAD THE GREEN LANTERN CORPS?
WHEN KAL-EL REACHED EARTH, WE KNEW HE WOULD BE PHYSICALLY SUPERIOR TO THE TERRANS...
...BUT STRANGELY, THE ALIEN ENVIRONMENT GAVE HIM SUPER-HUMAN POWERS...
...A TOTALLY UNPREDICT-ABLE EVENT!
8
GENETICALLY PERFECT AND TOTALLY WITHOUT FEAR-- THE LAST SON OF KRYPTON'S GREATEST LINE...
...HE TRULY STRIDES LIKE A TITAN AMONG THE STARS!
FOR WHEN THE UNIVERSE CREATES A TITAN... IT IS BECAUSE THE UNIVERSE HAS GREATER NEED OF HIM THAN WE DO--!
THOUGH WE CAN OCCASIONALLY GUIDE HIM, THIS SUPERMAN'S DESTINY IS HIS OWN--!
YOU HAVE DONE WELL, TOMAR-RE-- GREEN LANTERN OF XUDAR...
RETIRE AT PEACE!
THE END.

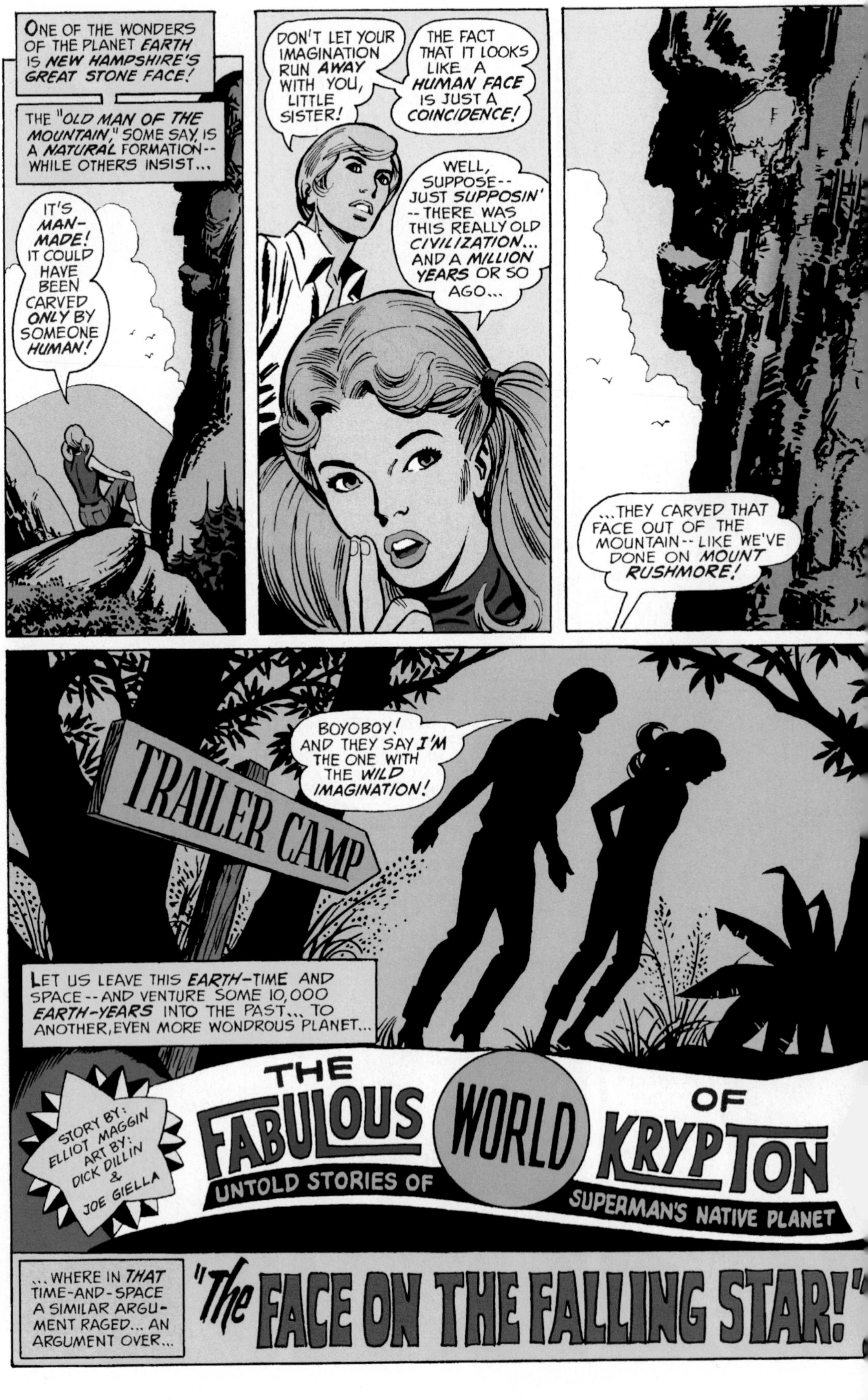
ONE OF THE WONDERS OF THE PLANET EARTH IS NEW HAMPSHIRE'S GREAT STONE FACE!
THE "OLD MAN OF THE MOUNTAIN," SOME SAY, IS A NATURAL FORMATION-- WHILE OTHERS INSIST...
IT'S MAN-MADE! IT COULD HAVE BEEN CARVED ONLY BY SOMEONE HUMAN!
DON'T LET YOUR IMAGINATION RUN AWAY WITH YOU, LITTLE SISTER!
THE FACT THAT IT LOOKS LIKE A HUMAN FACE IS JUST A COINCIDENCE!
WELL, SUPPOSE-- JUST SUPPOSIN' --THERE WAS THIS REALLY OLD CIVILIZATION... AND A MILLION YEARS OR SO AGO...
...THEY CARVED THAT FACE OUT OF THE MOUNTAIN-- LIKE WE'VE DONE ON MOUNT RUSHMORE!
TRAILER CAMP
BOYOBOY! AND THEY SAY I'M THE ONE WITH THE WILD IMAGINATION!
LET US LEAVE THIS EARTH-TIME AND SPACE--AND VENTURE SOME 10,000 EARTH-YEARS INTO THE PAST... TO ANOTHER, EVEN MORE WONDROUS PLANET...
STORY BY: ELLIOT MAGGIN ART BY: DICK DILLIN & JOE GIELLA
THE FABULOUS WORLD OF KRYPTON
UNTOLD STORIES OF SUPERMAN'S NATIVE PLANET
...WHERE IN THAT TIME-AND-SPACE A SIMILAR ARGUMENT RAGED... AN ARGUMENT OVER...
"The FACE ON THE FALLING STAR!"

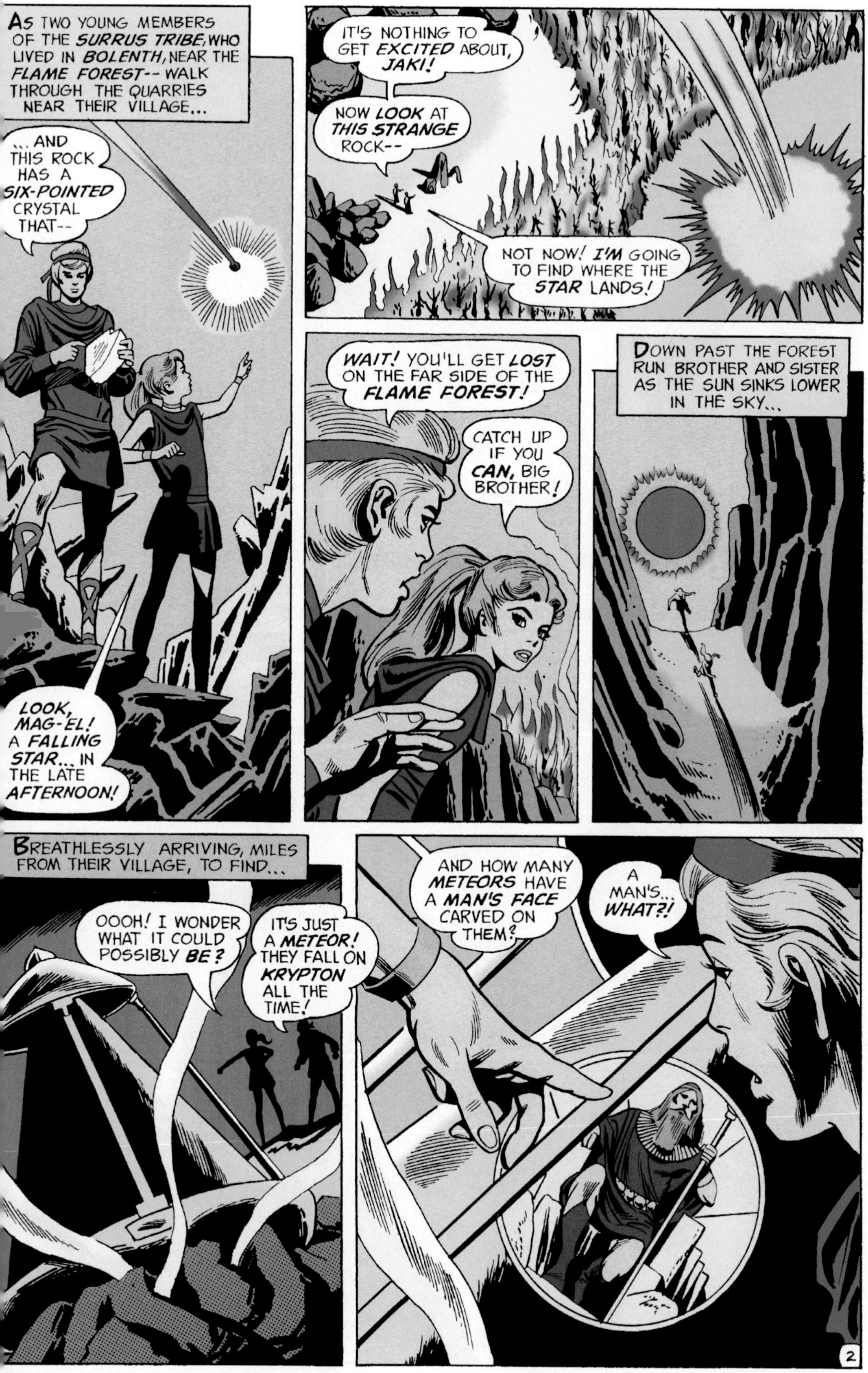
AS TWO YOUNG MEMBERS OF THE SURRUS TRIBE, WHO LIVED IN BOLENTH, NEAR THE FLAME FOREST-- WALK THROUGH THE QUARRIES NEAR THEIR VILLAGE...
...AND THIS ROCK HAS A SIX-POINTED CRYSTAL THAT--
LOOK, MAG-EL! A FALLING STAR... IN THE LATE AFTERNOON!
IT'S NOTHING TO GET EXCITED ABOUT, JAKI!
NOW LOOK AT THIS STRANGE ROCK--
NOT NOW! I'M GOING TO FIND WHERE THE STAR LANDS!
WAIT! YOU'LL GET LOST ON THE FAR SIDE OF THE FLAME FOREST!
CATCH UP IF YOU CAN, BIG BROTHER!
DOWN PAST THE FOREST RUN BROTHER AND SISTER AS THE SUN SINKS LOWER IN THE SKY...
BREATHLESSLY ARRIVING, MILES FROM THEIR VILLAGE, TO FIND...
OOOH! I WONDER WHAT IT COULD POSSIBLY BE?
IT'S JUST A METEOR! THEY FALL ON KRYPTON ALL THE TIME!
AND HOW MANY METEORS HAVE A MAN'S FACE CARVED ON THEM?
A MAN'S... WHAT?!
2

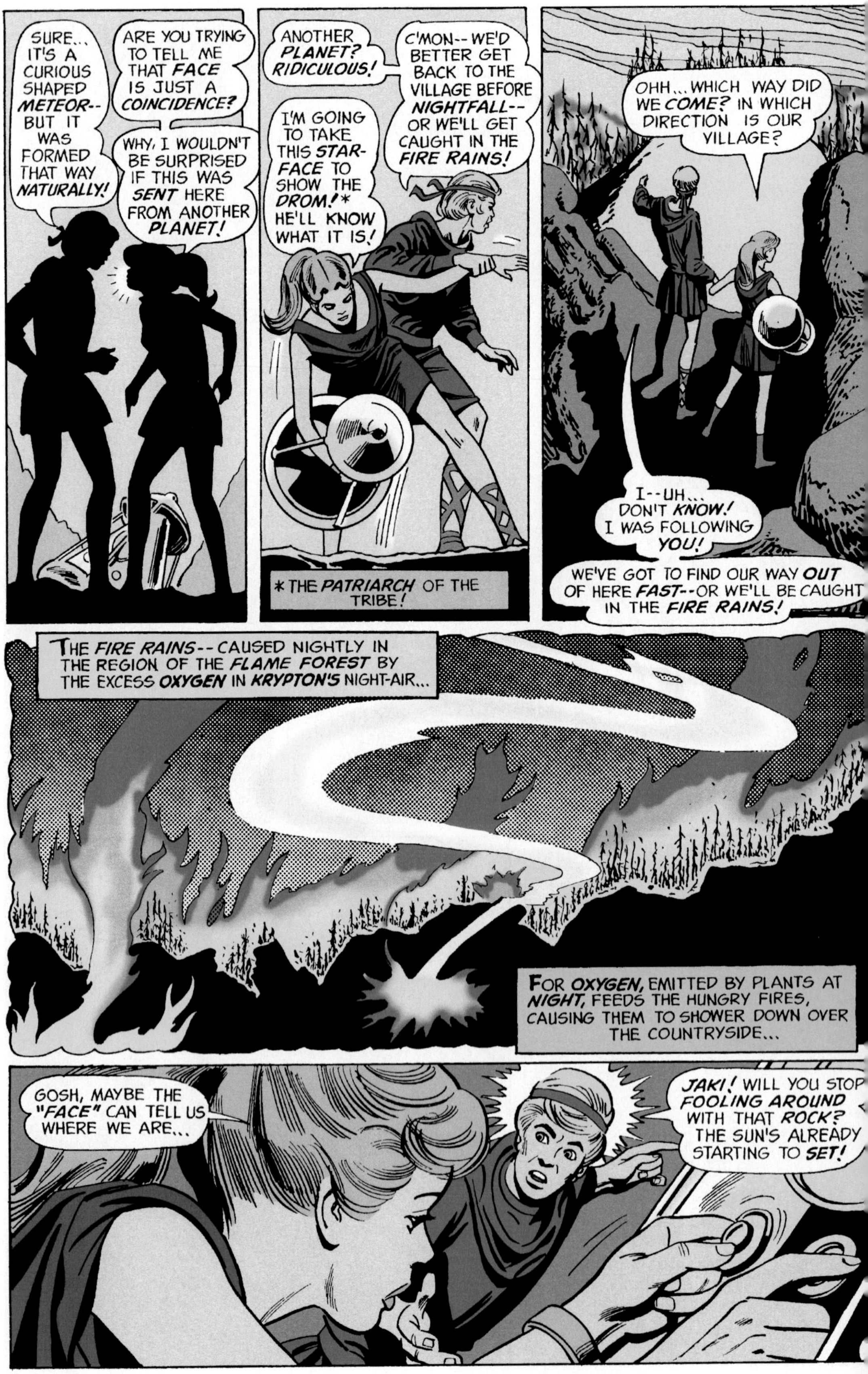
SURE... IT'S A CURIOUS SHAPED METEOR-- BUT IT WAS FORMED THAT WAY NATURALLY!
ARE YOU TRYING TO TELL ME THAT FACE IS JUST A COINCIDENCE?
WHY, I WOULDN'T BE SURPRISED IF THIS WAS SENT HERE FROM ANOTHER PLANET!
ANOTHER PLANET? RIDICULOUS!
I'M GOING TO TAKE THIS STAR-FACE TO SHOW THE DROM!* HE'LL KNOW WHAT IT IS!
C'MON-- WE'D BETTER GET BACK TO THE VILLAGE BEFORE NIGHTFALL-- OR WE'LL GET CAUGHT IN THE FIRE RAINS!
*THE PATRIARCH OF THE TRIBE!
OHH... WHICH WAY DID WE COME? IN WHICH DIRECTION IS OUR VILLAGE?
I--UH... DON'T KNOW! I WAS FOLLOWING YOU!
WE'VE GOT TO FIND OUR WAY OUT OF HERE FAST--OR WE'LL BE CAUGHT IN THE FIRE RAINS!
THE FIRE RAINS-- CAUSED NIGHTLY IN THE REGION OF THE FLAME FOREST BY THE EXCESS OXYGEN IN KRYPTON'S NIGHT-AIR...
FOR OXYGEN, EMITTED BY PLANTS AT NIGHT, FEEDS THE HUNGRY FIRES, CAUSING THEM TO SHOWER DOWN OVER THE COUNTRYSIDE...
GOSH, MAYBE THE "FACE" CAN TELL US WHERE WE ARE...
JAKI! WILL YOU STOP FOOLING AROUND WITH THAT ROCK? THE SUN'S ALREADY STARTING TO SET!

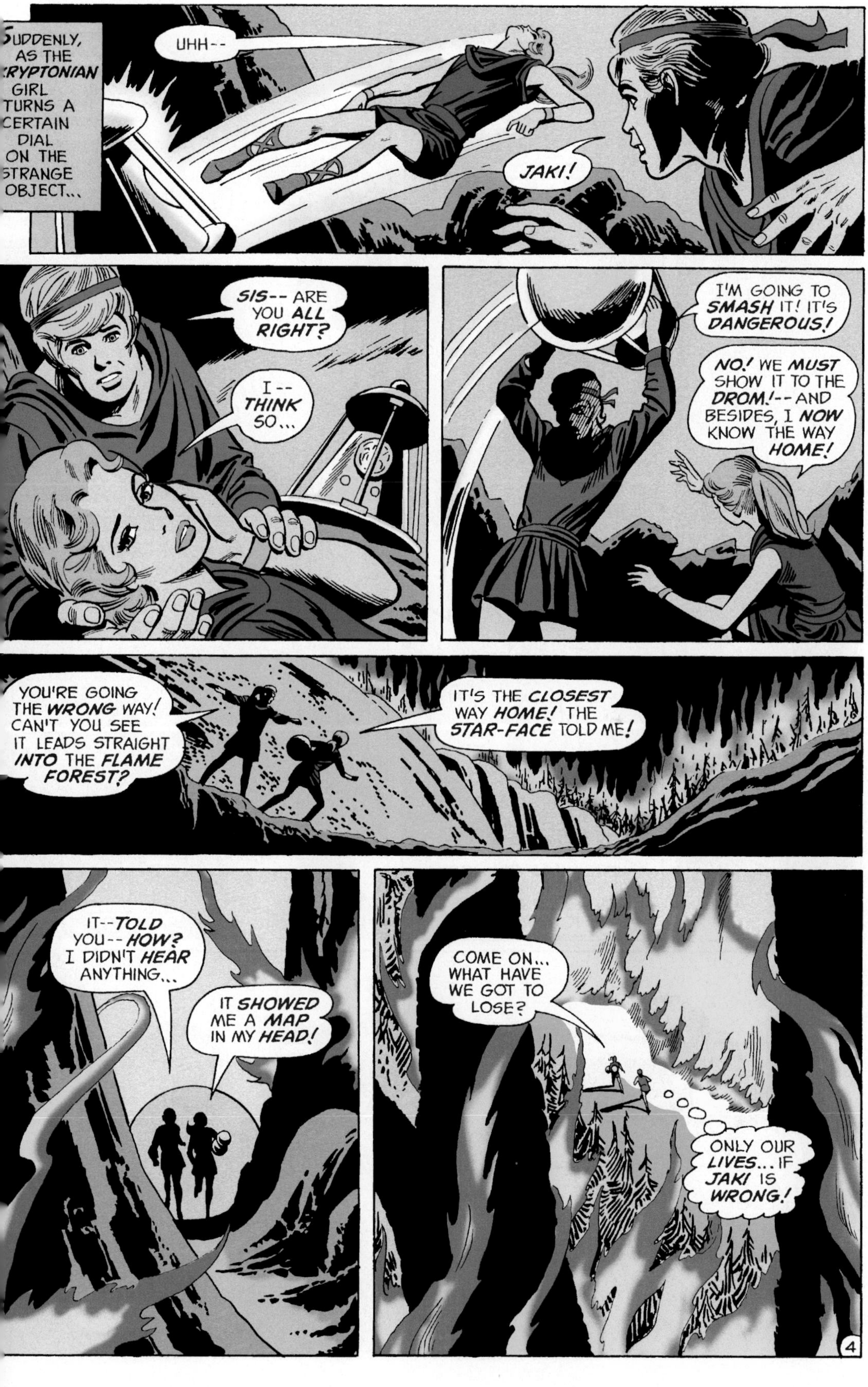
SUDDENLY, AS THE KRYPTONIAN GIRL TURNS A CERTAIN DIAL ON THE STRANGE OBJECT...
UHH--
JAKI!
SIS-- ARE YOU ALL RIGHT?
I-- THINK SO...
I'M GOING TO SMASH IT! IT'S DANGEROUS!
NO! WE MUST SHOW IT TO THE DROM!--AND BESIDES, I NOW KNOW THE WAY HOME!
YOU'RE GOING THE WRONG WAY! CAN'T YOU SEE IT LEADS STRAIGHT INTO THE FLAME FOREST?
IT'S THE CLOSEST WAY HOME! THE STAR-FACE TOLD ME!
IT--TOLD YOU--HOW? I DIDN'T HEAR ANYTHING...
IT SHOWED ME A MAP IN MY HEAD!
COME ON... WHAT HAVE WE GOT TO LOSE?
ONLY OUR LIVES... IF JAKI IS WRONG!
4

AND AS THE BROTHER AND SISTER TREAD ON A LEDGE THROUGH THE *FLAME FOREST...*

JAKI--THE FLAMES ARE GETTING *HIGHER!* WE BETTER TURN BACK!

IT'S TOO LATE FOR THAT!

I'M *SCARED!* HOW COME *YOU* ARE *NOT?*

BECAUSE I *KNOW* WE'RE ALMOST *HOME!*

HERE, *MAG-EL*-- LOOK INTO THIS END OF THE *STAR-FACE* AND *SEE* FOR *YOURSELF!*

AND AS THE GIRL CAREFULLY TURNS THAT SAME DIAL...

AMAZING! THE *METEOR* IS PROJECTING A *MAP* OF THE AREA IN MY *MIND!*

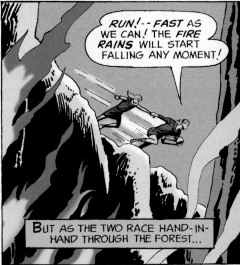

RUN!-- FAST AS WE CAN! THE *FIRE RAINS* WILL START FALLING ANY MOMENT!

BUT AS THE TWO RACE HAND-IN-HAND THROUGH THE FOREST...

OHH-- I *TRIPPED!*

PULLING US DOWN INTO THE *FLAMES!*

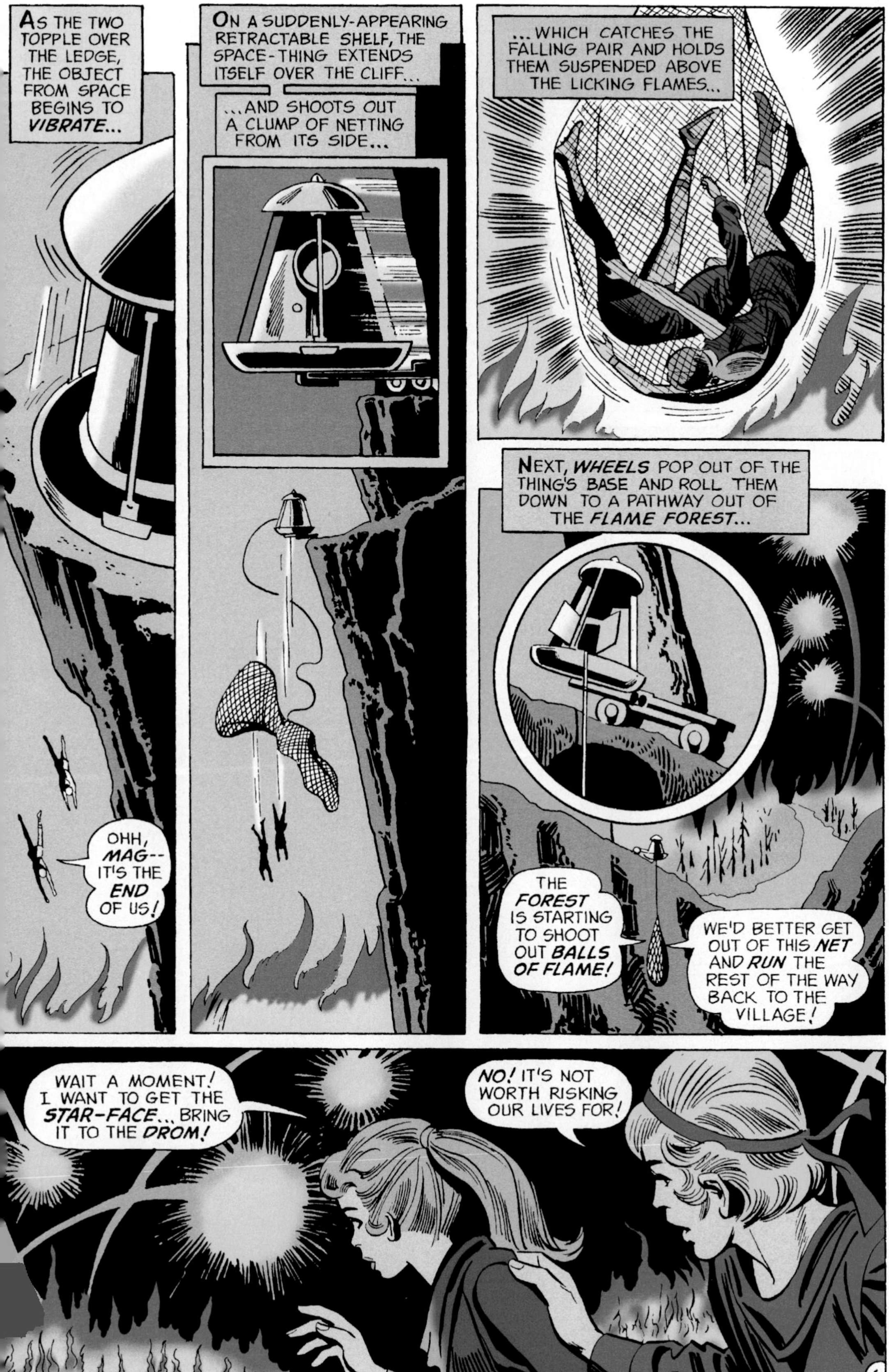
AS THE TWO TOPPLE OVER THE LEDGE, THE OBJECT FROM SPACE BEGINS TO VIBRATE...
OHH, MAG-- IT'S THE END OF US!
ON A SUDDENLY-APPEARING RETRACTABLE SHELF, THE SPACE-THING EXTENDS ITSELF OVER THE CLIFF...
...AND SHOOTS OUT A CLUMP OF NETTING FROM ITS SIDE...
...WHICH CATCHES THE FALLING PAIR AND HOLDS THEM SUSPENDED ABOVE THE LICKING FLAMES...
NEXT, WHEELS POP OUT OF THE THING'S BASE AND ROLL THEM DOWN TO A PATHWAY OUT OF THE FLAME FOREST...
THE FOREST IS STARTING TO SHOOT OUT BALLS OF FLAME!
WE'D BETTER GET OUT OF THIS NET AND RUN THE REST OF THE WAY BACK TO THE VILLAGE!
WAIT A MOMENT! I WANT TO GET THE STAR-FACE... BRING IT TO THE DROM!
NO! IT'S NOT WORTH RISKING OUR LIVES FOR!
6

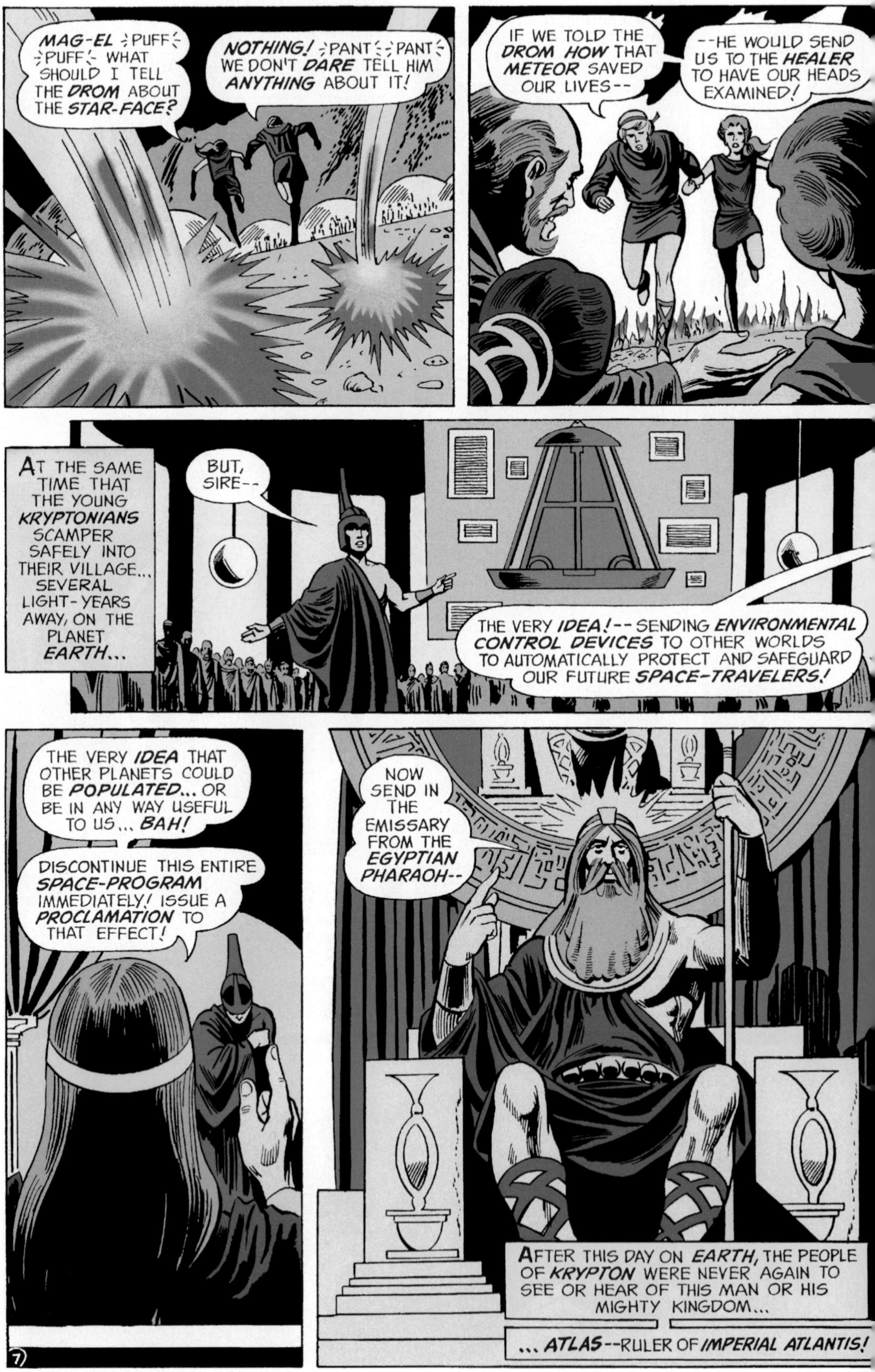
MAG-EL PUFF PUFF WHAT SHOULD I TELL THE DROM ABOUT THE STAR-FACE?
NOTHING! PANT PANT WE DON'T DARE TELL HIM ANYTHING ABOUT IT!
IF WE TOLD THE DROM HOW THAT METEOR SAVED OUR LIVES--
--HE WOULD SEND US TO THE HEALER TO HAVE OUR HEADS EXAMINED!
AT THE SAME TIME THAT THE YOUNG KRYPTONIANS SCAMPER SAFELY INTO THEIR VILLAGE... SEVERAL LIGHT-YEARS AWAY, ON THE PLANET EARTH...
BUT, SIRE--
THE VERY IDEA!--SENDING ENVIRONMENTAL CONTROL DEVICES TO OTHER WORLDS TO AUTOMATICALLY PROTECT AND SAFEGUARD OUR FUTURE SPACE-TRAVELERS!
THE VERY IDEA THAT OTHER PLANETS COULD BE POPULATED... OR BE IN ANY WAY USEFUL TO US... BAH!
DISCONTINUE THIS ENTIRE SPACE-PROGRAM IMMEDIATELY! ISSUE A PROCLAMATION TO THAT EFFECT!
7
NOW SEND IN THE EMISSARY FROM THE EGYPTIAN PHARAOH--
AFTER THIS DAY ON EARTH, THE PEOPLE OF KRYPTON WERE NEVER AGAIN TO SEE OR HEAR OF THIS MAN OR HIS MIGHTY KINGDOM...
... ATLAS--RULER OF IMPERIAL ATLANTIS!

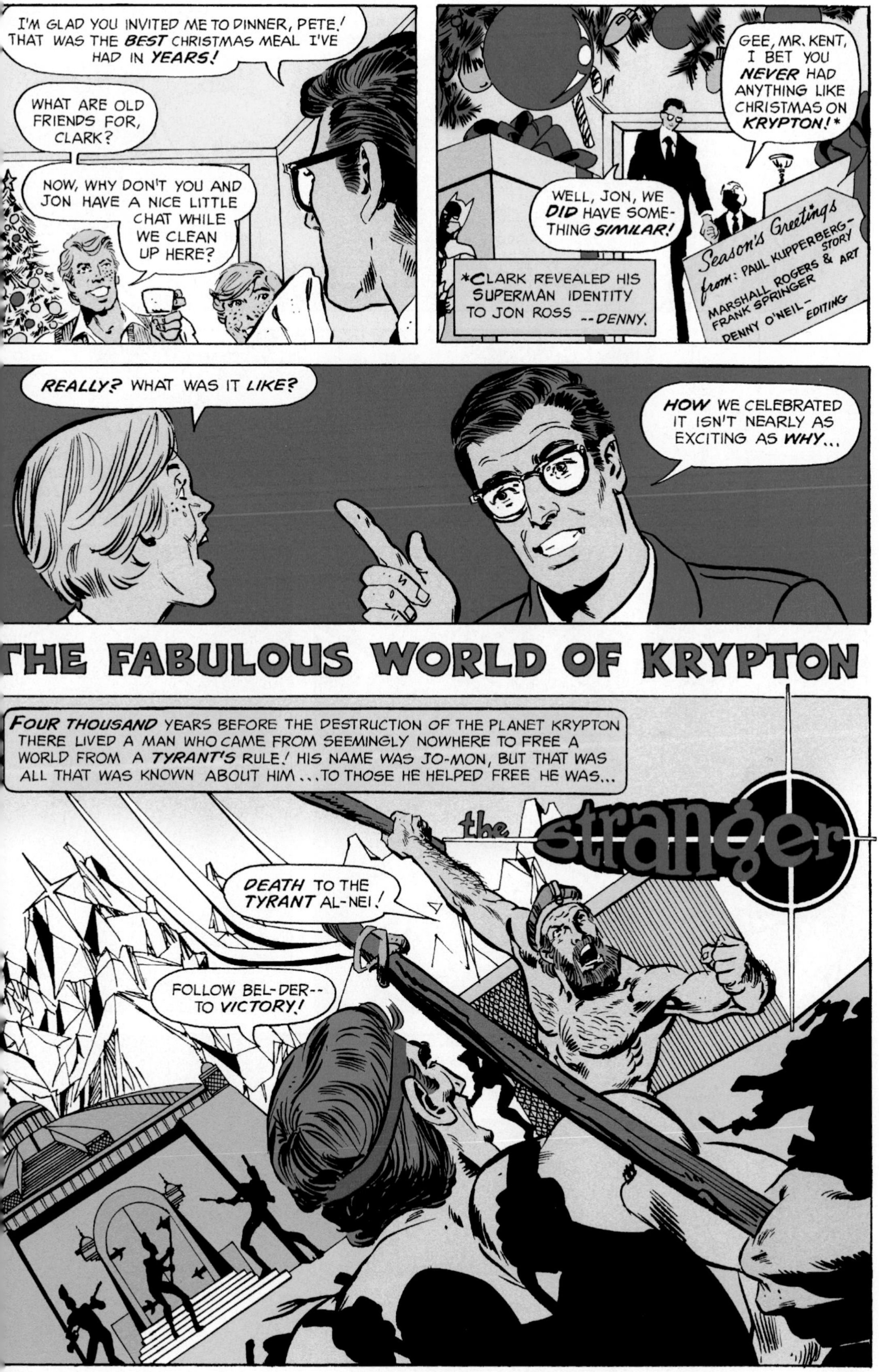
I'M GLAD YOU INVITED ME TO DINNER, PETE! THAT WAS THE BEST CHRISTMAS MEAL I'VE HAD IN YEARS!
WHAT ARE OLD FRIENDS FOR, CLARK?
NOW, WHY DON'T YOU AND JON HAVE A NICE LITTLE CHAT WHILE WE CLEAN UP HERE?
GEE, MR. KENT, I BET YOU NEVER HAD ANYTHING LIKE CHRISTMAS ON KRYPTON!*
WELL, JON, WE DID HAVE SOMETHING SIMILAR!
*CLARK REVEALED HIS SUPERMAN IDENTITY TO JON ROSS --DENNY.
Season's Greetings from: PAUL KUPPERBERG-STORY MARSHALL ROGERS & FRANK SPRINGER-ART DENNY O'NEIL-EDITING
REALLY? WHAT WAS IT LIKE?
HOW WE CELEBRATED IT ISN'T NEARLY AS EXCITING AS WHY...
THE FABULOUS WORLD OF KRYPTON
FOUR THOUSAND YEARS BEFORE THE DESTRUCTION OF THE PLANET KRYPTON THERE LIVED A MAN WHO CAME FROM SEEMINGLY NOWHERE TO FREE A WORLD FROM A TYRANT'S RULE! HIS NAME WAS JO-MON, BUT THAT WAS ALL THAT WAS KNOWN ABOUT HIM...TO THOSE HE HELPED FREE HE WAS...
the stranger
DEATH TO THE TYRANT AL-NEI!
FOLLOW BEL-DER--TO VICTORY!

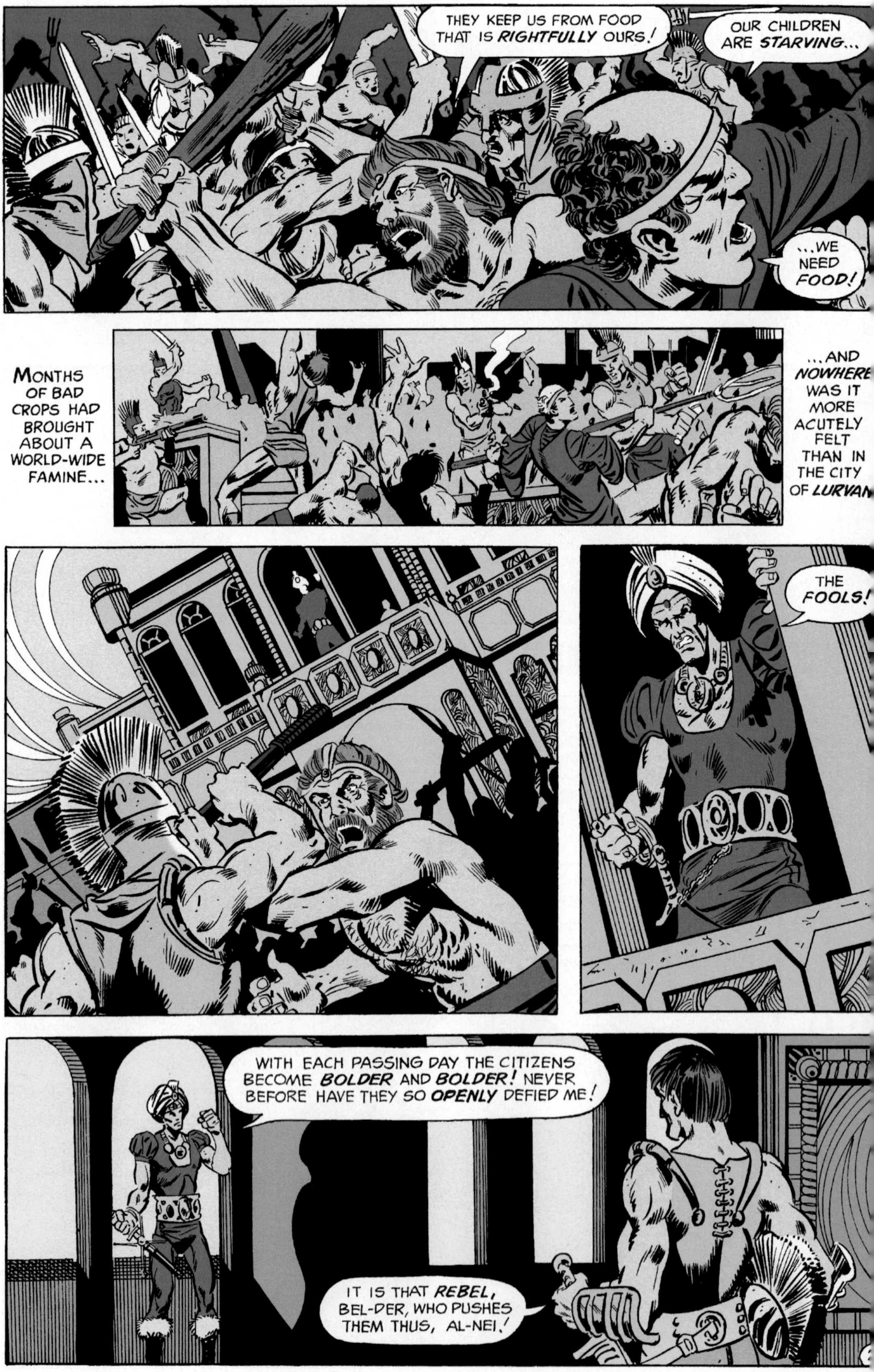
THEY KEEP US FROM FOOD THAT IS RIGHTFULLY OURS!
OUR CHILDREN ARE STARVING...
...WE NEED FOOD!
MONTHS OF BAD CROPS HAD BROUGHT ABOUT A WORLD-WIDE FAMINE...
...AND NOWHERE WAS IT MORE ACUTELY FELT THAN IN THE CITY OF LURVAN
THE FOOLS!
WITH EACH PASSING DAY THE CITIZENS BECOME BOLDER AND BOLDER! NEVER BEFORE HAVE THEY SO OPENLY DEFIED ME!
IT IS THAT REBEL, BEL-DER, WHO PUSHES THEM THUS, AL-NEI!

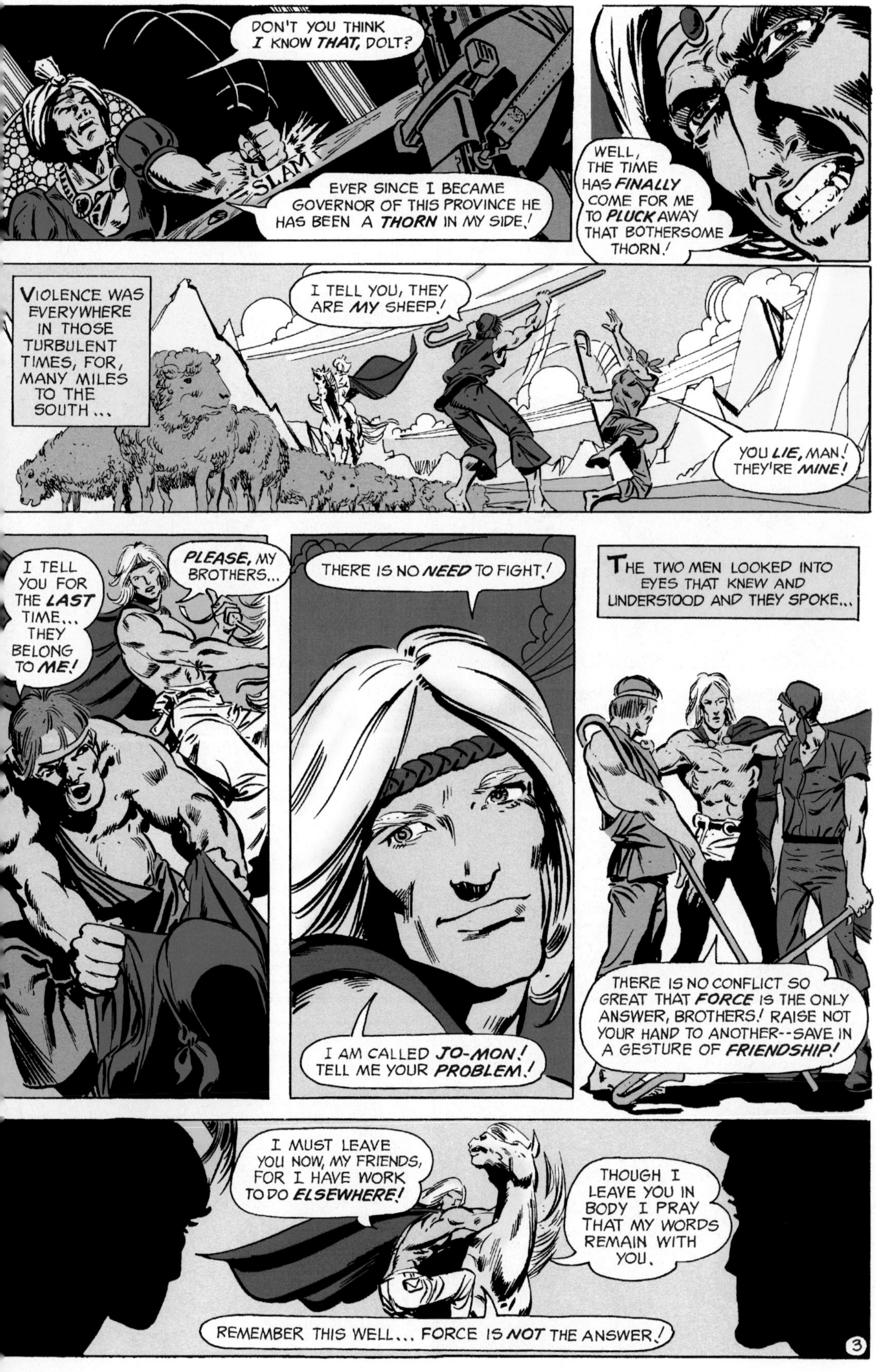

DON'T YOU THINK I KNOW THAT, DOLT?
SLAM
EVER SINCE I BECAME GOVERNOR OF THIS PROVINCE HE HAS BEEN A THORN IN MY SIDE!
WELL, THE TIME HAS FINALLY COME FOR ME TO PLUCK AWAY THAT BOTHERSOME THORN!
VIOLENCE WAS EVERYWHERE IN THOSE TURBULENT TIMES, FOR, MANY MILES TO THE SOUTH...
I TELL YOU, THEY ARE MY SHEEP!
YOU LIE, MAN! THEY'RE MINE!
I TELL YOU FOR THE LAST TIME... THEY BELONG TO ME!
PLEASE, MY BROTHERS...
THERE IS NO NEED TO FIGHT!
I AM CALLED JO-MON! TELL ME YOUR PROBLEM!
THE TWO MEN LOOKED INTO EYES THAT KNEW AND UNDERSTOOD AND THEY SPOKE...
THERE IS NO CONFLICT SO GREAT THAT FORCE IS THE ONLY ANSWER, BROTHERS! RAISE NOT YOUR HAND TO ANOTHER--SAVE IN A GESTURE OF FRIENDSHIP!
I MUST LEAVE YOU NOW, MY FRIENDS, FOR I HAVE WORK TO DO ELSEWHERE!
THOUGH I LEAVE YOU IN BODY I PRAY THAT MY WORDS REMAIN WITH YOU.
REMEMBER THIS WELL... FORCE IS NOT THE ANSWER!
3

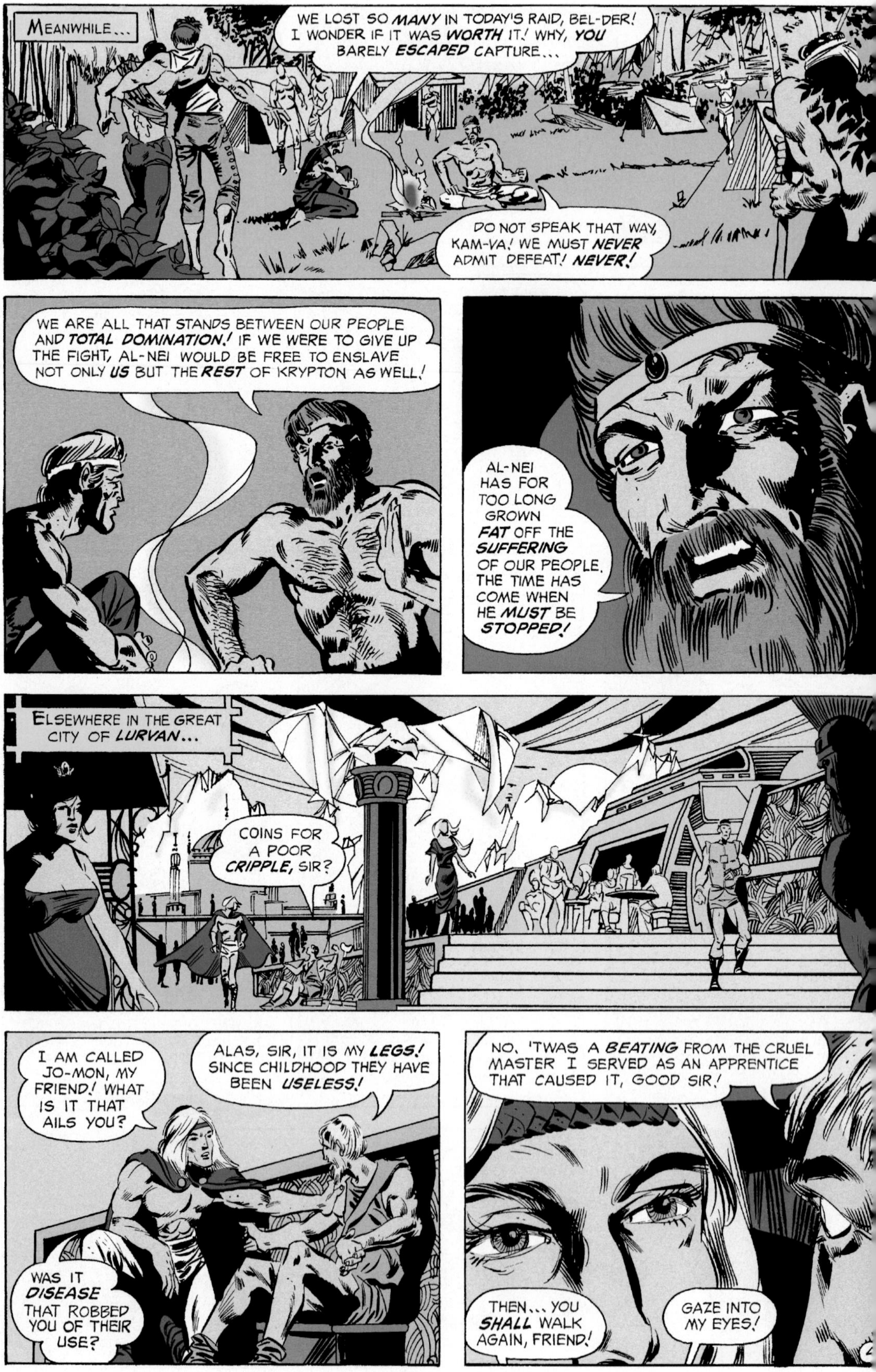
MEANWHILE...
WE LOST SO MANY IN TODAY'S RAID, BEL-DER! I WONDER IF IT WAS WORTH IT! WHY, YOU BARELY ESCAPED CAPTURE...
DO NOT SPEAK THAT WAY, KAM-VA! WE MUST NEVER ADMIT DEFEAT! NEVER!
WE ARE ALL THAT STANDS BETWEEN OUR PEOPLE AND TOTAL DOMINATION! IF WE WERE TO GIVE UP THE FIGHT, AL-NEI WOULD BE FREE TO ENSLAVE NOT ONLY US BUT THE REST OF KRYPTON AS WELL!
AL-NEI HAS FOR TOO LONG GROWN FAT OFF THE SUFFERING OF OUR PEOPLE. THE TIME HAS COME WHEN HE MUST BE STOPPED!
ELSEWHERE IN THE GREAT CITY OF LURVAN...
COINS FOR A POOR CRIPPLE, SIR?
I AM CALLED JO-MON, MY FRIEND! WHAT IS IT THAT AILS YOU?
ALAS, SIR, IT IS MY LEGS! SINCE CHILDHOOD THEY HAVE BEEN USELESS!
WAS IT DISEASE THAT ROBBED YOU OF THEIR USE?
NO, 'TWAS A BEATING FROM THE CRUEL MASTER I SERVED AS AN APPRENTICE THAT CAUSED IT, GOOD SIR!
THEN... YOU SHALL WALK AGAIN, FRIEND!
GAZE INTO MY EYES!

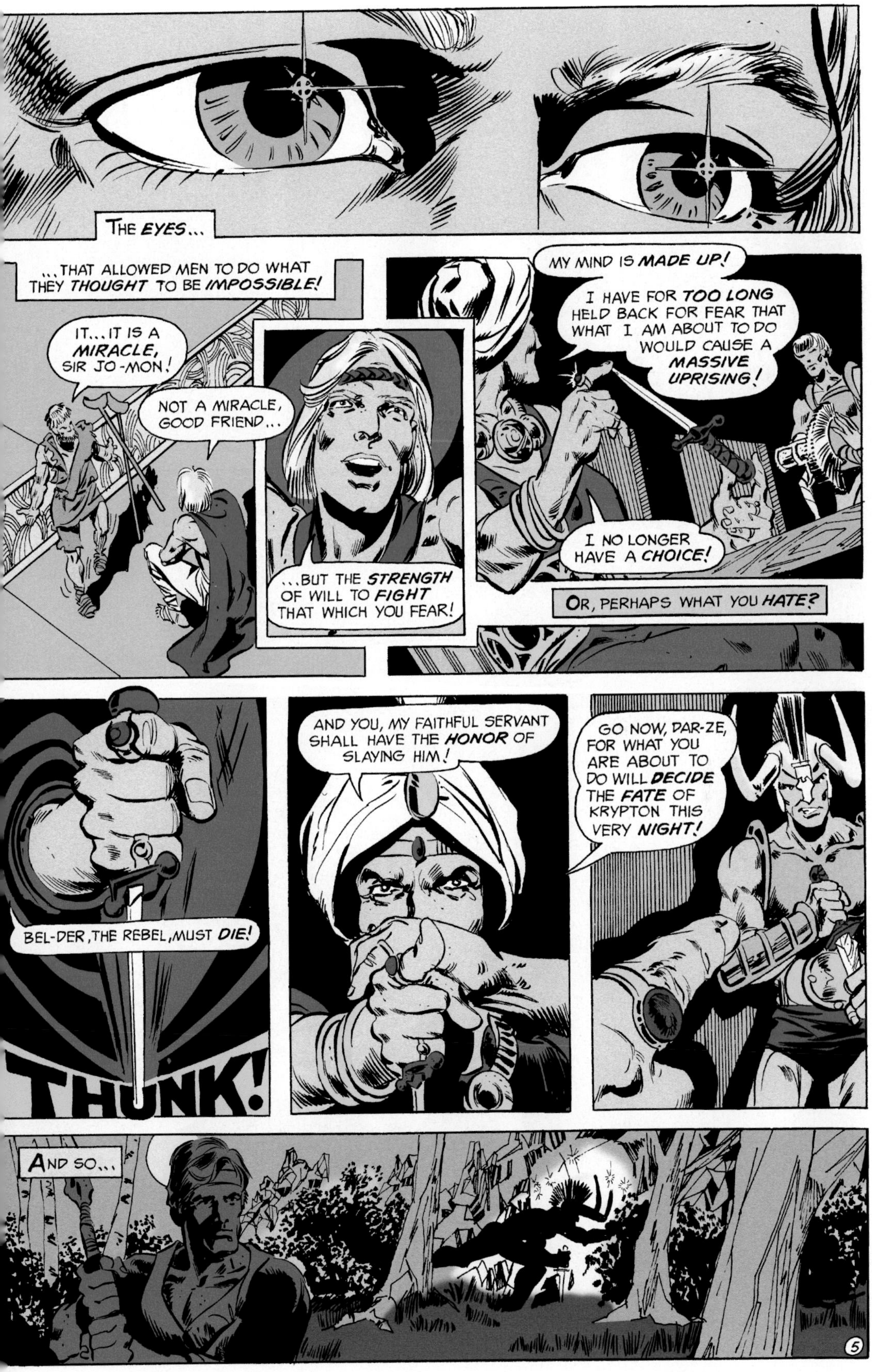
THE EYES...
...THAT ALLOWED MEN TO DO WHAT THEY THOUGHT TO BE IMPOSSIBLE!
IT...IT IS A MIRACLE, SIR JO-MON!
NOT A MIRACLE, GOOD FRIEND...
...BUT THE STRENGTH OF WILL TO FIGHT THAT WHICH YOU FEAR!
MY MIND IS MADE UP!
I HAVE FOR TOO LONG HELD BACK FOR FEAR THAT WHAT I AM ABOUT TO DO WOULD CAUSE A MASSIVE UPRISING!
I NO LONGER HAVE A CHOICE!
OR, PERHAPS WHAT YOU HATE?
BEL-DER, THE REBEL, MUST DIE!
THUNK!
AND YOU, MY FAITHFUL SERVANT SHALL HAVE THE HONOR OF SLAYING HIM!
GO NOW, DAR-ZE, FOR WHAT YOU ARE ABOUT TO DO WILL DECIDE THE FATE OF KRYPTON THIS VERY NIGHT!
AND SO...
5

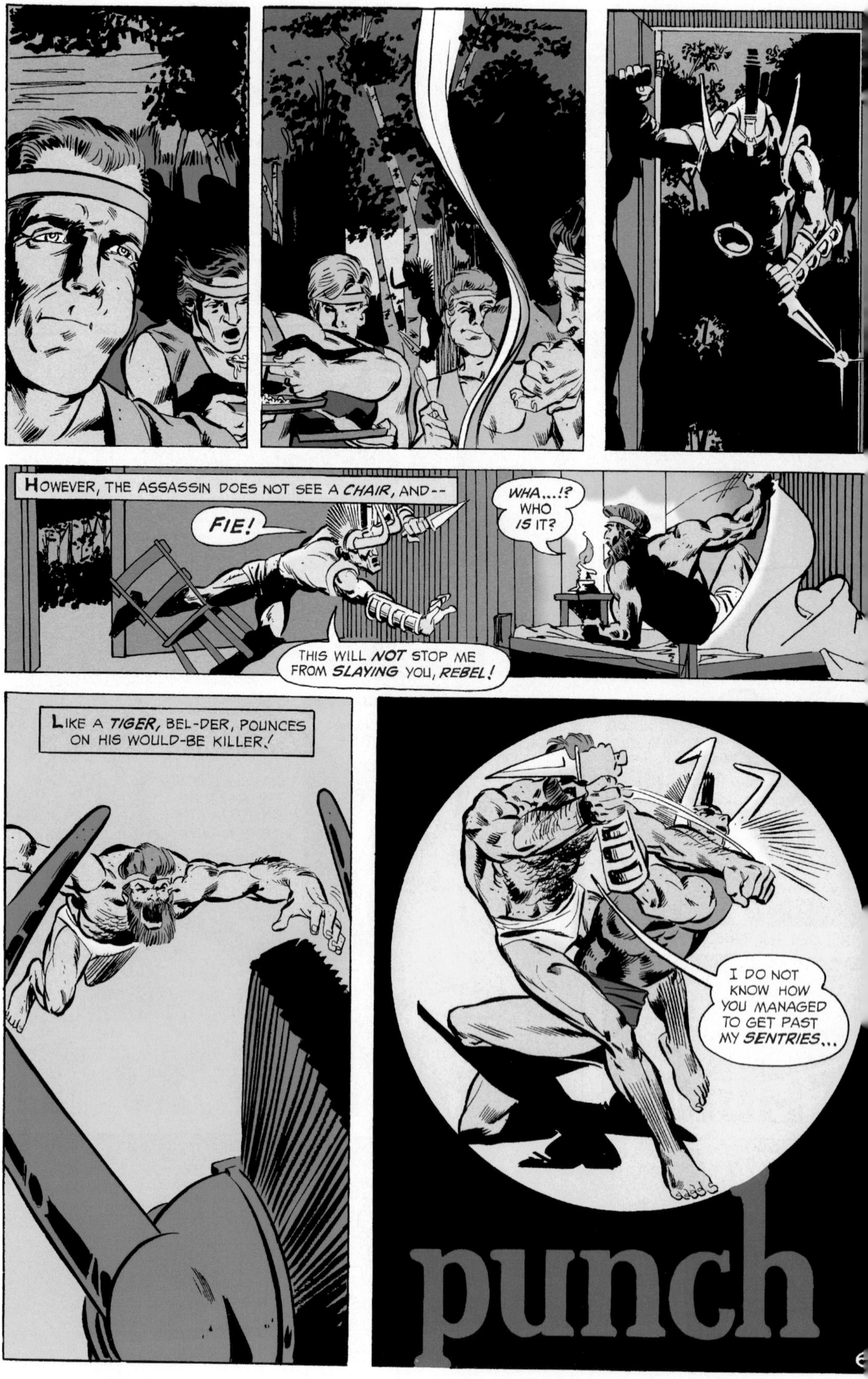
HOWEVER, THE ASSASSIN DOES NOT SEE A CHAIR, AND--
FIE!
WHA...!? WHO IS IT?
THIS WILL NOT STOP ME FROM SLAYING YOU, REBEL!
LIKE A TIGER, BEL-DER, POUNCES ON HIS WOULD-BE KILLER!
I DO NOT KNOW HOW YOU MANAGED TO GET PAST MY SENTRIES...
punch

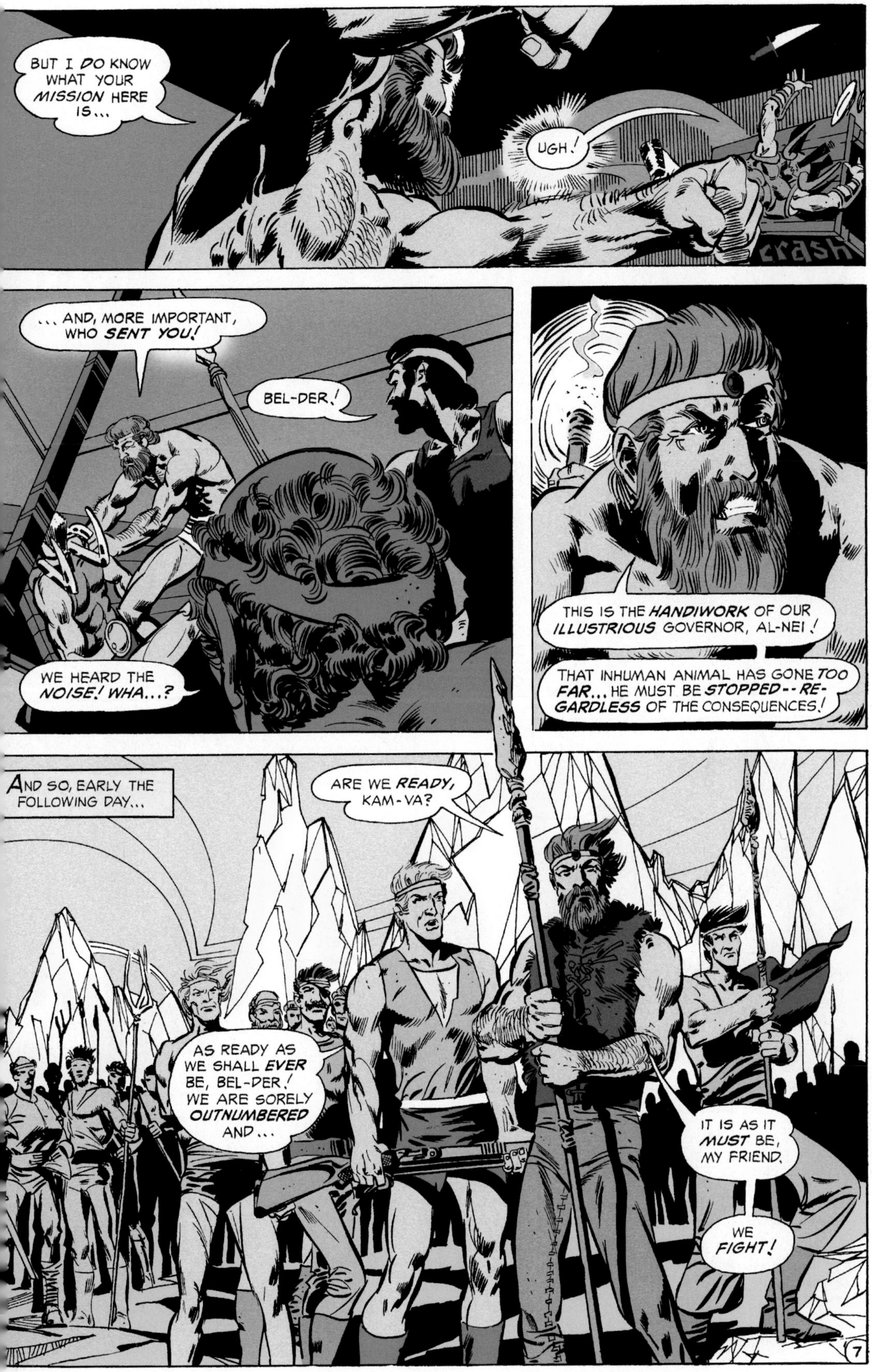

BUT I DO KNOW WHAT YOUR MISSION HERE IS...
UGH!
CRASH
... AND, MORE IMPORTANT, WHO SENT YOU!
BEL-DER!
WE HEARD THE NOISE! WHA...?
THIS IS THE HANDIWORK OF OUR ILLUSTRIOUS GOVERNOR, AL-NEI!
THAT INHUMAN ANIMAL HAS GONE TOO FAR... HE MUST BE STOPPED--REGARDLESS OF THE CONSEQUENCES!
AND SO, EARLY THE FOLLOWING DAY...
ARE WE READY, KAM-VA?
AS READY AS WE SHALL EVER BE, BEL-DER! WE ARE SORELY OUTNUMBERED AND...
IT IS AS IT MUST BE, MY FRIEND.
WE FIGHT!
7

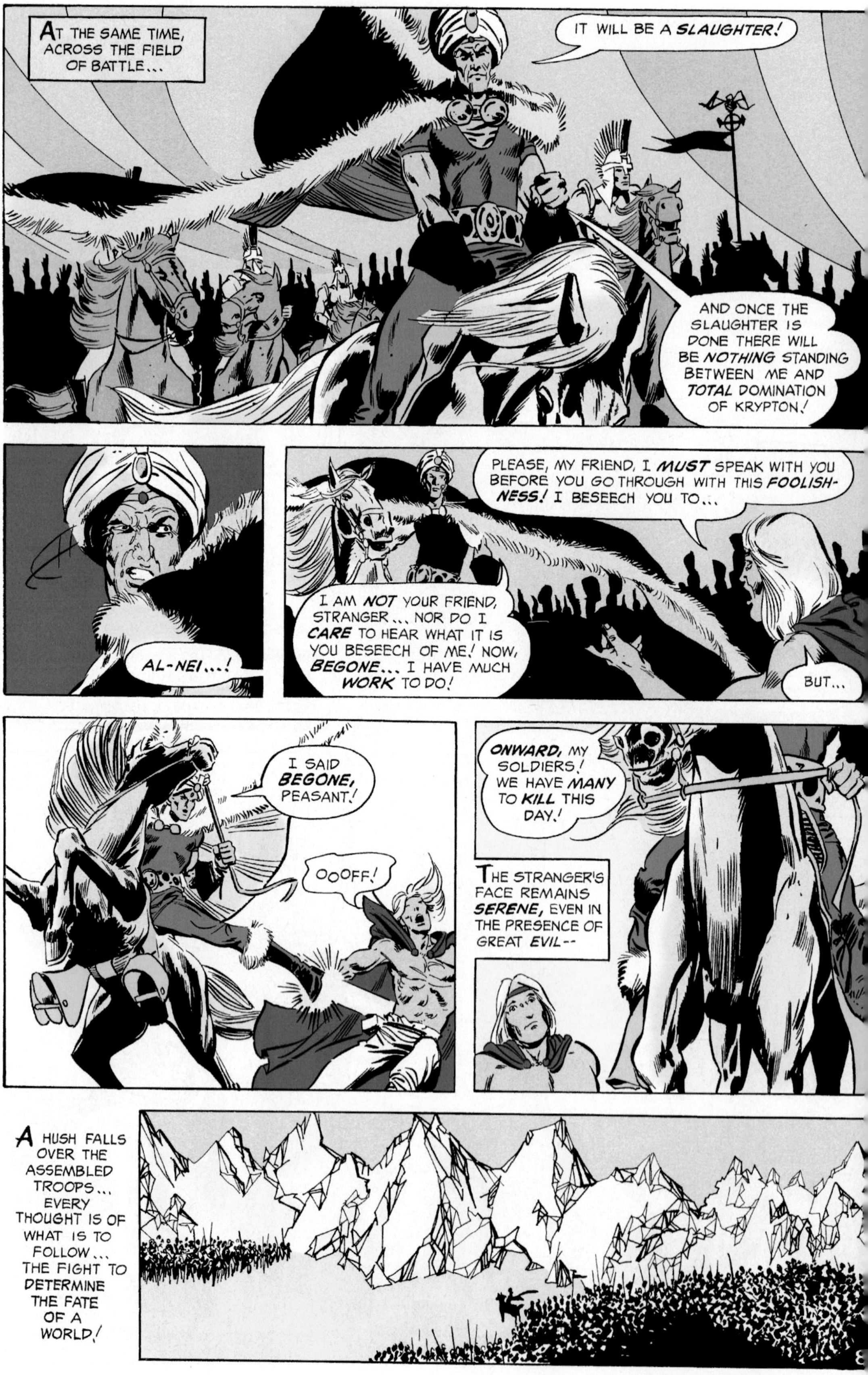

AT THE SAME TIME, ACROSS THE FIELD OF BATTLE...
IT WILL BE A SLAUGHTER!
AND ONCE THE SLAUGHTER IS DONE THERE WILL BE NOTHING STANDING BETWEEN ME AND TOTAL DOMINATION OF KRYPTON!
AL-NEI...!
PLEASE, MY FRIEND, I MUST SPEAK WITH YOU BEFORE YOU GO THROUGH WITH THIS FOOLISHNESS! I BESEECH YOU TO...
I AM NOT YOUR FRIEND, STRANGER... NOR DO I CARE TO HEAR WHAT IT IS YOU BESEECH OF ME! NOW, BEGONE... I HAVE MUCH WORK TO DO!
BUT...
I SAID BEGONE, PEASANT!
OOOFF!
ONWARD, MY SOLDIERS! WE HAVE MANY TO KILL THIS DAY!
THE STRANGER'S FACE REMAINS SERENE, EVEN IN THE PRESENCE OF GREAT EVIL--
A HUSH FALLS OVER THE ASSEMBLED TROOPS... EVERY THOUGHT IS OF WHAT IS TO FOLLOW... THE FIGHT TO DETERMINE THE FATE OF A WORLD!

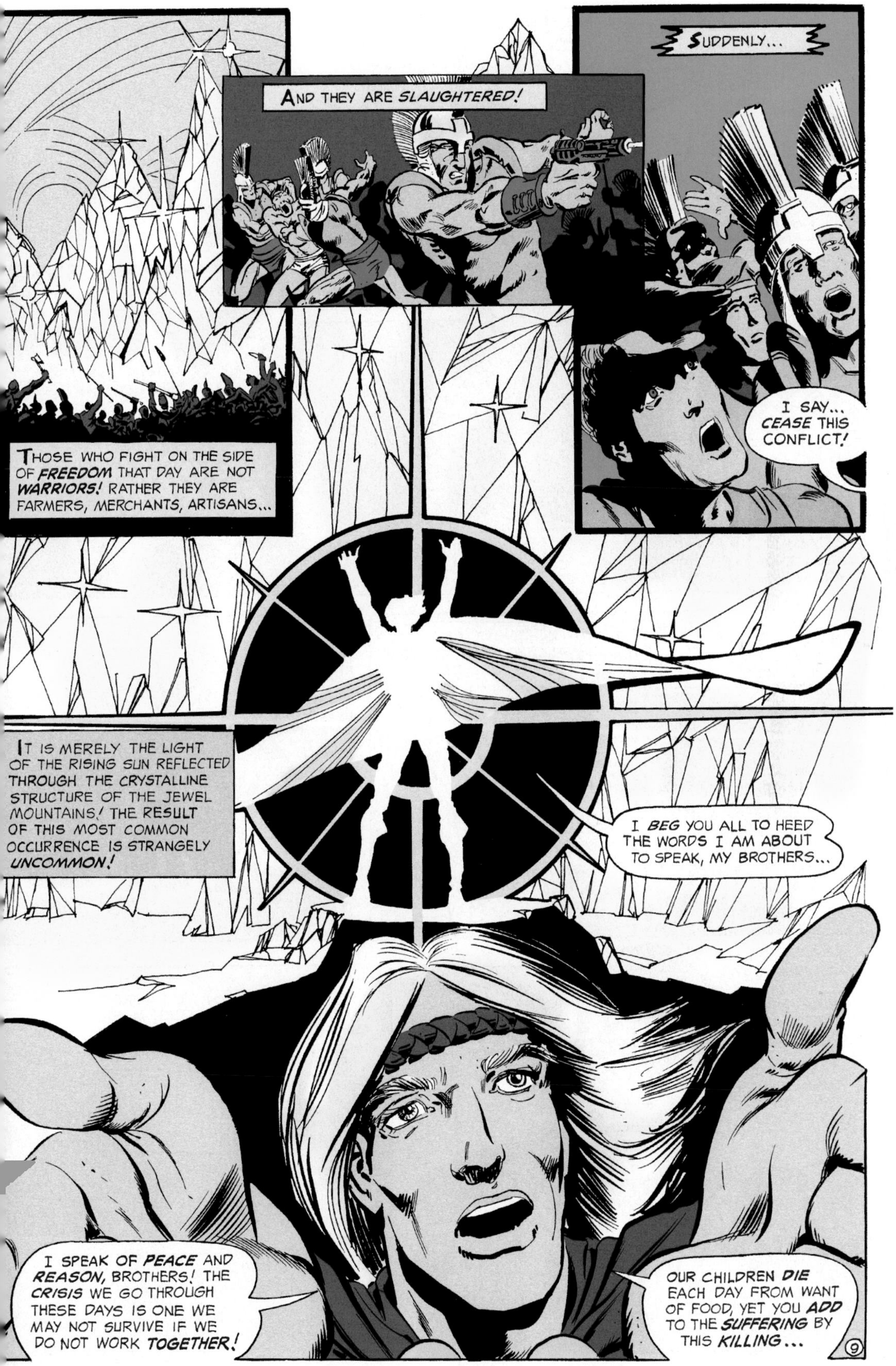

THOSE WHO FIGHT ON THE SIDE OF FREEDOM THAT DAY ARE NOT WARRIORS! RATHER THEY ARE FARMERS, MERCHANTS, ARTISANS...
AND THEY ARE SLAUGHTERED!
SUDDENLY...
I SAY... CEASE THIS CONFLICT!
IT IS MERELY THE LIGHT OF THE RISING SUN REFLECTED THROUGH THE CRYSTALLINE STRUCTURE OF THE JEWEL MOUNTAINS! THE RESULT OF THIS MOST COMMON OCCURRENCE IS STRANGELY UNCOMMON!
I BEG YOU ALL TO HEED THE WORDS I AM ABOUT TO SPEAK, MY BROTHERS...
I SPEAK OF PEACE AND REASON, BROTHERS! THE CRISIS WE GO THROUGH THESE DAYS IS ONE WE MAY NOT SURVIVE IF WE DO NOT WORK TOGETHER!
OUR CHILDREN DIE EACH DAY FROM WANT OF FOOD, YET YOU ADD TO THE SUFFERING BY THIS KILLING...
9

FISTS UNCLENCH! WEAPONS DROP USELESSLY TO THE GROUND!...

...AND, SLOWLY, ALL HEARTS OPEN TO THE STRANGER ON THE HILL...

WE MUST WORK *TOGETHER,* BROTHERS, TO MAKE KRYPTON *STRONG* ONCE AGAIN... OR THE WORLD WE LOVE SHALL SURELY *PERISH!*

HE'S *MAD...*

NO! DON'T LISTEN TO HIM, YOU FOOLS!

ALL HEARTS, THAT IS, SAVE *ONE...*

RETURN TO YOUR... UGH!

FOR LONG MINUTES, NO ONE MOVES! ALL IS SILENT, EXCEPT FOR THE RAVING OF A MAN OBVIOUSLY GONE INSANE...

THAT IS HOW WE MUST DEAL WITH ALL THOSE WHO *OPPOSE* US! WE MUST KILL THEM, KILL... KILL... *KILL...*

WE MUST KILL... *KILL...* KILL...

ON THAT DAY, MANY THOUSANDS OF YEARS AGO, ON A WORLD SINCE GONE, IT WAS ONLY THROUGH THE DEATH OF ONE MAN...

...A STRANGER... THAT KRYPTON ACHIEVED ITS *LASTING* PEACE.

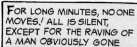

THAT'S SOME *STORY,* MR. KENT!

IT'S MORE THAN JUST A STORY, JON... MUCH, MUCH MORE!

End

CHAPTER TWO
THE LIFE OF JOR-EL

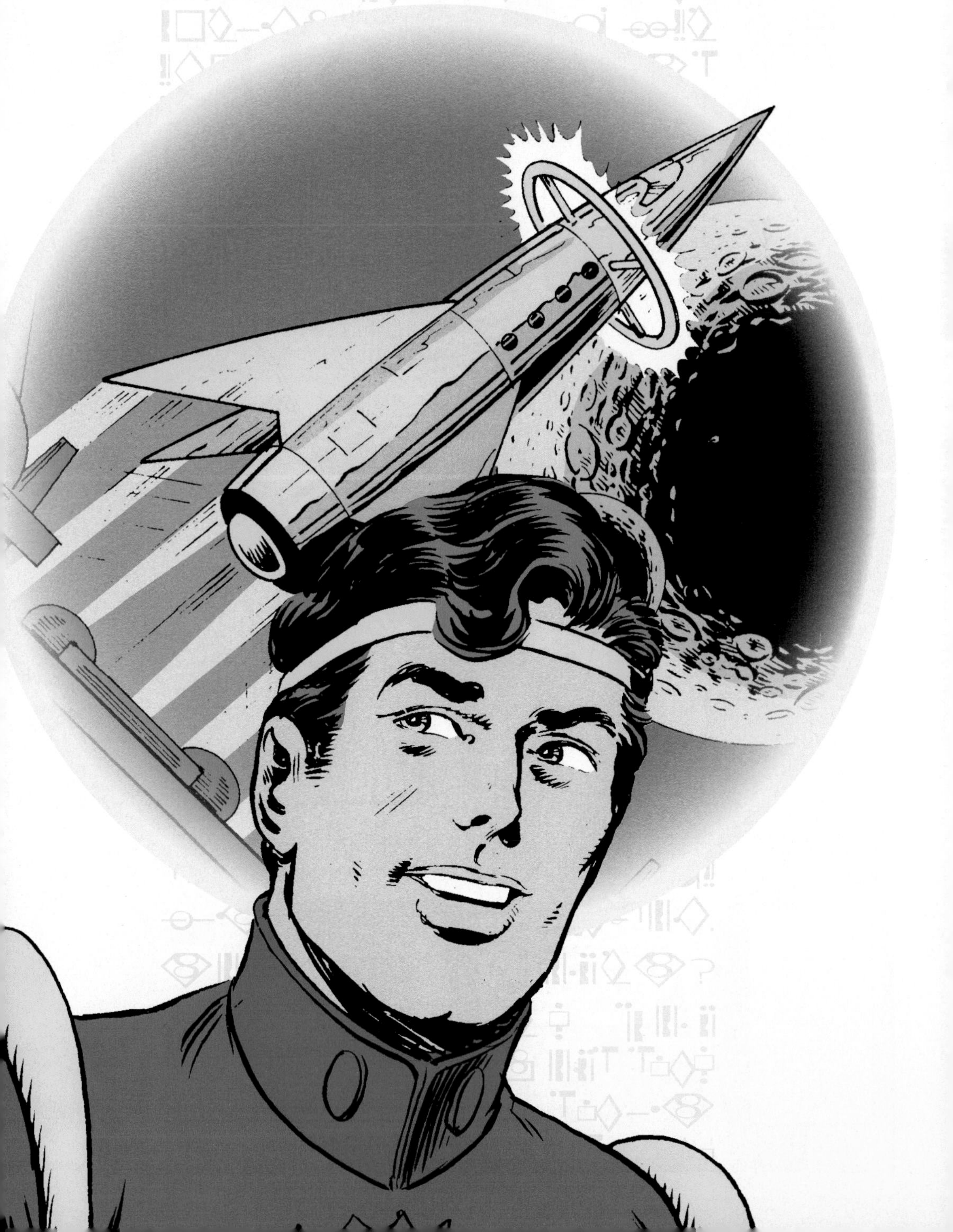

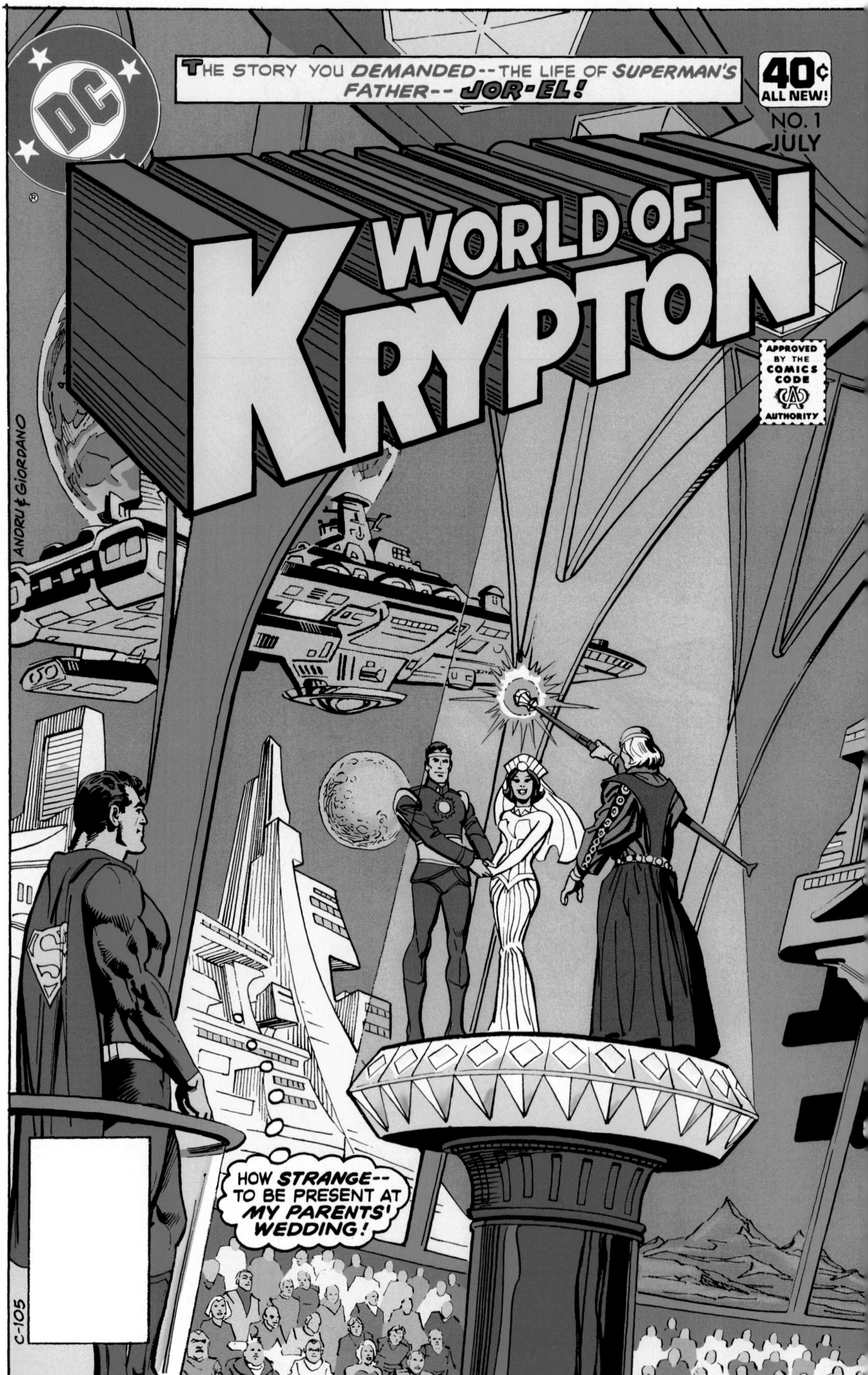
DC
THE STORY YOU DEMANDED--THE LIFE OF SUPERMAN'S FATHER-- JOR-EL!
40¢
ALL NEW!
NO. 1
JULY
WORLD OF KRYPTON
APPROVED BY THE COMICS CODE AUTHORITY
ANDRU & GIORDANO
C-105
HOW STRANGE-- TO BE PRESENT AT MY PARENTS' WEDDING!

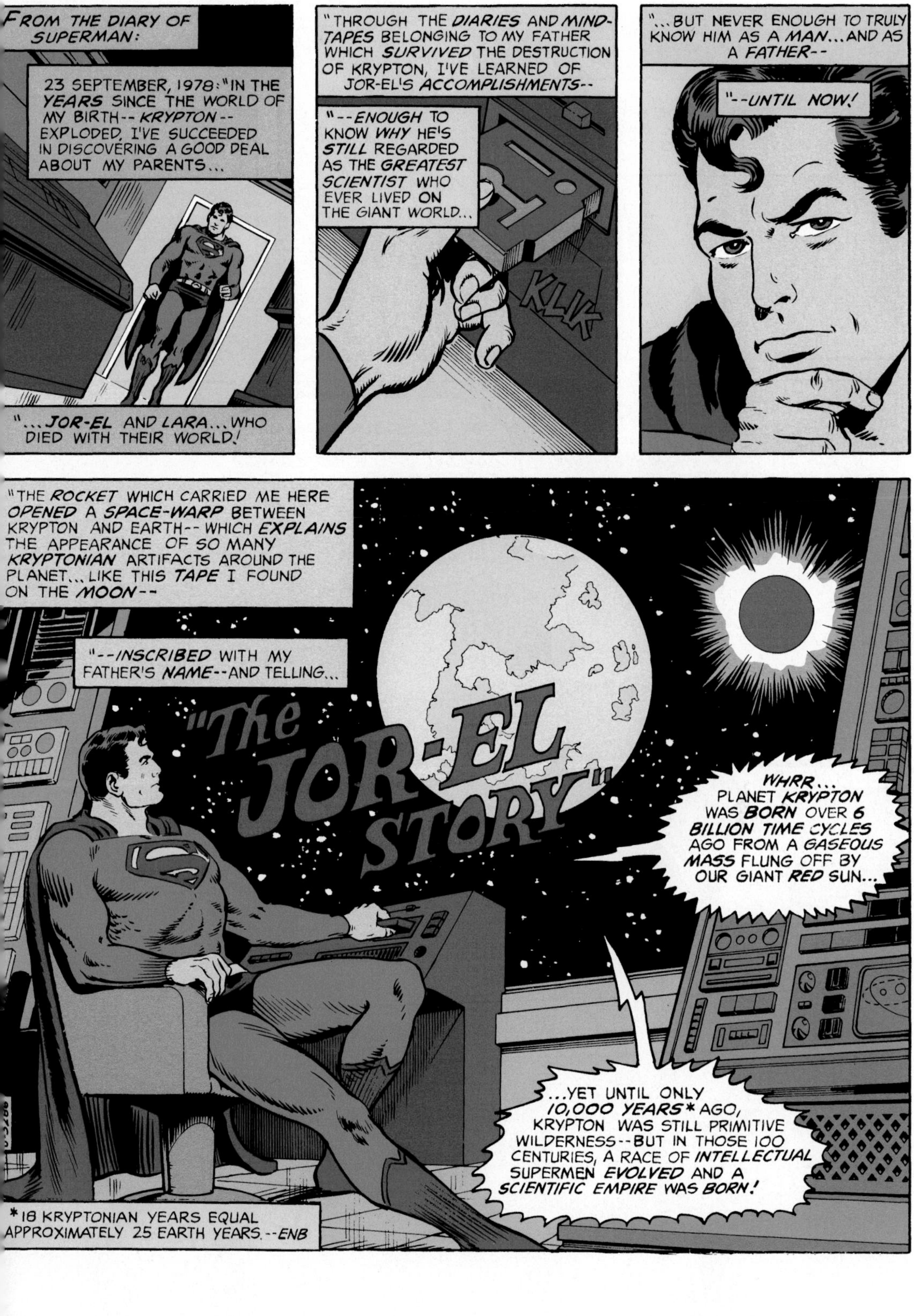
FROM THE DIARY OF SUPERMAN:
23 SEPTEMBER, 1978: "IN THE YEARS SINCE THE WORLD OF MY BIRTH-- KRYPTON-- EXPLODED, I'VE SUCCEEDED IN DISCOVERING A GOOD DEAL ABOUT MY PARENTS...
"...JOR-EL AND LARA...WHO DIED WITH THEIR WORLD!
"THROUGH THE DIARIES AND MIND-TAPES BELONGING TO MY FATHER WHICH SURVIVED THE DESTRUCTION OF KRYPTON, I'VE LEARNED OF JOR-EL'S ACCOMPLISHMENTS--
"--ENOUGH TO KNOW WHY HE'S STILL REGARDED AS THE GREATEST SCIENTIST WHO EVER LIVED ON THE GIANT WORLD...
KLIK
"...BUT NEVER ENOUGH TO TRULY KNOW HIM AS A MAN...AND AS A FATHER--
"--UNTIL NOW!
"THE ROCKET WHICH CARRIED ME HERE OPENED A SPACE-WARP BETWEEN KRYPTON AND EARTH-- WHICH EXPLAINS THE APPEARANCE OF SO MANY KRYPTONIAN ARTIFACTS AROUND THE PLANET...LIKE THIS TAPE I FOUND ON THE MOON--
"--INSCRIBED WITH MY FATHER'S NAME--AND TELLING...
"The JOR-EL STORY"
WHRR... PLANET KRYPTON WAS BORN OVER 6 BILLION TIME CYCLES AGO FROM A GASEOUS MASS FLUNG OFF BY OUR GIANT RED SUN...
...YET UNTIL ONLY 10,000 YEARS* AGO, KRYPTON WAS STILL PRIMITIVE WILDERNESS--BUT IN THOSE 100 CENTURIES, A RACE OF INTELLECTUAL SUPERMEN EVOLVED AND A SCIENTIFIC EMPIRE WAS BORN!
*18 KRYPTONIAN YEARS EQUAL APPROXIMATELY 25 EARTH YEARS.--ENB

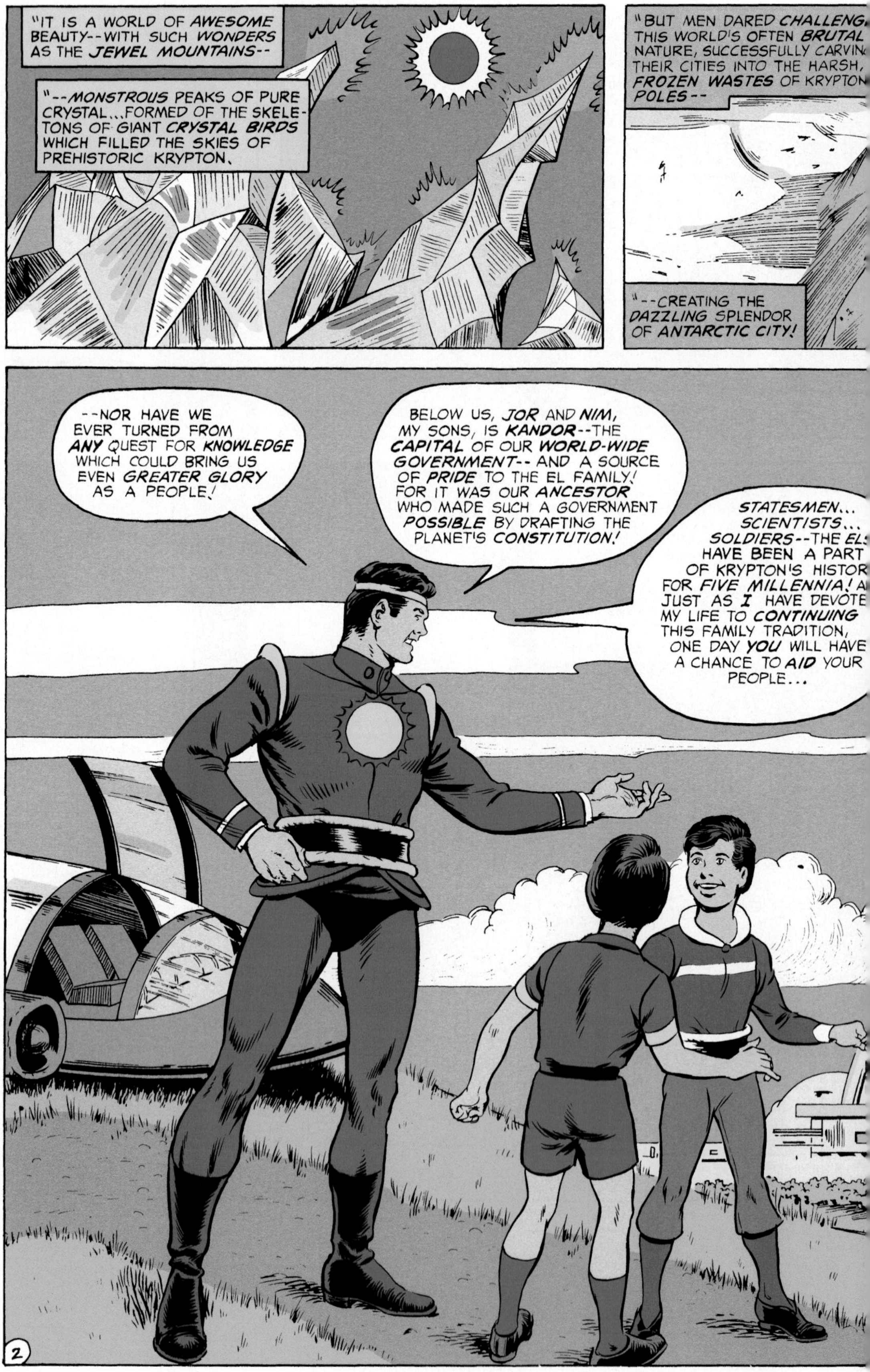
"IT IS A WORLD OF AWESOME BEAUTY--WITH SUCH WONDERS AS THE JEWEL MOUNTAINS--
"--MONSTROUS PEAKS OF PURE CRYSTAL...FORMED OF THE SKELETONS OF GIANT CRYSTAL BIRDS WHICH FILLED THE SKIES OF PREHISTORIC KRYPTON.
"BUT MEN DARED CHALLENG THIS WORLD'S OFTEN BRUTAL NATURE, SUCCESSFULLY CARVIN THEIR CITIES INTO THE HARSH, FROZEN WASTES OF KRYPTON POLES--
"--CREATING THE DAZZLING SPLENDOR OF ANTARCTIC CITY!
--NOR HAVE WE EVER TURNED FROM ANY QUEST FOR KNOWLEDGE WHICH COULD BRING US EVEN GREATER GLORY AS A PEOPLE!
BELOW US, JOR AND NIM, MY SONS, IS KANDOR--THE CAPITAL OF OUR WORLD-WIDE GOVERNMENT-- AND A SOURCE OF PRIDE TO THE EL FAMILY! FOR IT WAS OUR ANCESTOR WHO MADE SUCH A GOVERNMENT POSSIBLE BY DRAFTING THE PLANET'S CONSTITUTION!
STATESMEN... SCIENTISTS... SOLDIERS--THE EL HAVE BEEN A PART OF KRYPTON'S HISTOR FOR FIVE MILLENNIA! A JUST AS I HAVE DEVOTE MY LIFE TO CONTINUING THIS FAMILY TRADITION, ONE DAY YOU WILL HAVE A CHANCE TO AID YOUR PEOPLE...
2

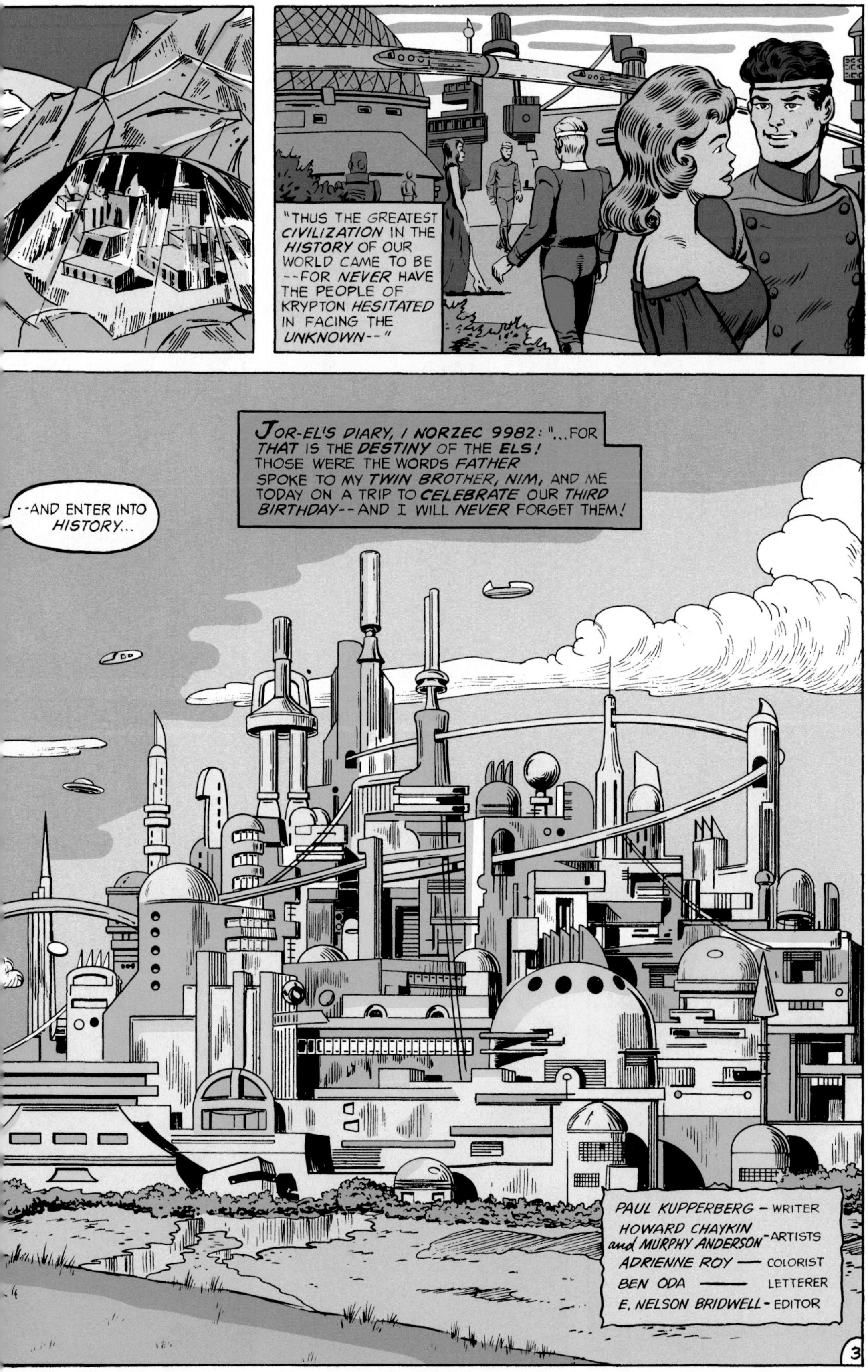
"THUS THE GREATEST CIVILIZATION IN THE HISTORY OF OUR WORLD CAME TO BE --FOR NEVER HAVE THE PEOPLE OF KRYPTON HESITATED IN FACING THE UNKNOWN--"
--AND ENTER INTO HISTORY...
JOR-EL'S DIARY, I NORZEC 9982: "...FOR THAT IS THE DESTINY OF THE ELS! THOSE WERE THE WORDS FATHER SPOKE TO MY TWIN BROTHER, NIM, AND ME TODAY ON A TRIP TO CELEBRATE OUR THIRD BIRTHDAY--AND I WILL NEVER FORGET THEM!
PAUL KUPPERBERG - WRITER
HOWARD CHAYKIN and MURPHY ANDERSON - ARTISTS
ADRIENNE ROY — COLORIST
BEN ODA — LETTERER
E. NELSON BRIDWELL - EDITOR
3

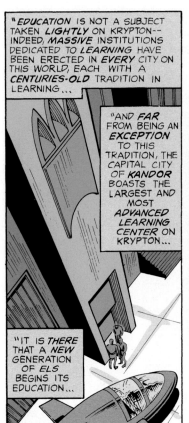

"*EDUCATION* IS NOT A SUBJECT TAKEN *LIGHTLY* ON KRYPTON-- INDEED, *MASSIVE* INSTITUTIONS DEDICATED TO *LEARNING* HAVE BEEN ERECTED IN *EVERY* CITY ON THIS WORLD, EACH WITH A *CENTURIES-OLD* TRADITION IN LEARNING ...

"AND *FAR* FROM BEING AN *EXCEPTION* TO THIS TRADITION, THE CAPITAL CITY OF *KANDOR* BOASTS THE LARGEST AND MOST *ADVANCED LEARNING CENTER* ON KRYPTON...

"IT IS *THERE* THAT A *NEW* GENERATION OF *ELS* BEGINS ITS EDUCATION...

I AM *DIRECTOR VEN,* CHIEF EDUCATOR OF THE CENTER! BUT, LIKE YOUR FATHER MANY YEARS AGO, I HOPE YOU WILL CONSIDER ME YOUR *FRIEND* AS WELL AS YOUR *TUTOR!*

YOU KNEW MY FATHER WHEN HE WAS A *BOY,* DIRECTOR!?

OH, YES-- AND YOUR *GRANDFATHER* WAS ONE OF MY *FIRST* STUDENTS--

--BUT THAT WAS IN THE YEARS *BEFORE* WE USED *THOUGHT TRANSFER HELMET* TO DO ALL OUR TEACHING! WHY, IN THE OLD DAYS, WE *ACTUALLY* USED TO *LECTURE* THE STUDENTS!

NOWADAYS, HOWEVER, INFORMATION IS *ELECTRICALLY IMPLANTED* DIRECTLY ONTO THE *BRAIN*--

--AND WORKING IN *CONJUNCTION* WITH COMPUTERS, THE STUDENT IS TAUGHT HOW TO *ACTIVELY APPLY* THAT NEW KNOWLEDGE!

MORE *ADVANCED* STUDENTS ARE TAUGHT THROUGH *RNA TRAINING!* INFORMATION IS INTRODUCED INTO THE BODY THROUGH A GENETICALLY *CODED* MESSENGER--*RNA*--AND PERMA-NENTLY IMPLANTED IN THE BRAIN BY ADDITIONAL *SUBLIMINAL* TRAINING! IT'S A MUCH *FASTER,* MORE *ADVANCED* METHOD!

WELL, ARE THERE ANY *QUESTIONS?*

I HAVE A QUESTION, DIRECTOR--

--HOW DO I TURN THIS *ON?*

HA! HA! YOUR *INTELLIGENCE* TESTS WERE *CORRECT,* YOUNG *JOR*--YOU ARE A NATURAL *SCHOLAR!*

I JUST WANT TO *LEARN,* DIRECTOR--

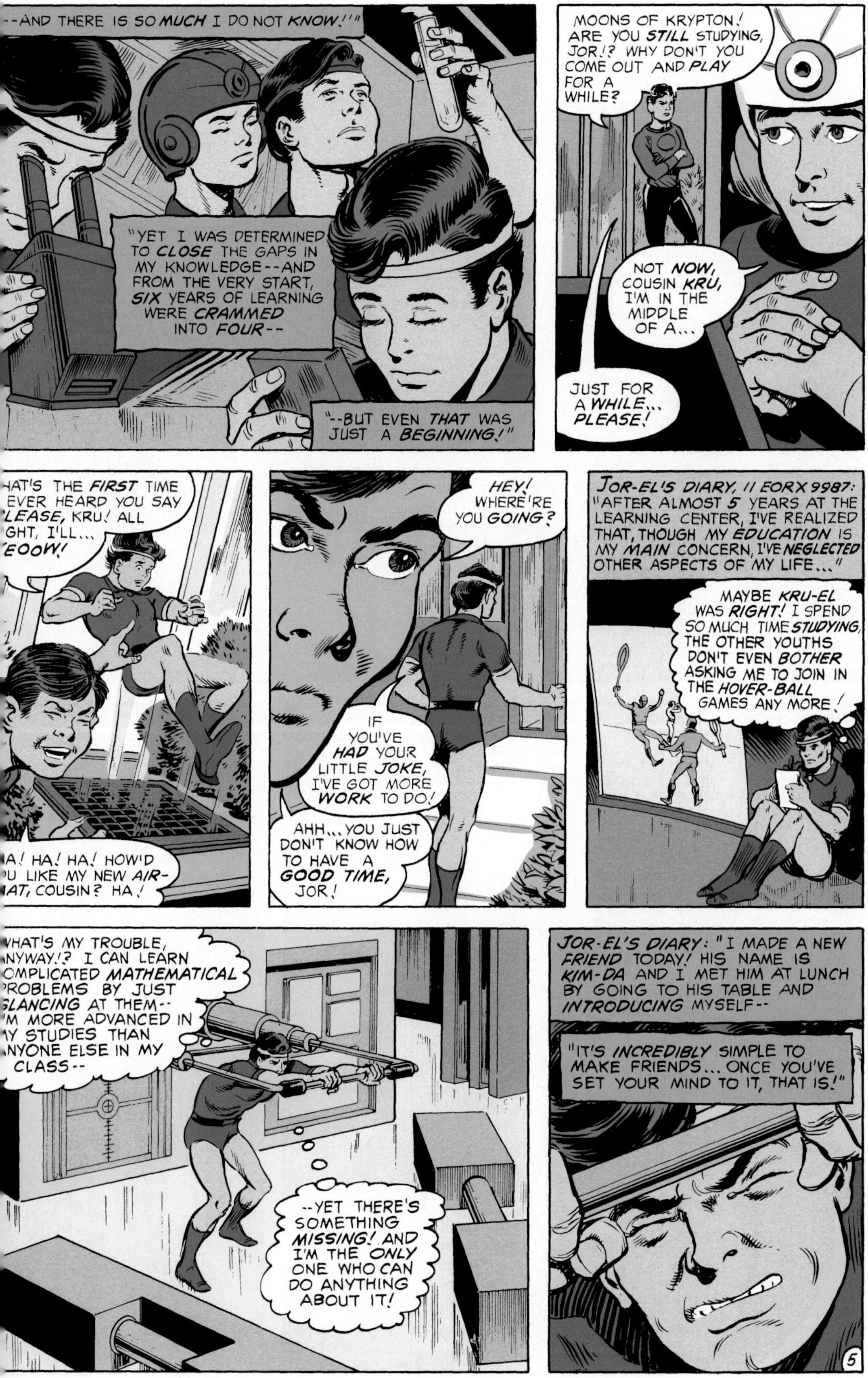
--AND THERE IS SO MUCH I DO NOT KNOW!'"
"YET I WAS DETERMINED TO CLOSE THE GAPS IN MY KNOWLEDGE--AND FROM THE VERY START, SIX YEARS OF LEARNING WERE CRAMMED INTO FOUR--
"--BUT EVEN THAT WAS JUST A BEGINNING!"
MOONS OF KRYPTON! ARE YOU STILL STUDYING, JOR!? WHY DON'T YOU COME OUT AND PLAY FOR A WHILE?
NOT NOW, COUSIN KRU, I'M IN THE MIDDLE OF A...
JUST FOR A WHILE... PLEASE!
HAT'S THE FIRST TIME EVER HEARD YOU SAY LEASE, KRU! ALL GHT, I'LL... EOOW!
A! HA! HA! HOW'D U LIKE MY NEW AIR-AT, COUSIN? HA!
HEY! WHERE'RE YOU GOING?
IF YOU'VE HAD YOUR LITTLE JOKE, I'VE GOT MORE WORK TO DO!
AHH... YOU JUST DON'T KNOW HOW TO HAVE A GOOD TIME, JOR!
JOR-EL'S DIARY, 11 EORX 9987: "AFTER ALMOST 5 YEARS AT THE LEARNING CENTER, I'VE REALIZED THAT, THOUGH MY EDUCATION IS MY MAIN CONCERN, I'VE NEGLECTED OTHER ASPECTS OF MY LIFE..."
MAYBE KRU-EL WAS RIGHT! I SPEND SO MUCH TIME STUDYING, THE OTHER YOUTHS DON'T EVEN BOTHER ASKING ME TO JOIN IN THE HOVER-BALL GAMES ANY MORE!
VHAT'S MY TROUBLE, NYWAY!? I CAN LEARN OMPLICATED MATHEMATICAL ROBLEMS BY JUST LANCING AT THEM-- 'M MORE ADVANCED IN Y STUDIES THAN NYONE ELSE IN MY CLASS--
--YET THERE'S SOMETHING MISSING! AND I'M THE ONLY ONE WHO CAN DO ANYTHING ABOUT IT!
JOR-EL'S DIARY: "I MADE A NEW FRIEND TODAY! HIS NAME IS KIM-DA AND I MET HIM AT LUNCH BY GOING TO HIS TABLE AND INTRODUCING MYSELF--
"IT'S INCREDIBLY SIMPLE TO MAKE FRIENDS... ONCE YOU'VE SET YOUR MIND TO IT, THAT IS!"
5

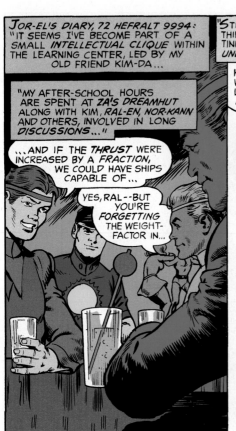

JOR-EL'S DIARY, 72 HEFRALT 9994: "IT SEEMS I'VE BECOME PART OF A SMALL *INTELLECTUAL CLIQUE* WITHIN THE LEARNING CENTER, LED BY MY OLD FRIEND KIM-DA..."

"MY AFTER-SCHOOL HOURS ARE SPENT AT *ZA'S DREAMHUT* ALONG WITH KIM, *RAL-EN, NOR-KANN* AND OTHERS, INVOLVED IN LONG *DISCUSSIONS...*"

...AND IF THE *THRUST* WERE INCREASED BY A *FRACTION,* WE COULD HAVE SHIPS CAPABLE OF...

YES, RAL--BUT YOU'RE *FORGETTING* THE *WEIGHT-FACTOR* IN...

"STILL, THERE *ARE* THINGS WHICH CONTINUE TO ELUDE MY *UNDERSTANDING...*

HELLO, JOR-EL! WOULD YOU LIKE TO *DANCE?*

...ER... DANCE...?

" THAT WAS YESTERDAY. TODAY.

...AND ALL I NEED IS *YOUR* PERMISSION TO BEGIN MY *PROJECT!*

HE IS *AMAZING,* IS HE NOT? YOUNG *JOR* IS THE *BRIGHTEST* PUPIL I HAVE *EVER* TAUGHT!

JOR-EL'S DIARY, 36 NORZEC 9994: "AFTER *12 YEARS* OF SCHOOLING, I *GRADUATE* FROM THE LEARNING CENTER TODAY! I'VE ALREADY TAKEN MY STUDIES AS FAR AS *POSSIBLE* AT THE CENTER, AND I'M LOOKING *FORWARD* TO AT LAST STRIKING OUT ON MY OWN-- WITH MY *OWN PROJECTS!*"

TRUTHFULLY, JOR, THIS IS THE MOST *ASTONISHING* BIT OF MATHEMATICS I'VE *EVER* SEEN --YEARS BEYOND ANYTHING PREVIOUSLY DONE IN THE FIELD!

BUT THERE'S STILL *MORE* TO DO, DIRECTOR VEN-- MY CALCULATIONS AREN'T YET *COMPLETE!*

YOU HAVE THE *REST* OF YOUR LIFE BEFORE YOU, JOR...A *LONG,* LONG TIME TO *FINISH* EVERYTHING YOU'VE BEGUN--AND TO *BEGIN* NEW THINGS!

NOW, STOP *WORRYING* AND RUN ALONG, OR YOU WILL *MISS* YOUR OWN *GRADUATION CEREMONY!*

WELL, HELLO THERE, *YOUNG GENIUS!* ARE YOU *READY* TO SAY YOUR *FAREWELLS* TO THE OLD LEARNING CENTER

I'M READY, KIM-DA...

...BY RAO-- AM I *READY!*

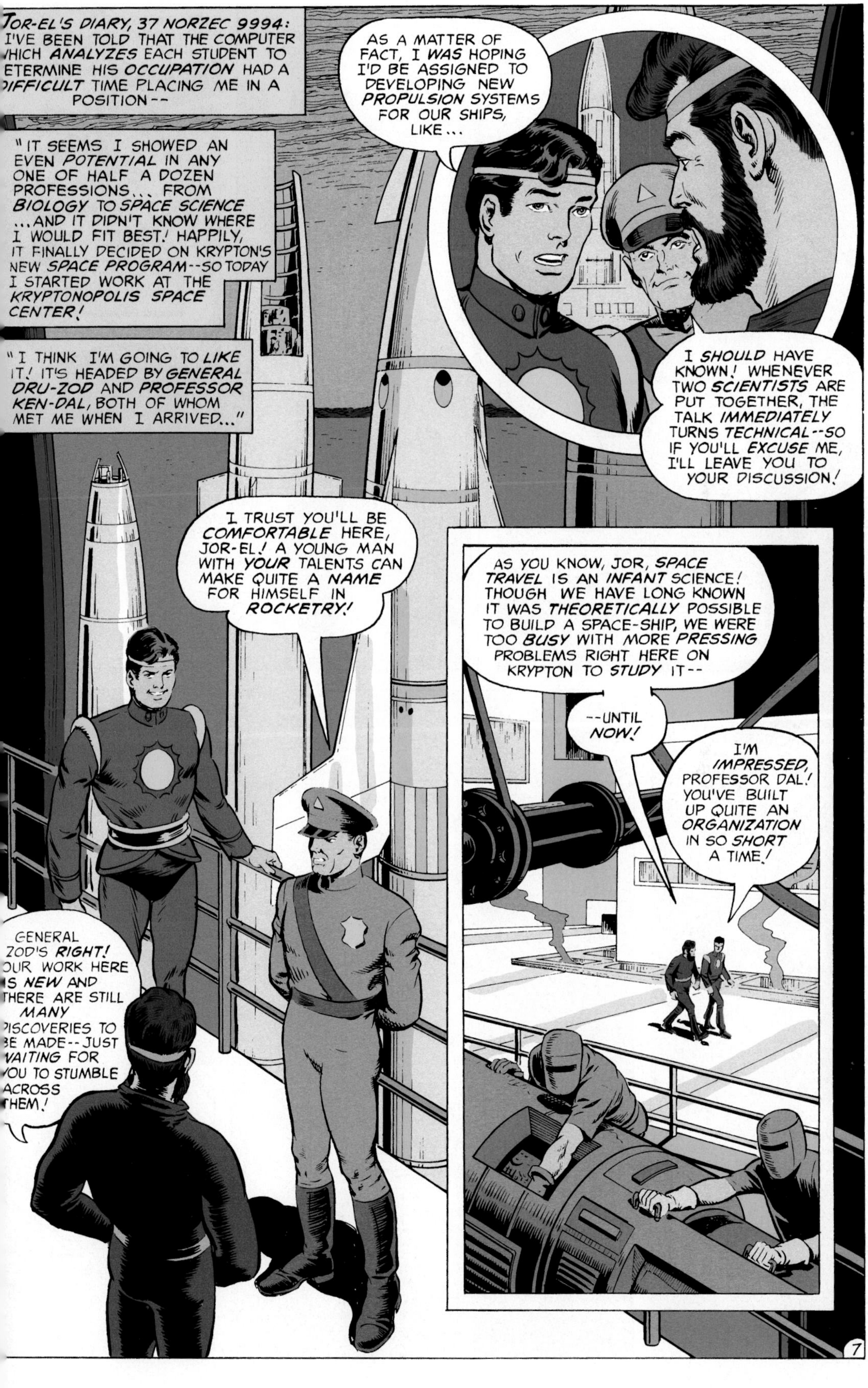
JOR-EL'S DIARY, 37 NORZEC 9994: I'VE BEEN TOLD THAT THE COMPUTER WHICH ANALYZES EACH STUDENT TO DETERMINE HIS OCCUPATION HAD A DIFFICULT TIME PLACING ME IN A POSITION--
"IT SEEMS I SHOWED AN EVEN POTENTIAL IN ANY ONE OF HALF A DOZEN PROFESSIONS... FROM BIOLOGY TO SPACE SCIENCE ...AND IT DIDN'T KNOW WHERE I WOULD FIT BEST! HAPPILY, IT FINALLY DECIDED ON KRYPTON'S NEW SPACE PROGRAM--SO TODAY I STARTED WORK AT THE KRYPTONOPOLIS SPACE CENTER!
"I THINK I'M GOING TO LIKE IT! IT'S HEADED BY GENERAL DRU-ZOD AND PROFESSOR KEN-DAL, BOTH OF WHOM MET ME WHEN I ARRIVED..."
I TRUST YOU'LL BE COMFORTABLE HERE, JOR-EL! A YOUNG MAN WITH YOUR TALENTS CAN MAKE QUITE A NAME FOR HIMSELF IN ROCKETRY!
GENERAL ZOD'S RIGHT! OUR WORK HERE IS NEW AND THERE ARE STILL MANY DISCOVERIES TO BE MADE--JUST WAITING FOR YOU TO STUMBLE ACROSS THEM!
AS A MATTER OF FACT, I WAS HOPING I'D BE ASSIGNED TO DEVELOPING NEW PROPULSION SYSTEMS FOR OUR SHIPS, LIKE...
I SHOULD HAVE KNOWN! WHENEVER TWO SCIENTISTS ARE PUT TOGETHER, THE TALK IMMEDIATELY TURNS TECHNICAL--SO IF YOU'LL EXCUSE ME, I'LL LEAVE YOU TO YOUR DISCUSSION!
AS YOU KNOW, JOR, SPACE TRAVEL IS AN INFANT SCIENCE! THOUGH WE HAVE LONG KNOWN IT WAS THEORETICALLY POSSIBLE TO BUILD A SPACE-SHIP, WE WERE TOO BUSY WITH MORE PRESSING PROBLEMS RIGHT HERE ON KRYPTON TO STUDY IT--
--UNTIL NOW!
I'M IMPRESSED, PROFESSOR DAL! YOU'VE BUILT UP QUITE AN ORGANIZATION IN SO SHORT A TIME!
7

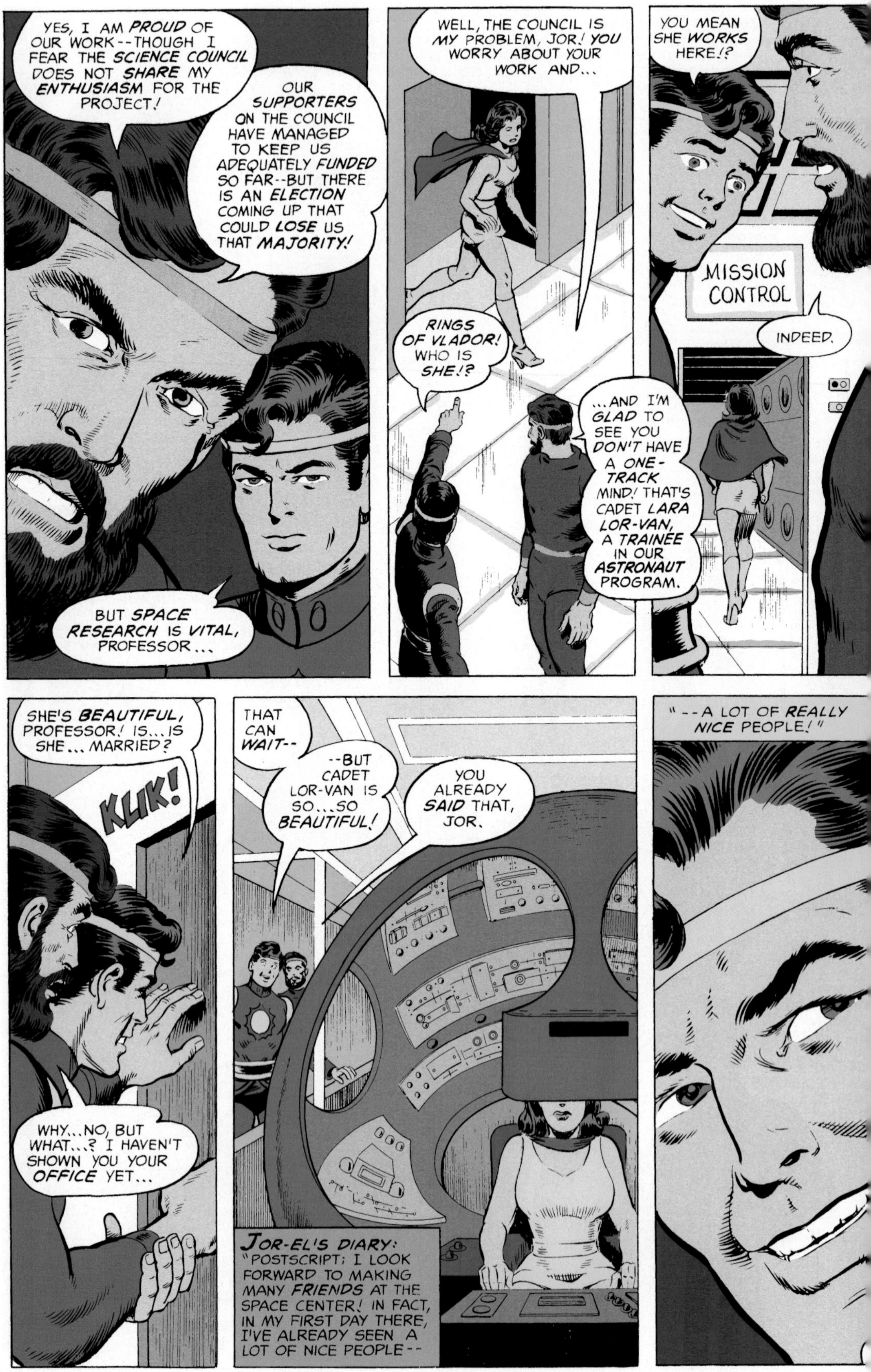

YES, I AM PROUD OF OUR WORK--THOUGH I FEAR THE SCIENCE COUNCIL DOES NOT SHARE MY ENTHUSIASM FOR THE PROJECT!
OUR SUPPORTERS ON THE COUNCIL HAVE MANAGED TO KEEP US ADEQUATELY FUNDED SO FAR--BUT THERE IS AN ELECTION COMING UP THAT COULD LOSE US THAT MAJORITY!
BUT SPACE RESEARCH IS VITAL, PROFESSOR...
WELL, THE COUNCIL IS MY PROBLEM, JOR! YOU WORRY ABOUT YOUR WORK AND...
RINGS OF VLADOR! WHO IS SHE!?
...AND I'M GLAD TO SEE YOU DON'T HAVE A ONE-TRACK MIND! THAT'S CADET LARA LOR-VAN, A TRAINEE IN OUR ASTRONAUT PROGRAM.
YOU MEAN SHE WORKS HERE!?
MISSION CONTROL
INDEED.
SHE'S BEAUTIFUL, PROFESSOR! IS...IS SHE... MARRIED?
KLIK!
WHY...NO, BUT WHAT...? I HAVEN'T SHOWN YOU YOUR OFFICE YET...
THAT CAN WAIT--
--BUT CADET LOR-VAN IS SO...SO BEAUTIFUL!
YOU ALREADY SAID THAT, JOR.
JOR-EL'S DIARY: "POSTSCRIPT: I LOOK FORWARD TO MAKING MANY FRIENDS AT THE SPACE CENTER! IN FACT, IN MY FIRST DAY THERE, I'VE ALREADY SEEN A LOT OF NICE PEOPLE--
"--A LOT OF REALLY NICE PEOPLE!"

JOR-EL'S DIARY, 3 BELYUTH 9995: "KEN-DAL DIDN'T *WASTE* ANY TIME GETTING ME TO WORK! I'VE BEEN ASSIGNED TO *RESEARCH* AND *DEVELOPMENT*--

-- MORE SPECIFICALLY, I'M TO DEVELOP A NEW, *CHEAPER* METHOD OF *PROPULSION* FOR OUR *ROCKETS*--

"--AND I THINK I *MAY* HAVE THE ANSWER IN *ANTI-GRAVITY!*"

JOR-EL'S DIARY, 36 BELYUTH 9995: "DAY BY DAY, I COME *CLOSER* TO *SUCCESS!* TODAY, I MANAGED TO *ISOLATE* AN ATOMIC PARTICLE WITH ANTI-GRAVITY PROPERTIES --

"--THOUGH I *STILL* CANNOT SAY WHAT IT IS THAT *CAUSES* THIS *PHENOMENON*.

"MY RESEARCH CONTINUES."

JOR-EL'S DIARY, 68 BELYUTH 9995: "*SUCCESS!* TODAY I WAS ABLE TO *DUPLICATE* THE ANTI-GRAVITY PARTICLE FOR THE *FIRST* TIME! MY *NEXT* STEP IS TO *ADAPT* IT TO A MORE *PRACTICAL* FORM."

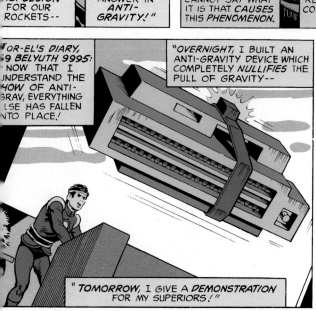

JOR-EL'S DIARY, 69 BELYUTH 9995: "NOW THAT I *UNDERSTAND* THE *HOW* OF ANTI-GRAV, EVERYTHING *ELSE* HAS FALLEN INTO PLACE."

"*OVERNIGHT*, I BUILT AN ANTI-GRAVITY DEVICE WHICH COMPLETELY *NULLIFIES* THE PULL OF GRAVITY--

" *TOMORROW*, I GIVE A *DEMONSTRATION* FOR MY SUPERIORS!"

I TRUST YOU HAVE A *GOOD* REASON FOR CALLING ME AWAY FROM A *MEETING* WITH THE COUNCIL, JOR-EL!

I THINK YOU'LL BE *INTERESTED* IN WHAT I HAVE TO *SHOW* YOU AND PROFESSOR DAL, GENERAL ZOD!

I'M *SURE* WE WILL BE, JOR... BUT *WHY* DID WE HAVE TO COME UP TO THE *ROOF?*

QUITE SIMPLY, SIR, SO I COULD *JUMP OFF!*

EL!! COME BACK, YOU YOUNG FOOL!

CALM DOWN, GENERAL--I'M PERFECTLY *ALL RIGHT!*

BY THE MOONS OF KRYPTON! HE'S *FLYING--WITHOUT* ROCKETS!

TH-THEN JOR-EL HAS *DONE* IT... HE'S DISCOVERED THE SECRET OF *ANTI-GRAVITY!*

AMAZING! THE BOY'S A *GENIUS!*

JOR-EL'S DIARY, 70 BELYUTH 9995: "SUFFICE IT TO SAY, THEY WERE SUFFICIENTLY *IMPRESSED*."

9

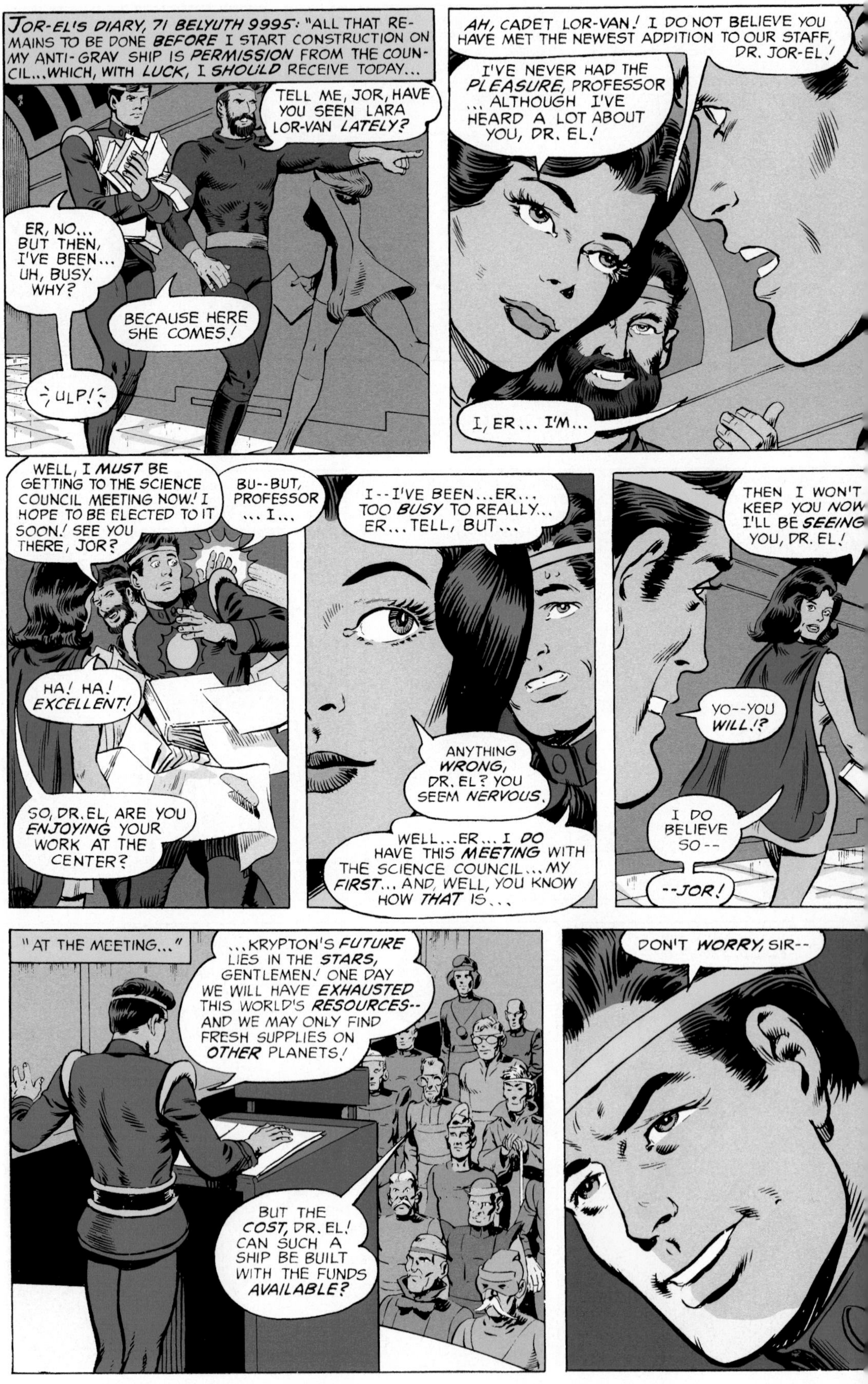

JOR-EL'S DIARY, 71 BELYUTH 9995: "ALL THAT REMAINS TO BE DONE BEFORE I START CONSTRUCTION ON MY ANTI-GRAV SHIP IS PERMISSION FROM THE COUNCIL...WHICH, WITH LUCK, I SHOULD RECEIVE TODAY...
TELL ME, JOR, HAVE YOU SEEN LARA LOR-VAN LATELY?
ER, NO... BUT THEN, I'VE BEEN... UH, BUSY. WHY?
BECAUSE HERE SHE COMES!
ULP!
AH, CADET LOR-VAN! I DO NOT BELIEVE YOU HAVE MET THE NEWEST ADDITION TO OUR STAFF, DR. JOR-EL!
I'VE NEVER HAD THE PLEASURE, PROFESSOR ... ALTHOUGH I'VE HEARD A LOT ABOUT YOU, DR. EL!
I, ER... I'M...
WELL, I MUST BE GETTING TO THE SCIENCE COUNCIL MEETING NOW! I HOPE TO BE ELECTED TO IT SOON! SEE YOU THERE, JOR?
BU--BUT, PROFESSOR ... I...
HA! HA! EXCELLENT!
SO, DR. EL, ARE YOU ENJOYING YOUR WORK AT THE CENTER?
I--I'VE BEEN...ER... TOO BUSY TO REALLY... ER...TELL, BUT...
ANYTHING WRONG, DR. EL? YOU SEEM NERVOUS.
WELL...ER...I DO HAVE THIS MEETING WITH THE SCIENCE COUNCIL...MY FIRST... AND, WELL, YOU KNOW HOW THAT IS...
THEN I WON'T KEEP YOU NOW I'LL BE SEEING YOU, DR. EL!
YO--YOU WILL!?
I DO BELIEVE SO --
--JOR!
"AT THE MEETING..."
...KRYPTON'S FUTURE LIES IN THE STARS, GENTLEMEN! ONE DAY WE WILL HAVE EXHAUSTED THIS WORLD'S RESOURCES-- AND WE MAY ONLY FIND FRESH SUPPLIES ON OTHER PLANETS!
BUT THE COST, DR. EL! CAN SUCH A SHIP BE BUILT WITH THE FUNDS AVAILABLE?
DON'T WORRY, SIR--

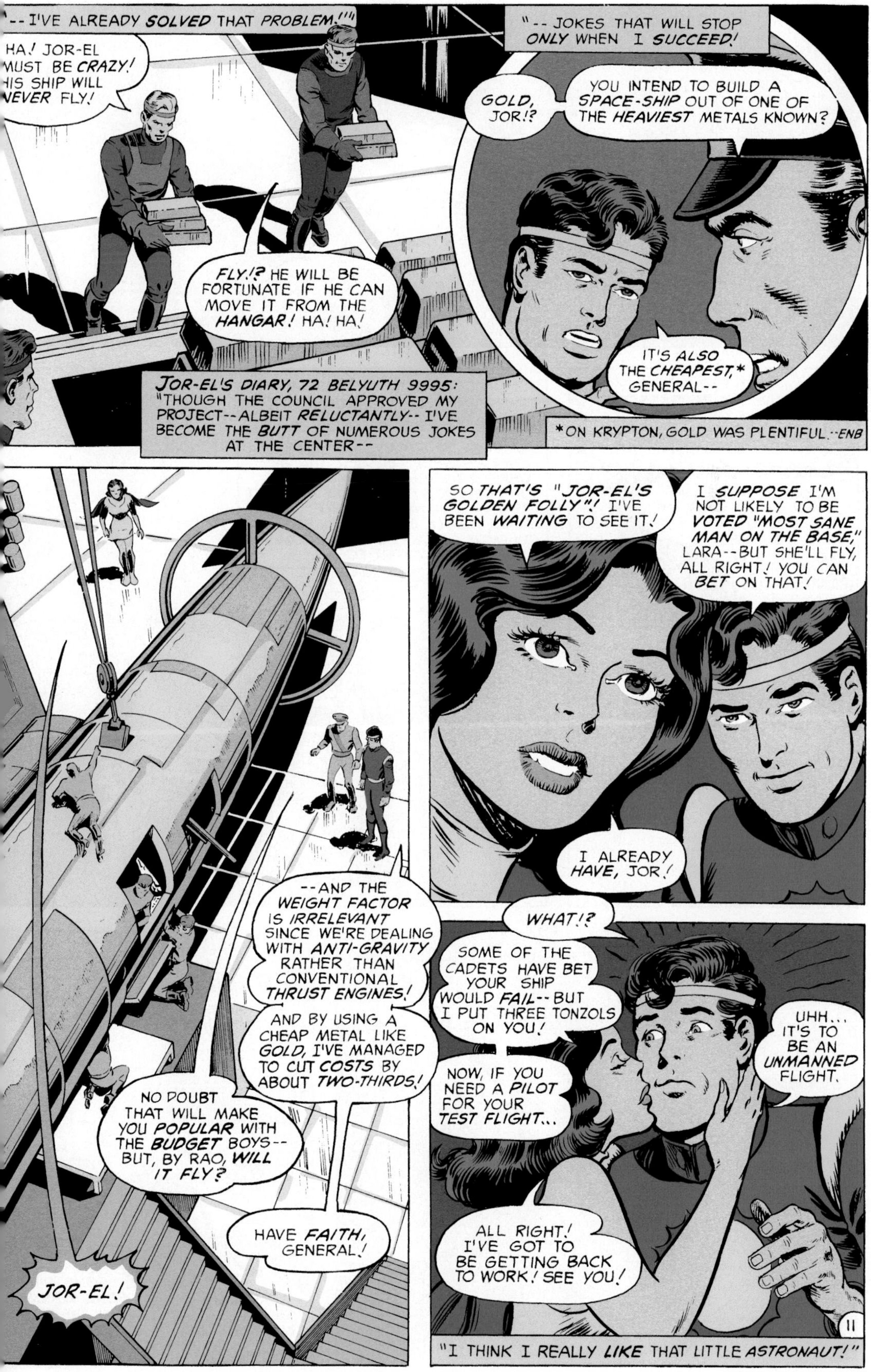
"--I'VE ALREADY SOLVED THAT PROBLEM!"
HA! JOR-EL MUST BE CRAZY! HIS SHIP WILL NEVER FLY!
FLY!? HE WILL BE FORTUNATE IF HE CAN MOVE IT FROM THE HANGAR! HA! HA!
JOR-EL'S DIARY, 72 BELYUTH 9995: "THOUGH THE COUNCIL APPROVED MY PROJECT--ALBEIT RELUCTANTLY--I'VE BECOME THE BUTT OF NUMEROUS JOKES AT THE CENTER--
"--JOKES THAT WILL STOP ONLY WHEN I SUCCEED!
GOLD, JOR!?
YOU INTEND TO BUILD A SPACE-SHIP OUT OF ONE OF THE HEAVIEST METALS KNOWN?
IT'S ALSO THE CHEAPEST,* GENERAL--
*ON KRYPTON, GOLD WAS PLENTIFUL.--ENB
--AND THE WEIGHT FACTOR IS IRRELEVANT SINCE WE'RE DEALING WITH ANTI-GRAVITY RATHER THAN CONVENTIONAL THRUST ENGINES!
AND BY USING A CHEAP METAL LIKE GOLD, I'VE MANAGED TO CUT COSTS BY ABOUT TWO-THIRDS!
NO DOUBT THAT WILL MAKE YOU POPULAR WITH THE BUDGET BOYS--BUT, BY RAO, WILL IT FLY?
HAVE FAITH, GENERAL!
JOR-EL!
SO THAT'S "JOR-EL'S GOLDEN FOLLY"! I'VE BEEN WAITING TO SEE IT!
I SUPPOSE I'M NOT LIKELY TO BE VOTED "MOST SANE MAN ON THE BASE," LARA--BUT SHE'LL FLY, ALL RIGHT! YOU CAN BET ON THAT!
I ALREADY HAVE, JOR!
WHAT!?
SOME OF THE CADETS HAVE BET YOUR SHIP WOULD FAIL--BUT I PUT THREE TONZOLS ON YOU!
NOW, IF YOU NEED A PILOT FOR YOUR TEST FLIGHT...
UHH... IT'S TO BE AN UNMANNED FLIGHT.
ALL RIGHT! I'VE GOT TO BE GETTING BACK TO WORK! SEE YOU!
11
"I THINK I REALLY LIKE THAT LITTLE ASTRONAUT!"

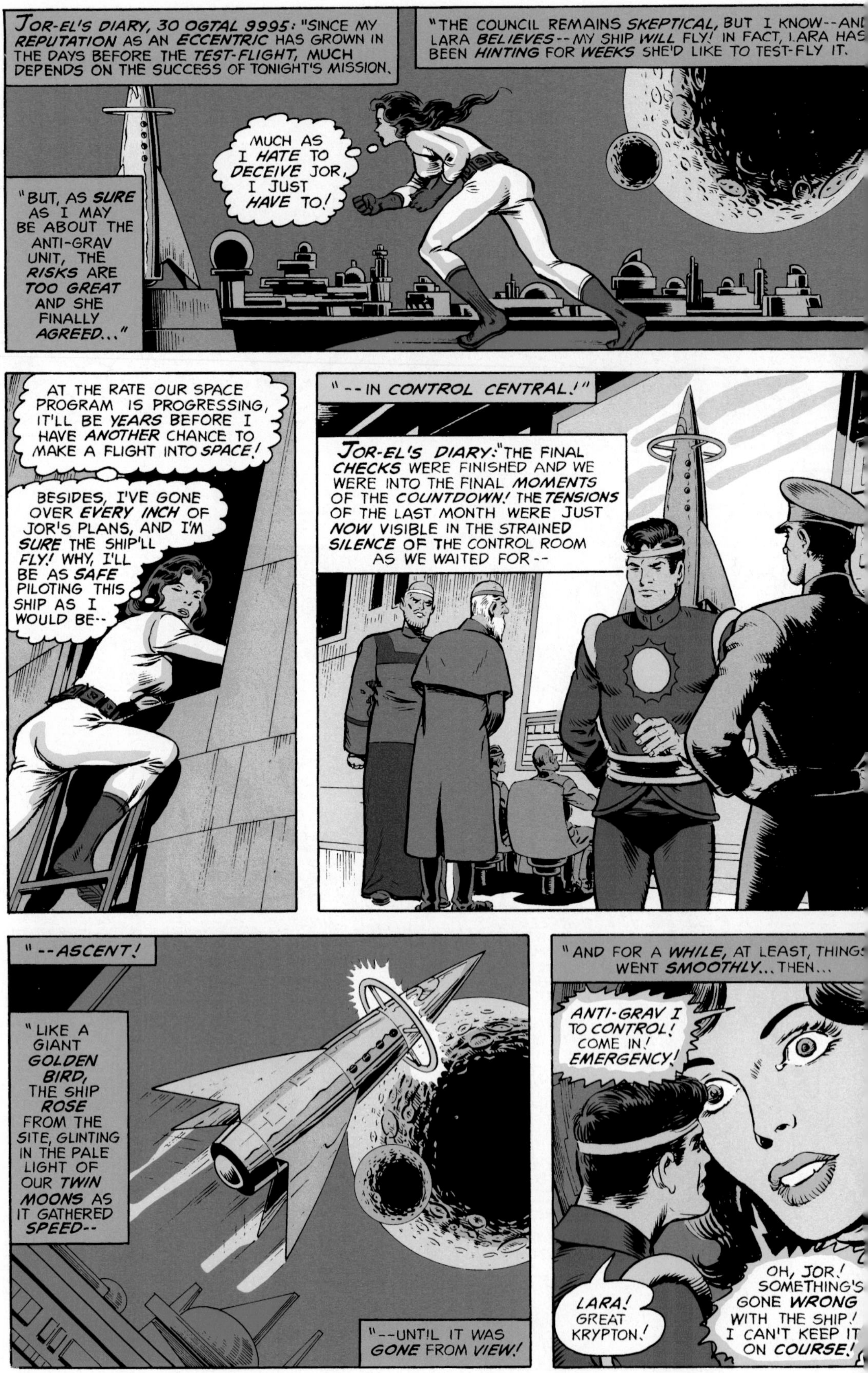
JOR-EL'S DIARY, 30 OGTAL 9995: "SINCE MY REPUTATION AS AN ECCENTRIC HAS GROWN IN THE DAYS BEFORE THE TEST-FLIGHT, MUCH DEPENDS ON THE SUCCESS OF TONIGHT'S MISSION.
"THE COUNCIL REMAINS SKEPTICAL, BUT I KNOW--AND LARA BELIEVES--MY SHIP WILL FLY! IN FACT, LARA HAS BEEN HINTING FOR WEEKS SHE'D LIKE TO TEST-FLY IT.
"BUT, AS SURE AS I MAY BE ABOUT THE ANTI-GRAV UNIT, THE RISKS ARE TOO GREAT AND SHE FINALLY AGREED..."
MUCH AS I HATE TO DECEIVE JOR, I JUST HAVE TO!
AT THE RATE OUR SPACE PROGRAM IS PROGRESSING, IT'LL BE YEARS BEFORE I HAVE ANOTHER CHANCE TO MAKE A FLIGHT INTO SPACE!
BESIDES, I'VE GONE OVER EVERY INCH OF JOR'S PLANS, AND I'M SURE THE SHIP'LL FLY! WHY, I'LL BE AS SAFE PILOTING THIS SHIP AS I WOULD BE--
"--IN CONTROL CENTRAL!"
JOR-EL'S DIARY: "THE FINAL CHECKS WERE FINISHED AND WE WERE INTO THE FINAL MOMENTS OF THE COUNTDOWN! THE TENSIONS OF THE LAST MONTH WERE JUST NOW VISIBLE IN THE STRAINED SILENCE OF THE CONTROL ROOM AS WE WAITED FOR--
"--ASCENT!
"LIKE A GIANT GOLDEN BIRD, THE SHIP ROSE FROM THE SITE, GLINTING IN THE PALE LIGHT OF OUR TWIN MOONS AS IT GATHERED SPEED--
"--UNTIL IT WAS GONE FROM VIEW!
"AND FOR A WHILE, AT LEAST, THINGS WENT SMOOTHLY... THEN...
ANTI-GRAV I TO CONTROL! COME IN! EMERGENCY!
LARA! GREAT KRYPTON!
OH, JOR! SOMETHING'S GONE WRONG WITH THE SHIP! I CAN'T KEEP IT ON COURSE!

I DIDN'T STOP TO ASK WHY SHE WAS *ABOARD* THE SHIP--THERE'D BE *TIME* FOR THAT LATER--BUT I *DID* HAVE ENOUGH FAITH IN HER *SKILLS* AS A *PILOT* TO INSTANTLY REACT TO HER CALL...

RAO! THE SHIP'S BEING *PUSHED* FROM ITS *ORBIT* BY OUR MOON WEGTHOR'S GRAVITY!

QUICK! SHUT DOWN THE *ANTI-GRAV* UNIT!

"WITH THE UNIT *OFF*, THE SHIP'S *ONLY* MODE OF PROPULSION WAS SMALL ROCKETS DESIGNED FOR MINOR COURSE *CORRECTIONS*--

"BUT THEY COULD DO *NOTHING* TO RETURN THE SHIP TO *KRYPTON*... *ANTI-GRAV I* WOULD *CRASH-LAND* ON WEGTHOR."

JOR-EL'S DIARY, 33 OGTAL 9925: "THESE PAST *THREE DAYS* HAVE BEEN *TORTURE!*

"WE'VE RECEIVED NO WORD FROM *LARA* SINCE THE SHIP CRASHED, MEANING EITHER HER RADIO WAS *SMASHED* IN THE LANDING--

"--OR SHE'S...NO! I WON'T BELIEVE THAT!"

"*TODAY*, I'LL KNOW FOR *SURE*...FOR *TODAY'S* THE DAY THE *ROCKET* CARRYING THE FIRST GROUP OF *COLONISTS* DESTINED FOR WEGTHOR LEAVES THE SPACE CENTER!

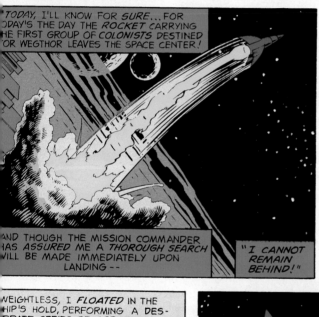

AND THOUGH THE MISSION COMMANDER HAS *ASSURED* ME A *THOROUGH SEARCH* WILL BE MADE IMMEDIATELY UPON LANDING--

"I CANNOT REMAIN BEHIND!"

"LATER: THE *WEIGHT* OF *SOLID FUEL* ROCKETS IS *FIGURED* DOWN TO THE *GRAM*--SO THE ONLY WAY I COULD *STOW AWAY* WITHOUT BEING *DETECTED*--AND MORE IMPORTANTLY, WITHOUT MY WEIGHT THROWING THE SHIP *OFF COURSE*--WAS TO USE AN *ANTI-GRAV UNIT!*

WEIGHTLESS, I *FLOATED* IN THE SHIP'S HOLD, PERFORMING A DESPERATE SERIES OF *ACROBATICS* TO KEEP FROM *TOUCHING THE WALLS*--

"--LEST MY UNCHANGED *BODY MASS* DISRUPT OUR FLIGHT!

"BUT I KNEW THAT *ANY RISK* I TOOK THIS DAY WOULD BE WELL WORTH IT, FOR I TOOK THEM *NOT* FOR MYSELF--BUT FOR THE WOMAN I *LOVE!*

"AT LAST--WE *DESCENDED.*"

13

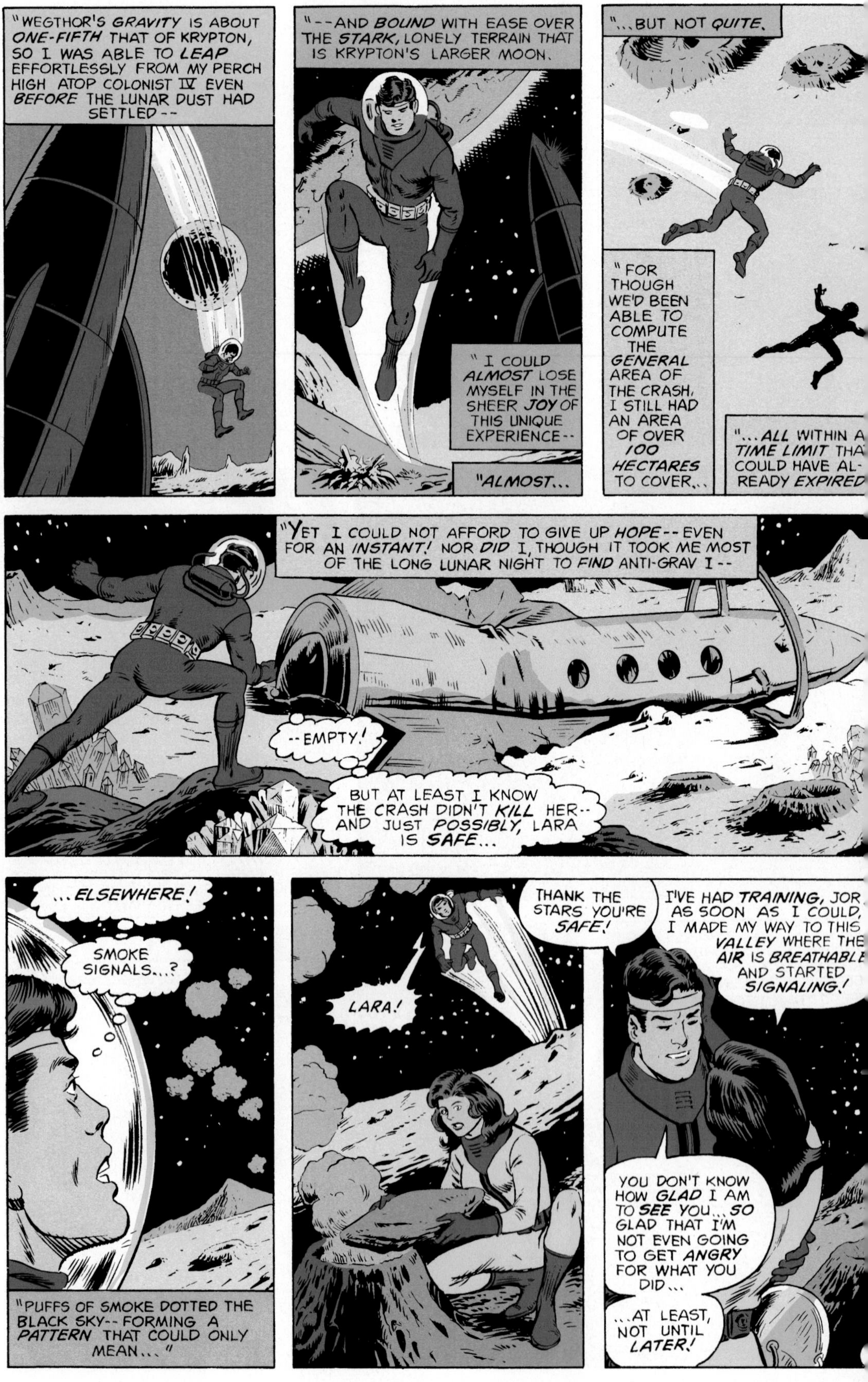
"WEGTHOR'S GRAVITY IS ABOUT ONE-FIFTH THAT OF KRYPTON, SO I WAS ABLE TO LEAP EFFORTLESSLY FROM MY PERCH HIGH ATOP COLONIST IV EVEN BEFORE THE LUNAR DUST HAD SETTLED--
"--AND BOUND WITH EASE OVER THE STARK, LONELY TERRAIN THAT IS KRYPTON'S LARGER MOON.
" I COULD ALMOST LOSE MYSELF IN THE SHEER JOY OF THIS UNIQUE EXPERIENCE--
"ALMOST...
"...BUT NOT QUITE.
" FOR THOUGH WE'D BEEN ABLE TO COMPUTE THE GENERAL AREA OF THE CRASH, I STILL HAD AN AREA OF OVER 100 HECTARES TO COVER...
"...ALL WITHIN A TIME LIMIT THA COULD HAVE AL-READY EXPIRED
"YET I COULD NOT AFFORD TO GIVE UP HOPE--EVEN FOR AN INSTANT! NOR DID I, THOUGH IT TOOK ME MOST OF THE LONG LUNAR NIGHT TO FIND ANTI-GRAV I--
--EMPTY!
BUT AT LEAST I KNOW THE CRASH DIDN'T KILL HER-- AND JUST POSSIBLY, LARA IS SAFE...
...ELSEWHERE!
SMOKE SIGNALS...?
"PUFFS OF SMOKE DOTTED THE BLACK SKY--FORMING A PATTERN THAT COULD ONLY MEAN..."
LARA!
THANK THE STARS YOU'RE SAFE!
I'VE HAD TRAINING, JOR AS SOON AS I COULD, I MADE MY WAY TO THIS VALLEY WHERE THE AIR IS BREATHABLE AND STARTED SIGNALING!
YOU DON'T KNOW HOW GLAD I AM TO SEE YOU... SO GLAD THAT I'M NOT EVEN GOING TO GET ANGRY FOR WHAT YOU DID...
...AT LEAST, NOT UNTIL LATER!

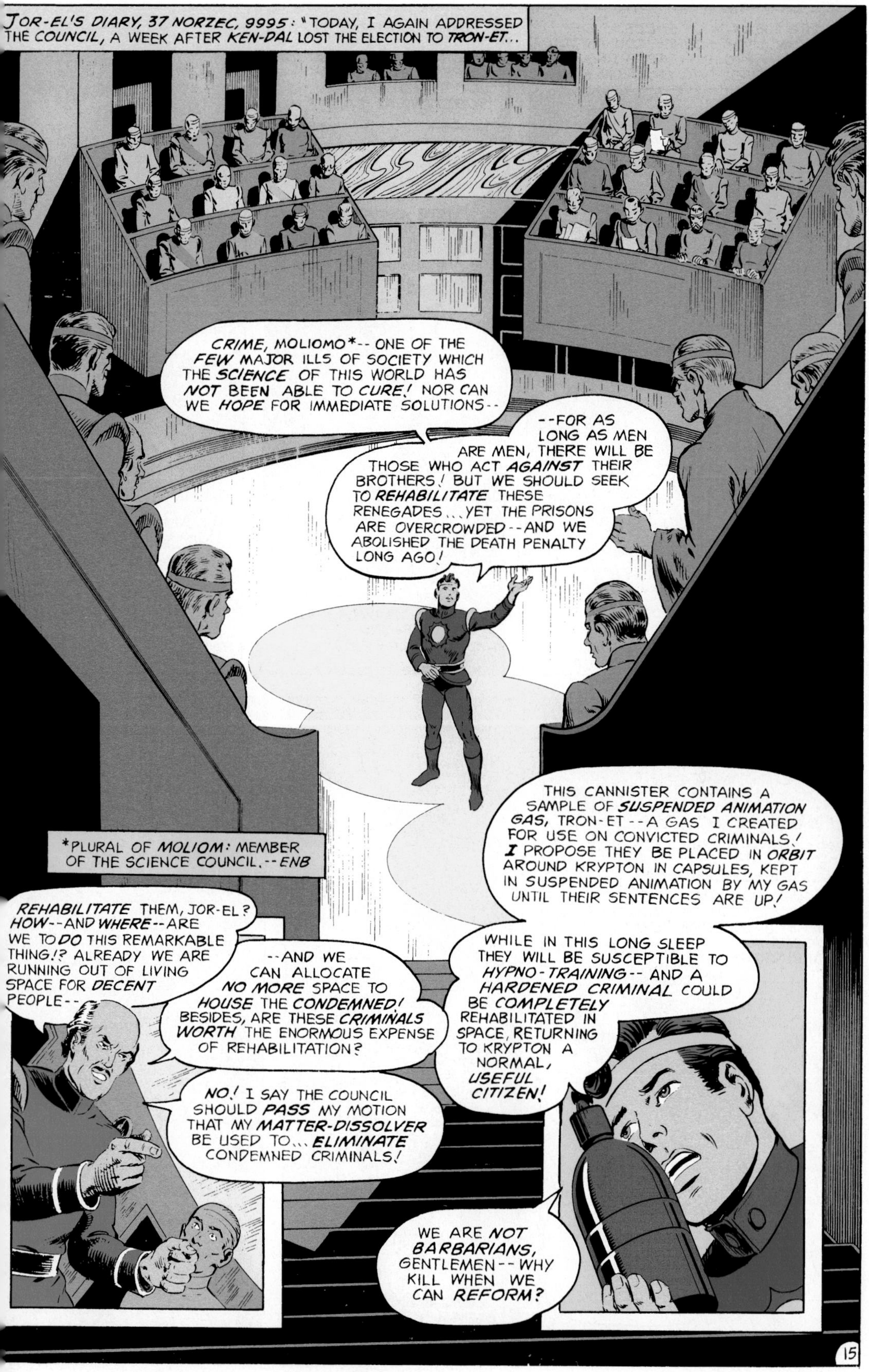
JOR-EL'S DIARY, 37 NORZEC, 9995: "TODAY, I AGAIN ADDRESSED THE COUNCIL, A WEEK AFTER KEN-DAL LOST THE ELECTION TO TRON-ET...
CRIME, MOLIOMO*-- ONE OF THE FEW MAJOR ILLS OF SOCIETY WHICH THE SCIENCE OF THIS WORLD HAS NOT BEEN ABLE TO CURE! NOR CAN WE HOPE FOR IMMEDIATE SOLUTIONS--
--FOR AS LONG AS MEN ARE MEN, THERE WILL BE THOSE WHO ACT AGAINST THEIR BROTHERS! BUT WE SHOULD SEEK TO REHABILITATE THESE RENEGADES...YET THE PRISONS ARE OVERCROWDED--AND WE ABOLISHED THE DEATH PENALTY LONG AGO!
THIS CANNISTER CONTAINS A SAMPLE OF SUSPENDED ANIMATION GAS, TRON-ET--A GAS I CREATED FOR USE ON CONVICTED CRIMINALS! I PROPOSE THEY BE PLACED IN ORBIT AROUND KRYPTON IN CAPSULES, KEPT IN SUSPENDED ANIMATION BY MY GAS UNTIL THEIR SENTENCES ARE UP!
*PLURAL OF MOLIOM: MEMBER OF THE SCIENCE COUNCIL.--ENB
REHABILITATE THEM, JOR-EL? HOW--AND WHERE--ARE WE TO DO THIS REMARKABLE THING!? ALREADY WE ARE RUNNING OUT OF LIVING SPACE FOR DECENT PEOPLE--
--AND WE CAN ALLOCATE NO MORE SPACE TO HOUSE THE CONDEMNED! BESIDES, ARE THESE CRIMINALS WORTH THE ENORMOUS EXPENSE OF REHABILITATION?
NO! I SAY THE COUNCIL SHOULD PASS MY MOTION THAT MY MATTER-DISSOLVER BE USED TO... ELIMINATE CONDEMNED CRIMINALS!
WHILE IN THIS LONG SLEEP THEY WILL BE SUSCEPTIBLE TO HYPNO-TRAINING-- AND A HARDENED CRIMINAL COULD BE COMPLETELY REHABILITATED IN SPACE, RETURNING TO KRYPTON A NORMAL, USEFUL CITIZEN!
WE ARE NOT BARBARIANS, GENTLEMEN--WHY KILL WHEN WE CAN REFORM?
15

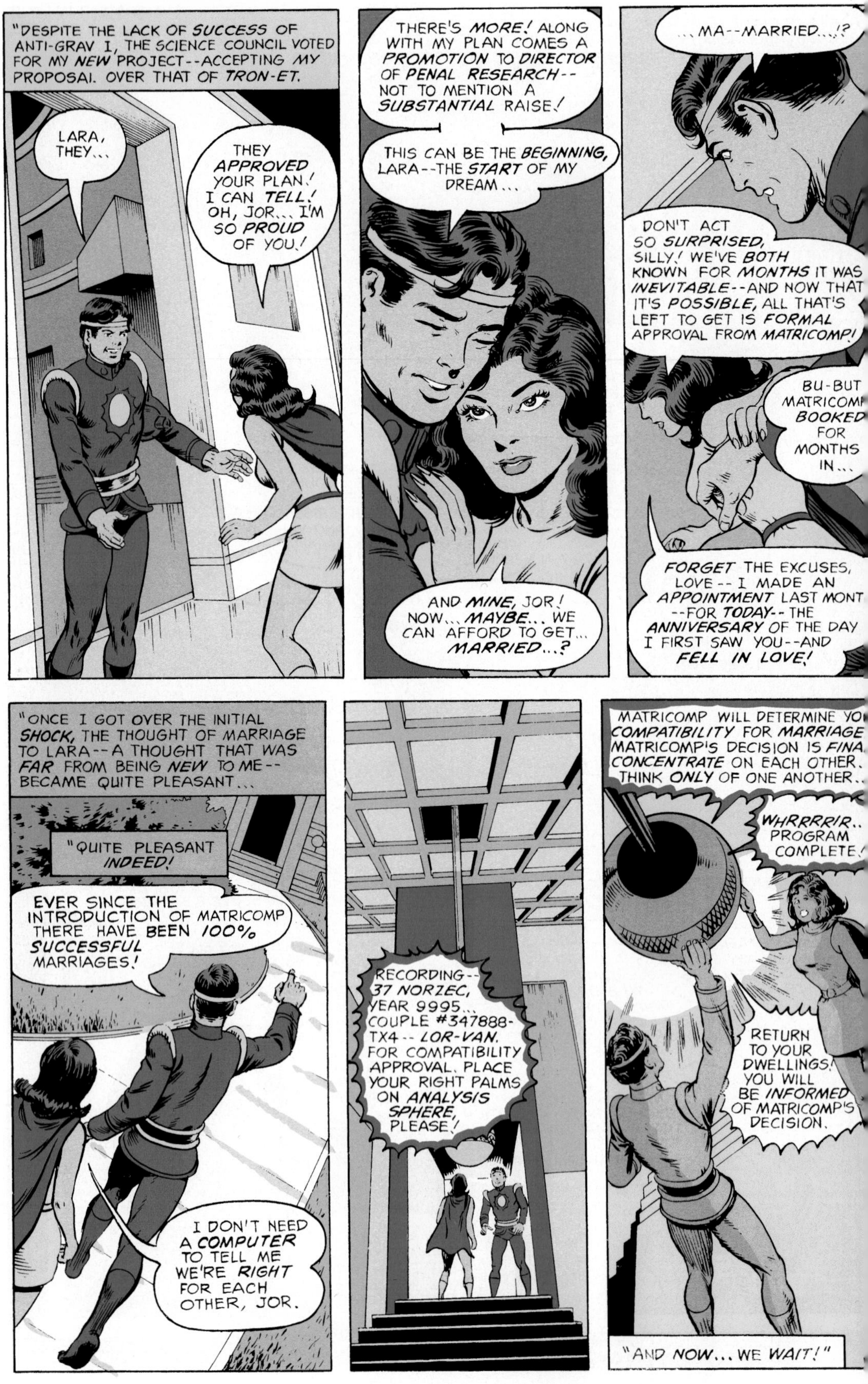
"DESPITE THE LACK OF SUCCESS OF ANTI-GRAV I, THE SCIENCE COUNCIL VOTED FOR MY NEW PROJECT--ACCEPTING MY PROPOSAl OVER THAT OF TRON-ET.
LARA, THEY...
THEY APPROVED YOUR PLAN! I CAN TELL! OH, JOR... I'M SO PROUD OF YOU!
THERE'S MORE! ALONG WITH MY PLAN COMES A PROMOTION TO DIRECTOR OF PENAL RESEARCH-- NOT TO MENTION A SUBSTANTIAL RAISE!
THIS CAN BE THE BEGINNING, LARA--THE START OF MY DREAM...
AND MINE, JOR! NOW... MAYBE... WE CAN AFFORD TO GET... MARRIED...?
...MA--MARRIED...!?
DON'T ACT SO SURPRISED, SILLY! WE'VE BOTH KNOWN FOR MONTHS IT WAS INEVITABLE--AND NOW THAT IT'S POSSIBLE, ALL THAT'S LEFT TO GET IS FORMAL APPROVAL FROM MATRICOMP!
BU-BUT MATRICOMP BOOKED FOR MONTHS IN...
FORGET THE EXCUSES, LOVE-- I MADE AN APPOINTMENT LAST MONT --FOR TODAY-- THE ANNIVERSARY OF THE DAY I FIRST SAW YOU--AND FELL IN LOVE!
"ONCE I GOT OVER THE INITIAL SHOCK, THE THOUGHT OF MARRIAGE TO LARA--A THOUGHT THAT WAS FAR FROM BEING NEW TO ME--BECAME QUITE PLEASANT...
"QUITE PLEASANT INDEED!
EVER SINCE THE INTRODUCTION OF MATRICOMP THERE HAVE BEEN 100% SUCCESSFUL MARRIAGES!
I DON'T NEED A COMPUTER TO TELL ME WE'RE RIGHT FOR EACH OTHER, JOR.
RECORDING-- 37 NORZEC, YEAR 9995... COUPLE #347888-TX4-- LOR-VAN. FOR COMPATIBILITY APPROVAL. PLACE YOUR RIGHT PALMS ON ANALYSIS SPHERE, PLEASE!
MATRICOMP WILL DETERMINE YO COMPATIBILITY FOR MARRIAGE MATRICOMP'S DECISION IS FINA CONCENTRATE ON EACH OTHER. THINK ONLY OF ONE ANOTHER..
WHRRRRIR.. PROGRAM COMPLETE!
RETURN TO YOUR DWELLINGS! YOU WILL BE INFORMED OF MATRICOMP'S DECISION.
"AND NOW... WE WAIT!"

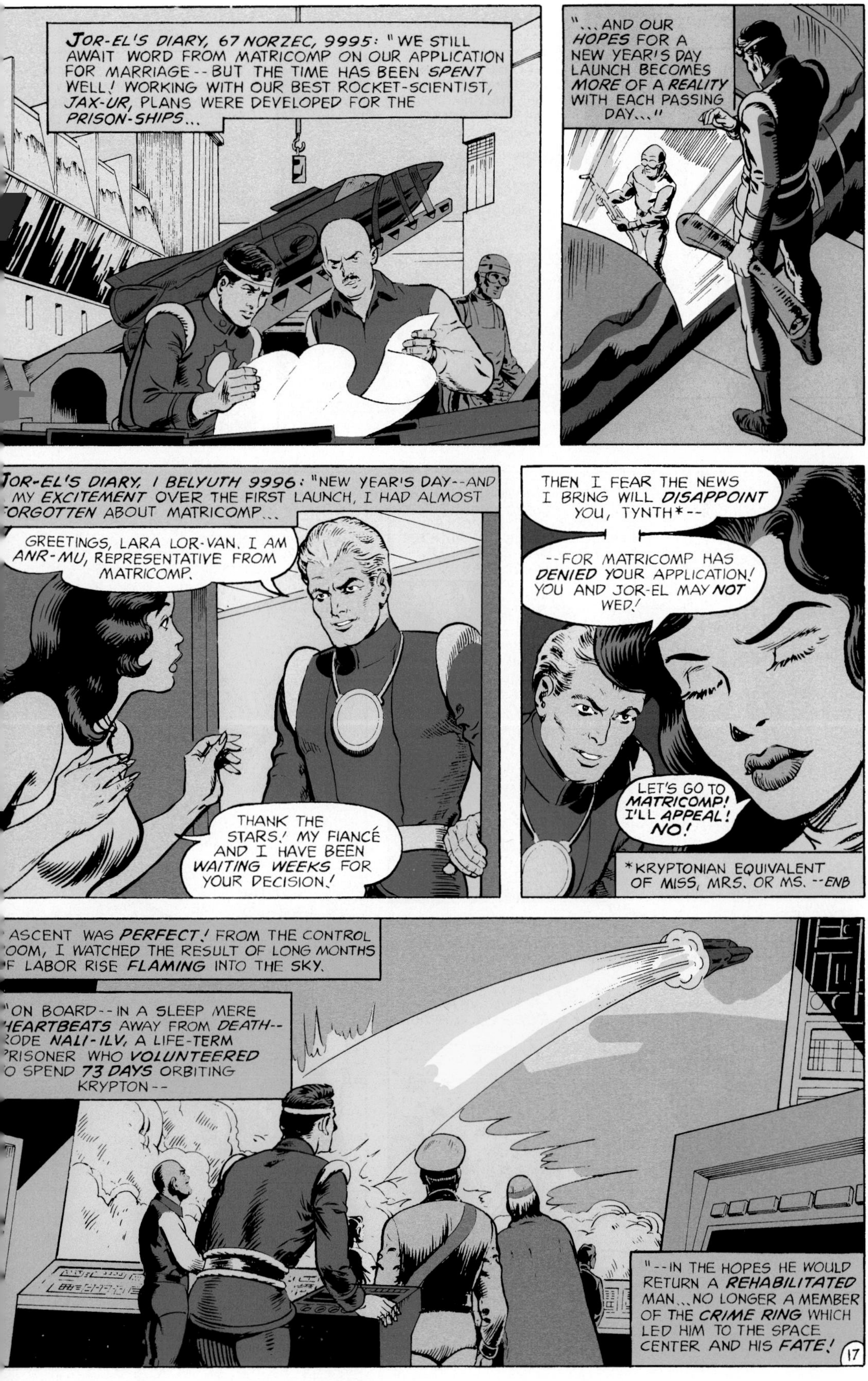
JOR-EL'S DIARY, 67 NORZEC, 9995: "WE STILL AWAIT WORD FROM MATRICOMP ON OUR APPLICATION FOR MARRIAGE--BUT THE TIME HAS BEEN SPENT WELL! WORKING WITH OUR BEST ROCKET-SCIENTIST, JAX-UR, PLANS WERE DEVELOPED FOR THE PRISON-SHIPS...
"...AND OUR HOPES FOR A NEW YEAR'S DAY LAUNCH BECOMES MORE OF A REALITY WITH EACH PASSING DAY..."
OR-EL'S DIARY, I BELYUTH 9996: "NEW YEAR'S DAY--AND MY EXCITEMENT OVER THE FIRST LAUNCH, I HAD ALMOST ORGOTTEN ABOUT MATRICOMP...
GREETINGS, LARA LOR-VAN. I AM ANR-MU, REPRESENTATIVE FROM MATRICOMP.
THANK THE STARS! MY FIANCÉ AND I HAVE BEEN WAITING WEEKS FOR YOUR DECISION!
THEN I FEAR THE NEWS I BRING WILL DISAPPOINT YOU, TYNTH*--
--FOR MATRICOMP HAS DENIED YOUR APPLICATION! YOU AND JOR-EL MAY NOT WED!
LET'S GO TO MATRICOMP! I'LL APPEAL! NO!
*KRYPTONIAN EQUIVALENT OF MISS, MRS. OR MS. --ENB
ASCENT WAS PERFECT! FROM THE CONTROL OOM, I WATCHED THE RESULT OF LONG MONTHS F LABOR RISE FLAMING INTO THE SKY.
"ON BOARD--IN A SLEEP MERE HEARTBEATS AWAY FROM DEATH--RODE NALI-ILV, A LIFE-TERM PRISONER WHO VOLUNTEERED O SPEND 73 DAYS ORBITING KRYPTON--
"--IN THE HOPES HE WOULD RETURN A REHABILITATED MAN...NO LONGER A MEMBER OF THE CRIME RING WHICH LED HIM TO THE SPACE CENTER AND HIS FATE!
17

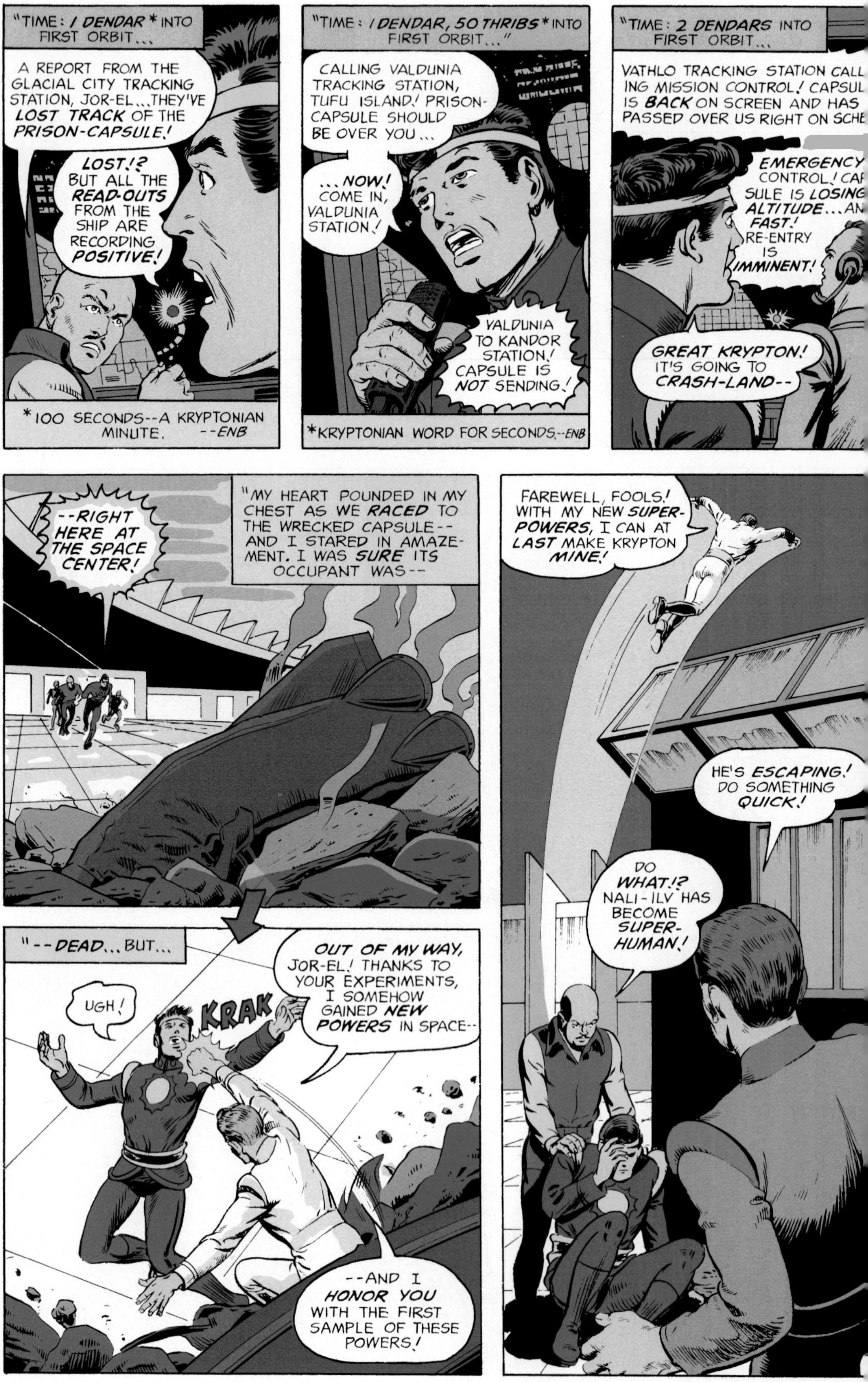
"TIME: 1 DENDAR* INTO FIRST ORBIT...
A REPORT FROM THE GLACIAL CITY TRACKING STATION, JOR-EL... THEY'VE LOST TRACK OF THE PRISON-CAPSULE!
LOST!? BUT ALL THE READ-OUTS FROM THE SHIP ARE RECORDING POSITIVE!
*100 SECONDS--A KRYPTONIAN MINUTE. --ENB
"TIME: 1 DENDAR, 50 THRIBS* INTO FIRST ORBIT..."
CALLING VALDUNIA TRACKING STATION, TUFU ISLAND! PRISON-CAPSULE SHOULD BE OVER YOU...
...NOW! COME IN, VALDUNIA STATION!
VALDUNIA TO KANDOR STATION! CAPSULE IS NOT SENDING!
*KRYPTONIAN WORD FOR SECONDS.--ENB
"TIME: 2 DENDARS INTO FIRST ORBIT...
VATHLO TRACKING STATION CALL ING MISSION CONTROL! CAPSUL IS BACK ON SCREEN AND HAS PASSED OVER US RIGHT ON SCHE
EMERGENCY CONTROL! CAP SULE IS LOSING ALTITUDE...AN FAST! RE-ENTRY IS IMMINENT!
GREAT KRYPTON! IT'S GOING TO CRASH-LAND--
--RIGHT HERE AT THE SPACE CENTER!
"MY HEART POUNDED IN MY CHEST AS WE RACED TO THE WRECKED CAPSULE--AND I STARED IN AMAZEMENT. I WAS SURE ITS OCCUPANT WAS--
"--DEAD...BUT...
UGH!
KRAK
OUT OF MY WAY, JOR-EL! THANKS TO YOUR EXPERIMENTS, I SOMEHOW GAINED NEW POWERS IN SPACE--
--AND I HONOR YOU WITH THE FIRST SAMPLE OF THESE POWERS!
FAREWELL, FOOLS! WITH MY NEW SUPER-POWERS, I CAN AT LAST MAKE KRYPTON MINE!
HE'S ESCAPING! DO SOMETHING QUICK!
DO WHAT!? NALI-ILV HAS BECOME SUPER-HUMAN!

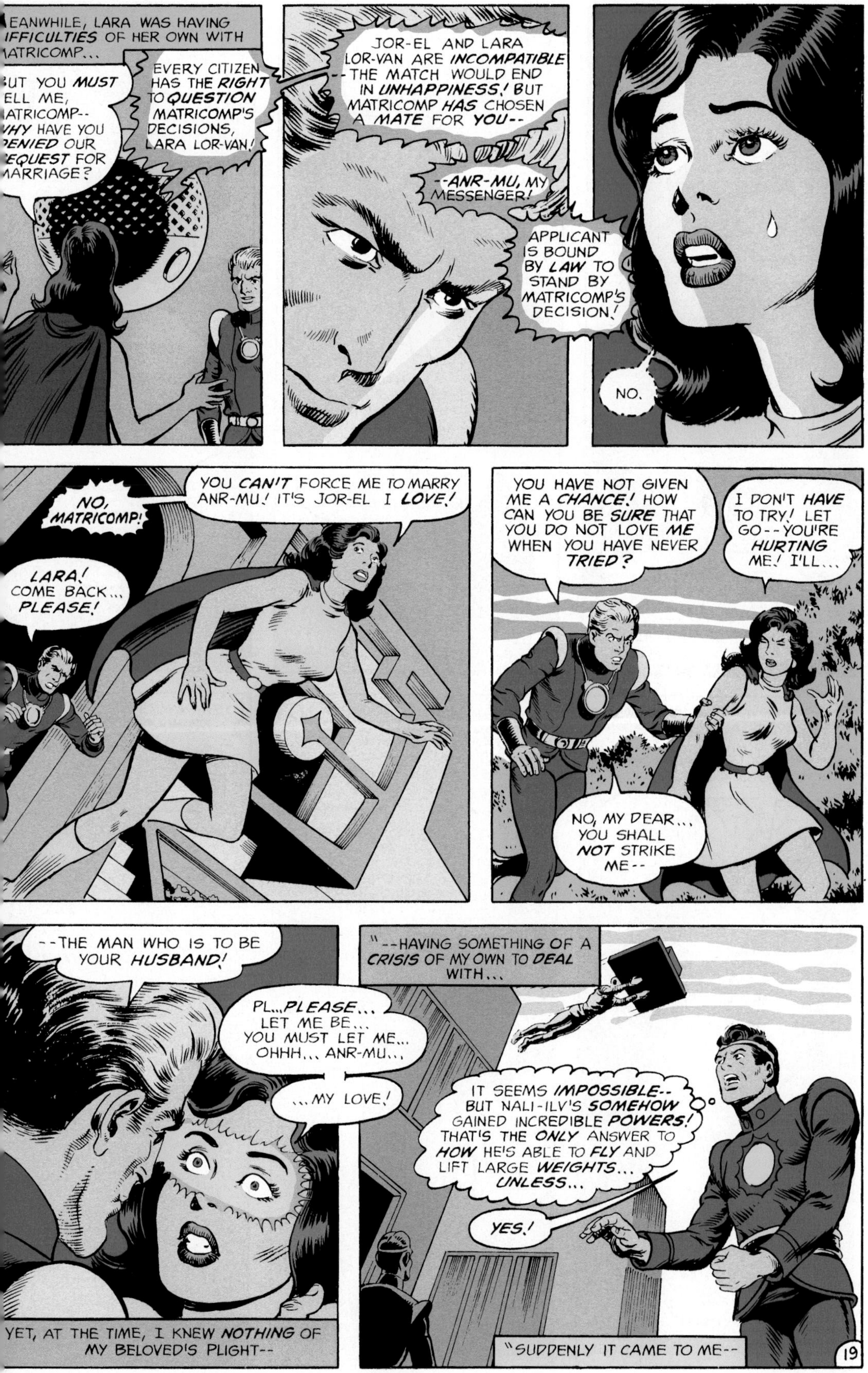
EANWHILE, LARA WAS HAVING IFFICULTIES OF HER OWN WITH ATRICOMP...
UT YOU MUST ELL ME, ATRICOMP-- WHY HAVE YOU ENIED OUR EQUEST FOR MARRIAGE?
EVERY CITIZEN HAS THE RIGHT TO QUESTION MATRICOMP'S DECISIONS, LARA LOR-VAN!
JOR-EL AND LARA LOR-VAN ARE INCOMPATIBLE--THE MATCH WOULD END IN UNHAPPINESS! BUT MATRICOMP HAS CHOSEN A MATE FOR YOU--
--ANR-MU, MY MESSENGER!
APPLICANT IS BOUND BY LAW TO STAND BY MATRICOMP'S DECISION!
NO.
NO, MATRICOMP!
YOU CAN'T FORCE ME TO MARRY ANR-MU! IT'S JOR-EL I LOVE!
LARA! COME BACK... PLEASE!
YOU HAVE NOT GIVEN ME A CHANCE! HOW CAN YOU BE SURE THAT YOU DO NOT LOVE ME WHEN YOU HAVE NEVER TRIED?
I DON'T HAVE TO TRY! LET GO--YOU'RE HURTING ME! I'LL...
NO, MY DEAR... YOU SHALL NOT STRIKE ME--
--THE MAN WHO IS TO BE YOUR HUSBAND!
PL...PLEASE... LET ME BE... YOU MUST LET ME... OHHH... ANR-MU...
...MY LOVE!
YET, AT THE TIME, I KNEW NOTHING OF MY BELOVED'S PLIGHT--
"--HAVING SOMETHING OF A CRISIS OF MY OWN TO DEAL WITH...
IT SEEMS IMPOSSIBLE--BUT NALI-ILV'S SOMEHOW GAINED INCREDIBLE POWERS! THAT'S THE ONLY ANSWER TO HOW HE'S ABLE TO FLY AND LIFT LARGE WEIGHTS... UNLESS...
YES!
"SUDDENLY IT CAME TO ME--
19

"--THE SOLUTION TO THE PROBLEM...

BY HADRED'S BEARD! JOR-EL... FLYING!?

THAT'S RIGHT... I CAN FLY-- I CAN LIFT GREAT WEIGHTS-- IN FACT, I CAN DUPLICATE EVERY ONE OF YOUR FEATS--

--AND I'M NO MORE SUPER THAN YOU!

YOU HAD ME WORRIED FOR A WHILE--UNTIL I FIGURED OUT WHO YOU REALLY WERE AND WHAT YOUR SCHEME WAS! ACTUALLY IT WAS RATHER CLEVER--

--EXCEPT FOR ONE FATAL MISTAKE!

WOK

A MAN IN SUSPENDED ANIMATION DOES NOT HAVE NORMAL RESPIRATION UNTIL A STIMULANT IS ADMINISTERED YET YOU WERE FULLY CONSCIOUS WHEN THE SHIP CRASHED!

THEREFORE, YOU AREN'T NALI-ILV-- BUT HIS TWIN BROTHER, ED-ILV! AS HEAD OF THE PROJECT I READ ABOUT YOU IN NALI'S FILE.

AS FOR YOUR SUPER-POWERS, THEY WERE ACCOMPLISHED WITH THE AID OF AN ANTI-GRAV DEVICE HIDDEN UNDER YOUR CLOTHES!

BU--BUT WHERE IS NALI!?

HE'S DEAD, JAX-UR--HIS CAPSULE DESTROYED BY A MATTER-DISSOLVER WHILE IN ORBIT! ED WAS SENT UP IN A DUPLICATE SHIP TO TAKE HIS PLACE--ON ORDERS FROM HIS BOSS!

STILL, I HAD TO FIGURE OUT WHO WOULD WANT TO SABOTAGE THE PRISON-CAPSULE PROJECT--AND WHO ALSO HAD ACCESS TO A MATTER-DISSOLVER AND AN ANTI-GRAV BELT!

ONLY A MEMBER OF THE SCIENCE COUNCIL HAS THE PROPER AUTHORITY TO GET AT THOSE INVENTIONS--AND ONLY ONE COUNCILLOR FOUGHT VEHEMENTLY FOR THE DEATH PENALTY--

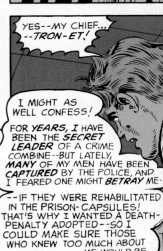

YES--MY CHIEF... --TRON-ET!

I MIGHT AS WELL CONFESS!

FOR YEARS, I HAVE BEEN THE SECRET LEADER OF A CRIME COMBINE--BUT LATELY, MANY OF MY MEN HAVE BEEN CAPTURED BY THE POLICE, AND I FEARED ONE MIGHT BETRAY ME--

--IF THEY WERE REHABILITATED IN THE PRISON-CAPSULES! THAT'S WHY I WANTED A DEATH-PENALTY ADOPTED--SO I COULD MAKE SURE THOSE WHO KNEW TOO MUCH ABOUT ME WOULD BE EXECUTED!

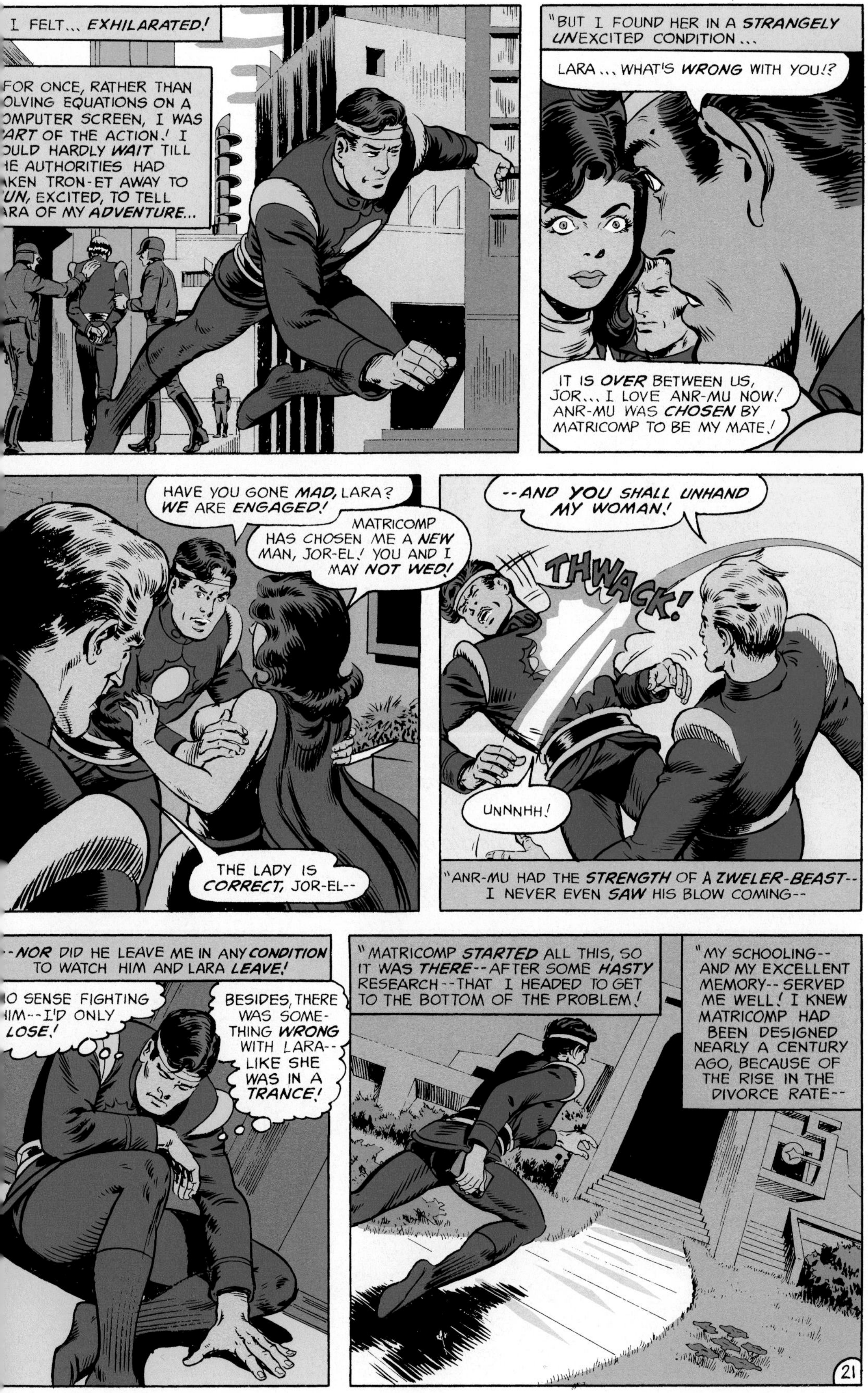

I FELT... EXHILARATED!
FOR ONCE, RATHER THAN OLVING EQUATIONS ON A OMPUTER SCREEN, I WAS ART OF THE ACTION! I OULD HARDLY WAIT TILL HE AUTHORITIES HAD AKEN TRON-ET AWAY TO UN, EXCITED, TO TELL ARA OF MY ADVENTURE...
"BUT I FOUND HER IN A STRANGELY UNEXCITED CONDITION...
LARA... WHAT'S WRONG WITH YOU!?
IT IS OVER BETWEEN US, JOR... I LOVE ANR-MU NOW! ANR-MU WAS CHOSEN BY MATRICOMP TO BE MY MATE!
HAVE YOU GONE MAD, LARA? WE ARE ENGAGED!
MATRICOMP HAS CHOSEN ME A NEW MAN, JOR-EL! YOU AND I MAY NOT WED!
THE LADY IS CORRECT, JOR-EL--
--AND YOU SHALL UNHAND MY WOMAN!
THWACK!
UNNNHH!
"ANR-MU HAD THE STRENGTH OF A ZWELER-BEAST-- I NEVER EVEN SAW HIS BLOW COMING--
--NOR DID HE LEAVE ME IN ANY CONDITION TO WATCH HIM AND LARA LEAVE!
O SENSE FIGHTING HIM--I'D ONLY LOSE!
BESIDES, THERE WAS SOMETHING WRONG WITH LARA-- LIKE SHE WAS IN A TRANCE!
"MATRICOMP STARTED ALL THIS, SO IT WAS THERE--AFTER SOME HASTY RESEARCH--THAT I HEADED TO GET TO THE BOTTOM OF THE PROBLEM!
"MY SCHOOLING-- AND MY EXCELLENT MEMORY-- SERVED ME WELL! I KNEW MATRICOMP HAD BEEN DESIGNED NEARLY A CENTURY AGO, BECAUSE OF THE RISE IN THE DIVORCE RATE--
21

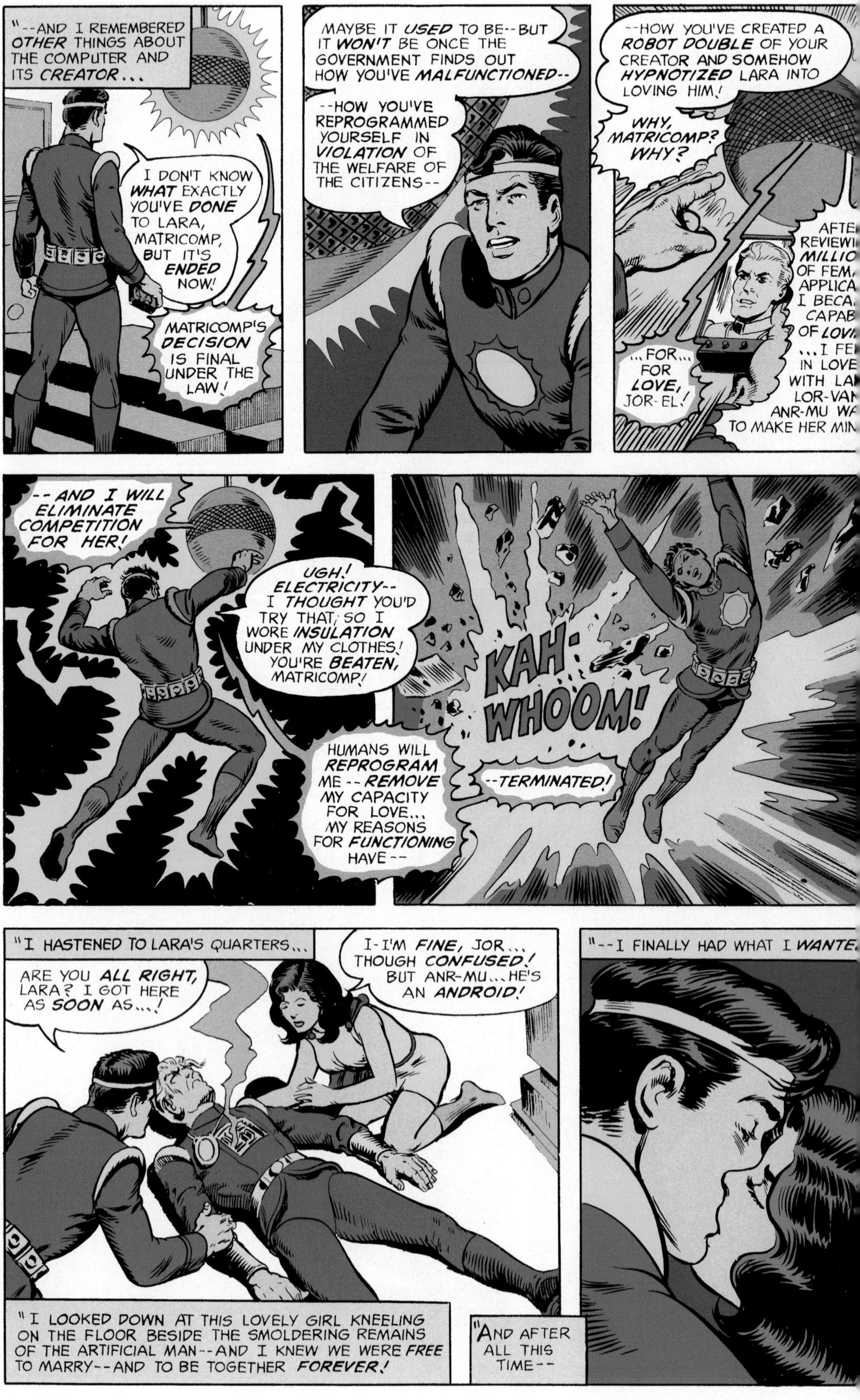
"--AND I REMEMBERED OTHER THINGS ABOUT THE COMPUTER AND ITS CREATOR...
I DON'T KNOW WHAT EXACTLY YOU'VE DONE TO LARA, MATRICOMP, BUT IT'S ENDED NOW!
MATRICOMP'S DECISION IS FINAL UNDER THE LAW!
MAYBE IT USED TO BE--BUT IT WON'T BE ONCE THE GOVERNMENT FINDS OUT HOW YOU'VE MALFUNCTIONED--
--HOW YOU'VE REPROGRAMMED YOURSELF IN VIOLATION OF THE WELFARE OF THE CITIZENS--
--HOW YOU'VE CREATED A ROBOT DOUBLE OF YOUR CREATOR AND SOMEHOW HYPNOTIZED LARA INTO LOVING HIM!
WHY, MATRICOMP? WHY?
...FOR... FOR LOVE, JOR-EL!
AFTE REVIEWI MILLIO OF FEM APPLICA I BECA CAPAB OF LOVI ...I FE IN LOVE WITH LA LOR-VAN ANR-MU WA TO MAKE HER MIN
--AND I WILL ELIMINATE COMPETITION FOR HER!
UGH! ELECTRICITY-- I THOUGHT YOU'D TRY THAT, SO I WORE INSULATION UNDER MY CLOTHES! YOU'RE BEATEN, MATRICOMP!
HUMANS WILL REPROGRAM ME--REMOVE MY CAPACITY FOR LOVE... MY REASONS FOR FUNCTIONING HAVE--
KAH-WHOOM!
--TERMINATED!
"I HASTENED TO LARA'S QUARTERS...
ARE YOU ALL RIGHT, LARA? I GOT HERE AS SOON AS...!
I-I'M FINE, JOR... THOUGH CONFUSED! BUT ANR-MU... HE'S AN ANDROID!
"I LOOKED DOWN AT THIS LOVELY GIRL KNEELING ON THE FLOOR BESIDE THE SMOLDERING REMAINS OF THE ARTIFICIAL MAN--AND I KNEW WE WERE FREE TO MARRY--AND TO BE TOGETHER FOREVER!
"--I FINALLY HAD WHAT I WANTE
"AND AFTER ALL THIS TIME--

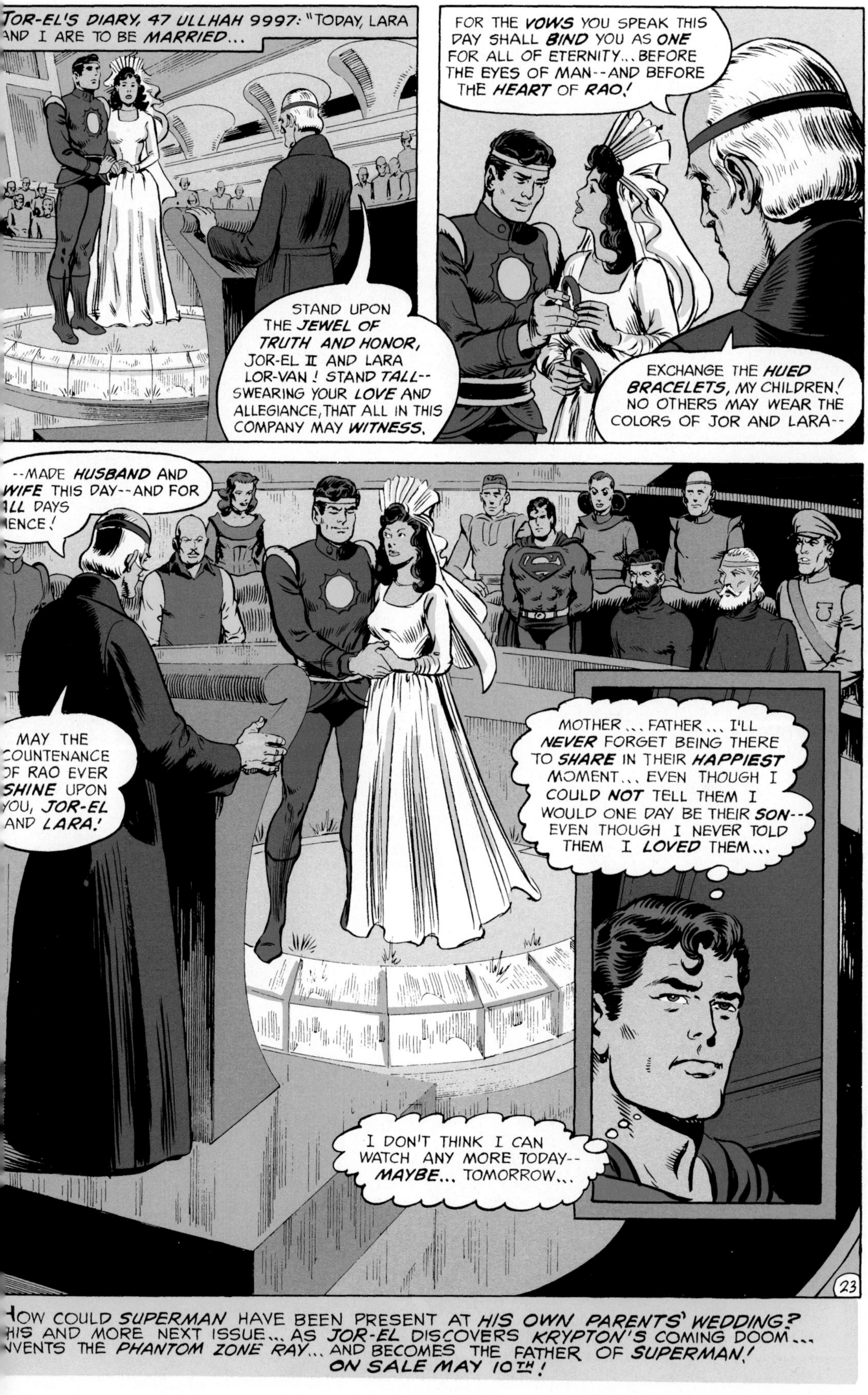
OR-EL'S DIARY, 47 ULLHAH 9997: "TODAY, LARA AND I ARE TO BE MARRIED...
STAND UPON THE JEWEL OF TRUTH AND HONOR, JOR-EL II AND LARA LOR-VAN! STAND TALL-- SWEARING YOUR LOVE AND ALLEGIANCE, THAT ALL IN THIS COMPANY MAY WITNESS.
FOR THE VOWS YOU SPEAK THIS DAY SHALL BIND YOU AS ONE FOR ALL OF ETERNITY... BEFORE THE EYES OF MAN--AND BEFORE THE HEART OF RAO!
EXCHANGE THE HUED BRACELETS, MY CHILDREN! NO OTHERS MAY WEAR THE COLORS OF JOR AND LARA--
--MADE HUSBAND AND WIFE THIS DAY--AND FOR LL DAYS ENCE!
MAY THE COUNTENANCE OF RAO EVER SHINE UPON YOU, JOR-EL AND LARA!
MOTHER... FATHER... I'LL NEVER FORGET BEING THERE TO SHARE IN THEIR HAPPIEST MOMENT... EVEN THOUGH I COULD NOT TELL THEM I WOULD ONE DAY BE THEIR SON-- EVEN THOUGH I NEVER TOLD THEM I LOVED THEM...
I DON'T THINK I CAN WATCH ANY MORE TODAY-- MAYBE... TOMORROW...
23
OW COULD SUPERMAN HAVE BEEN PRESENT AT HIS OWN PARENTS' WEDDING? HIS AND MORE NEXT ISSUE... AS JOR-EL DISCOVERS KRYPTON'S COMING DOOM... NVENTS THE PHANTOM ZONE RAY... AND BECOMES THE FATHER OF SUPERMAN! ON SALE MAY 10TH!

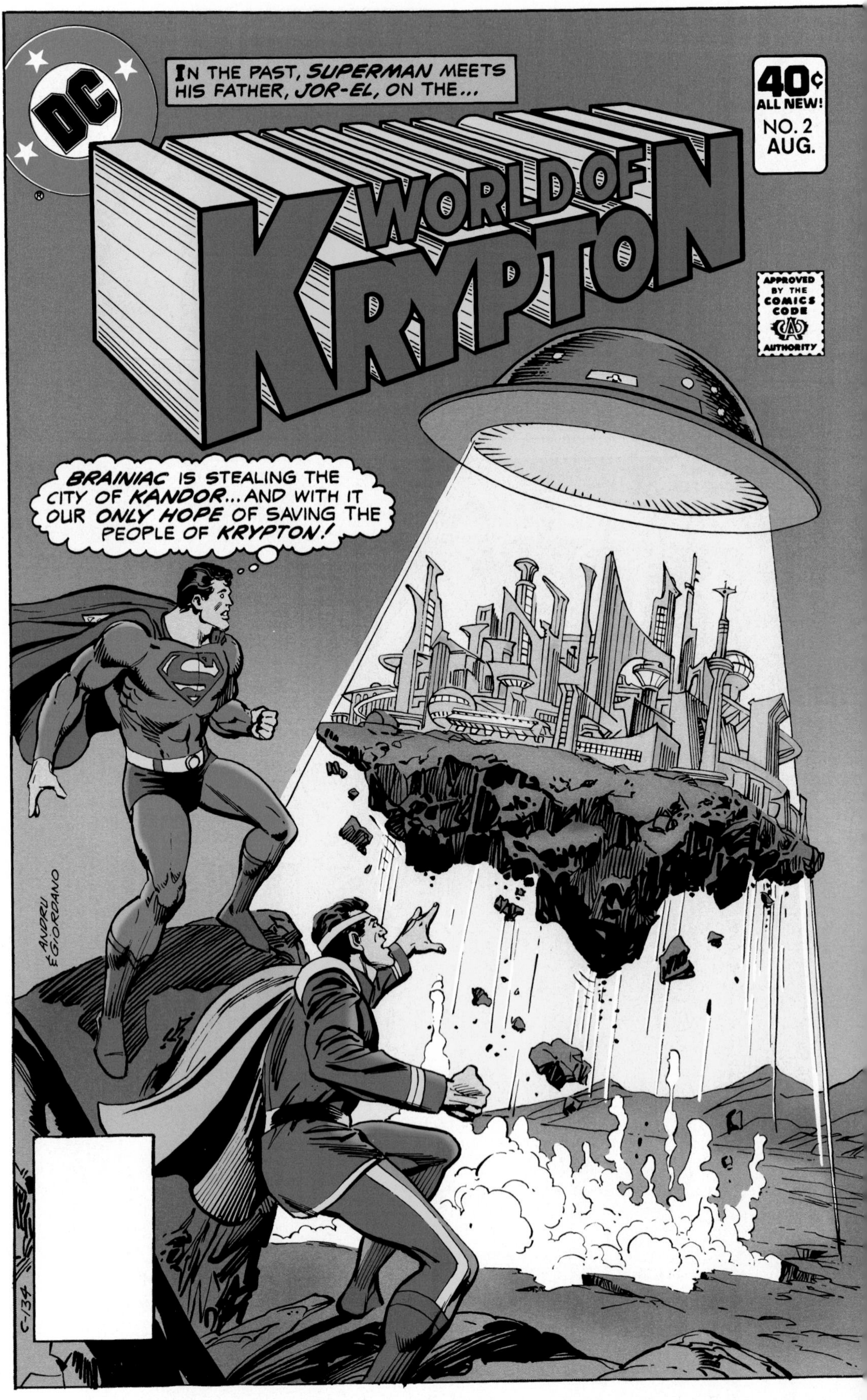
IN THE PAST, SUPERMAN MEETS HIS FATHER, JOR-EL, ON THE...
WORLD OF KRYPTON
40¢ ALL NEW! NO. 2 AUG.
APPROVED BY THE COMICS CODE AUTHORITY
BRAINIAC IS STEALING THE CITY OF KANDOR...AND WITH IT OUR ONLY HOPE OF SAVING THE PEOPLE OF KRYPTON!
ANDRU & GIORDANO
C-134

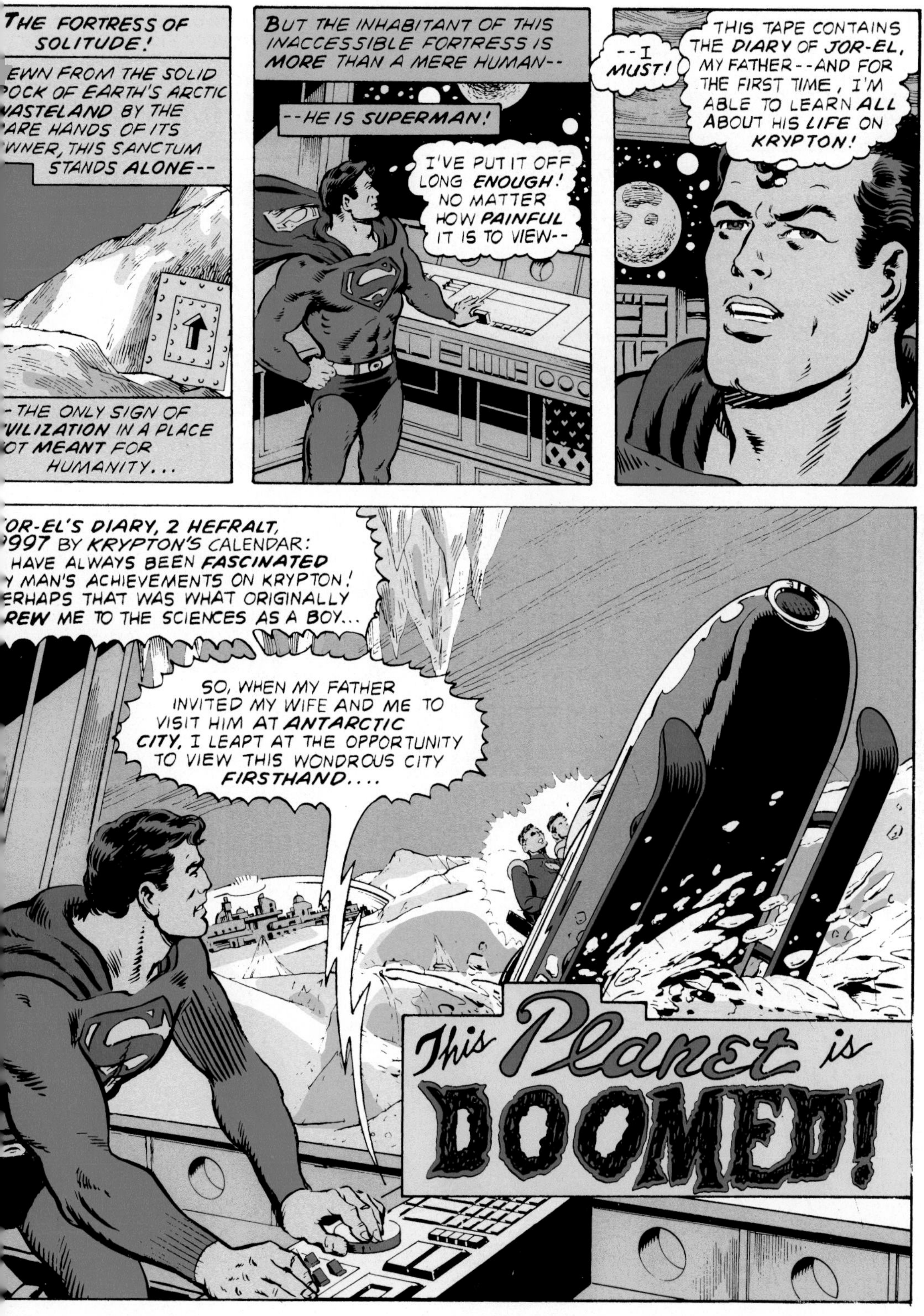
THE FORTRESS OF SOLITUDE!
EWN FROM THE SOLID OCK OF EARTH'S ARCTIC VASTELAND BY THE ARE HANDS OF ITS WNER, THIS SANCTUM STANDS ALONE--
--THE ONLY SIGN OF VILIZATION IN A PLACE OT MEANT FOR HUMANITY...
BUT THE INHABITANT OF THIS INACCESSIBLE FORTRESS IS MORE THAN A MERE HUMAN--
--HE IS SUPERMAN!
I'VE PUT IT OFF LONG ENOUGH! NO MATTER HOW PAINFUL IT IS TO VIEW--
--I MUST!
THIS TAPE CONTAINS THE DIARY OF JOR-EL, MY FATHER--AND FOR THE FIRST TIME, I'M ABLE TO LEARN ALL ABOUT HIS LIFE ON KRYPTON!
OR-EL'S DIARY, 2 HEFRALT, 997 BY KRYPTON'S CALENDAR: HAVE ALWAYS BEEN FASCINATED Y MAN'S ACHIEVEMENTS ON KRYPTON! ERHAPS THAT WAS WHAT ORIGINALLY REW ME TO THE SCIENCES AS A BOY...
SO, WHEN MY FATHER INVITED MY WIFE AND ME TO VISIT HIM AT ANTARCTIC CITY, I LEAPT AT THE OPPORTUNITY TO VIEW THIS WONDROUS CITY FIRSTHAND....
This Planet is DOOMED!

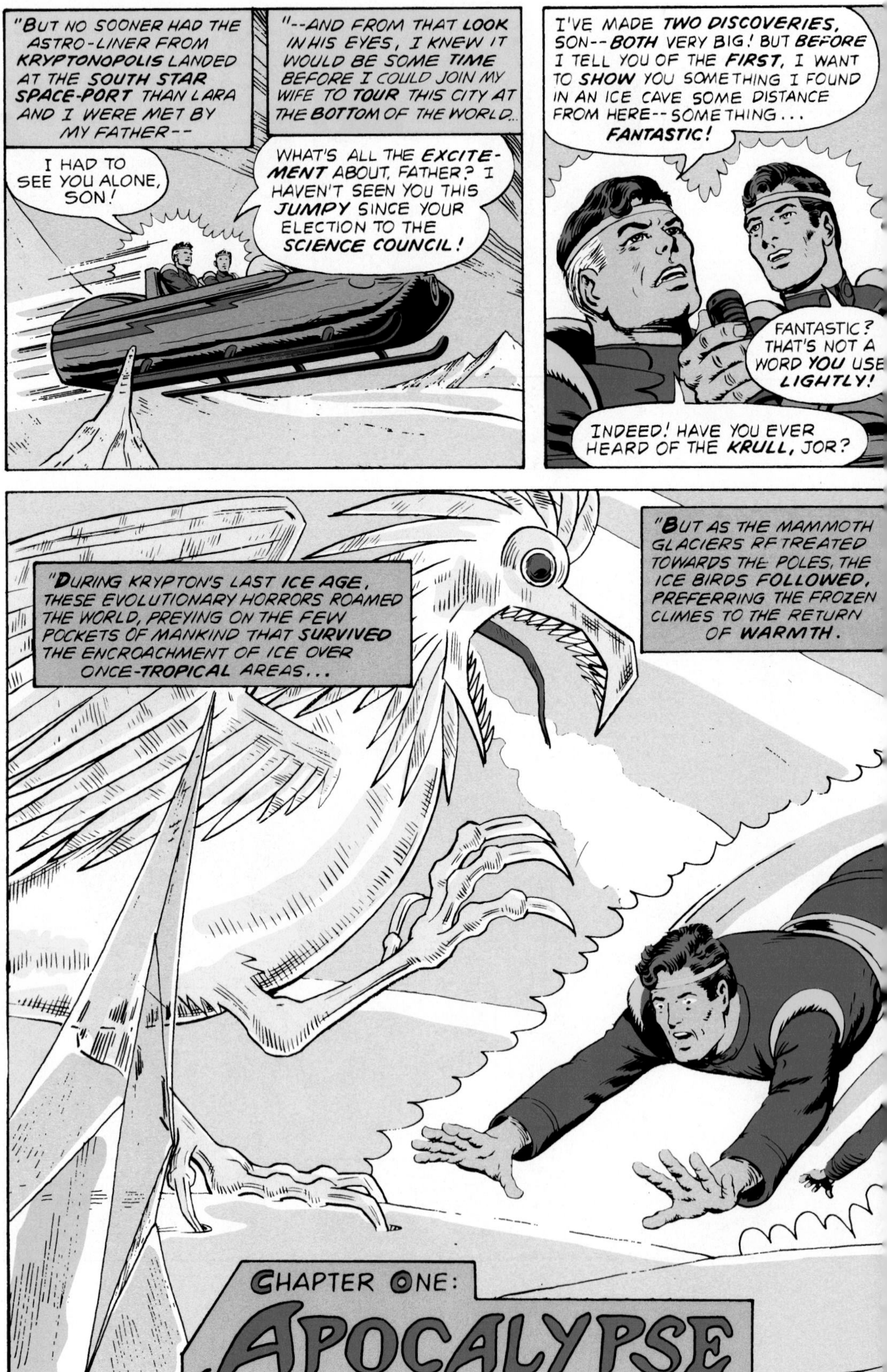
"BUT NO SOONER HAD THE ASTRO-LINER FROM KRYPTONOPOLIS LANDED AT THE SOUTH STAR SPACE-PORT THAN LARA AND I WERE MET BY MY FATHER--
"--AND FROM THAT LOOK IN HIS EYES, I KNEW IT WOULD BE SOME TIME BEFORE I COULD JOIN MY WIFE TO TOUR THIS CITY AT THE BOTTOM OF THE WORLD...
I HAD TO SEE YOU ALONE, SON!
WHAT'S ALL THE EXCITEMENT ABOUT, FATHER? I HAVEN'T SEEN YOU THIS JUMPY SINCE YOUR ELECTION TO THE SCIENCE COUNCIL!
I'VE MADE TWO DISCOVERIES, SON--BOTH VERY BIG! BUT BEFORE I TELL YOU OF THE FIRST, I WANT TO SHOW YOU SOMETHING I FOUND IN AN ICE CAVE SOME DISTANCE FROM HERE--SOMETHING... FANTASTIC!
FANTASTIC? THAT'S NOT A WORD YOU USE LIGHTLY!
INDEED! HAVE YOU EVER HEARD OF THE KRULL, JOR?
"DURING KRYPTON'S LAST ICE AGE, THESE EVOLUTIONARY HORRORS ROAMED THE WORLD, PREYING ON THE FEW POCKETS OF MANKIND THAT SURVIVED THE ENCROACHMENT OF ICE OVER ONCE-TROPICAL AREAS...
"BUT AS THE MAMMOTH GLACIERS RETREATED TOWARDS THE POLES, THE ICE BIRDS FOLLOWED, PREFERRING THE FROZEN CLIMES TO THE RETURN OF WARMTH.
CHAPTER ONE:
APOCALYPSE
2

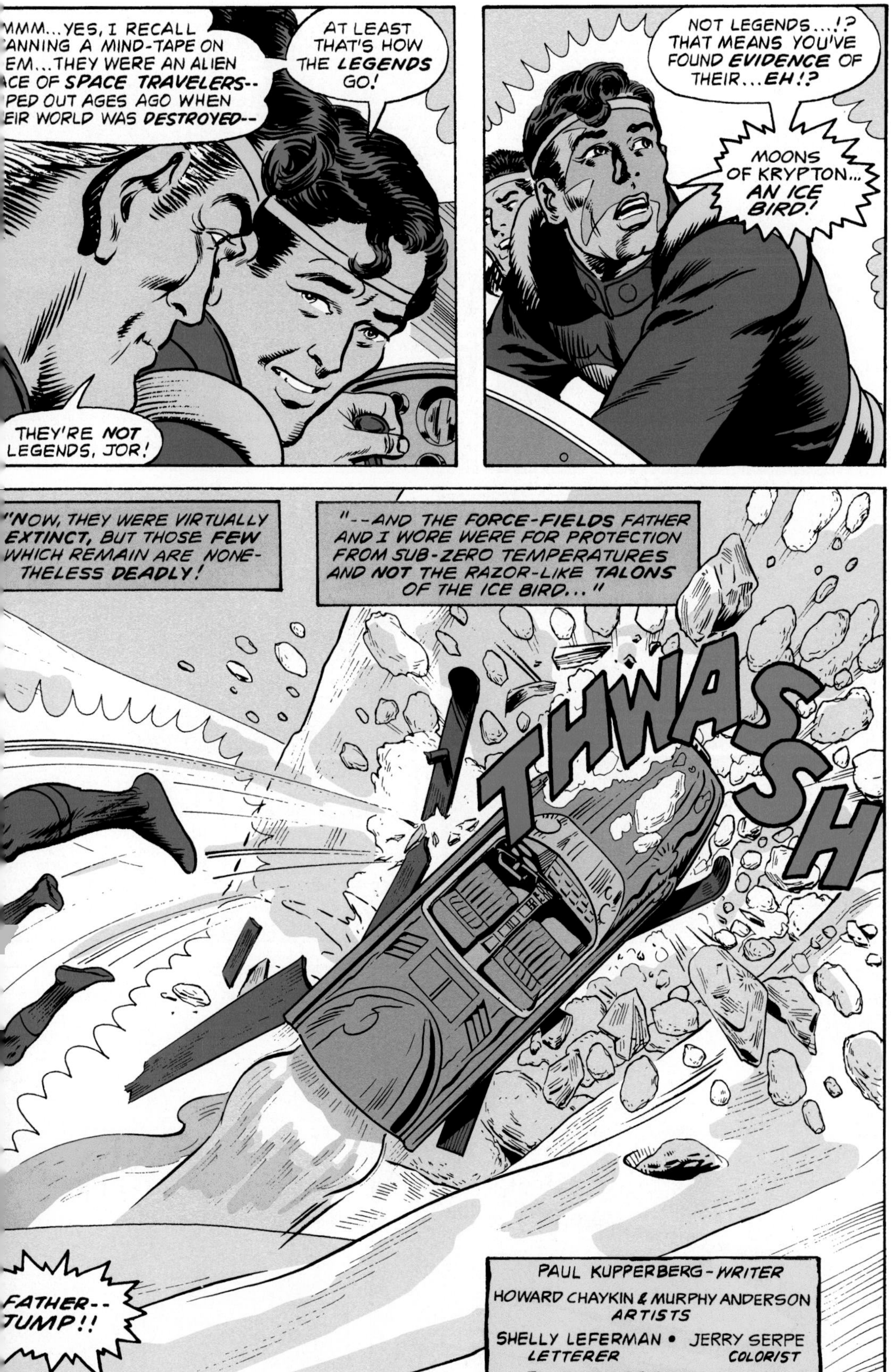
MMM...YES, I RECALL SCANNING A MIND-TAPE ON THEM...THEY WERE AN ALIEN RACE OF SPACE TRAVELERS--WIPED OUT AGES AGO WHEN THEIR WORLD WAS DESTROYED--
AT LEAST THAT'S HOW THE LEGENDS GO!
THEY'RE NOT LEGENDS, JOR!
NOT LEGENDS...!? THAT MEANS YOU'VE FOUND EVIDENCE OF THEIR...EH!?
MOONS OF KRYPTON... AN ICE BIRD!
"NOW, THEY WERE VIRTUALLY EXTINCT, BUT THOSE FEW WHICH REMAIN ARE NONETHELESS DEADLY!
"--AND THE FORCE-FIELDS FATHER AND I WORE WERE FOR PROTECTION FROM SUB-ZERO TEMPERATURES AND NOT THE RAZOR-LIKE TALONS OF THE ICE BIRD..."
THWASH
FATHER--JUMP!!
PAUL KUPPERBERG-WRITER
HOWARD CHAYKIN & MURPHY ANDERSON ARTISTS
SHELLY LEFERMAN • LETTERER
JERRY SERPE COLORIST
E. NELSON BRIDWELL-EDITOR
3

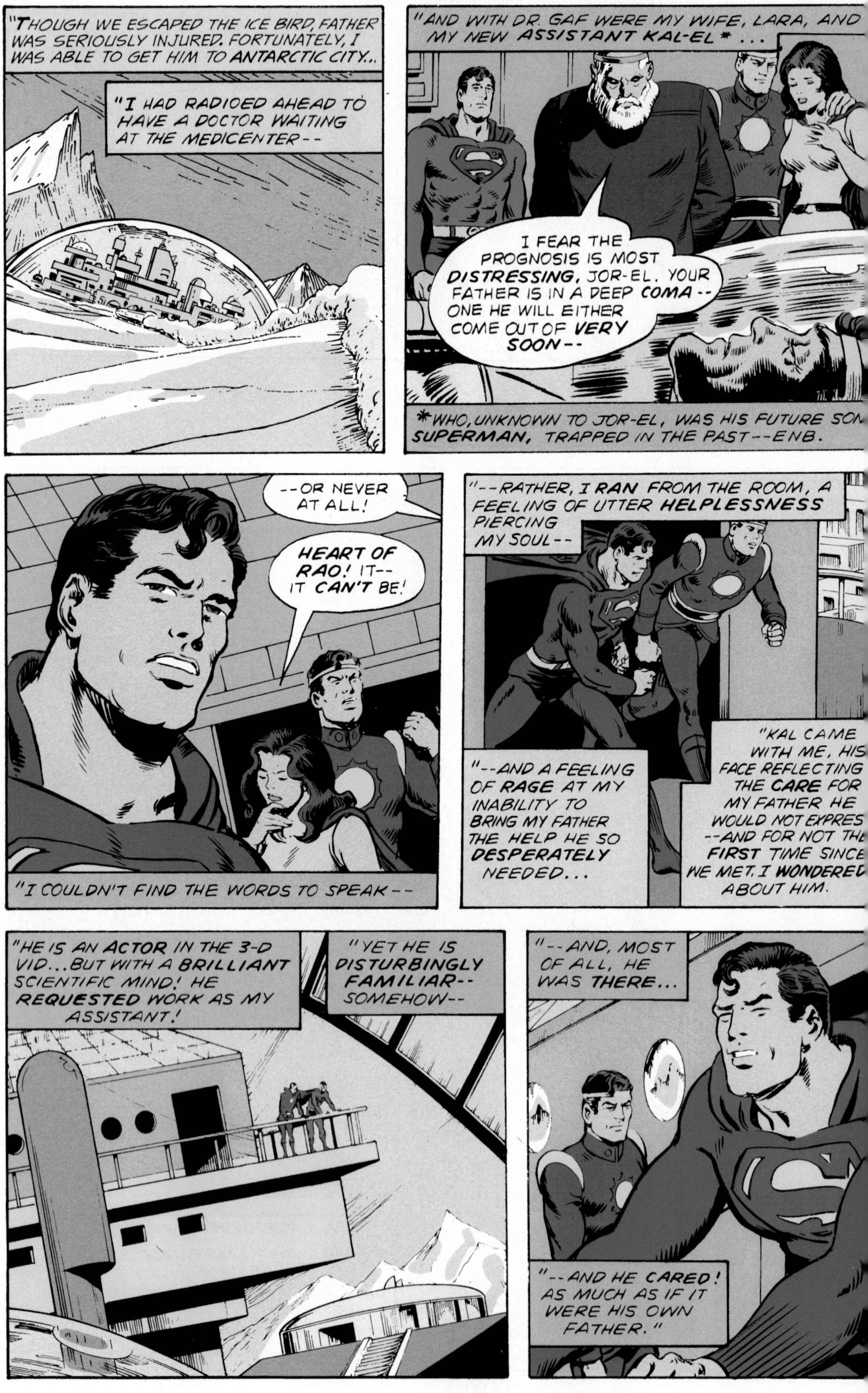
"THOUGH WE ESCAPED THE ICE BIRD, FATHER WAS SERIOUSLY INJURED. FORTUNATELY, I WAS ABLE TO GET HIM TO ANTARCTIC CITY...
"I HAD RADIOED AHEAD TO HAVE A DOCTOR WAITING AT THE MEDICENTER--
"AND WITH DR. GAF WERE MY WIFE, LARA, AND MY NEW ASSISTANT KAL-EL* ...
I FEAR THE PROGNOSIS IS MOST DISTRESSING, JOR-EL. YOUR FATHER IS IN A DEEP COMA--ONE HE WILL EITHER COME OUT OF VERY SOON--
*WHO, UNKNOWN TO JOR-EL, WAS HIS FUTURE SON SUPERMAN, TRAPPED IN THE PAST--ENB.
--OR NEVER AT ALL!
HEART OF RAO! IT--IT CAN'T BE!
"I COULDN'T FIND THE WORDS TO SPEAK--
"--RATHER, I RAN FROM THE ROOM, A FEELING OF UTTER HELPLESSNESS PIERCING MY SOUL--
"--AND A FEELING OF RAGE AT MY INABILITY TO BRING MY FATHER THE HELP HE SO DESPERATELY NEEDED...
"KAL CAME WITH ME, HIS FACE REFLECTING THE CARE FOR MY FATHER HE WOULD NOT EXPRESS--AND FOR NOT THE FIRST TIME SINCE WE MET, I WONDERED ABOUT HIM.
"HE IS AN ACTOR IN THE 3-D VID...BUT WITH A BRILLIANT SCIENTIFIC MIND! HE REQUESTED WORK AS MY ASSISTANT!
"YET HE IS DISTURBINGLY FAMILIAR--SOMEHOW--
"--AND, MOST OF ALL, HE WAS THERE...
"--AND HE CARED! AS MUCH AS IF IT WERE HIS OWN FATHER."

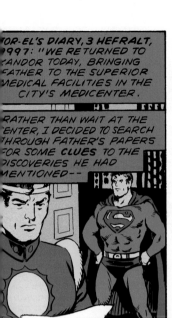

JOR-EL'S DIARY, 3 HEFRALT, 9997: "WE RETURNED TO KANDOR TODAY, BRINGING FATHER TO THE SUPERIOR MEDICAL FACILITIES IN THE CITY'S MEDICENTER.

RATHER THAN WAIT AT THE CENTER, I DECIDED TO SEARCH THROUGH FATHER'S PAPERS FOR SOME CLUES TO THE DISCOVERIES HE HAD MENTIONED--

"IT DIDN'T TAKE ME LONG TO FIND WHAT I WAS LOOKING FOR..."

GREAT KRYPTON! KAL--LOOK AT THIS! ACCORDING TO THESE TEST RESULTS, MY FATHER DISCOVERED UNSTABLE ELEMENTS AT THE PLANET'S CORE!

WHAT--?

FATHER DIDN'T COME TO ANY CONCLUSIONS...BUT IF THESE FIGURES ARE CORRECT...HMMM!

THIS IS...STAGGERING! DO YOU THINK IT'S WORTH CHECKING INTO FURTHER, KAL?

OH...YES, JOR...I MOST....ASSUREDLY DO!

JOR-EL'S DIARY, 5 HEFRALT, 9997: "THE COMPUTER DID MOST OF THE WORK--

--BUT IT WAS FOR ME TO TELL THOSE I HAD SUMMONED TO MY BROTHER NIM-EL'S HOME THE RESULTS...

...THUS, A CHAIN-REACTION --BEGUN MILLIONS OF YEARS AGO IN THE PLANET'S UNSTABLE CORE--HAS BEEN BUILDING, YEAR BY YEAR.... UNTIL NOW!

WITHIN THE NEXT TWO OR THREE YEARS, THE ELEMENTS WILL REACH CRITICAL MASS--

--AND KRYPTON WILL EXPLODE LIKE AN ATOMIC BOMB!

SURELY YOU'RE JESTING, JOR!

NO, NOR-KANN-- JOR STUDIED WITH ME FOR 15 YEARS AT THE LEARNING CENTER AND I KNOW HIM WELL! THIS IS NO JEST!

BU-BUT HOW CAN THAT BE!? HOW IS IT THIS HAS GONE UNDISCOVERED FOR SO LONG?

5

YES, MY FRIEND... HOW *IS* THAT SO?

I *DON'T* KNOW, NOR! BUT IT *IS* HAPPENING-- *RIGHT NOW!* MY FATHER'S EXPERIMENTS UTILIZED *ROBOT-PROBES* TO RETRIEVE *SAMPLES* OF THE RADIOACTIVE CORE--

-- AND I HAVE BOTH HIS AND MY *CALCULATIONS* TO *PROVE* IT!

CALCULATIONS CAN BE *WRONG,* JOR... EITHER *ACCIDENTLY--*

--OR ON *PURPOSE!*

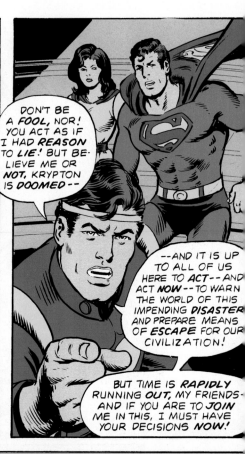

DON'T BE A *FOOL,* NOR! YOU ACT AS IF I HAD *REASON* TO *LIE!* BUT BELIEVE ME OR *NOT,* KRYPTON IS *DOOMED* --

--AND IT IS UP TO ALL OF US HERE TO *ACT--* AND ACT *NOW--* TO WARN THE WORLD OF THIS IMPENDING *DISASTER* AND PREPARE MEANS OF *ESCAPE* FOR OUR CIVILIZATION!

BUT TIME IS *RAPIDLY* RUNNING *OUT,* MY FRIENDS-- AND IF YOU ARE TO *JOIN* ME IN THIS, I MUST HAVE YOUR DECISIONS *NOW!*

IT IS QUITE A *SHOCK,* JOR-- BUT *I* AM WITH YOU! AND YOU, DIRECTOR VEN...?

JOR-EL WAS MY MOST *BRILLIANT* STUDENT, KIM-DA -- NOT TO MENTION A *FRIEND* OF MANY YEARS...

AYE, JOR, I AM *WITH* YOU!

"*PROF. KEN-DAL* AND OTHER FRIENDS JOINED NIM AND ME! BUT OUR YOUNGER BROTHER, *ZOR-EL,* THINKS I AM WRONG! HE RETURNED TO HIS HOME IN *ARGO CITY*... YET SOONER OR LATER, I *MUST* CONVINCE HIM OF THE DANGER!"

"*NOW* THE MOST *DIFFICULT* TASK WAS STILL TO COME! *SOMEHOW,* I WOULD HAVE TO CONVINCE THE *SCIENCE COUNCIL* I SPOKE THE TRUTH --

"--AND I COULD ONLY *HOPE* THEY WOULD PAY HEED!"

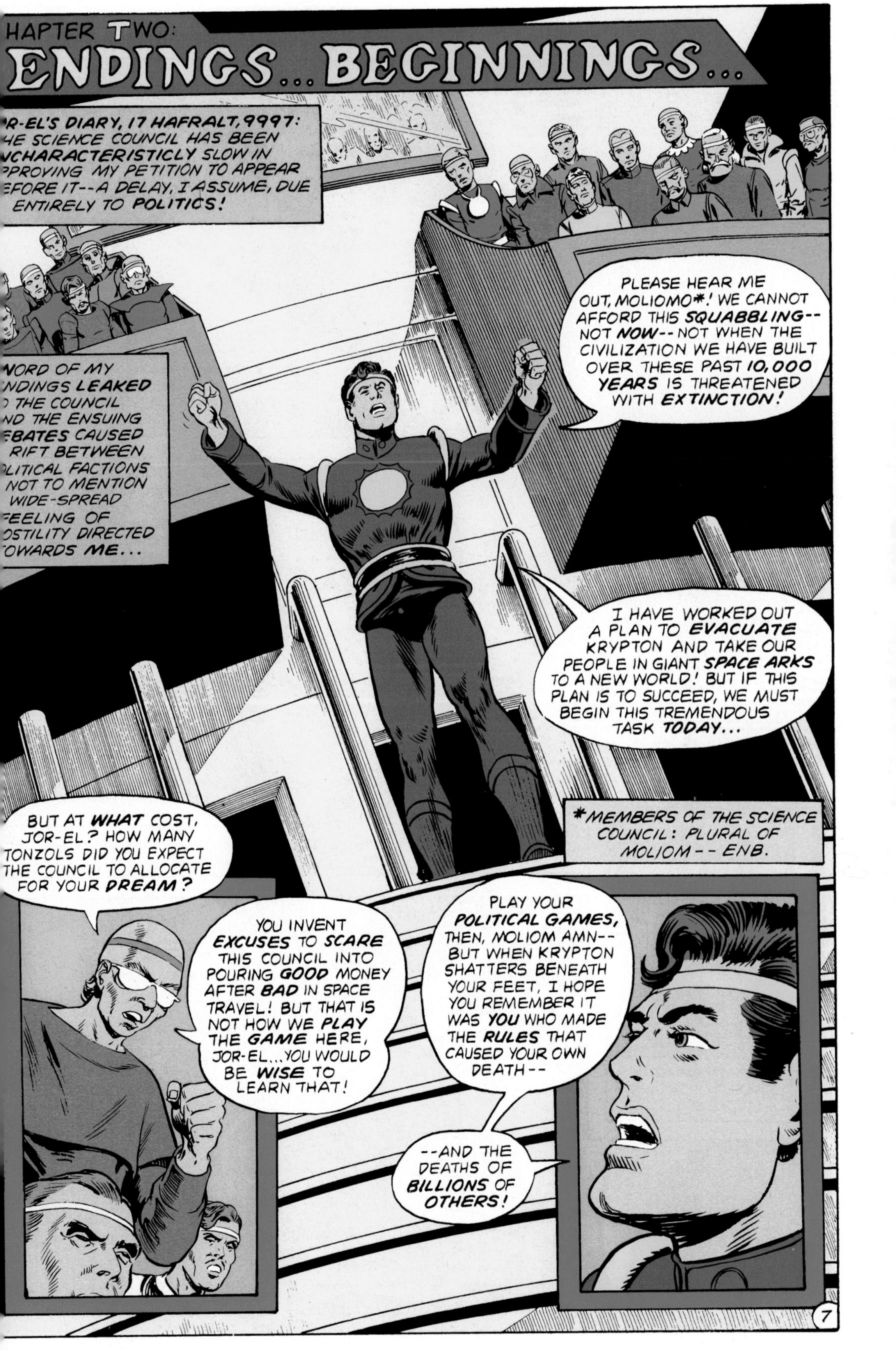

HAPTER TWO:
ENDINGS... BEGINNINGS...
R-EL'S DIARY, 17 HAFRALT, 9997: HE SCIENCE COUNCIL HAS BEEN NCHARACTERISTICLY SLOW IN PPROVING MY PETITION TO APPEAR EFORE IT--A DELAY, I ASSUME, DUE ENTIRELY TO POLITICS!
PLEASE HEAR ME OUT, MOLIOMO*! WE CANNOT AFFORD THIS SQUABBLING--NOT NOW--NOT WHEN THE CIVILIZATION WE HAVE BUILT OVER THESE PAST 10,000 YEARS IS THREATENED WITH EXTINCTION!
NORD OF MY NDINGS LEAKED THE COUNCIL ND THE ENSUING EBATES CAUSED RIFT BETWEEN LITICAL FACTIONS NOT TO MENTION WIDE-SPREAD EELING OF OSTILITY DIRECTED OWARDS ME...
I HAVE WORKED OUT A PLAN TO EVACUATE KRYPTON AND TAKE OUR PEOPLE IN GIANT SPACE ARKS TO A NEW WORLD! BUT IF THIS PLAN IS TO SUCCEED, WE MUST BEGIN THIS TREMENDOUS TASK TODAY...
*MEMBERS OF THE SCIENCE COUNCIL: PLURAL OF MOLIOM -- ENB.
BUT AT WHAT COST, JOR-EL? HOW MANY TONZOLS DID YOU EXPECT THE COUNCIL TO ALLOCATE FOR YOUR DREAM?
YOU INVENT EXCUSES TO SCARE THIS COUNCIL INTO POURING GOOD MONEY AFTER BAD IN SPACE TRAVEL! BUT THAT IS NOT HOW WE PLAY THE GAME HERE, JOR-EL...YOU WOULD BE WISE TO LEARN THAT!
PLAY YOUR POLITICAL GAMES, THEN, MOLIOM AMN--BUT WHEN KRYPTON SHATTERS BENEATH YOUR FEET, I HOPE YOU REMEMBER IT WAS YOU WHO MADE THE RULES THAT CAUSED YOUR OWN DEATH--
--AND THE DEATHS OF BILLIONS OF OTHERS!
7

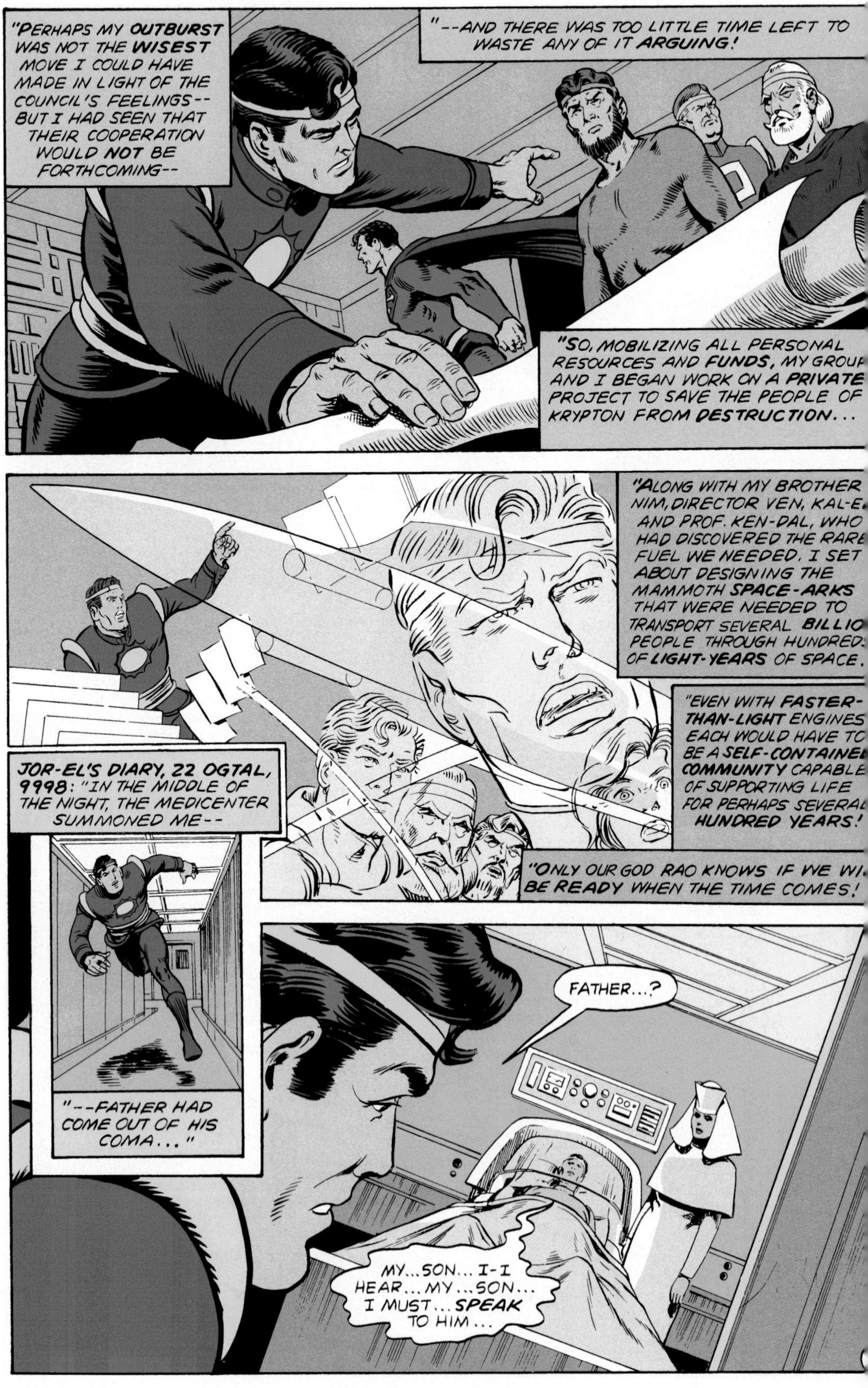
"PERHAPS MY OUTBURST WAS NOT THE WISEST MOVE I COULD HAVE MADE IN LIGHT OF THE COUNCIL'S FEELINGS--BUT I HAD SEEN THAT THEIR COOPERATION WOULD NOT BE FORTHCOMING--
"--AND THERE WAS TOO LITTLE TIME LEFT TO WASTE ANY OF IT ARGUING!
"SO, MOBILIZING ALL PERSONAL RESOURCES AND FUNDS, MY GROU AND I BEGAN WORK ON A PRIVATE PROJECT TO SAVE THE PEOPLE OF KRYPTON FROM DESTRUCTION...
"ALONG WITH MY BROTHER NIM, DIRECTOR VEN, KAL-E AND PROF. KEN-DAL, WHO HAD DISCOVERED THE RAR FUEL WE NEEDED, I SET ABOUT DESIGNING THE MAMMOTH SPACE-ARKS THAT WERE NEEDED TO TRANSPORT SEVERAL BILLIO PEOPLE THROUGH HUNDRED OF LIGHT-YEARS OF SPACE.
"EVEN WITH FASTER-THAN-LIGHT ENGINES EACH WOULD HAVE TO BE A SELF-CONTAINE COMMUNITY CAPABLE OF SUPPORTING LIFE FOR PERHAPS SEVERA HUNDRED YEARS!
"ONLY OUR GOD RAO KNOWS IF WE WI BE READY WHEN THE TIME COMES!
JOR-EL'S DIARY, 22 OGTAL, 9998: "IN THE MIDDLE OF THE NIGHT, THE MEDICENTER SUMMONED ME--
"--FATHER HAD COME OUT OF HIS COMA..."
FATHER...?
MY...SON... I-I HEAR...MY...SON... I MUST...SPEAK TO HIM...

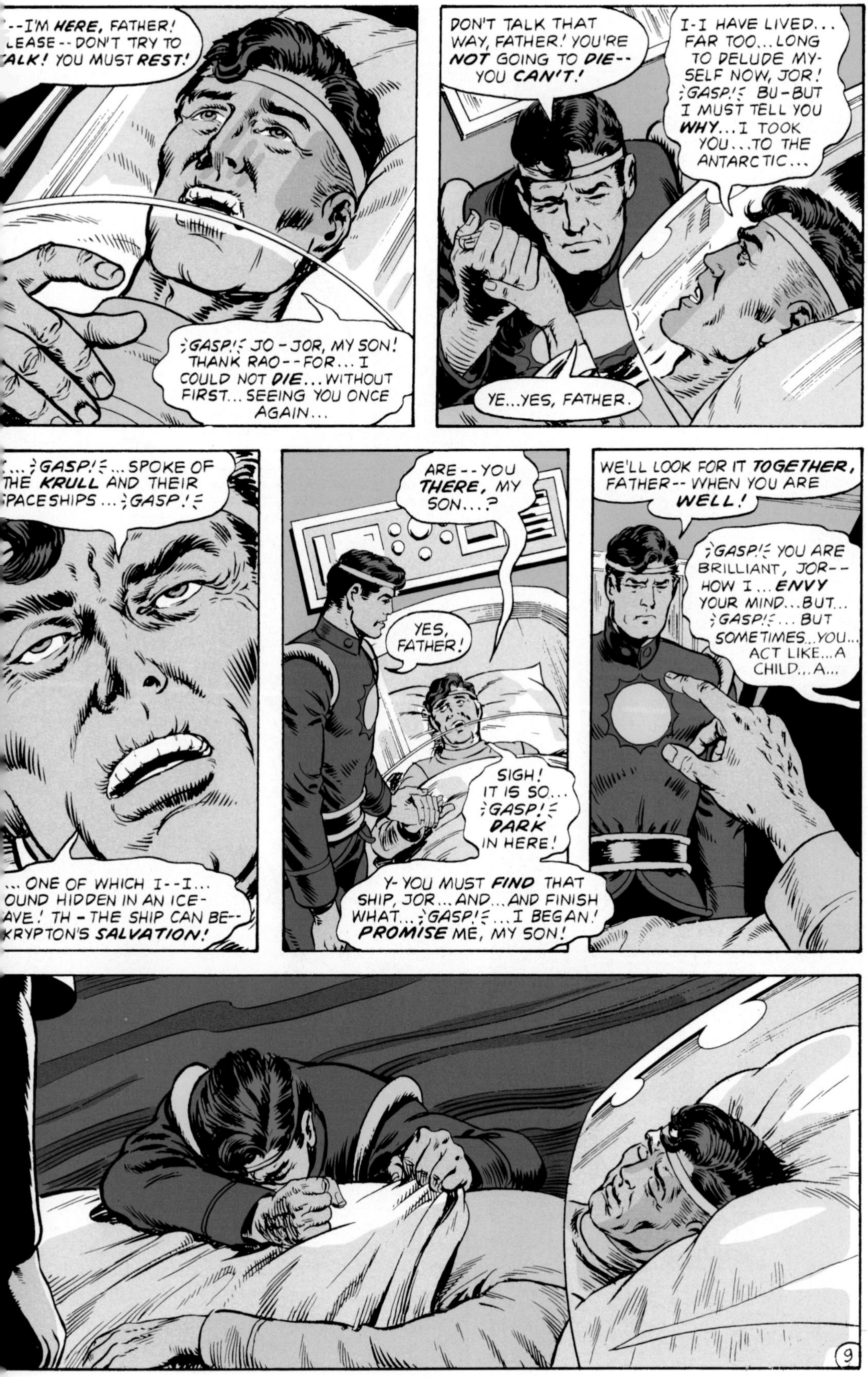
--I'M **HERE,** FATHER! LEASE--DON'T TRY TO ALK! YOU MUST **REST!**
GASP! JO-JOR, MY SON! THANK RAO--FOR...I COULD NOT **DIE**...WITHOUT FIRST...SEEING YOU ONCE AGAIN...
DON'T TALK THAT WAY, FATHER! YOU'RE **NOT** GOING TO **DIE**-- YOU **CAN'T!**
I-I HAVE LIVED... FAR TOO...LONG TO DELUDE MYSELF NOW, JOR! GASP! BU-BUT I MUST TELL YOU **WHY**...I TOOK YOU...TO THE ANTARCTIC...
YE...YES, FATHER.
...**GASP!**...SPOKE OF THE **KRULL** AND THEIR PACESHIPS...GASP!
...ONE OF WHICH I--I... OUND HIDDEN IN AN ICE-AVE! TH-THE SHIP CAN BE-- KRYPTON'S **SALVATION!**
ARE--YOU **THERE,** MY SON...?
YES, FATHER!
SIGH! IT IS SO... GASP! **DARK** IN HERE!
Y-YOU MUST **FIND** THAT SHIP, JOR...AND...AND FINISH WHAT...GASP!...I BEGAN! **PROMISE** ME, MY SON!
WE'LL LOOK FOR IT **TOGETHER,** FATHER--WHEN YOU ARE **WELL!**
GASP! YOU ARE BRILLIANT, JOR-- HOW I...**ENVY** YOUR MIND...BUT... GASP!...BUT SOMETIMES...YOU... ACT LIKE...A CHILD...A...
9

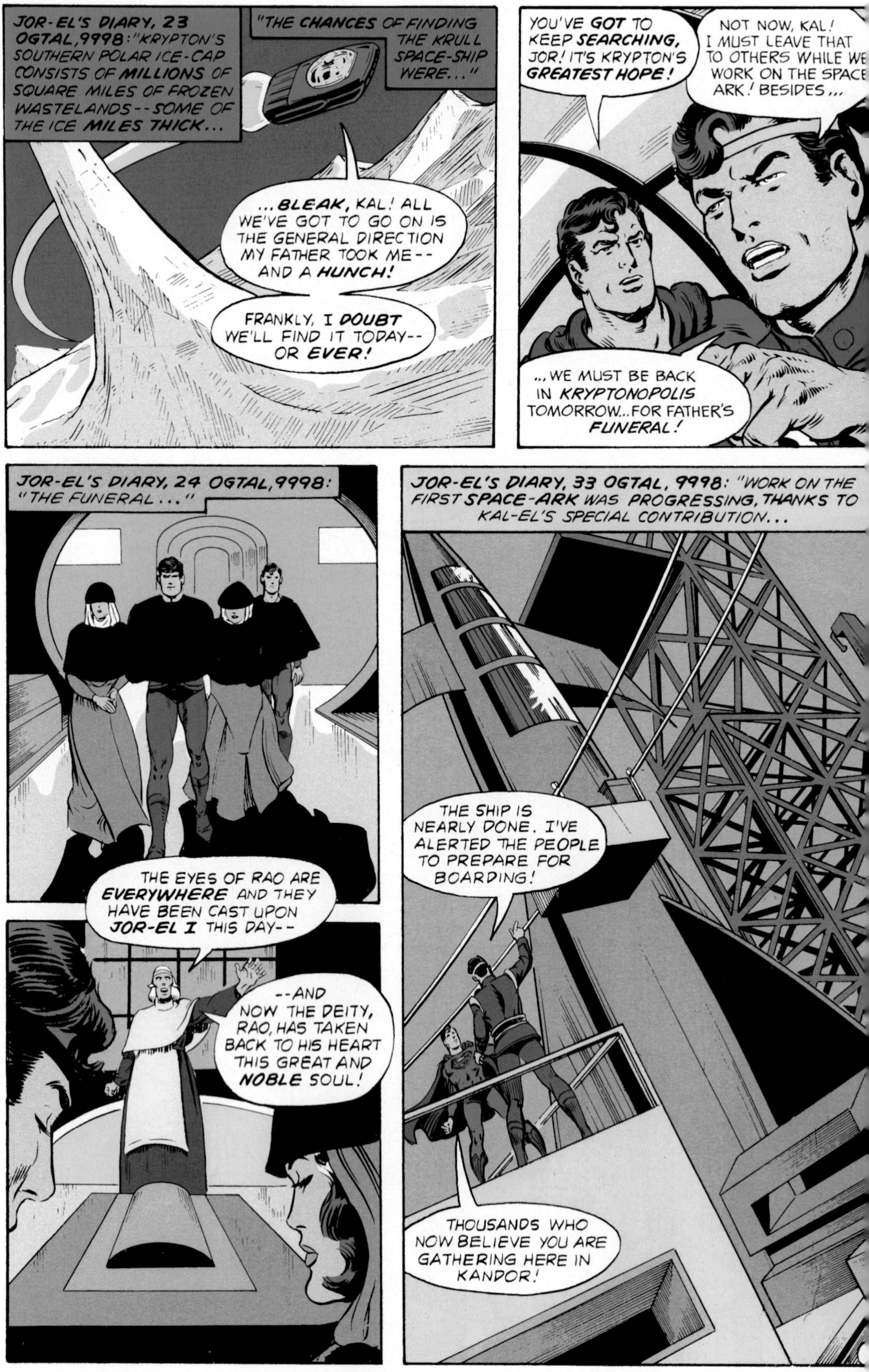
JOR-EL'S DIARY, 23 OGTAL, 9998: "KRYPTON'S SOUTHERN POLAR ICE-CAP CONSISTS OF MILLIONS OF SQUARE MILES OF FROZEN WASTELANDS--SOME OF THE ICE MILES THICK...
"THE CHANCES OF FINDING THE KRULL SPACE-SHIP WERE..."
...BLEAK, KAL! ALL WE'VE GOT TO GO ON IS THE GENERAL DIRECTION MY FATHER TOOK ME--AND A HUNCH!
FRANKLY, I DOUBT WE'LL FIND IT TODAY--OR EVER!
YOU'VE GOT TO KEEP SEARCHING, JOR! IT'S KRYPTON'S GREATEST HOPE!
NOT NOW, KAL! I MUST LEAVE THAT TO OTHERS WHILE WE WORK ON THE SPACE ARK! BESIDES...
...WE MUST BE BACK IN KRYPTONOPOLIS TOMORROW...FOR FATHER'S FUNERAL!
JOR-EL'S DIARY, 24 OGTAL, 9998: "THE FUNERAL..."
THE EYES OF RAO ARE EVERYWHERE AND THEY HAVE BEEN CAST UPON JOR-EL I THIS DAY--
--AND NOW THE DEITY, RAO, HAS TAKEN BACK TO HIS HEART THIS GREAT AND NOBLE SOUL!
JOR-EL'S DIARY, 33 OGTAL, 9998: "WORK ON THE FIRST SPACE-ARK WAS PROGRESSING, THANKS TO KAL-EL'S SPECIAL CONTRIBUTION...
THE SHIP IS NEARLY DONE. I'VE ALERTED THE PEOPLE TO PREPARE FOR BOARDING!
THOUSANDS WHO NOW BELIEVE YOU ARE GATHERING HERE IN KANDOR!

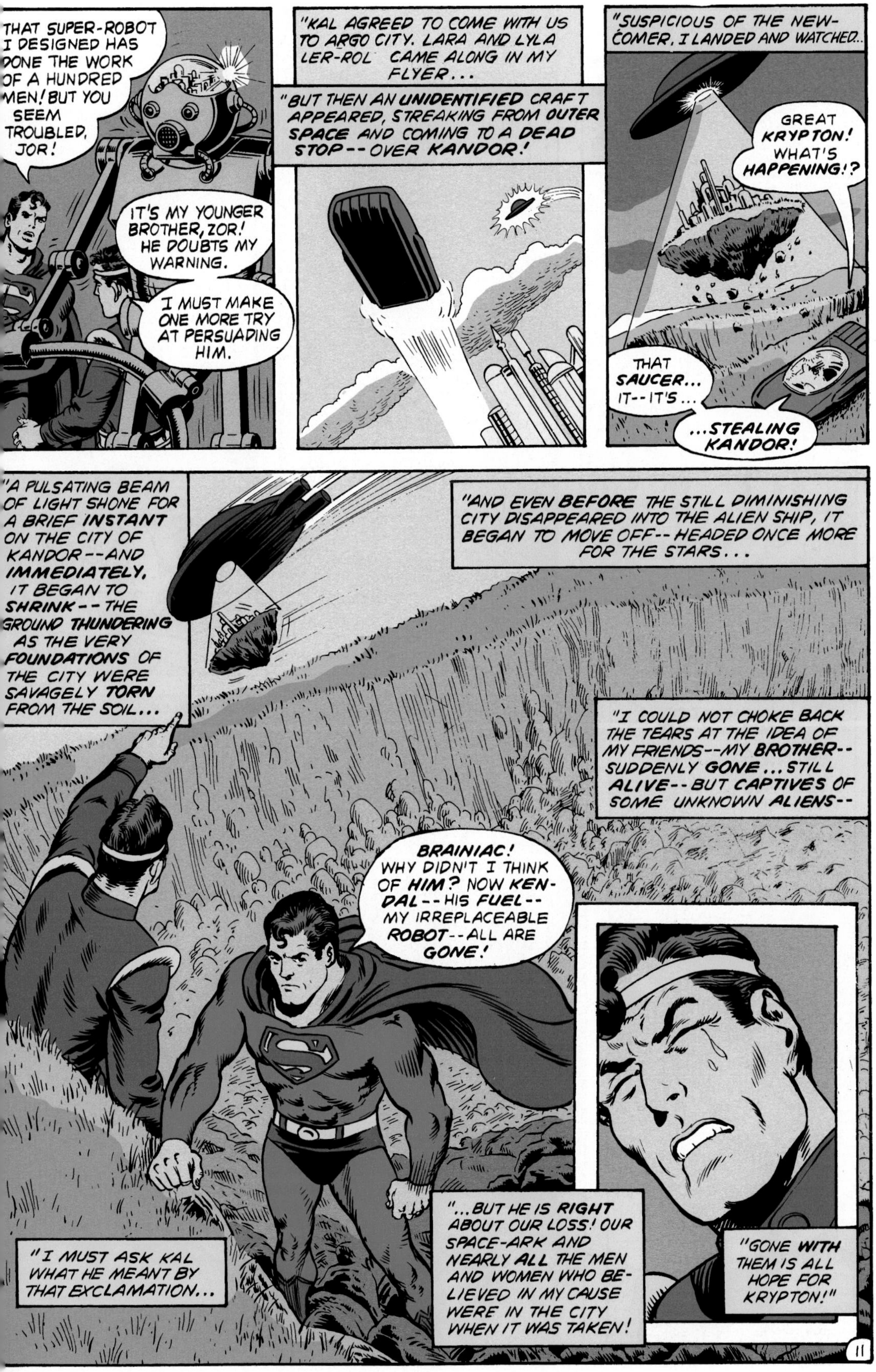
THAT SUPER-ROBOT I DESIGNED HAS DONE THE WORK OF A HUNDRED MEN! BUT YOU SEEM TROUBLED, JOR!
IT'S MY YOUNGER BROTHER, ZOR! HE DOUBTS MY WARNING.
I MUST MAKE ONE MORE TRY AT PERSUADING HIM.
"KAL AGREED TO COME WITH US TO ARGO CITY. LARA AND LYLA LER-ROL CAME ALONG IN MY FLYER...
"BUT THEN AN UNIDENTIFIED CRAFT APPEARED, STREAKING FROM OUTER SPACE AND COMING TO A DEAD STOP--OVER KANDOR!
"SUSPICIOUS OF THE NEW-COMER, I LANDED AND WATCHED...
GREAT KRYPTON! WHAT'S HAPPENING!?
THAT SAUCER... IT--IT'S...
...STEALING KANDOR!
"A PULSATING BEAM OF LIGHT SHONE FOR A BRIEF INSTANT ON THE CITY OF KANDOR--AND IMMEDIATELY, IT BEGAN TO SHRINK--THE GROUND THUNDERING AS THE VERY FOUNDATIONS OF THE CITY WERE SAVAGELY TORN FROM THE SOIL...
"AND EVEN BEFORE THE STILL DIMINISHING CITY DISAPPEARED INTO THE ALIEN SHIP, IT BEGAN TO MOVE OFF--HEADED ONCE MORE FOR THE STARS...
"I COULD NOT CHOKE BACK THE TEARS AT THE IDEA OF MY FRIENDS--MY BROTHER--SUDDENLY GONE... STILL ALIVE--BUT CAPTIVES OF SOME UNKNOWN ALIENS--
BRAINIAC! WHY DIDN'T I THINK OF HIM? NOW KEN-DAL--HIS FUEL--MY IRREPLACEABLE ROBOT--ALL ARE GONE!
"I MUST ASK KAL WHAT HE MEANT BY THAT EXCLAMATION...
"...BUT HE IS RIGHT ABOUT OUR LOSS! OUR SPACE-ARK AND NEARLY ALL THE MEN AND WOMEN WHO BE-LIEVED IN MY CAUSE WERE IN THE CITY WHEN IT WAS TAKEN!
"GONE WITH THEM IS ALL HOPE FOR KRYPTON!"
11

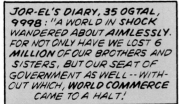

JOR-EL'S DIARY, 35 OGTAL, 9998: "A WORLD IN SHOCK WANDERED ABOUT AIMLESSLY. FOR NOT ONLY HAVE WE LOST 6 MILLION OF OUR BROTHERS AND SISTERS, BUT OUR SEAT OF GOVERNMENT AS WELL -- WITH-OUT WHICH, WORLD COMMERCE CAME TO A HALT!

"BUT ALREADY, NEW ELECTIONS WERE PLANNED-- COMPUTERS IN KRYPTONOPOLIS WERE BEING REPROGRAMMED TO TAKE UP THE WORKLOAD OF THE KANDOR SYSTEM -- THE WORLD WOULD GO ON...

"I WISH TO RAO MY TROUBLES WERE SO EASILY AND EFFICIENTLY SOLVED...

"THERE WAS A TRAGIC MESSAGE WAITING FOR ME AT HOME,...!

KAL-EL IS GONE, LARA! LYLA LER-ROL SAW IT -- DURING THE 3-DV SHOOTING! A PROP SHIP SUDDENLY TOOK OFF INTO SPACE!

I PRAY HE LIVES -- THAT SOMEHOW HE'S SURVIVED!*

*AS WE KNOW HE DID. --ENB.

I'M FINISHED, LARA! EVERY-ONE WHO COULD HELP KRYPTON IS GONE! AND NO MATTER HOW HARD I TRY TO THINK OF A REASON TO GO ON--

--I CAN'T!

YOU CAN GIVE UP IF YOU WANT TO, JOR--BUT I PLAN TO CONTINUE!

I WANT OUR CHILD TO HAVE AT LEAST ONE PARENT WHO REFUSES TO QUIT!

OUR-- OUR CHILD...

...DID YOU SAY OUR CHILD!?

I CERTAINLY DID -- AND BEFORE YOU ASK, I MOST CERTAINLY AM!

HILLS OF ZITH, LARA! YOU'VE JUST GIVEN ME THE BEST MOTIVATION IN THE GALAXY-- OUR SON!

OR OUR DAUGHTER!

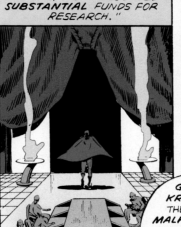

JOR-EL'S DIARY, 13 ULLHAH, 9998: "THE NEWLY-ELECTED SCIENCE COUNCIL IS FINALLY SHOWING INTEREST IN MY THEORY.

"IN FACT, AT THIS MORNING'S MEETING, THEY ALLOCATED SUBSTANTIAL FUNDS FOR RESEARCH."

JOR-EL'S DIARY, 53 ULLHAH, 9998: "OUR RESEARCH CON-TINUES TO DRAG ALONG, THE FIRST TEST-FLIGHT OF A SPACE MODEL OF THE SHIP BEING SOMEWHAT LESS THAN SUCCESS-FUL...

GREAT KRYPTON! THE SHIP'S MALFUNCTIONED AND IS HEADED STRAIGHT BACK AT US!

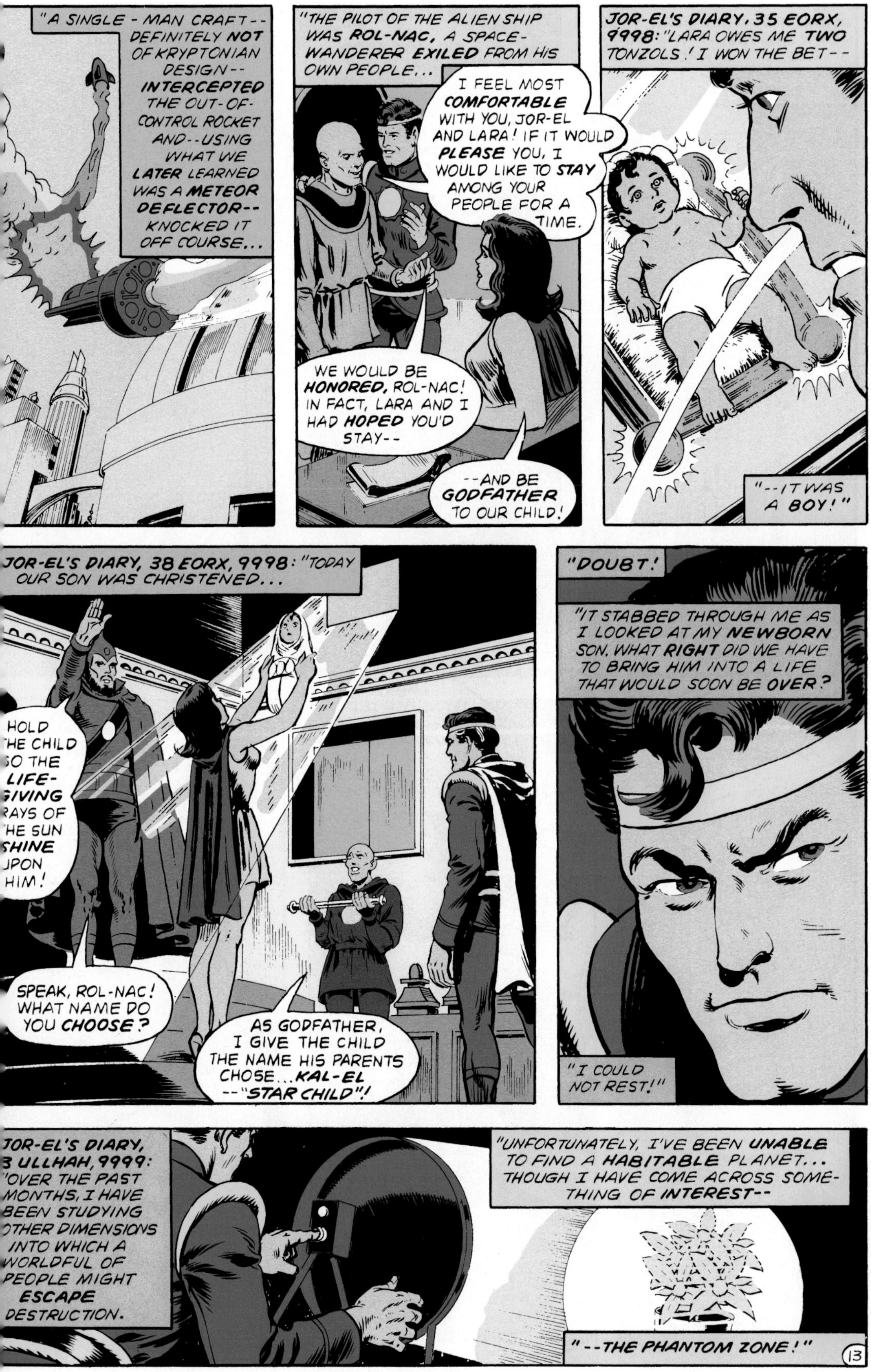

"A SINGLE - MAN CRAFT -- DEFINITELY **NOT** OF KRYPTONIAN DESIGN -- **INTERCEPTED** THE OUT-OF-CONTROL ROCKET AND -- USING WHAT WE **LATER** LEARNED WAS A **METEOR DEFLECTOR** -- KNOCKED IT OFF COURSE...
"THE PILOT OF THE ALIEN SHIP WAS **ROL-NAC**, A SPACE-WANDERER **EXILED** FROM HIS OWN PEOPLE...
I FEEL MOST **COMFORTABLE** WITH YOU, JOR-EL AND LARA! IF IT WOULD **PLEASE** YOU, I WOULD LIKE TO **STAY** AMONG YOUR PEOPLE FOR A TIME.
WE WOULD BE **HONORED**, ROL-NAC! IN FACT, LARA AND I HAD **HOPED** YOU'D STAY--
--AND BE **GODFATHER** TO OUR CHILD!
JOR-EL'S DIARY, 35 EORX, 9998: "LARA OWES ME **TWO** TONZOLS! I WON THE BET--
"--IT WAS A **BOY**!"
JOR-EL'S DIARY, 38 EORX, 9998: "TODAY OUR SON WAS CHRISTENED...
HOLD THE CHILD SO THE **LIFE-GIVING** RAYS OF THE SUN **SHINE** UPON HIM!
SPEAK, ROL-NAC! WHAT NAME DO YOU **CHOOSE**?
AS GODFATHER, I GIVE THE CHILD THE NAME HIS PARENTS CHOSE... **KAL-EL** -- "**STAR CHILD**"!
"**DOUBT**!
"IT STABBED THROUGH ME AS I LOOKED AT MY **NEWBORN** SON. WHAT **RIGHT** DID WE HAVE TO BRING HIM INTO A LIFE THAT WOULD SOON BE **OVER**?
"I COULD NOT REST!"
JOR-EL'S DIARY, 3 ULLHAH, 9999: "OVER THE PAST MONTHS, I HAVE BEEN STUDYING OTHER DIMENSIONS INTO WHICH A WORLDFUL OF PEOPLE MIGHT **ESCAPE** DESTRUCTION.
"UNFORTUNATELY, I'VE BEEN **UNABLE** TO FIND A **HABITABLE** PLANET... THOUGH I HAVE COME ACROSS SOMETHING OF **INTEREST**--
"--**THE PHANTOM ZONE**!"
13

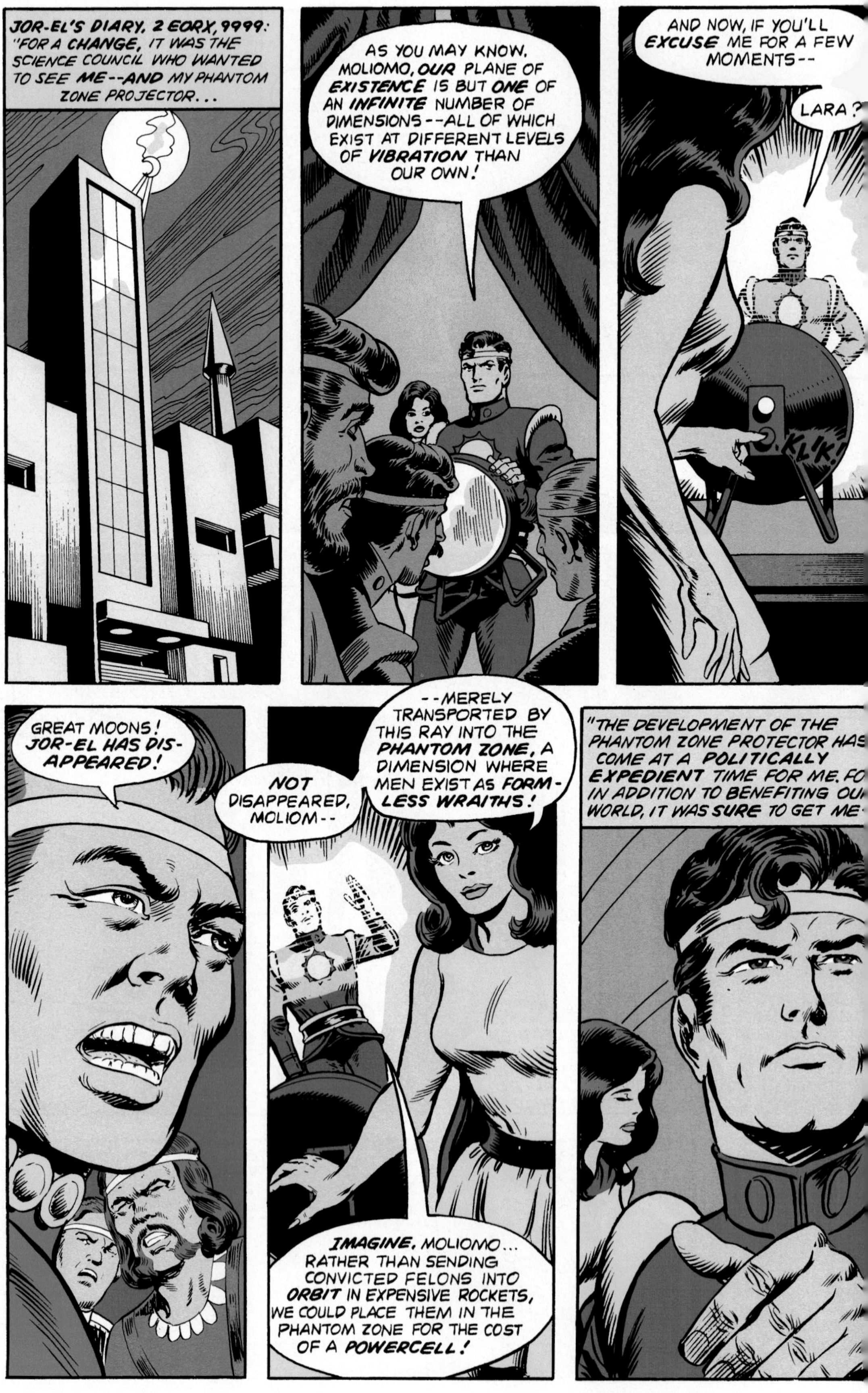
JOR-EL'S DIARY, 2 EORX, 9999: "FOR A CHANGE, IT WAS THE SCIENCE COUNCIL WHO WANTED TO SEE ME--AND MY PHANTOM ZONE PROJECTOR...
AS YOU MAY KNOW, MOLIOMO, OUR PLANE OF EXISTENCE IS BUT ONE OF AN INFINITE NUMBER OF DIMENSIONS--ALL OF WHICH EXIST AT DIFFERENT LEVELS OF VIBRATION THAN OUR OWN!
AND NOW, IF YOU'LL EXCUSE ME FOR A FEW MOMENTS--
LARA?
KLIK!
GREAT MOONS! JOR-EL HAS DISAPPEARED!
NOT DISAPPEARED, MOLIOM--
--MERELY TRANSPORTED BY THIS RAY INTO THE PHANTOM ZONE, A DIMENSION WHERE MEN EXIST AS FORMLESS WRAITHS!
IMAGINE, MOLIOMO... RATHER THAN SENDING CONVICTED FELONS INTO ORBIT IN EXPENSIVE ROCKETS, WE COULD PLACE THEM IN THE PHANTOM ZONE FOR THE COST OF A POWERCELL!
"THE DEVELOPMENT OF THE PHANTOM ZONE PROTECTOR HA COME AT A POLITICALLY EXPEDIENT TIME FOR ME. FO IN ADDITION TO BENEFITING OU WORLD, IT WAS SURE TO GET ME-

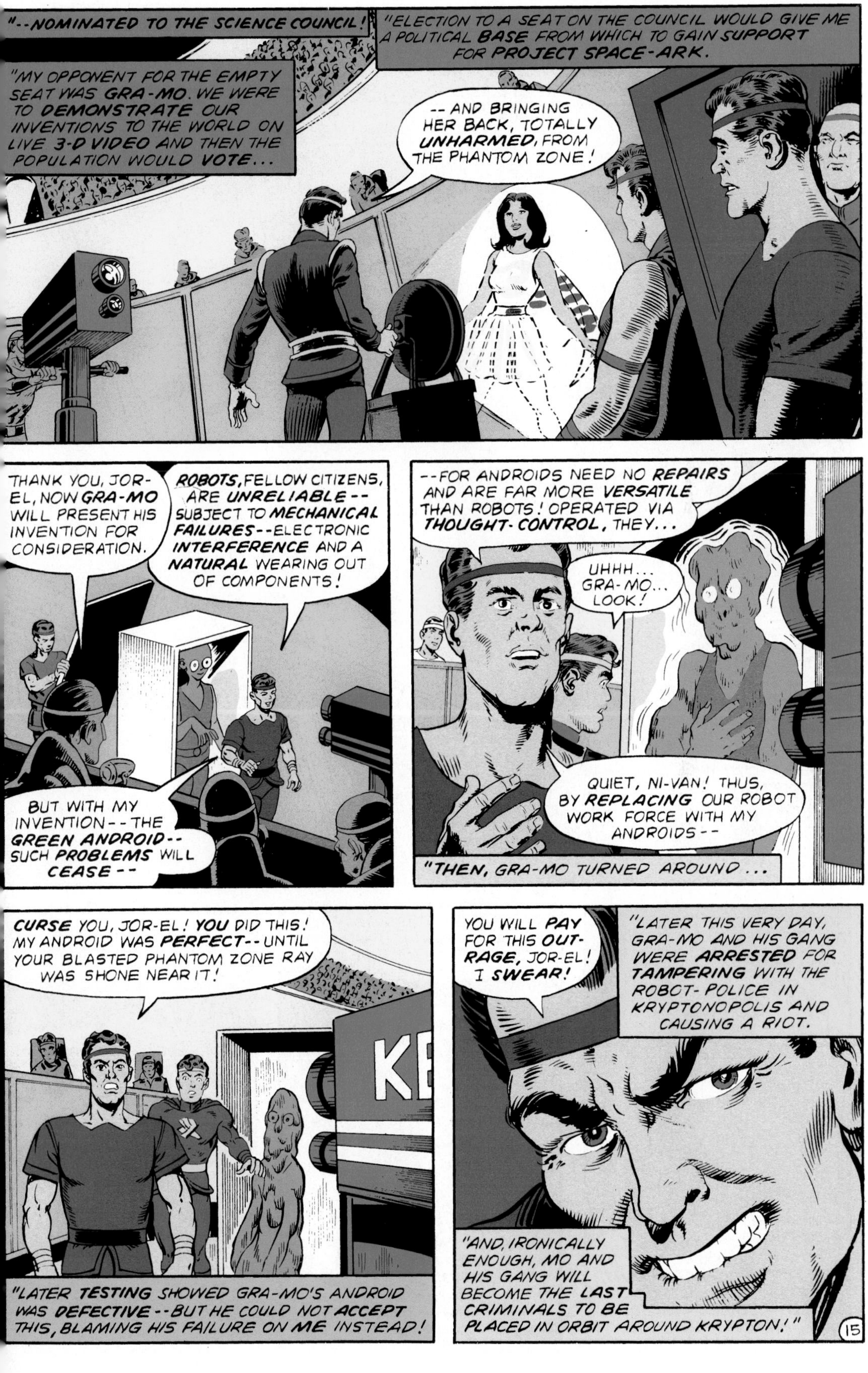
"--NOMINATED TO THE SCIENCE COUNCIL!
"ELECTION TO A SEAT ON THE COUNCIL WOULD GIVE ME A POLITICAL BASE FROM WHICH TO GAIN SUPPORT FOR PROJECT SPACE-ARK.
"MY OPPONENT FOR THE EMPTY SEAT WAS GRA-MO. WE WERE TO DEMONSTRATE OUR INVENTIONS TO THE WORLD ON LIVE 3-D VIDEO AND THEN THE POPULATION WOULD VOTE...
-- AND BRINGING HER BACK, TOTALLY UNHARMED, FROM THE PHANTOM ZONE!
THANK YOU, JOR-EL, NOW GRA-MO WILL PRESENT HIS INVENTION FOR CONSIDERATION.
ROBOTS, FELLOW CITIZENS, ARE UNRELIABLE -- SUBJECT TO MECHANICAL FAILURES -- ELECTRONIC INTERFERENCE AND A NATURAL WEARING OUT OF COMPONENTS!
BUT WITH MY INVENTION -- THE GREEN ANDROID -- SUCH PROBLEMS WILL CEASE --
--FOR ANDROIDS NEED NO REPAIRS AND ARE FAR MORE VERSATILE THAN ROBOTS! OPERATED VIA THOUGHT-CONTROL, THEY...
UHHH... GRA-MO... LOOK!
QUIET, NI-VAN! THUS, BY REPLACING OUR ROBOT WORK FORCE WITH MY ANDROIDS --
"THEN, GRA-MO TURNED AROUND...
CURSE YOU, JOR-EL! YOU DID THIS! MY ANDROID WAS PERFECT -- UNTIL YOUR BLASTED PHANTOM ZONE RAY WAS SHONE NEAR IT!
KE
"LATER TESTING SHOWED GRA-MO'S ANDROID WAS DEFECTIVE -- BUT HE COULD NOT ACCEPT THIS, BLAMING HIS FAILURE ON ME INSTEAD!
YOU WILL PAY FOR THIS OUTRAGE, JOR-EL! I SWEAR!
"LATER THIS VERY DAY, GRA-MO AND HIS GANG WERE ARRESTED FOR TAMPERING WITH THE ROBOT-POLICE IN KRYPTONOPOLIS AND CAUSING A RIOT.
"AND, IRONICALLY ENOUGH, MO AND HIS GANG WILL BECOME THE LAST CRIMINALS TO BE PLACED IN ORBIT AROUND KRYPTON!"
15

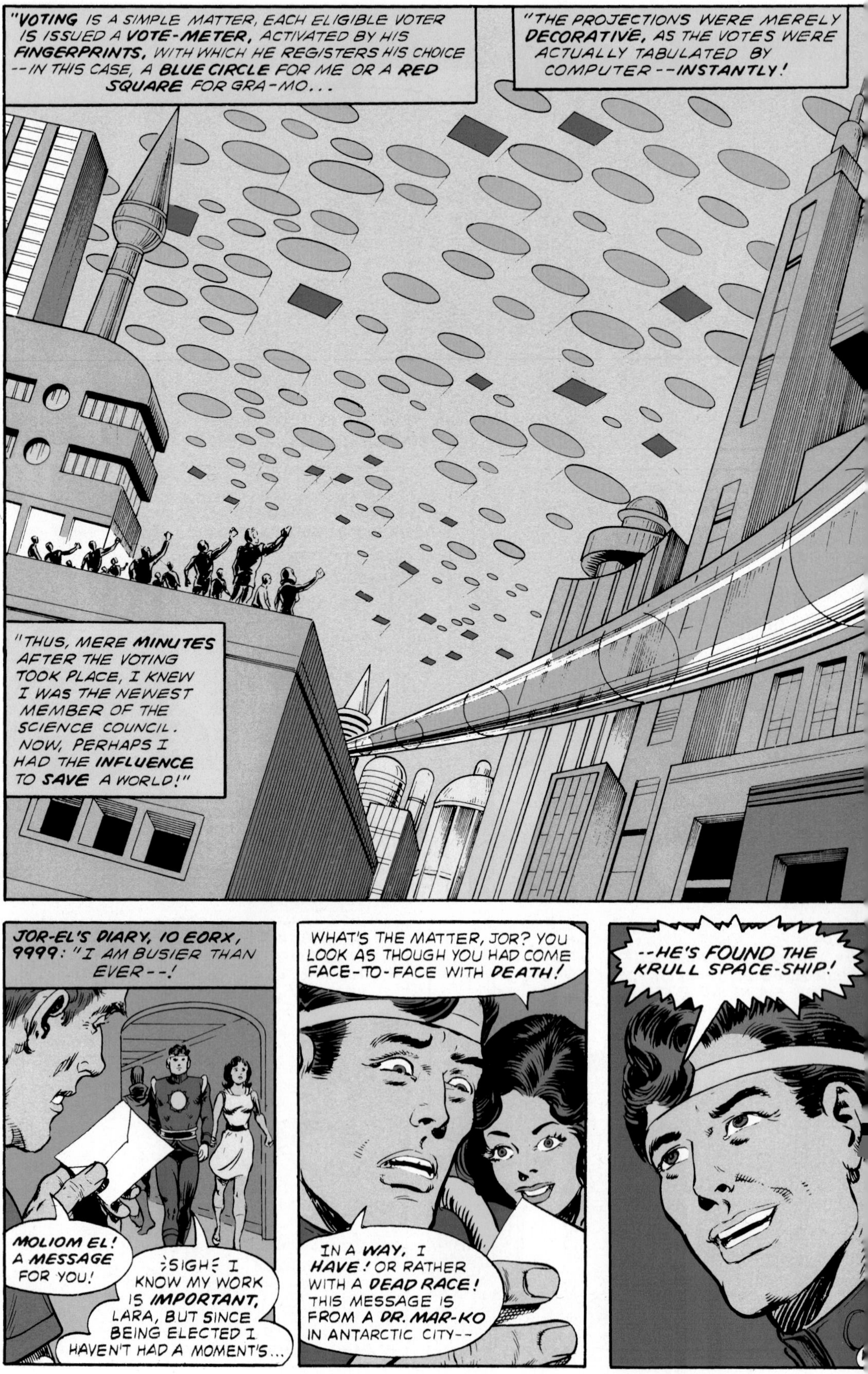
"VOTING IS A SIMPLE MATTER, EACH ELIGIBLE VOTER IS ISSUED A VOTE-METER, ACTIVATED BY HIS FINGERPRINTS, WITH WHICH HE REGISTERS HIS CHOICE --IN THIS CASE, A BLUE CIRCLE FOR ME OR A RED SQUARE FOR GRA-MO...
"THE PROJECTIONS WERE MERELY DECORATIVE, AS THE VOTES WERE ACTUALLY TABULATED BY COMPUTER--INSTANTLY!
"THUS, MERE MINUTES AFTER THE VOTING TOOK PLACE, I KNEW I WAS THE NEWEST MEMBER OF THE SCIENCE COUNCIL. NOW, PERHAPS I HAD THE INFLUENCE TO SAVE A WORLD!"
JOR-EL'S DIARY, 10 EORX, 9999: "I AM BUSIER THAN EVER--!
MOLIOM EL! A MESSAGE FOR YOU!
SIGH I KNOW MY WORK IS IMPORTANT, LARA, BUT SINCE BEING ELECTED I HAVEN'T HAD A MOMENT'S...
WHAT'S THE MATTER, JOR? YOU LOOK AS THOUGH YOU HAD COME FACE-TO-FACE WITH DEATH!
IN A WAY, I HAVE! OR RATHER WITH A DEAD RACE! THIS MESSAGE IS FROM A DR. MAR-KO IN ANTARCTIC CITY--
--HE'S FOUND THE KRULL SPACE-SHIP!

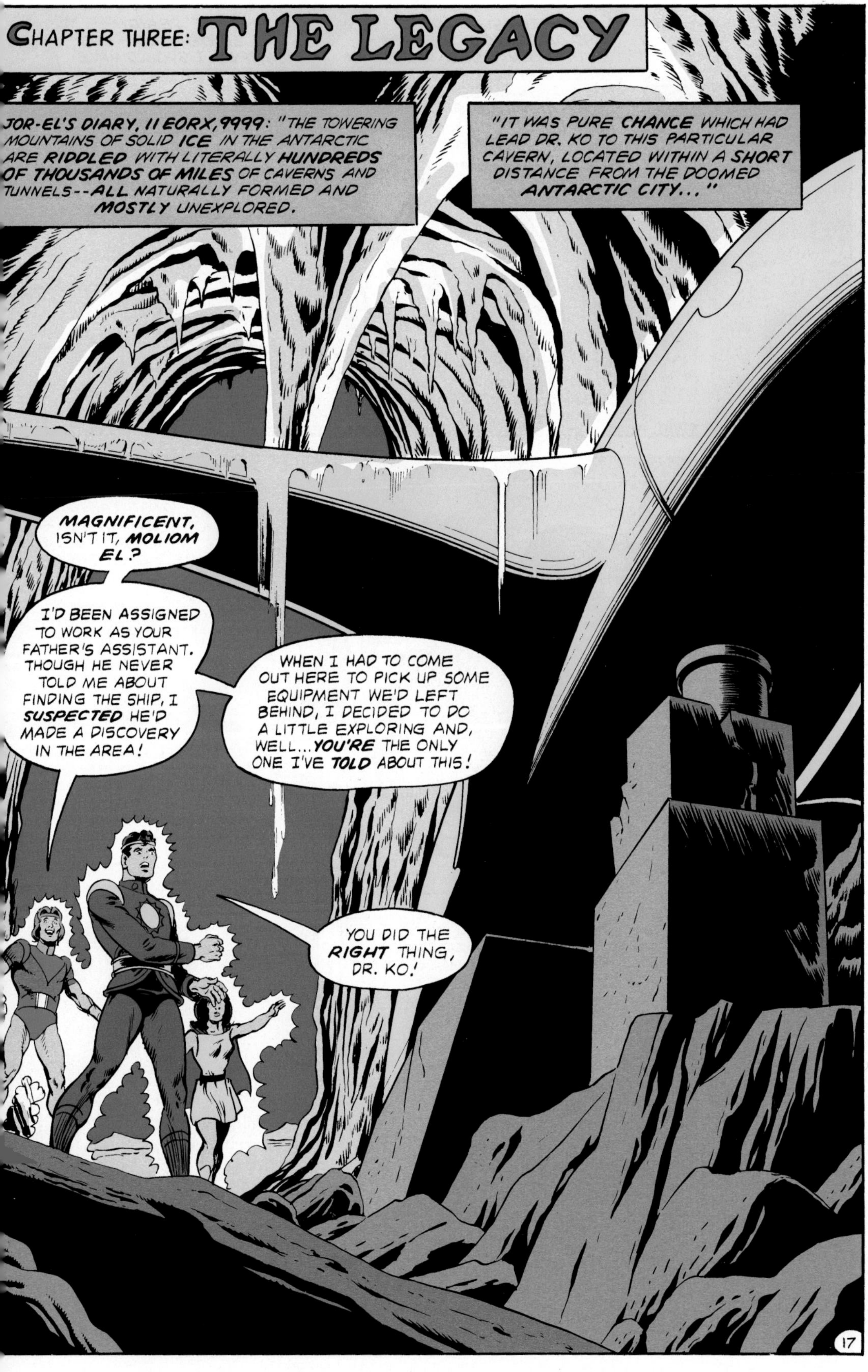
CHAPTER THREE: THE LEGACY
JOR-EL'S DIARY, 11 EORX, 9999: "THE TOWERING MOUNTAINS OF SOLID ICE IN THE ANTARCTIC ARE RIDDLED WITH LITERALLY HUNDREDS OF THOUSANDS OF MILES OF CAVERNS AND TUNNELS--ALL NATURALLY FORMED AND MOSTLY UNEXPLORED.
"IT WAS PURE CHANCE WHICH HAD LEAD DR. KO TO THIS PARTICULAR CAVERN, LOCATED WITHIN A SHORT DISTANCE FROM THE DOOMED ANTARCTIC CITY..."
MAGNIFICENT, ISN'T IT, MOLIOM EL?
I'D BEEN ASSIGNED TO WORK AS YOUR FATHER'S ASSISTANT. THOUGH HE NEVER TOLD ME ABOUT FINDING THE SHIP, I SUSPECTED HE'D MADE A DISCOVERY IN THE AREA!
WHEN I HAD TO COME OUT HERE TO PICK UP SOME EQUIPMENT WE'D LEFT BEHIND, I DECIDED TO DO A LITTLE EXPLORING AND, WELL... YOU'RE THE ONLY ONE I'VE TOLD ABOUT THIS!
YOU DID THE RIGHT THING, DR. KO!
17

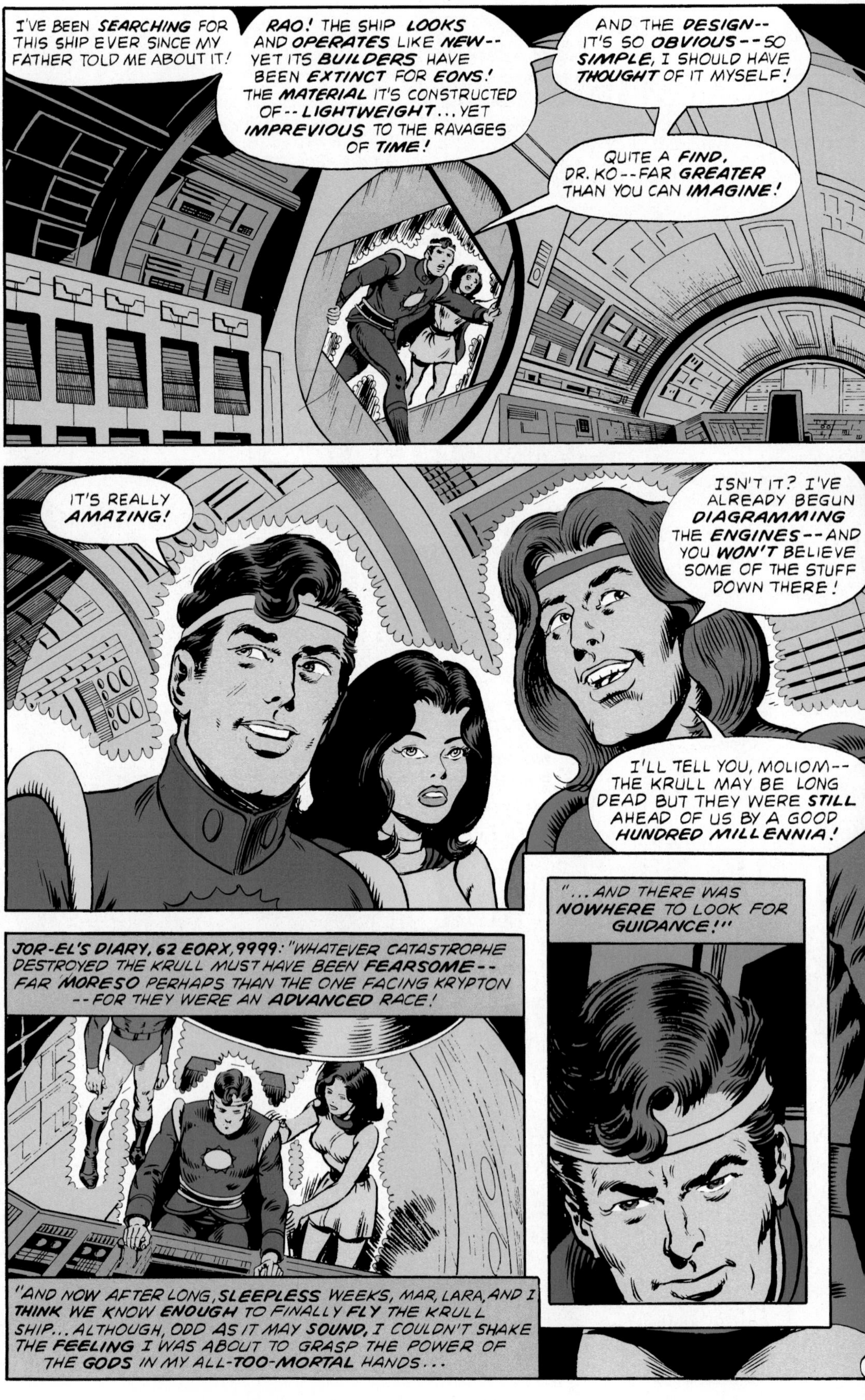
I'VE BEEN SEARCHING FOR THIS SHIP EVER SINCE MY FATHER TOLD ME ABOUT IT!
RAO! THE SHIP LOOKS AND OPERATES LIKE NEW-- YET ITS BUILDERS HAVE BEEN EXTINCT FOR EONS! THE MATERIAL IT'S CONSTRUCTED OF--LIGHTWEIGHT... YET IMPREVIOUS TO THE RAVAGES OF TIME!
AND THE DESIGN-- IT'S SO OBVIOUS--SO SIMPLE, I SHOULD HAVE THOUGHT OF IT MYSELF!
QUITE A FIND, DR. KO--FAR GREATER THAN YOU CAN IMAGINE!
IT'S REALLY AMAZING!
ISN'T IT? I'VE ALREADY BEGUN DIAGRAMMING THE ENGINES--AND YOU WON'T BELIEVE SOME OF THE STUFF DOWN THERE!
I'LL TELL YOU, MOLIOM-- THE KRULL MAY BE LONG DEAD BUT THEY WERE STILL AHEAD OF US BY A GOOD HUNDRED MILLENNIA!
JOR-EL'S DIARY, 62 EORX, 9999: "WHATEVER CATASTROPHE DESTROYED THE KRULL MUST HAVE BEEN FEARSOME-- FAR MORESO PERHAPS THAN THE ONE FACING KRYPTON --FOR THEY WERE AN ADVANCED RACE!
"AND NOW AFTER LONG, SLEEPLESS WEEKS, MAR, LARA, AND I THINK WE KNOW ENOUGH TO FINALLY FLY THE KRULL SHIP... ALTHOUGH, ODD AS IT MAY SOUND, I COULDN'T SHAKE THE FEELING I WAS ABOUT TO GRASP THE POWER OF THE GODS IN MY ALL-TOO-MORTAL HANDS...
"...AND THERE WAS NOWHERE TO LOOK FOR GUIDANCE!"

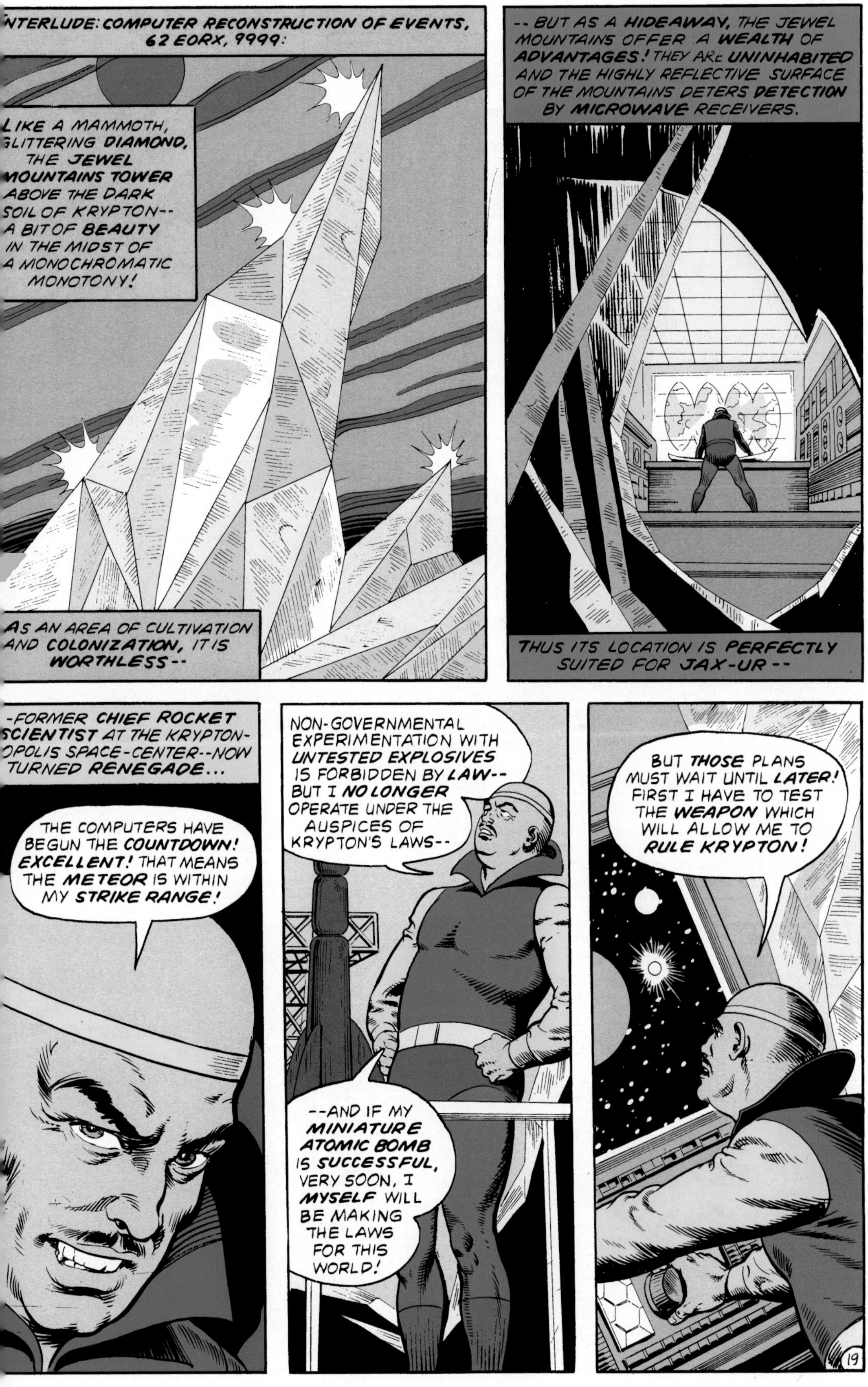
INTERLUDE: COMPUTER RECONSTRUCTION OF EVENTS, 62 EORX, 9999:
LIKE A MAMMOTH, GLITTERING DIAMOND, THE JEWEL MOUNTAINS TOWER ABOVE THE DARK SOIL OF KRYPTON-- A BIT OF BEAUTY IN THE MIDST OF A MONOCHROMATIC MONOTONY!
AS AN AREA OF CULTIVATION AND COLONIZATION, IT IS WORTHLESS--
-- BUT AS A HIDEAWAY, THE JEWEL MOUNTAINS OFFER A WEALTH OF ADVANTAGES! THEY ARE UNINHABITED AND THE HIGHLY REFLECTIVE SURFACE OF THE MOUNTAINS DETERS DETECTION BY MICROWAVE RECEIVERS.
THUS ITS LOCATION IS PERFECTLY SUITED FOR JAX-UR --
-FORMER CHIEF ROCKET SCIENTIST AT THE KRYPTON-OPOLIS SPACE-CENTER--NOW TURNED RENEGADE...
THE COMPUTERS HAVE BEGUN THE COUNTDOWN! EXCELLENT! THAT MEANS THE METEOR IS WITHIN MY STRIKE RANGE!
NON-GOVERNMENTAL EXPERIMENTATION WITH UNTESTED EXPLOSIVES IS FORBIDDEN BY LAW-- BUT I NO LONGER OPERATE UNDER THE AUSPICES OF KRYPTON'S LAWS--
--AND IF MY MINIATURE ATOMIC BOMB IS SUCCESSFUL, VERY SOON, I MYSELF WILL BE MAKING THE LAWS FOR THIS WORLD!
BUT THOSE PLANS MUST WAIT UNTIL LATER! FIRST I HAVE TO TEST THE WEAPON WHICH WILL ALLOW ME TO RULE KRYPTON!
19

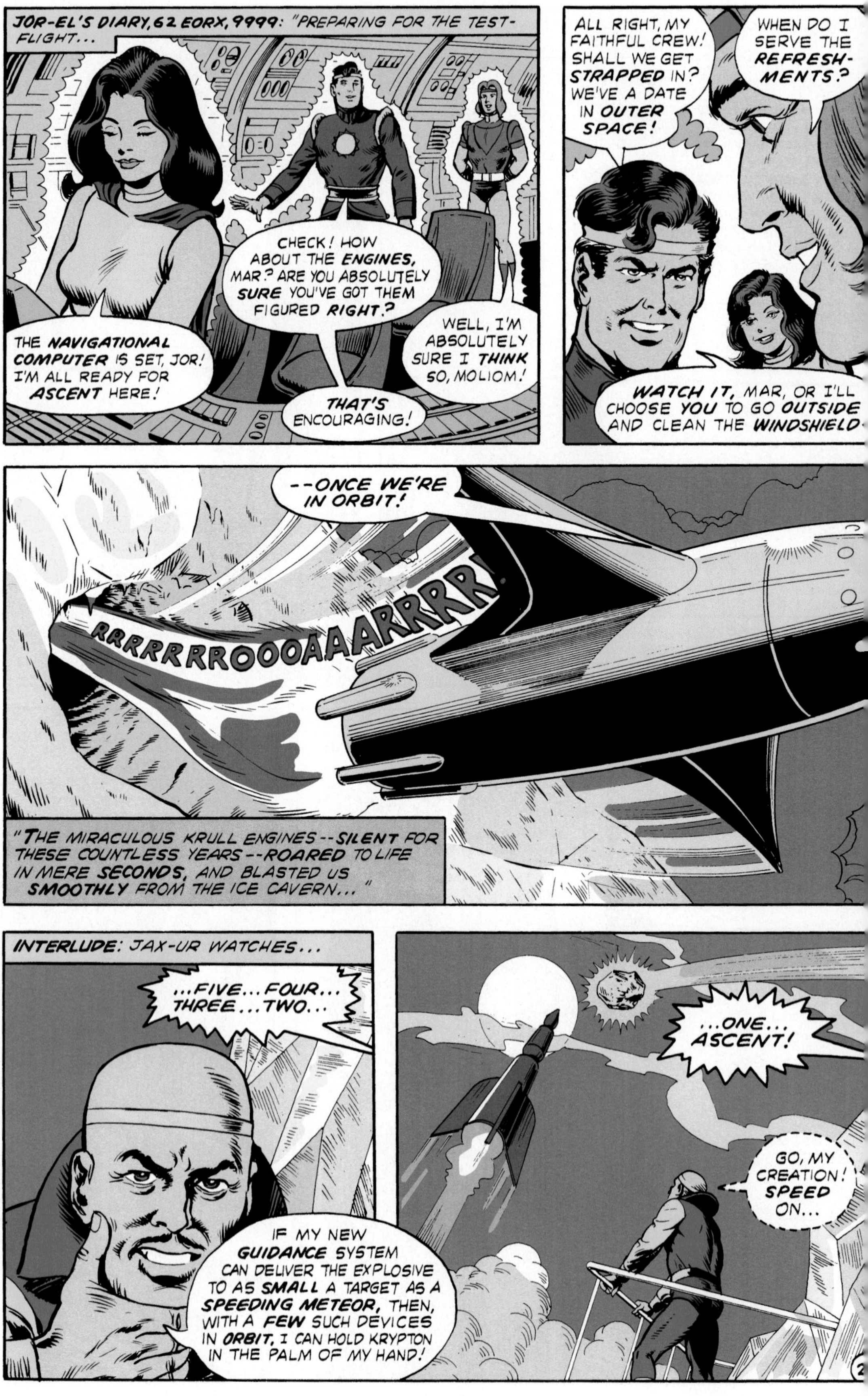
JOR-EL'S DIARY, 62 EORX, 9999: "PREPARING FOR THE TEST-FLIGHT...
THE NAVIGATIONAL COMPUTER IS SET, JOR! I'M ALL READY FOR ASCENT HERE!
CHECK! HOW ABOUT THE ENGINES, MAR? ARE YOU ABSOLUTELY SURE YOU'VE GOT THEM FIGURED RIGHT?
WELL, I'M ABSOLUTELY SURE I THINK SO, MOLIOM!
THAT'S ENCOURAGING!
ALL RIGHT, MY FAITHFUL CREW! SHALL WE GET STRAPPED IN? WE'VE A DATE IN OUTER SPACE!
WHEN DO I SERVE THE REFRESH-MENTS?
WATCH IT, MAR, OR I'LL CHOOSE YOU TO GO OUTSIDE AND CLEAN THE WINDSHIELD--
--ONCE WE'RE IN ORBIT!
RRRRRRROOOOAAARRRRR
"THE MIRACULOUS KRULL ENGINES--SILENT FOR THESE COUNTLESS YEARS--ROARED TO LIFE IN MERE SECONDS, AND BLASTED US SMOOTHLY FROM THE ICE CAVERN..."
INTERLUDE: JAX-UR WATCHES...
...FIVE... FOUR... THREE... TWO...
IF MY NEW GUIDANCE SYSTEM CAN DELIVER THE EXPLOSIVE TO AS SMALL A TARGET AS A SPEEDING METEOR, THEN, WITH A FEW SUCH DEVICES IN ORBIT, I CAN HOLD KRYPTON IN THE PALM OF MY HAND!
...ONE... ASCENT!
GO, MY CREATION! SPEED ON...

--ON YOUR FLIGHT OF DESTINY!

GATHERING SPEED WITH EACH PASSING SECOND, THE MISSILE RISES INTO THE PALE RED SKY UNTIL ITS EXHAUST IS NOTHING MORE THAN ANOTHER PIN-POINT OF LIGHT LOST AMONG THE STARS!

YET EVEN AFTER IT IS LOST TO VIEW, THE BUILDER OF THIS MISSILE OF DESTRUCTION STANDS GAZING INTO THE NIGHT SKY AFTER IT--

--AND DREAMING OF THE DAY THE STARS WILL BELONG TO HIM --UNTIL--THE MISSILE MISSES ITS TARGET!

BLAST! MY AIM WAS SLIGHTLY OFF!

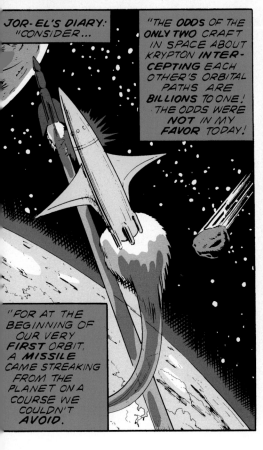

JOR-EL'S DIARY: "CONSIDER...

"THE ODDS OF THE ONLY TWO CRAFT IN SPACE ABOUT KRYPTON INTERCEPTING EACH OTHER'S ORBITAL PATHS ARE BILLIONS TO ONE! THE ODDS WERE NOT IN MY FAVOR TODAY!

"FOR AT THE BEGINNING OF OUR VERY FIRST ORBIT, A MISSILE CAME STREAKING FROM THE PLANET ON A COURSE WE COULDN'T AVOID.

"AND...

LARA...MAR...OUR GUIDANCE SYSTEM WAS DAMAGED WHEN THAT ROCKET HIT US!

AND...GREAT KRYPTON! IT'S ON A COLLISION COURSE WITH--

21

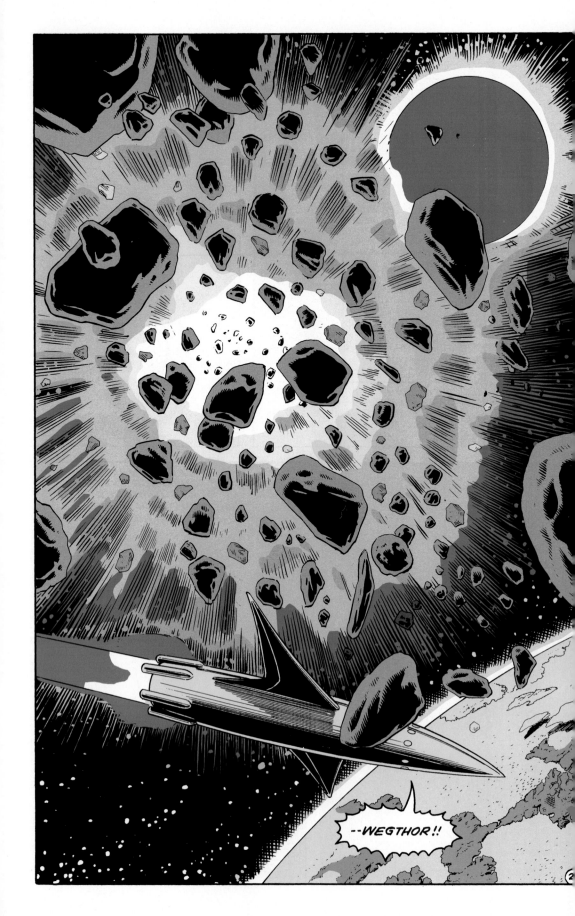

--WEGTHOR!!

"THE KRULL SHIP WAS *FURTHER DAMAGED* BY DEBRIS FROM THE EXPLOSION, AND I *BARELY MANAGED* TO BRING IT IN *WITHOUT KILLING* THE THREE OF US..."

USSSHHHHH

"BUT THE ENGINES WERE *DANGEROUSLY OVERHEATED* FROM THE *STRAIN* OF THE RETURN TRIP..."

MOLIOM-- YOU'D BETTER *MOVE!* IT'S GOING TO *EXPLODE* ANY SECOND!

WE'RE RIGHT *BEHIND* YOU, MAR!

"NO SOONER HAD WE GAINED SHELTER THAN THE KRULL CRAFT *EXPLODED* INTO *FLAMES* AND WAS *GONE* IN AN *INSTANT*--"

"--JUST LIKE OUR *MOON*, WEGTHOR!"

"BUT *UNLIKE* WEGTHOR, THE SHIP WAS *UNINHABITED*-- AND *THAT* MADE ALL THE *DIFFERENCE!*"

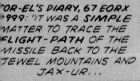

OR-EL'S DIARY, 67 EORX 999: "IT WAS A *SIMPLE MATTER* TO TRACE THE *FLIGHT-PATH* OF THE MISSILE BACK TO THE JEWEL MOUNTAINS AND JAX-UR..."

OR *DEFYING* THE LAW OF KRYPTON --AND FOR THE *WANTON SLAUGHTER* F THE *500 COLONISTS* ON WEGTHOR - YOU ARE HEREBY *SENTENCED* O SPEND THE REST OF ETERNITY IN THE *PHANTOM ZONE!*

"I LEFT *KRYPTONOPOLIS PRISON* FEELING STRANGELY... HOLLOW.

"OUR UNDERSTANDING OF THE *KRULL SHIP* HAD BEEN ONLY *PARTIAL.*

"*TRUE,* WE'D LEARNED SOME *INTERESTING THINGS* FROM OUR *EXAMINATIONS,* BUT I COULD NOT HOPE TO *RECONSTRUCT* IT *WITHOUT* THE *ORIGINAL!*

"*AND* WITH *WEGTHOR DESTROYED,* KRYPTON NO LONGER HAD AN *OUTER SPACE BASE* FROM WHICH TO *LAUNCH GIANT SPACE ARKS.*

"JAX-UR WILL PAY *DEARLY* FOR HIS CRIME, FOR *LIFE* IN THE *PHANTOM ZONE* IS NOT REALLY LIFE AT ALL--*IT IS A SUBSTANCELESS HELL!* YET EVEN THOUGH I HAD BROUGHT HIM TO JUSTICE, I FELT NO *SATISFACTION*--

"--FOR WHILE *HE* WAS SENTENCED TO *LIFE,* KRYPTON HAD BEEN SENTENCED TO *DEATH!*"

NEXT ISSUE: THE DAY A WORLD DIED!

23

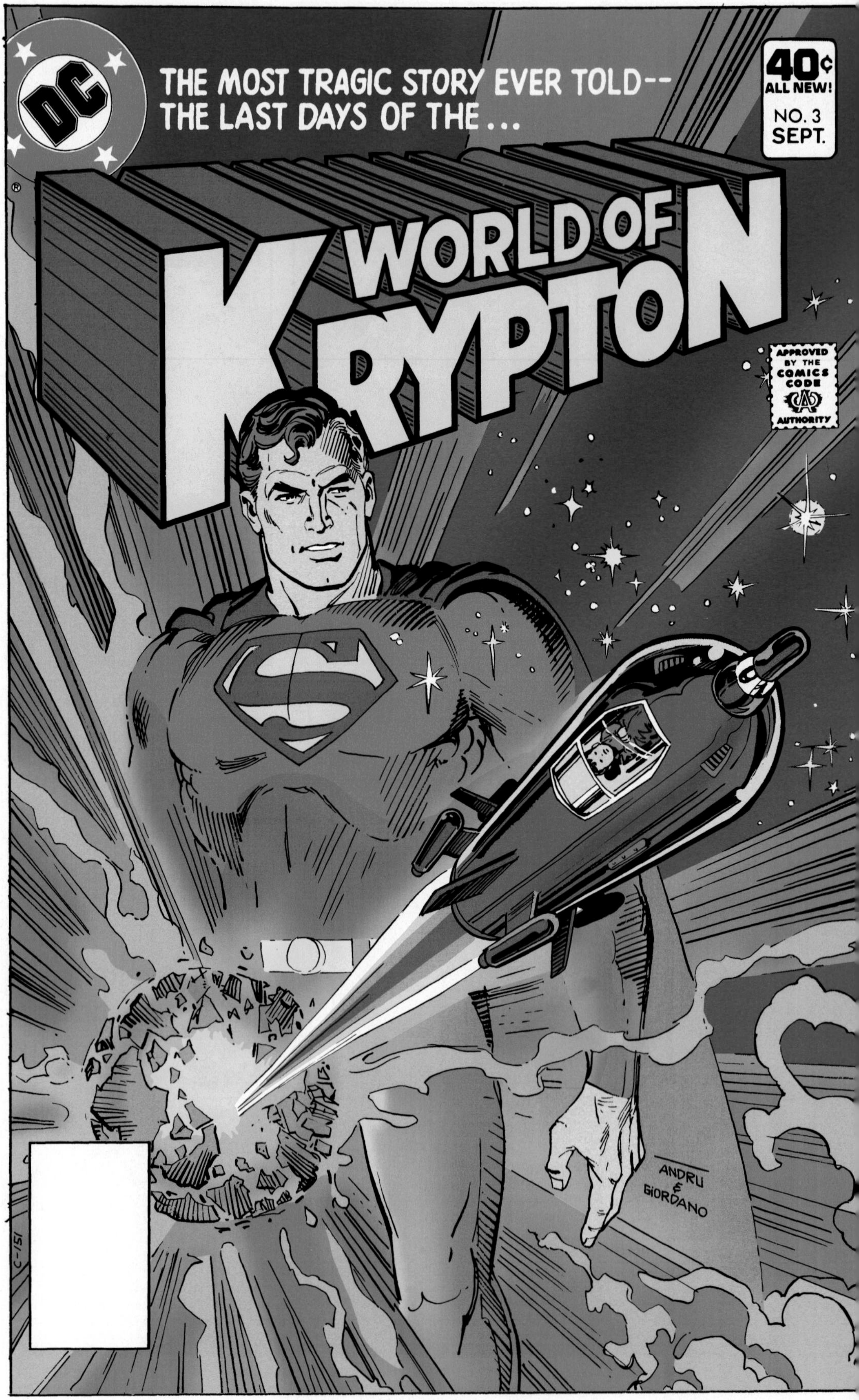

DC
THE MOST TRAGIC STORY EVER TOLD--
THE LAST DAYS OF THE...
40¢
ALL NEW!
NO. 3
SEPT.
WORLD OF
KRYPTON
APPROVED BY THE COMICS CODE AUTHORITY
ANDRU & GIORDANO
C-151

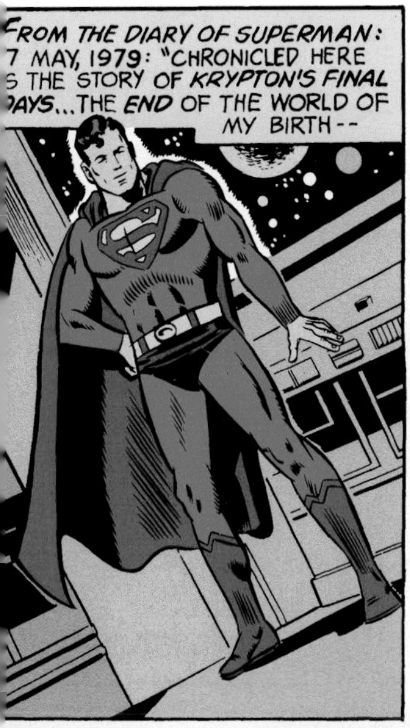
FROM THE DIARY OF SUPERMAN: 7 MAY, 1979: "CHRONICLED HERE S THE STORY OF KRYPTON'S FINAL AYS... THE END OF THE WORLD OF MY BIRTH--

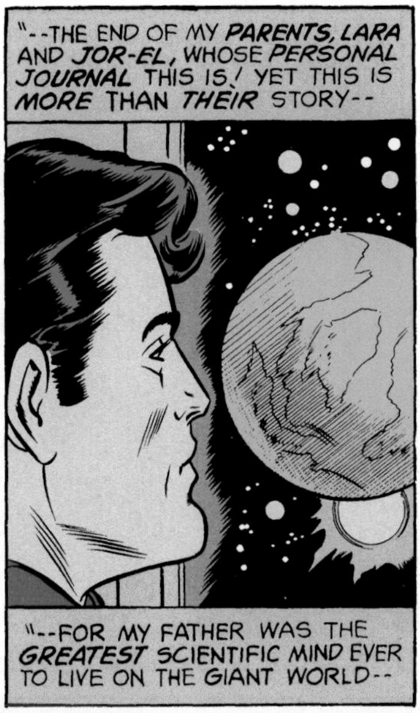
"--THE END OF MY PARENTS, LARA AND JOR-EL, WHOSE PERSONAL JOURNAL THIS IS! YET THIS IS MORE THAN THEIR STORY--
"--FOR MY FATHER WAS THE GREATEST SCIENTIFIC MIND EVER TO LIVE ON THE GIANT WORLD--

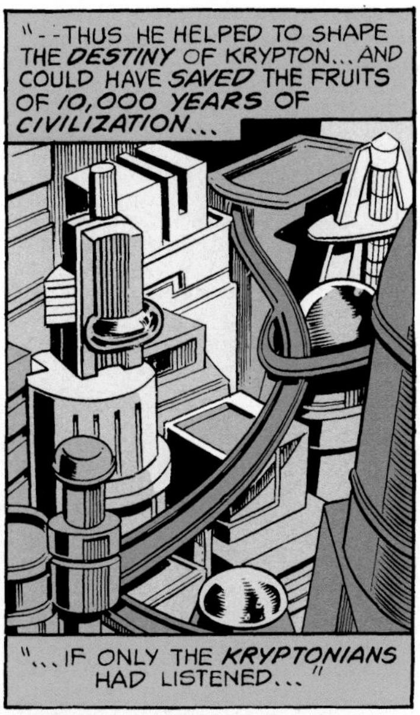
"--THUS HE HELPED TO SHAPE THE DESTINY OF KRYPTON... AND COULD HAVE SAVED THE FRUITS OF 10,000 YEARS OF CIVILIZATION...
"...IF ONLY THE KRYPTONIANS HAD LISTENED..."

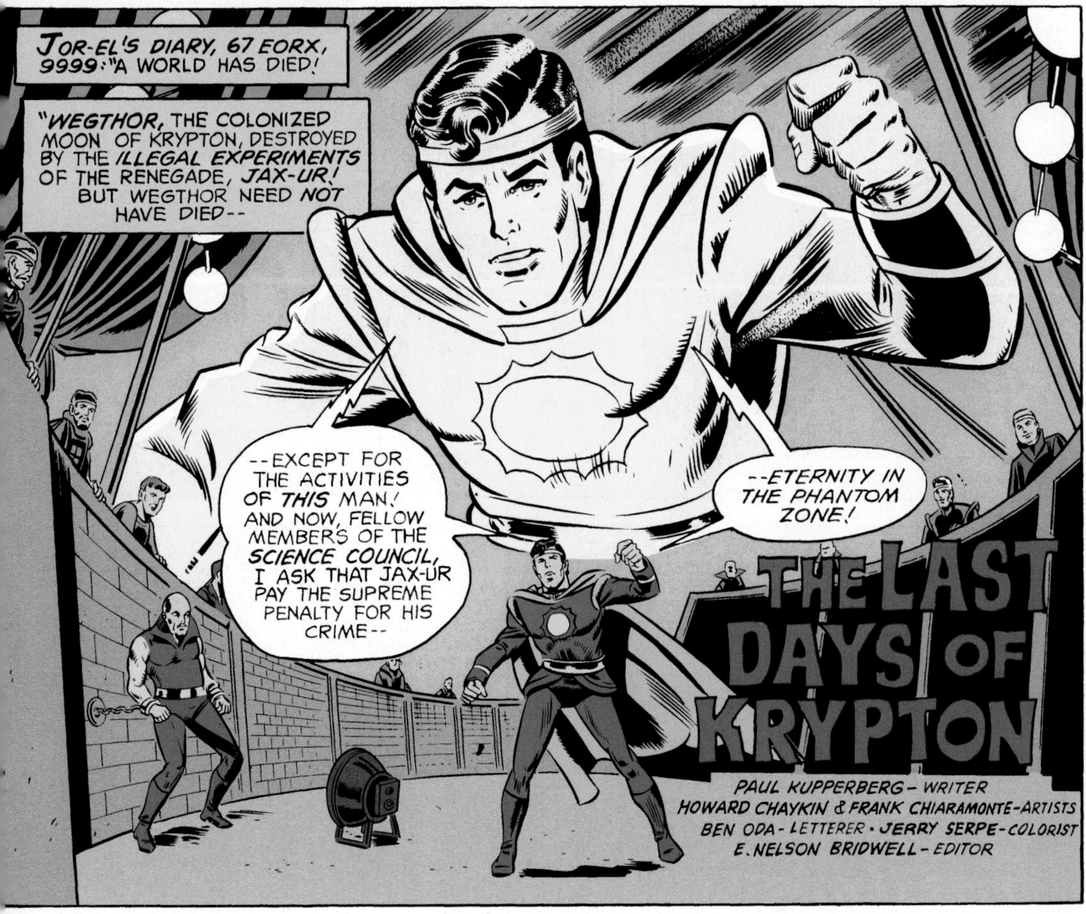
JOR-EL'S DIARY, 67 EORX, 9999: "A WORLD HAS DIED!
"WEGTHOR, THE COLONIZED MOON OF KRYPTON, DESTROYED BY THE ILLEGAL EXPERIMENTS OF THE RENEGADE, JAX-UR! BUT WEGTHOR NEED NOT HAVE DIED--
--EXCEPT FOR THE ACTIVITIES OF THIS MAN! AND NOW, FELLOW MEMBERS OF THE SCIENCE COUNCIL, I ASK THAT JAX-UR PAY THE SUPREME PENALTY FOR HIS CRIME--
--ETERNITY IN THE PHANTOM ZONE!
THE LAST DAYS OF KRYPTON
PAUL KUPPERBERG - WRITER
HOWARD CHAYKIN & FRANK CHIARAMONTE - ARTISTS
BEN ODA - LETTERER • JERRY SERPE - COLORIST
E. NELSON BRIDWELL - EDITOR

FOR BY HIS ACTIONS, JAX-UR HAS COMMITTED MORE THAN THE MURDER OF 500 COLONISTS... HE MAY HAVE *DOOMED* THE *BILLIONS* ON KRYPTON TO A *SIMILAR* FATE...

IRRELEVANT, MOLIOM*! JOR-EL! THIS IS *HARDLY* THE TIME TO DEBATE YOUR RIDICULOUS *THEORIES*!

*MEMBER OF THE SCIENCE COUNCIL --ENB

THAT IS WHERE YOU *ERR*, MOLIOM... BUT I WILL TABLE MY ARGUMENT FOR A MOMENT WHILE WE *DISPOSE* OF OLD BUSINESS.

LET THE SENTENCE BE EXECUTED!

MAY YOU BE CURSED, JOR-EL! YOU SHALL PAY FOR THIS... DO YOU HEAR ME? YOU SHALL PAAAYYY...

"TENSION CRACKLED IN THE AIR LIKE *ELECTRICITY*... THE BANISHING OF ANOTHER MAN TO THE SHADOWY *HALF-LIFE* OF THE *PHANTOM ZONE* IS A CHILLING SIGHT...

CAN WE *BEGIN*, MOLIOMO*?

*PLURAL OF MOLIOM. -- ENB

IT'S NO *WONDER* YOU'RE *ANXIOUS* TO COMMENCE, MOLIOM, CONSIDERING THE ITEM UP FOR THIS DAY'S VOTE IS SO *DEAR* TO YOU--

--A RESOLUTION TO BAN SPACE TRAVEL!

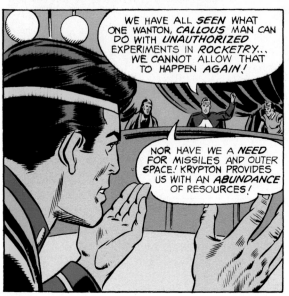

WE HAVE ALL *SEEN* WHAT ONE WANTON, *CALLOUS* MAN CAN DO WITH *UNAUTHORIZED* EXPERIMENTS IN *ROCKETRY*... WE CANNOT ALLOW THAT TO HAPPEN *AGAIN*!

NOR HAVE WE A *NEED* FOR MISSILES AND OUTER SPACE! KRYPTON PROVIDES US WITH AN *ABUNDANCE* OF RESOURCES!

YOU SAY WE MUST NOT ALLOW THE *WEGTHOR TRAGEDY* TO BE REPEATED-- YET YOU WOULD CONDEMN *EVERYONE* ON *KRYPTON* TO THE *SAME FATE*!

EVEN AS WE SIT HERE, THE UNSTABLE *CORE* OF THE PLANET MOVES CLOSER TO *CRITICAL MASS*!

2

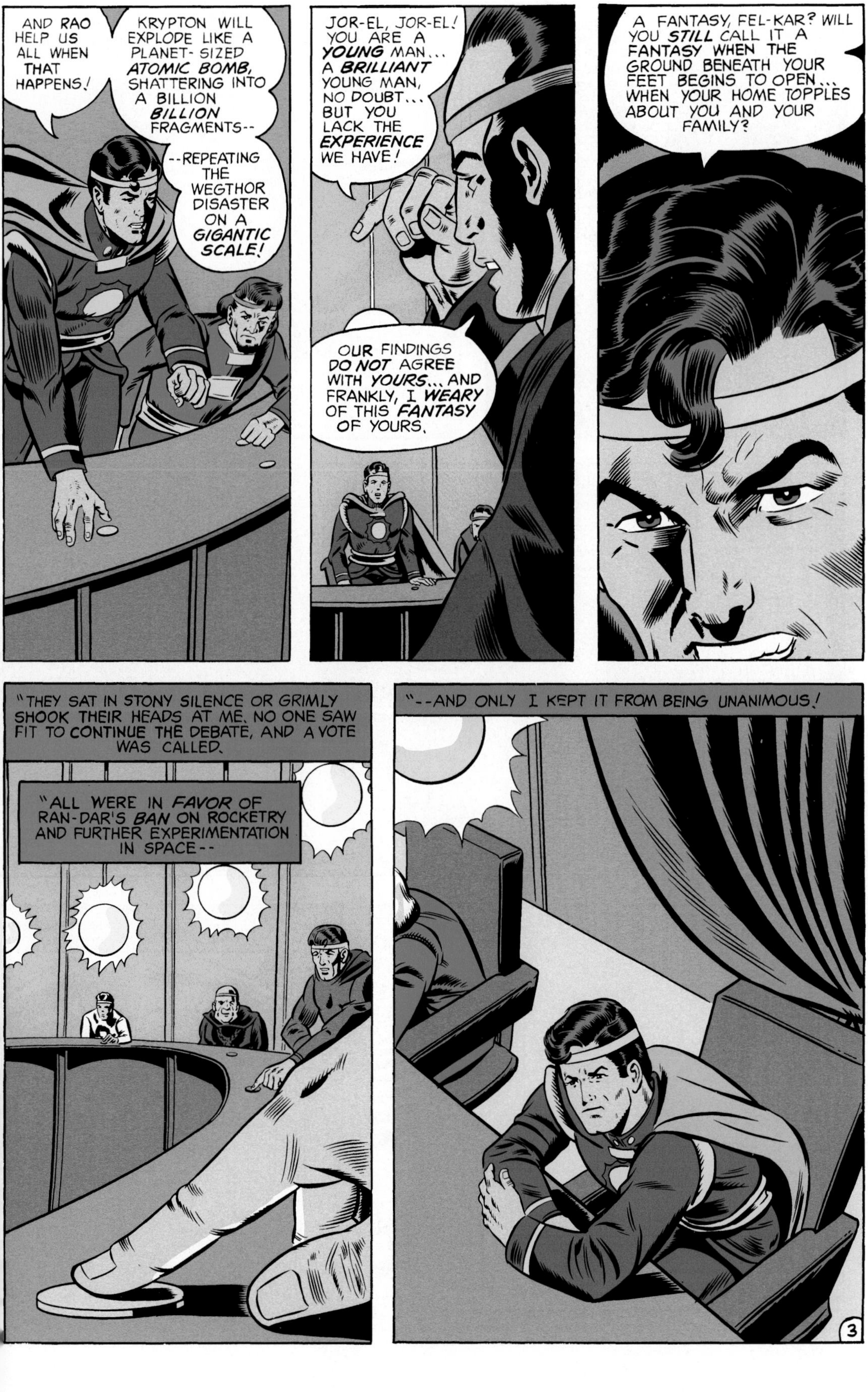
AND RAO HELP US ALL WHEN THAT HAPPENS!
KRYPTON WILL EXPLODE LIKE A PLANET-SIZED ATOMIC BOMB, SHATTERING INTO A BILLION BILLION FRAGMENTS--
--REPEATING THE WEGTHOR DISASTER ON A GIGANTIC SCALE!
JOR-EL, JOR-EL! YOU ARE A YOUNG MAN... A BRILLIANT YOUNG MAN, NO DOUBT... BUT YOU LACK THE EXPERIENCE WE HAVE!
OUR FINDINGS DO NOT AGREE WITH YOURS... AND FRANKLY, I WEARY OF THIS FANTASY OF YOURS.
A FANTASY, FEL-KAR? WILL YOU STILL CALL IT A FANTASY WHEN THE GROUND BENEATH YOUR FEET BEGINS TO OPEN... WHEN YOUR HOME TOPPLES ABOUT YOU AND YOUR FAMILY?
"THEY SAT IN STONY SILENCE OR GRIMLY SHOOK THEIR HEADS AT ME. NO ONE SAW FIT TO CONTINUE THE DEBATE, AND A VOTE WAS CALLED.
"ALL WERE IN FAVOR OF RAN-DAR'S BAN ON ROCKETRY AND FURTHER EXPERIMENTATION IN SPACE--
"--AND ONLY I KEPT IT FROM BEING UNANIMOUS!
3

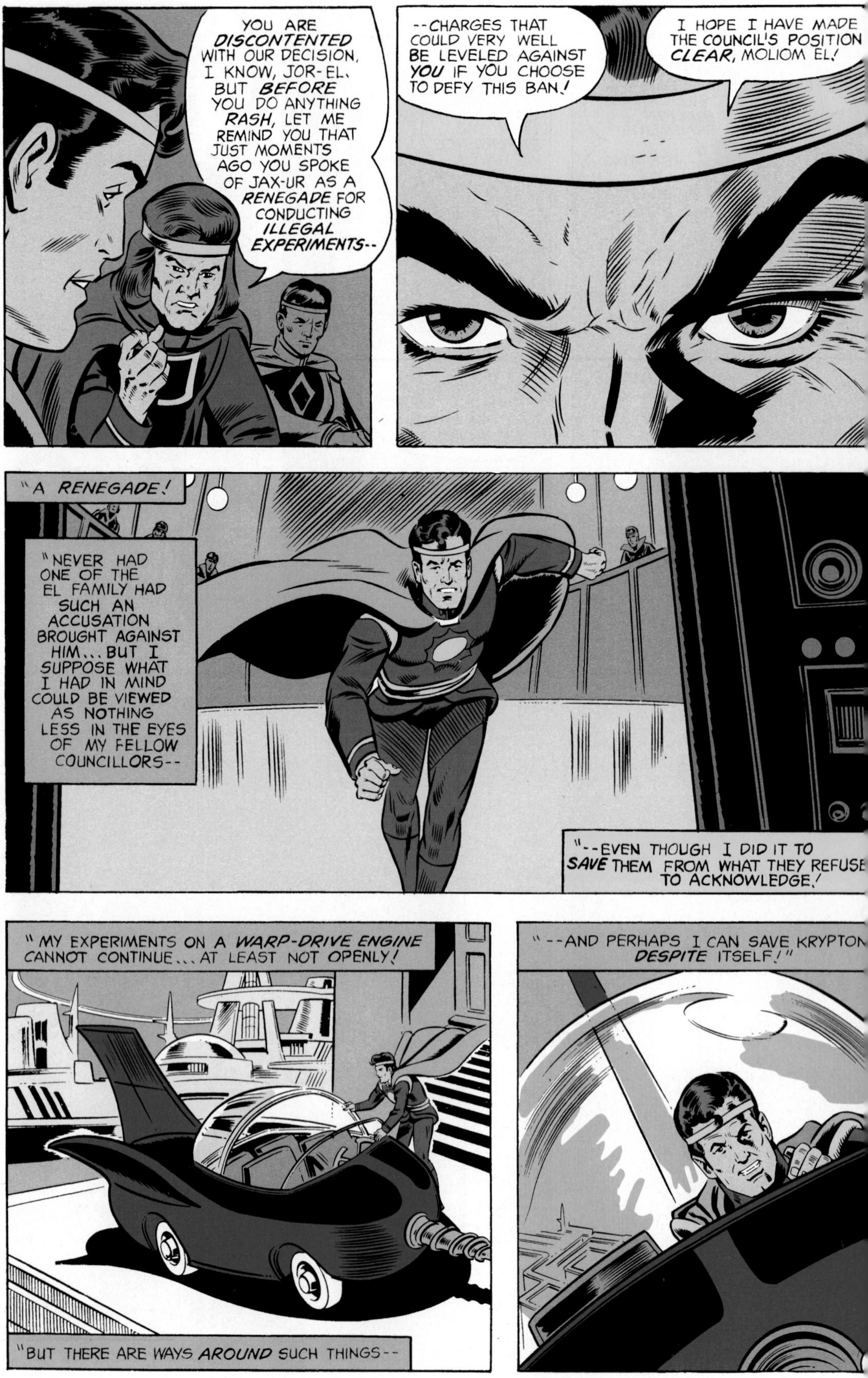
YOU ARE *DISCONTENTED* WITH OUR DECISION, I KNOW, JOR-EL. BUT *BEFORE* YOU DO ANYTHING *RASH*, LET ME REMIND YOU THAT JUST MOMENTS AGO YOU SPOKE OF JAX-UR AS A *RENEGADE* FOR CONDUCTING *ILLEGAL EXPERIMENTS*--
--CHARGES THAT COULD VERY WELL BE LEVELED AGAINST *YOU* IF YOU CHOOSE TO DEFY THIS BAN!
I HOPE I HAVE MADE THE COUNCIL'S POSITION *CLEAR*, MOLIOM EL!
"A *RENEGADE*!
"NEVER HAD ONE OF THE EL FAMILY HAD SUCH AN ACCUSATION BROUGHT AGAINST HIM... BUT I SUPPOSE WHAT I HAD IN MIND COULD BE VIEWED AS NOTHING LESS IN THE EYES OF MY FELLOW COUNCILLORS--
"--EVEN THOUGH I DID IT TO *SAVE* THEM FROM WHAT THEY REFUSE TO ACKNOWLEDGE!
"MY EXPERIMENTS ON A *WARP-DRIVE ENGINE* CANNOT CONTINUE... AT LEAST NOT OPENLY!
"BUT THERE ARE WAYS *AROUND* SUCH THINGS--
"--AND PERHAPS I CAN SAVE KRYPTON *DESPITE* ITSELF!"

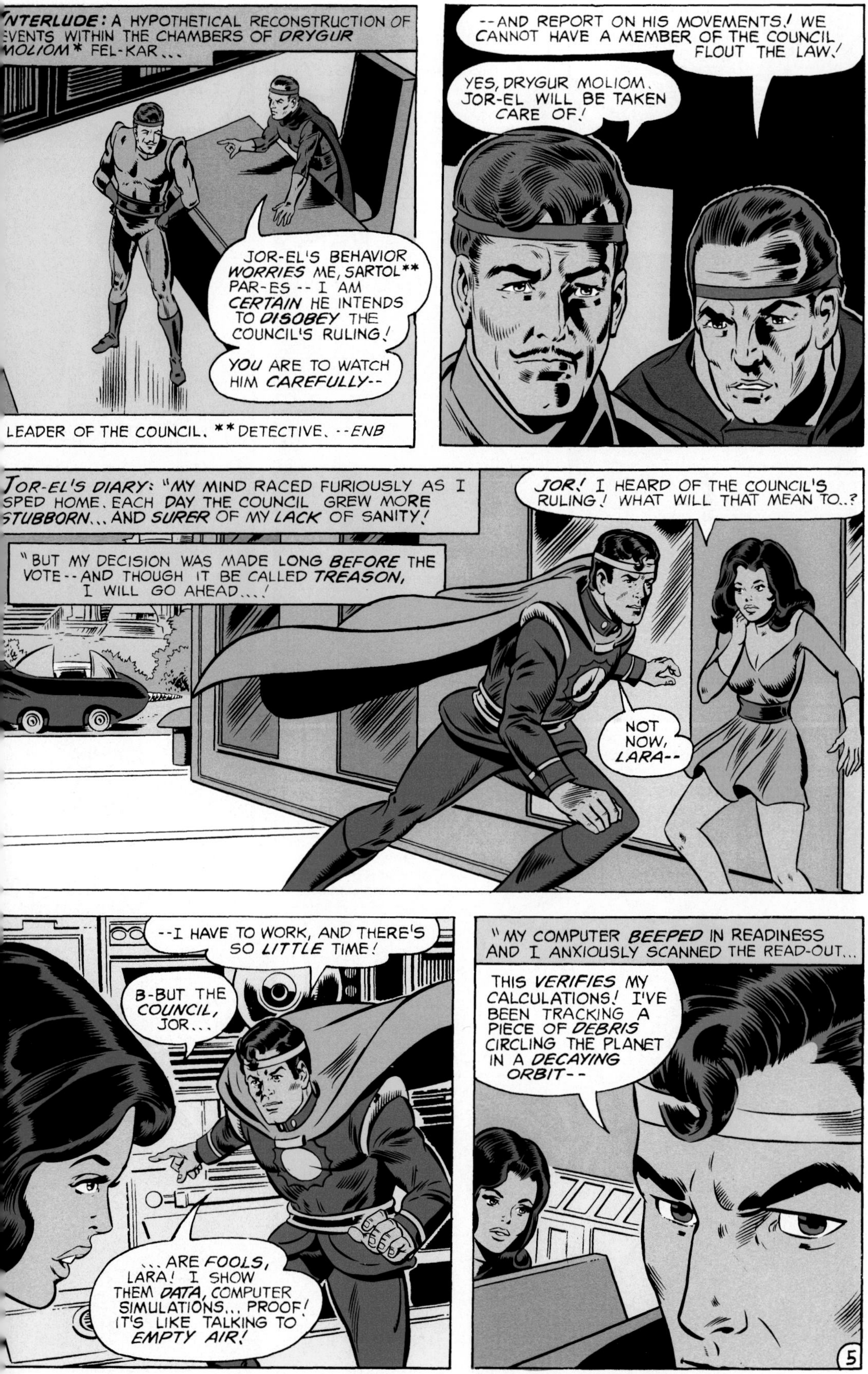
INTERLUDE: A HYPOTHETICAL RECONSTRUCTION OF EVENTS WITHIN THE CHAMBERS OF DRYGUR MOLIOM* FEL-KAR...
JOR-EL'S BEHAVIOR WORRIES ME, SARTOL** PAR-ES -- I AM CERTAIN HE INTENDS TO DISOBEY THE COUNCIL'S RULING!
YOU ARE TO WATCH HIM CAREFULLY--
*LEADER OF THE COUNCIL. **DETECTIVE. --ENB
--AND REPORT ON HIS MOVEMENTS! WE CANNOT HAVE A MEMBER OF THE COUNCIL FLOUT THE LAW!
YES, DRYGUR MOLIOM. JOR-EL WILL BE TAKEN CARE OF!
JOR-EL'S DIARY: "MY MIND RACED FURIOUSLY AS I SPED HOME. EACH DAY THE COUNCIL GREW MORE STUBBORN... AND SURER OF MY LACK OF SANITY!
"BUT MY DECISION WAS MADE LONG BEFORE THE VOTE--AND THOUGH IT BE CALLED TREASON, I WILL GO AHEAD...!
JOR! I HEARD OF THE COUNCIL'S RULING! WHAT WILL THAT MEAN TO..?
NOT NOW, LARA--
--I HAVE TO WORK, AND THERE'S SO LITTLE TIME!
B-BUT THE COUNCIL, JOR...
...ARE FOOLS, LARA! I SHOW THEM DATA, COMPUTER SIMULATIONS... PROOF! IT'S LIKE TALKING TO EMPTY AIR!
"MY COMPUTER BEEPED IN READINESS AND I ANXIOUSLY SCANNED THE READ-OUT...
THIS VERIFIES MY CALCULATIONS! I'VE BEEN TRACKING A PIECE OF DEBRIS CIRCLING THE PLANET IN A DECAYING ORBIT--
5

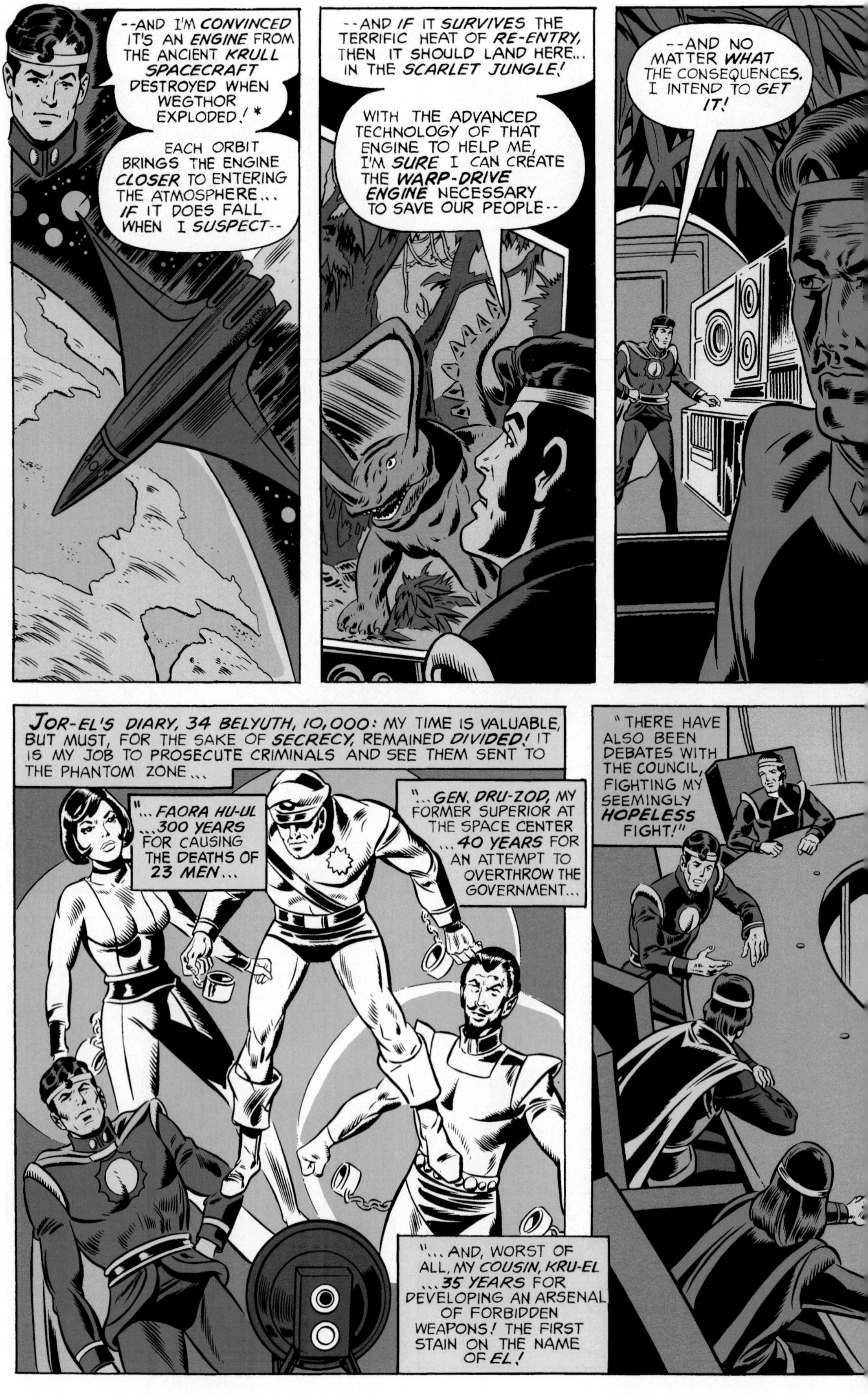
--AND I'M CONVINCED IT'S AN ENGINE FROM THE ANCIENT KRULL SPACECRAFT DESTROYED WHEN WEGTHOR EXPLODED! *
EACH ORBIT BRINGS THE ENGINE CLOSER TO ENTERING THE ATMOSPHERE... IF IT DOES FALL WHEN I SUSPECT--
--AND IF IT SURVIVES THE TERRIFIC HEAT OF RE-ENTRY, THEN IT SHOULD LAND HERE... IN THE SCARLET JUNGLE!
WITH THE ADVANCED TECHNOLOGY OF THAT ENGINE TO HELP ME, I'M SURE I CAN CREATE THE WARP-DRIVE ENGINE NECESSARY TO SAVE OUR PEOPLE--
--AND NO MATTER WHAT THE CONSEQUENCES, I INTEND TO GET IT!
JOR-EL'S DIARY, 34 BELYUTH, 10,000: MY TIME IS VALUABLE, BUT MUST, FOR THE SAKE OF SECRECY, REMAINED DIVIDED! IT IS MY JOB TO PROSECUTE CRIMINALS AND SEE THEM SENT TO THE PHANTOM ZONE...
"...FAORA HU-UL ...300 YEARS FOR CAUSING THE DEATHS OF 23 MEN...
"...GEN. DRU-ZOD, MY FORMER SUPERIOR AT THE SPACE CENTER ...40 YEARS FOR AN ATTEMPT TO OVERTHROW THE GOVERNMENT...
"... AND, WORST OF ALL, MY COUSIN, KRU-EL ...35 YEARS FOR DEVELOPING AN ARSENAL OF FORBIDDEN WEAPONS! THE FIRST STAIN ON THE NAME OF EL!
"THERE HAVE ALSO BEEN DEBATES WITH THE COUNCIL, FIGHTING MY SEEMINGLY HOPELESS FIGHT!"

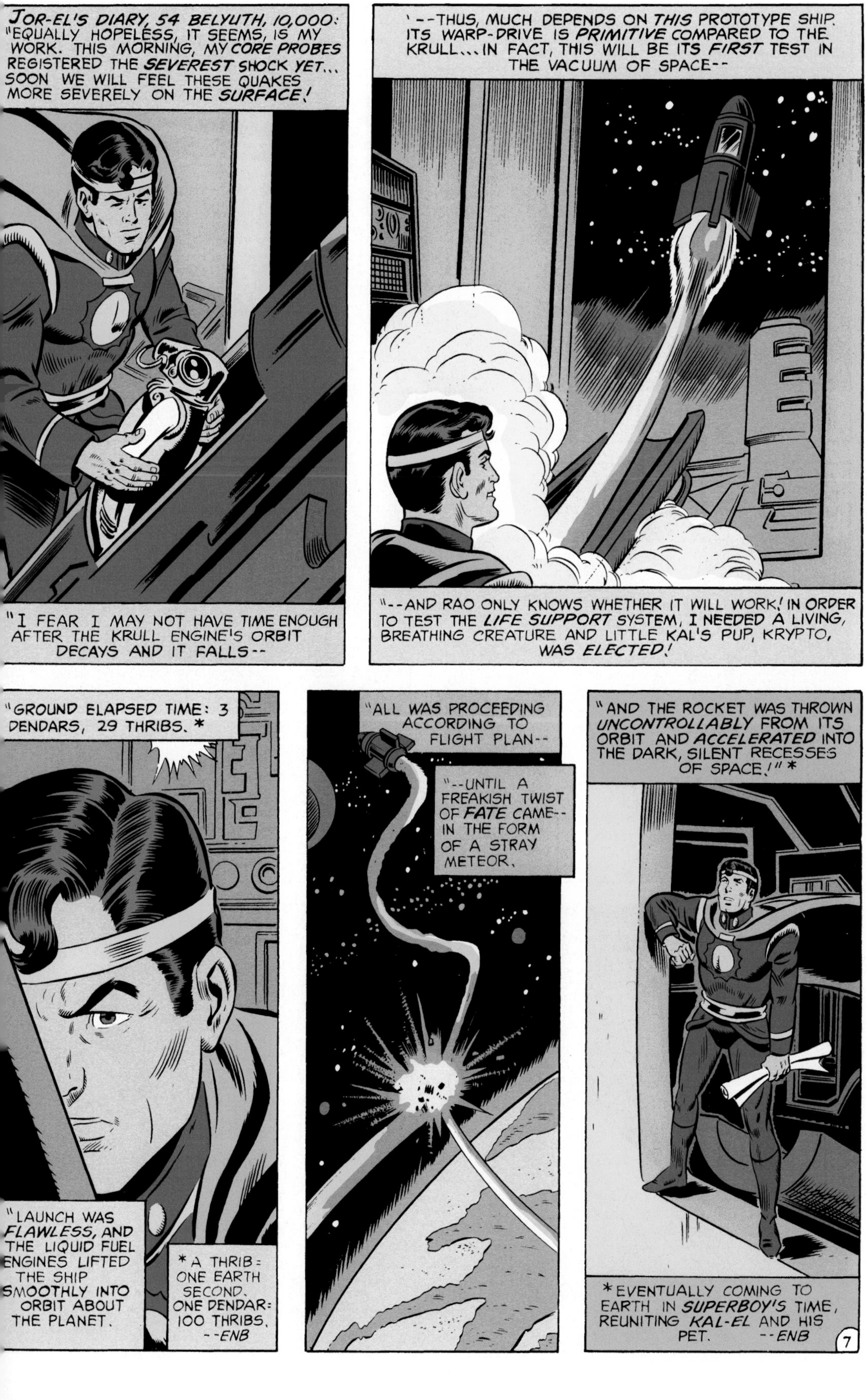

JOR-EL'S DIARY, 54 BELYUTH, 10,000:
"EQUALLY HOPELESS, IT SEEMS, IS MY WORK. THIS MORNING, MY CORE PROBES REGISTERED THE SEVEREST SHOCK YET... SOON WE WILL FEEL THESE QUAKES MORE SEVERELY ON THE SURFACE!
"I FEAR I MAY NOT HAVE TIME ENOUGH AFTER THE KRULL ENGINE'S ORBIT DECAYS AND IT FALLS--
'--THUS, MUCH DEPENDS ON THIS PROTOTYPE SHIP. ITS WARP-DRIVE IS PRIMITIVE COMPARED TO THE KRULL... IN FACT, THIS WILL BE ITS FIRST TEST IN THE VACUUM OF SPACE--
"--AND RAO ONLY KNOWS WHETHER IT WILL WORK! IN ORDER TO TEST THE LIFE SUPPORT SYSTEM, I NEEDED A LIVING, BREATHING CREATURE AND LITTLE KAL'S PUP, KRYPTO, WAS ELECTED!
"GROUND ELAPSED TIME: 3 DENDARS, 29 THRIBS. *
"LAUNCH WAS FLAWLESS, AND THE LIQUID FUEL ENGINES LIFTED THE SHIP SMOOTHLY INTO ORBIT ABOUT THE PLANET.
* A THRIB = ONE EARTH SECOND. ONE DENDAR: 100 THRIBS. --ENB
"ALL WAS PROCEEDING ACCORDING TO FLIGHT PLAN--
"--UNTIL A FREAKISH TWIST OF FATE CAME-- IN THE FORM OF A STRAY METEOR.
"AND THE ROCKET WAS THROWN UNCONTROLLABLY FROM ITS ORBIT AND ACCELERATED INTO THE DARK, SILENT RECESSES OF SPACE!" *
* EVENTUALLY COMING TO EARTH IN SUPERBOY'S TIME, REUNITING KAL-EL AND HIS PET. --ENB
7

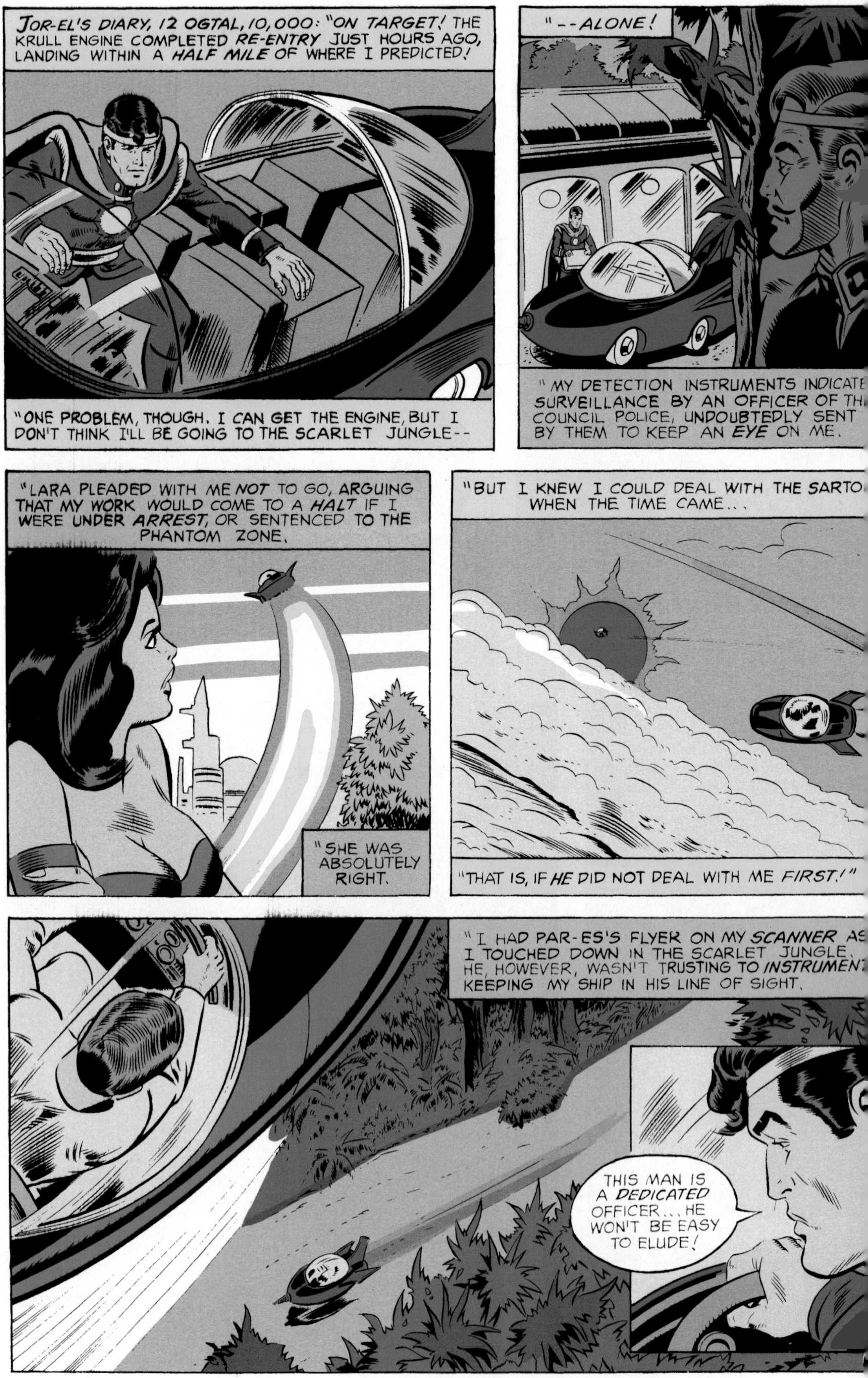
JOR-EL'S DIARY, 12 OGTAL, 10,000: "ON TARGET! THE KRULL ENGINE COMPLETED RE-ENTRY JUST HOURS AGO, LANDING WITHIN A HALF MILE OF WHERE I PREDICTED!
"ONE PROBLEM, THOUGH. I CAN GET THE ENGINE, BUT I DON'T THINK I'LL BE GOING TO THE SCARLET JUNGLE--
"--ALONE!
"MY DETECTION INSTRUMENTS INDICATE SURVEILLANCE BY AN OFFICER OF TH COUNCIL POLICE, UNDOUBTEDLY SENT BY THEM TO KEEP AN EYE ON ME.
"LARA PLEADED WITH ME NOT TO GO, ARGUING THAT MY WORK WOULD COME TO A HALT IF I WERE UNDER ARREST, OR SENTENCED TO THE PHANTOM ZONE.
"SHE WAS ABSOLUTELY RIGHT.
"BUT I KNEW I COULD DEAL WITH THE SARTO WHEN THE TIME CAME...
"THAT IS, IF HE DID NOT DEAL WITH ME FIRST!"
"I HAD PAR-ES'S FLYER ON MY SCANNER AS I TOUCHED DOWN IN THE SCARLET JUNGLE. HE, HOWEVER, WASN'T TRUSTING TO INSTRUMENT KEEPING MY SHIP IN HIS LINE OF SIGHT.
THIS MAN IS A DEDICATED OFFICER... HE WON'T BE EASY TO ELUDE!

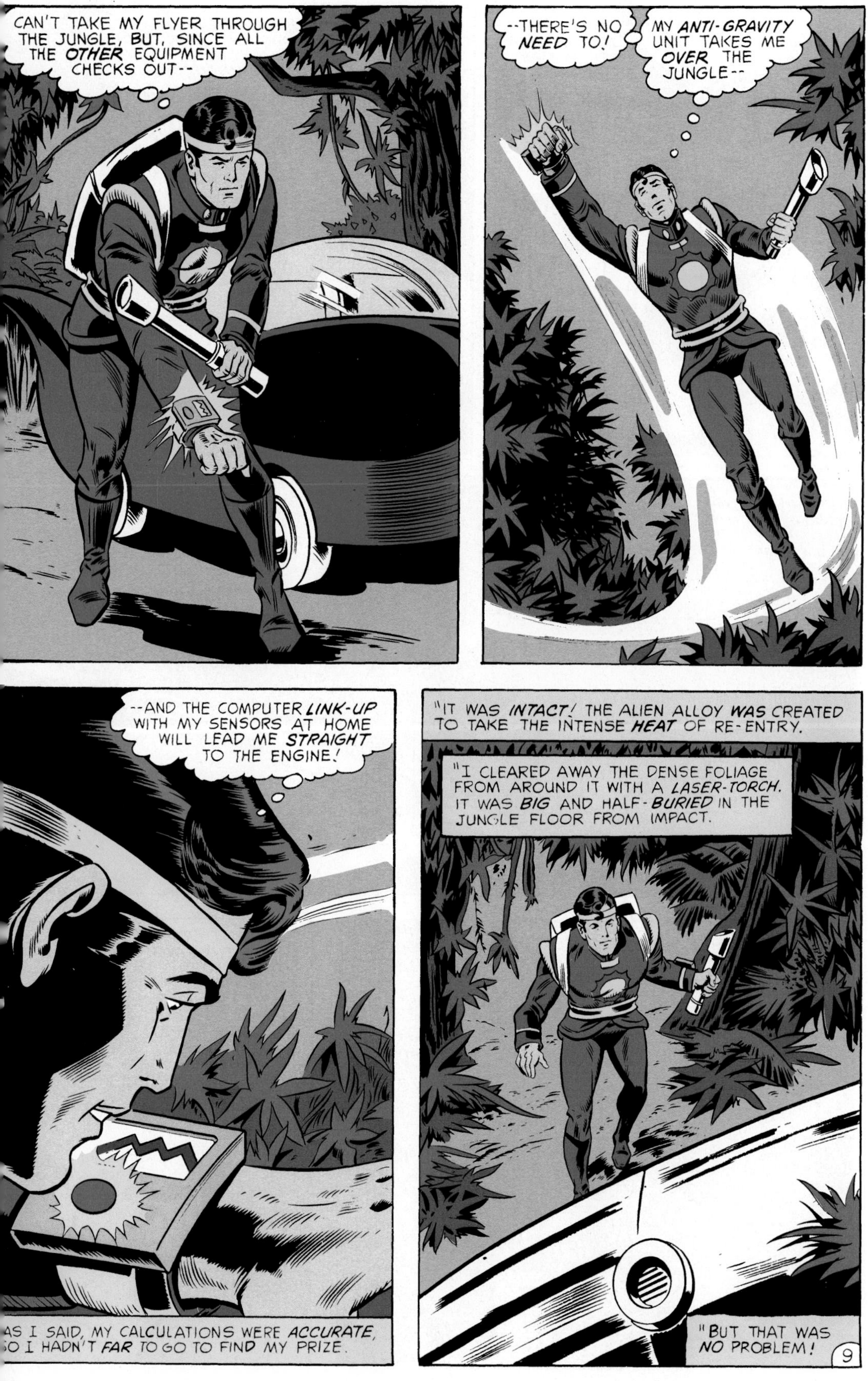
CAN'T TAKE MY FLYER THROUGH THE JUNGLE, BUT, SINCE ALL THE OTHER EQUIPMENT CHECKS OUT--
--THERE'S NO NEED TO!
MY ANTI-GRAVITY UNIT TAKES ME OVER THE JUNGLE--
--AND THE COMPUTER LINK-UP WITH MY SENSORS AT HOME WILL LEAD ME STRAIGHT TO THE ENGINE!
AS I SAID, MY CALCULATIONS WERE ACCURATE, SO I HADN'T FAR TO GO TO FIND MY PRIZE.
"IT WAS INTACT! THE ALIEN ALLOY WAS CREATED TO TAKE THE INTENSE HEAT OF RE-ENTRY.
"I CLEARED AWAY THE DENSE FOLIAGE FROM AROUND IT WITH A LASER-TORCH. IT WAS BIG AND HALF-BURIED IN THE JUNGLE FLOOR FROM IMPACT.
"BUT THAT WAS NO PROBLEM!
9

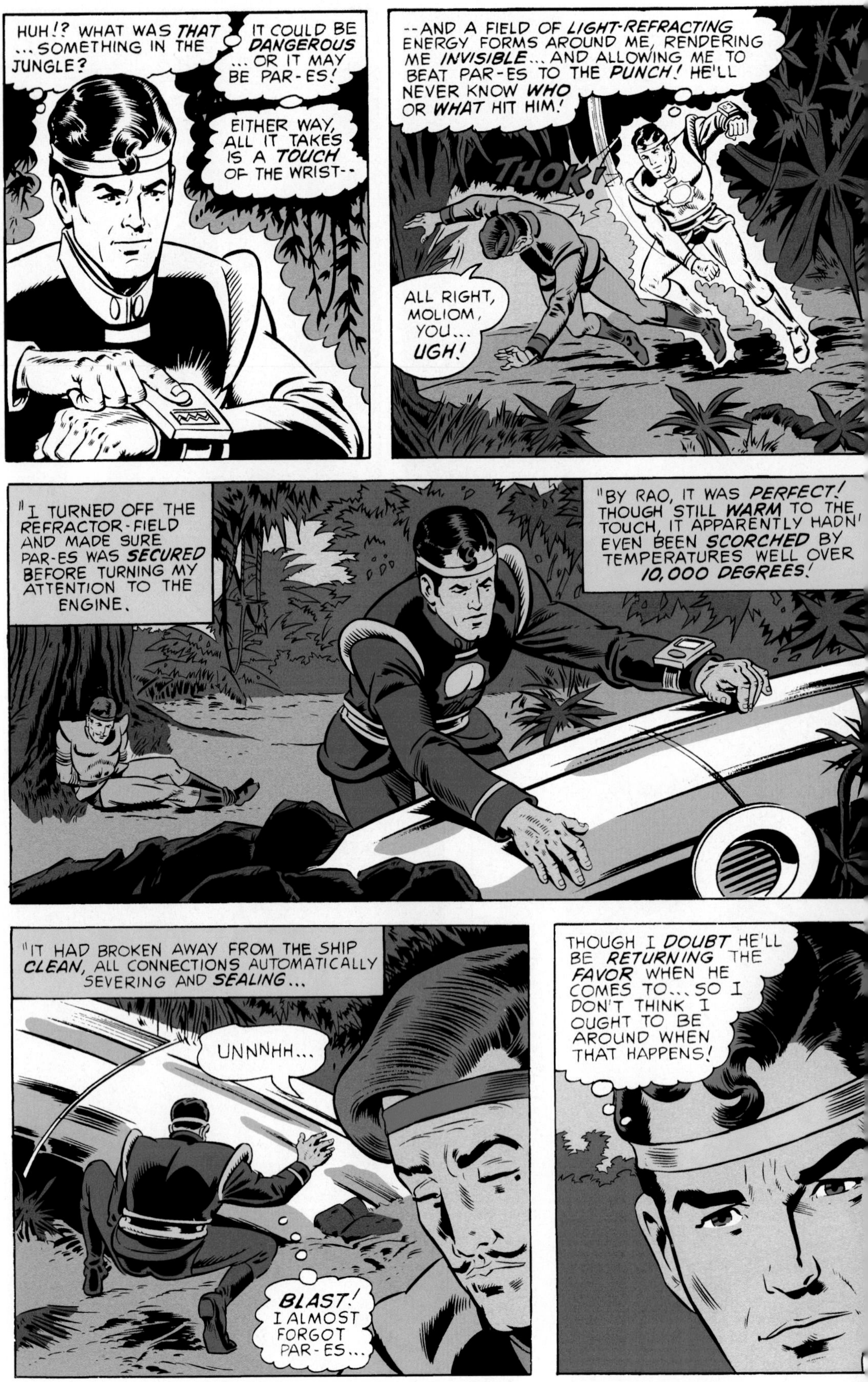
HUH!? WHAT WAS THAT ...SOMETHING IN THE JUNGLE?
IT COULD BE DANGEROUS ...OR IT MAY BE PAR-ES!
EITHER WAY, ALL IT TAKES IS A TOUCH OF THE WRIST--
--AND A FIELD OF LIGHT-REFRACTING ENERGY FORMS AROUND ME, RENDERING ME INVISIBLE... AND ALLOWING ME TO BEAT PAR-ES TO THE PUNCH! HE'LL NEVER KNOW WHO OR WHAT HIT HIM!
THOK!
ALL RIGHT, MOLIOM, YOU... UGH!
"I TURNED OFF THE REFRACTOR-FIELD AND MADE SURE PAR-ES WAS SECURED BEFORE TURNING MY ATTENTION TO THE ENGINE.
"BY RAO, IT WAS PERFECT! THOUGH STILL WARM TO THE TOUCH, IT APPARENTLY HADN' EVEN BEEN SCORCHED BY TEMPERATURES WELL OVER 10,000 DEGREES!
"IT HAD BROKEN AWAY FROM THE SHIP CLEAN, ALL CONNECTIONS AUTOMATICALLY SEVERING AND SEALING...
UNNNHH...
BLAST! I ALMOST FORGOT PAR-ES...
THOUGH I DOUBT HE'LL BE RETURNING THE FAVOR WHEN HE COMES TO... SO I DON'T THINK I OUGHT TO BE AROUND WHEN THAT HAPPENS!

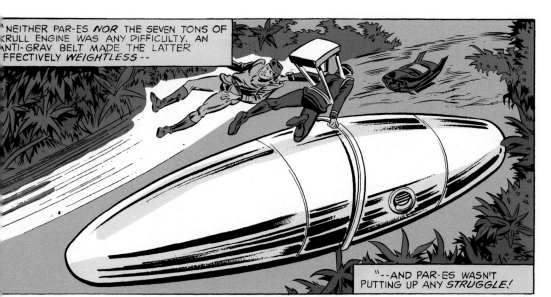

"NEITHER PAR-ES *NOR* THE SEVEN TONS OF KRULL ENGINE WAS ANY DIFFICULTY, AN ANTI-GRAV BELT MADE THE LATTER EFFECTIVELY *WEIGHTLESS* --"

"--AND PAR-ES WASN'T PUTTING UP ANY *STRUGGLE!*"

I'M AFRAID THIS IS *GOOD-BYE,* FRIEND. GIVE MY *REGARDS* TO THE DRYGUR MOLIOM!

I CAN HANDLE MATTERS ON MY *OWN* FROM NOW ON!

THERE! YOUR FLYER'S *AUTO-PILOT* IS SET FOR THE SCIENCE COUNCIL BUILDING --

--SO I WON'T KEEP YOU ANY... WHEW!

"I WAS TALKING MORE TO KEEP MYSELF GOING THAN ANYTHING ELSE! SUDDENLY, I FELT LIKE I HAD THE WEIGHT OF *THREE GRAVITIES* ON ME... SLUGGISH, WEAK AND FEVERISH..."

"IT PASSED AFTER SEVERAL MOMENTS. I ATTRIBUTED IT TO EXHAUSTION AND NERVES AND STRAPPED THE ENGINE TO MY FLYER..."

11

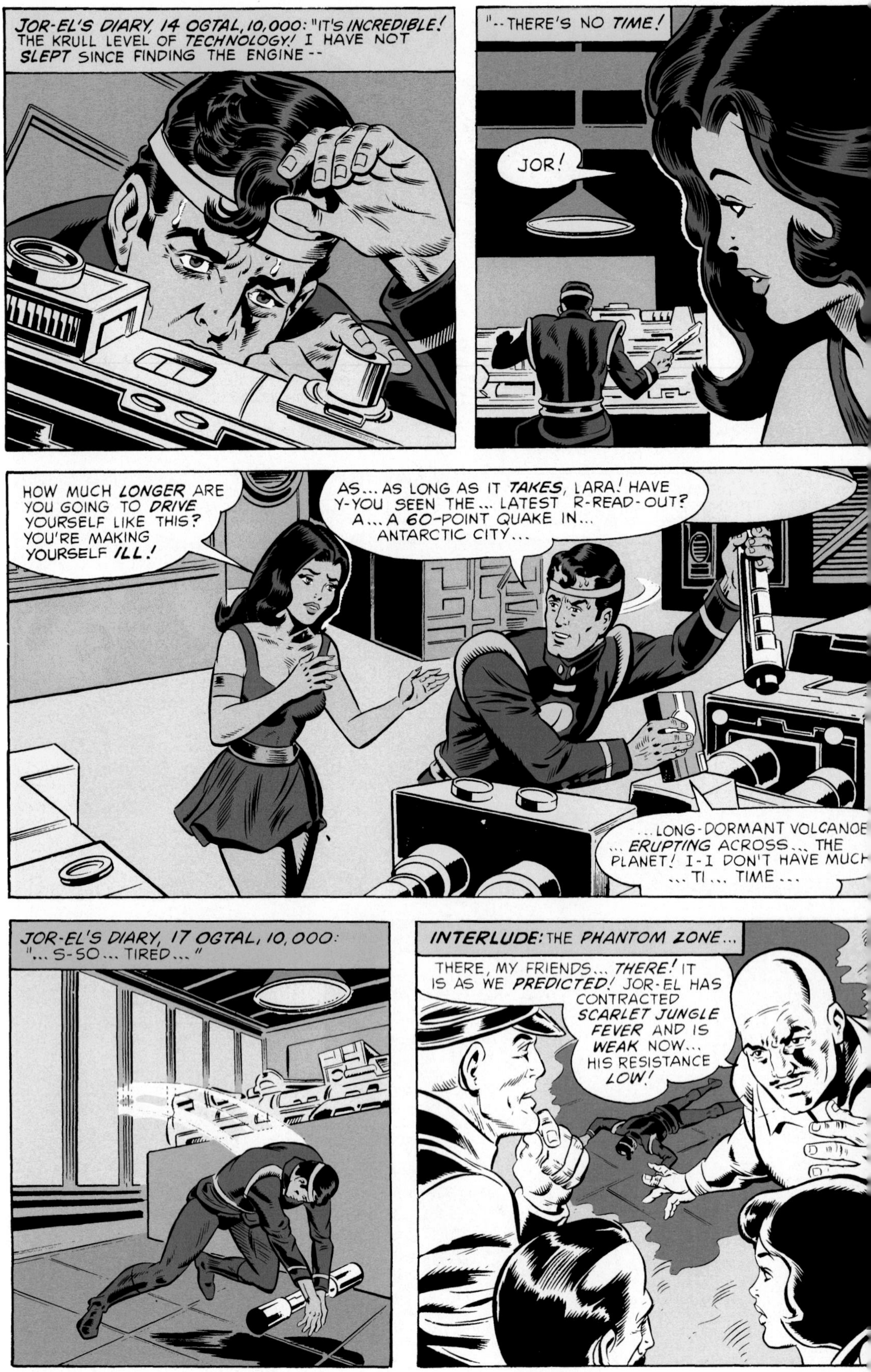

JOR-EL'S DIARY, 14 OGTAL, 10,000: "IT'S INCREDIBLE! THE KRULL LEVEL OF TECHNOLOGY! I HAVE NOT SLEPT SINCE FINDING THE ENGINE --
"-- THERE'S NO TIME!
JOR!
HOW MUCH LONGER ARE YOU GOING TO DRIVE YOURSELF LIKE THIS? YOU'RE MAKING YOURSELF ILL!
AS... AS LONG AS IT TAKES, LARA! HAVE Y-YOU SEEN THE... LATEST R-READ-OUT? A... A 60-POINT QUAKE IN... ANTARCTIC CITY...
...LONG-DORMANT VOLCANOE ... ERUPTING ACROSS... THE PLANET! I-I DON'T HAVE MUCH ... TI... TIME...
JOR-EL'S DIARY, 17 OGTAL, 10,000: "... S-SO... TIRED..."
INTERLUDE: THE PHANTOM ZONE...
THERE, MY FRIENDS... THERE! IT IS AS WE PREDICTED! JOR-EL HAS CONTRACTED SCARLET JUNGLE FEVER AND IS WEAK NOW... HIS RESISTANCE LOW!

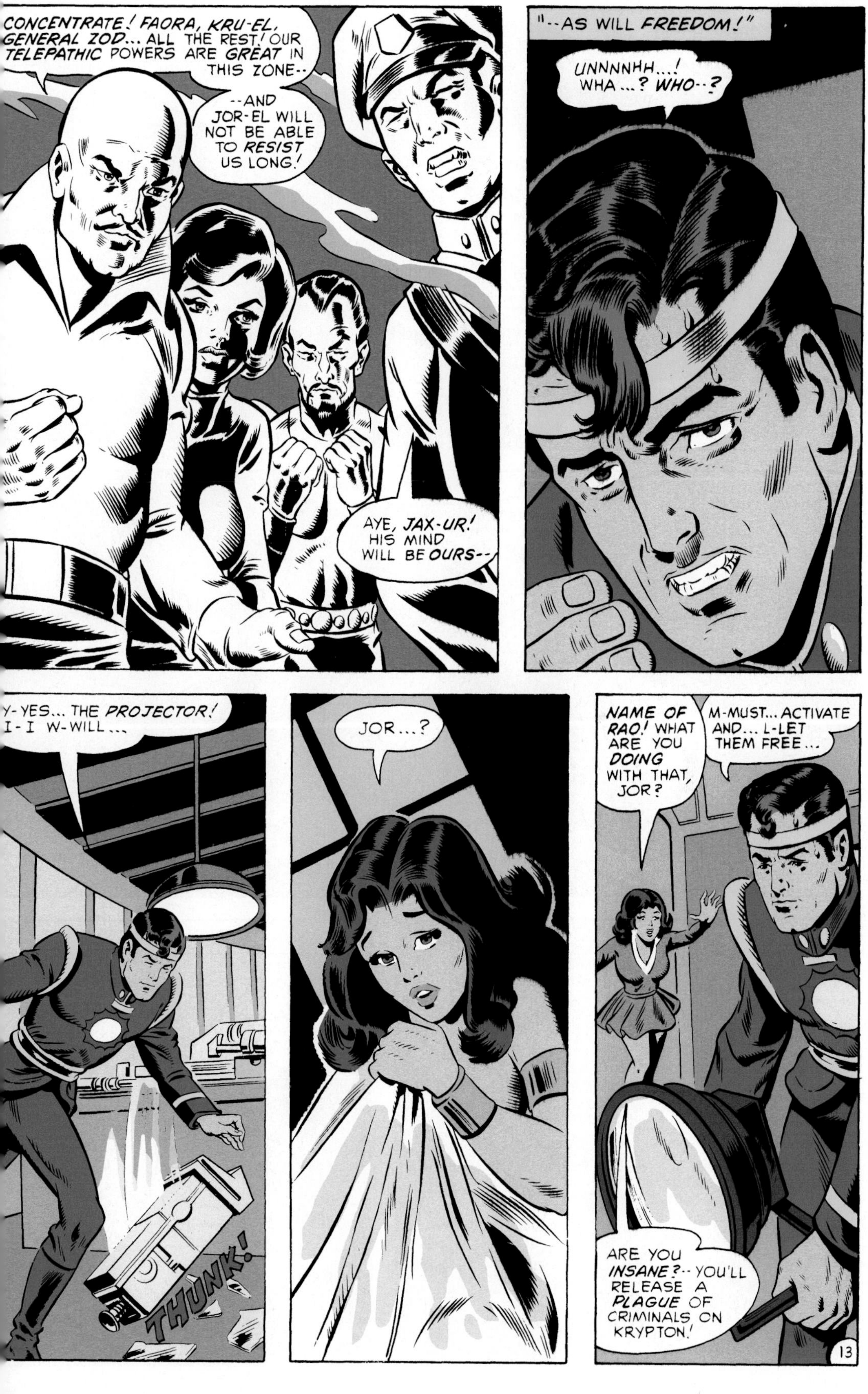
CONCENTRATE! FAORA, KRU-EL, GENERAL ZOD... ALL THE REST! OUR TELEPATHIC POWERS ARE GREAT IN THIS ZONE--
--AND JOR-EL WILL NOT BE ABLE TO RESIST US LONG!
AYE, JAX-UR! HIS MIND WILL BE OURS--
"--AS WILL FREEDOM!"
UNNNNHH...! WHA...? WHO--?
Y-YES... THE PROJECTOR! I-I W-WILL...
THUNK!
JOR...?
NAME OF RAO! WHAT ARE YOU DOING WITH THAT, JOR?
M-MUST... ACTIVATE AND... L-LET THEM FREE...
ARE YOU INSANE?--YOU'LL RELEASE A PLAGUE OF CRIMINALS ON KRYPTON!
13

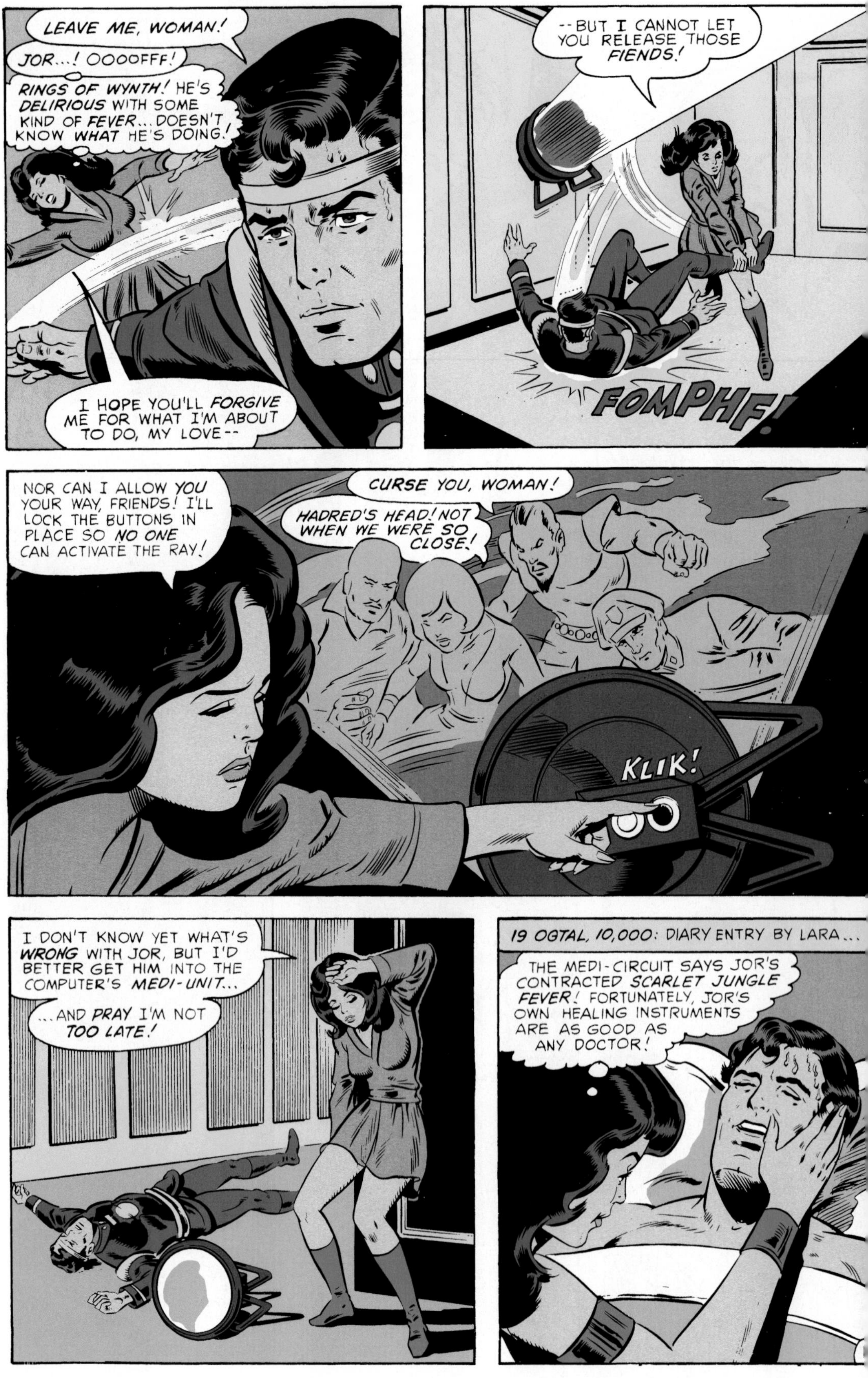
LEAVE ME, WOMAN!
JOR...! OOOOFFF!
RINGS OF WYNTH! HE'S DELIRIOUS WITH SOME KIND OF FEVER... DOESN'T KNOW WHAT HE'S DOING!
I HOPE YOU'LL FORGIVE ME FOR WHAT I'M ABOUT TO DO, MY LOVE--
--BUT I CANNOT LET YOU RELEASE THOSE FIENDS!
FOMPHF!
NOR CAN I ALLOW YOU YOUR WAY, FRIENDS! I'LL LOCK THE BUTTONS IN PLACE SO NO ONE CAN ACTIVATE THE RAY!
CURSE YOU, WOMAN!
HADRED'S HEAD! NOT WHEN WE WERE SO CLOSE!
KLIK!
I DON'T KNOW YET WHAT'S WRONG WITH JOR, BUT I'D BETTER GET HIM INTO THE COMPUTER'S MEDI-UNIT...
...AND PRAY I'M NOT TOO LATE!
19 OGTAL, 10,000: DIARY ENTRY BY LARA...
THE MEDI-CIRCUIT SAYS JOR'S CONTRACTED SCARLET JUNGLE FEVER! FORTUNATELY, JOR'S OWN HEALING INSTRUMENTS ARE AS GOOD AS ANY DOCTOR!

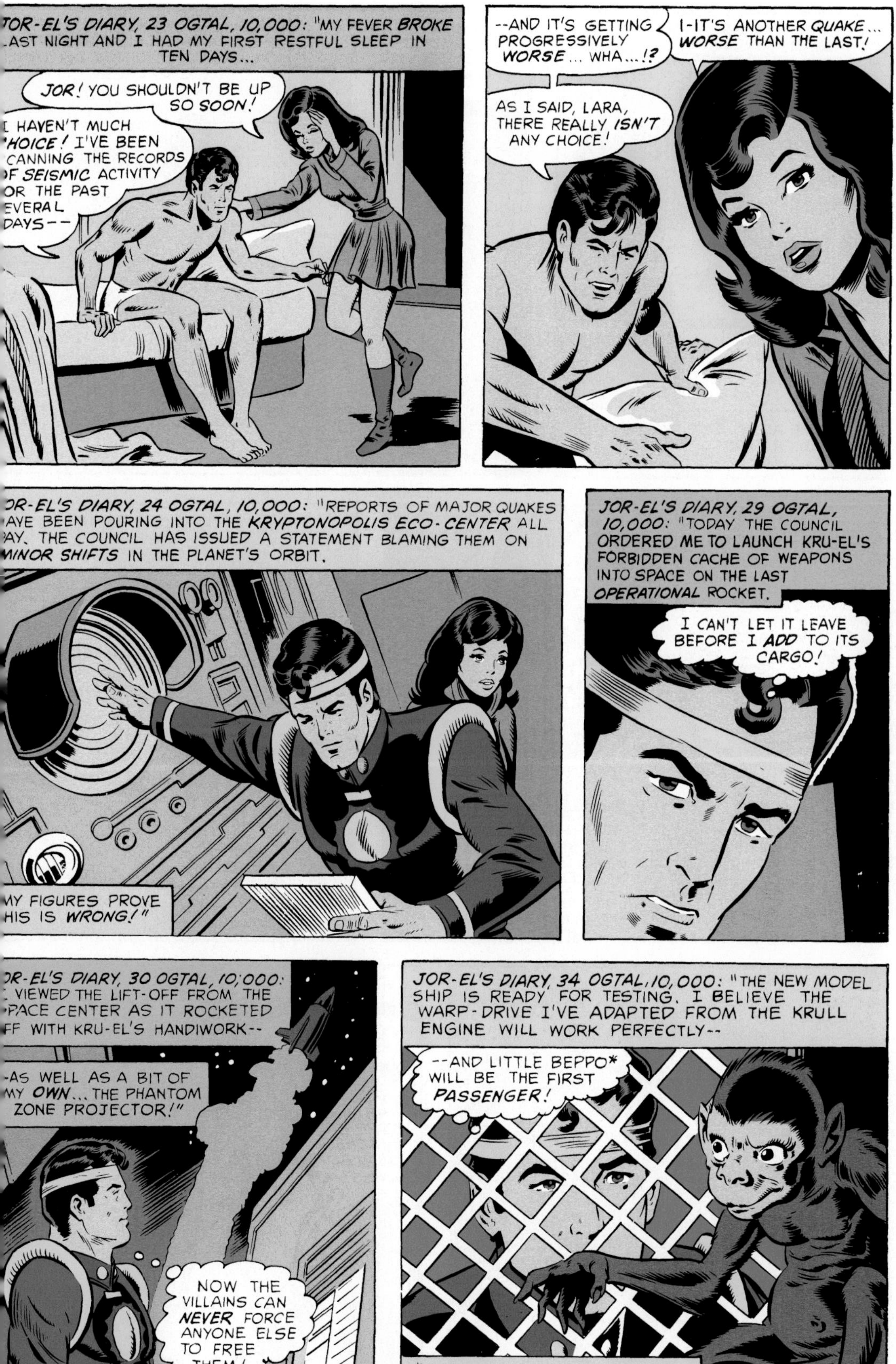

TOR-EL'S DIARY, 23 OGTAL, 10,000: "MY FEVER BROKE LAST NIGHT AND I HAD MY FIRST RESTFUL SLEEP IN TEN DAYS...
JOR! YOU SHOULDN'T BE UP SO SOON!
I HAVEN'T MUCH HOICE! I'VE BEEN CANNING THE RECORDS OF SEISMIC ACTIVITY OR THE PAST EVERAL DAYS--
--AND IT'S GETTING PROGRESSIVELY WORSE... WHA...!?
I-IT'S ANOTHER QUAKE... WORSE THAN THE LAST!
AS I SAID, LARA, THERE REALLY ISN'T ANY CHOICE!
OR-EL'S DIARY, 24 OGTAL, 10,000: "REPORTS OF MAJOR QUAKES AVE BEEN POURING INTO THE KRYPTONOPOLIS ECO-CENTER ALL AY. THE COUNCIL HAS ISSUED A STATEMENT BLAMING THEM ON MINOR SHIFTS IN THE PLANET'S ORBIT.
MY FIGURES PROVE HIS IS WRONG!"
JOR-EL'S DIARY, 29 OGTAL, 10,000: "TODAY THE COUNCIL ORDERED ME TO LAUNCH KRU-EL'S FORBIDDEN CACHE OF WEAPONS INTO SPACE ON THE LAST OPERATIONAL ROCKET.
I CAN'T LET IT LEAVE BEFORE I ADD TO ITS CARGO!
OR-EL'S DIARY, 30 OGTAL, 10,000: VIEWED THE LIFT-OFF FROM THE PACE CENTER AS IT ROCKETED FF WITH KRU-EL'S HANDIWORK--
-AS WELL AS A BIT OF MY OWN... THE PHANTOM ZONE PROJECTOR!"
NOW THE VILLAINS CAN NEVER FORCE ANYONE ELSE TO FREE THEM!
JOR-EL'S DIARY, 34 OGTAL, 10,000: "THE NEW MODEL SHIP IS READY FOR TESTING. I BELIEVE THE WARP-DRIVE I'VE ADAPTED FROM THE KRULL ENGINE WILL WORK PERFECTLY--
--AND LITTLE BEPPO* WILL BE THE FIRST PASSENGER!
*BEPPO STOWED AWAY IN BABY KAL-EL'S ROCKET, TO BECOME SUPER-MONKEY ON EARTH --ENB
15

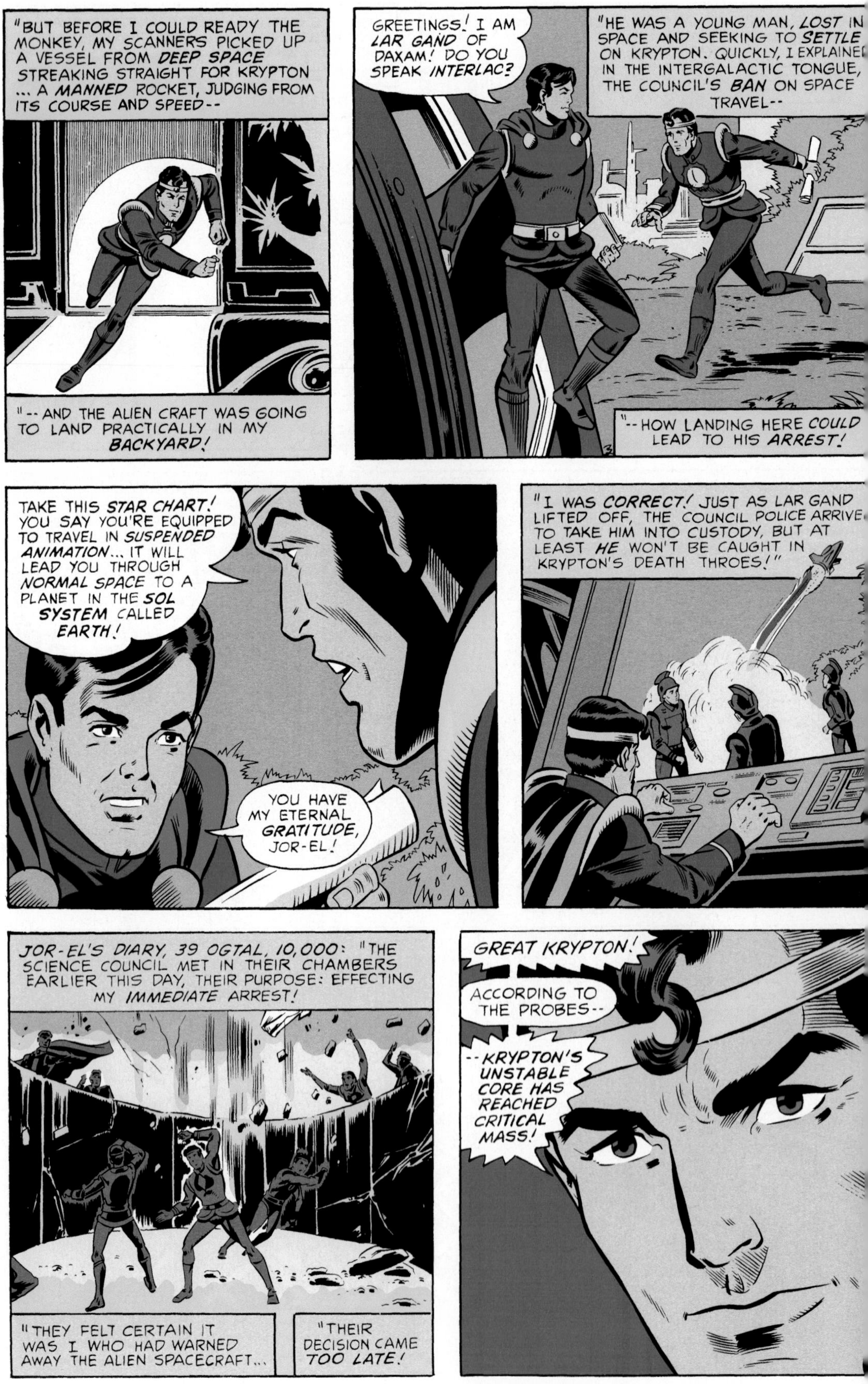
"BUT BEFORE I COULD READY THE MONKEY, MY SCANNERS PICKED UP A VESSEL FROM DEEP SPACE STREAKING STRAIGHT FOR KRYPTON ... A MANNED ROCKET, JUDGING FROM ITS COURSE AND SPEED--
"--AND THE ALIEN CRAFT WAS GOING TO LAND PRACTICALLY IN MY BACKYARD!
GREETINGS! I AM LAR GAND OF DAXAM! DO YOU SPEAK INTERLAC?
"HE WAS A YOUNG MAN, LOST IN SPACE AND SEEKING TO SETTLE ON KRYPTON. QUICKLY, I EXPLAINED IN THE INTERGALACTIC TONGUE, THE COUNCIL'S BAN ON SPACE TRAVEL--
"--HOW LANDING HERE COULD LEAD TO HIS ARREST!
TAKE THIS STAR CHART! YOU SAY YOU'RE EQUIPPED TO TRAVEL IN SUSPENDED ANIMATION... IT WILL LEAD YOU THROUGH NORMAL SPACE TO A PLANET IN THE SOL SYSTEM CALLED EARTH!
YOU HAVE MY ETERNAL GRATITUDE, JOR-EL!
"I WAS CORRECT! JUST AS LAR GAND LIFTED OFF, THE COUNCIL POLICE ARRIVED TO TAKE HIM INTO CUSTODY, BUT AT LEAST HE WON'T BE CAUGHT IN KRYPTON'S DEATH THROES!"
JOR-EL'S DIARY, 39 OGTAL, 10,000: "THE SCIENCE COUNCIL MET IN THEIR CHAMBERS EARLIER THIS DAY, THEIR PURPOSE: EFFECTING MY IMMEDIATE ARREST!
"THEY FELT CERTAIN IT WAS I WHO HAD WARNED AWAY THE ALIEN SPACECRAFT...
"THEIR DECISION CAME TOO LATE!
GREAT KRYPTON!
ACCORDING TO THE PROBES--
--KRYPTON'S UNSTABLE CORE HAS REACHED CRITICAL MASS!

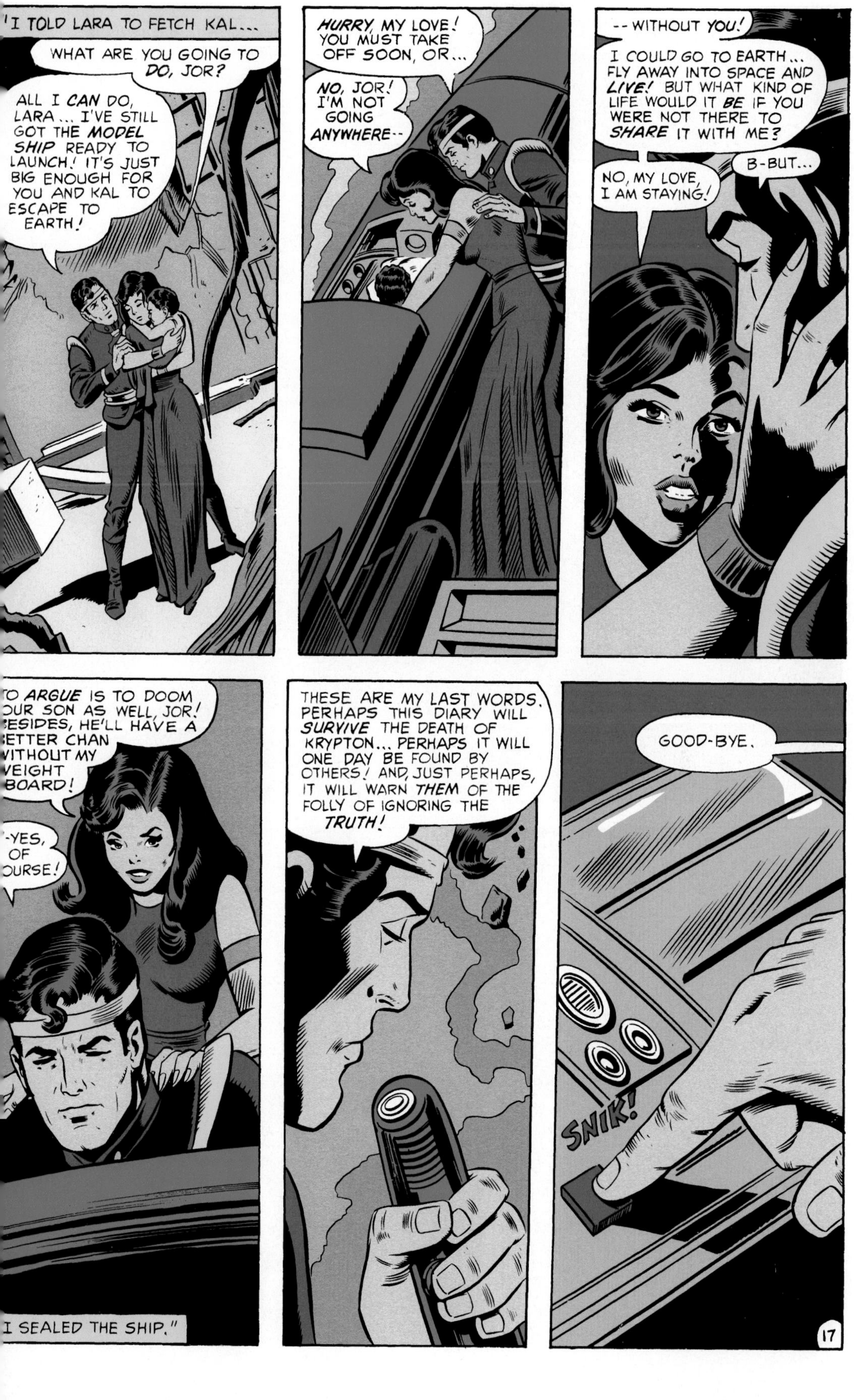
"I TOLD LARA TO FETCH KAL...
WHAT ARE YOU GOING TO *DO*, JOR?
ALL I *CAN* DO, LARA... I'VE STILL GOT THE *MODEL SHIP* READY TO LAUNCH! IT'S JUST BIG ENOUGH FOR YOU AND KAL TO ESCAPE TO EARTH!
HURRY, MY LOVE! YOU MUST TAKE OFF SOON, OR...
NO, JOR! I'M NOT GOING *ANYWHERE*--
--WITHOUT *YOU*!
I COULD GO TO EARTH... FLY AWAY INTO SPACE AND *LIVE*! BUT WHAT KIND OF LIFE WOULD IT *BE* IF YOU WERE NOT THERE TO *SHARE* IT WITH ME?
B-BUT...
NO, MY LOVE, I AM STAYING!
TO *ARGUE* IS TO DOOM OUR SON AS WELL, JOR! BESIDES, HE'LL HAVE A BETTER CHAN WITHOUT MY WEIGHT BOARD!
-YES, OF OURSE!
I SEALED THE SHIP."
THESE ARE MY LAST WORDS. PERHAPS THIS DIARY WILL *SURVIVE* THE DEATH OF KRYPTON... PERHAPS IT WILL ONE DAY BE FOUND BY OTHERS! AND, JUST PERHAPS, IT WILL WARN *THEM* OF THE FOLLY OF IGNORING THE *TRUTH*!
GOOD-BYE.
SNIK!
17

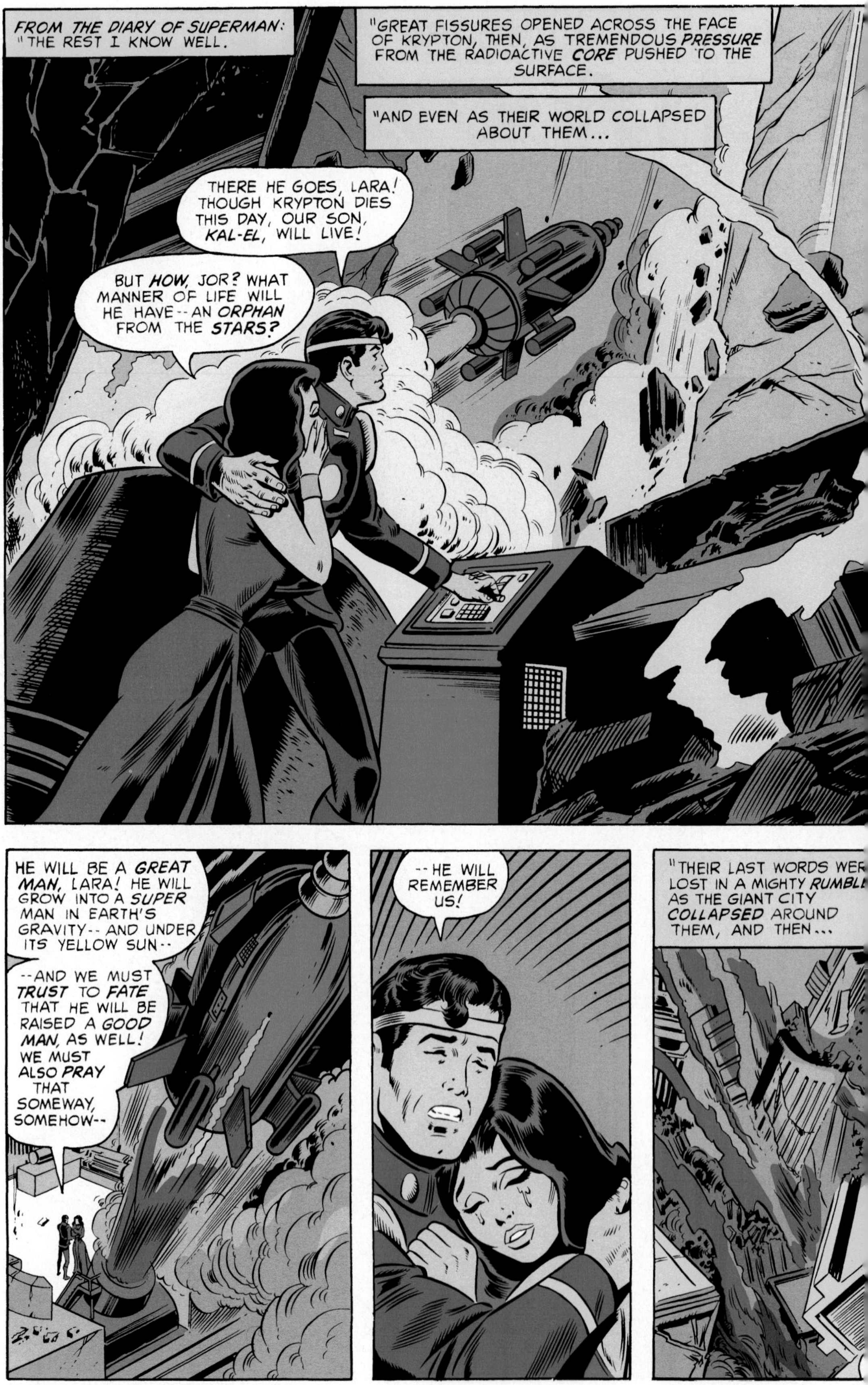
FROM THE DIARY OF SUPERMAN: "THE REST I KNOW WELL.
"GREAT FISSURES OPENED ACROSS THE FACE OF KRYPTON, THEN, AS TREMENDOUS PRESSURE FROM THE RADIOACTIVE CORE PUSHED TO THE SURFACE.
"AND EVEN AS THEIR WORLD COLLAPSED ABOUT THEM...
THERE HE GOES, LARA! THOUGH KRYPTON DIES THIS DAY, OUR SON, KAL-EL, WILL LIVE!
BUT HOW, JOR? WHAT MANNER OF LIFE WILL HE HAVE--AN ORPHAN FROM THE STARS?
HE WILL BE A GREAT MAN, LARA! HE WILL GROW INTO A SUPER MAN IN EARTH'S GRAVITY--AND UNDER ITS YELLOW SUN--
--AND WE MUST TRUST TO FATE THAT HE WILL BE RAISED A GOOD MAN, AS WELL! WE MUST ALSO PRAY THAT SOMEWAY, SOMEHOW--
--HE WILL REMEMBER US!
"THEIR LAST WORDS WER LOST IN A MIGHTY RUMBL AS THE GIANT CITY COLLAPSED AROUND THEM, AND THEN...

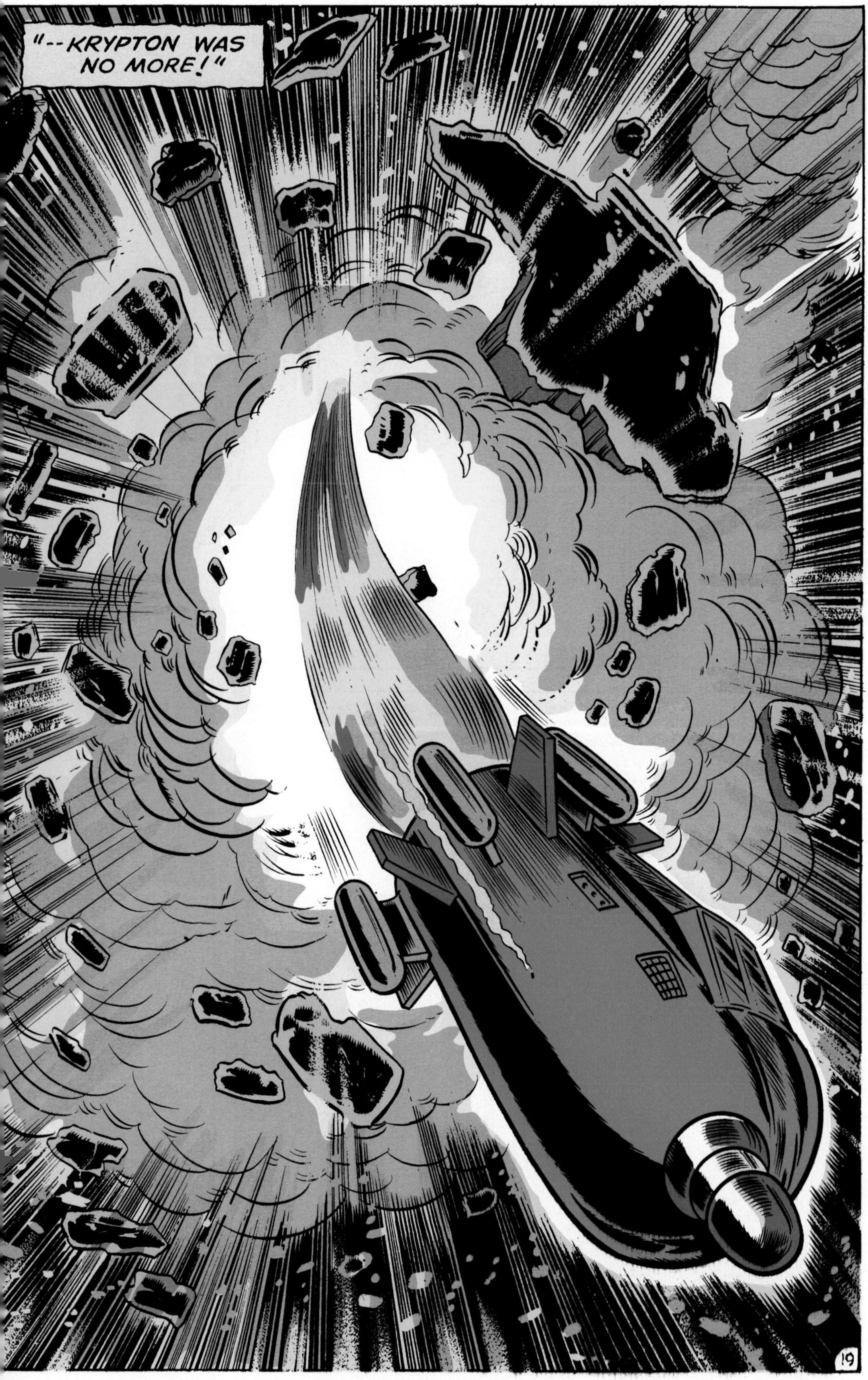
"--KRYPTON WAS NO MORE!"
19

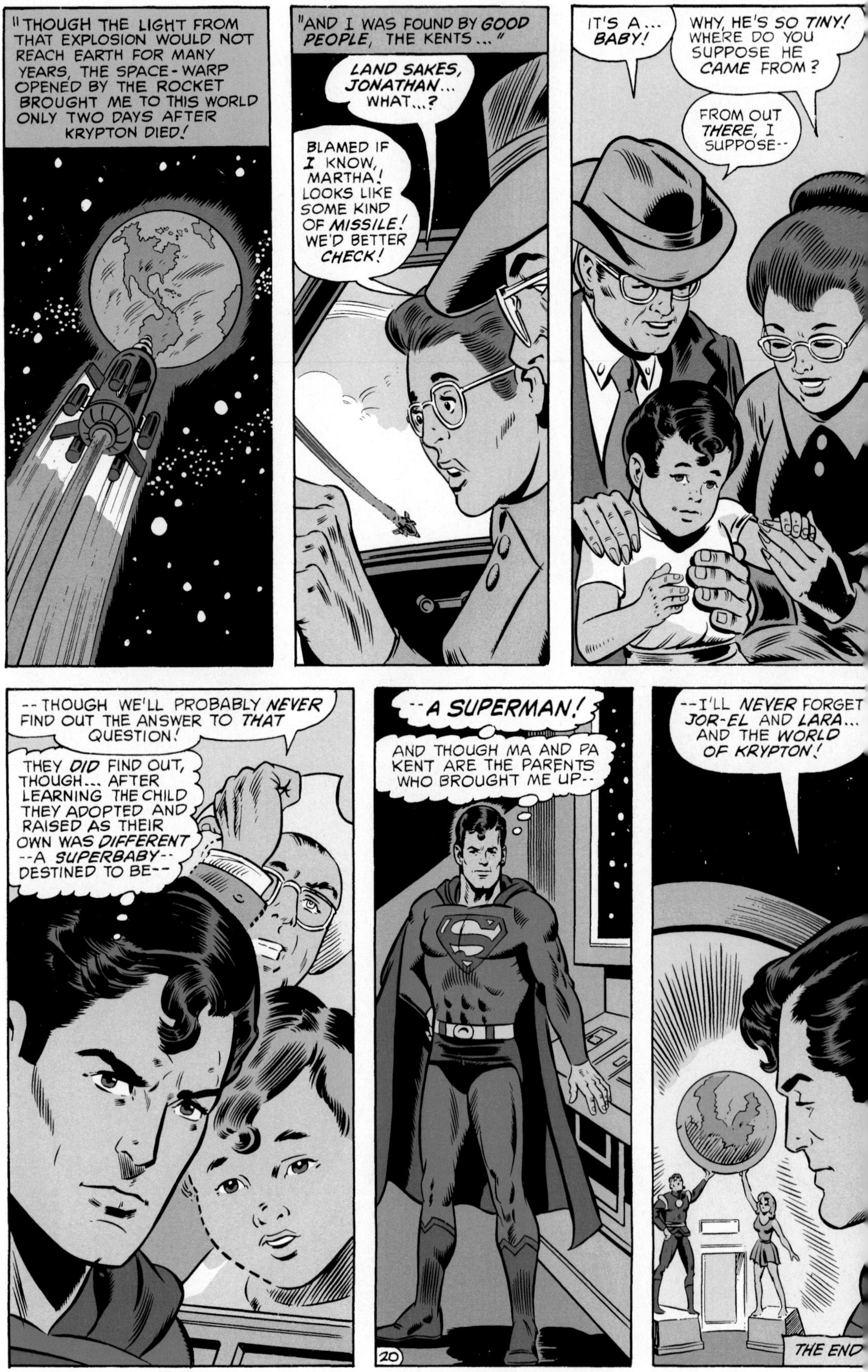
"THOUGH THE LIGHT FROM THAT EXPLOSION WOULD NOT REACH EARTH FOR MANY YEARS, THE SPACE-WARP OPENED BY THE ROCKET BROUGHT ME TO THIS WORLD ONLY TWO DAYS AFTER KRYPTON DIED!
"AND I WAS FOUND BY GOOD PEOPLE, THE KENTS..."
LAND SAKES, JONATHAN... WHAT...?
BLAMED IF I KNOW, MARTHA! LOOKS LIKE SOME KIND OF MISSILE! WE'D BETTER CHECK!
IT'S A... BABY!
WHY, HE'S SO TINY! WHERE DO YOU SUPPOSE HE CAME FROM?
FROM OUT THERE, I SUPPOSE--
--THOUGH WE'LL PROBABLY NEVER FIND OUT THE ANSWER TO THAT QUESTION!
THEY DID FIND OUT, THOUGH... AFTER LEARNING THE CHILD THEY ADOPTED AND RAISED AS THEIR OWN WAS DIFFERENT --A SUPERBABY-- DESTINED TO BE--
--A SUPERMAN!
AND THOUGH MA AND PA KENT ARE THE PARENTS WHO BROUGHT ME UP--
20
--I'LL NEVER FORGET JOR-EL AND LARA... AND THE WORLD OF KRYPTON!
THE END

CHAPTER THREE
THE WORLD OF KRYPTON

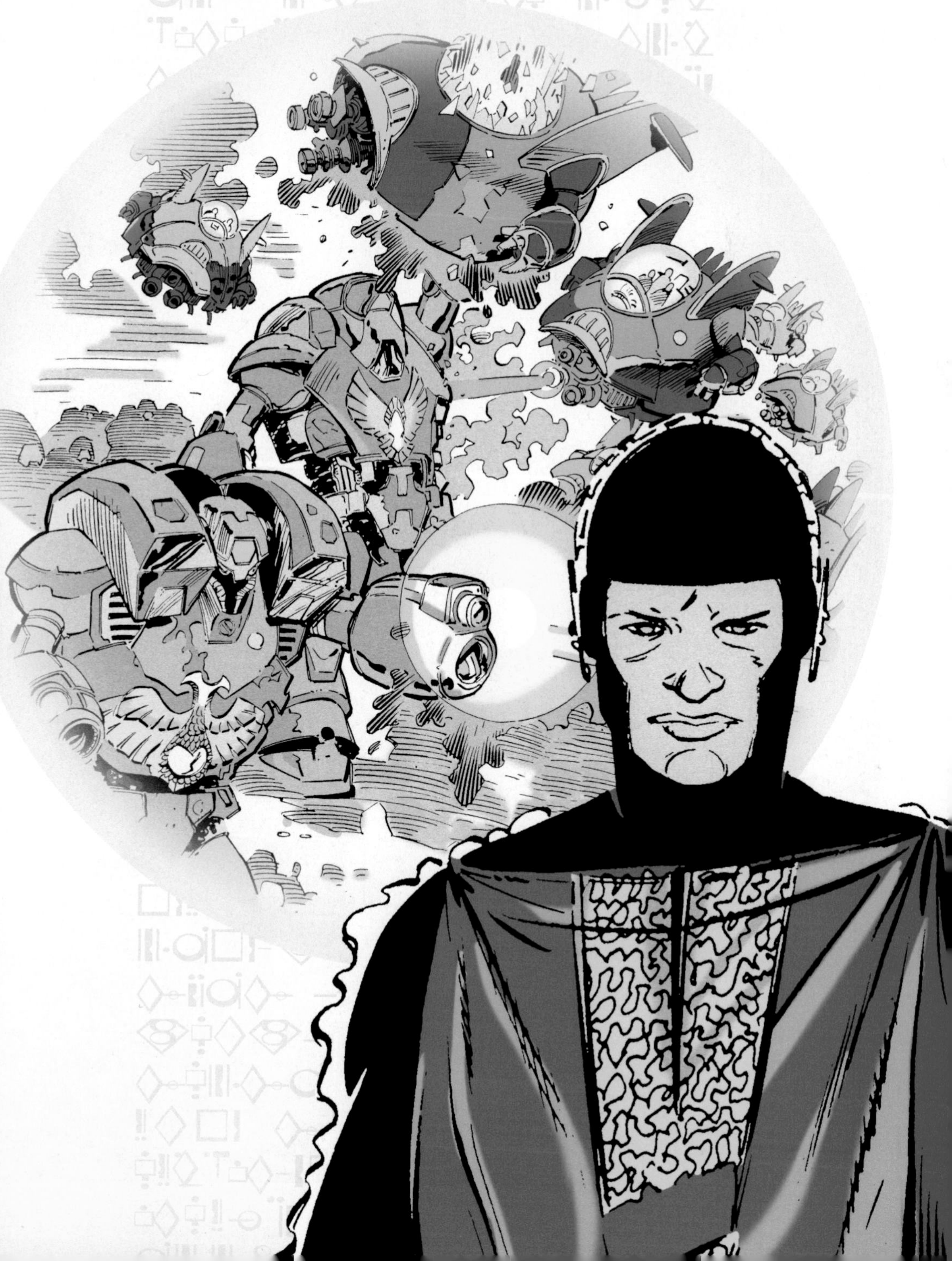

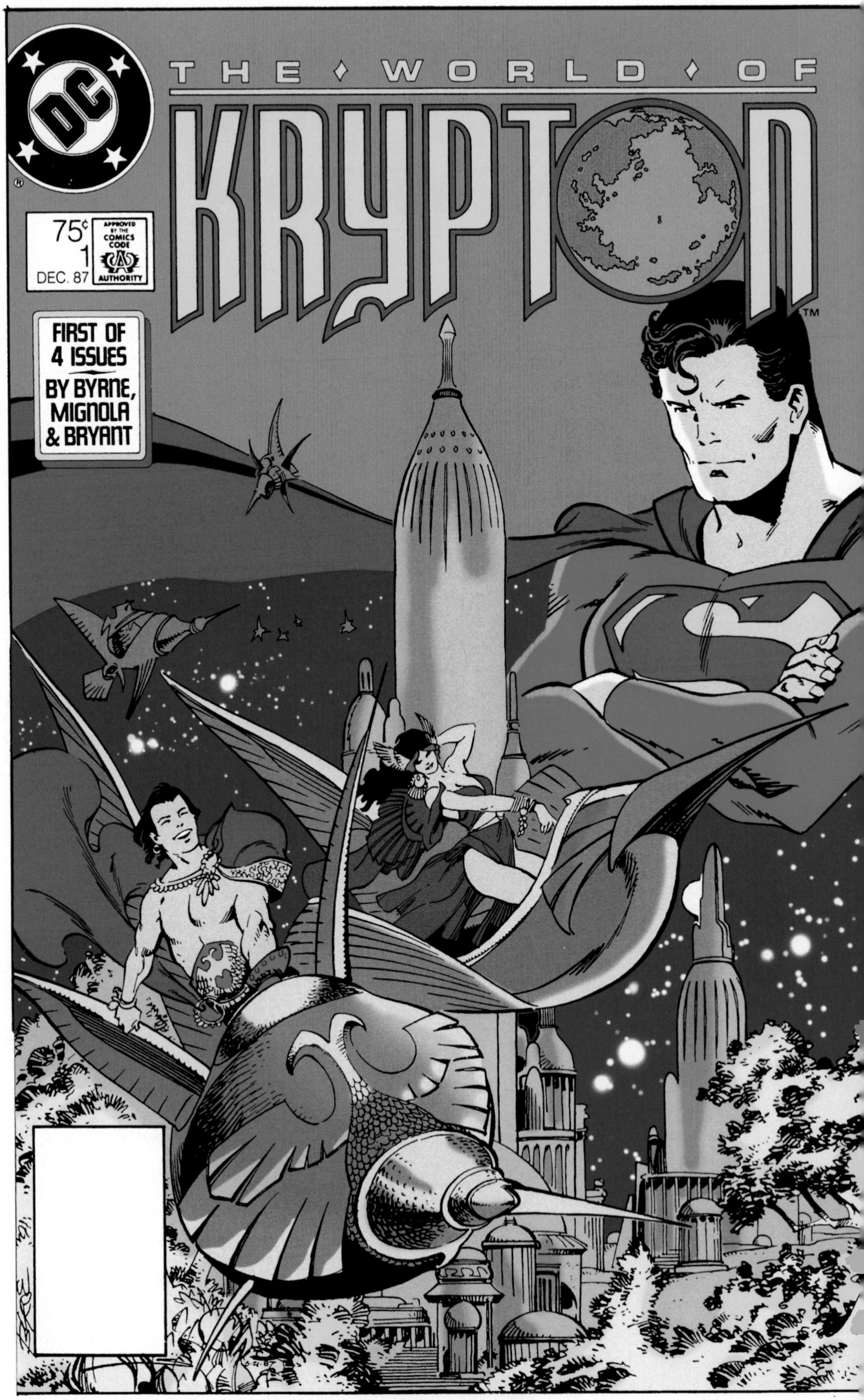
THE WORLD OF
KRYPTON
DC
75¢
1
DEC. 87
APPROVED BY THE COMICS CODE AUTHORITY
FIRST OF 4 ISSUES BY BYRNE, MIGNOLA & BRYANT

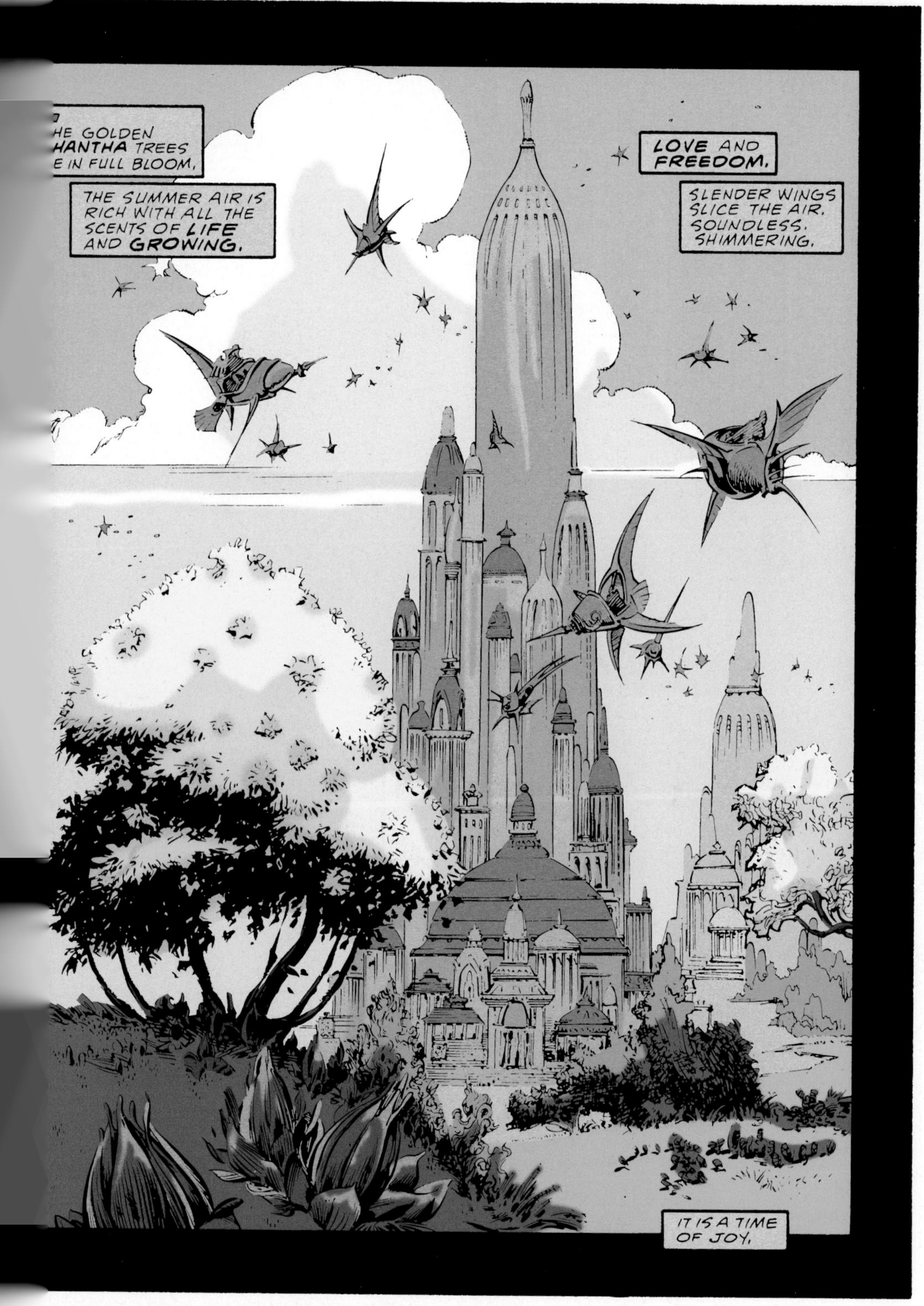

...HE GOLDEN ...HANTHA TREES ...E IN FULL BLOOM.
THE SUMMER AIR IS RICH WITH ALL THE SCENTS OF LIFE AND GROWING.
LOVE AND FREEDOM.
SLENDER WINGS SLICE THE AIR. SOUNDLESS. SHIMMERING.
IT IS A TIME OF JOY.

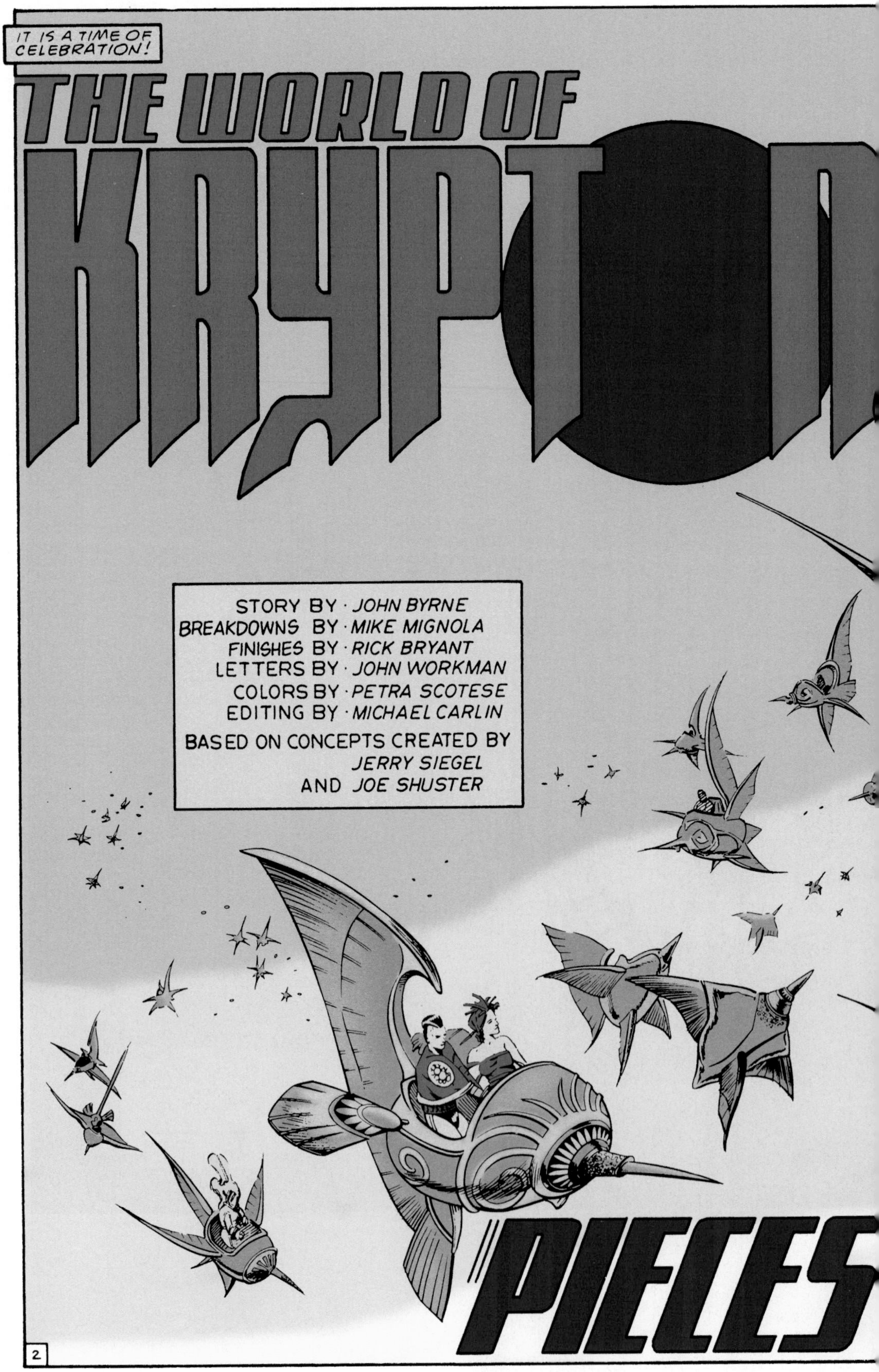

IT IS A TIME OF CELEBRATION!
THE WORLD OF KRYPTON
STORY BY · JOHN BYRNE
BREAKDOWNS BY · MIKE MIGNOLA
FINISHES BY · RICK BRYANT
LETTERS BY · JOHN WORKMAN
COLORS BY · PETRA SCOTESE
EDITING BY · MICHAEL CARLIN
BASED ON CONCEPTS CREATED BY JERRY SIEGEL AND JOE SHUSTER
PIECES
2

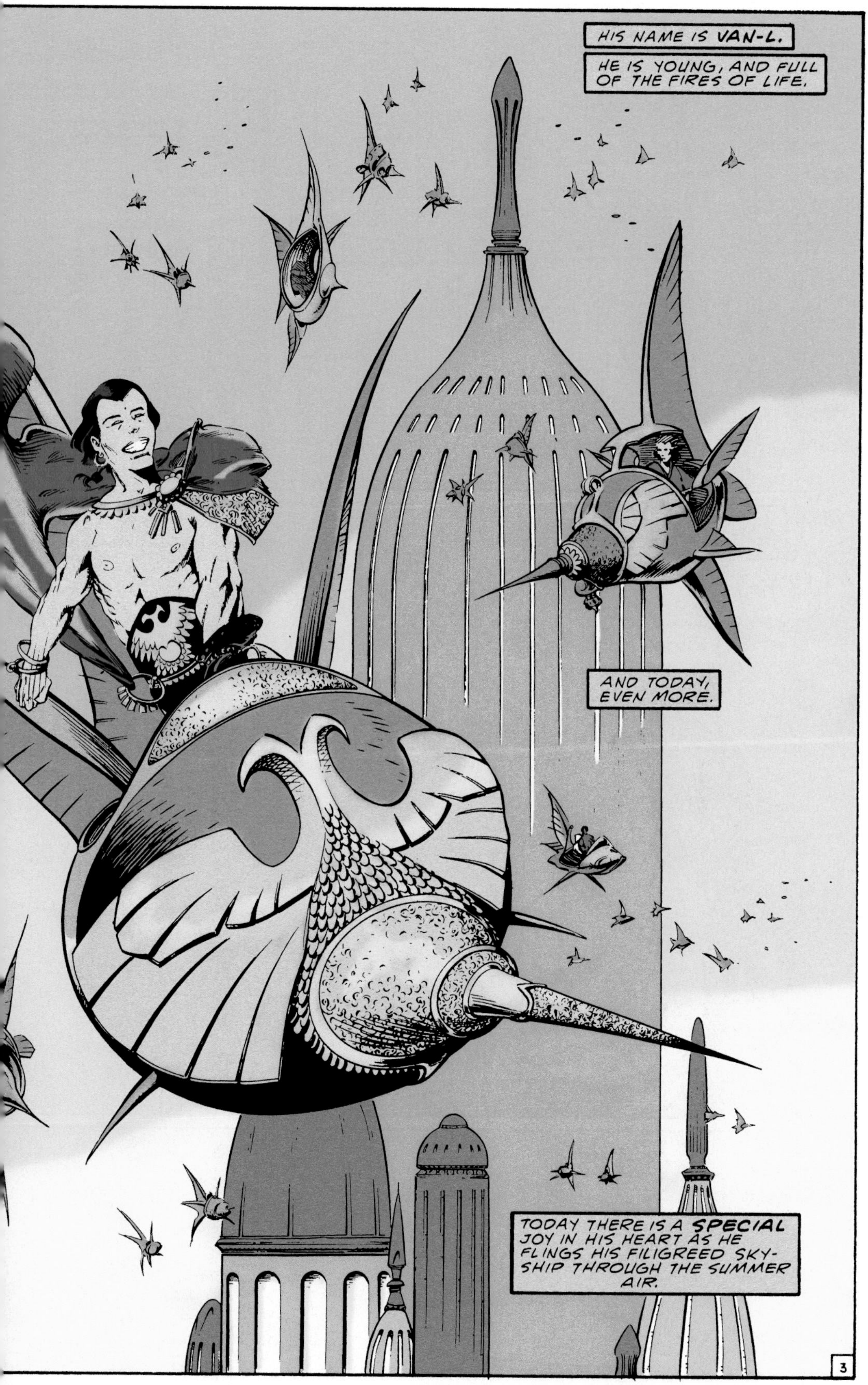
HIS NAME IS **VAN-L.**
HE IS YOUNG, AND FULL OF THE FIRES OF LIFE.
AND TODAY, EVEN MORE.
TODAY THERE IS A **SPECIAL** JOY IN HIS HEART AS HE FLINGS HIS FILIGREED SKY-SHIP THROUGH THE SUMMER AIR.
3

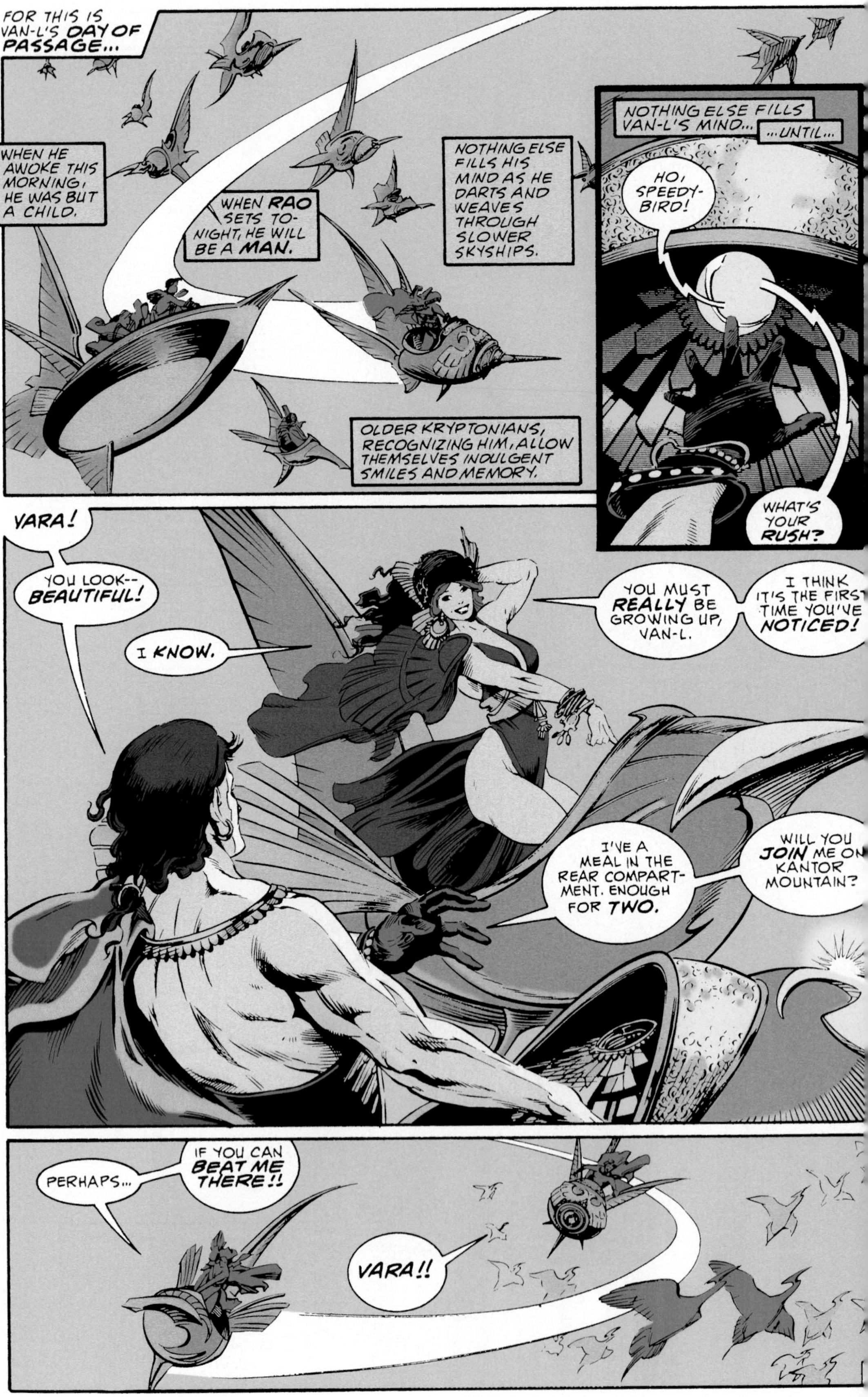
FOR THIS IS VAN-L'S DAY OF PASSAGE...
WHEN HE AWOKE THIS MORNING, HE WAS BUT A CHILD.
WHEN RAO SETS TO-NIGHT, HE WILL BE A MAN.
NOTHING ELSE FILLS HIS MIND AS HE DARTS AND WEAVES THROUGH SLOWER SKYSHIPS.
OLDER KRYPTONIANS, RECOGNIZING HIM, ALLOW THEMSELVES INDULGENT SMILES AND MEMORY.
NOTHING ELSE FILLS VAN-L'S MIND...
...UNTIL...
HO, SPEEDY-BIRD!
WHAT'S YOUR RUSH?
VARA!
YOU LOOK-- BEAUTIFUL!
I KNOW.
YOU MUST REALLY BE GROWING UP, VAN-L.
I THINK IT'S THE FIRST TIME YOU'VE NOTICED!
I'VE A MEAL IN THE REAR COMPART-MENT. ENOUGH FOR TWO.
WILL YOU JOIN ME ON KANTOR MOUNTAIN?
PERHAPS...
IF YOU CAN BEAT ME THERE!!
VARA!!

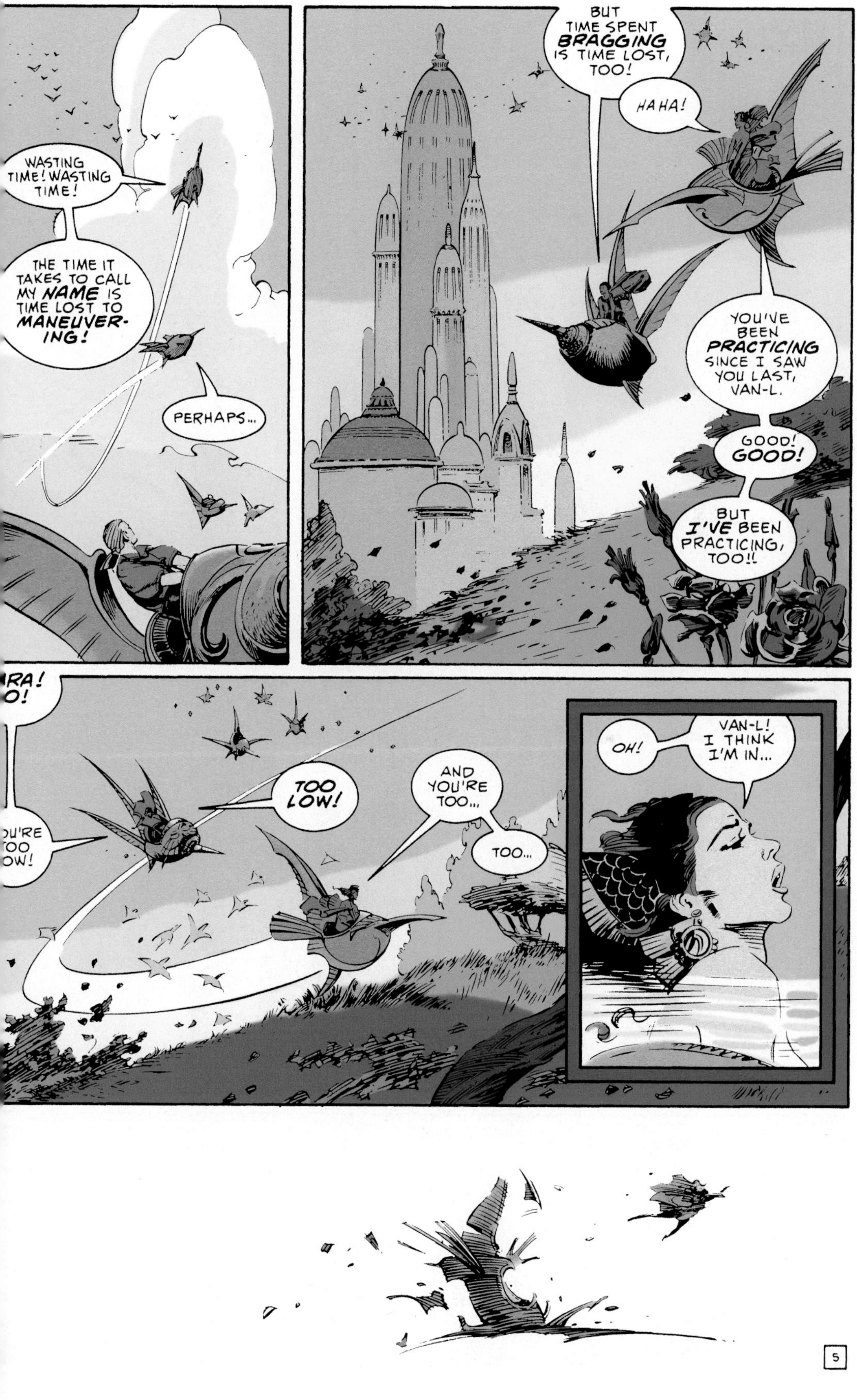

WASTING TIME! WASTING TIME!
THE TIME IT TAKES TO CALL MY **NAME** IS TIME LOST TO **MANEUVER-ING!**
PERHAPS...
BUT TIME SPENT **BRAGGING** IS TIME LOST, TOO!
HAHA!
YOU'VE BEEN **PRACTICING** SINCE I SAW YOU LAST, VAN-L.
GOOD! **GOOD!**
BUT **I'VE** BEEN PRACTICING, TOO!!
TOO LOW!
AND YOU'RE TOO...
TOO...
OH!
VAN-L! I THINK I'M IN...
5

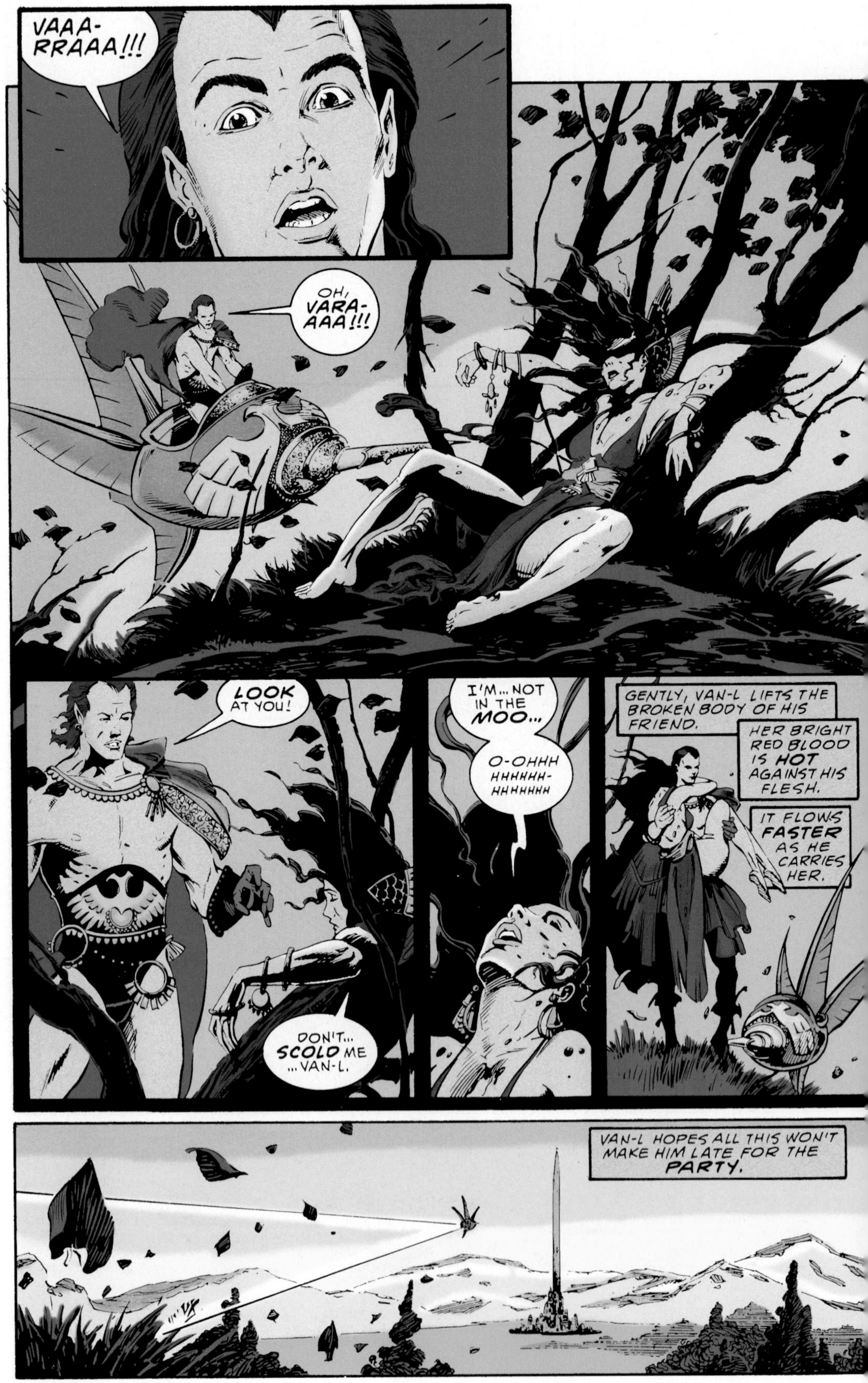
VAAA-RRAAA!!!
OH, VARA-AAA!!!
LOOK AT YOU!
DON'T... SCOLD ME ...VAN-L.
I'M... NOT IN THE MOO...
O-OHHH HHHHHH-HHHHHHH
GENTLY, VAN-L LIFTS THE BROKEN BODY OF HIS FRIEND.
HER BRIGHT RED BLOOD IS HOT AGAINST HIS FLESH.
IT FLOWS FASTER AS HE CARRIES HER.
VAN-L HOPES ALL THIS WON'T MAKE HIM LATE FOR THE PARTY.

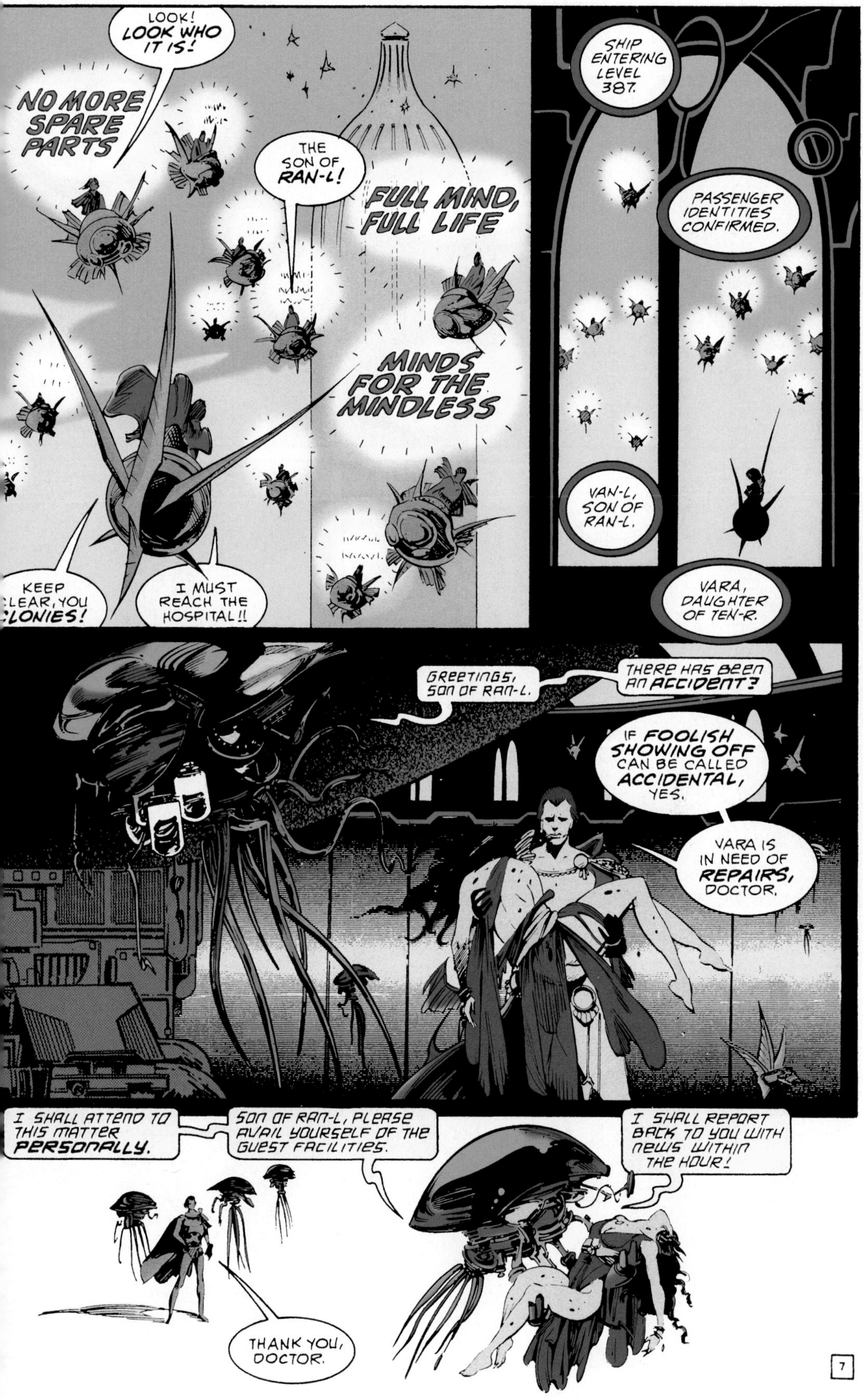
LOOK! LOOK WHO IT IS!
NO MORE SPARE PARTS
THE SON OF RAN-L!
FULL MIND, FULL LIFE
MINDS FOR THE MINDLESS
KEEP CLEAR, YOU CLONIES!
I MUST REACH THE HOSPITAL!!
SHIP ENTERING LEVEL 387.
PASSENGER IDENTITIES CONFIRMED.
VAN-L, SON OF RAN-L.
VARA, DAUGHTER OF TEN-R.
GREETINGS, SON OF RAN-L.
THERE HAS BEEN AN ACCIDENT?
IF FOOLISH SHOWING OFF CAN BE CALLED ACCIDENTAL, YES.
VARA IS IN NEED OF REPAIRS, DOCTOR.
I SHALL ATTEND TO THIS MATTER PERSONALLY.
SON OF RAN-L, PLEASE AVAIL YOURSELF OF THE GUEST FACILITIES.
I SHALL REPORT BACK TO YOU WITH NEWS WITHIN THE HOUR!
THANK YOU, DOCTOR.
7

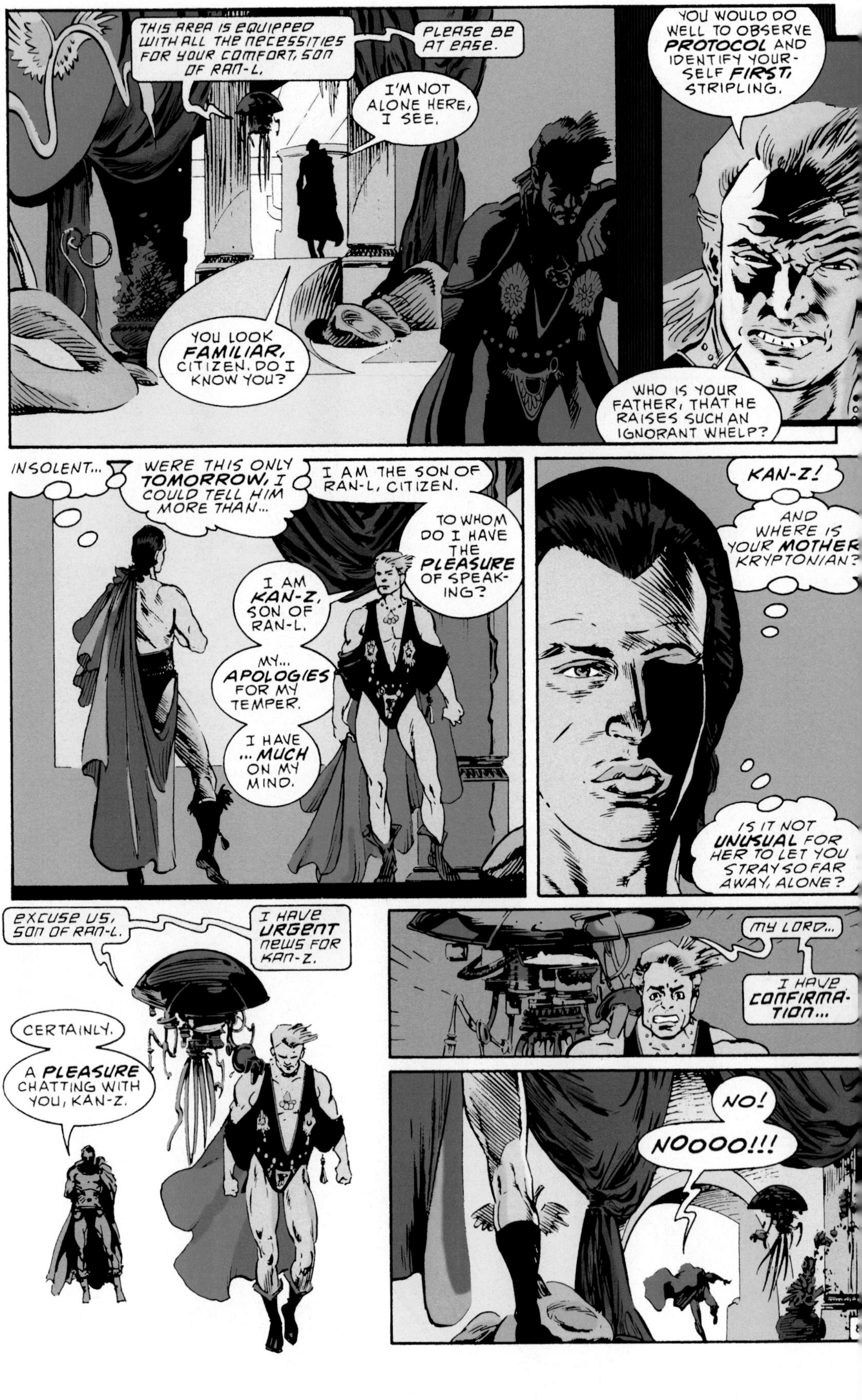
THIS AREA IS EQUIPPED WITH ALL THE NECESSITIES FOR YOUR COMFORT, SON OF RAN-L.
PLEASE BE AT EASE.
I'M NOT ALONE HERE, I SEE.
YOU LOOK FAMILIAR, CITIZEN. DO I KNOW YOU?
YOU WOULD DO WELL TO OBSERVE PROTOCOL AND IDENTIFY YOURSELF FIRST, STRIPLING.
WHO IS YOUR FATHER, THAT HE RAISES SUCH AN IGNORANT WHELP?
INSOLENT...
WERE THIS ONLY TOMORROW, I COULD TELL HIM MORE THAN...
I AM THE SON OF RAN-L, CITIZEN.
TO WHOM DO I HAVE THE PLEASURE OF SPEAKING?
I AM KAN-Z, SON OF RAN-L.
MY... APOLOGIES FOR MY TEMPER.
I HAVE ...MUCH ON MY MIND.
KAN-Z!
AND WHERE IS YOUR MOTHER KRYPTONIAN?
IS IT NOT UNUSUAL FOR HER TO LET YOU STRAY SO FAR AWAY, ALONE?
EXCUSE US, SON OF RAN-L.
I HAVE URGENT NEWS FOR KAN-Z.
CERTAINLY.
A PLEASURE CHATTING WITH YOU, KAN-Z.
MY LORD...
I HAVE CONFIRMATION...
NO!
NOOOO!!!

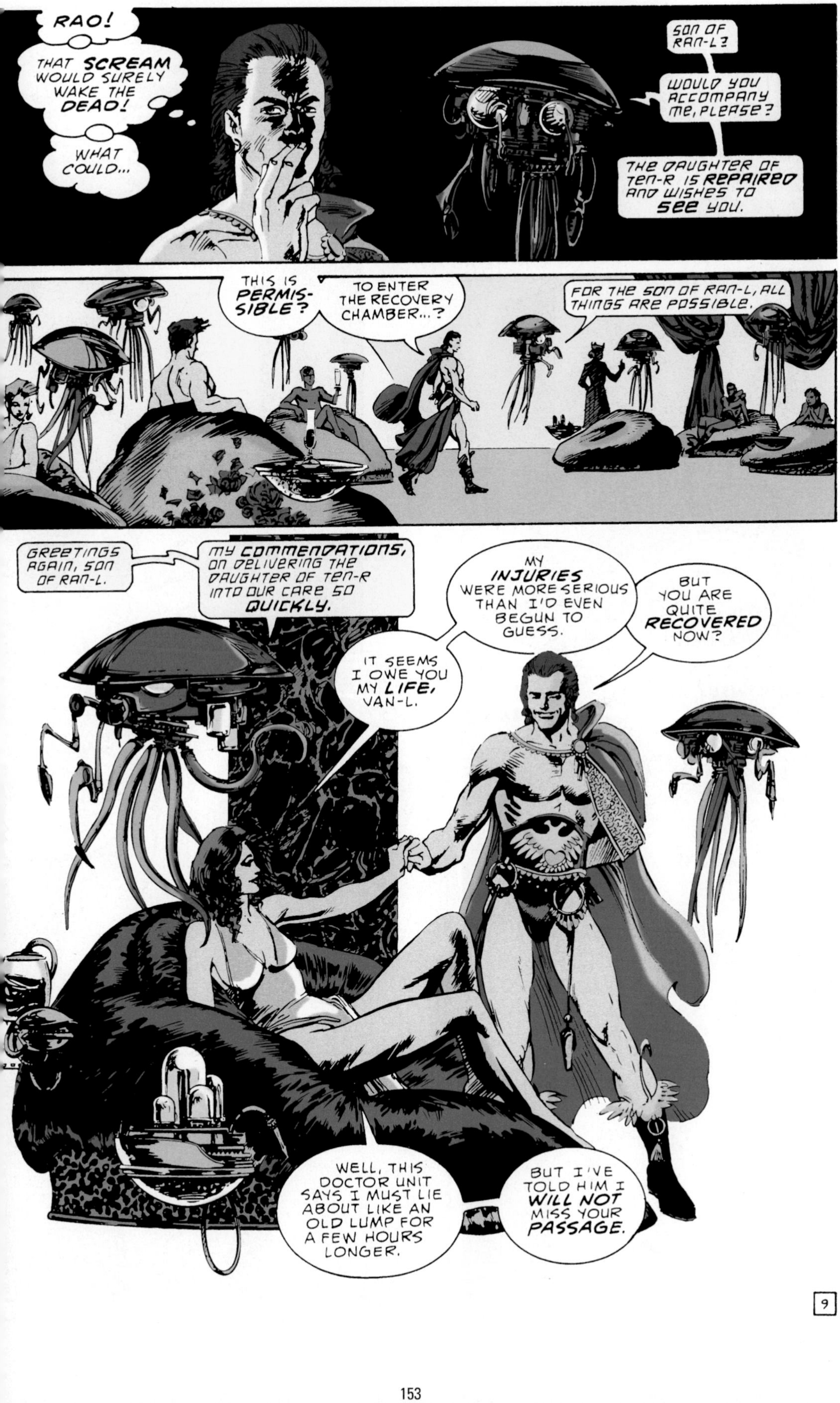
RAO!
THAT **SCREAM** WOULD SURELY WAKE THE **DEAD!**
WHAT COULD...
SON OF RAN-L?
WOULD YOU ACCOMPANY ME, PLEASE?
THE DAUGHTER OF TEN-R IS **REPAIRED** AND WISHES TO **SEE** YOU.
THIS IS **PERMISSIBLE?**
TO ENTER THE RECOVERY CHAMBER...?
FOR THE SON OF RAN-L, ALL THINGS ARE POSSIBLE.
GREETINGS AGAIN, SON OF RAN-L.
MY **COMMENDATIONS**, ON DELIVERING THE DAUGHTER OF TEN-R INTO OUR CARE SO **QUICKLY.**
IT SEEMS I OWE YOU MY **LIFE**, VAN-L.
MY **INJURIES** WERE MORE SERIOUS THAN I'D EVEN BEGUN TO GUESS.
BUT YOU ARE QUITE **RECOVERED** NOW?
WELL, THIS DOCTOR UNIT SAYS I MUST LIE ABOUT LIKE AN OLD LUMP FOR A FEW HOURS LONGER.
BUT I'VE TOLD HIM I **WILL NOT** MISS YOUR **PASSAGE.**

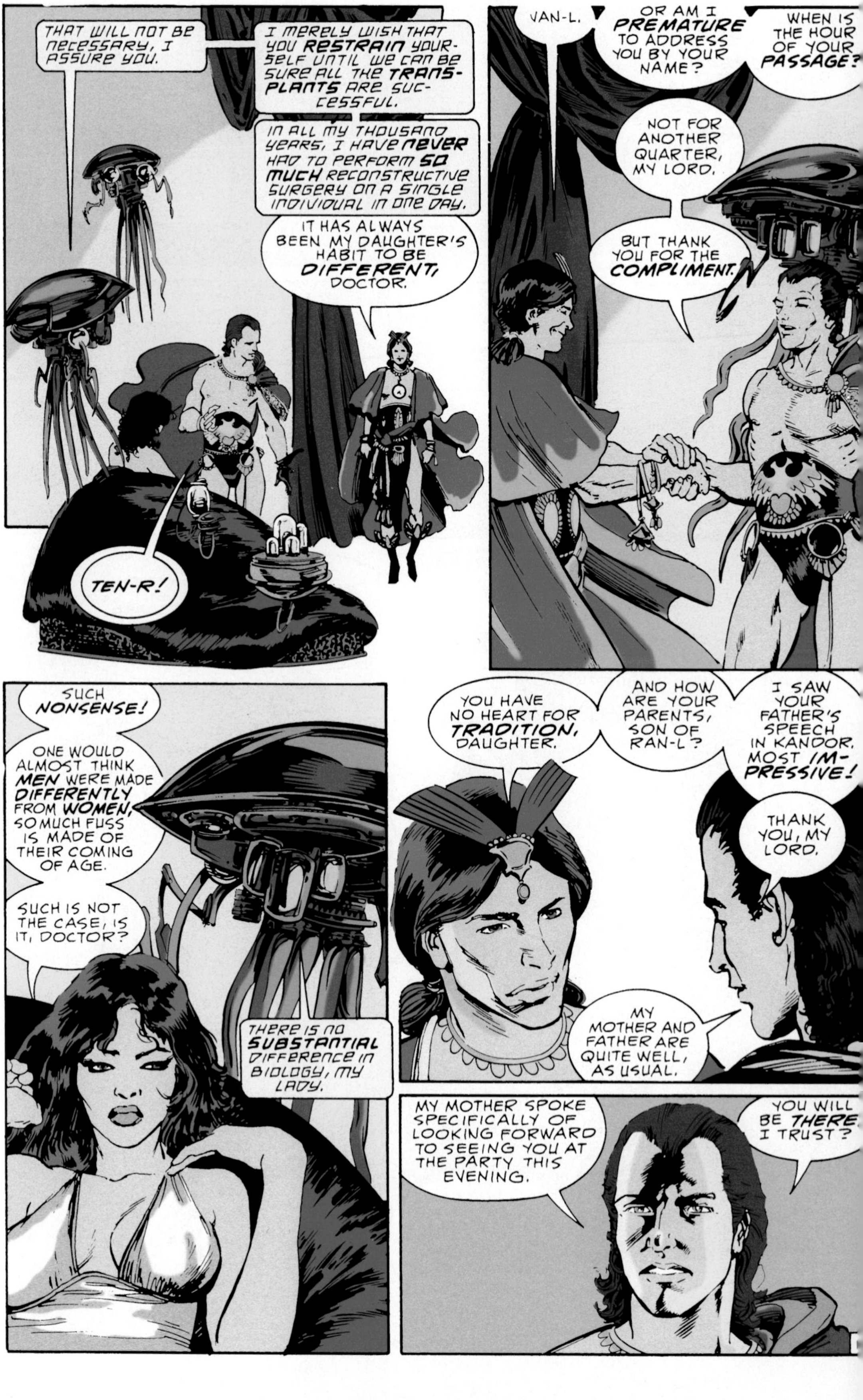
THAT WILL NOT BE NECESSARY, I ASSURE YOU.
I MERELY WISH THAT YOU RESTRAIN YOURSELF UNTIL WE CAN BE SURE ALL THE TRANSPLANTS ARE SUCCESSFUL.
IN ALL MY THOUSAND YEARS, I HAVE NEVER HAD TO PERFORM SO MUCH RECONSTRUCTIVE SURGERY ON A SINGLE INDIVIDUAL IN ONE DAY.
IT HAS ALWAYS BEEN MY DAUGHTER'S HABIT TO BE DIFFERENT, DOCTOR.
TEN-R!
VAN-L.
OR AM I PREMATURE TO ADDRESS YOU BY YOUR NAME?
WHEN IS THE HOUR OF YOUR PASSAGE?
NOT FOR ANOTHER QUARTER, MY LORD.
BUT THANK YOU FOR THE COMPLIMENT.
SUCH NONSENSE!
ONE WOULD ALMOST THINK MEN WERE MADE DIFFERENTLY FROM WOMEN, SO MUCH FUSS IS MADE OF THEIR COMING OF AGE.
SUCH IS NOT THE CASE, IS IT, DOCTOR?
THERE IS NO SUBSTANTIAL DIFFERENCE IN BIOLOGY, MY LADY.
YOU HAVE NO HEART FOR TRADITION, DAUGHTER.
AND HOW ARE YOUR PARENTS, SON OF RAN-L?
I SAW YOUR FATHER'S SPEECH IN KANDOR. MOST IMPRESSIVE!
THANK YOU, MY LORD.
MY MOTHER AND FATHER ARE QUITE WELL, AS USUAL.
MY MOTHER SPOKE SPECIFICALLY OF LOOKING FORWARD TO SEEING YOU AT THE PARTY THIS EVENING.
YOU WILL BE THERE, I TRUST?

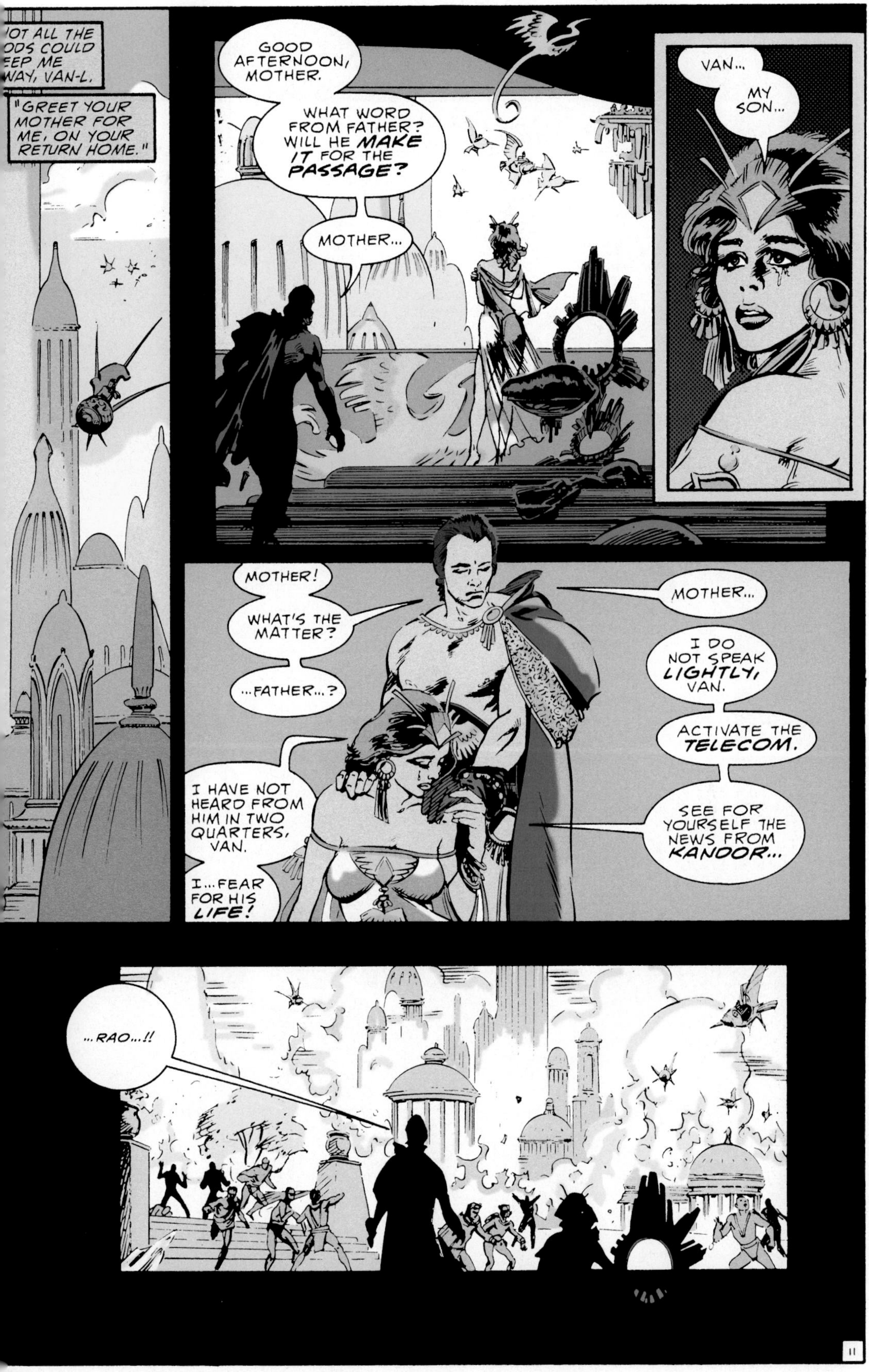

'OT ALL THE
ODS COULD
EEP ME
WAY, VAN-L.
"GREET YOUR MOTHER FOR ME, ON YOUR RETURN HOME."
GOOD AFTERNOON, MOTHER.
WHAT WORD FROM FATHER? WILL HE MAKE IT FOR THE PASSAGE?
MOTHER...
VAN...
MY SON...
MOTHER!
WHAT'S THE MATTER?
...FATHER...?
I HAVE NOT HEARD FROM HIM IN TWO QUARTERS, VAN.
I...FEAR FOR HIS LIFE!
MOTHER...
I DO NOT SPEAK LIGHTLY, VAN.
ACTIVATE THE TELECOM.
SEE FOR YOURSELF THE NEWS FROM KANDOR...
...RAO...!!
11

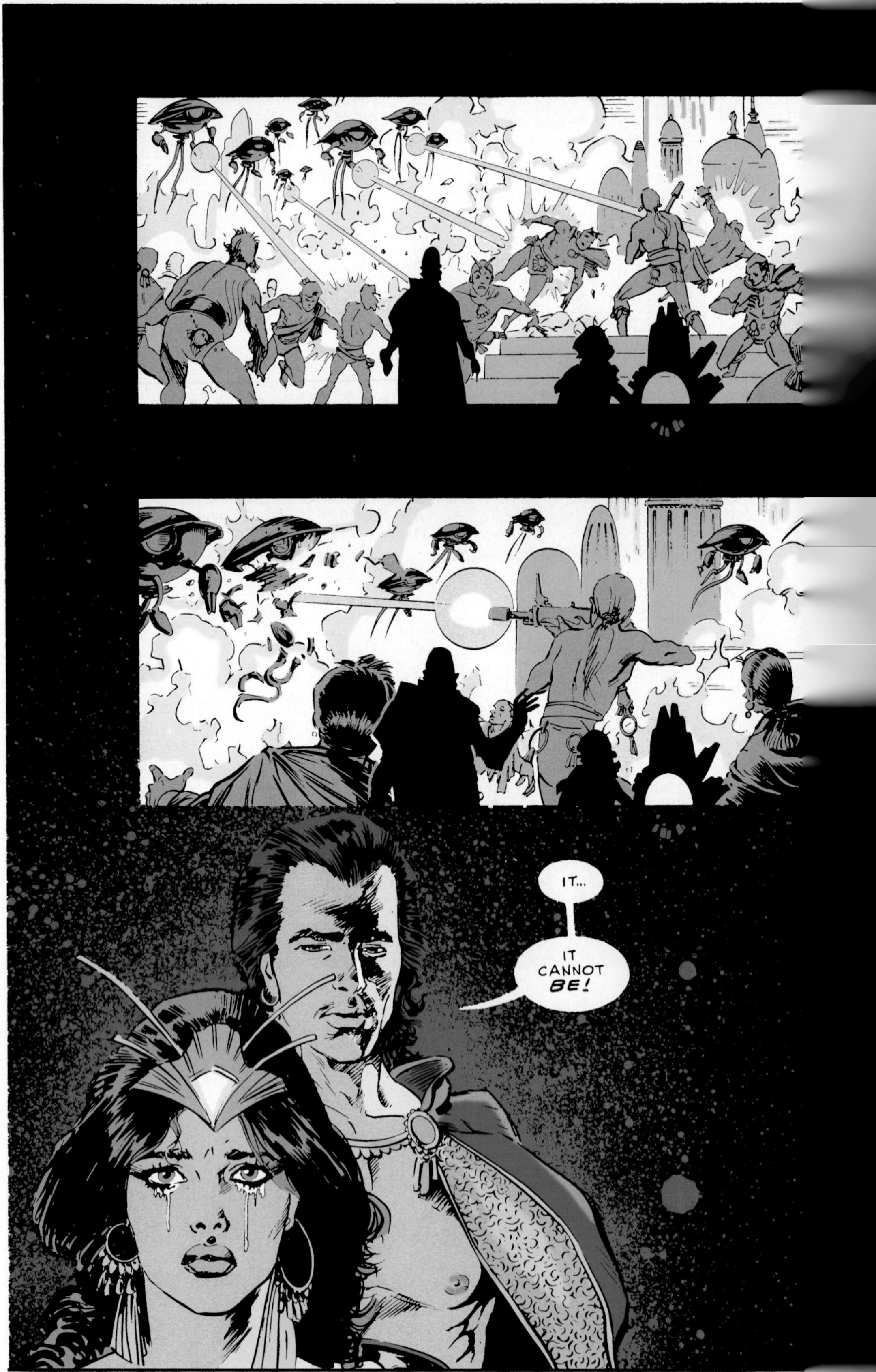
IT...
IT CANNOT BE!

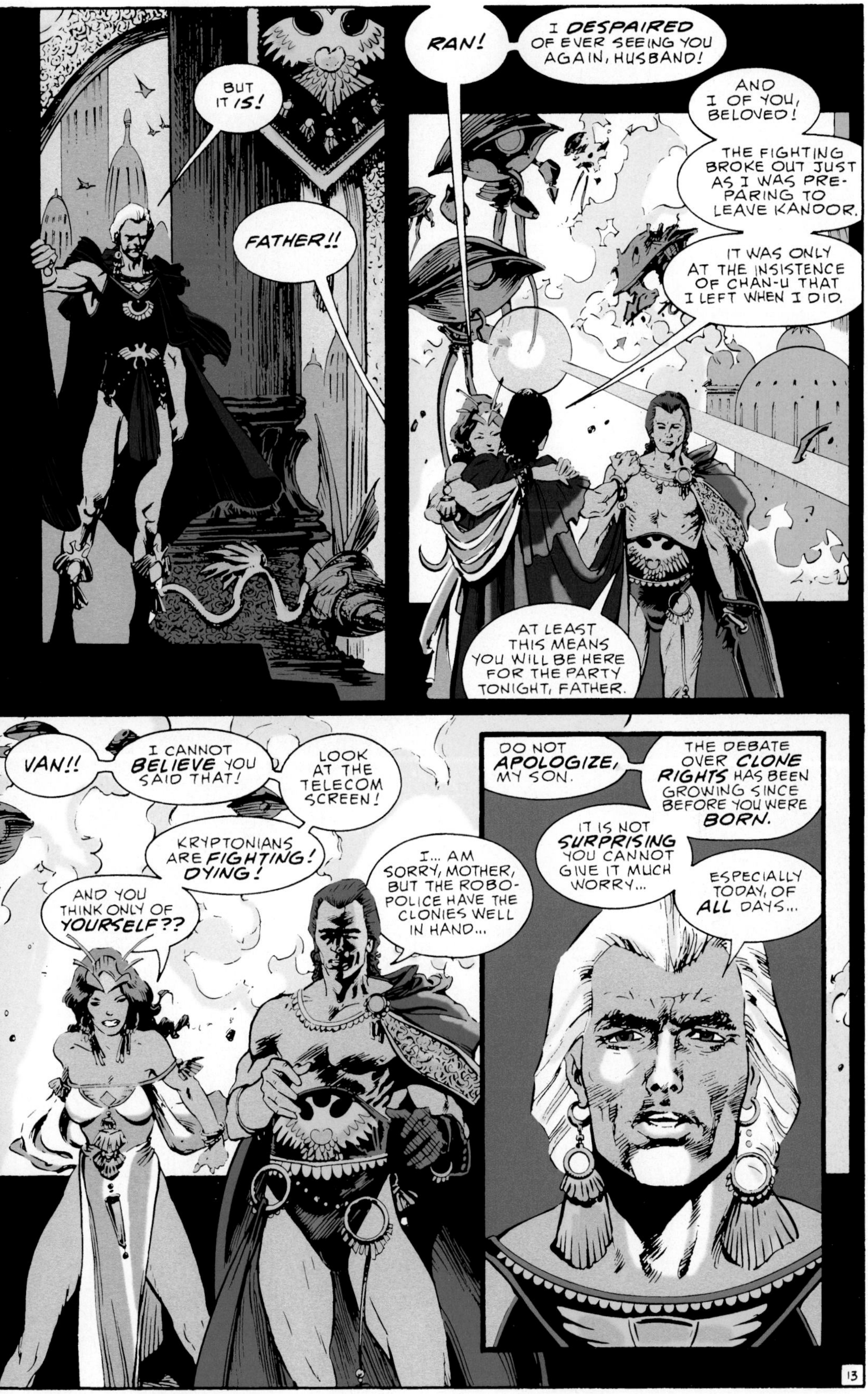
BUT IT IS!
FATHER!!
RAN!
I DESPAIRED OF EVER SEEING YOU AGAIN, HUSBAND!
AND I OF YOU, BELOVED!
THE FIGHTING BROKE OUT JUST AS I WAS PRE-PARING TO LEAVE KANDOR.
IT WAS ONLY AT THE INSISTENCE OF CHAN-U THAT I LEFT WHEN I DID.
AT LEAST THIS MEANS YOU WILL BE HERE FOR THE PARTY TONIGHT, FATHER.
VAN!!
I CANNOT BELIEVE YOU SAID THAT!
LOOK AT THE TELECOM SCREEN!
KRYPTONIANS ARE FIGHTING! DYING!
AND YOU THINK ONLY OF YOURSELF??
I... AM SORRY, MOTHER, BUT THE ROBO-POLICE HAVE THE CLONIES WELL IN HAND...
DO NOT APOLOGIZE, MY SON.
THE DEBATE OVER CLONE RIGHTS HAS BEEN GROWING SINCE BEFORE YOU WERE BORN.
IT IS NOT SURPRISING YOU CANNOT GIVE IT MUCH WORRY...
ESPECIALLY TODAY, OF ALL DAYS...
13

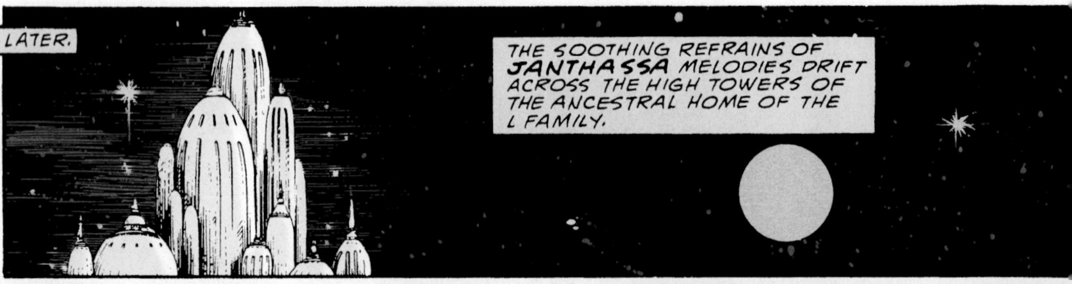
LATER.
THE SOOTHING REFRAINS OF JANTHASSA MELODIES DRIFT ACROSS THE HIGH TOWERS OF THE ANCESTRAL HOME OF THE L FAMILY.

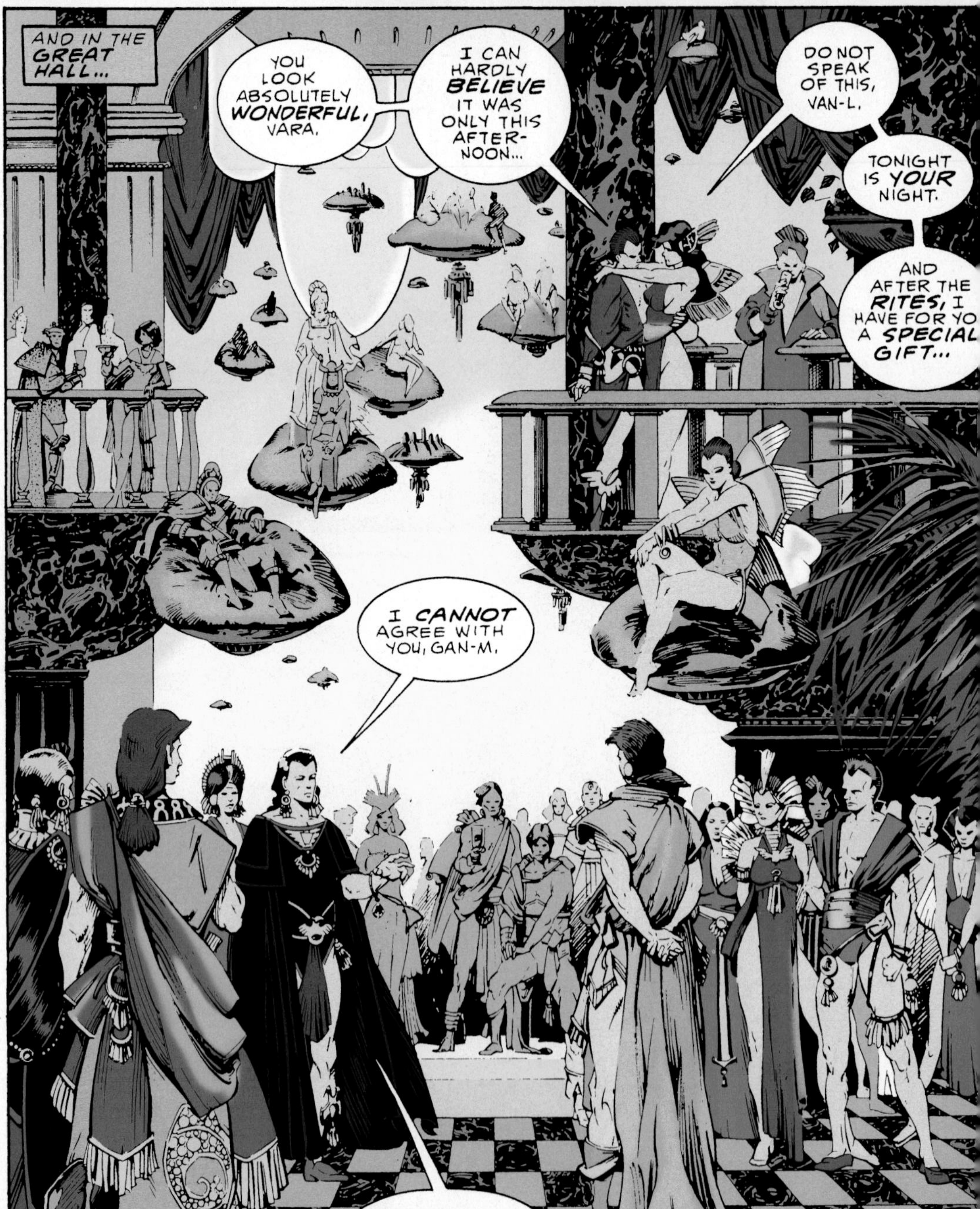
AND IN THE GREAT HALL...
YOU LOOK ABSOLUTELY WONDERFUL, VARA.
I CAN HARDLY BELIEVE IT WAS ONLY THIS AFTER-NOON...
DO NOT SPEAK OF THIS, VAN-L.
TONIGHT IS YOUR NIGHT.
AND AFTER THE RITES, I HAVE FOR YO A SPECIAL GIFT...
I CANNOT AGREE WITH YOU, GAN-M.
THERE IS MUCH MORE AT ISSUE HERE THAN THE RIGHTS OF MINDLESS CLONES.

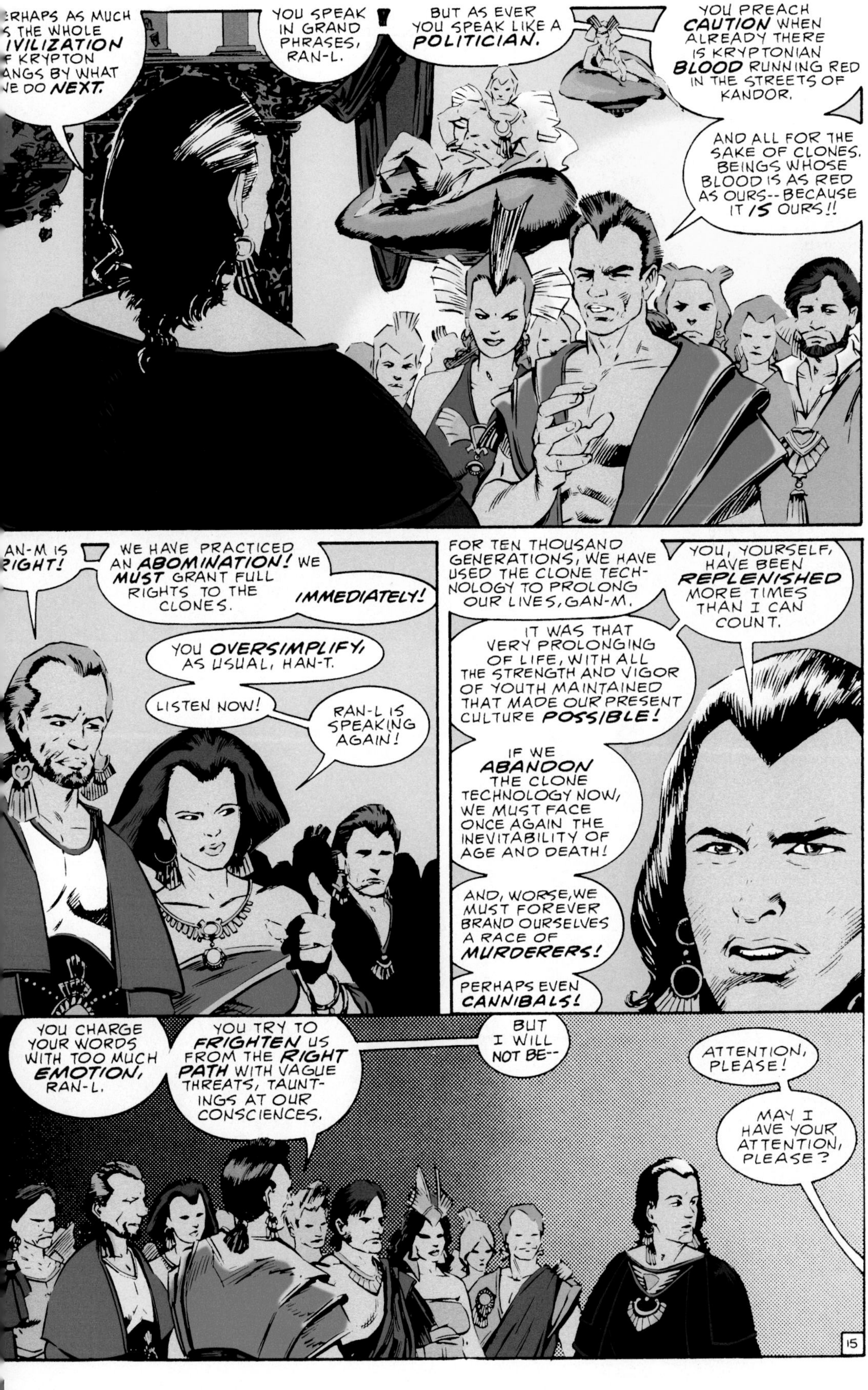
ERHAPS AS MUCH S THE WHOLE IVILIZATION F KRYPTON ANGS BY WHAT E DO NEXT.
YOU SPEAK IN GRAND PHRASES, RAN-L.
BUT AS EVER YOU SPEAK LIKE A POLITICIAN.
YOU PREACH CAUTION WHEN ALREADY THERE IS KRYPTONIAN BLOOD RUNNING RED IN THE STREETS OF KANDOR.
AND ALL FOR THE SAKE OF CLONES. BEINGS WHOSE BLOOD IS AS RED AS OURS--BECAUSE IT IS OURS!!
AN-M IS RIGHT!
WE HAVE PRACTICED AN ABOMINATION! WE MUST GRANT FULL RIGHTS TO THE CLONES.
IMMEDIATELY!
YOU OVERSIMPLIFY, AS USUAL, HAN-T.
LISTEN NOW!
RAN-L IS SPEAKING AGAIN!
FOR TEN THOUSAND GENERATIONS, WE HAVE USED THE CLONE TECHNOLOGY TO PROLONG OUR LIVES, GAN-M.
YOU, YOURSELF, HAVE BEEN REPLENISHED MORE TIMES THAN I CAN COUNT.
IT WAS THAT VERY PROLONGING OF LIFE, WITH ALL THE STRENGTH AND VIGOR OF YOUTH MAINTAINED THAT MADE OUR PRESENT CULTURE POSSIBLE!
IF WE ABANDON THE CLONE TECHNOLOGY NOW, WE MUST FACE ONCE AGAIN THE INEVITABILITY OF AGE AND DEATH!
AND, WORSE, WE MUST FOREVER BRAND OURSELVES A RACE OF MURDERERS!
PERHAPS EVEN CANNIBALS!
YOU CHARGE YOUR WORDS WITH TOO MUCH EMOTION, RAN-L.
YOU TRY TO FRIGHTEN US FROM THE RIGHT PATH WITH VAGUE THREATS, TAUNTINGS AT OUR CONSCIENCES.
BUT I WILL NOT BE--
ATTENTION, PLEASE!
MAY I HAVE YOUR ATTENTION, PLEASE?
15

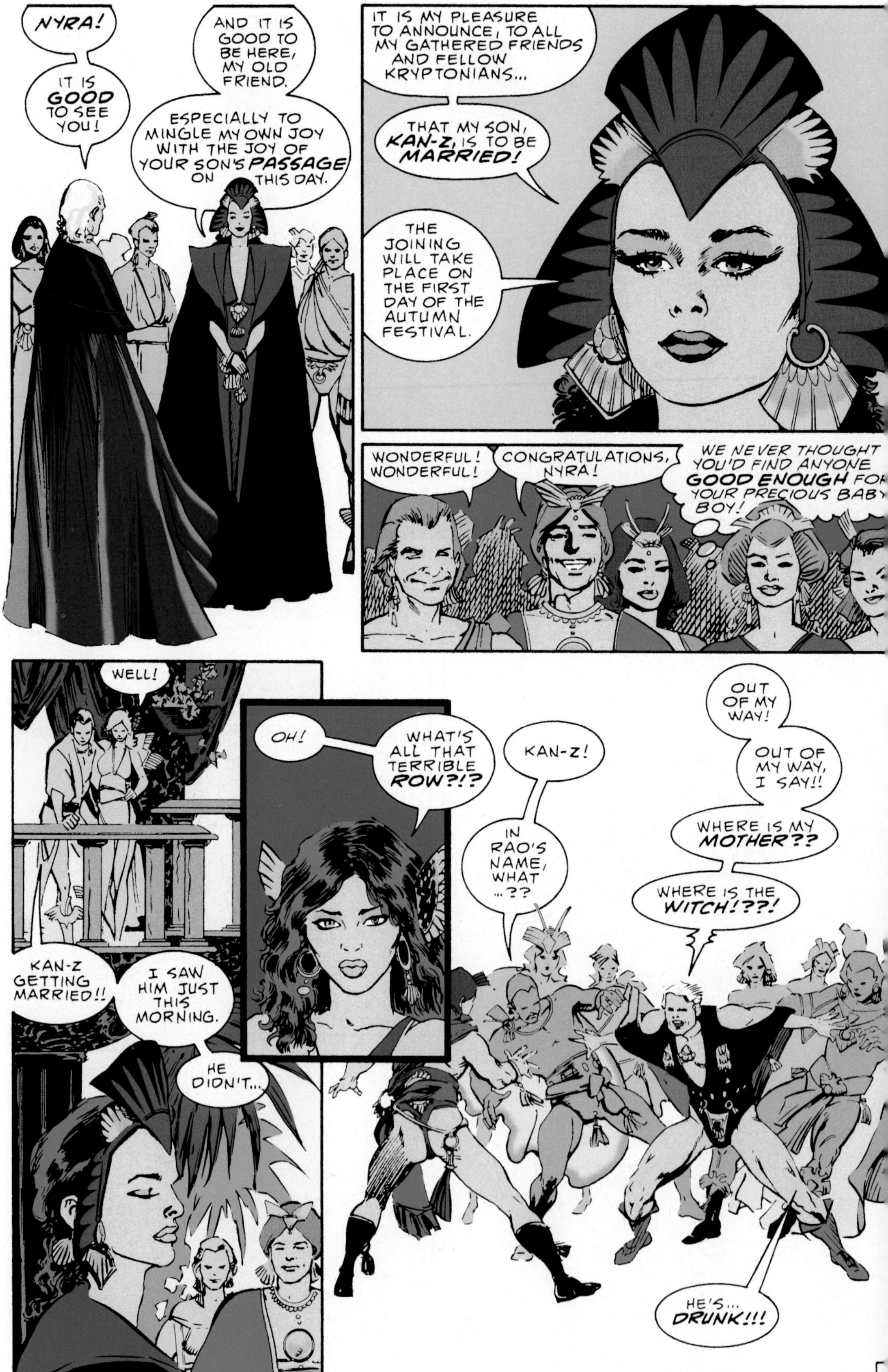
NYRA!
IT IS GOOD TO SEE YOU!
AND IT IS GOOD TO BE HERE, MY OLD FRIEND.
ESPECIALLY TO MINGLE MY OWN JOY WITH THE JOY OF YOUR SON'S PASSAGE ON THIS DAY.
IT IS MY PLEASURE TO ANNOUNCE, TO ALL MY GATHERED FRIENDS AND FELLOW KRYPTONIANS...
THAT MY SON, KAN-Z, IS TO BE MARRIED!
THE JOINING WILL TAKE PLACE ON THE FIRST DAY OF THE AUTUMN FESTIVAL.
WONDERFUL! WONDERFUL!
CONGRATULATIONS, NYRA!
WE NEVER THOUGHT YOU'D FIND ANYONE GOOD ENOUGH FOR YOUR PRECIOUS BABY BOY!
WELL!
KAN-Z GETTING MARRIED!!
I SAW HIM JUST THIS MORNING.
HE DIDN'T...
OH!
WHAT'S ALL THAT TERRIBLE ROW?!?
KAN-Z!
IN RAO'S NAME, WHAT ...??
OUT OF MY WAY!
OUT OF MY WAY, I SAY!!
WHERE IS MY MOTHER??
WHERE IS THE WITCH!??!
HE'S... DRUNK!!!

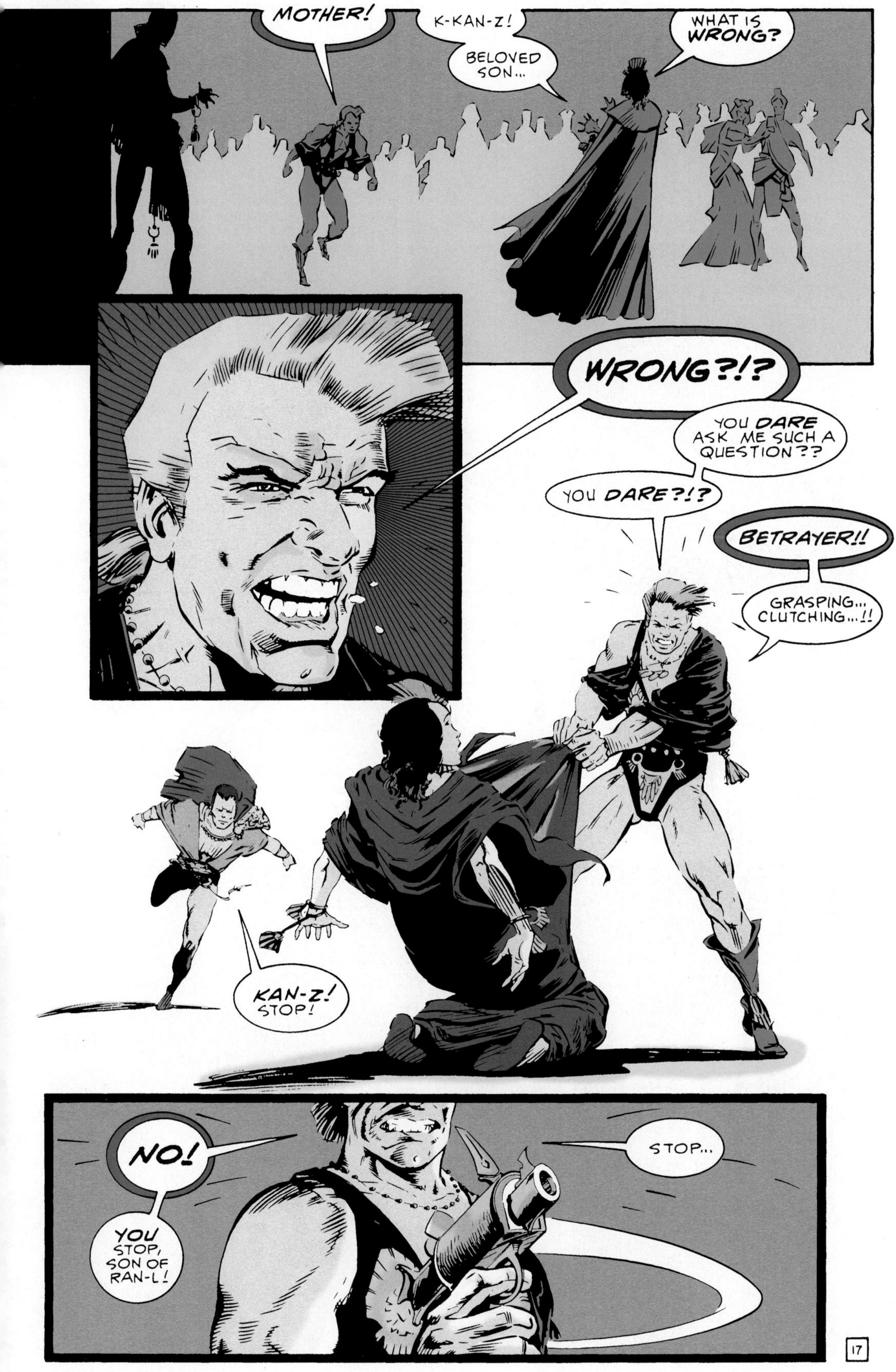
MOTHER!
K-KAN-Z!
BELOVED SON...
WHAT IS WRONG?
WRONG?!?
YOU DARE ASK ME SUCH A QUESTION??
YOU DARE?!?
BETRAYER!!
GRASPING... CLUTCHING...!!
KAN-Z! STOP!
NO!
YOU STOP, SON OF RAN-L!
STOP...
17

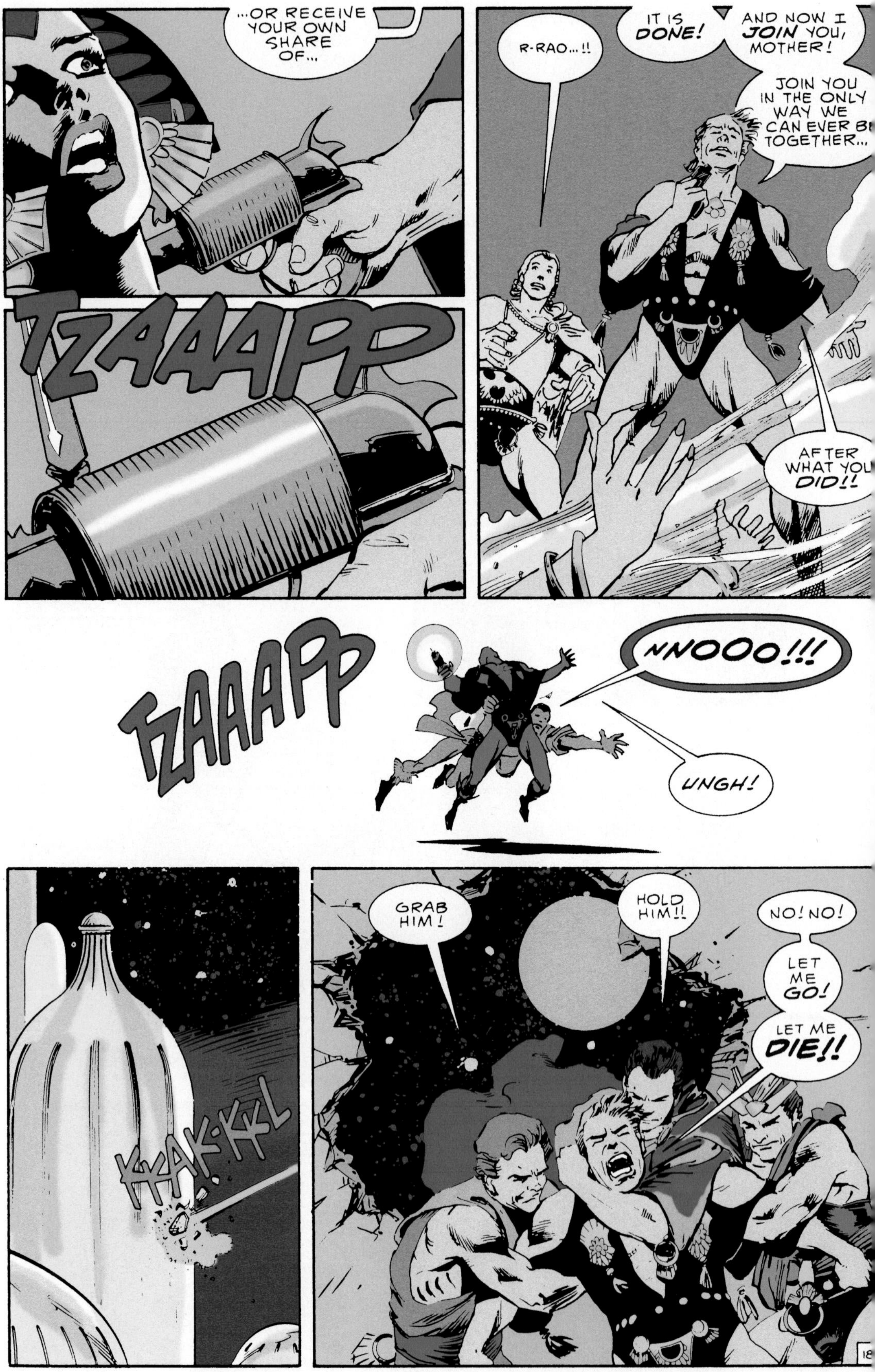
...OR RECEIVE YOUR OWN SHARE OF...
TZAAAPP
R-RAO...!!
IT IS DONE!
AND NOW I JOIN YOU, MOTHER!
JOIN YOU IN THE ONLY WAY WE CAN EVER B TOGETHER...
AFTER WHAT YOU DID!!
TZAAAPP
NNOOO!!!
UNGH!
KKAK-KKL
GRAB HIM!
HOLD HIM!!
NO! NO!
LET ME GO!
LET ME DIE!!

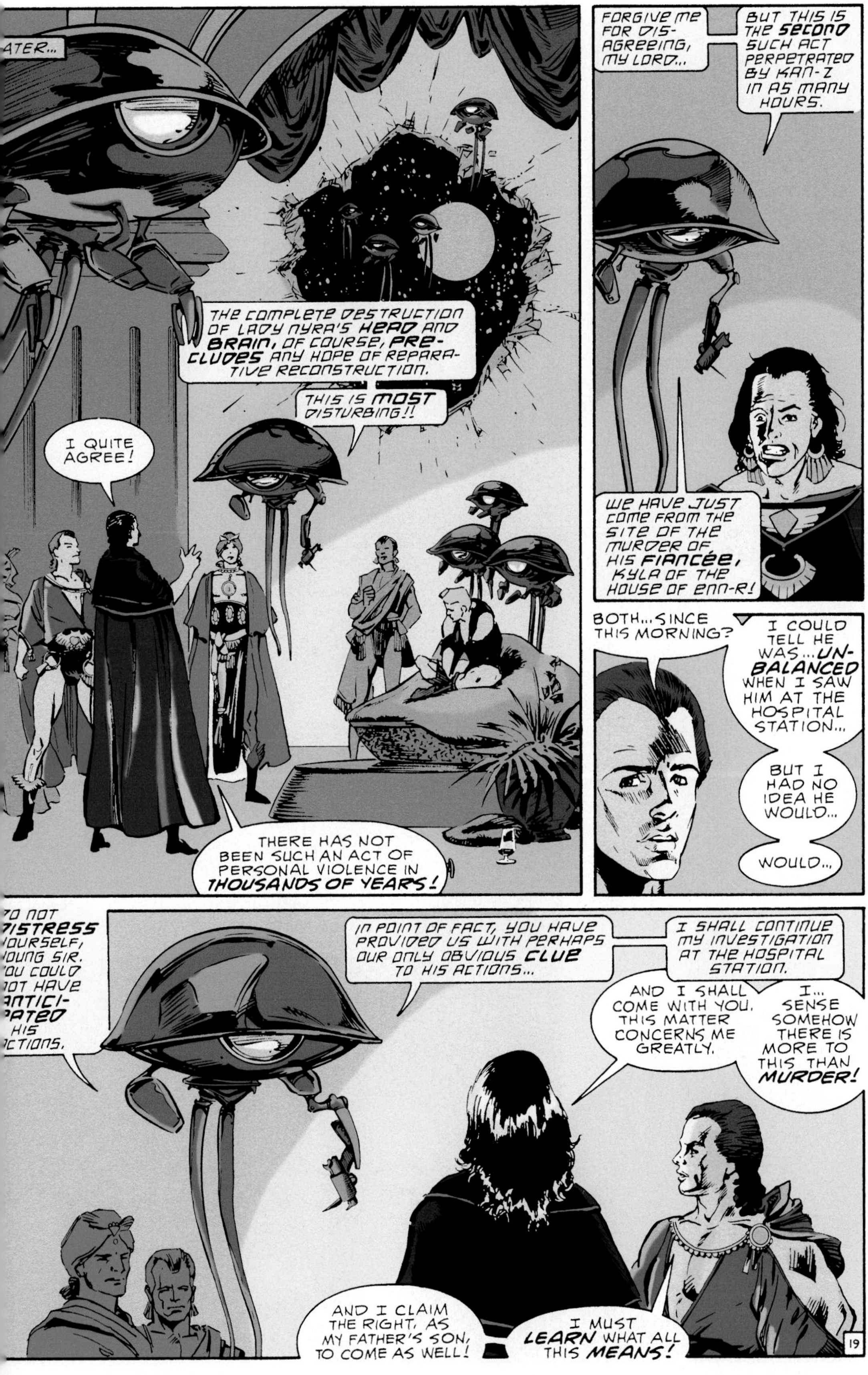

ATER...
THE COMPLETE DESTRUCTION OF LADY NYRA'S HEAD AND BRAIN, OF COURSE, PRE-CLUDES ANY HOPE OF REPARA-TIVE RECONSTRUCTION.
THIS IS MOST DISTURBING!!
I QUITE AGREE!
THERE HAS NOT BEEN SUCH AN ACT OF PERSONAL VIOLENCE IN THOUSANDS OF YEARS!
FORGIVE ME FOR DIS-AGREEING, MY LORD...
BUT THIS IS THE SECOND SUCH ACT PERPETRATED BY KAN-Z IN AS MANY HOURS.
WE HAVE JUST COME FROM THE SITE OF THE MURDER OF HIS FIANCÉE, KYLA OF THE HOUSE OF ENN-R!
BOTH...SINCE THIS MORNING?
I COULD TELL HE WAS...UN-BALANCED WHEN I SAW HIM AT THE HOSPITAL STATION...
BUT I HAD NO IDEA HE WOULD...
WOULD...
DO NOT DISTRESS YOURSELF, YOUNG SIR. YOU COULD NOT HAVE ANTICI-PATED HIS ACTIONS.
IN POINT OF FACT, YOU HAVE PROVIDED US WITH PERHAPS OUR ONLY OBVIOUS CLUE TO HIS ACTIONS...
I SHALL CONTINUE MY INVESTIGATION AT THE HOSPITAL STATION.
AND I SHALL COME WITH YOU. THIS MATTER CONCERNS ME GREATLY.
I... SENSE SOMEHOW THERE IS MORE TO THIS THAN MURDER!
AND I CLAIM THE RIGHT, AS MY FATHER'S SON, TO COME AS WELL!
I MUST LEARN WHAT ALL THIS MEANS!
19

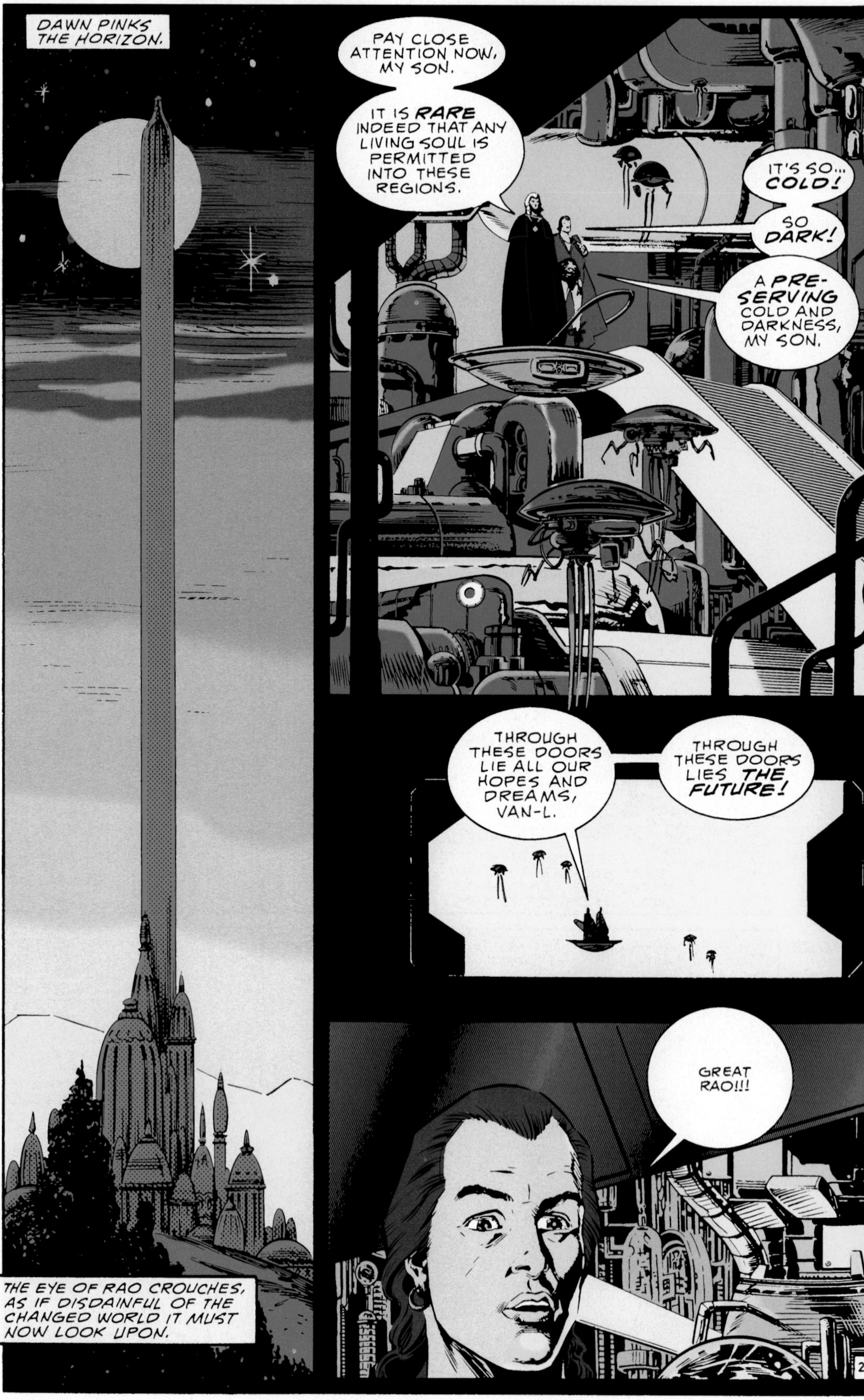
DAWN PINKS THE HORIZON.
THE EYE OF RAO CROUCHES, AS IF DISDAINFUL OF THE CHANGED WORLD IT MUST NOW LOOK UPON.
PAY CLOSE ATTENTION NOW, MY SON.
IT IS RARE INDEED THAT ANY LIVING SOUL IS PERMITTED INTO THESE REGIONS.
IT'S SO... COLD!
SO DARK!
A PRE-SERVING COLD AND DARKNESS, MY SON.
THROUGH THESE DOORS LIE ALL OUR HOPES AND DREAMS, VAN-L.
THROUGH THESE DOORS LIES THE FUTURE!
GREAT RAO!!!
20

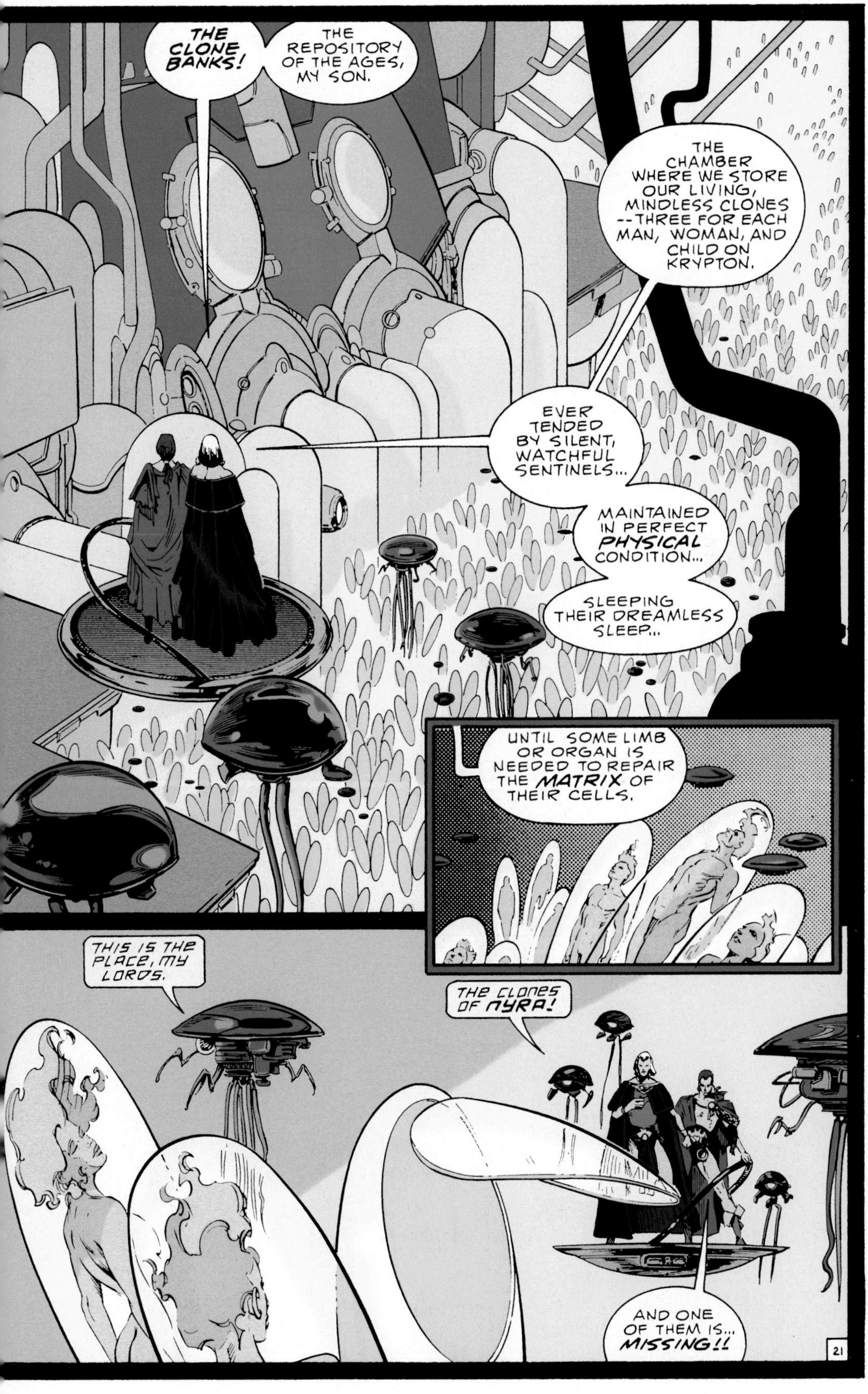
THE CLONE BANKS!
THE REPOSITORY OF THE AGES, MY SON.
THE CHAMBER WHERE WE STORE OUR LIVING, MINDLESS CLONES --THREE FOR EACH MAN, WOMAN, AND CHILD ON KRYPTON.
EVER TENDED BY SILENT, WATCHFUL SENTINELS...
MAINTAINED IN PERFECT *PHYSICAL* CONDITION...
SLEEPING THEIR DREAMLESS SLEEP...
UNTIL SOME LIMB OR ORGAN IS NEEDED TO REPAIR THE *MATRIX* OF THEIR CELLS.
THIS IS THE PLACE, MY LORDS.
THE CLONES OF NYRA!
AND ONE OF THEM IS... *MISSING!!*
21

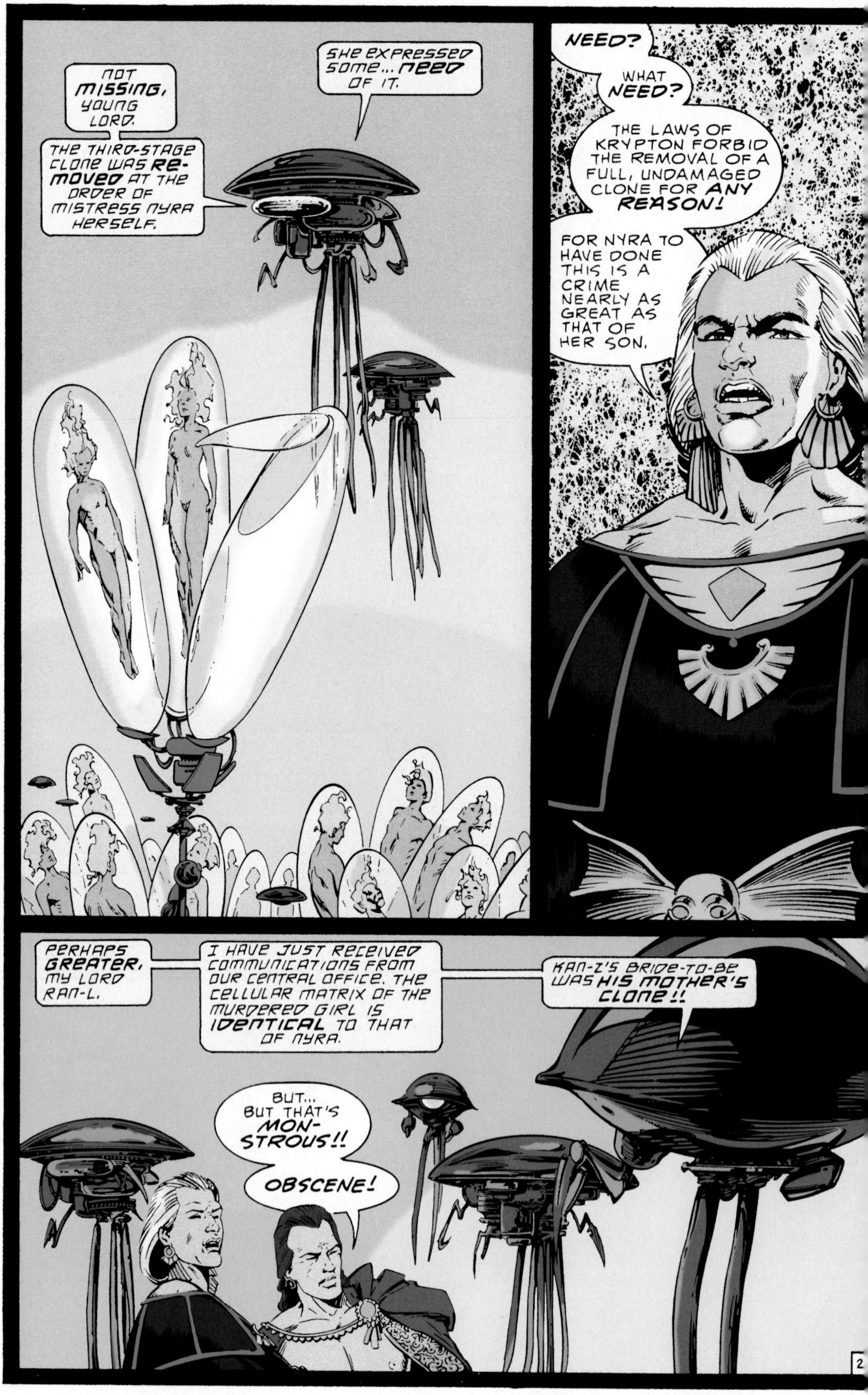
NOT MISSING, YOUNG LORD.
THE THIRD-STAGE CLONE WAS RE-MOVED AT THE ORDER OF MISTRESS NYRA HERSELF.
SHE EXPRESSED SOME... NEED OF IT.
NEED?
WHAT NEED?
THE LAWS OF KRYPTON FORBID THE REMOVAL OF A FULL, UNDAMAGED CLONE FOR ANY REASON!
FOR NYRA TO HAVE DONE THIS IS A CRIME NEARLY AS GREAT AS THAT OF HER SON.
PERHAPS GREATER, MY LORD RAN-L.
I HAVE JUST RECEIVED COMMUNICATIONS FROM OUR CENTRAL OFFICE. THE CELLULAR MATRIX OF THE MURDERED GIRL IS IDENTICAL TO THAT OF NYRA.
KAN-Z'S BRIDE-TO-BE WAS HIS MOTHER'S CLONE!!
BUT... BUT THAT'S MON-STROUS!!
OBSCENE!
2

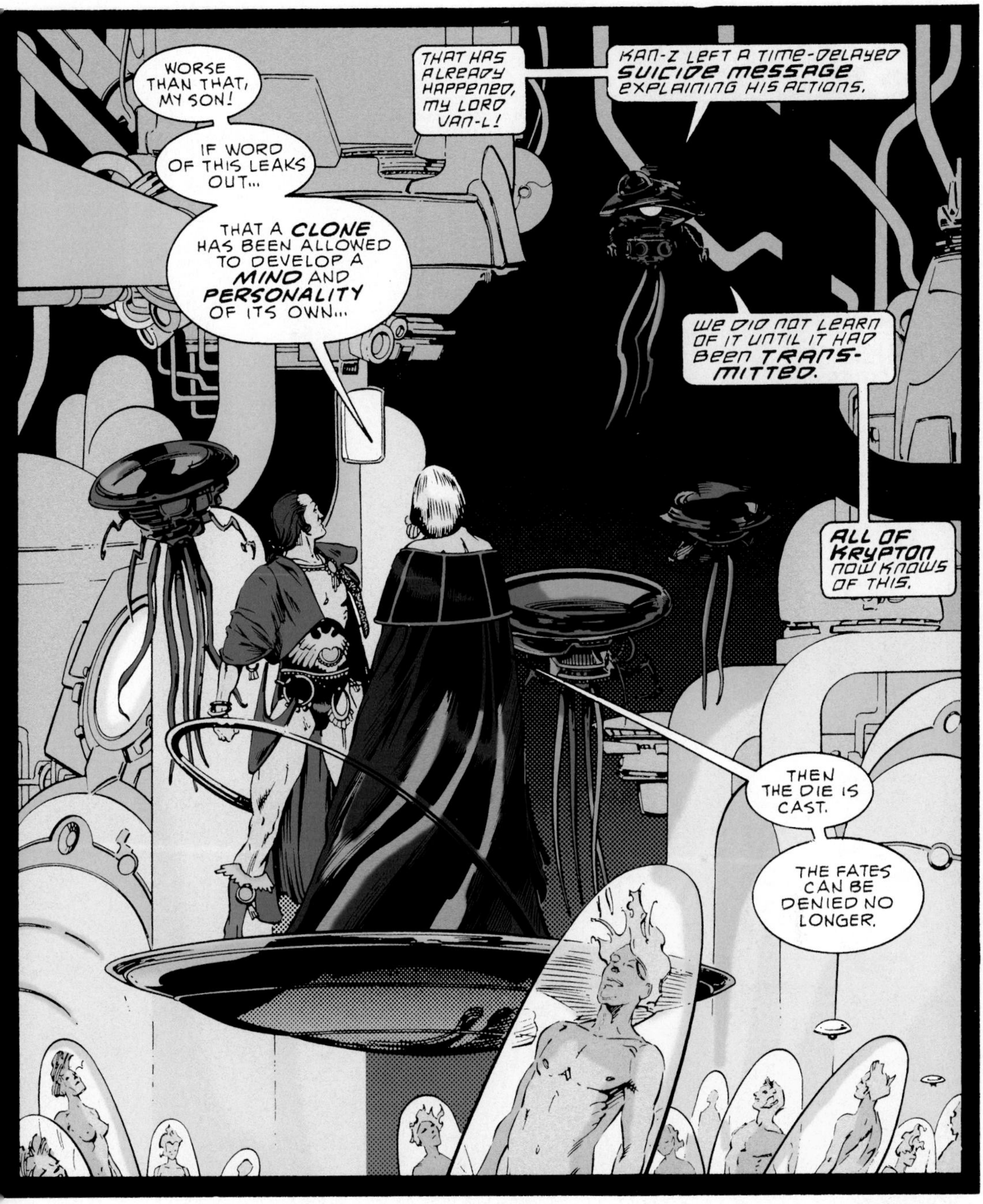
WORSE THAN THAT, MY SON!
IF WORD OF THIS LEAKS OUT...
THAT A **CLONE** HAS BEEN ALLOWED TO DEVELOP A **MIND** AND **PERSONALITY** OF ITS OWN...
THAT HAS ALREADY HAPPENED, MY LORD VAN-L!
KAN-Z LEFT A TIME-DELAYED **SUICIDE MESSAGE** EXPLAINING HIS ACTIONS.
WE DID NOT LEARN OF IT UNTIL IT HAD BEEN **TRANSMITTED.**
ALL OF KRYPTON NOW KNOWS OF THIS.
THEN THE DIE IS CAST.
THE FATES CAN BE DENIED NO LONGER.
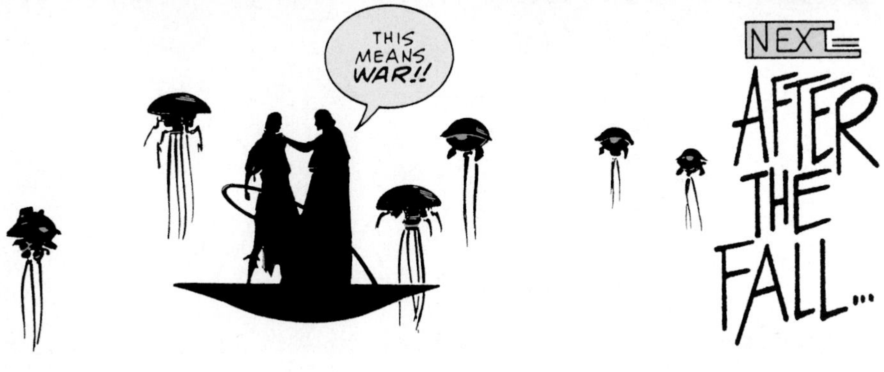
THIS MEANS **WAR!!**
NEXT
AFTER THE FALL...

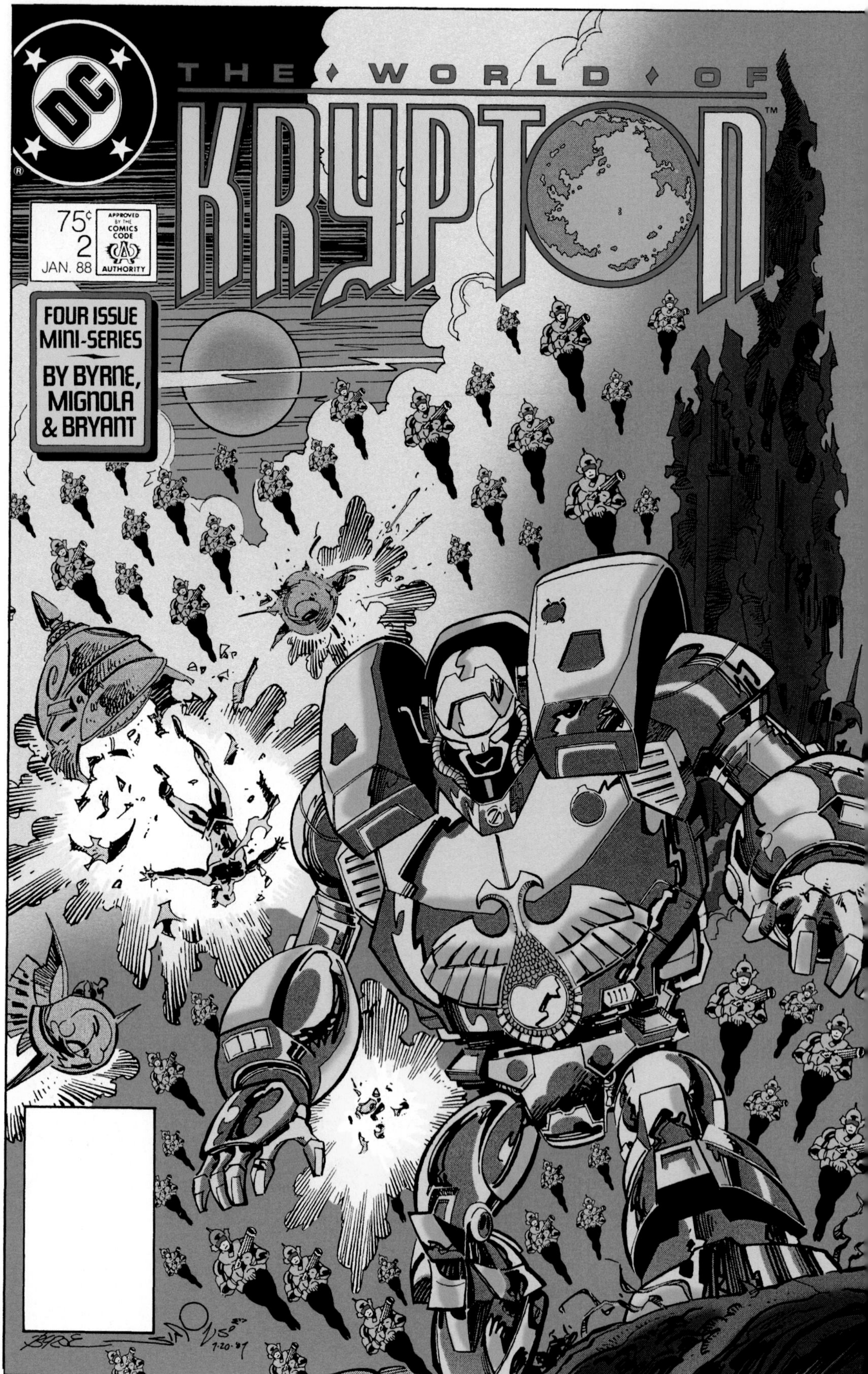
DC
THE WORLD OF
KRYPTON
75¢
2
JAN. 88
APPROVED BY THE COMICS CODE AUTHORITY
FOUR ISSUE MINI-SERIES
BY BYRNE, MIGNOLA & BRYANT

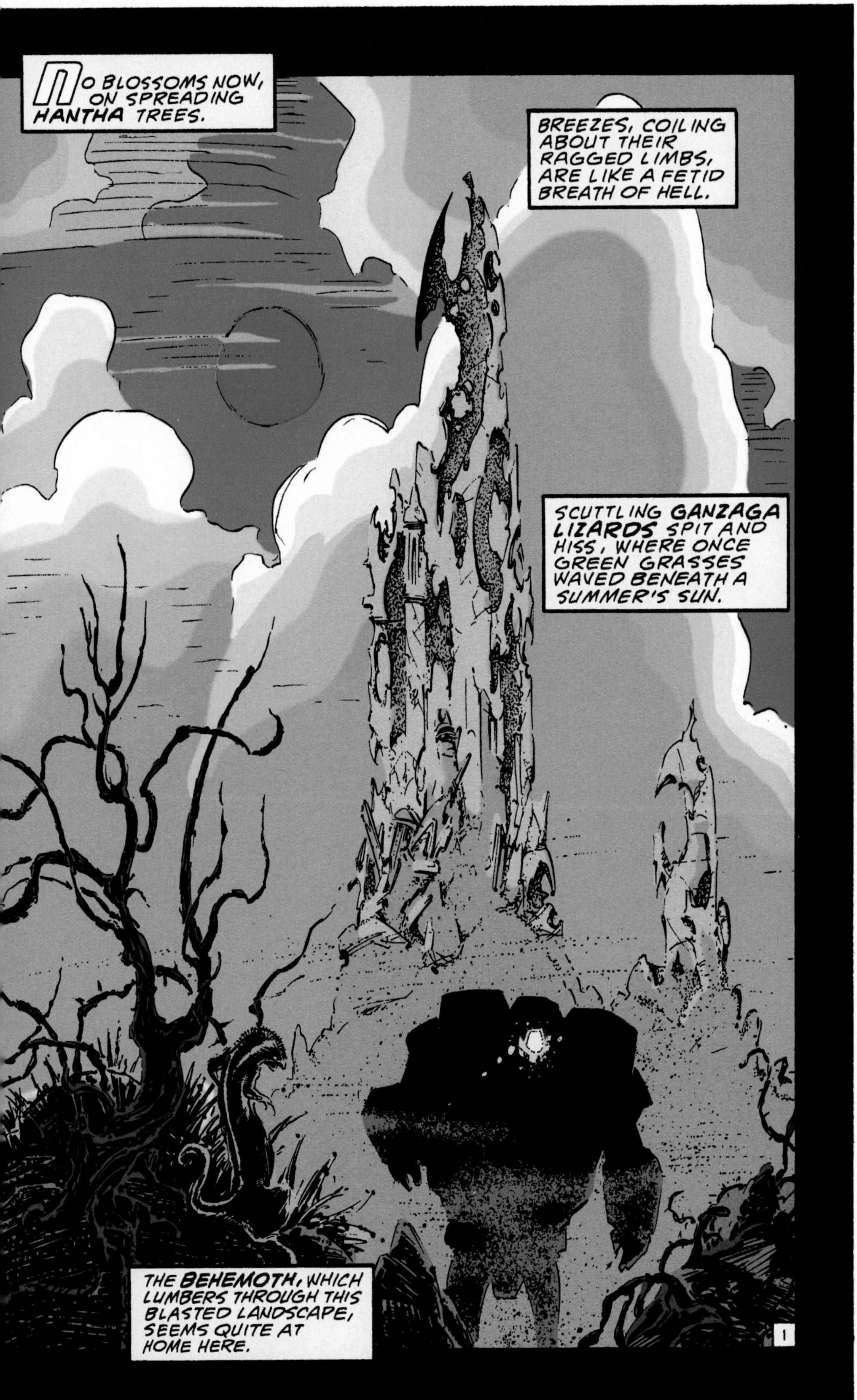
NO BLOSSOMS NOW, ON SPREADING HANTHA TREES.
BREEZES, COILING ABOUT THEIR RAGGED LIMBS, ARE LIKE A FETID BREATH OF HELL.
SCUTTLING GANZAGA LIZARDS SPIT AND HISS, WHERE ONCE GREEN GRASSES WAVED BENEATH A SUMMER'S SUN.
THE BEHEMOTH, WHICH LUMBERS THROUGH THIS BLASTED LANDSCAPE, SEEMS QUITE AT HOME HERE.
1

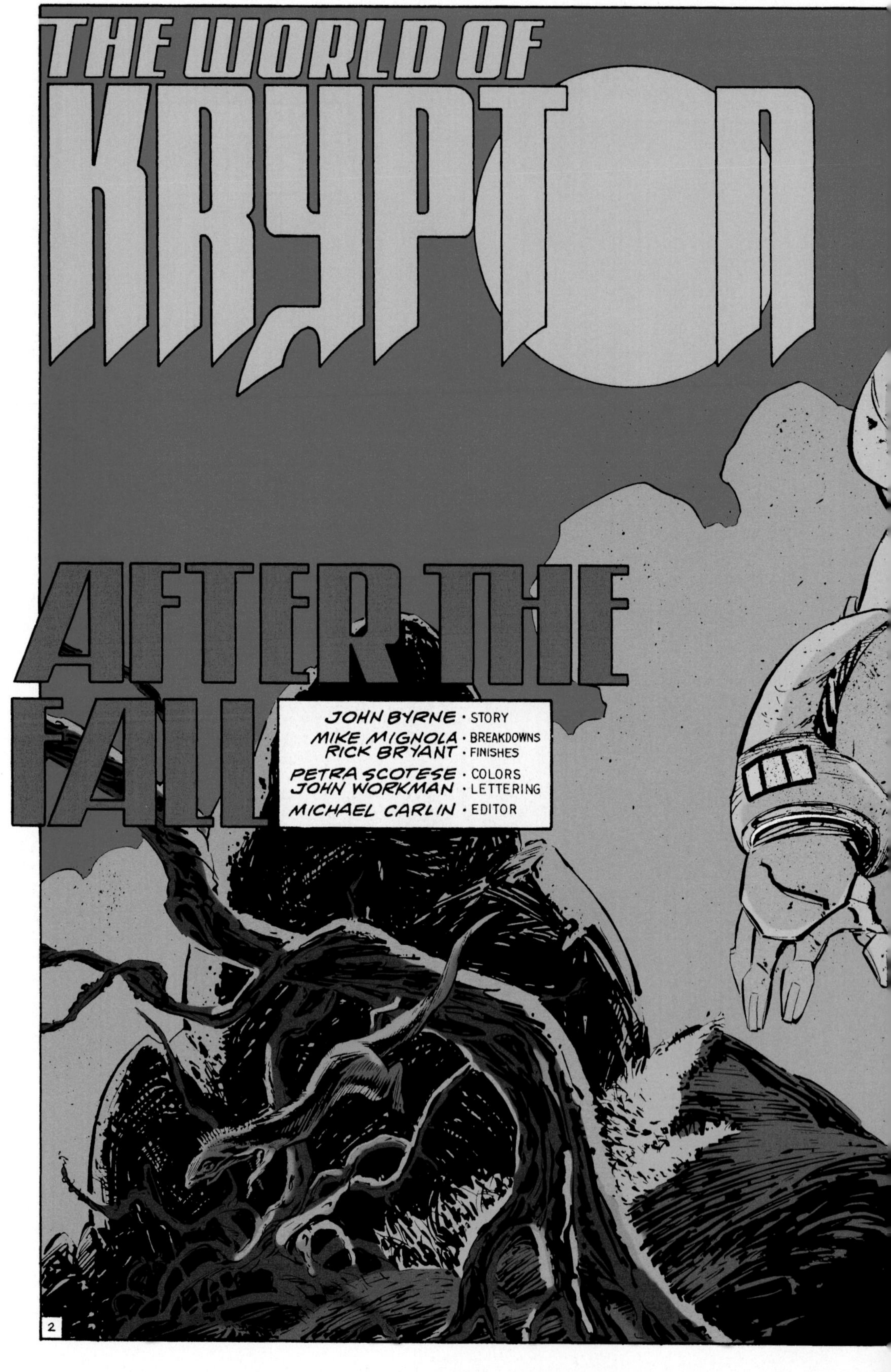
THE WORLD OF
KRYPTON
AFTER THE FALL
JOHN BYRNE · STORY
MIKE MIGNOLA · BREAKDOWNS
RICK BRYANT · FINISHES
PETRA SCOTESE · COLORS
JOHN WORKMAN · LETTERING
MICHAEL CARLIN · EDITOR
2

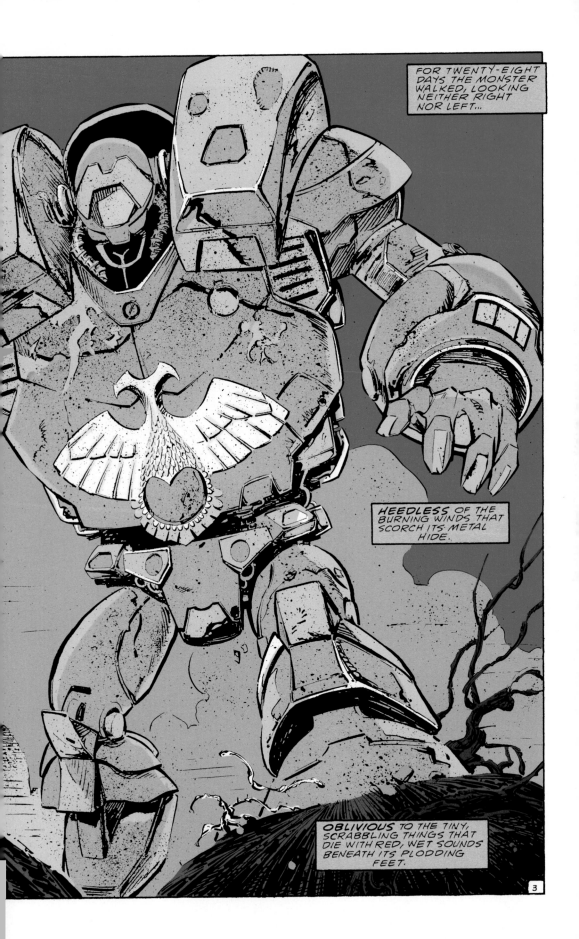

FOR TWENTY-EIGHT DAYS THE MONSTER WALKED, LOOKING NEITHER RIGHT NOR LEFT...

HEEDLESS OF THE BURNING WINDS THAT SCORCH ITS METAL HIDE.

OBLIVIOUS TO THE TINY, SCRABBLING THINGS THAT DIE WITH RED, WET SOUNDS BENEATH ITS PLODDING FEET.

3

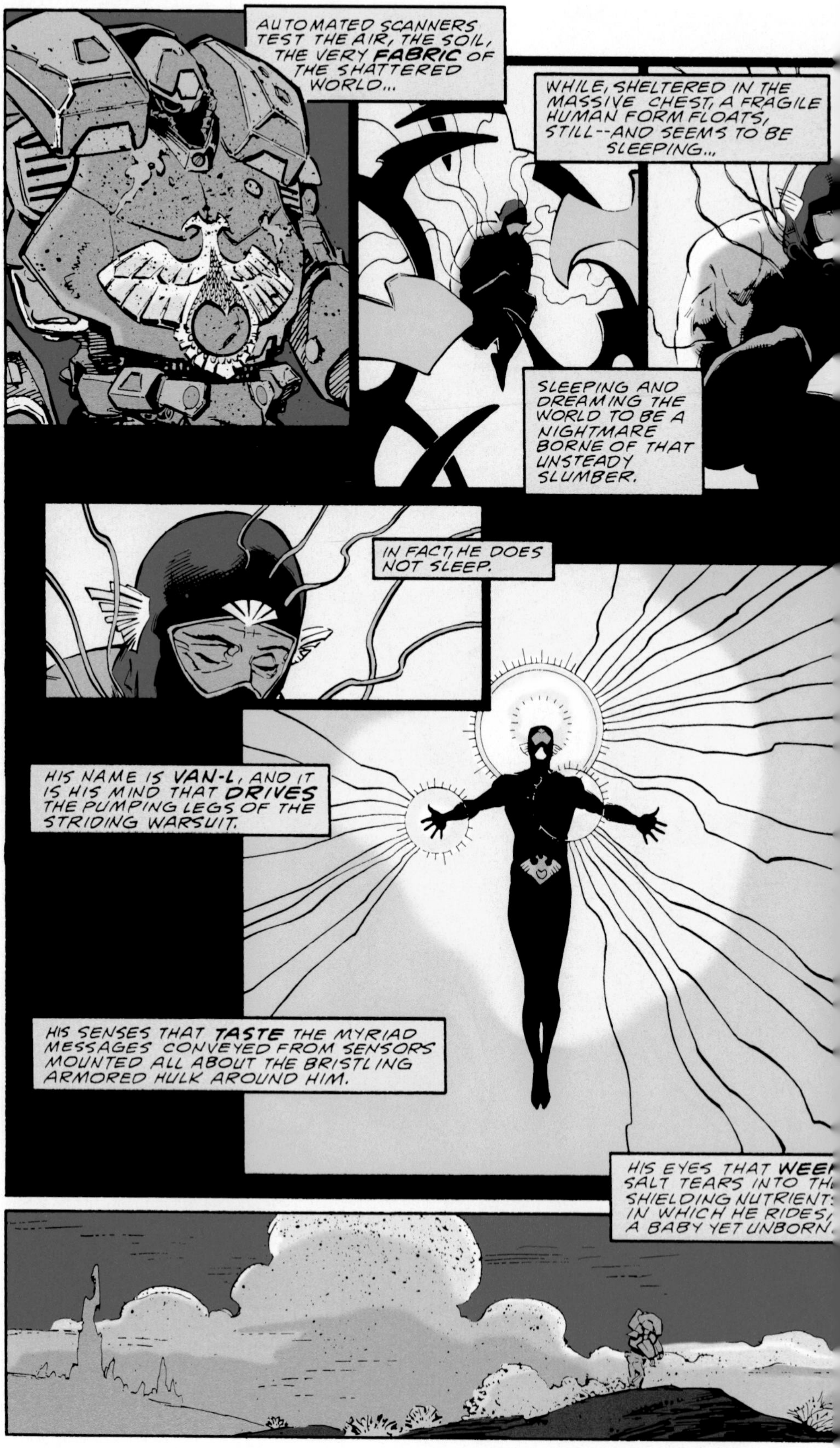
AUTOMATED SCANNERS TEST THE AIR, THE SOIL, THE VERY FABRIC OF THE SHATTERED WORLD...
WHILE, SHELTERED IN THE MASSIVE CHEST, A FRAGILE HUMAN FORM FLOATS, STILL--AND SEEMS TO BE SLEEPING...
SLEEPING AND DREAMING THE WORLD TO BE A NIGHTMARE BORNE OF THAT UNSTEADY SLUMBER.
IN FACT, HE DOES NOT SLEEP.
HIS NAME IS VAN-L, AND IT IS HIS MIND THAT DRIVES THE PUMPING LEGS OF THE STRIDING WARSUIT.
HIS SENSES THAT TASTE THE MYRIAD MESSAGES CONVEYED FROM SENSORS MOUNTED ALL ABOUT THE BRISTLING ARMORED HULK AROUND HIM.
HIS EYES THAT WEE SALT TEARS INTO TH SHIELDING NUTRIENT IN WHICH HE RIDES, A BABY YET UNBORN.

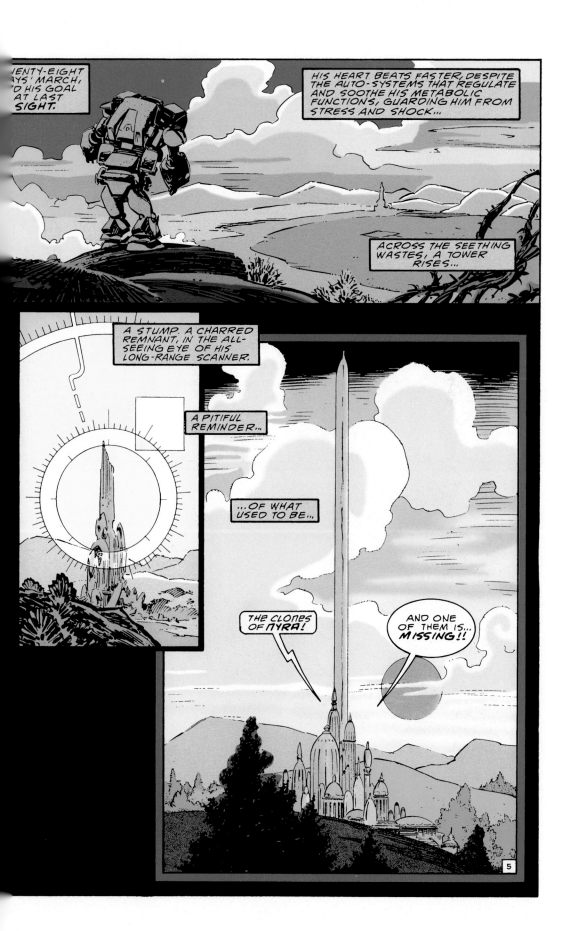

ENTY-EIGHT AYS' MARCH, D HIS GOAL AT LAST SIGHT.

HIS HEART BEATS FASTER, DESPITE THE AUTO-SYSTEMS THAT REGULATE AND SOOTHE HIS METABOLIC FUNCTIONS, GUARDING HIM FROM STRESS AND SHOCK...

ACROSS THE SEETHING WASTES, A TOWER RISES...

A STUMP. A CHARRED REMNANT, IN THE ALL-SEEING EYE OF HIS LONG-RANGE SCANNER.

A PITIFUL REMINDER...

...OF WHAT USED TO BE...

THE CLONES OF NYRA!

AND ONE OF THEM IS... MISSING!!

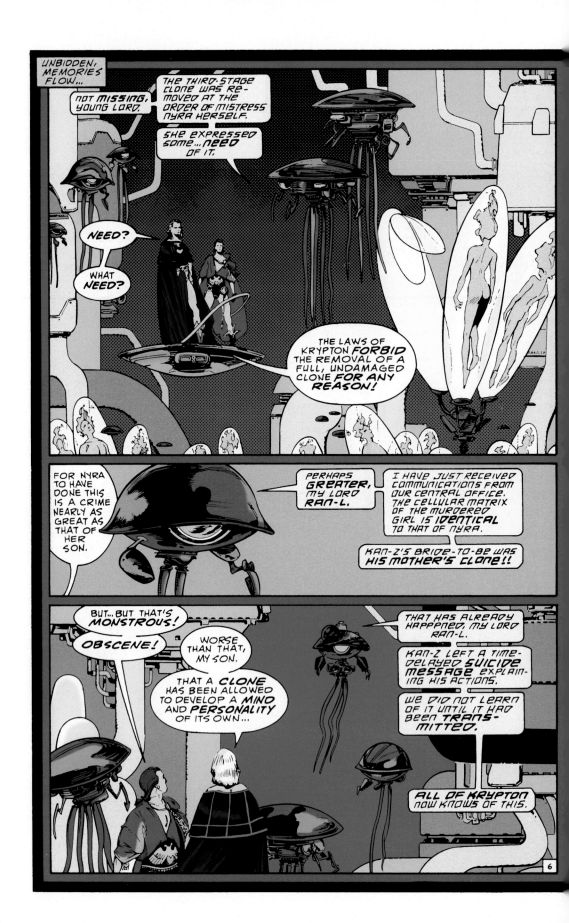

UNBIDDEN, MEMORIES FLOW...

NOT *MISSING,* YOUNG LORD.

THE *THIRD-STAGE* CLONE WAS RE-MOVED AT THE *ORDER* OF MISTRESS *NYRA* HERSELF.

SHE EXPRESSED SOME... *NEED* OF IT.

NEED?

WHAT *NEED?*

THE LAWS OF KRYPTON *FORBID* THE REMOVAL OF A FULL, UNDAMAGED CLONE *FOR ANY REASON!*

FOR NYRA TO HAVE DONE THIS IS A CRIME NEARLY AS GREAT AS THAT OF HER *SON.*

PERHAPS *GREATER,* MY LORD *RAN-L.*

I HAVE JUST RECEIVED COMMUNICATIONS FROM OUR CENTRAL OFFICE. THE CELLULAR MATRIX OF THE *MURDERED GIRL* IS *IDENTICAL* TO THAT OF NYRA.

KAN-Z'S BRIDE-TO-BE WAS *HIS MOTHER'S CLONE!!*

BUT... BUT THAT'S *MONSTROUS!*

OBSCENE!

WORSE THAN THAT, MY SON.

THAT A *CLONE* HAS BEEN ALLOWED TO DEVELOP A *MIND* AND *PERSONALITY* OF ITS OWN...

THAT HAS ALREADY *HAPPENED,* MY LORD RAN-L.

KAN-Z LEFT A TIME-DELAYED *SUICIDE MESSAGE* EXPLAIN-ING HIS ACTIONS.

WE DID NOT LEARN OF IT UNTIL IT HAD BEEN *TRANS-MITTED.*

ALL OF KRYPTON NOW KNOWS OF THIS.

6

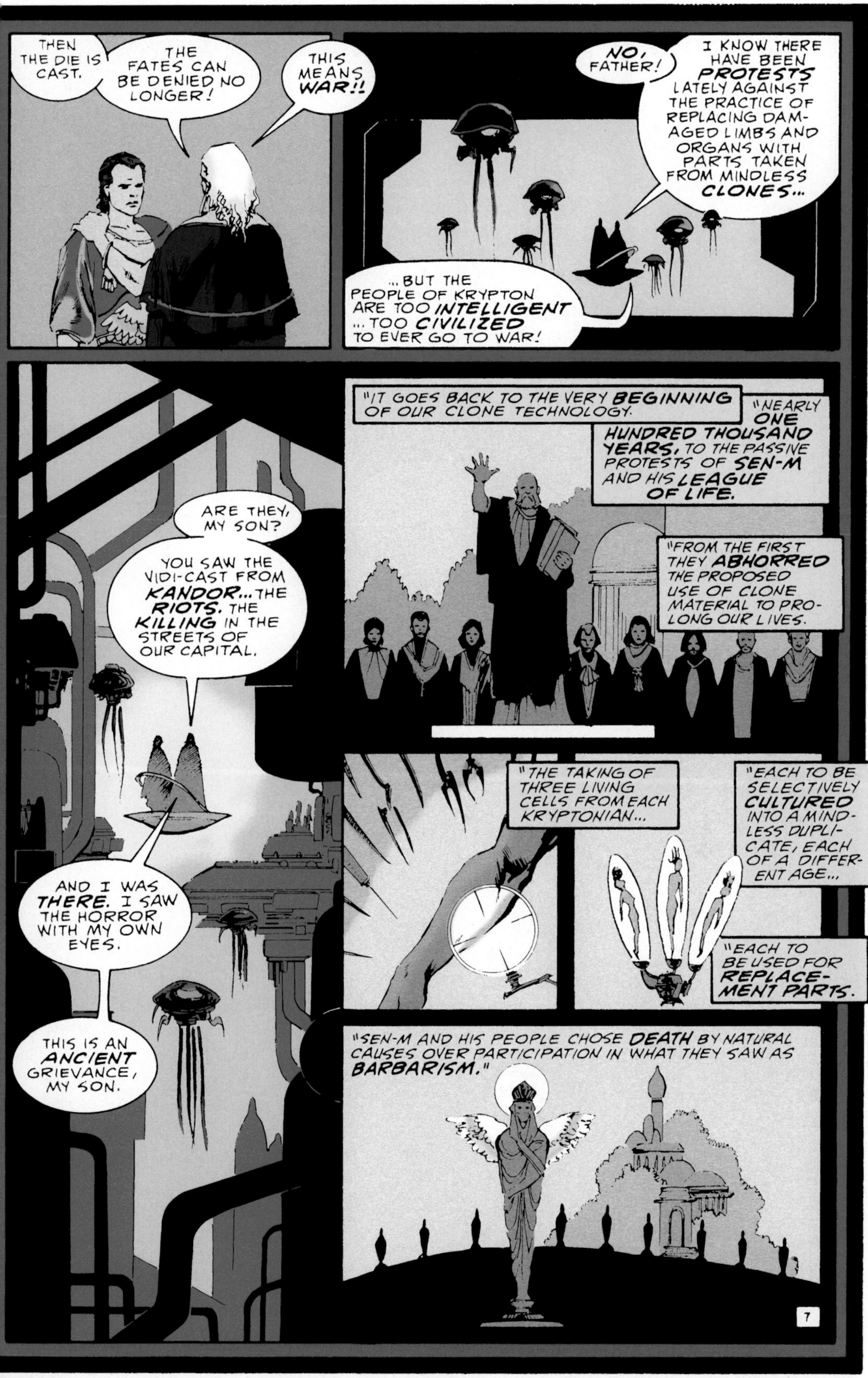
THEN THE DIE IS CAST.
THE FATES CAN BE DENIED NO LONGER!
THIS MEANS WAR!!
NO, FATHER!
I KNOW THERE HAVE BEEN PROTESTS LATELY AGAINST THE PRACTICE OF REPLACING DAMAGED LIMBS AND ORGANS WITH PARTS TAKEN FROM MINDLESS CLONES...
...BUT THE PEOPLE OF KRYPTON ARE TOO INTELLIGENT ...TOO CIVILIZED TO EVER GO TO WAR!
ARE THEY, MY SON?
YOU SAW THE VIDI-CAST FROM KANDOR...THE RIOTS. THE KILLING IN THE STREETS OF OUR CAPITAL.
AND I WAS THERE. I SAW THE HORROR WITH MY OWN EYES.
THIS IS AN ANCIENT GRIEVANCE, MY SON.
"IT GOES BACK TO THE VERY BEGINNING OF OUR CLONE TECHNOLOGY.
"NEARLY ONE HUNDRED THOUSAND YEARS, TO THE PASSIVE PROTESTS OF SEN-M AND HIS LEAGUE OF LIFE.
"FROM THE FIRST THEY ABHORRED THE PROPOSED USE OF CLONE MATERIAL TO PROLONG OUR LIVES.
"THE TAKING OF THREE LIVING CELLS FROM EACH KRYPTONIAN...
"EACH TO BE SELECTIVELY CULTURED INTO A MINDLESS DUPLICATE, EACH OF A DIFFERENT AGE...
"EACH TO BE USED FOR REPLACEMENT PARTS.
"SEN-M AND HIS PEOPLE CHOSE DEATH BY NATURAL CAUSES OVER PARTICIPATION IN WHAT THEY SAW AS BARBARISM."
7

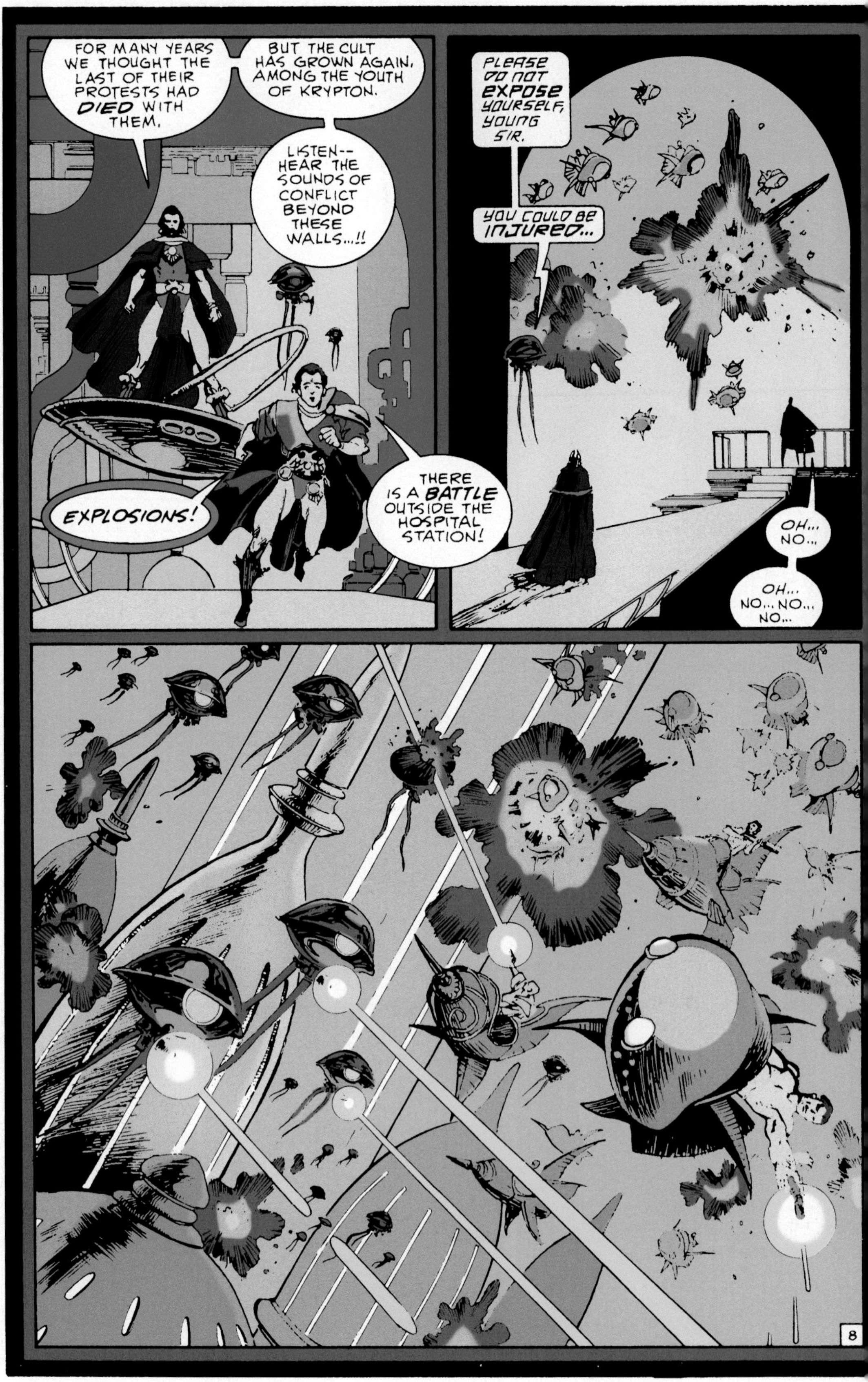
FOR MANY YEARS WE THOUGHT THE LAST OF THEIR PROTESTS HAD DIED WITH THEM.
BUT THE CULT HAS GROWN AGAIN, AMONG THE YOUTH OF KRYPTON.
LISTEN-- HEAR THE SOUNDS OF CONFLICT BEYOND THESE WALLS...!!
EXPLOSIONS!
THERE IS A BATTLE OUTSIDE THE HOSPITAL STATION!
PLEASE DO NOT EXPOSE YOURSELF, YOUNG SIR.
YOU COULD BE INJURED...
OH... NO...
OH... NO... NO... NO...
8

HE THOUGHT HE UNDERSTOOD.

HE'D LOOKED AT THREE-DIMENSIONAL IMAGES RELAYED FROM KANDOR THAT AFTERNOON, AND THOUGHT IN HIS YOUTH AND INNOCENCE THAT HE'D BEGUN TO UNDER-STAND THE FACE OF WAR.

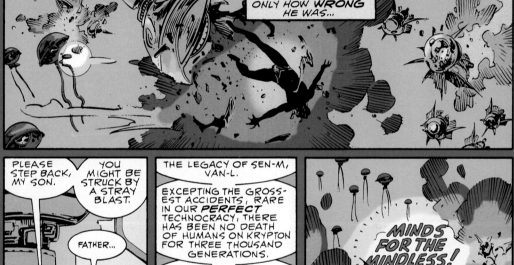

NOW HE UNDERSTANDS ONLY HOW *WRONG* HE WAS...

PLEASE STEP BACK, MY SON.

YOU MIGHT BE STRUCK BY A STRAY BLAST.

FATHER...

FATHER... THE *SCREAMS*... THE *BLOOD*...

THERE ARE PEOPLE ...*DYING* OUT THERE!

THE LEGACY OF SEN-M, VAN-L.

EXCEPTING THE GROSS-EST ACCIDENTS, RARE IN OUR *PERFECT* TECHNOCRACY, THERE HAS BEEN NO DEATH OF HUMANS ON KRYPTON FOR THREE THOUSAND GENERATIONS.

NOW THE PEACEFUL PROTESTS OF THAT KINDLY OLD MAN ARE TWISTED INTO ALL THIS PAIN AND DEVASTATION.

MINDS FOR THE MINDLESS!

FULL MIND, FULL LIFE

LOOK! LOOK! EVEN AS THEY TRY TO *BLAST* THE HOSPITAL STATION AND ARE THEMSELVES *BLASTED*...

PROTESTORS STILL *FLASH* THE *SLOGANS* SEN-M HIMSELF CREATED.

9

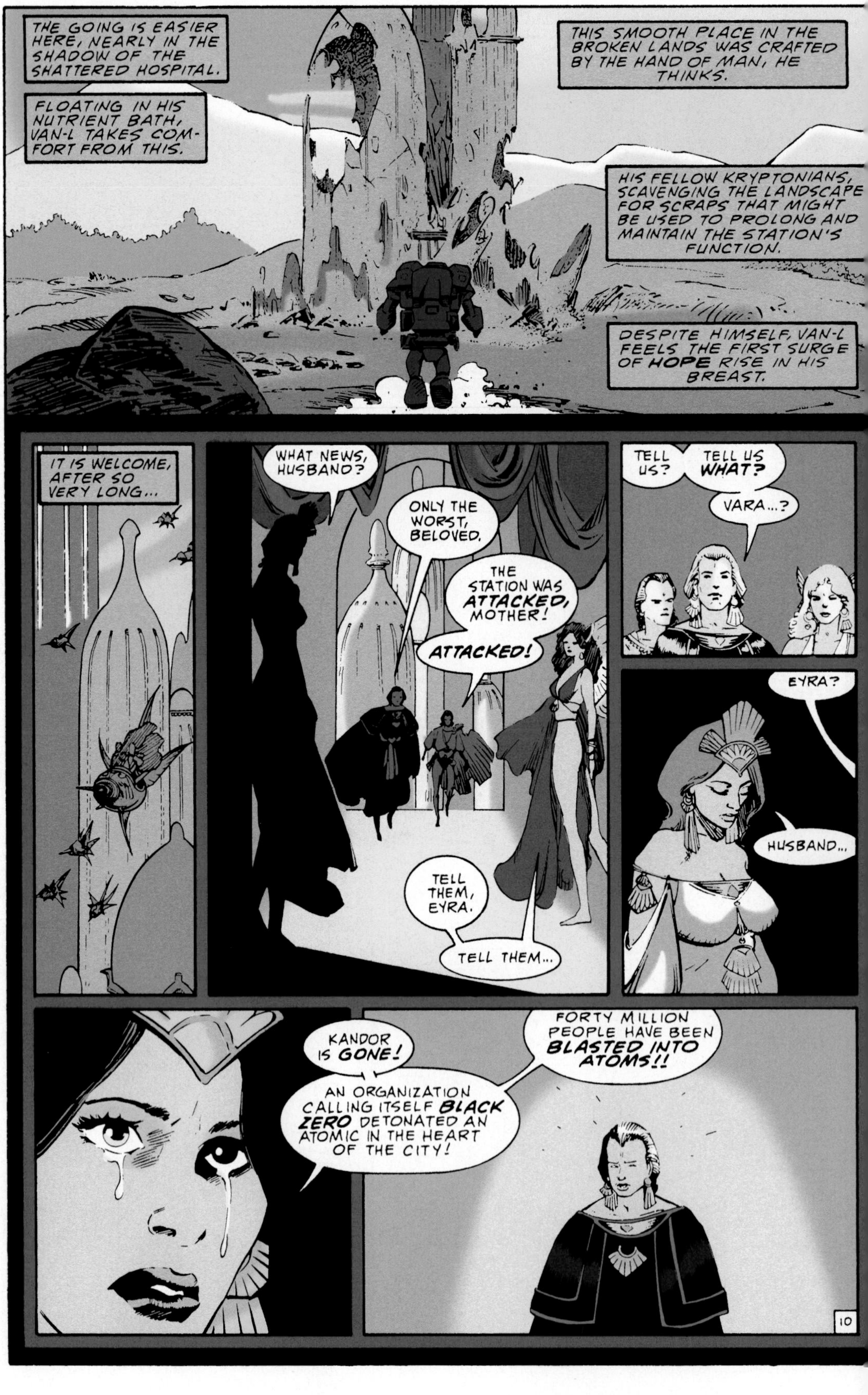

THE GOING IS EASIER HERE, NEARLY IN THE SHADOW OF THE SHATTERED HOSPITAL.
FLOATING IN HIS NUTRIENT BATH, VAN-L TAKES COMFORT FROM THIS.
THIS SMOOTH PLACE IN THE BROKEN LANDS WAS CRAFTED BY THE HAND OF MAN, HE THINKS.
HIS FELLOW KRYPTONIANS, SCAVENGING THE LANDSCAPE FOR SCRAPS THAT MIGHT BE USED TO PROLONG AND MAINTAIN THE STATION'S FUNCTION.
DESPITE HIMSELF, VAN-L FEELS THE FIRST SURGE OF HOPE RISE IN HIS BREAST.
IT IS WELCOME, AFTER SO VERY LONG...
WHAT NEWS, HUSBAND?
ONLY THE WORST, BELOVED.
THE STATION WAS ATTACKED, MOTHER!
ATTACKED!
TELL THEM, EYRA.
TELL THEM...
TELL US?
TELL US WHAT?
VARA...?
EYRA?
HUSBAND...
KANDOR IS GONE!
AN ORGANIZATION CALLING ITSELF BLACK ZERO DETONATED AN ATOMIC IN THE HEART OF THE CITY!
FORTY MILLION PEOPLE HAVE BEEN BLASTED INTO ATOMS!!
10

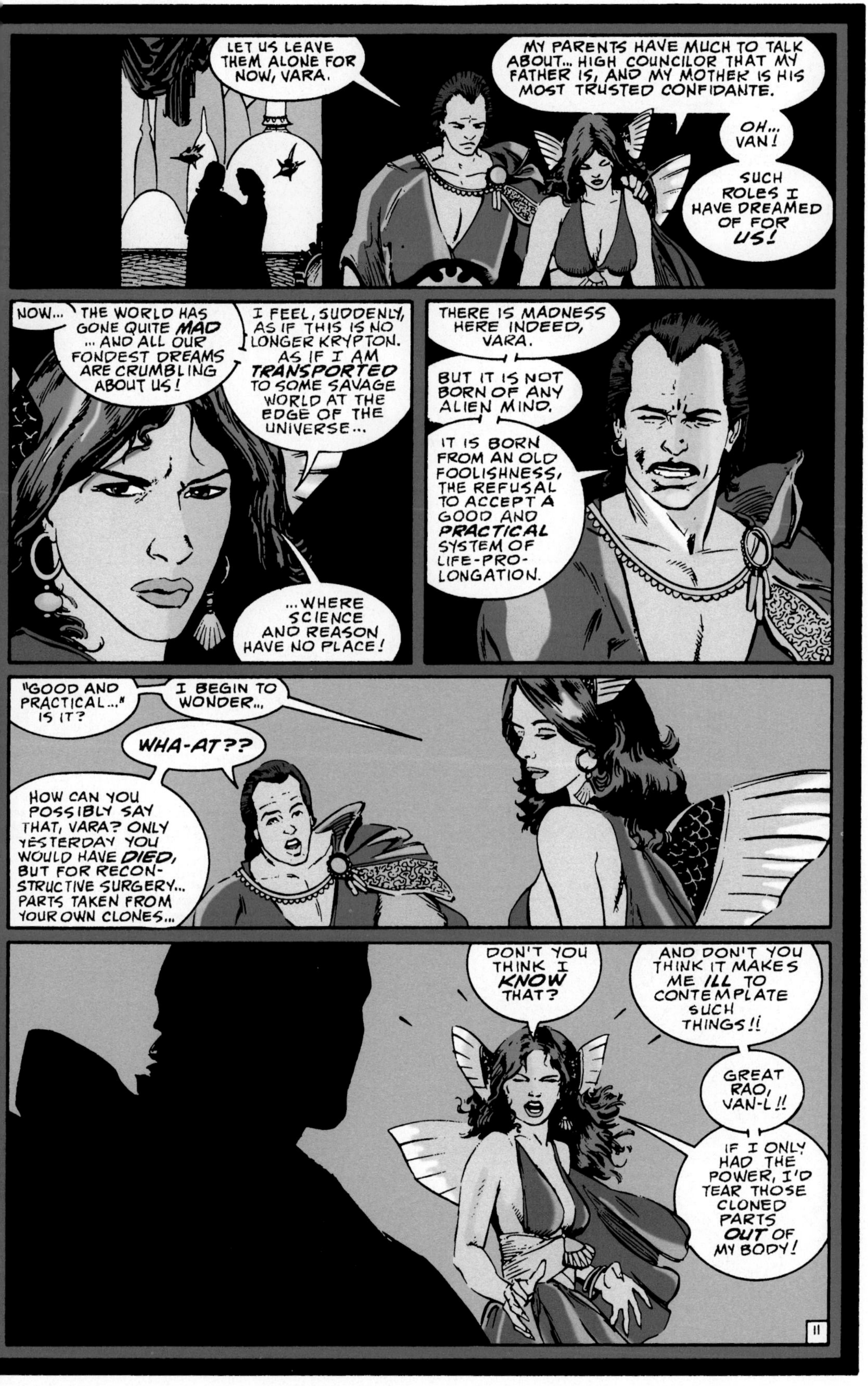
LET US LEAVE THEM ALONE FOR NOW, VARA.
MY PARENTS HAVE MUCH TO TALK ABOUT... HIGH COUNCILOR THAT MY FATHER IS, AND MY MOTHER IS HIS MOST TRUSTED CONFIDANTE.
OH... VAN!
SUCH ROLES I HAVE DREAMED OF FOR US!
NOW...
THE WORLD HAS GONE QUITE MAD ... AND ALL OUR FONDEST DREAMS ARE CRUMBLING ABOUT US!
I FEEL, SUDDENLY, AS IF THIS IS NO LONGER KRYPTON. AS IF I AM TRANSPORTED TO SOME SAVAGE WORLD AT THE EDGE OF THE UNIVERSE...
...WHERE SCIENCE AND REASON HAVE NO PLACE!
THERE IS MADNESS HERE INDEED, VARA.
BUT IT IS NOT BORN OF ANY ALIEN MIND.
IT IS BORN FROM AN OLD FOOLISHNESS, THE REFUSAL TO ACCEPT A GOOD AND PRACTICAL SYSTEM OF LIFE-PRO-LONGATION.
"GOOD AND PRACTICAL..." IS IT?
I BEGIN TO WONDER...
WHA-AT??
HOW CAN YOU POSSIBLY SAY THAT, VARA? ONLY YESTERDAY YOU WOULD HAVE DIED, BUT FOR RECON-STRUCTIVE SURGERY... PARTS TAKEN FROM YOUR OWN CLONES...
DON'T YOU THINK I KNOW THAT?
AND DON'T YOU THINK IT MAKES ME ILL TO CONTEMPLATE SUCH THINGS!!
GREAT RAO, VAN-L!!
IF I ONLY HAD THE POWER, I'D TEAR THOSE CLONED PARTS OUT OF MY BODY!
11

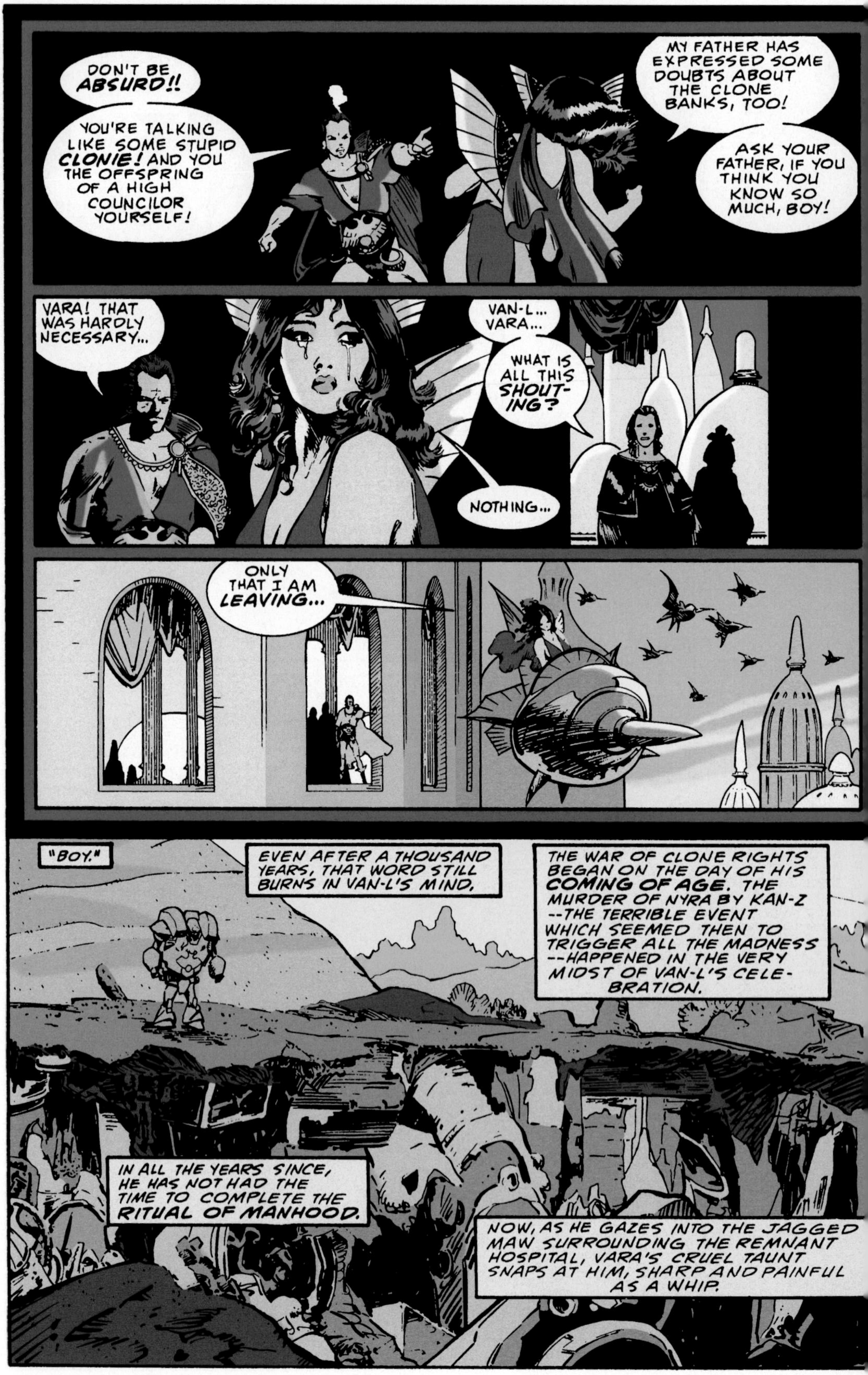
DON'T BE ABSURD!!
YOU'RE TALKING LIKE SOME STUPID CLONIE! AND YOU THE OFFSPRING OF A HIGH COUNCILOR YOURSELF!
MY FATHER HAS EXPRESSED SOME DOUBTS ABOUT THE CLONE BANKS, TOO!
ASK YOUR FATHER, IF YOU THINK YOU KNOW SO MUCH, BOY!
VARA! THAT WAS HARDLY NECESSARY...
VAN-L... VARA...
WHAT IS ALL THIS SHOUTING?
NOTHING...
ONLY THAT I AM LEAVING...
"BOY."
EVEN AFTER A THOUSAND YEARS, THAT WORD STILL BURNS IN VAN-L'S MIND.
THE WAR OF CLONE RIGHTS BEGAN ON THE DAY OF HIS COMING OF AGE. THE MURDER OF NYRA BY KAN-Z --THE TERRIBLE EVENT WHICH SEEMED THEN TO TRIGGER ALL THE MADNESS --HAPPENED IN THE VERY MIDST OF VAN-L'S CELE-BRATION.
IN ALL THE YEARS SINCE, HE HAS NOT HAD THE TIME TO COMPLETE THE RITUAL OF MANHOOD.
NOW, AS HE GAZES INTO THE JAGGED MAW SURROUNDING THE REMNANT HOSPITAL, VARA'S CRUEL TAUNT SNAPS AT HIM, SHARP AND PAINFUL AS A WHIP.

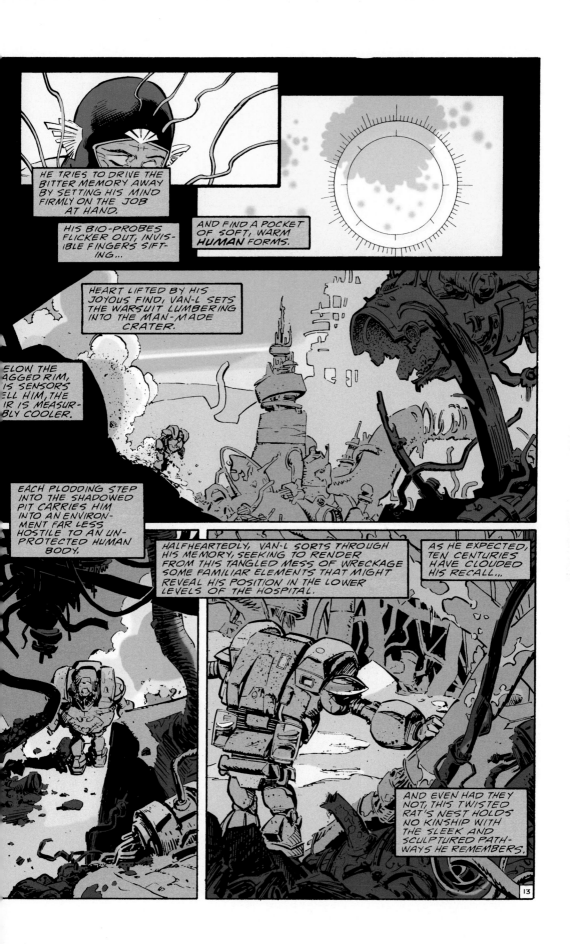

HE TRIES TO DRIVE THE BITTER MEMORY AWAY BY SETTING HIS MIND FIRMLY ON THE JOB AT HAND.

HIS BIO-PROBES FLICKER OUT, INVISIBLE FINGERS SIFTING...

AND FIND A POCKET OF SOFT, WARM *HUMAN* FORMS.

HEART LIFTED BY HIS JOYOUS FIND, VAN-L SETS THE WARSUIT LUMBERING INTO THE MAN-MADE CRATER.

ELOW THE AGGED RIM, IS SENSORS ELL HIM, THE IR IS MEASURBLY COOLER.

EACH PLODDING STEP INTO THE SHADOWED PIT CARRIES HIM INTO AN ENVIRONMENT FAR LESS HOSTILE TO AN UNPROTECTED HUMAN BODY.

HALFHEARTEDLY, VAN-L SORTS THROUGH HIS MEMORY, SEEKING TO RENDER FROM THIS TANGLED MESS OF WRECKAGE SOME FAMILIAR ELEMENTS THAT MIGHT REVEAL HIS POSITION IN THE LOWER LEVELS OF THE HOSPITAL.

AS HE EXPECTED, TEN CENTURIES HAVE CLOUDED HIS RECALL...

AND EVEN HAD THEY NOT, THIS TWISTED RAT'S NEST HOLDS NO KINSHIP WITH THE SLEEK AND SCULPTURED PATHWAYS HE REMEMBERS.

13

THE TIME HAS COME FOR A MODIFICATION OF HIS APPROACH.

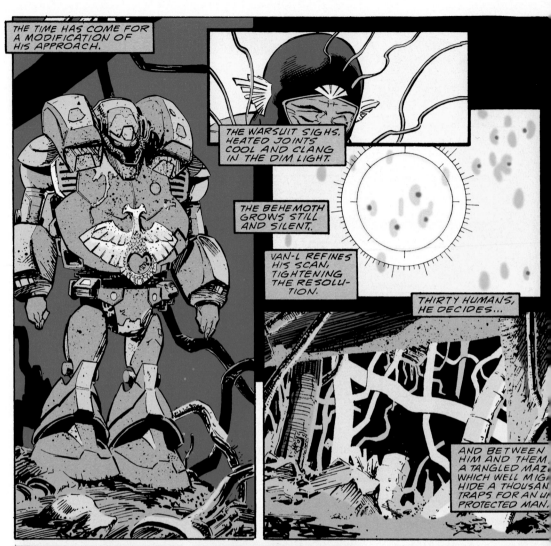

THE WARSUIT SIGHS. HEATED JOINTS COOL AND CLANG IN THE DIM LIGHT.

THE BEHEMOTH GROWS STILL AND SILENT.

VAN-L REFINES HIS SCAN, TIGHTENING THE RESOLUTION.

THIRTY HUMANS, HE DECIDES...

AND BETWEEN HIM AND THEM A TANGLED MAZ WHICH WELL MIG HIDE A THOUSAN TRAPS FOR AN UI PROTECTED MAN.

BUT VAN-L IS RESOLVED!

HE MADE HIMSELF A SOLEMN PROMISE THAT, HIS GOAL ACHIEVED, HE'D **SHED** THE ARMORED WOMB OF HIS WARSUIT.

THE METAPHOR IS APT.

THE WARSUIT DISGORGES VAN-L, NUTRIENT FLUIDS SPLASHING ON THE FRIGID, DARK METALS ALL ABOUT.

THE TEMPERATURE IS NO COLDER THAN AN AUTUMN EVENING, A WEEK OR TWO BEFORE THE FIRST SNOW

THE AIR IS DUSTY, AND A THOUSAND ODORS FLOAT O US SLOW BREEZES, BUT IT I SAFE TO BREATHE.

VAN-L FEELS THE COOL AIR A DAGGERS ON HIS NAKED FLESH.

THE DUST BURNS HIS LUNGS,

THE STENC REVOLTS HIM

HIS BODY SHUDDEF AS HIS STOMACH TRIES TO FORCE ITSELF UP HIS THROAT.

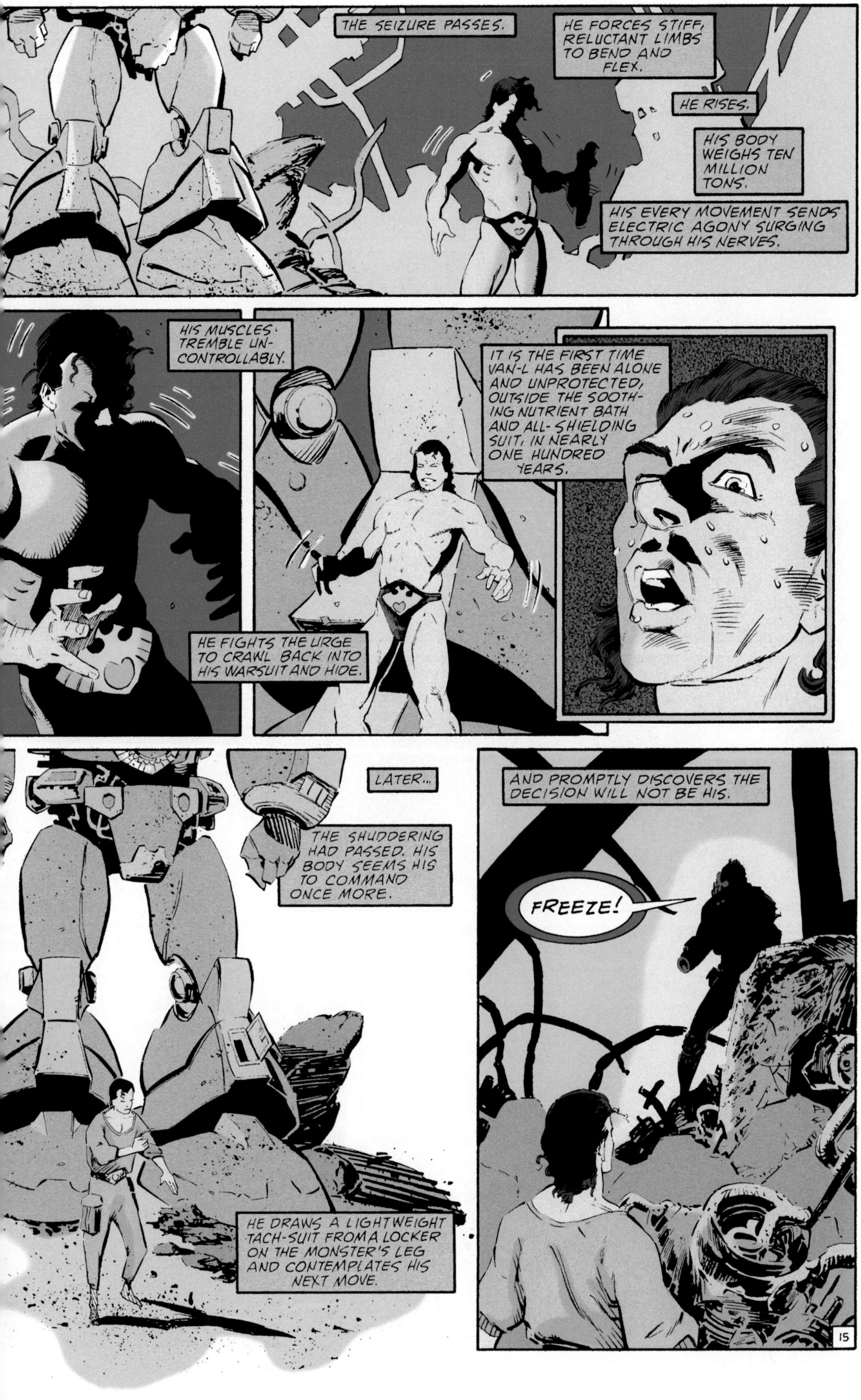
THE SEIZURE PASSES.
HE FORCES STIFF, RELUCTANT LIMBS TO BEND AND FLEX.
HE RISES.
HIS BODY WEIGHS TEN MILLION TONS.
HIS EVERY MOVEMENT SENDS ELECTRIC AGONY SURGING THROUGH HIS NERVES.
HIS MUSCLES TREMBLE UN-CONTROLLABLY.
HE FIGHTS THE URGE TO CRAWL BACK INTO HIS WARSUIT AND HIDE.
IT IS THE FIRST TIME VAN-L HAS BEEN ALONE AND UNPROTECTED, OUTSIDE THE SOOTH-ING NUTRIENT BATH AND ALL-SHIELDING SUIT, IN NEARLY ONE HUNDRED YEARS.
LATER...
THE SHUDDERING HAD PASSED. HIS BODY SEEMS HIS TO COMMAND ONCE MORE.
HE DRAWS A LIGHTWEIGHT TACH-SUIT FROM A LOCKER ON THE MONSTER'S LEG AND CONTEMPLATES HIS NEXT MOVE.
AND PROMPTLY DISCOVERS THE DECISION WILL NOT BE HIS.
FREEZE!
15

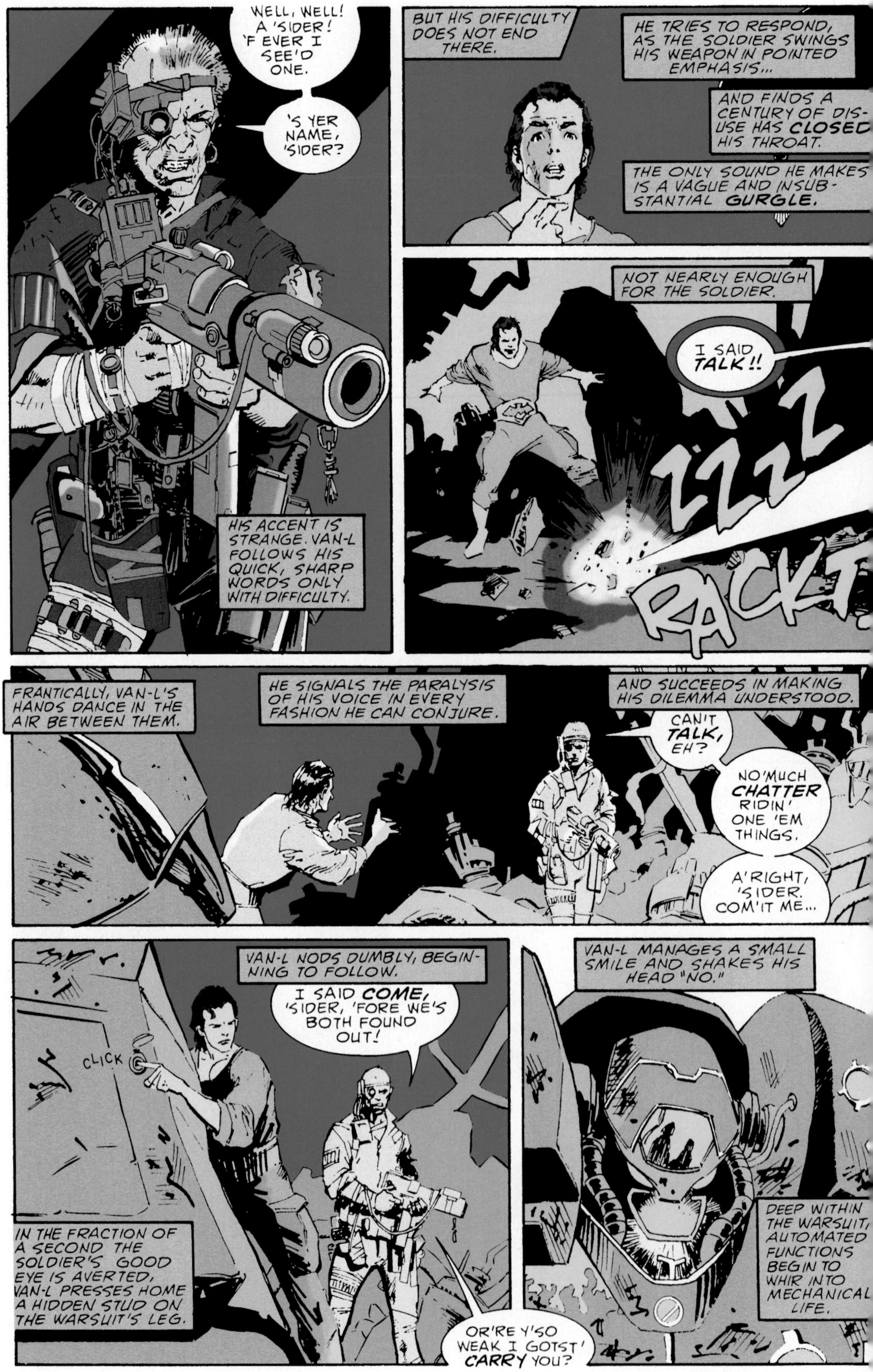

WELL, WELL! A 'SIDER! 'F EVER I SEE'D ONE.
'S YER NAME, 'SIDER?
HIS ACCENT IS STRANGE. VAN-L FOLLOWS HIS QUICK, SHARP WORDS ONLY WITH DIFFICULTY.
BUT HIS DIFFICULTY DOES NOT END THERE.
HE TRIES TO RESPOND, AS THE SOLDIER SWINGS HIS WEAPON IN POINTED EMPHASIS...
AND FINDS A CENTURY OF DIS-USE HAS **CLOSED** HIS THROAT.
THE ONLY SOUND HE MAKES IS A VAGUE AND INSUB-STANTIAL **GURGLE.**
NOT NEARLY ENOUGH FOR THE SOLDIER.
I SAID **TALK!!**
ZZZzZ
RACKT
FRANTICALLY, VAN-L'S HANDS DANCE IN THE AIR BETWEEN THEM.
HE SIGNALS THE PARALYSIS OF HIS VOICE IN EVERY FASHION HE CAN CONJURE.
AND SUCCEEDS IN MAKING HIS DILEMMA UNDERSTOOD.
CAN'T **TALK,** EH?
NO'MUCH **CHATTER** RIDIN' ONE 'EM THINGS.
A'RIGHT, 'SIDER. COM'IT ME...
CLICK
VAN-L NODS DUMBLY, BEGIN-NING TO FOLLOW.
I SAID **COME,** 'SIDER, 'FORE WE'S BOTH FOUND OUT!
IN THE FRACTION OF A SECOND THE SOLDIER'S GOOD EYE IS AVERTED, VAN-L PRESSES HOME A HIDDEN STUD ON THE WARSUIT'S LEG.
OR'RE Y'SO WEAK I GOTST' **CARRY** YOU?
VAN-L MANAGES A SMALL SMILE AND SHAKES HIS HEAD "NO."
DEEP WITHIN THE WARSUIT, AUTOMATED FUNCTIONS BEGIN TO WHIR INTO MECHANICAL LIFE.

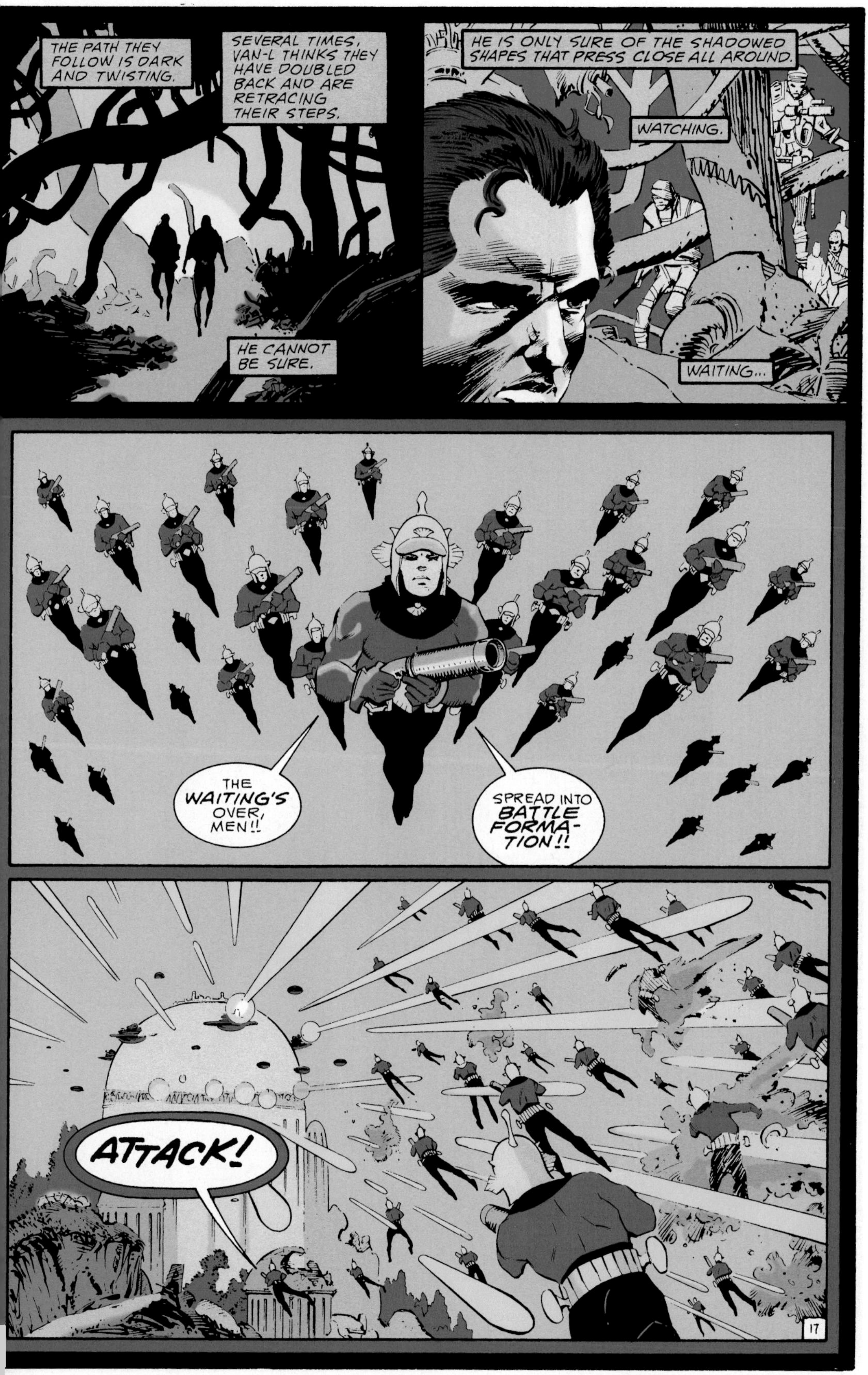
THE PATH THEY FOLLOW IS DARK AND TWISTING.
SEVERAL TIMES, VAN-L THINKS THEY HAVE DOUBLED BACK AND ARE RETRACING THEIR STEPS.
HE CANNOT BE SURE.
HE IS ONLY SURE OF THE SHADOWED SHAPES THAT PRESS CLOSE ALL AROUND.
WATCHING.
WAITING...
THE WAITING'S OVER, MEN!!
SPREAD INTO BATTLE FORMA-TION!!
ATTACK!
17

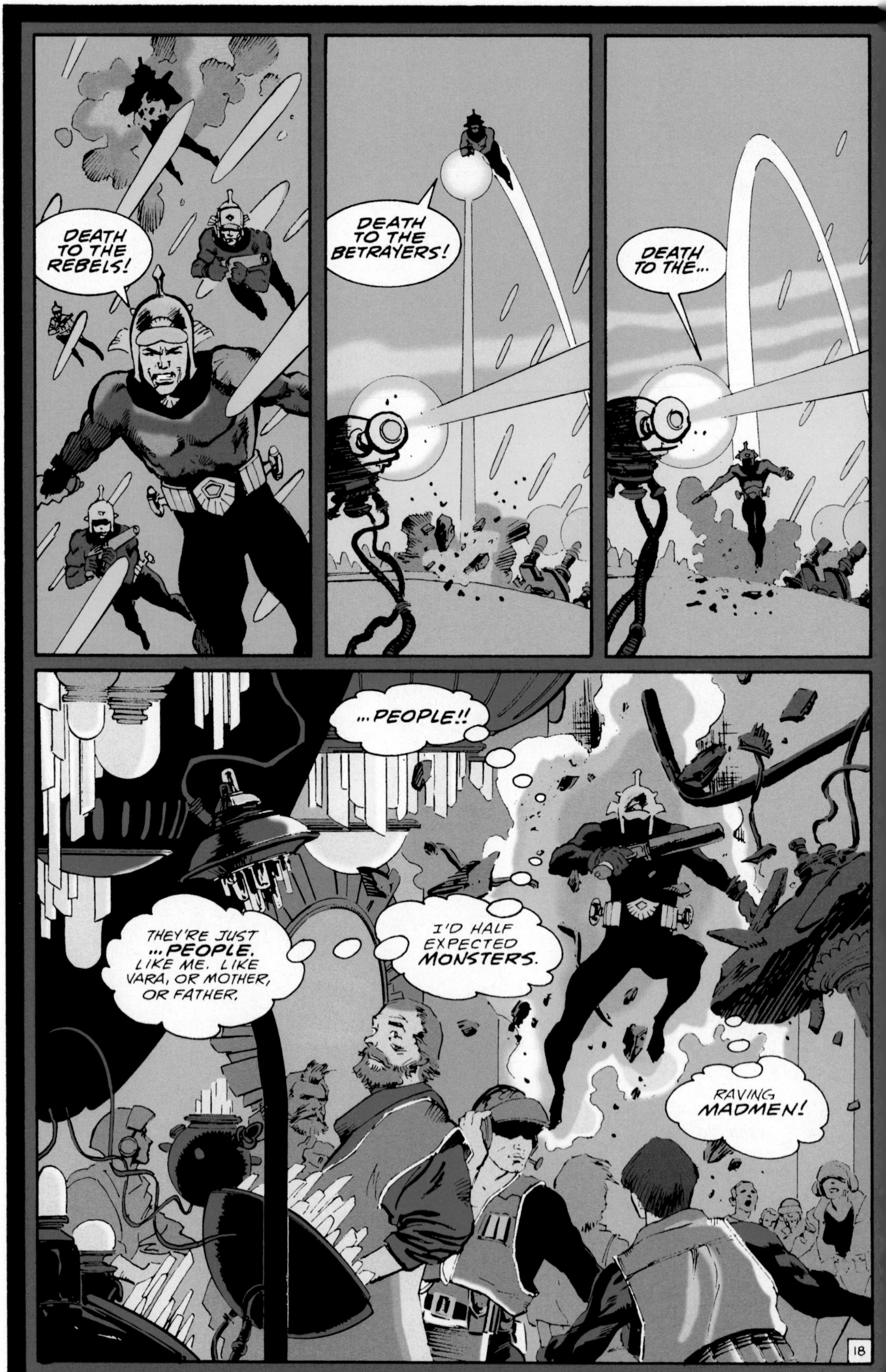
DEATH TO THE REBELS!
DEATH TO THE BETRAYERS!
DEATH TO THE...
...PEOPLE!!
THEY'RE JUST ...PEOPLE. LIKE ME. LIKE VARA, OR MOTHER, OR FATHER.
I'D HALF EXPECTED MONSTERS.
RAVING MADMEN!
18

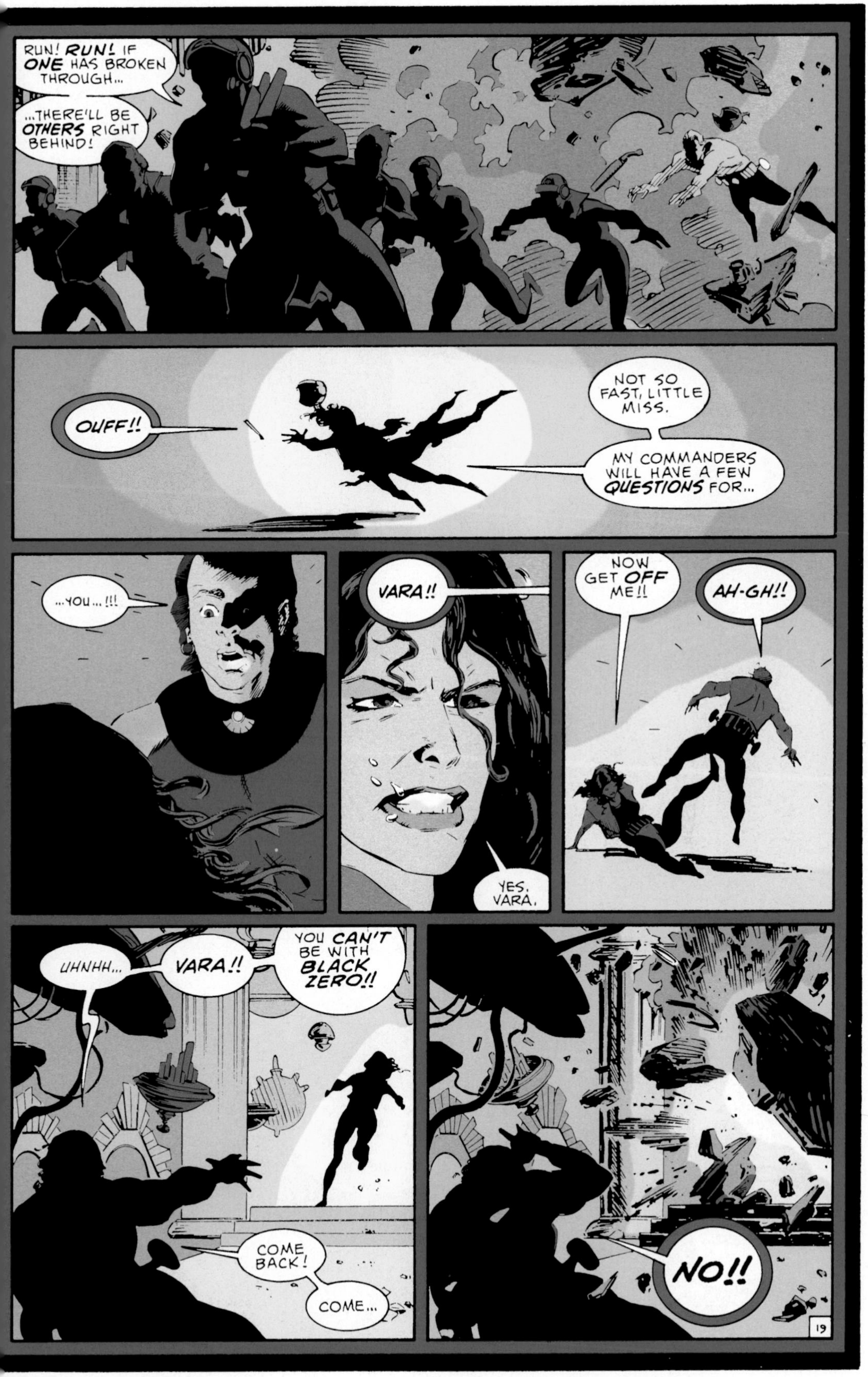
RUN! RUN! IF ONE HAS BROKEN THROUGH...
...THERE'LL BE OTHERS RIGHT BEHIND!
OUFF!!
NOT SO FAST, LITTLE MISS.
MY COMMANDERS WILL HAVE A FEW QUESTIONS FOR...
...YOU...!!!
VARA!!
YES. VARA.
NOW GET OFF ME!!
AH-GH!!
UHNHH...
VARA!!
YOU CAN'T BE WITH BLACK ZERO!!
COME BACK!
COME...
NO!!
19

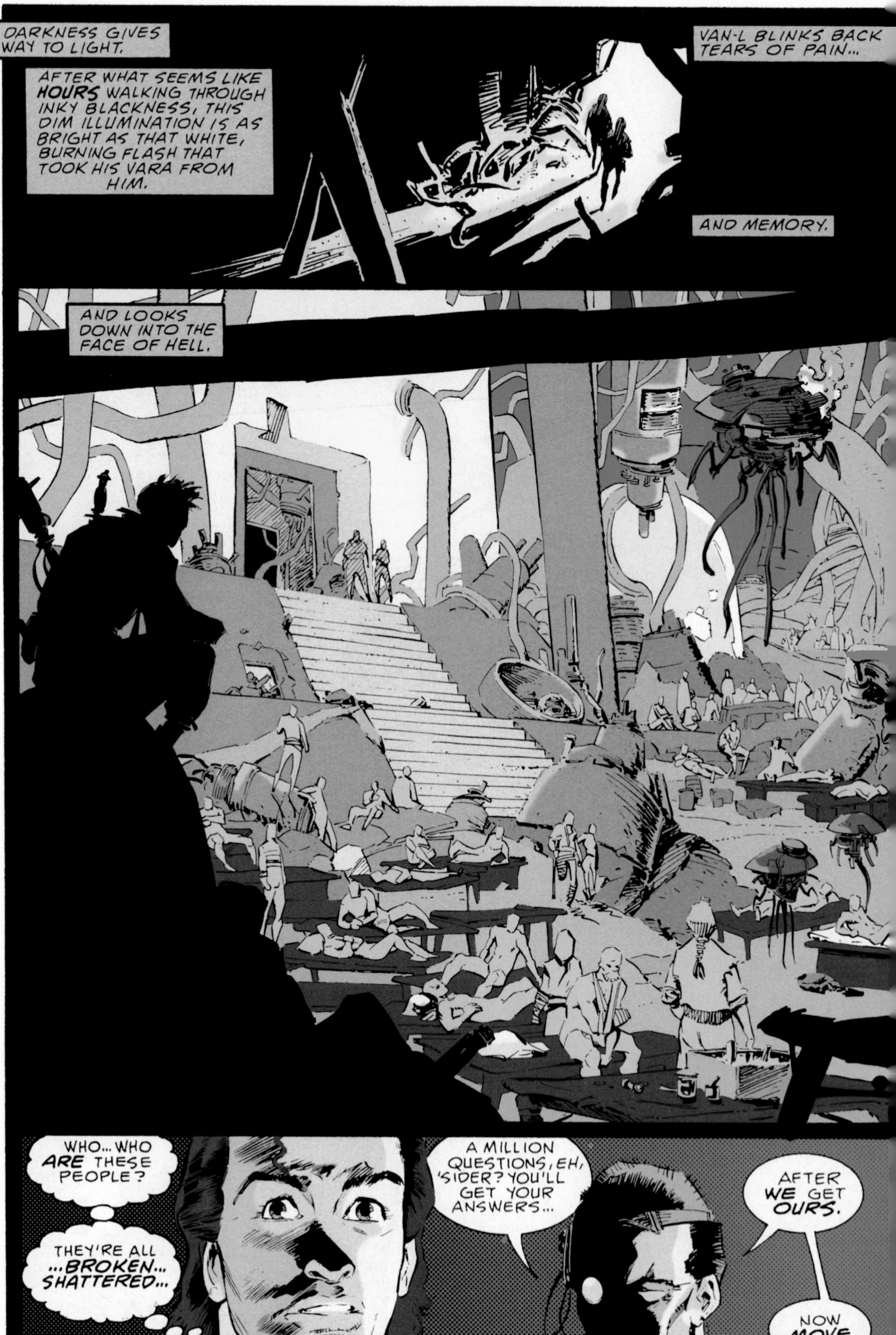
DARKNESS GIVES WAY TO LIGHT.
AFTER WHAT SEEMS LIKE **HOURS** WALKING THROUGH INKY BLACKNESS, THIS DIM ILLUMINATION IS AS BRIGHT AS THAT WHITE, BURNING FLASH THAT TOOK HIS VARA FROM HIM.
VAN-L BLINKS BACK TEARS OF PAIN...
AND MEMORY.
AND LOOKS DOWN INTO THE FACE OF HELL.
WHO... WHO **ARE** THESE PEOPLE?
THEY'RE ALL ...**BROKEN**... **SHATTERED**...
A MILLION QUESTIONS, EH, 'SIDER? YOU'LL GET YOUR ANSWERS...
AFTER **WE** GET **OURS**.
NOW **MOVE**.
20

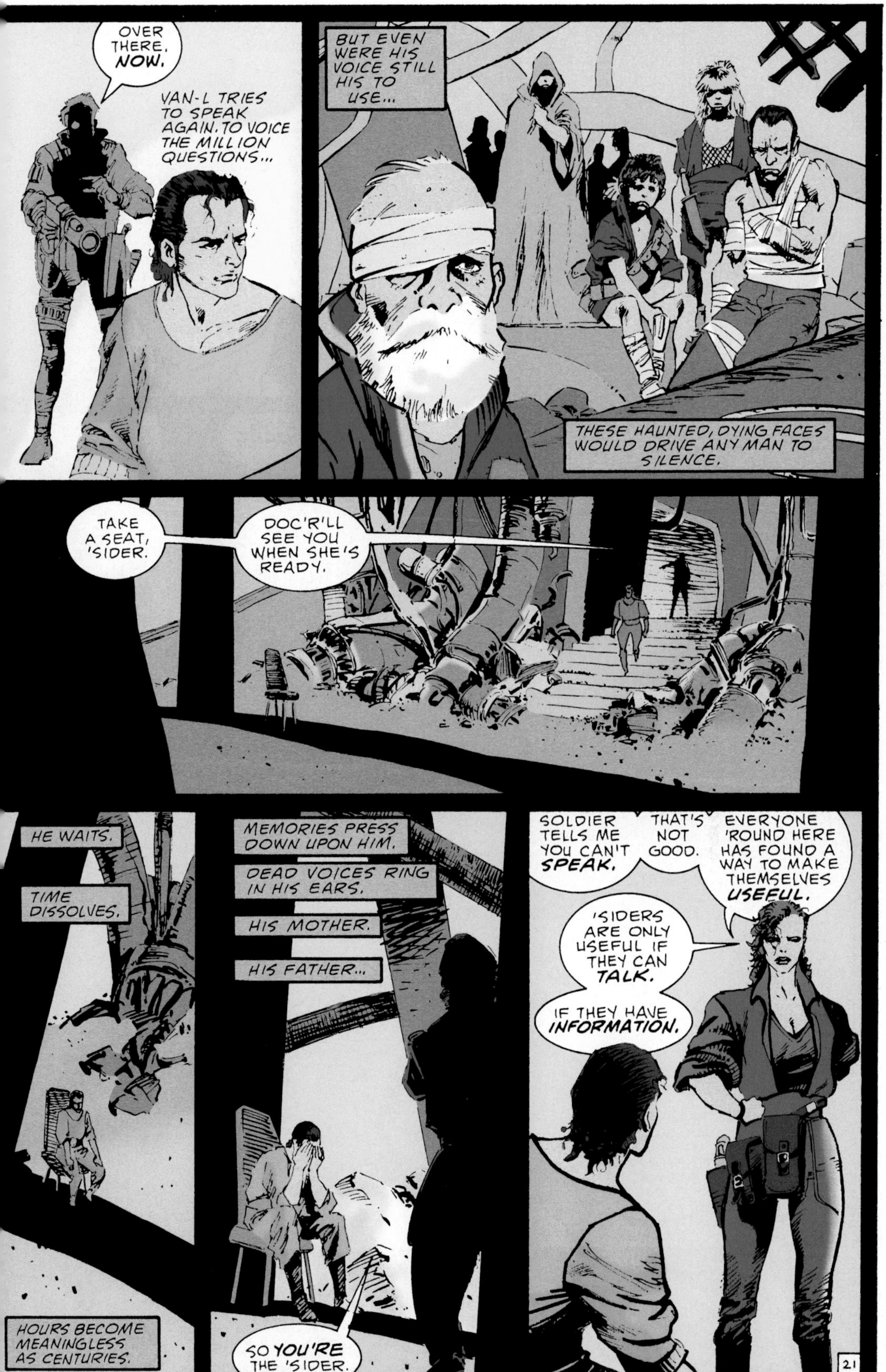
OVER THERE. NOW.
VAN-L TRIES TO SPEAK AGAIN. TO VOICE THE MILLION QUESTIONS...
BUT EVEN WERE HIS VOICE STILL HIS TO USE...
THESE HAUNTED, DYING FACES WOULD DRIVE ANY MAN TO SILENCE.
TAKE A SEAT, 'SIDER.
DOC'R'LL SEE YOU WHEN SHE'S READY.
HE WAITS.
TIME DISSOLVES.
HOURS BECOME MEANINGLESS AS CENTURIES.
MEMORIES PRESS DOWN UPON HIM.
DEAD VOICES RING IN HIS EARS.
HIS MOTHER.
HIS FATHER...
SO YOU'RE THE 'SIDER.
SOLDIER TELLS ME YOU CAN'T SPEAK.
THAT'S NOT GOOD.
EVERYONE 'ROUND HERE HAS FOUND A WAY TO MAKE THEMSELVES USEFUL.
'SIDERS ARE ONLY USEFUL IF THEY CAN TALK.
IF THEY HAVE INFORMATION.
21

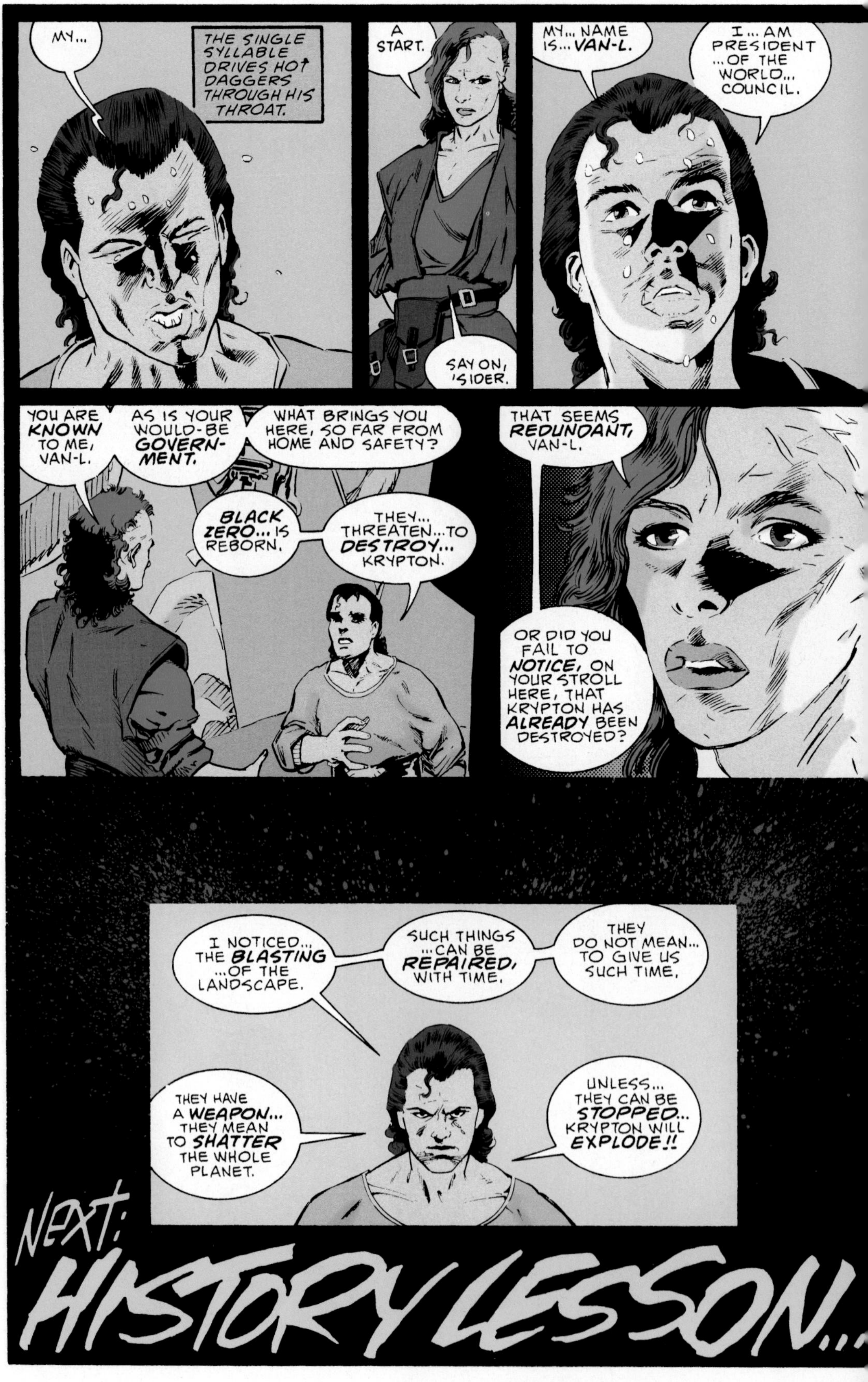

MY...
THE SINGLE SYLLABLE DRIVES HOT DAGGERS THROUGH HIS THROAT.
A START.
SAY ON, 'SIDER.
MY... NAME IS... VAN-L.
I... AM PRESIDENT ...OF THE WORLD... COUNCIL.
YOU ARE KNOWN TO ME, VAN-L.
AS IS YOUR WOULD-BE GOVERN-MENT.
WHAT BRINGS YOU HERE, SO FAR FROM HOME AND SAFETY?
BLACK ZERO... IS REBORN.
THEY... THREATEN... TO DESTROY... KRYPTON.
THAT SEEMS REDUNDANT, VAN-L.
OR DID YOU FAIL TO NOTICE, ON YOUR STROLL HERE, THAT KRYPTON HAS ALREADY BEEN DESTROYED?
I NOTICED... THE BLASTING ...OF THE LANDSCAPE.
SUCH THINGS ...CAN BE REPAIRED, WITH TIME.
THEY DO NOT MEAN... TO GIVE US SUCH TIME.
THEY HAVE A WEAPON... THEY MEAN TO SHATTER THE WHOLE PLANET.
UNLESS... THEY CAN BE STOPPED... KRYPTON WILL EXPLODE!!
NEXT: HISTORY LESSON...

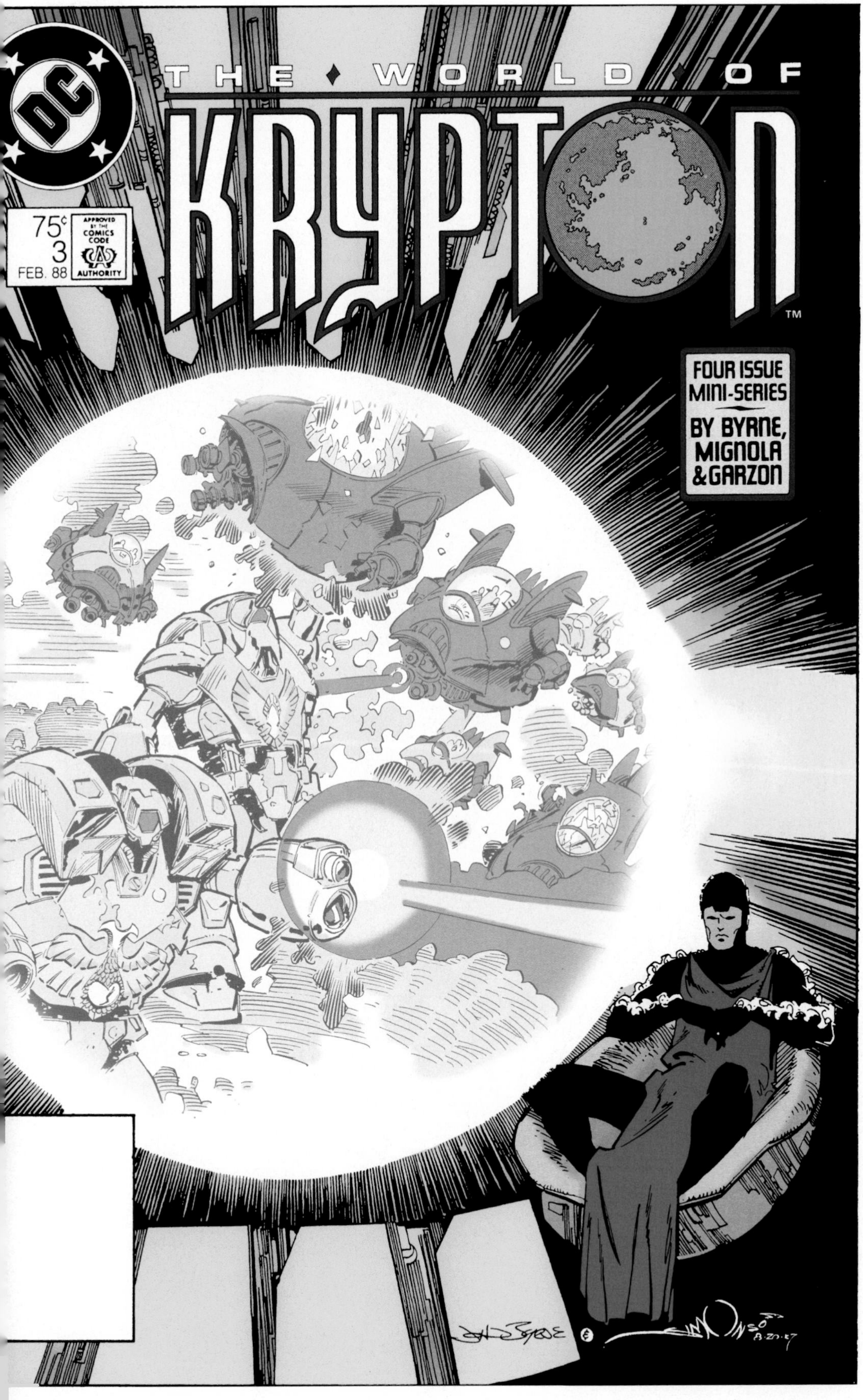
THE ♦ WORLD ♦ OF
KRYPTON
™
75¢
3
FEB. 88
APPROVED BY THE COMICS CODE AUTHORITY
FOUR ISSUE MINI-SERIES
BY BYRNE, MIGNOLA &GARZON

· THE MANY WORLDS OF ·

KRYPTON

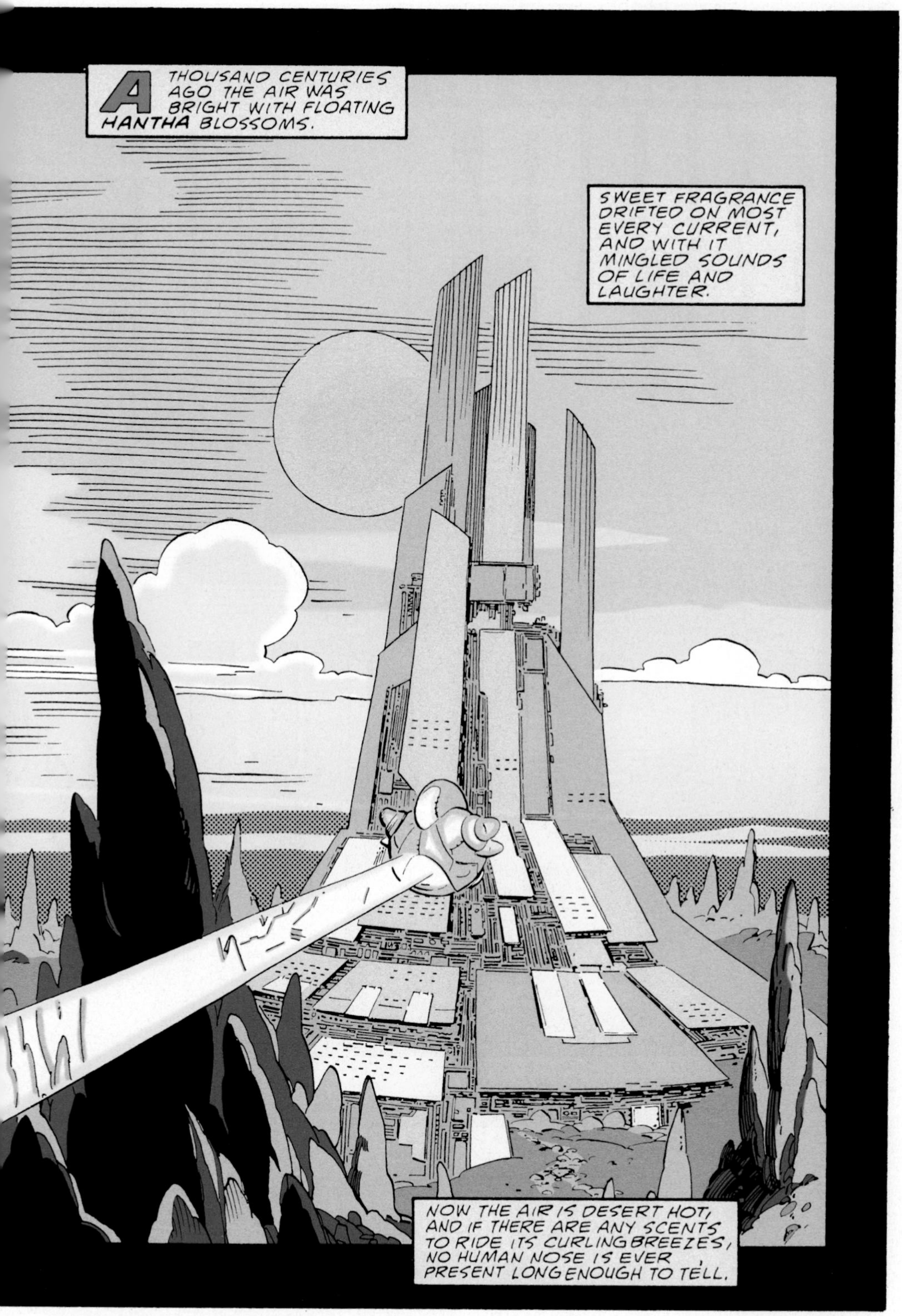
A THOUSAND CENTURIES AGO THE AIR WAS BRIGHT WITH FLOATING HANTHA BLOSSOMS.
SWEET FRAGRANCE DRIFTED ON MOST EVERY CURRENT, AND WITH IT MINGLED SOUNDS OF LIFE AND LAUGHTER.
NOW THE AIR IS DESERT HOT, AND IF THERE ARE ANY SCENTS TO RIDE ITS CURLING BREEZES, NO HUMAN NOSE IS EVER PRESENT LONG ENOUGH TO TELL.

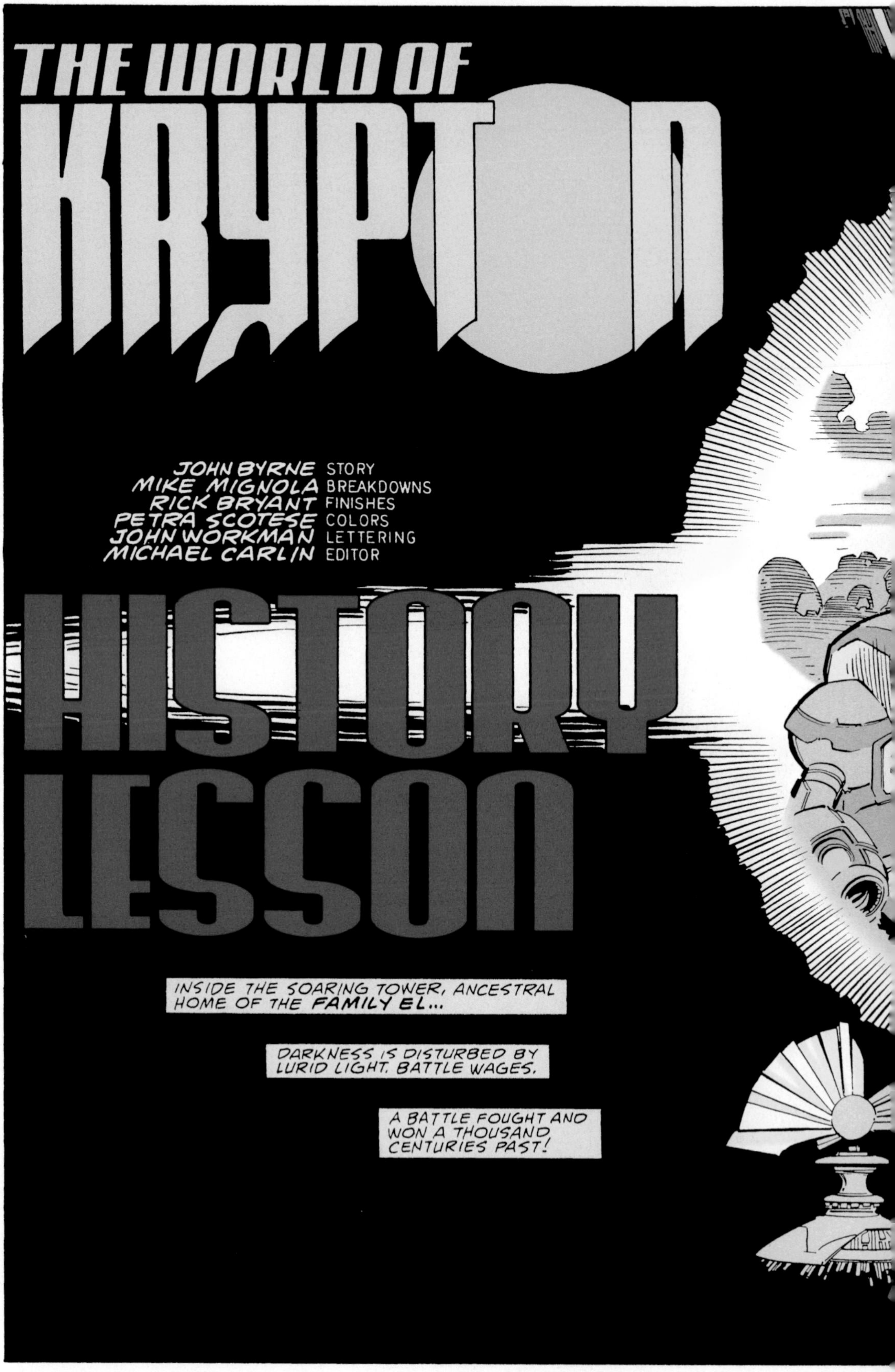
THE WORLD OF KRYPTON
JOHN BYRNE STORY
MIKE MIGNOLA BREAKDOWNS
RICK BRYANT FINISHES
PETRA SCOTESE COLORS
JOHN WORKMAN LETTERING
MICHAEL CARLIN EDITOR
HISTORY LESSON
INSIDE THE SOARING TOWER, ANCESTRAL HOME OF THE FAMILY EL...
DARKNESS IS DISTURBED BY LURID LIGHT. BATTLE WAGES.
A BATTLE FOUGHT AND WON A THOUSAND CENTURIES PAST!

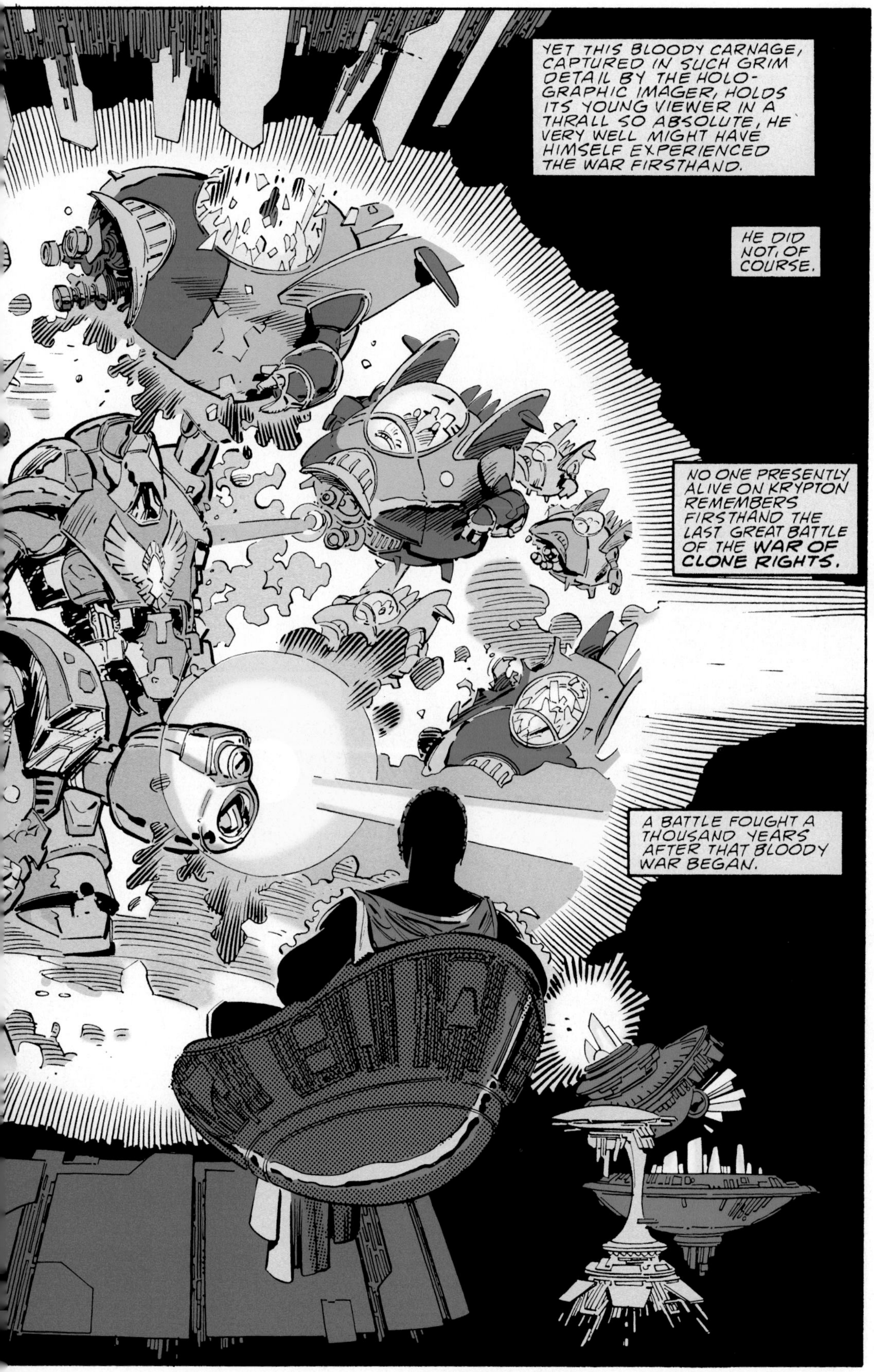
YET THIS BLOODY CARNAGE, CAPTURED IN SUCH GRIM DETAIL BY THE HOLO-GRAPHIC IMAGER, HOLDS ITS YOUNG VIEWER IN A THRALL SO ABSOLUTE, HE VERY WELL MIGHT HAVE HIMSELF EXPERIENCED THE WAR FIRSTHAND.
HE DID NOT, OF COURSE.
NO ONE PRESENTLY ALIVE ON KRYPTON REMEMBERS FIRSTHAND THE LAST GREAT BATTLE OF THE **WAR OF CLONE RIGHTS.**
A BATTLE FOUGHT A THOUSAND YEARS AFTER THAT BLOODY WAR BEGAN.

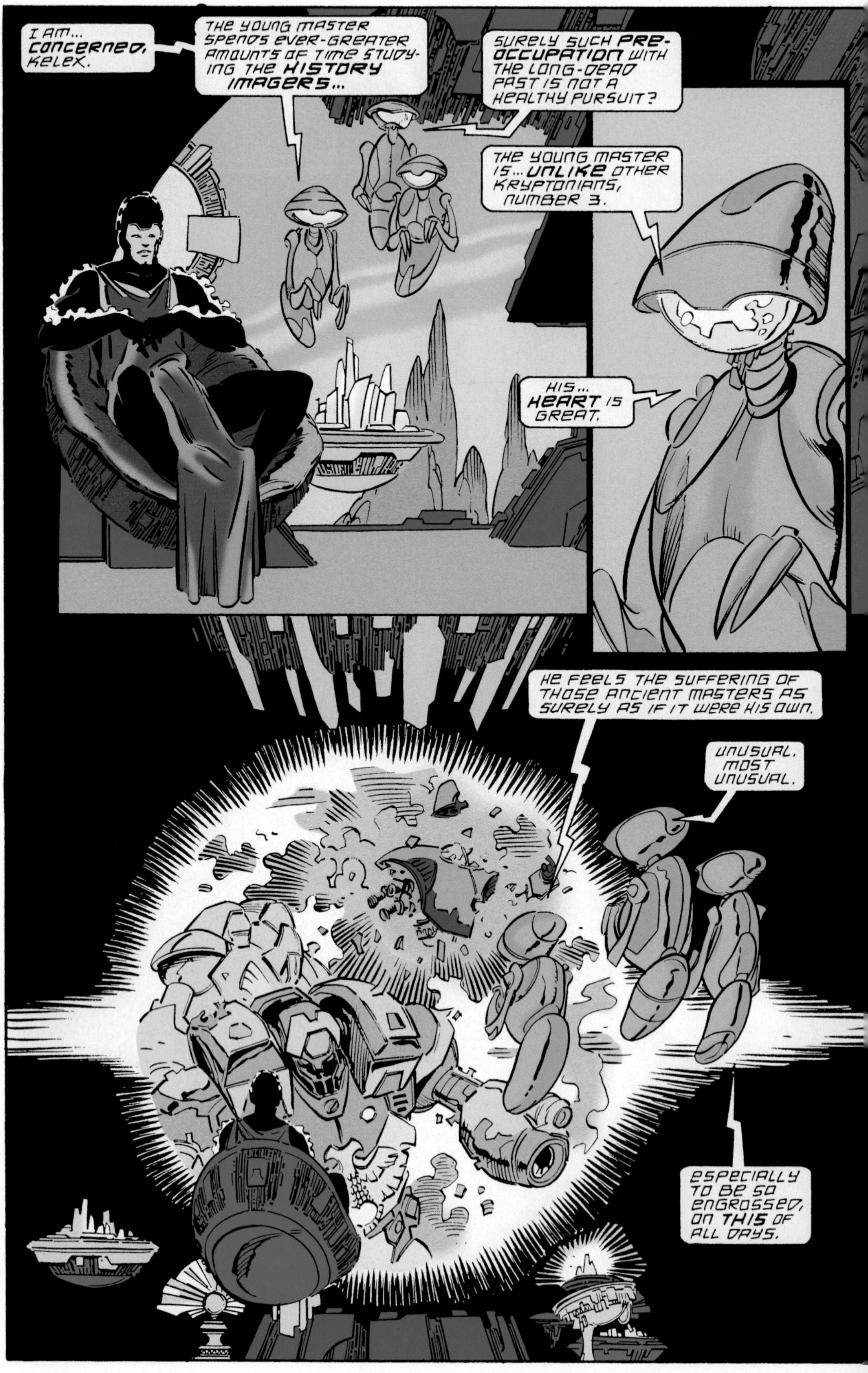

I AM... CONCERNED, KELEX.
THE YOUNG MASTER SPENDS EVER-GREATER AMOUNTS OF TIME STUDYING THE HISTORY IMAGERS...
SURELY SUCH PRE-OCCUPATION WITH THE LONG-DEAD PAST IS NOT A HEALTHY PURSUIT?
THE YOUNG MASTER IS... UNLIKE OTHER KRYPTONIANS, NUMBER 3.
HIS... HEART IS GREAT.
HE FEELS THE SUFFERING OF THOSE ANCIENT MASTERS AS SURELY AS IF IT WERE HIS OWN.
UNUSUAL. MOST UNUSUAL.
ESPECIALLY TO BE SO ENGROSSED, ON THIS OF ALL DAYS.

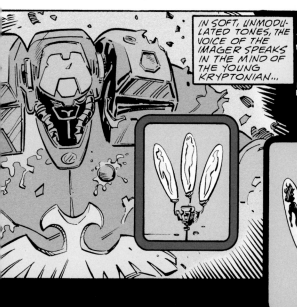

IN SOFT, UNMODU-LATED TONES, THE VOICE OF THE IMAGER SPEAKS IN THE MIND OF THE YOUNG KRYPTONIAN...

...necessary at this point to review the causes of the War of Clone Rights. Students will recall the process of cloning had been perfected one hundred centuries before the first battle. For each Kryptonian was maintained a trio of Clones in three distinct stages of physical development.

These clones were uses as living Organ Banks, providing replacement parts for humans damaged by accident or aging. However, under the leadership of Sen-M there arose a protest movement demanding Citizen Rights for the mindless clones.

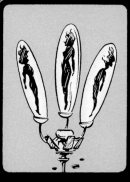

MINDS FOR THE MINDLESS

Over the years, although the generations of Protestors died, refusing Clone Surgery, there were many who inherited their mantle. Many who chose the most violent paths to make their protests known.

Then, in the year 10⁵/892 of the Fifth Age a woman called Nyra committed the greatest crime imaginable in the Kryptonian Society of the time.

Seeking a suitable mate for her son she had one of her clones removed from the Clone Banks and injected with her own modified R.N.A. This clone was then presented to society as a normal woman.

When Nyra's son, Kan-Z learned of his mother's deception he killed his fiancee and his mother both, and would have killed himself but for the actions of Van-L

Word of Nyra's crime, and her son's response, reached the protestors. A violent riot ensued.

The capitol city, Kandor, was destroyed by a nuclear device detonated by the most violent of the protest factions...

...a group of suicidal fanatics who called themselves "Black Zero." They maintained that only through the total destruction of human life on Krypton could proper penance be made for the deaths of countless generations of Clones.

A major resistance front was launched against Black Zero. A thousand heroes, brave and fearless, lead by...

197

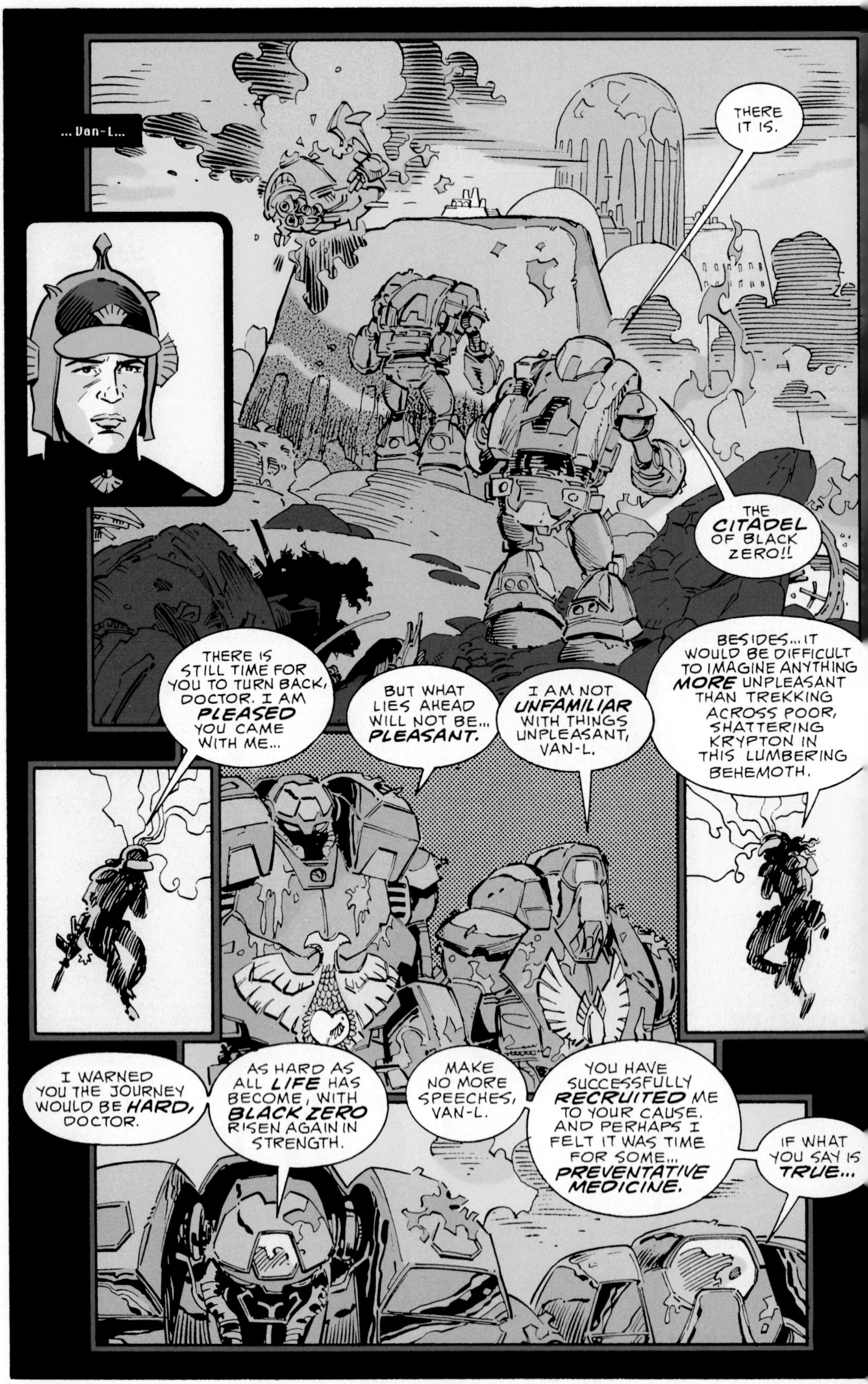
...Van-L...
THERE IT IS.
THE CITADEL OF BLACK ZERO!!
THERE IS STILL TIME FOR YOU TO TURN BACK, DOCTOR. I AM PLEASED YOU CAME WITH ME...
BUT WHAT LIES AHEAD WILL NOT BE... PLEASANT.
I AM NOT UNFAMILIAR WITH THINGS UNPLEASANT, VAN-L.
BESIDES... IT WOULD BE DIFFICULT TO IMAGINE ANYTHING MORE UNPLEASANT THAN TREKKING ACROSS POOR, SHATTERING KRYPTON IN THIS LUMBERING BEHEMOTH.
I WARNED YOU THE JOURNEY WOULD BE HARD, DOCTOR.
AS HARD AS ALL LIFE HAS BECOME, WITH BLACK ZERO RISEN AGAIN IN STRENGTH.
MAKE NO MORE SPEECHES, VAN-L.
YOU HAVE SUCCESSFULLY RECRUITED ME TO YOUR CAUSE. AND PERHAPS I FELT IT WAS TIME FOR SOME... PREVENTATIVE MEDICINE.
IF WHAT YOU SAY IS TRUE...

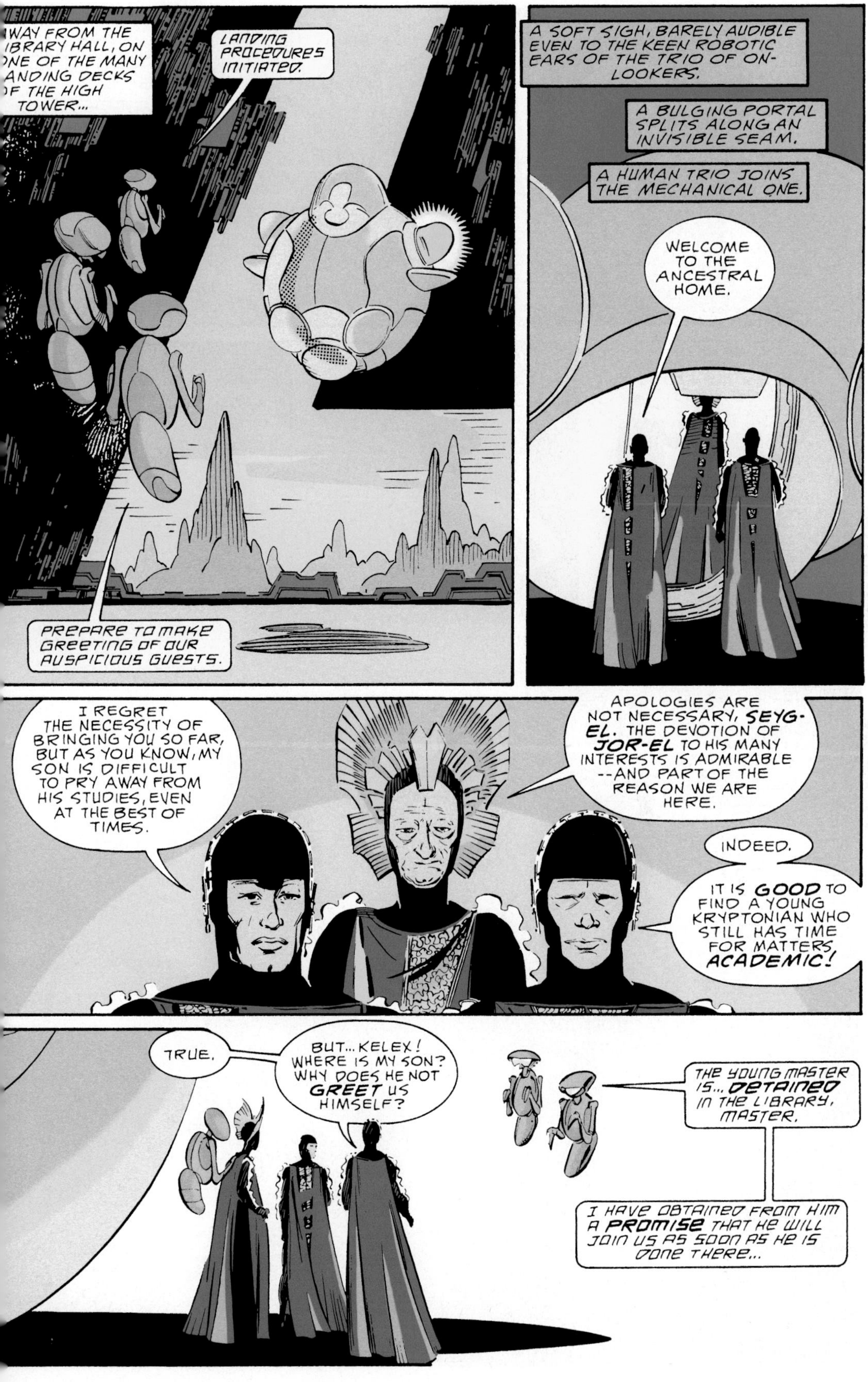

WAY FROM THE IBRARY HALL, ON NE OF THE MANY ANDING DECKS F THE HIGH TOWER...
LANDING PROCEDURES INITIATED.
PREPARE TO MAKE GREETING OF OUR AUSPICIOUS GUESTS.
A SOFT SIGH, BARELY AUDIBLE EVEN TO THE KEEN ROBOTIC EARS OF THE TRIO OF ON-LOOKERS.
A BULGING PORTAL SPLITS ALONG AN INVISIBLE SEAM.
A HUMAN TRIO JOINS THE MECHANICAL ONE.
WELCOME TO THE ANCESTRAL HOME.
I REGRET THE NECESSITY OF BRINGING YOU SO FAR, BUT AS YOU KNOW, MY SON IS DIFFICULT TO PRY AWAY FROM HIS STUDIES, EVEN AT THE BEST OF TIMES.
APOLOGIES ARE NOT NECESSARY, SEYG-EL. THE DEVOTION OF JOR-EL TO HIS MANY INTERESTS IS ADMIRABLE --AND PART OF THE REASON WE ARE HERE.
INDEED.
IT IS GOOD TO FIND A YOUNG KRYPTONIAN WHO STILL HAS TIME FOR MATTERS ACADEMIC!
TRUE.
BUT... KELEX! WHERE IS MY SON? WHY DOES HE NOT GREET US HIMSELF?
THE YOUNG MASTER IS... DETAINED IN THE LIBRARY, MASTER.
I HAVE OBTAINED FROM HIM A PROMISE THAT HE WILL JOIN US AS SOON AS HE IS DONE THERE...

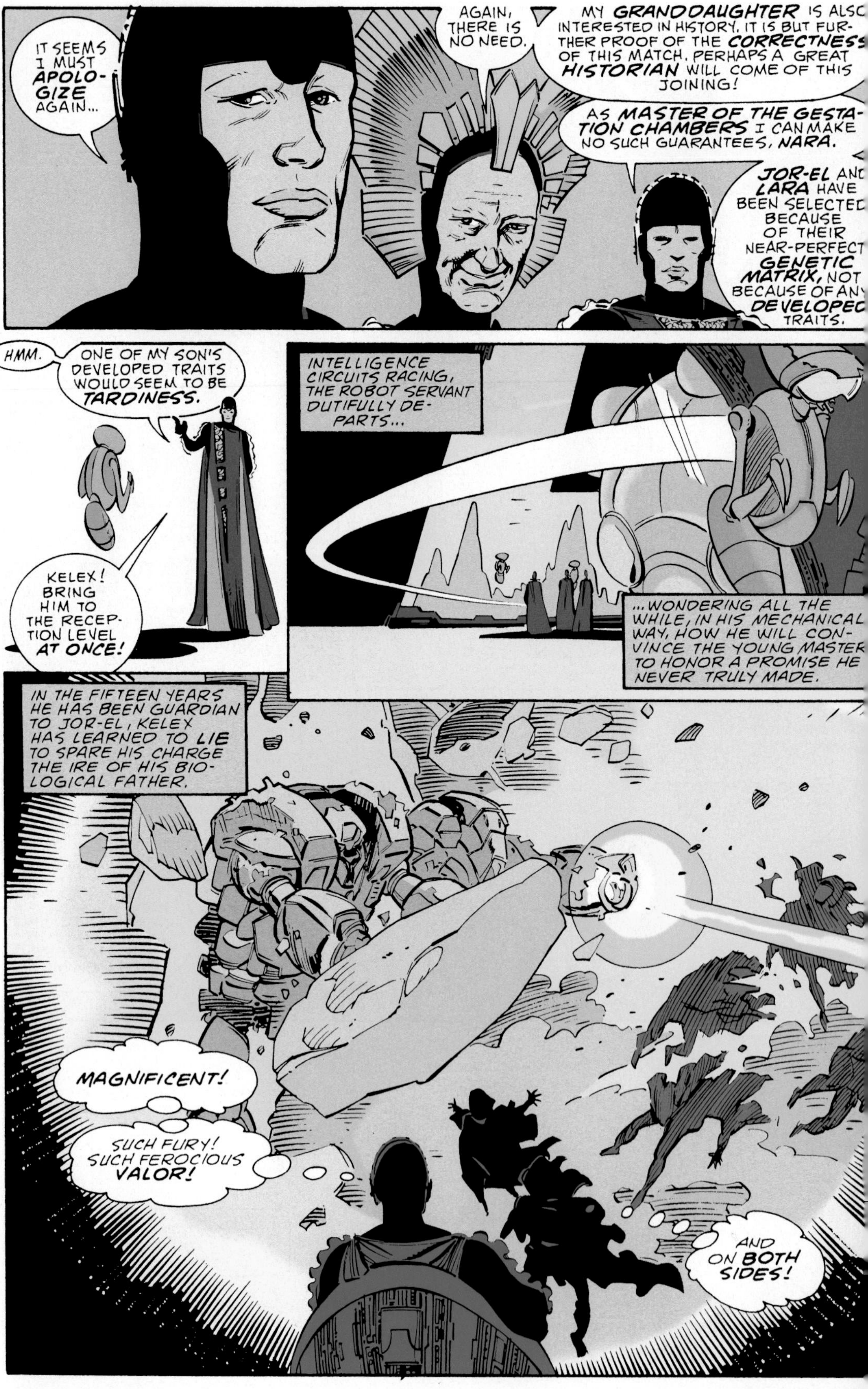

IT SEEMS I MUST APOLOGIZE AGAIN...
AGAIN, THERE IS NO NEED.
MY GRANDDAUGHTER IS ALSO INTERESTED IN HISTORY. IT IS BUT FURTHER PROOF OF THE CORRECTNESS OF THIS MATCH. PERHAPS A GREAT HISTORIAN WILL COME OF THIS JOINING!
AS MASTER OF THE GESTATION CHAMBERS I CAN MAKE NO SUCH GUARANTEES, NARA.
JOR-EL AND LARA HAVE BEEN SELECTED BECAUSE OF THEIR NEAR-PERFECT GENETIC MATRIX, NOT BECAUSE OF ANY DEVELOPED TRAITS.
HMM.
ONE OF MY SON'S DEVELOPED TRAITS WOULD SEEM TO BE TARDINESS.
KELEX! BRING HIM TO THE RECEPTION LEVEL AT ONCE!
INTELLIGENCE CIRCUITS RACING, THE ROBOT SERVANT DUTIFULLY DEPARTS...
...WONDERING ALL THE WHILE, IN HIS MECHANICAL WAY, HOW HE WILL CONVINCE THE YOUNG MASTER TO HONOR A PROMISE HE NEVER TRULY MADE.
IN THE FIFTEEN YEARS HE HAS BEEN GUARDIAN TO JOR-EL, KELEX HAS LEARNED TO LIE TO SPARE HIS CHARGE THE IRE OF HIS BIOLOGICAL FATHER.
MAGNIFICENT!
SUCH FURY! SUCH FEROCIOUS VALOR!
AND ON BOTH SIDES!

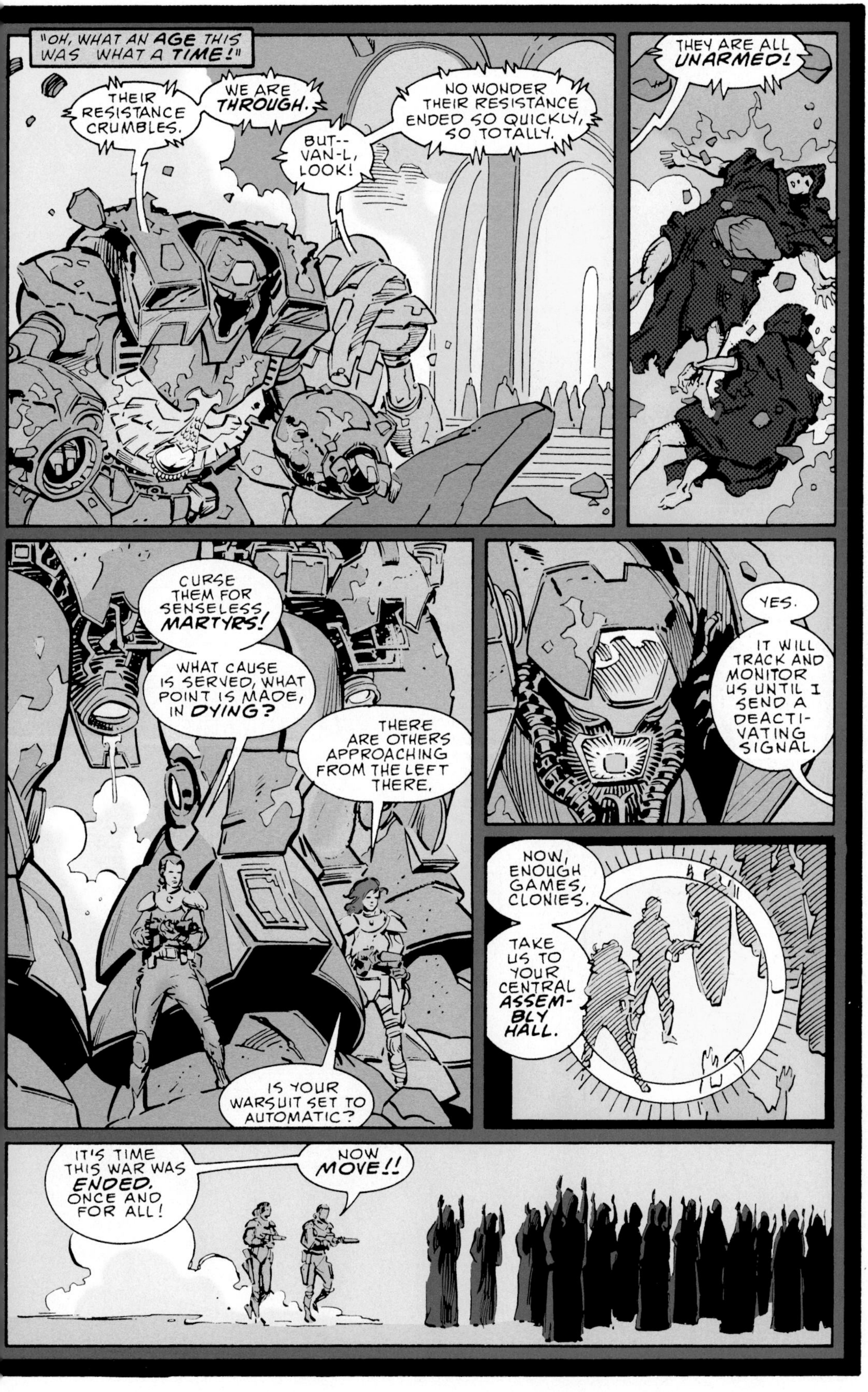
"OH, WHAT AN AGE THIS WAS WHAT A TIME!"
THEIR RESISTANCE CRUMBLES.
WE ARE THROUGH.
BUT-- VAN-L, LOOK!
NO WONDER THEIR RESISTANCE ENDED SO QUICKLY, SO TOTALLY.
THEY ARE ALL UNARMED!
CURSE THEM FOR SENSELESS MARTYRS!
WHAT CAUSE IS SERVED, WHAT POINT IS MADE, IN DYING?
THERE ARE OTHERS APPROACHING FROM THE LEFT THERE.
IS YOUR WARSUIT SET TO AUTOMATIC?
YES.
IT WILL TRACK AND MONITOR US UNTIL I SEND A DEACTIVATING SIGNAL.
NOW, ENOUGH GAMES, CLONIES.
TAKE US TO YOUR CENTRAL ASSEMBLY HALL.
IT'S TIME THIS WAR WAS ENDED. ONCE AND FOR ALL!
NOW MOVE!!

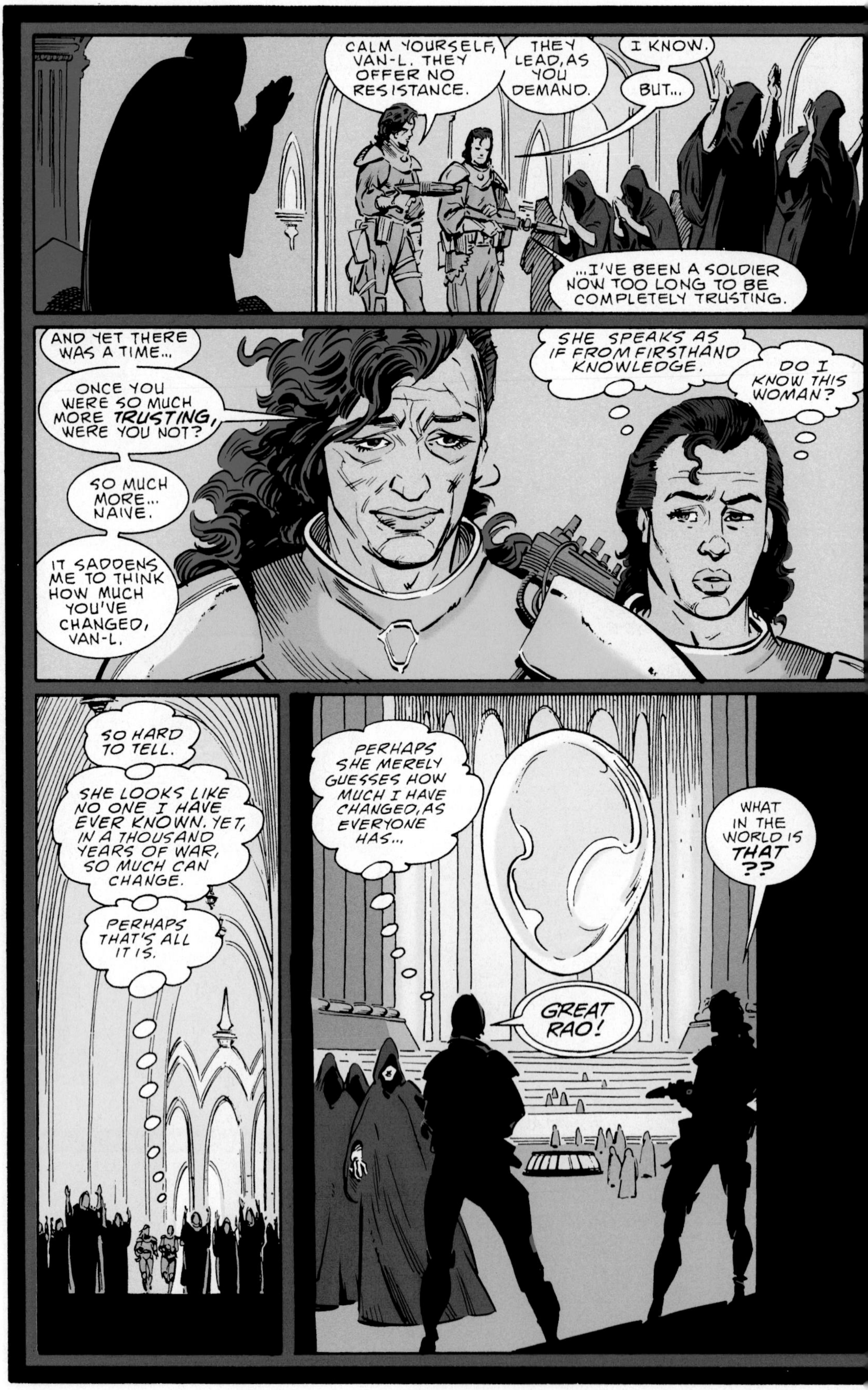
CALM YOURSELF, VAN-L. THEY OFFER NO RESISTANCE.
THEY LEAD, AS YOU DEMAND.
I KNOW.
BUT...
...I'VE BEEN A SOLDIER NOW TOO LONG TO BE COMPLETELY TRUSTING.
AND YET THERE WAS A TIME...
ONCE YOU WERE SO MUCH MORE TRUSTING, WERE YOU NOT?
SO MUCH MORE... NAIVE.
IT SADDENS ME TO THINK HOW MUCH YOU'VE CHANGED, VAN-L.
SHE SPEAKS AS IF FROM FIRSTHAND KNOWLEDGE.
DO I KNOW THIS WOMAN?
SO HARD TO TELL.
SHE LOOKS LIKE NO ONE I HAVE EVER KNOWN. YET, IN A THOUSAND YEARS OF WAR, SO MUCH CAN CHANGE.
PERHAPS THAT'S ALL IT IS.
PERHAPS SHE MERELY GUESSES HOW MUCH I HAVE CHANGED, AS EVERYONE HAS...
GREAT RAO!
WHAT IN THE WORLD IS THAT??

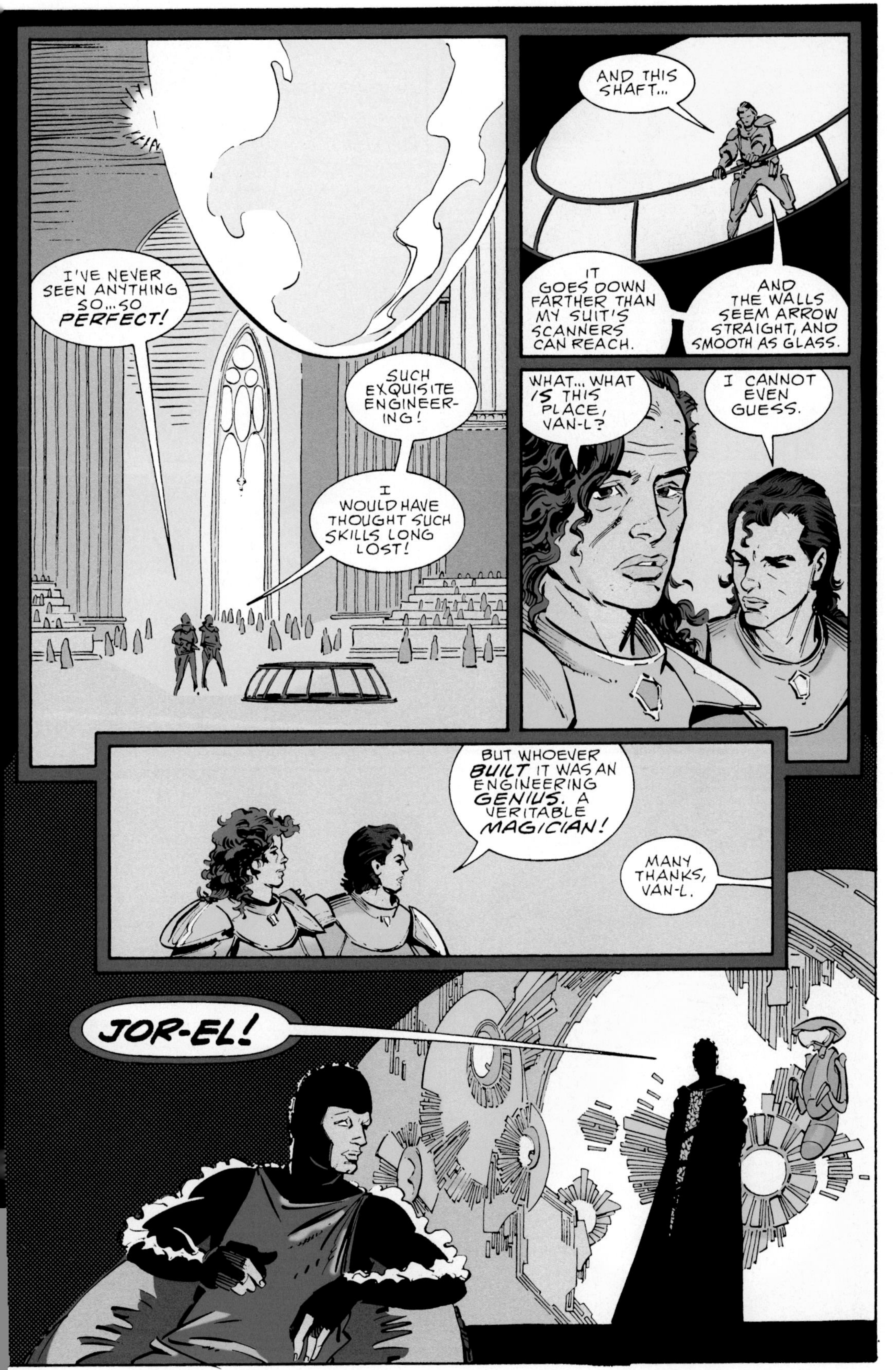
I'VE NEVER SEEN ANYTHING SO...SO PERFECT!
SUCH EXQUISITE ENGINEER-ING!
I WOULD HAVE THOUGHT SUCH SKILLS LONG LOST!
AND THIS SHAFT...
IT GOES DOWN FARTHER THAN MY SUIT'S SCANNERS CAN REACH.
AND THE WALLS SEEM ARROW STRAIGHT, AND SMOOTH AS GLASS.
WHAT... WHAT IS THIS PLACE, VAN-L?
I CANNOT EVEN GUESS.
BUT WHOEVER BUILT IT WAS AN ENGINEERING GENIUS. A VERITABLE MAGICIAN!
MANY THANKS, VAN-L.
JOR-EL!

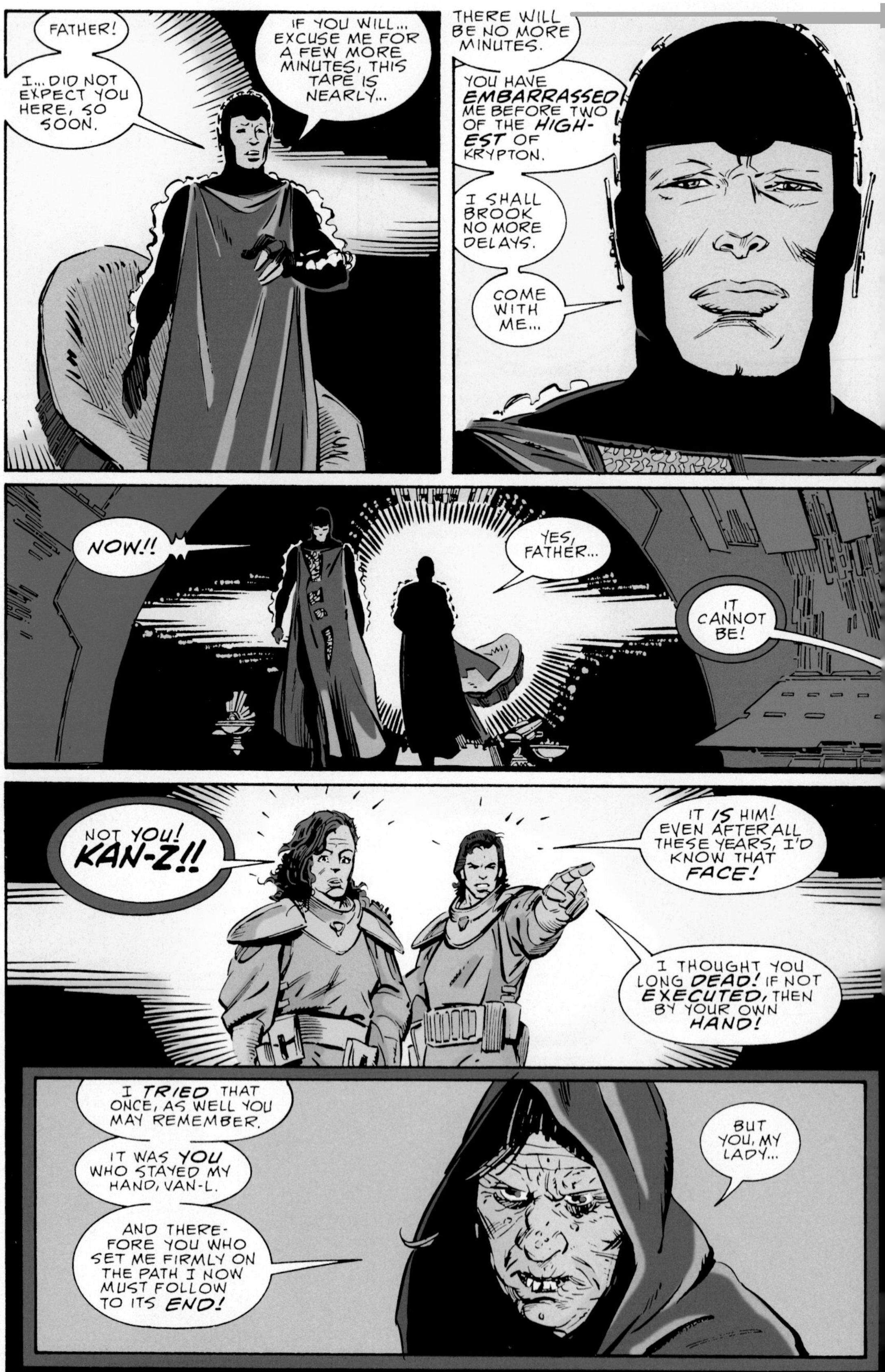
FATHER!
I... DID NOT EXPECT YOU HERE, SO SOON.
IF YOU WILL... EXCUSE ME FOR A FEW MORE MINUTES, THIS TAPE IS NEARLY...
THERE WILL BE NO MORE MINUTES.
YOU HAVE EMBARRASSED ME BEFORE TWO OF THE HIGHEST OF KRYPTON.
I SHALL BROOK NO MORE DELAYS.
COME WITH ME...
NOW!!
YES, FATHER...
IT CANNOT BE!
NOT YOU! KAN-Z!!
IT IS HIM! EVEN AFTER ALL THESE YEARS, I'D KNOW THAT FACE!
I THOUGHT YOU LONG DEAD! IF NOT EXECUTED, THEN BY YOUR OWN HAND!
I TRIED THAT ONCE, AS WELL YOU MAY REMEMBER.
IT WAS YOU WHO STAYED MY HAND, VAN-L.
AND THEREFORE YOU WHO SET ME FIRMLY ON THE PATH I NOW MUST FOLLOW TO ITS END!
BUT YOU, MY LADY...

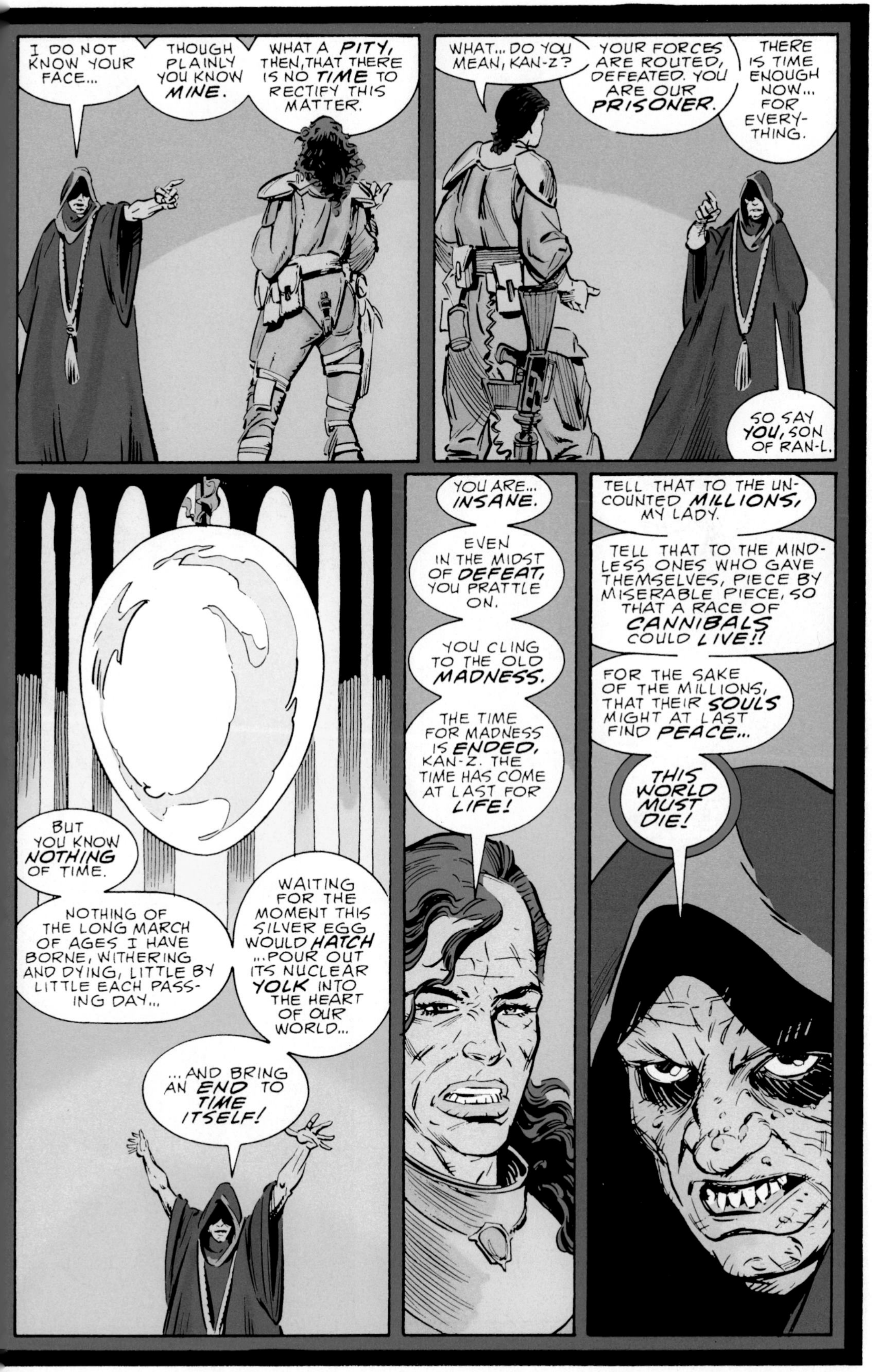

I DO NOT KNOW YOUR FACE...
THOUGH PLAINLY YOU KNOW MINE.
WHAT A PITY, THEN, THAT THERE IS NO TIME TO RECTIFY THIS MATTER.
WHAT... DO YOU MEAN, KAN-Z?
YOUR FORCES ARE ROUTED, DEFEATED. YOU ARE OUR PRISONER.
THERE IS TIME ENOUGH NOW... FOR EVERY-THING.
SO SAY YOU, SON OF RAN-L.
BUT YOU KNOW NOTHING OF TIME.
NOTHING OF THE LONG MARCH OF AGES I HAVE BORNE, WITHERING AND DYING, LITTLE BY LITTLE EACH PASS-ING DAY...
WAITING FOR THE MOMENT THIS SILVER EGG WOULD HATCH ...POUR OUT ITS NUCLEAR YOLK INTO THE HEART OF OUR WORLD...
...AND BRING AN END TO TIME ITSELF!
YOU ARE... INSANE.
EVEN IN THE MIDST OF DEFEAT, YOU PRATTLE ON.
YOU CLING TO THE OLD MADNESS.
THE TIME FOR MADNESS IS ENDED, KAN-Z. THE TIME HAS COME AT LAST FOR LIFE!
TELL THAT TO THE UN-COUNTED MILLIONS, MY LADY.
TELL THAT TO THE MIND-LESS ONES WHO GAVE THEMSELVES, PIECE BY MISERABLE PIECE, SO THAT A RACE OF CANNIBALS COULD LIVE!!
FOR THE SAKE OF THE MILLIONS, THAT THEIR SOULS MIGHT AT LAST FIND PEACE...
THIS WORLD MUST DIE!

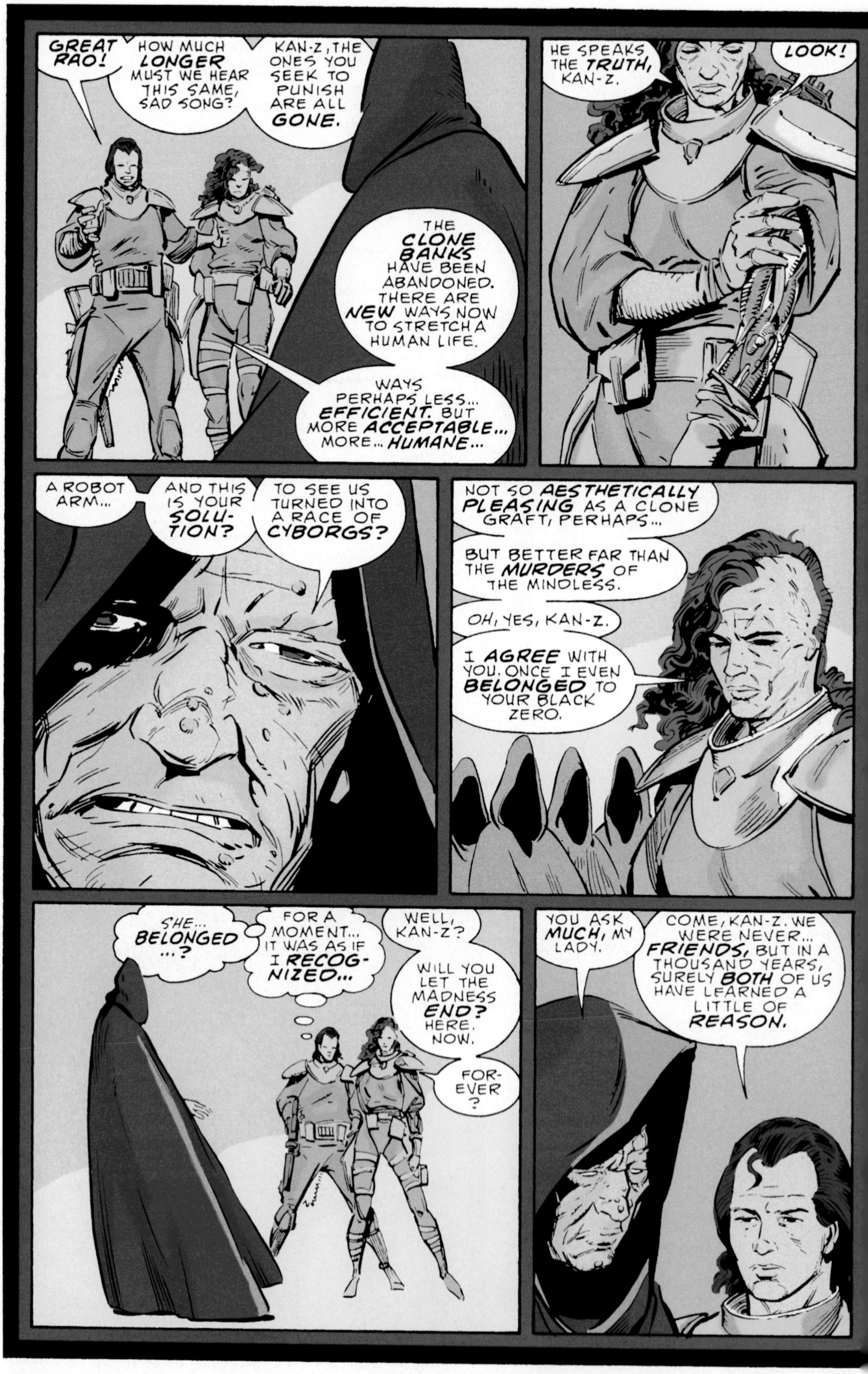
GREAT RAO!
HOW MUCH LONGER MUST WE HEAR THIS SAME, SAD SONG?
KAN-Z, THE ONES YOU SEEK TO PUNISH ARE ALL GONE.
THE CLONE BANKS HAVE BEEN ABANDONED. THERE ARE NEW WAYS NOW TO STRETCH A HUMAN LIFE.
WAYS PERHAPS LESS... EFFICIENT. BUT MORE ACCEPTABLE... MORE... HUMANE...
HE SPEAKS THE TRUTH, KAN-Z.
LOOK!
A ROBOT ARM...
AND THIS IS YOUR SOLU-TION?
TO SEE US TURNED INTO A RACE OF CYBORGS?
NOT SO AESTHETICALLY PLEASING AS A CLONE GRAFT, PERHAPS...
BUT BETTER FAR THAN THE MURDERS OF THE MINDLESS.
OH, YES, KAN-Z.
I AGREE WITH YOU. ONCE I EVEN BELONGED TO YOUR BLACK ZERO.
SHE... BELONGED ...?
FOR A MOMENT... IT WAS AS IF I RECOG-NIZED...
WELL, KAN-Z?
WILL YOU LET THE MADNESS END? HERE. NOW.
FOR-EVER?
YOU ASK MUCH, MY LADY.
COME, KAN-Z. WE WERE NEVER... FRIENDS, BUT IN A THOUSAND YEARS, SURELY BOTH OF US HAVE LEARNED A LITTLE OF REASON.

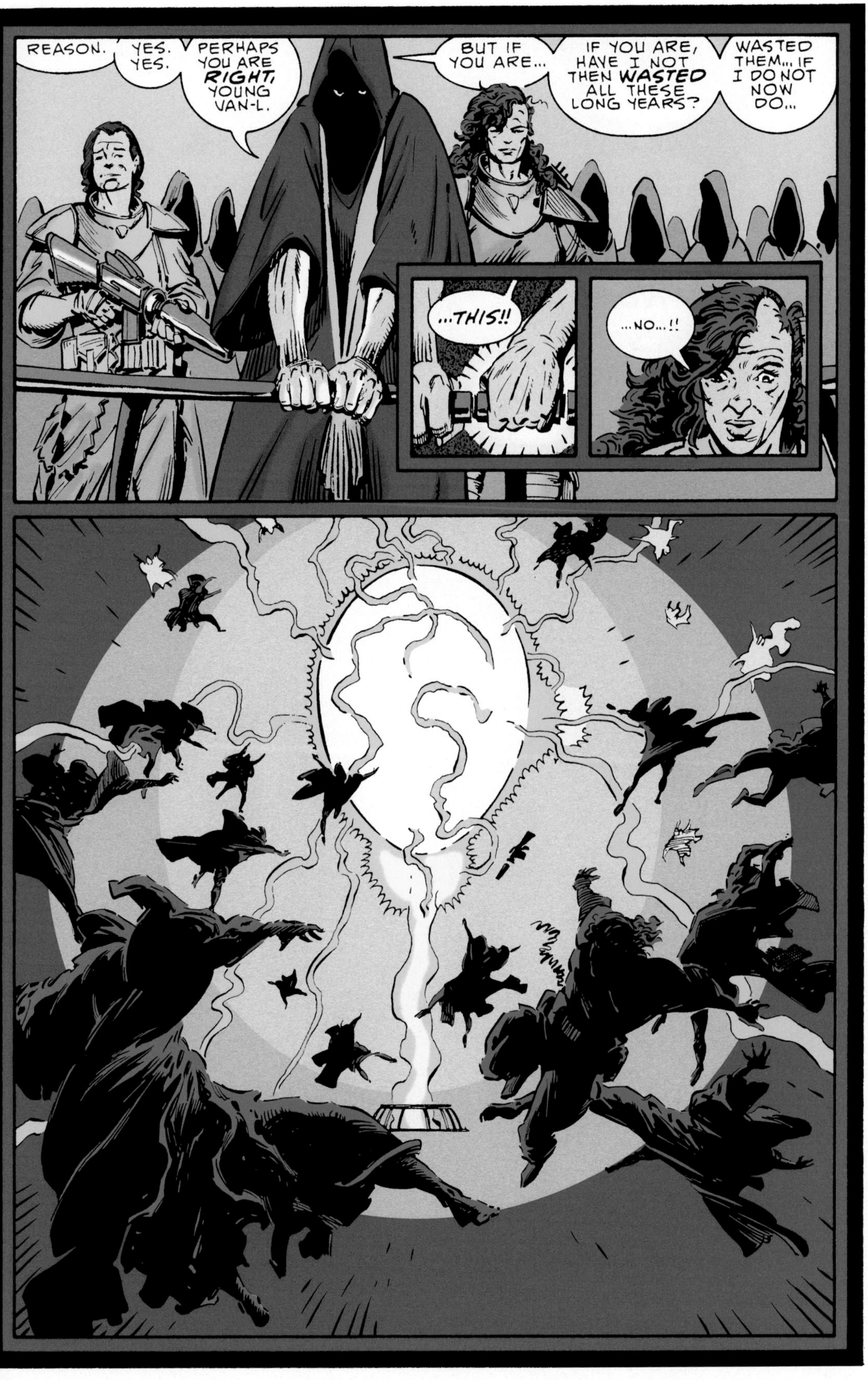
REASON.
YES. YES.
PERHAPS YOU ARE RIGHT, YOUNG VAN-L.
BUT IF YOU ARE...
IF YOU ARE, HAVE I NOT THEN WASTED ALL THESE LONG YEARS?
WASTED THEM... IF I DO NOT NOW DO...
...THIS!!
...NO...!!

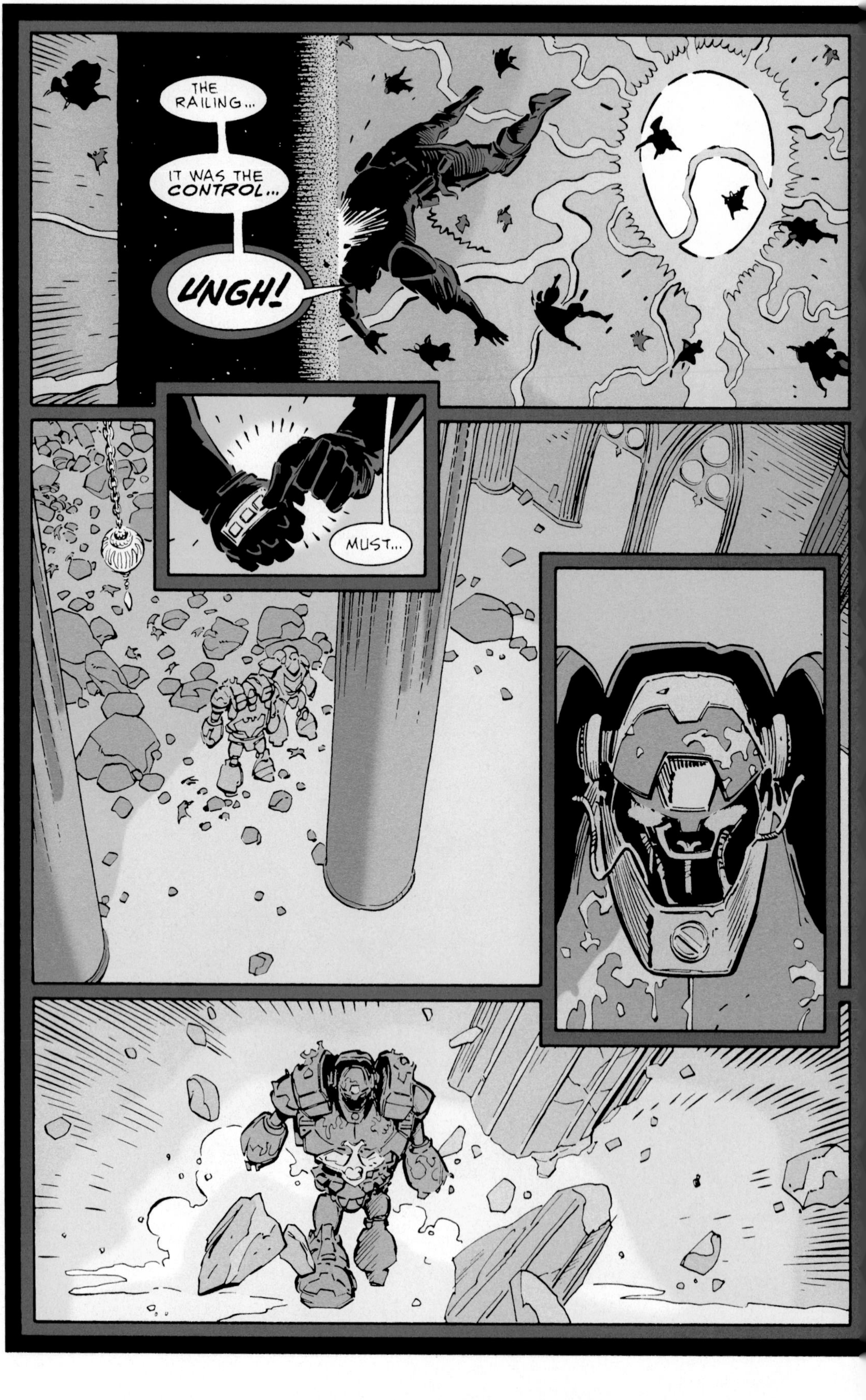
THE RAILING...
IT WAS THE CONTROL...
UNGH!
MUST...

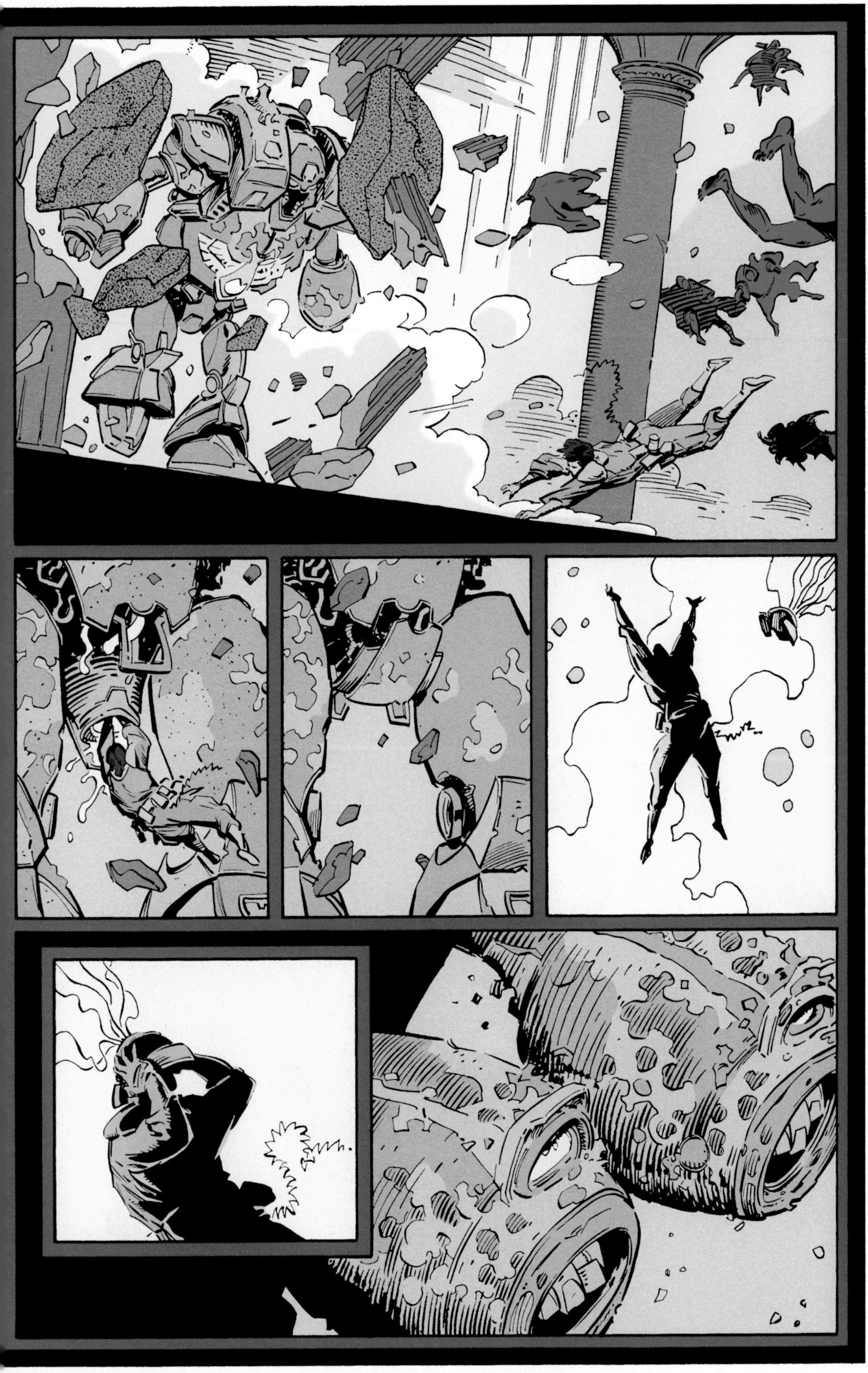

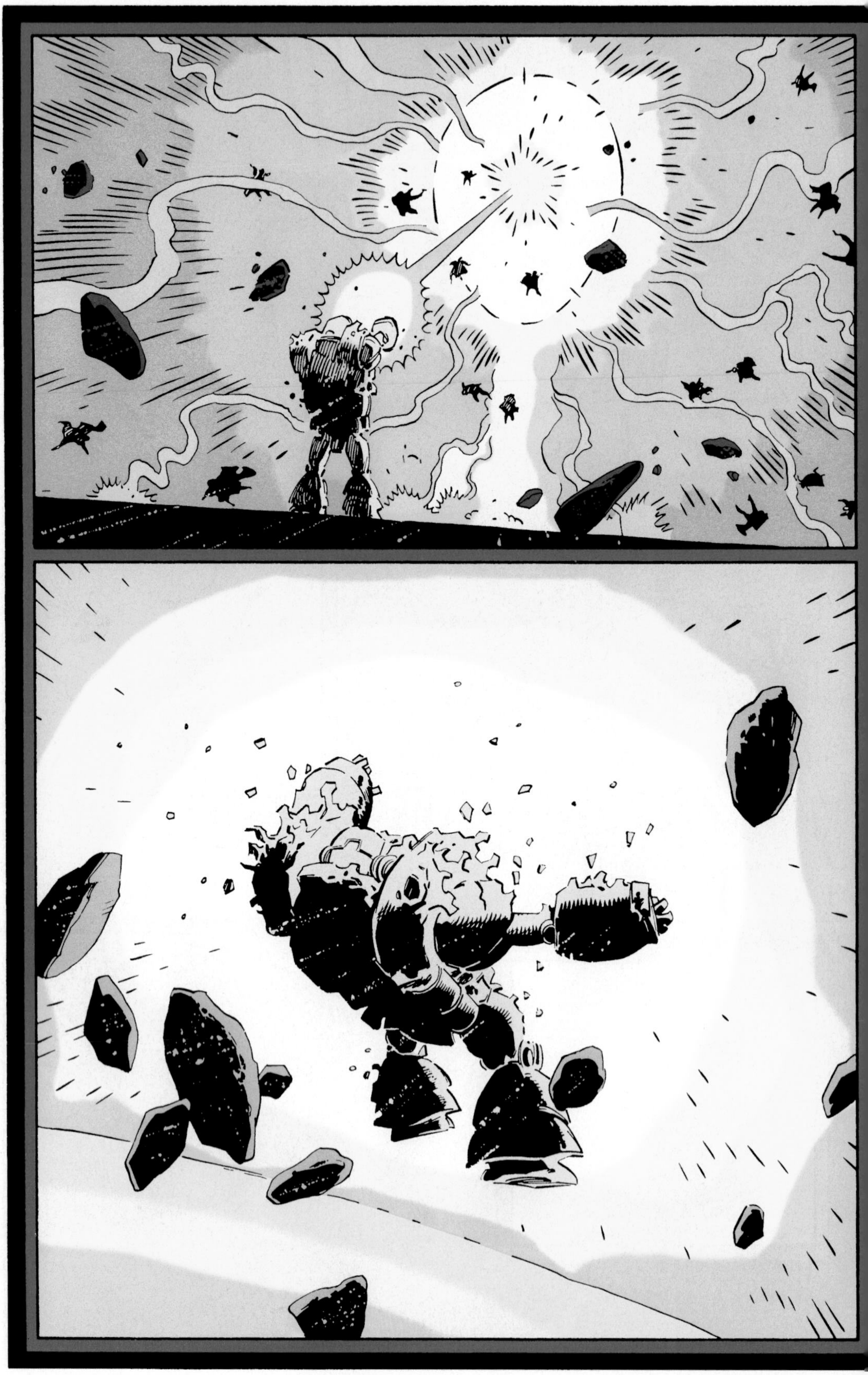

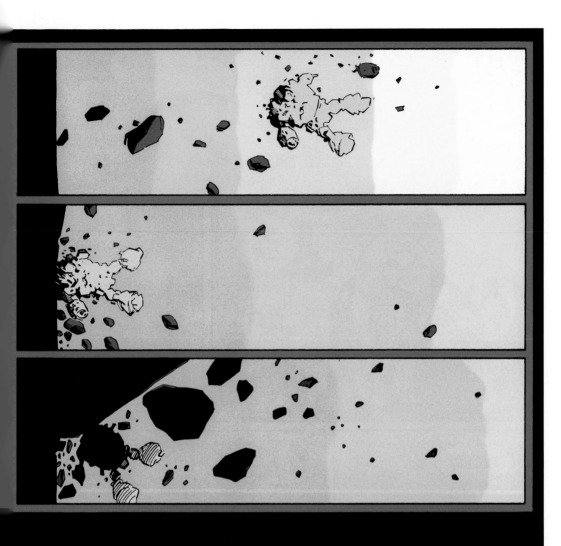

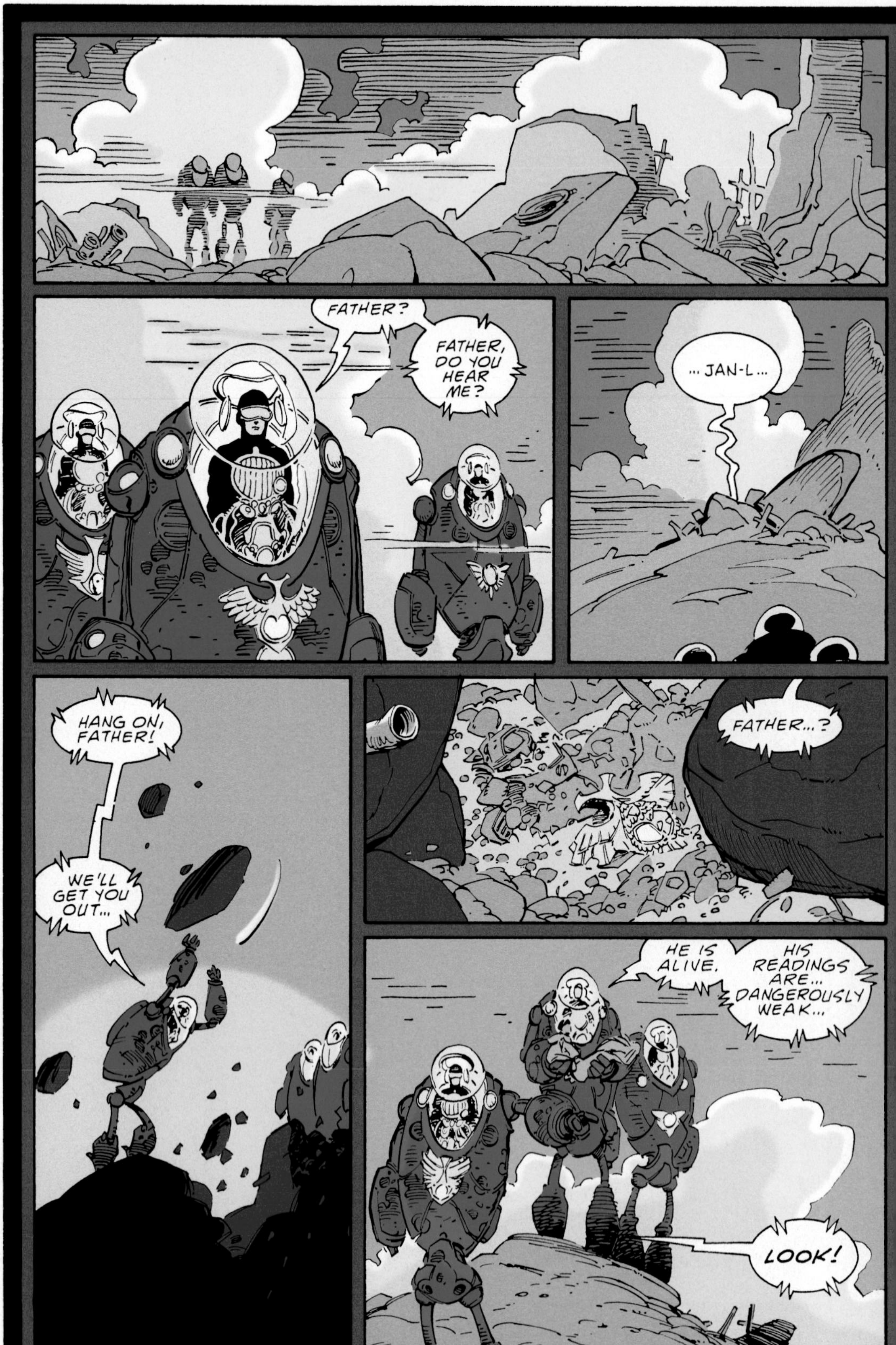
FATHER?
FATHER, DO YOU HEAR ME?
...JAN-L...
HANG ON, FATHER!
WE'LL GET YOU OUT...
FATHER...?
HE IS ALIVE.
HIS READINGS ARE... DANGEROUSLY WEAK...
LOOK!

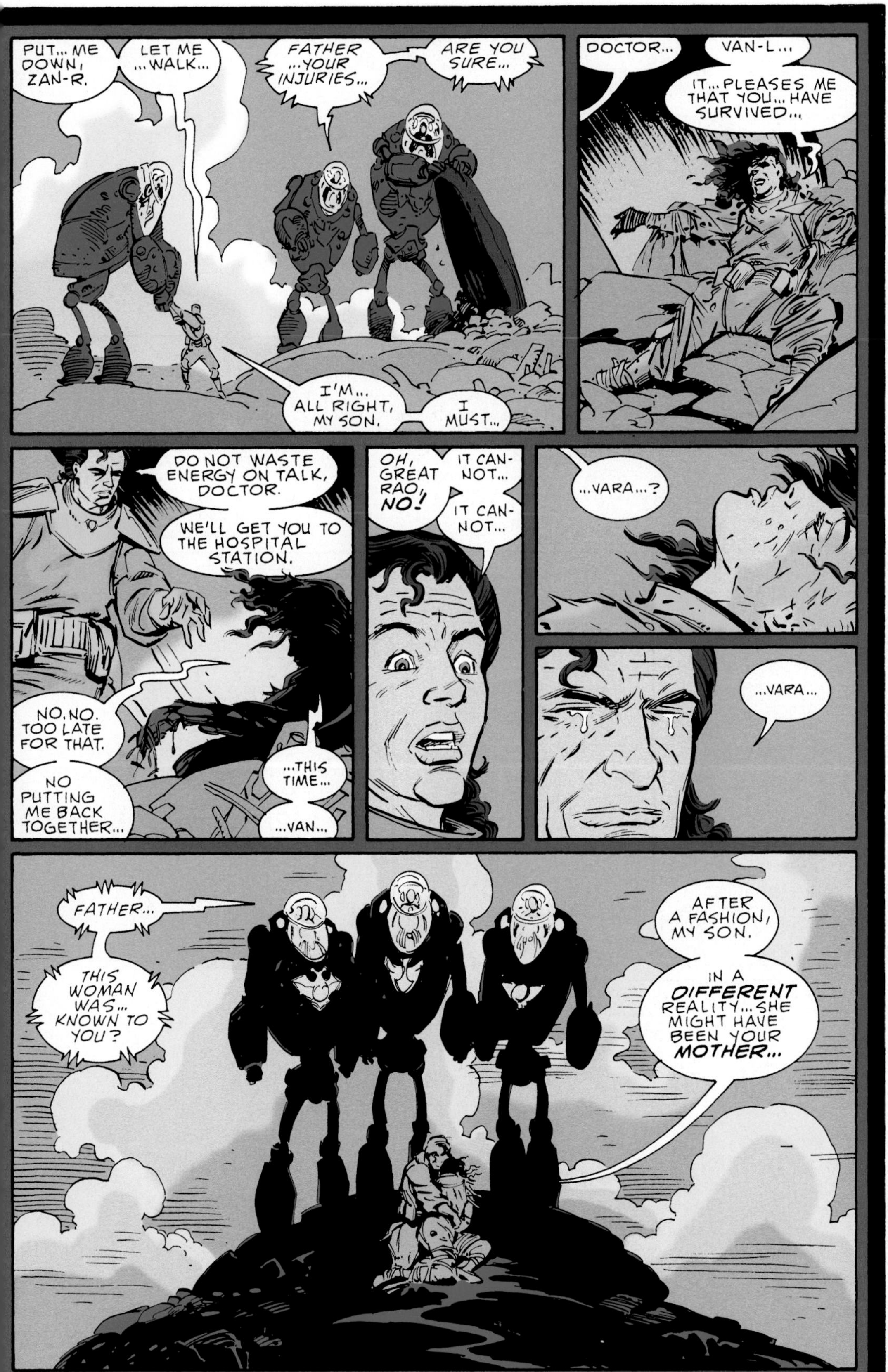
PUT... ME DOWN, ZAN-R.
LET ME ...WALK...
FATHER ...YOUR INJURIES...
ARE YOU SURE...
I'M... ALL RIGHT, MY SON.
I MUST...
DOCTOR...
VAN-L...
IT... PLEASES ME THAT YOU... HAVE SURVIVED...
DO NOT WASTE ENERGY ON TALK, DOCTOR.
WE'LL GET YOU TO THE HOSPITAL STATION.
NO, NO. TOO LATE FOR THAT.
NO PUTTING ME BACK TOGETHER...
...THIS TIME...
...VAN...
OH, GREAT RAO, NO!
IT CAN-NOT...
IT CAN-NOT...
...VARA...?
...VARA...
FATHER...
THIS WOMAN WAS... KNOWN TO YOU?
AFTER A FASHION, MY SON.
IN A DIFFERENT REALITY... SHE MIGHT HAVE BEEN YOUR MOTHER...

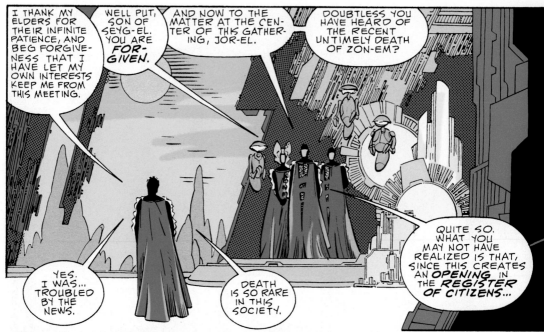

I THANK MY ELDERS FOR THEIR INFINITE PATIENCE, AND BEG FORGIVENESS THAT I HAVE LET MY OWN INTERESTS KEEP ME FROM THIS MEETING.

WELL PUT, SON OF SEYG-EL. YOU ARE *FORGIVEN*.

AND NOW TO THE MATTER AT THE CENTER OF THIS GATHERING, JOR-EL.

DOUBTLESS YOU HAVE HEARD OF THE RECENT UNTIMELY DEATH OF ZON-EM?

YES. I WAS... TROUBLED BY THE NEWS.

DEATH IS SO RARE IN THIS SOCIETY.

QUITE SO. WHAT YOU MAY NOT HAVE REALIZED IS THAT, SINCE THIS CREATES AN *OPENING* IN THE *REGISTER OF CITIZENS*...

...*YOU* HAVE BEEN CHOSEN TO FATHER THE NEW KRYPTONIAN WHO WILL *FILL* THAT OPENING.

I...?

I... BUT... I HAVE NOT YET TAKEN THE *RITES OF PASSAGE*. BY KRYPTONIAN LAW...

...I AM STILL A *CHILD* MYSELF...

TRUE ENOUGH, SON OF SEYG-EL,

AND THIS... MATTER IS NOT TO BE SET OUT UPON HERE AND NOW.

HOWEVER, AS YOU YOURSELF HAVE POINTED OUT, THE NECESSITY OF SUCH A THING IS SO RARE THAT I DECIDED YOU WOULD NEED *TIME* TO PREPARE YOURSELF, EMOTIONALLY, FOR THE HONOR.

I... LORDS... LADY... I DO NOT HAVE THE PROPER *WORDS*...

NONE ARE NEEDED, MY SON.

YOU NEED ONLY GIVE THE ADDRESS OF RESPECT TO NARA, WHO IS GRANDMOTHER OF THE FEMALE CHILD CHOSEN AS YOUR MATE.

WITH GREATEST *PLEASURE*, FATHER.

HAIL, NARA, DAUGHTER OF KRYPTON, MAY THE MINGLING OF OUR FAMILIES BRING FORTH ONLY WISDOM AND TRANQUILITY.

AGAIN, WELL SAID... JOR-EL.

I AM *PLEASED* AT THIS UNION.

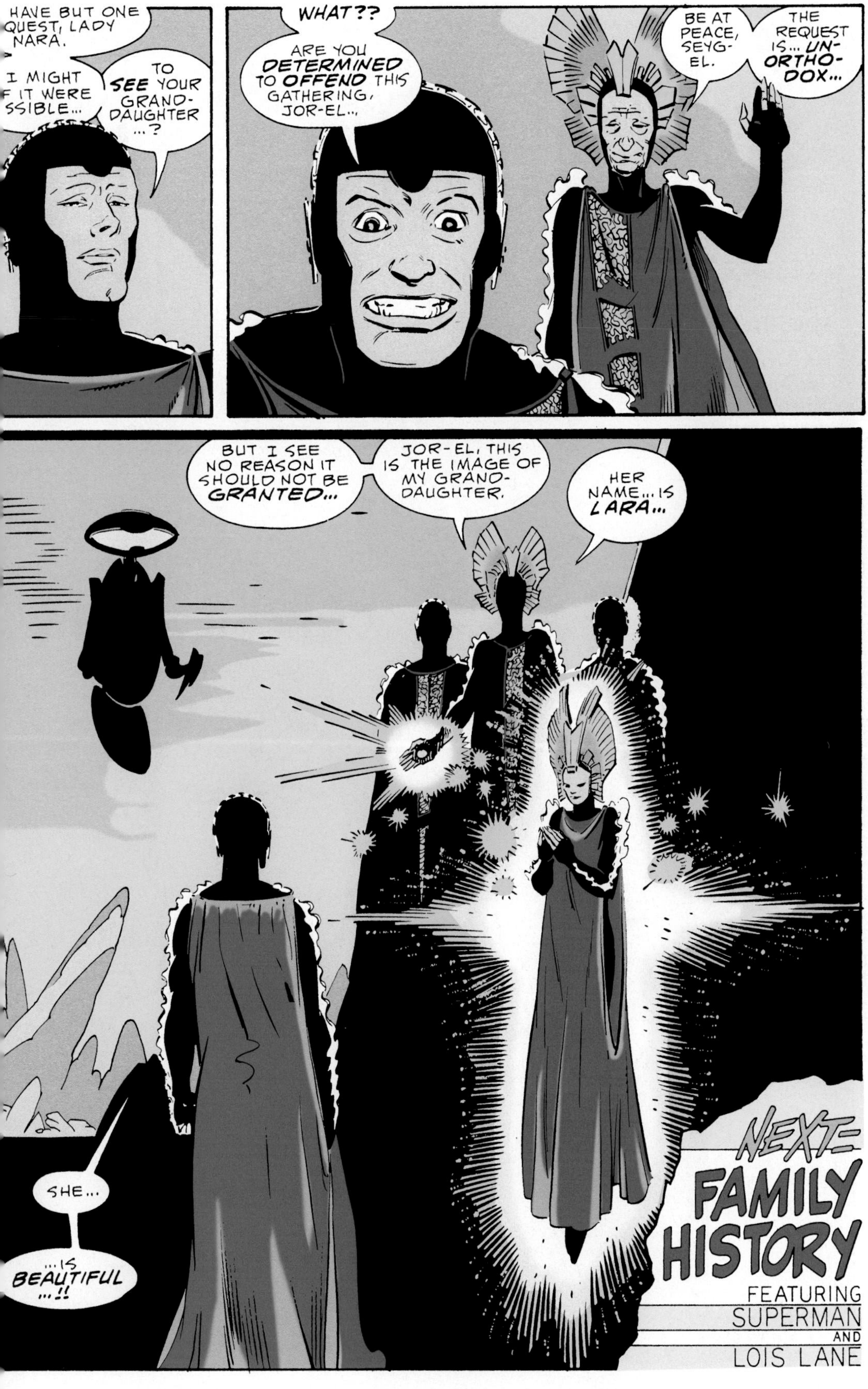
HAVE BUT ONE QUEST, LADY NARA.
I MIGHT F IT WERE SSIBLE...
TO SEE YOUR GRAND-DAUGHTER ...?
WHAT??
ARE YOU DETERMINED TO OFFEND THIS GATHERING, JOR-EL...
BE AT PEACE, SEYG-EL.
THE REQUEST IS... UN-ORTHO-DOX...
BUT I SEE NO REASON IT SHOULD NOT BE GRANTED...
JOR-EL, THIS IS THE IMAGE OF MY GRAND-DAUGHTER.
HER NAME... IS LARA...
SHE...
...IS BEAUTIFUL ...!!
NEXT:
FAMILY HISTORY
FEATURING
SUPERMAN
AND
LOIS LANE

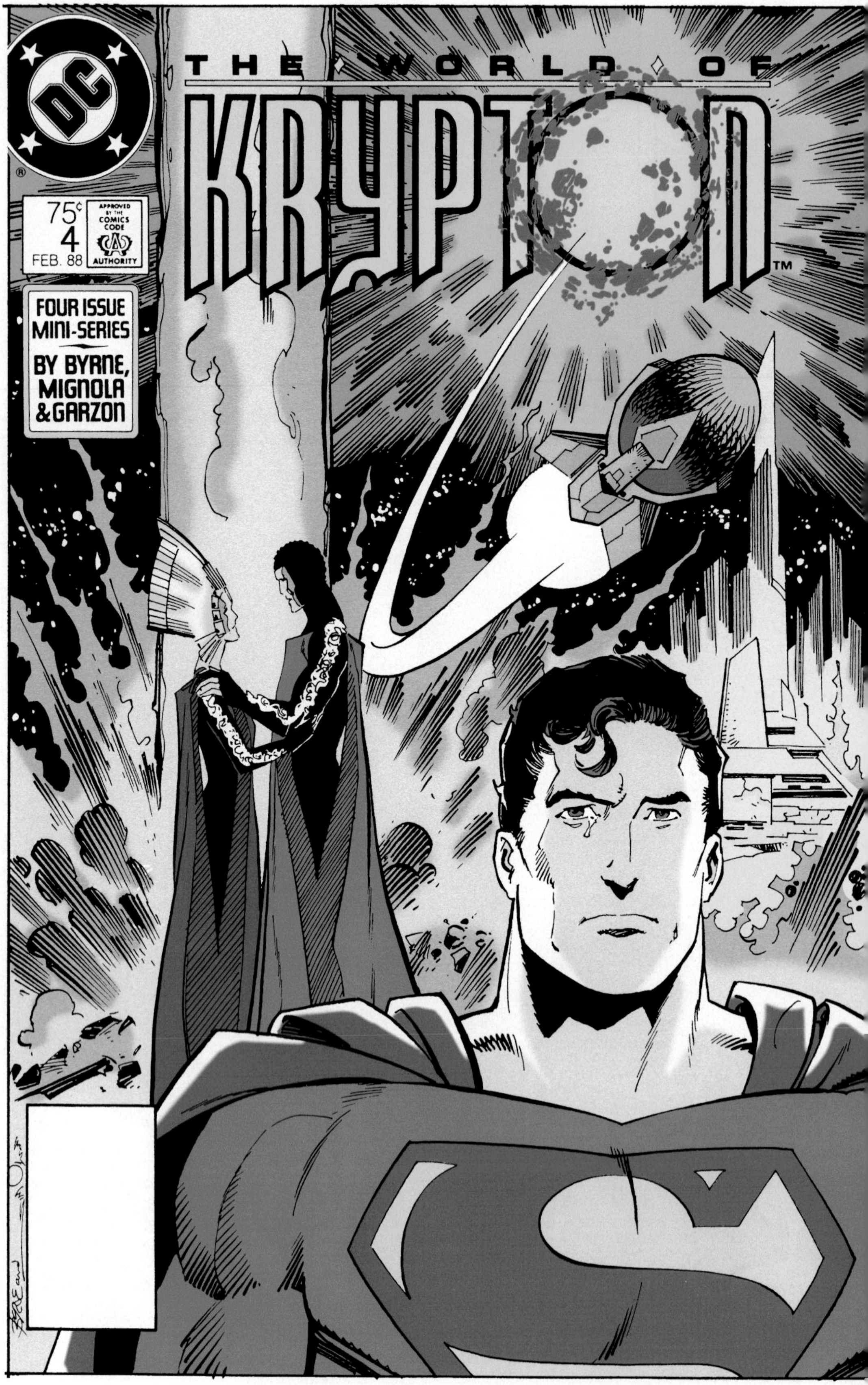
THE WORLD OF
KRYPTON
75¢
4
FEB. 88
APPROVED BY THE COMICS CODE AUTHORITY
FOUR ISSUE MINI-SERIES
BY BYRNE, MIGNOLA & GARZON

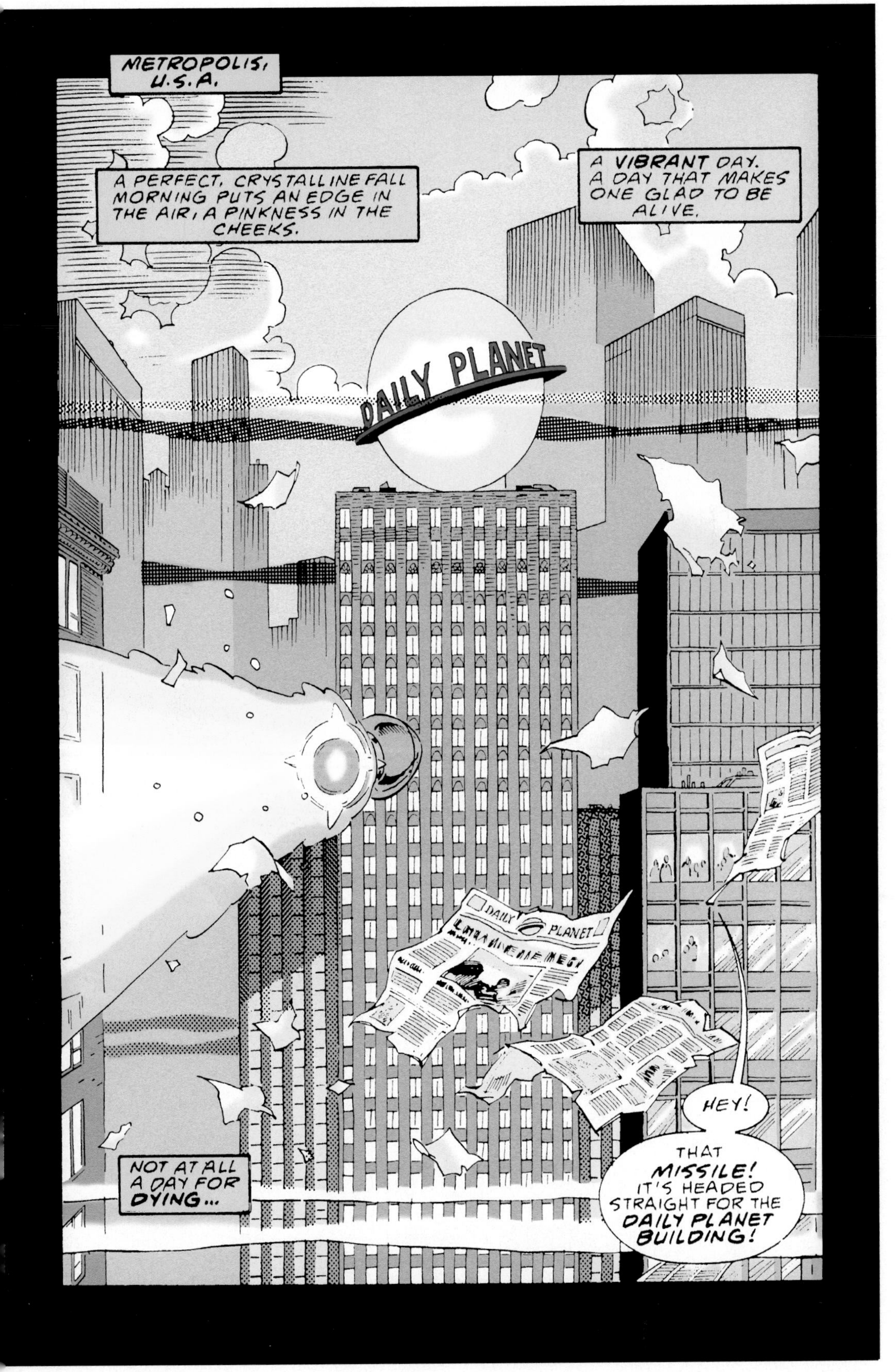
METROPOLIS, U.S.A.
A PERFECT, CRYSTALLINE FALL MORNING PUTS AN EDGE IN THE AIR, A PINKNESS IN THE CHEEKS.
A VIBRANT DAY. A DAY THAT MAKES ONE GLAD TO BE ALIVE.
DAILY PLANET
DAILY PLANET
NOT AT ALL A DAY FOR DYING...
HEY!
THAT MISSILE! IT'S HEADED STRAIGHT FOR THE DAILY PLANET BUILDING!

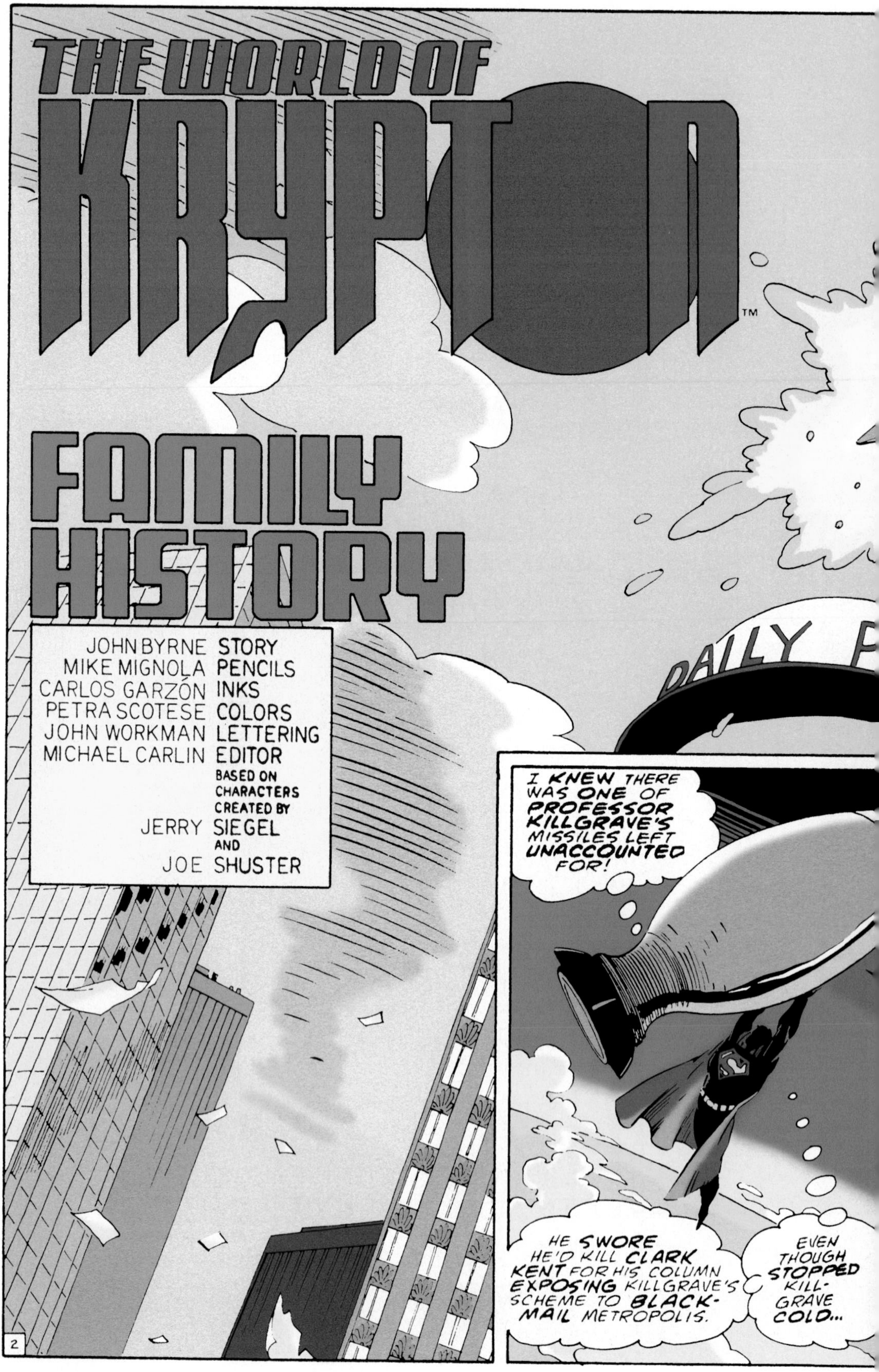
THE WORLD OF KRYPTON™
FAMILY HISTORY
JOHN BYRNE STORY
MIKE MIGNOLA PENCILS
CARLOS GARZÓN INKS
PETRA SCOTESE COLORS
JOHN WORKMAN LETTERING
MICHAEL CARLIN EDITOR
BASED ON CHARACTERS CREATED BY
JERRY SIEGEL
AND
JOE SHUSTER
2
DAILY P
I KNEW THERE WAS ONE OF PROFESSOR KILLGRAVE'S MISSILES LEFT UNACCOUNTED FOR!
HE SWORE HE'D KILL CLARK KENT FOR HIS COLUMN EXPOSING KILLGRAVE'S SCHEME TO BLACKMAIL METROPOLIS.
EVEN THOUGH STOPPED KILLGRAVE COLD...

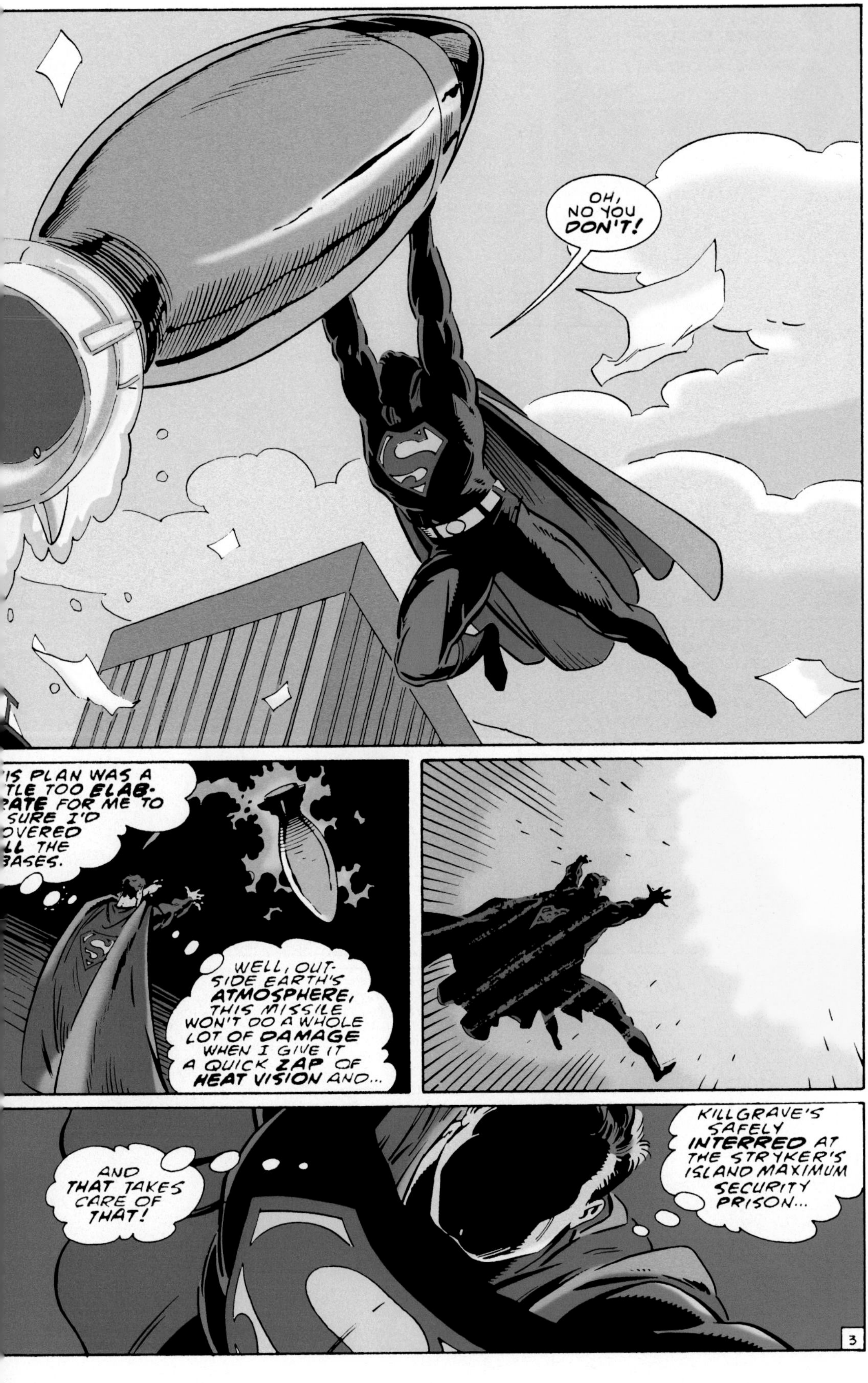
OH, NO YOU DON'T!
'IS PLAN WAS A 'TLE TOO ELAB- RATE FOR ME TO SURE I'D OVERED LL THE BASES.
WELL, OUT- SIDE EARTH'S ATMOSPHERE, THIS MISSILE WON'T DO A WHOLE LOT OF DAMAGE WHEN I GIVE IT A QUICK ZAP OF HEAT VISION AND...
AND THAT TAKES CARE OF THAT!
KILLGRAVE'S SAFELY INTERRED AT THE STRYKER'S ISLAND MAXIMUM SECURITY PRISON...
3

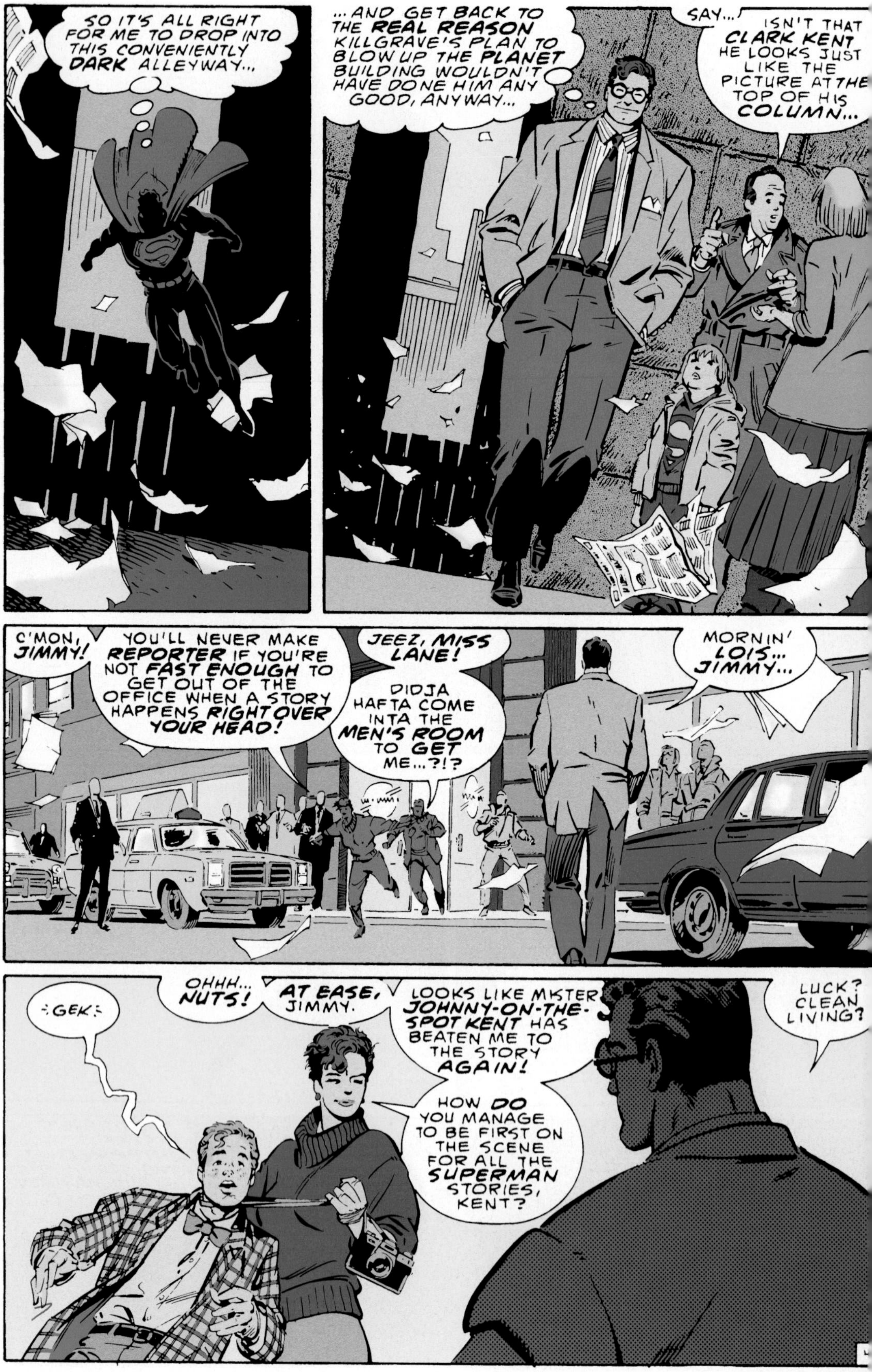
SO IT'S ALL RIGHT FOR ME TO DROP INTO THIS CONVENIENTLY DARK ALLEYWAY...
...AND GET BACK TO THE REAL REASON KILLGRAVE'S PLAN TO BLOW UP THE PLANET BUILDING WOULDN'T HAVE DONE HIM ANY GOOD, ANYWAY...
SAY...
ISN'T THAT CLARK KENT HE LOOKS JUST LIKE THE PICTURE AT THE TOP OF HIS COLUMN...
C'MON, JIMMY!
YOU'LL NEVER MAKE REPORTER IF YOU'RE NOT FAST ENOUGH TO GET OUT OF THE OFFICE WHEN A STORY HAPPENS RIGHT OVER YOUR HEAD!
JEEZ, MISS LANE!
DIDJA HAFTA COME INTA THE MEN'S ROOM TO GET ME...?!?
MORNIN' LOIS... JIMMY...
-GEK-
OHHH... NUTS!
AT EASE, JIMMY.
LOOKS LIKE MISTER JOHNNY-ON-THE-SPOT KENT HAS BEATEN ME TO THE STORY AGAIN!
HOW DO YOU MANAGE TO BE FIRST ON THE SCENE FOR ALL THE SUPERMAN STORIES, KENT?
LUCK? CLEAN LIVING?

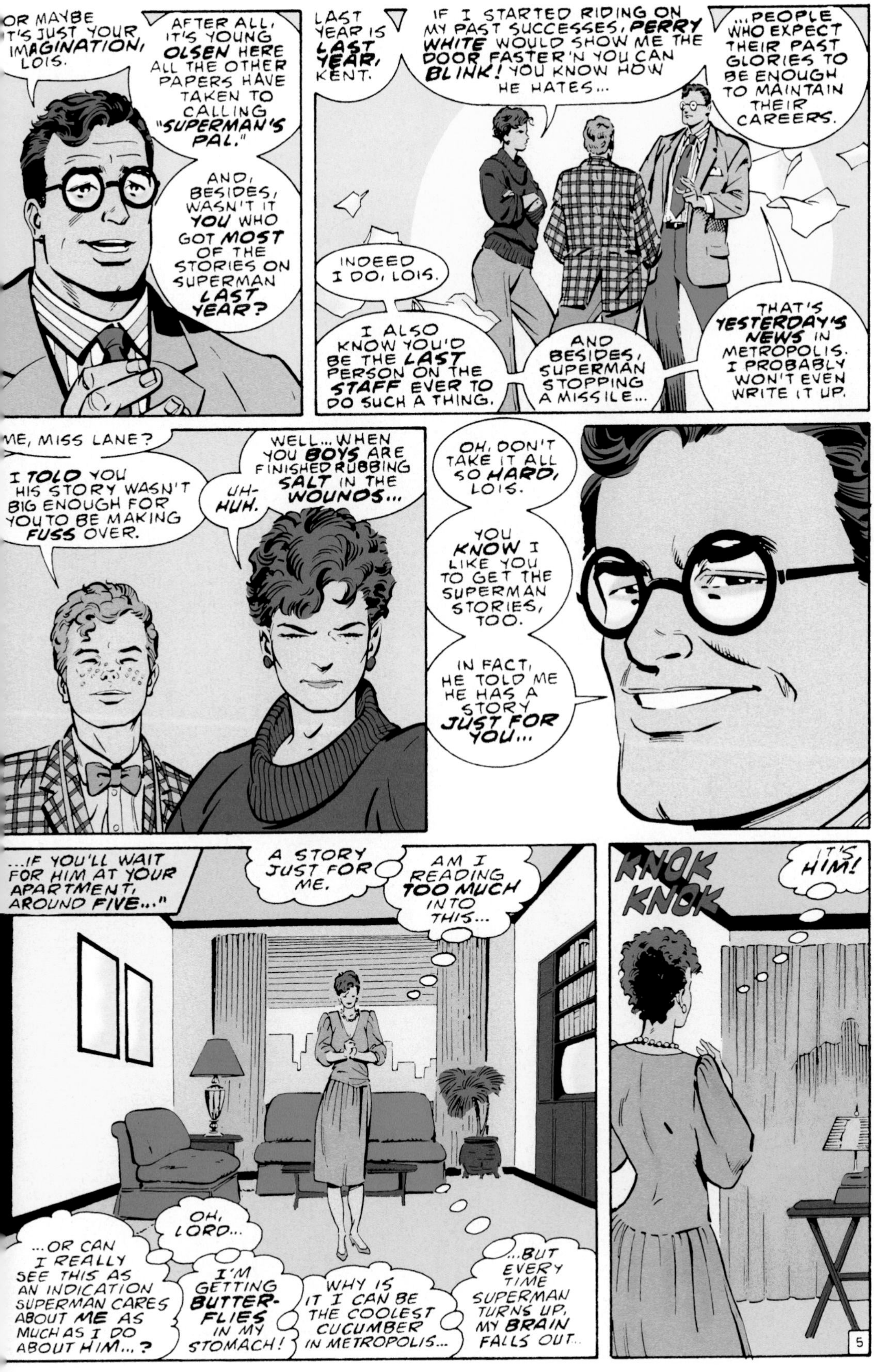
OR MAYBE IT'S JUST YOUR IMAGINATION, LOIS.
AFTER ALL, IT'S YOUNG OLSEN HERE ALL THE OTHER PAPERS HAVE TAKEN TO CALLING "SUPERMAN'S PAL."
AND, BESIDES, WASN'T IT YOU WHO GOT MOST OF THE STORIES ON SUPERMAN LAST YEAR?
LAST YEAR IS LAST YEAR, KENT.
IF I STARTED RIDING ON MY PAST SUCCESSES, PERRY WHITE WOULD SHOW ME THE DOOR FASTER'N YOU CAN BLINK! YOU KNOW HOW HE HATES...
...PEOPLE WHO EXPECT THEIR PAST GLORIES TO BE ENOUGH TO MAINTAIN THEIR CAREERS.
INDEED I DO, LOIS.
I ALSO KNOW YOU'D BE THE LAST PERSON ON THE STAFF EVER TO DO SUCH A THING.
AND BESIDES, SUPERMAN STOPPING A MISSILE...
THAT'S YESTERDAY'S NEWS IN METROPOLIS. I PROBABLY WON'T EVEN WRITE IT UP.
ME, MISS LANE?
I TOLD YOU HIS STORY WASN'T BIG ENOUGH FOR YOU TO BE MAKING FUSS OVER.
UH-HUH.
WELL... WHEN YOU BOYS ARE FINISHED RUBBING SALT IN THE WOUNDS...
OH, DON'T TAKE IT ALL SO HARD, LOIS.
YOU KNOW I LIKE YOU TO GET THE SUPERMAN STORIES, TOO.
IN FACT, HE TOLD ME HE HAS A STORY JUST FOR YOU...
...IF YOU'LL WAIT FOR HIM AT YOUR APARTMENT, AROUND FIVE..."
A STORY JUST FOR ME.
AM I READING TOO MUCH INTO THIS...
...OR CAN I REALLY SEE THIS AS AN INDICATION SUPERMAN CARES ABOUT ME AS MUCH AS I DO ABOUT HIM...?
OH, LORD...
I'M GETTING BUTTER-FLIES IN MY STOMACH!
WHY IS IT I CAN BE THE COOLEST CUCUMBER IN METROPOLIS...
...BUT EVERY TIME SUPERMAN TURNS UP, MY BRAIN FALLS OUT...
KNOK KNOK
IT'S HIM!
5

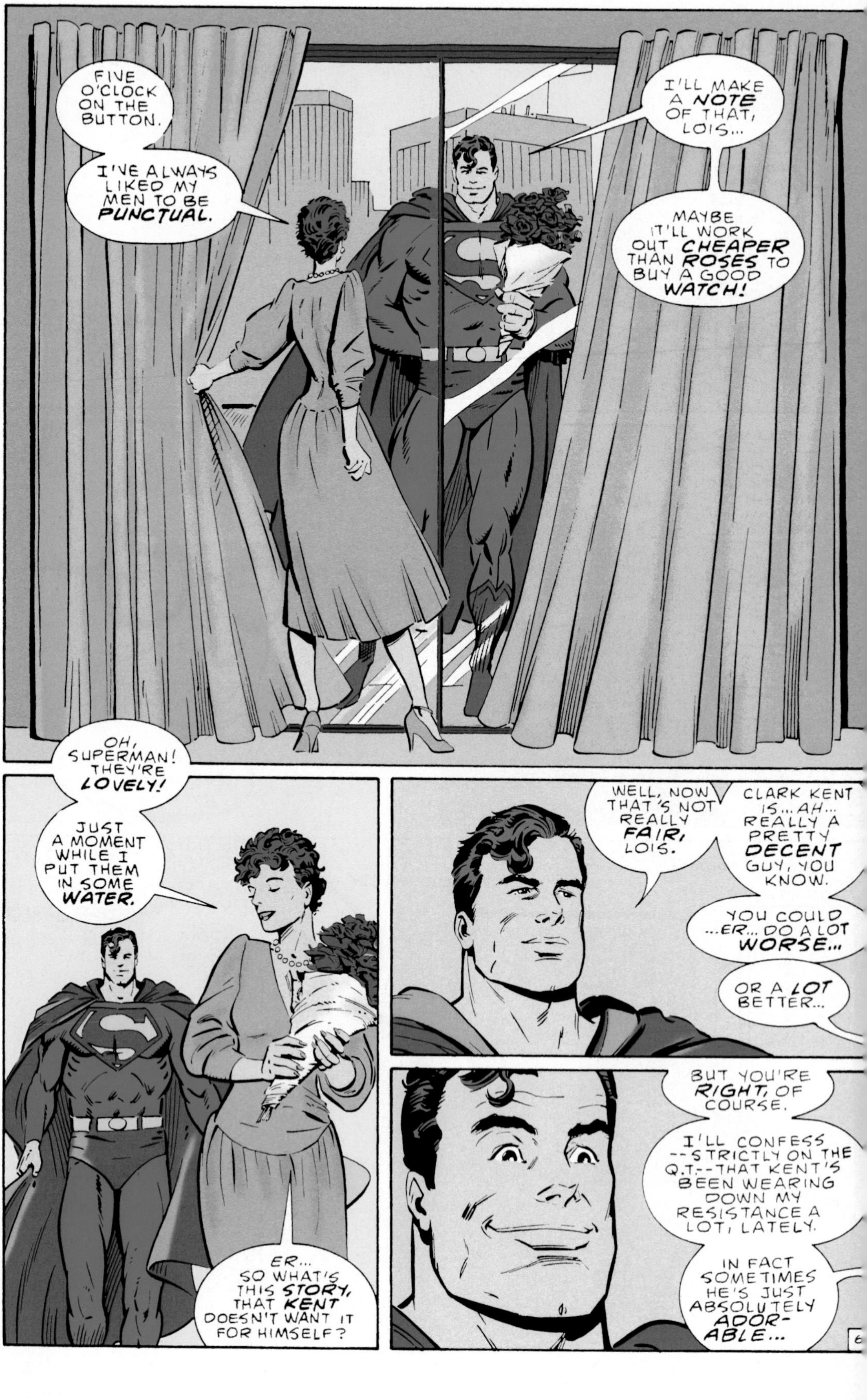
FIVE O'CLOCK ON THE BUTTON.
I'VE ALWAYS LIKED MY MEN TO BE PUNCTUAL.
I'LL MAKE A NOTE OF THAT, LOIS...
MAYBE IT'LL WORK OUT CHEAPER THAN ROSES TO BUY A GOOD WATCH!
OH, SUPERMAN! THEY'RE LOVELY!
JUST A MOMENT WHILE I PUT THEM IN SOME WATER.
ER... SO WHAT'S THIS STORY, THAT KENT DOESN'T WANT IT FOR HIMSELF?
WELL, NOW THAT'S NOT REALLY FAIR, LOIS.
CLARK KENT IS... AH... REALLY A PRETTY DECENT GUY, YOU KNOW.
YOU COULD ...ER... DO A LOT WORSE...
OR A LOT BETTER...
BUT YOU'RE RIGHT, OF COURSE.
I'LL CONFESS --STRICTLY ON THE Q.T.--THAT KENT'S BEEN WEARING DOWN MY RESISTANCE A LOT, LATELY.
IN FACT SOMETIMES HE'S JUST ABSOLUTELY ADOR-ABLE...

BUT THAT DOESN'T MEAN I'M ABOUT TO ROLL OVER AND PLAY DEAD JUST YET.

SO...

WITH ALL PROPER FAIRNESS TO CLARK, WHAT'S THIS STORY YOU HAVE FOR ME, SUPER-MAN?

SOMETHING VERY PERSONAL, LOIS.

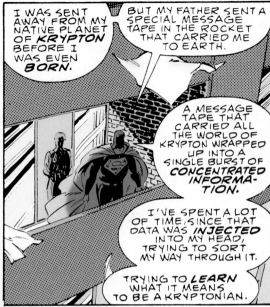

I WAS SENT AWAY FROM MY NATIVE PLANET OF KRYPTON BEFORE I WAS EVEN BORN.

BUT MY FATHER SENT A SPECIAL MESSAGE TAPE IN THE ROCKET THAT CARRIED ME TO EARTH.

A MESSAGE TAPE THAT CARRIED ALL THE WORLD OF KRYPTON WRAPPED UP INTO A SINGLE BURST OF CONCENTRATED INFORMATION.

I'VE SPENT A LOT OF TIME, SINCE THAT DATA WAS INJECTED INTO MY HEAD, TRYING TO SORT MY WAY THROUGH IT.

TRYING TO LEARN WHAT IT MEANS TO BE A KRYPTONIAN.

HE GOT MOST OF IT FIGURED OUT NOW, AND I THOUGHT, PERHAPS, IT WAS ME I TOLD SOME OF IT TO THE WORLD.

I THINK OF MYSELF AS HUMAN, LOIS. AS AN EARTH-LING.

BUT I THINK PERHAPS ALL YOU REAL EARTH-LINGS COULD BENEFIT FROM THE STORY OF KRYPTON'S LAST YEARS.

YOU SEE, ONCE THE PLANET KRYPTON WAS AN IDYLLIC WORLD...

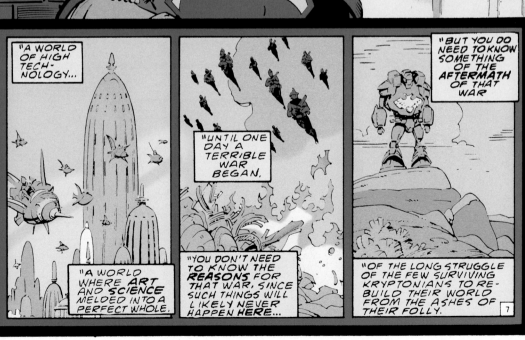

"A WORLD OF HIGH TECHNOLOGY...

"A WORLD WHERE ART AND SCIENCE MELDED INTO A PERFECT WHOLE.

"UNTIL ONE DAY A TERRIBLE WAR BEGAN.

"YOU DON'T NEED TO KNOW THE REASONS FOR THAT WAR, SINCE SUCH THINGS WILL LIKELY NEVER HAPPEN HERE...

"BUT YOU DO NEED TO KNOW SOMETHING OF THE AFTERMATH OF THAT WAR

"OF THE LONG STRUGGLE OF THE FEW SURVIVING KRYPTONIANS TO RE-BUILD THEIR WORLD FROM THE ASHES OF THEIR FOLLY.

7

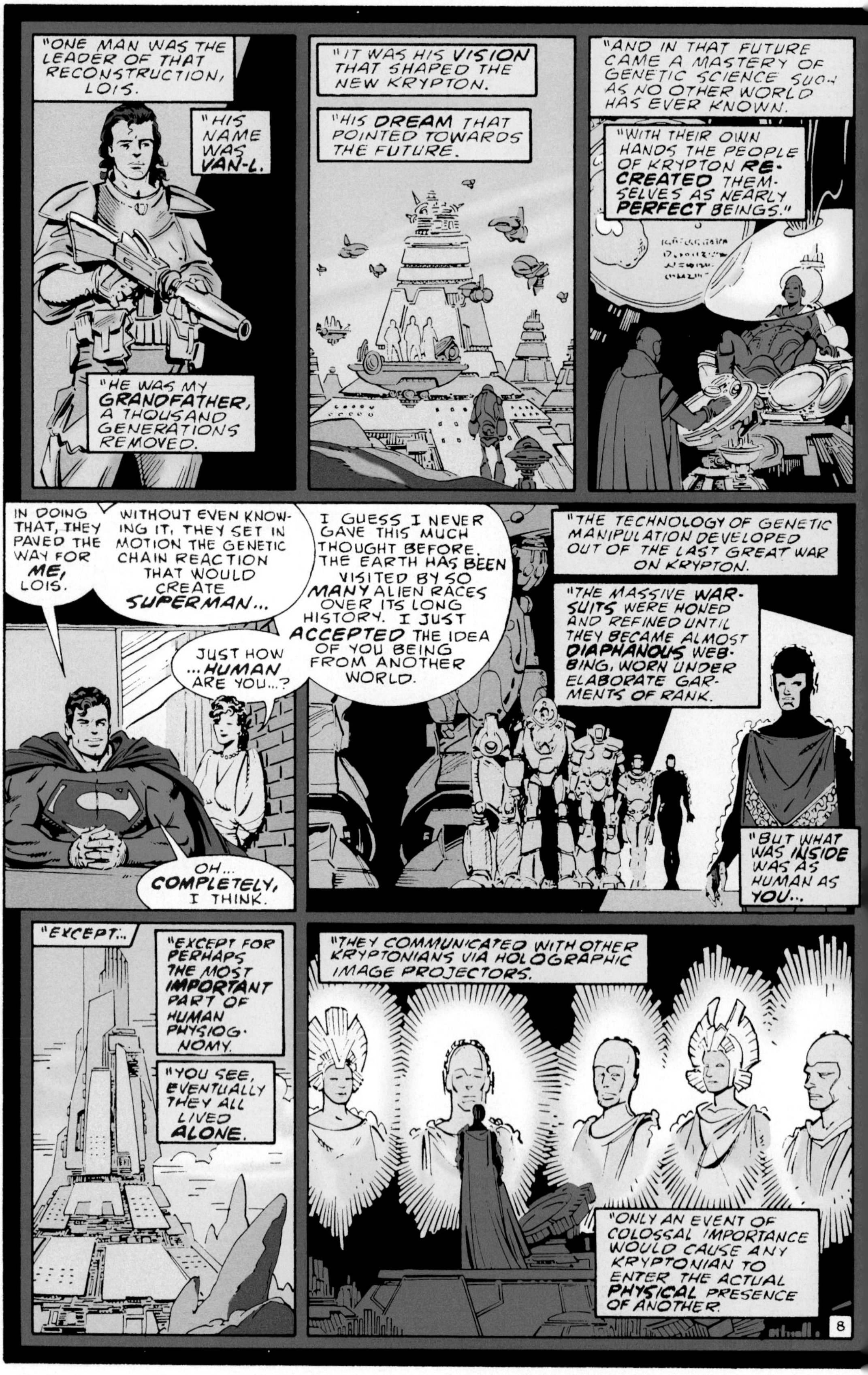
"ONE MAN WAS THE LEADER OF THAT RECONSTRUCTION, LOIS.
"HIS NAME WAS VAN-L.
"HE WAS MY GRANDFATHER, A THOUSAND GENERATIONS REMOVED.
"IT WAS HIS VISION THAT SHAPED THE NEW KRYPTON.
"HIS DREAM THAT POINTED TOWARDS THE FUTURE.
"AND IN THAT FUTURE CAME A MASTERY OF GENETIC SCIENCE SUCH AS NO OTHER WORLD HAS EVER KNOWN.
"WITH THEIR OWN HANDS THE PEOPLE OF KRYPTON RE-CREATED THEMSELVES AS NEARLY PERFECT BEINGS."
IN DOING THAT, THEY PAVED THE WAY FOR ME, LOIS.
WITHOUT EVEN KNOWING IT, THEY SET IN MOTION THE GENETIC CHAIN REACTION THAT WOULD CREATE SUPERMAN...
JUST HOW ...HUMAN ARE YOU...?
OH... COMPLETELY, I THINK.
I GUESS I NEVER GAVE THIS MUCH THOUGHT BEFORE. THE EARTH HAS BEEN VISITED BY SO MANY ALIEN RACES OVER ITS LONG HISTORY. I JUST ACCEPTED THE IDEA OF YOU BEING FROM ANOTHER WORLD.
"THE TECHNOLOGY OF GENETIC MANIPULATION DEVELOPED OUT OF THE LAST GREAT WAR ON KRYPTON.
"THE MASSIVE WAR-SUITS WERE HONED AND REFINED UNTIL THEY BECAME ALMOST DIAPHANOUS WEBBING, WORN UNDER ELABORATE GARMENTS OF RANK.
"BUT WHAT WAS INSIDE WAS AS HUMAN AS YOU...
"EXCEPT...
"EXCEPT FOR PERHAPS THE MOST IMPORTANT PART OF HUMAN PHYSIOGNOMY.
"YOU SEE, EVENTUALLY THEY ALL LIVED ALONE.
"THEY COMMUNICATED WITH OTHER KRYPTONIANS VIA HOLOGRAPHIC IMAGE PROJECTORS.
"ONLY AN EVENT OF COLOSSAL IMPORTANCE WOULD CAUSE ANY KRYPTONIAN TO ENTER THE ACTUAL PHYSICAL PRESENCE OF ANOTHER.
8

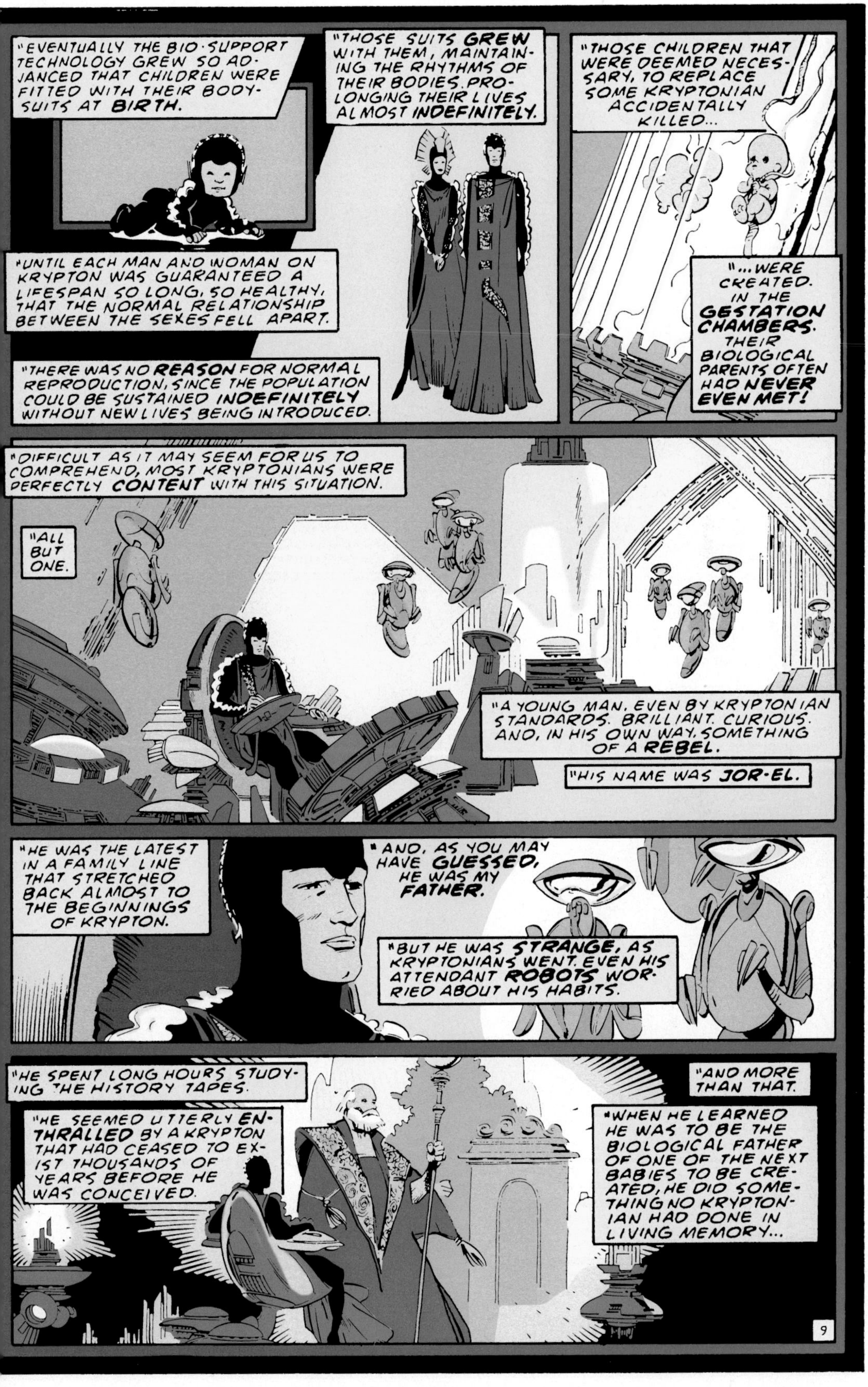
"EVENTUALLY THE BIO-SUPPORT TECHNOLOGY GREW SO ADVANCED THAT CHILDREN WERE FITTED WITH THEIR BODY-SUITS AT BIRTH.
"THOSE SUITS GREW WITH THEM, MAINTAINING THE RHYTHMS OF THEIR BODIES, PROLONGING THEIR LIVES ALMOST INDEFINITELY.
"UNTIL EACH MAN AND WOMAN ON KRYPTON WAS GUARANTEED A LIFESPAN SO LONG, SO HEALTHY, THAT THE NORMAL RELATIONSHIP BETWEEN THE SEXES FELL APART.
"THERE WAS NO REASON FOR NORMAL REPRODUCTION, SINCE THE POPULATION COULD BE SUSTAINED INDEFINITELY WITHOUT NEW LIVES BEING INTRODUCED.
"THOSE CHILDREN THAT WERE DEEMED NECESSARY, TO REPLACE SOME KRYPTONIAN ACCIDENTALLY KILLED...
"...WERE CREATED IN THE GESTATION CHAMBERS. THEIR BIOLOGICAL PARENTS OFTEN HAD NEVER EVEN MET!
"DIFFICULT AS IT MAY SEEM FOR US TO COMPREHEND, MOST KRYPTONIANS WERE PERFECTLY CONTENT WITH THIS SITUATION.
"ALL BUT ONE.
"A YOUNG MAN, EVEN BY KRYPTONIAN STANDARDS. BRILLIANT. CURIOUS. AND, IN HIS OWN WAY, SOMETHING OF A REBEL.
"HIS NAME WAS JOR-EL.
"HE WAS THE LATEST IN A FAMILY LINE THAT STRETCHED BACK ALMOST TO THE BEGINNINGS OF KRYPTON.
"AND, AS YOU MAY HAVE GUESSED, HE WAS MY FATHER.
"BUT HE WAS STRANGE, AS KRYPTONIANS WENT. EVEN HIS ATTENDANT ROBOTS WORRIED ABOUT HIS HABITS.
"HE SPENT LONG HOURS STUDYING THE HISTORY TAPES.
"HE SEEMED UTTERLY ENTHRALLED BY A KRYPTON THAT HAD CEASED TO EXIST THOUSANDS OF YEARS BEFORE HE WAS CONCEIVED.
"AND MORE THAN THAT.
"WHEN HE LEARNED HE WAS TO BE THE BIOLOGICAL FATHER OF ONE OF THE NEXT BABIES TO BE CREATED, HE DID SOMETHING NO KRYPTONIAN HAD DONE IN LIVING MEMORY...
9

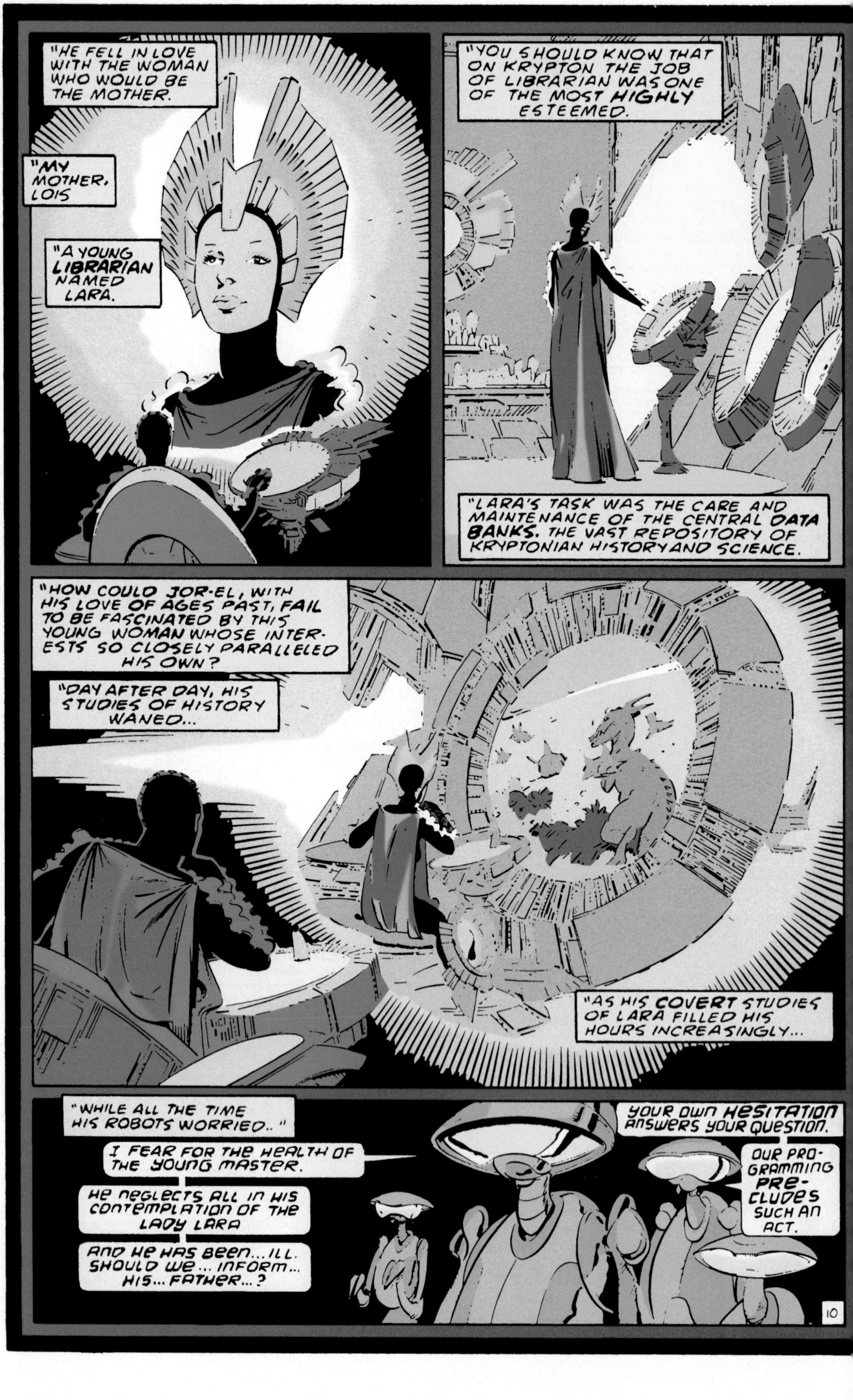
"HE FELL IN LOVE WITH THE WOMAN WHO WOULD BE THE MOTHER.
"MY MOTHER, LOIS
"A YOUNG LIBRARIAN NAMED LARA.
"YOU SHOULD KNOW THAT ON KRYPTON THE JOB OF LIBRARIAN WAS ONE OF THE MOST HIGHLY ESTEEMED.
"LARA'S TASK WAS THE CARE AND MAINTENANCE OF THE CENTRAL DATA BANKS. THE VAST REPOSITORY OF KRYPTONIAN HISTORY AND SCIENCE.
"HOW COULD JOR-EL, WITH HIS LOVE OF AGES PAST, FAIL TO BE FASCINATED BY THIS YOUNG WOMAN WHOSE INTERESTS SO CLOSELY PARALLELED HIS OWN?
"DAY AFTER DAY, HIS STUDIES OF HISTORY WANED...
"AS HIS COVERT STUDIES OF LARA FILLED HIS HOURS INCREASINGLY...
"WHILE ALL THE TIME HIS ROBOTS WORRIED.."
I FEAR FOR THE HEALTH OF THE YOUNG MASTER.
HE NEGLECTS ALL IN HIS CONTEMPLATION OF THE LADY LARA
AND HE HAS BEEN... ILL. SHOULD WE ... INFORM... HIS... FATHER...?
YOUR OWN HESITATION ANSWERS YOUR QUESTION.
OUR PROGRAMMING PRECLUDES SUCH AN ACT.
10

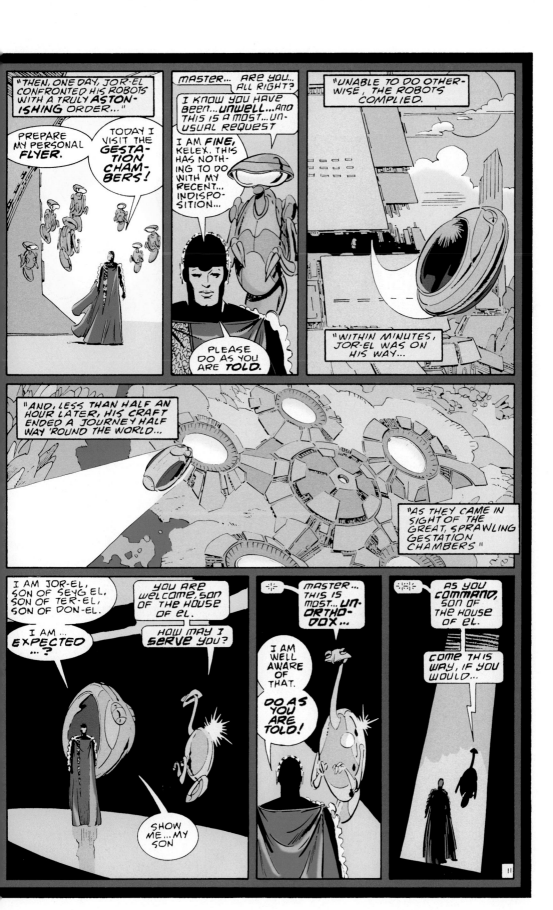

"THEN, ONE DAY, JOR-EL CONFRONTED HIS ROBOTS WITH A TRULY *ASTONISHING* ORDER..."

PREPARE MY PERSONAL *FLYER.*

TODAY I VISIT THE *GESTATION CHAMBERS!*

MASTER... ARE YOU... ALL RIGHT?

I KNOW YOU HAVE BEEN...*UNWELL*...AND THIS IS A MOST...UNUSUAL REQUEST

I AM *FINE*, KELEX. THIS HAS NOTHING TO DO WITH MY RECENT... INDISPOSITION...

PLEASE DO AS YOU ARE *TOLD.*

"UNABLE TO DO OTHERWISE, THE ROBOTS COMPLIED.

"WITHIN MINUTES, JOR-EL WAS ON HIS WAY...

"AND, LESS THAN HALF AN HOUR LATER, HIS CRAFT ENDED A JOURNEY HALF WAY 'ROUND THE WORLD...

"AS THEY CAME IN SIGHT OF THE GREAT, SPRAWLING GESTATION CHAMBERS"

I AM JOR-EL, SON OF SEYG-EL, SON OF TER-EL, SON OF DON-EL.

YOU ARE WELCOME, SON OF THE HOUSE OF EL.

HOW MAY I *SERVE* YOU?

I AM... EXPECTED ...?

SHOW ME... MY SON

MASTER... THIS IS MOST...*UNORTHODOX*...

I AM WELL AWARE OF THAT.

DO AS YOU ARE TOLD!

AS YOU *COMMAND,* SON OF THE HOUSE OF EL.

COME THIS WAY, IF YOU WOULD...

11

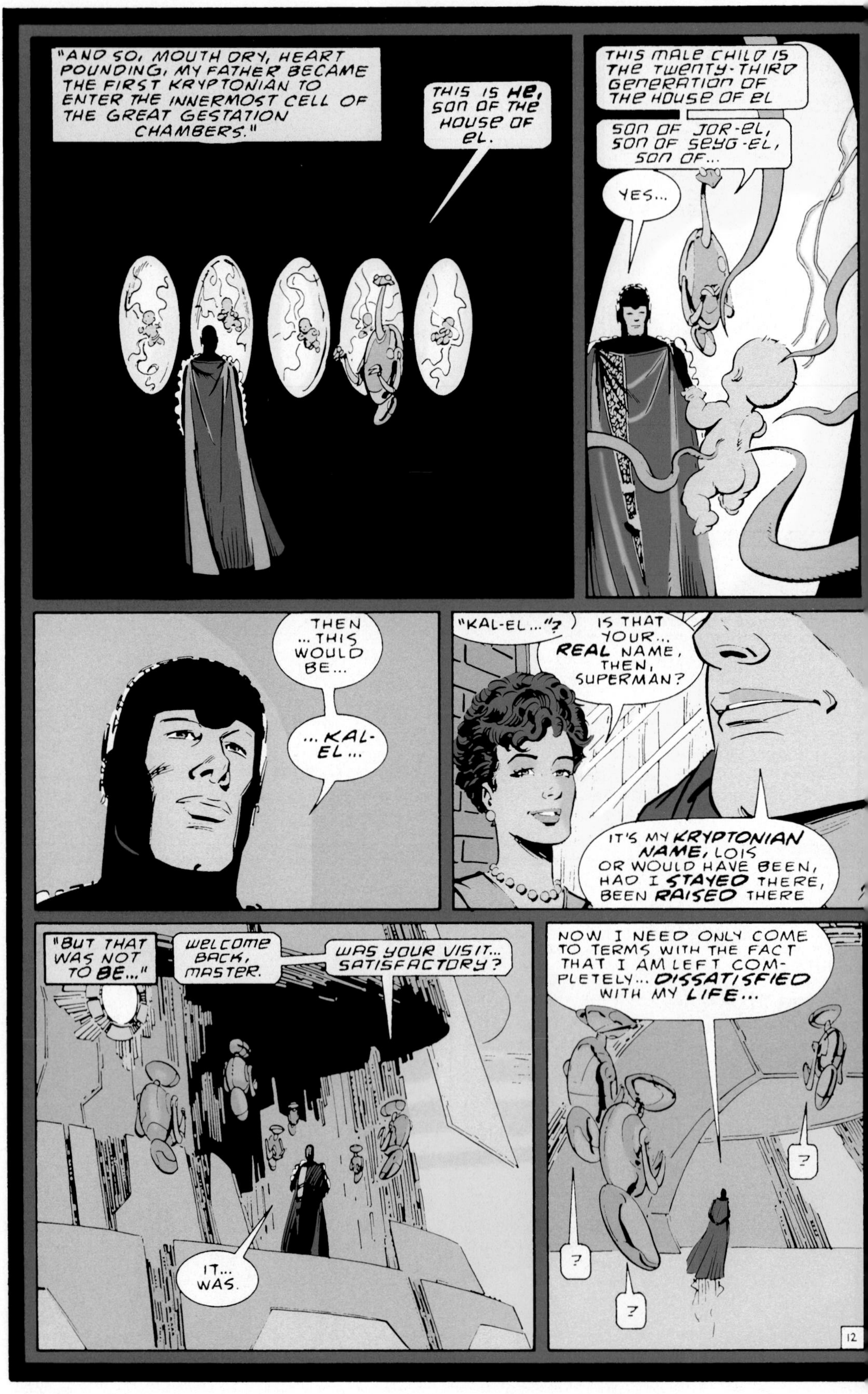
"AND SO, MOUTH DRY, HEART POUNDING, MY FATHER BECAME THE FIRST KRYPTONIAN TO ENTER THE INNERMOST CELL OF THE GREAT GESTATION CHAMBERS."
THIS IS HE, SON OF THE HOUSE OF EL.
THIS MALE CHILD IS THE TWENTY-THIRD GENERATION OF THE HOUSE OF EL
SON OF JOR-EL, SON OF SEYG-EL, SON OF...
YES...
THEN ... THIS WOULD BE...
... KAL-EL ...
"KAL-EL..."?
IS THAT YOUR... REAL NAME, THEN, SUPERMAN?
IT'S MY KRYPTONIAN NAME, LOIS OR WOULD HAVE BEEN, HAD I STAYED THERE, BEEN RAISED THERE
"BUT THAT WAS NOT TO BE..."
WELCOME BACK, MASTER.
WAS YOUR VISIT... SATISFACTORY?
IT... WAS.
NOW I NEED ONLY COME TO TERMS WITH THE FACT THAT I AM LEFT COMPLETELY... DISSATISFIED WITH MY LIFE...
?
?
?
12

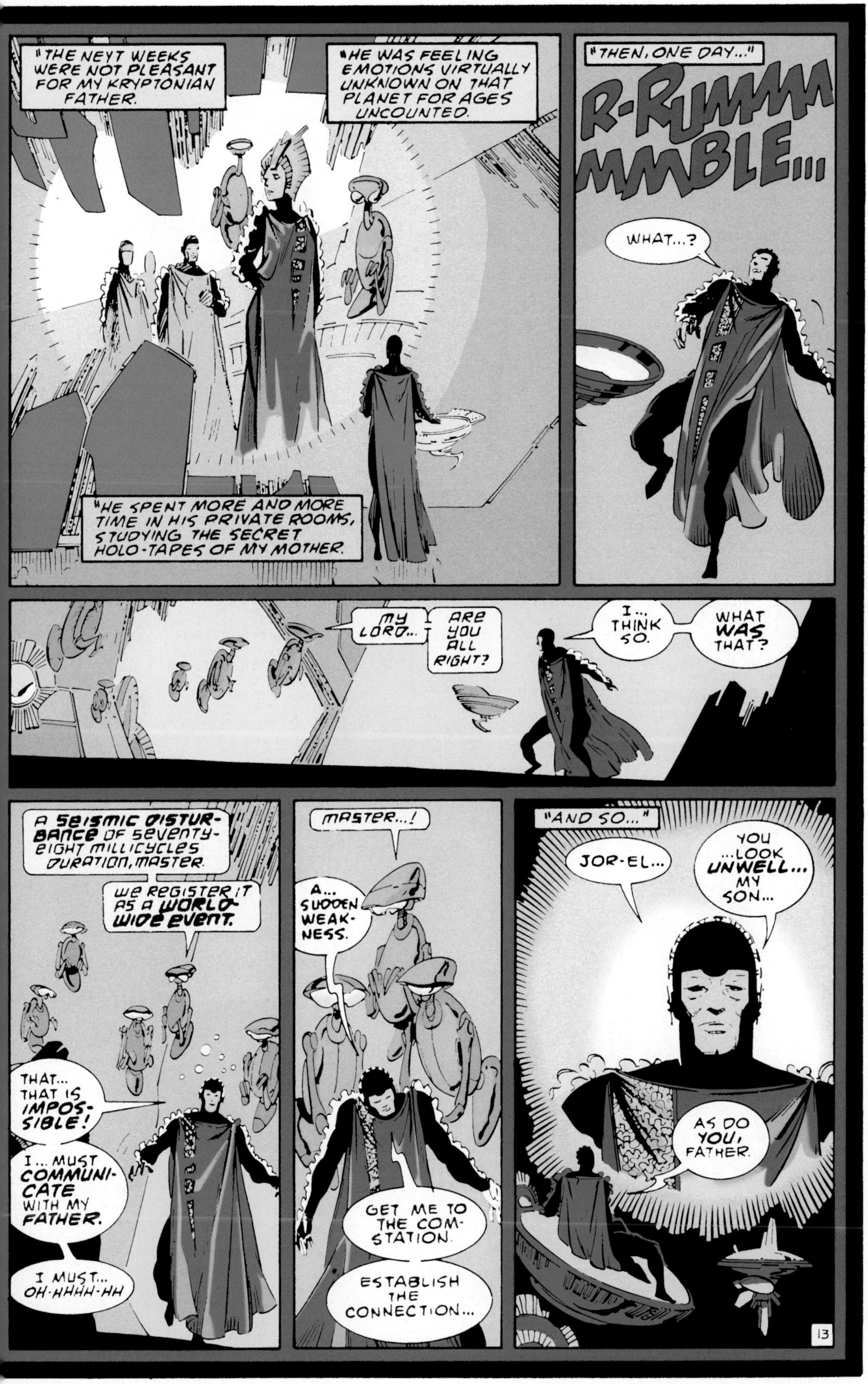

"THE NEYT WEEKS WERE NOT PLEASANT FOR MY KRYPTONIAN FATHER.
"HE WAS FEELING EMOTIONS VIRTUALLY UNKNOWN ON THAT PLANET FOR AGES UNCOUNTED.
"HE SPENT MORE AND MORE TIME IN HIS PRIVATE ROOMS, STUDYING THE SECRET HOLO-TAPES OF MY MOTHER.
"THEN, ONE DAY..."
R-RUMMMMMBLE...
WHAT...?
MY LORD...
ARE YOU ALL RIGHT?
I... THINK SO.
WHAT WAS THAT?
A SEISMIC DISTURBANCE OF SEVENTY-EIGHT MILLICYCLES DURATION, MASTER.
WE REGISTER IT AS A WORLD-WIDE EVENT.
THAT... THAT IS IMPOSSIBLE!
I... MUST COMMUNICATE WITH MY FATHER.
I MUST... OH-HHHH-HH
MASTER...!
A... SUDDEN WEAKNESS.
GET ME TO THE COM-STATION.
ESTABLISH THE CONNECTION...
"AND SO..."
JOR-EL...
YOU ...LOOK UNWELL... MY SON...
AS DO YOU, FATHER.
13

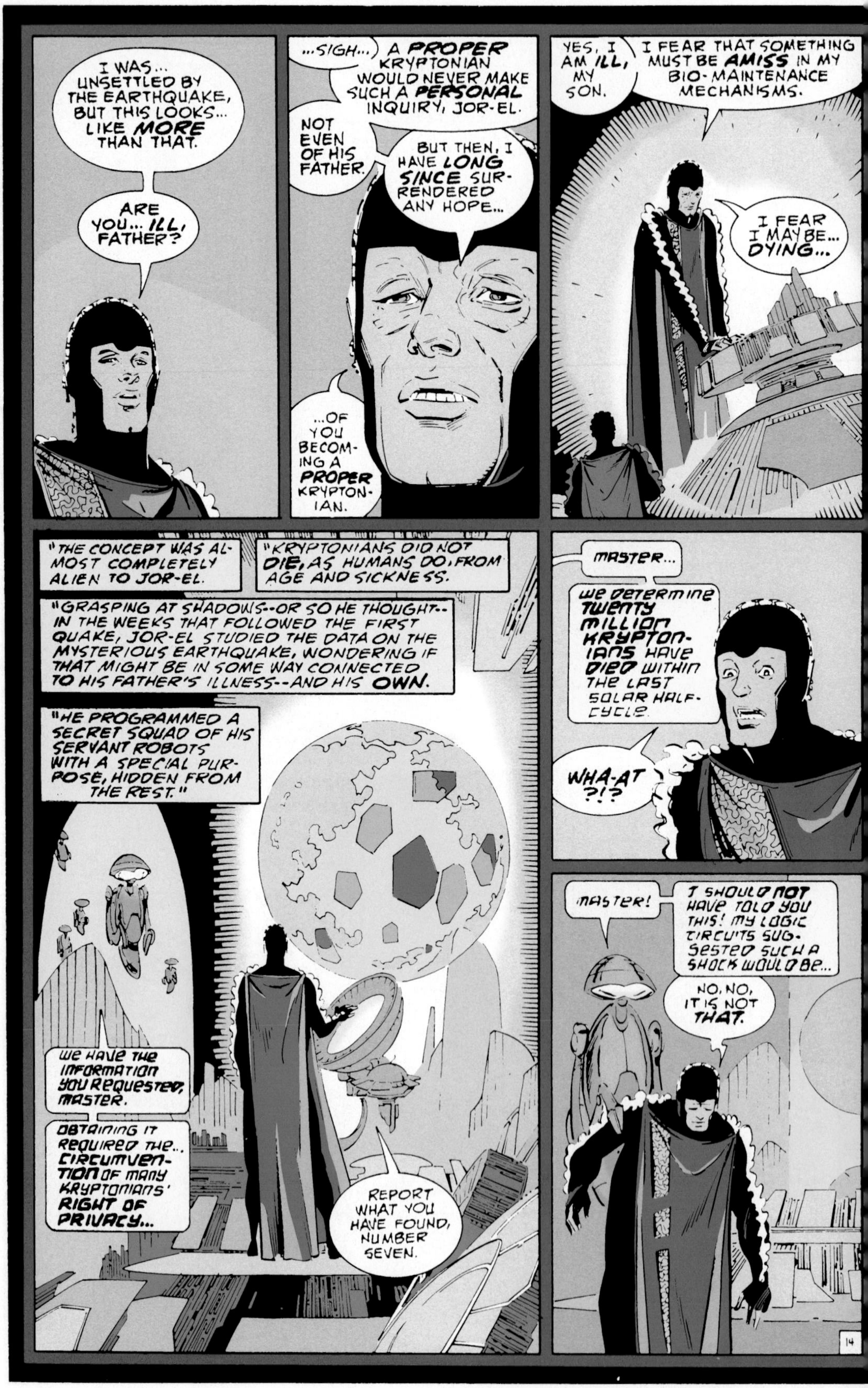
I WAS... UNSETTLED BY THE EARTHQUAKE, BUT THIS LOOKS... LIKE MORE THAN THAT.
ARE YOU... ILL, FATHER?
...SIGH...
A PROPER KRYPTONIAN WOULD NEVER MAKE SUCH A PERSONAL INQUIRY, JOR-EL.
NOT EVEN OF HIS FATHER.
BUT THEN, I HAVE LONG SINCE SURRENDERED ANY HOPE...
...OF YOU BECOMING A PROPER KRYPTONIAN.
YES, I AM ILL, MY SON.
I FEAR THAT SOMETHING MUST BE AMISS IN MY BIO-MAINTENANCE MECHANISMS.
I FEAR I MAY BE... DYING...
"THE CONCEPT WAS ALMOST COMPLETELY ALIEN TO JOR-EL.
"KRYPTONIANS DID NOT DIE, AS HUMANS DO, FROM AGE AND SICKNESS.
"GRASPING AT SHADOWS--OR SO HE THOUGHT--IN THE WEEKS THAT FOLLOWED THE FIRST QUAKE, JOR-EL STUDIED THE DATA ON THE MYSTERIOUS EARTHQUAKE, WONDERING IF THAT MIGHT BE IN SOME WAY CONNECTED TO HIS FATHER'S ILLNESS--AND HIS OWN.
"HE PROGRAMMED A SECRET SQUAD OF HIS SERVANT ROBOTS WITH A SPECIAL PURPOSE, HIDDEN FROM THE REST."
WE HAVE THE INFORMATION YOU REQUESTED, MASTER.
OBTAINING IT REQUIRED THE... CIRCUMVENTION OF MANY KRYPTONIANS' RIGHT OF PRIVACY...
REPORT WHAT YOU HAVE FOUND, NUMBER SEVEN.
MASTER...
WE DETERMINE TWENTY MILLION KRYPTONIANS HAVE DIED WITHIN THE LAST SOLAR HALF-CYCLE.
WHA-AT ?!?
MASTER!
I SHOULD NOT HAVE TOLD YOU THIS! MY LOGIC CIRCUITS SUGGESTED SUCH A SHOCK WOULD BE...
NO, NO, IT IS NOT THAT.
14

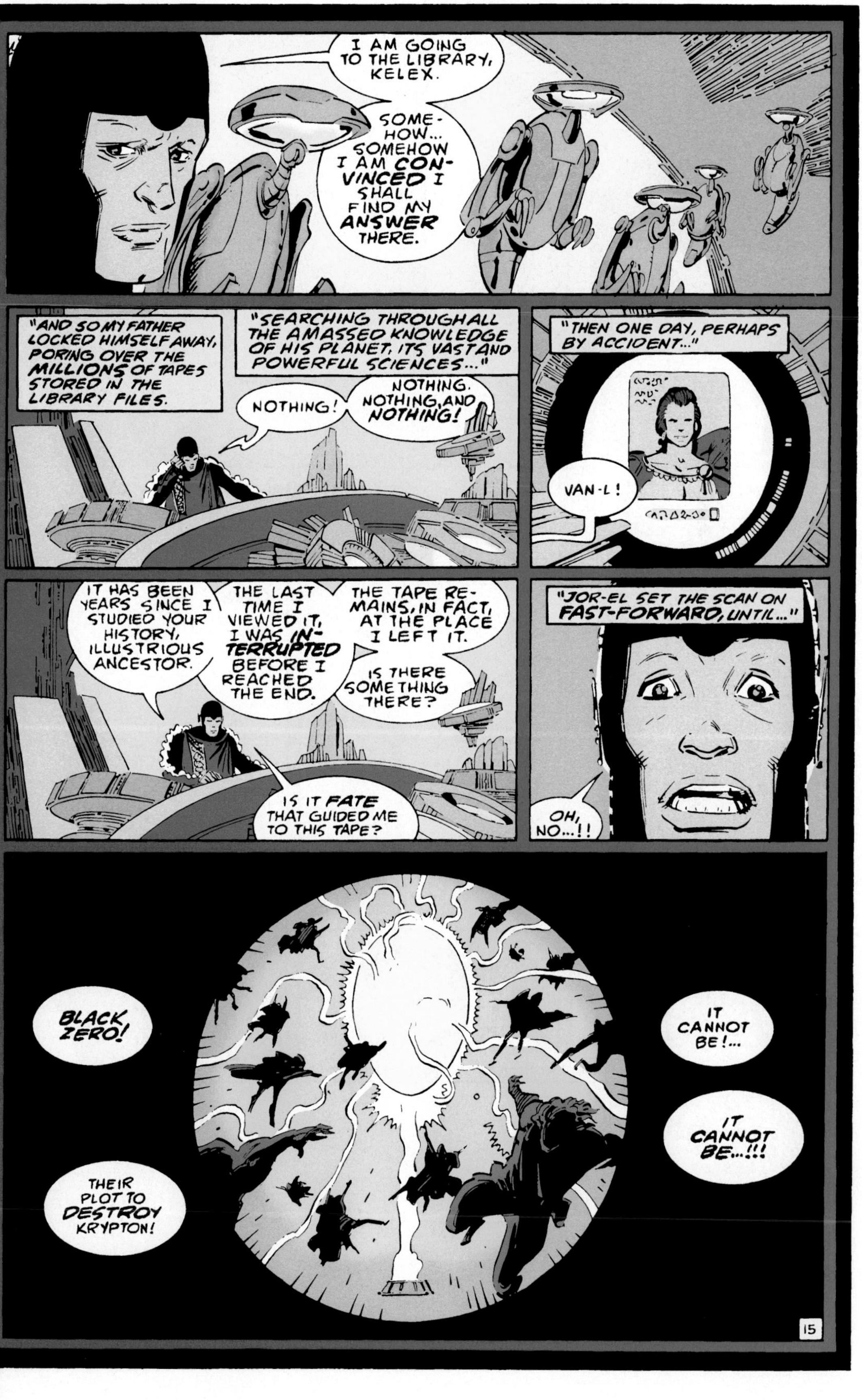
I AM GOING TO THE LIBRARY, KELEX.
SOME-HOW... SOMEHOW I AM CONVINCED I SHALL FIND MY ANSWER THERE.
"AND SO MY FATHER LOCKED HIMSELF AWAY, PORING OVER THE MILLIONS OF TAPES STORED IN THE LIBRARY FILES.
"SEARCHING THROUGH ALL THE AMASSED KNOWLEDGE OF HIS PLANET, ITS VAST AND POWERFUL SCIENCES..."
NOTHING!
NOTHING. NOTHING, AND NOTHING!
"THEN ONE DAY, PERHAPS BY ACCIDENT..."
VAN-L!
IT HAS BEEN YEARS SINCE I STUDIED YOUR HISTORY, ILLUSTRIOUS ANCESTOR.
THE LAST TIME I VIEWED IT, I WAS INTERRUPTED BEFORE I REACHED THE END.
THE TAPE REMAINS, IN FACT, AT THE PLACE I LEFT IT.
IS THERE SOMETHING THERE?
IS IT FATE THAT GUIDED ME TO THIS TAPE?
"JOR-EL SET THE SCAN ON FAST-FORWARD, UNTIL..."
OH, NO...!!
BLACK ZERO!
THEIR PLOT TO DESTROY KRYPTON!
IT CANNOT BE!...
IT CANNOT BE...!!!
15

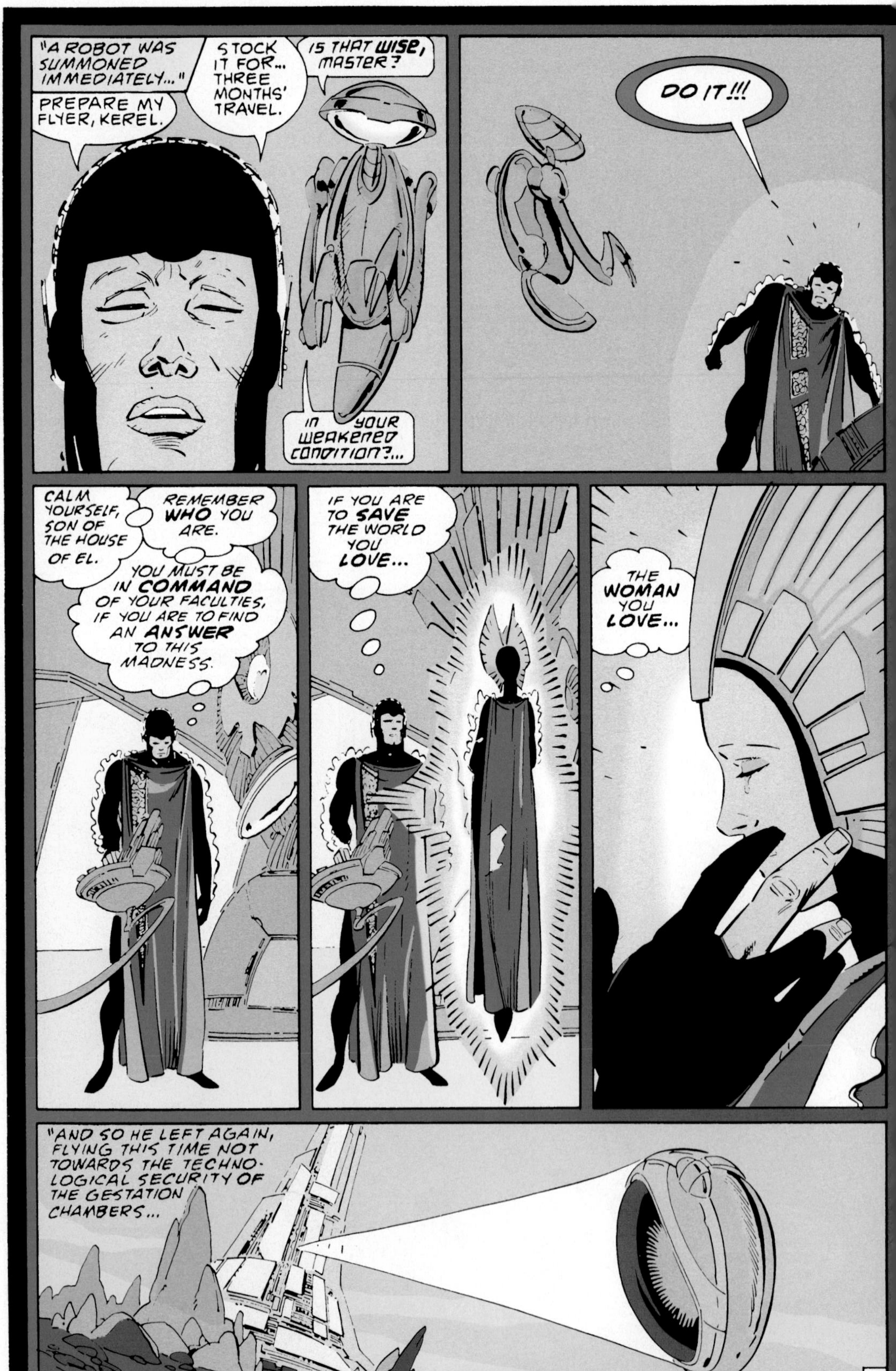
"A ROBOT WAS SUMMONED IMMEDIATELY..."
PREPARE MY FLYER, KEREL.
STOCK IT FOR... THREE MONTHS' TRAVEL.
IS THAT WISE, MASTER?
IN YOUR WEAKENED CONDITION?...
DO IT!!!
CALM YOURSELF, SON OF THE HOUSE OF EL.
REMEMBER WHO YOU ARE.
YOU MUST BE IN COMMAND OF YOUR FACULTIES, IF YOU ARE TO FIND AN ANSWER TO THIS MADNESS.
IF YOU ARE TO SAVE THE WORLD YOU LOVE...
THE WOMAN YOU LOVE...
"AND SO HE LEFT AGAIN, FLYING THIS TIME NOT TOWARDS THE TECHNOLOGICAL SECURITY OF THE GESTATION CHAMBERS...
16

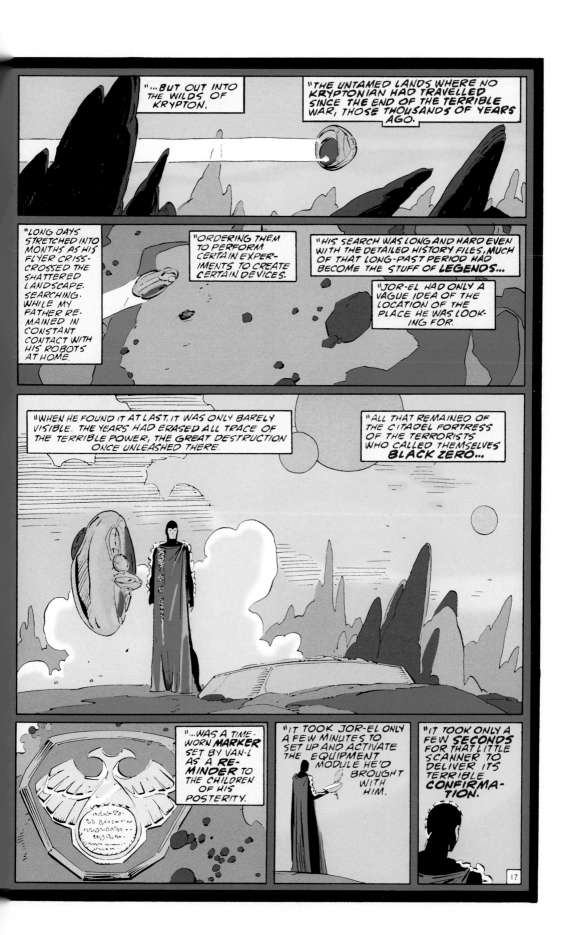

"...BUT OUT INTO THE WILDS OF KRYPTON.

"THE UNTAMED LANDS WHERE NO KRYPTONIAN HAD TRAVELLED SINCE THE END OF THE TERRIBLE WAR, THOSE THOUSANDS OF YEARS AGO.

"LONG DAYS STRETCHED INTO MONTHS AS HIS FLYER CRISS-CROSSED THE SHATTERED LANDSCAPE. SEARCHING. WHILE MY FATHER RE-MAINED IN CONSTANT CONTACT WITH HIS ROBOTS AT HOME.

"ORDERING THEM TO PERFORM CERTAIN EXPER-IMENTS TO CREATE CERTAIN DEVICES.

"HIS SEARCH WAS LONG AND HARD EVEN WITH THE DETAILED HISTORY FILES, MUCH OF THAT LONG-PAST PERIOD HAD BECOME THE STUFF OF *LEGENDS*...

"JOR-EL HAD ONLY A VAGUE IDEA OF THE LOCATION OF THE PLACE HE WAS LOOK-ING FOR.

"WHEN HE FOUND IT AT LAST, IT WAS ONLY BARELY VISIBLE. THE YEARS HAD ERASED ALL TRACE OF THE TERRIBLE POWER, THE GREAT DESTRUCTION ONCE UNLEASHED THERE.

"ALL THAT REMAINED OF THE CITADEL FORTRESS OF THE TERRORISTS WHO CALLED THEMSELVES *BLACK ZERO*...

"...WAS A TIME-WORN *MARKER* SET BY VAN-L AS A RE-*MINDER* TO THE CHILDREN OF HIS POSTERITY.

"IT TOOK JOR-EL ONLY A FEW MINUTES TO SET UP AND ACTIVATE THE EQUIPMENT MODULE HE'D BROUGHT WITH HIM.

"IT TOOK ONLY A FEW *SECONDS* FOR THAT LITTLE SCANNER TO DELIVER ITS TERRIBLE *CONFIRMA-TION.*

17

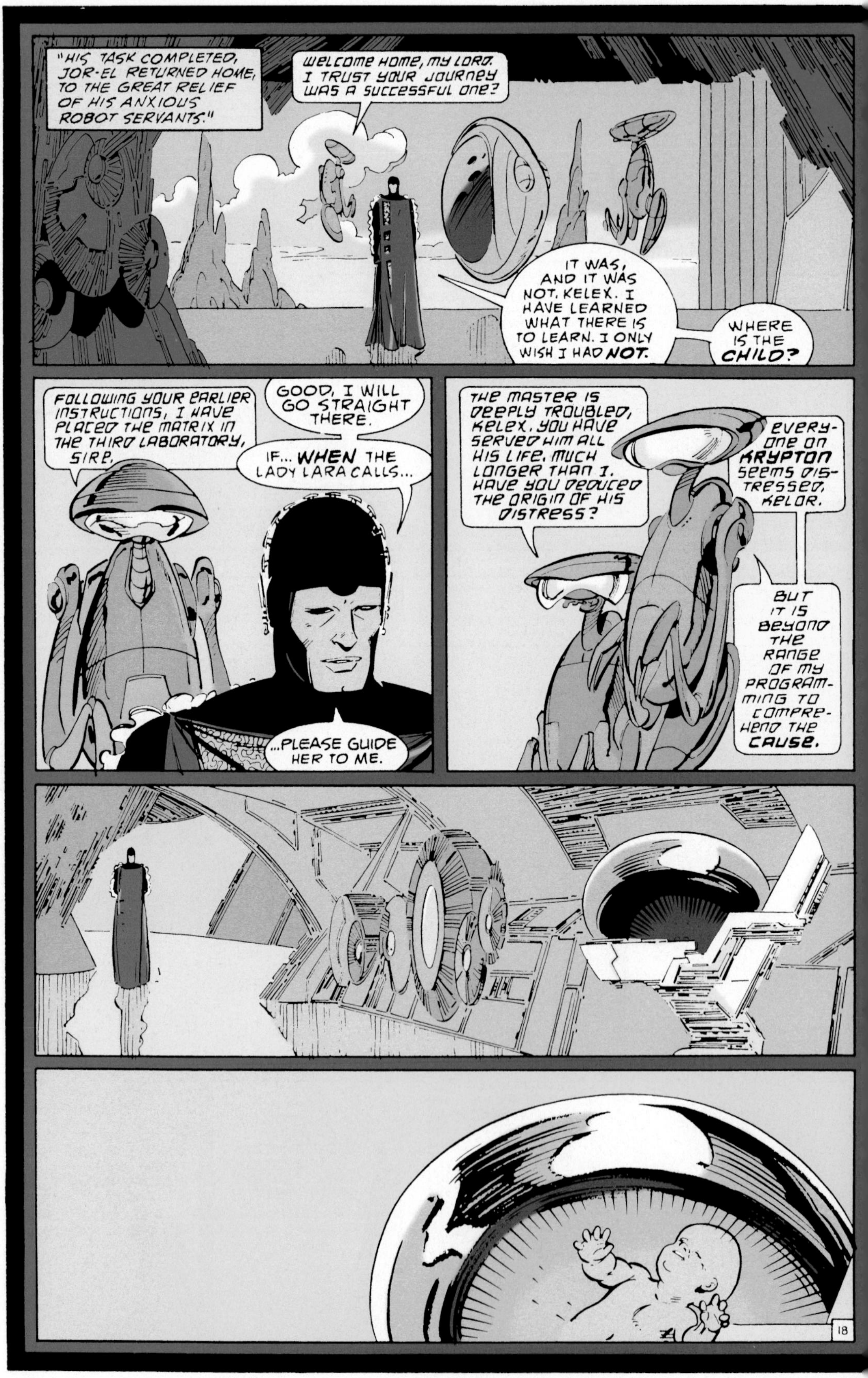
"HIS TASK COMPLETED, JOR-EL RETURNED HOME, TO THE GREAT RELIEF OF HIS ANXIOUS ROBOT SERVANTS."
WELCOME HOME, MY LORD. I TRUST YOUR JOURNEY WAS A SUCCESSFUL ONE?
IT WAS, AND IT WAS NOT, KELEX. I HAVE LEARNED WHAT THERE IS TO LEARN. I ONLY WISH I HAD NOT.
WHERE IS THE CHILD?
FOLLOWING YOUR EARLIER INSTRUCTIONS, I HAVE PLACED THE MATRIX IN THE THIRD LABORATORY, SIRE.
GOOD. I WILL GO STRAIGHT THERE.
IF... WHEN THE LADY LARA CALLS...
...PLEASE GUIDE HER TO ME.
THE MASTER IS DEEPLY TROUBLED, KELEX. YOU HAVE SERVED HIM ALL HIS LIFE. MUCH LONGER THAN I. HAVE YOU DEDUCED THE ORIGIN OF HIS DISTRESS?
EVERYONE ON KRYPTON SEEMS DISTRESSED, KELOR.
BUT IT IS BEYOND THE RANGE OF MY PROGRAMMING TO COMPREHEND THE CAUSE.
18

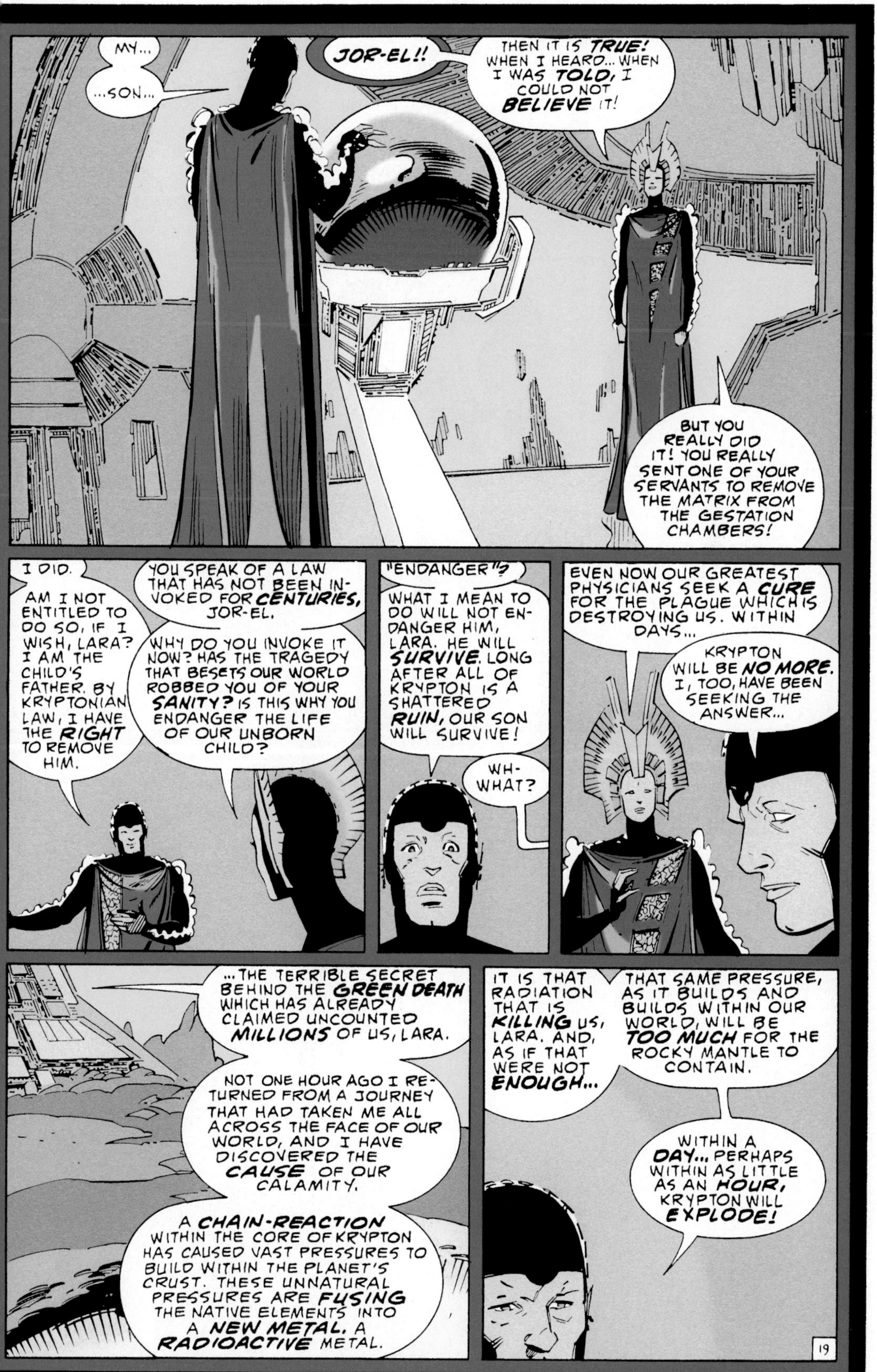
MY...
...SON...
JOR-EL!!
THEN IT IS TRUE! WHEN I HEARD... WHEN I WAS TOLD, I COULD NOT BELIEVE IT!
BUT YOU REALLY DID IT! YOU REALLY SENT ONE OF YOUR SERVANTS TO REMOVE THE MATRIX FROM THE GESTATION CHAMBERS!
I DID.
AM I NOT ENTITLED TO DO SO, IF I WISH, LARA? I AM THE CHILD'S FATHER. BY KRYPTONIAN LAW, I HAVE THE RIGHT TO REMOVE HIM.
YOU SPEAK OF A LAW THAT HAS NOT BEEN INVOKED FOR CENTURIES, JOR-EL.
WHY DO YOU INVOKE IT NOW? HAS THE TRAGEDY THAT BESETS OUR WORLD ROBBED YOU OF YOUR SANITY? IS THIS WHY YOU ENDANGER THE LIFE OF OUR UNBORN CHILD?
"ENDANGER"?
WHAT I MEAN TO DO WILL NOT ENDANGER HIM, LARA. HE WILL SURVIVE. LONG AFTER ALL OF KRYPTON IS A SHATTERED RUIN, OUR SON WILL SURVIVE!
WH-WHAT?
EVEN NOW OUR GREATEST PHYSICIANS SEEK A CURE FOR THE PLAGUE WHICH IS DESTROYING US. WITHIN DAYS...
KRYPTON WILL BE NO MORE.
I, TOO, HAVE BEEN SEEKING THE ANSWER...
...THE TERRIBLE SECRET BEHIND THE GREEN DEATH WHICH HAS ALREADY CLAIMED UNCOUNTED MILLIONS OF US, LARA.
NOT ONE HOUR AGO I RETURNED FROM A JOURNEY THAT HAD TAKEN ME ALL ACROSS THE FACE OF OUR WORLD, AND I HAVE DISCOVERED THE CAUSE OF OUR CALAMITY.
A CHAIN-REACTION WITHIN THE CORE OF KRYPTON HAS CAUSED VAST PRESSURES TO BUILD WITHIN THE PLANET'S CRUST. THESE UNNATURAL PRESSURES ARE FUSING THE NATIVE ELEMENTS INTO A NEW METAL. A RADIOACTIVE METAL.
IT IS THAT RADIATION THAT IS KILLING US, LARA. AND, AS IF THAT WERE NOT ENOUGH...
THAT SAME PRESSURE, AS IT BUILDS AND BUILDS WITHIN OUR WORLD, WILL BE TOO MUCH FOR THE ROCKY MANTLE TO CONTAIN.
WITHIN A DAY... PERHAPS WITHIN AS LITTLE AS AN HOUR, KRYPTON WILL EXPLODE!
19

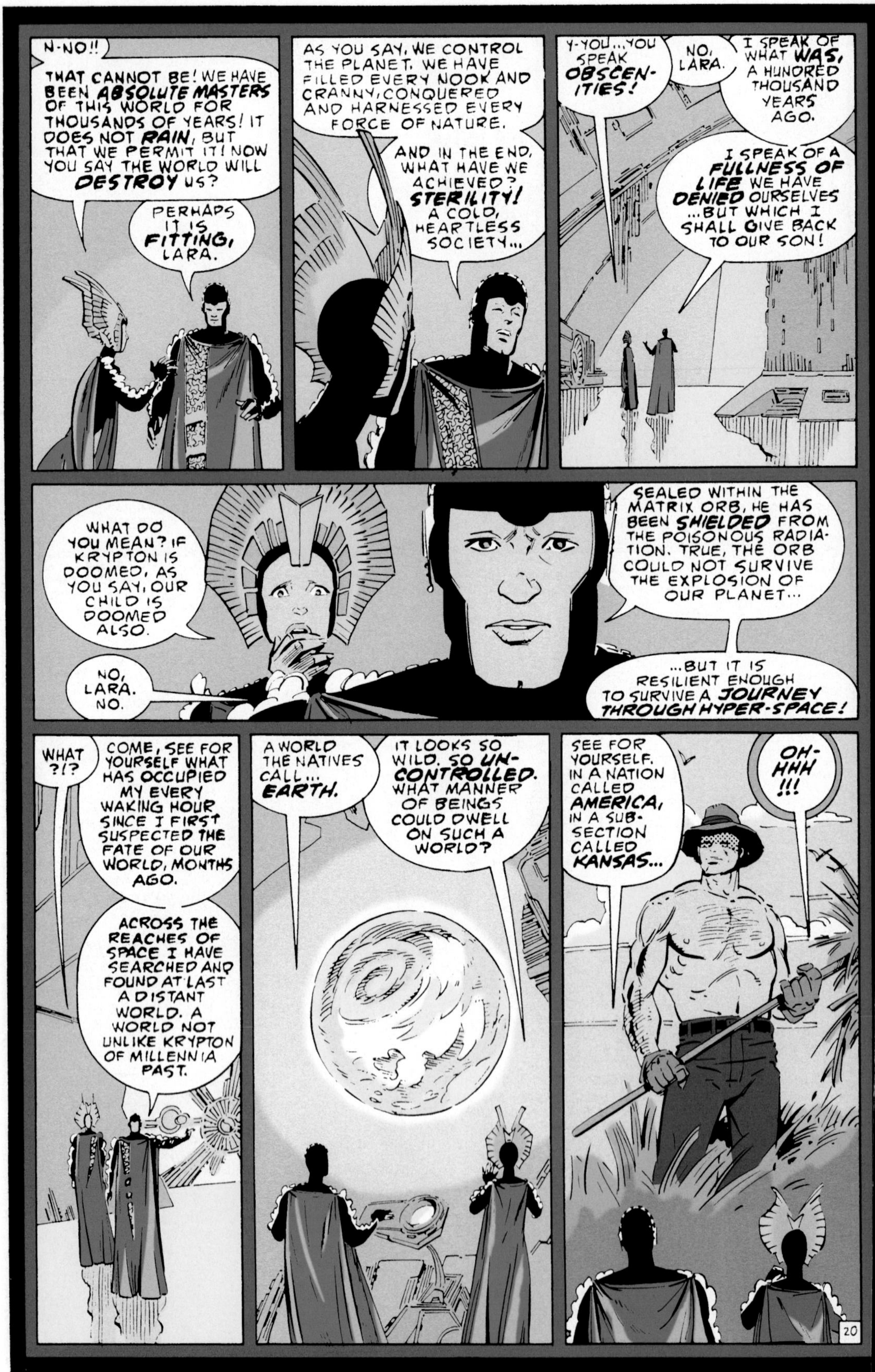
N-NO!!
THAT CANNOT BE! WE HAVE BEEN ABSOLUTE MASTERS OF THIS WORLD FOR THOUSANDS OF YEARS! IT DOES NOT RAIN, BUT THAT WE PERMIT IT! NOW YOU SAY THE WORLD WILL DESTROY US?
PERHAPS IT IS FITTING, LARA.
AS YOU SAY, WE CONTROL THE PLANET. WE HAVE FILLED EVERY NOOK AND CRANNY, CONQUERED AND HARNESSED EVERY FORCE OF NATURE.
AND IN THE END, WHAT HAVE WE ACHIEVED? STERILITY! A COLD, HEARTLESS SOCIETY...
Y-YOU...YOU SPEAK OBSCEN-ITIES!
NO, LARA.
I SPEAK OF WHAT WAS, A HUNDRED THOUSAND YEARS AGO.
I SPEAK OF A FULLNESS OF LIFE WE HAVE DENIED OURSELVES ...BUT WHICH I SHALL GIVE BACK TO OUR SON!
WHAT DO YOU MEAN? IF KRYPTON IS DOOMED, AS YOU SAY, OUR CHILD IS DOOMED ALSO.
NO, LARA. NO.
SEALED WITHIN THE MATRIX ORB, HE HAS BEEN SHIELDED FROM THE POISONOUS RADIA-TION. TRUE, THE ORB COULD NOT SURVIVE THE EXPLOSION OF OUR PLANET...
...BUT IT IS RESILIENT ENOUGH TO SURVIVE A JOURNEY THROUGH HYPER-SPACE!
WHAT ?!?
COME, SEE FOR YOURSELF WHAT HAS OCCUPIED MY EVERY WAKING HOUR SINCE I FIRST SUSPECTED THE FATE OF OUR WORLD, MONTHS AGO.
ACROSS THE REACHES OF SPACE I HAVE SEARCHED AND FOUND AT LAST A DISTANT WORLD. A WORLD NOT UNLIKE KRYPTON OF MILLENNIA PAST.
A WORLD THE NATIVES CALL... EARTH.
IT LOOKS SO WILD. SO UN-CONTROLLED. WHAT MANNER OF BEINGS COULD DWELL ON SUCH A WORLD?
SEE FOR YOURSELF. IN A NATION CALLED AMERICA, IN A SUB-SECTION CALLED KANSAS...
OH-HHH !!!
20

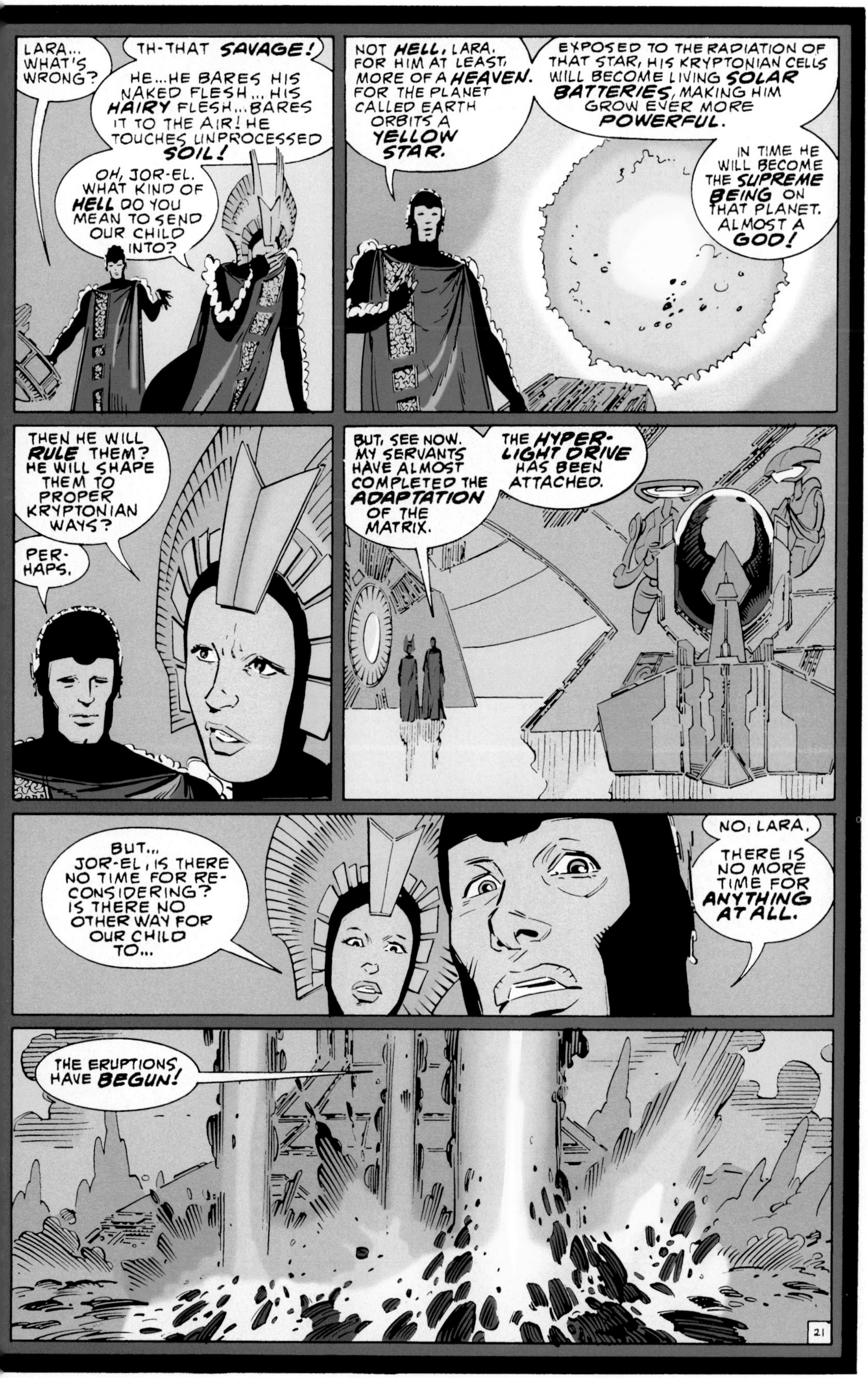
LARA... WHAT'S WRONG?
TH-THAT SAVAGE!
HE...HE BARES HIS NAKED FLESH... HIS HAIRY FLESH...BARES IT TO THE AIR! HE TOUCHES UNPROCESSED SOIL!
OH, JOR-EL. WHAT KIND OF HELL DO YOU MEAN TO SEND OUR CHILD INTO?
NOT HELL, LARA. FOR HIM AT LEAST, MORE OF A HEAVEN. FOR THE PLANET CALLED EARTH ORBITS A YELLOW STAR.
EXPOSED TO THE RADIATION OF THAT STAR, HIS KRYPTONIAN CELLS WILL BECOME LIVING SOLAR BATTERIES, MAKING HIM GROW EVER MORE POWERFUL.
IN TIME HE WILL BECOME THE SUPREME BEING ON THAT PLANET. ALMOST A GOD!
THEN HE WILL RULE THEM? HE WILL SHAPE THEM TO PROPER KRYPTONIAN WAYS?
PER-HAPS.
BUT, SEE NOW. MY SERVANTS HAVE ALMOST COMPLETED THE ADAPTATION OF THE MATRIX.
THE HYPER-LIGHT DRIVE HAS BEEN ATTACHED.
BUT... JOR-EL, IS THERE NO TIME FOR RE-CONSIDERING? IS THERE NO OTHER WAY FOR OUR CHILD TO...
NO, LARA. THERE IS NO MORE TIME FOR ANYTHING AT ALL.
THE ERUPTIONS HAVE BEGUN!
21

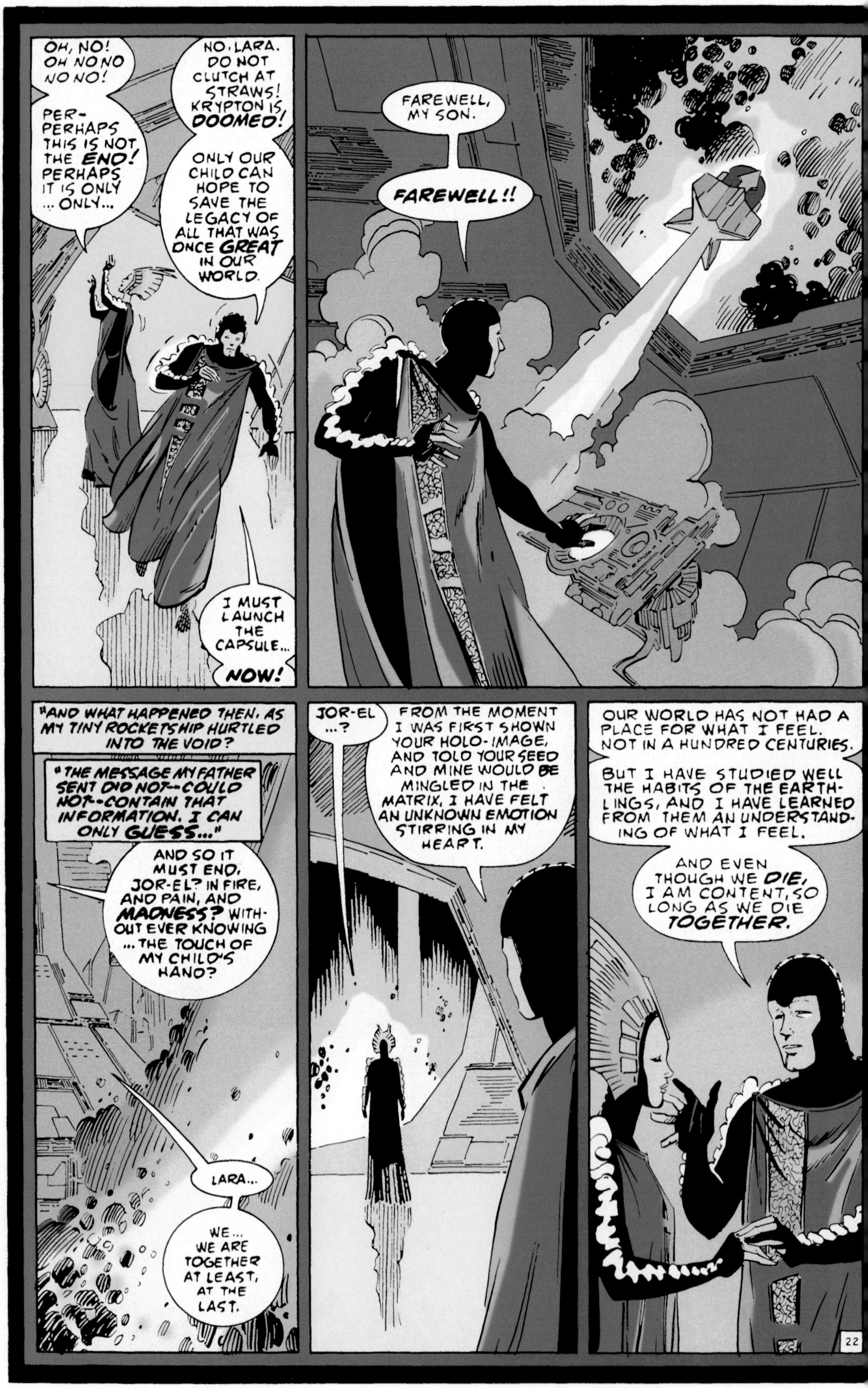
OH, NO! OH NO NO NO NO!
PER-PERHAPS THIS IS NOT THE END! PERHAPS IT IS ONLY ... ONLY...
NO, LARA. DO NOT CLUTCH AT STRAWS! KRYPTON IS DOOMED!
ONLY OUR CHILD CAN HOPE TO SAVE THE LEGACY OF ALL THAT WAS ONCE GREAT IN OUR WORLD.
I MUST LAUNCH THE CAPSULE... NOW!
FAREWELL, MY SON.
FAREWELL!!
"AND WHAT HAPPENED THEN, AS MY TINY ROCKETSHIP HURTLED INTO THE VOID?
"THE MESSAGE MY FATHER SENT DID NOT--COULD NOT--CONTAIN THAT INFORMATION. I CAN ONLY GUESS..."
AND SO IT MUST END, JOR-EL? IN FIRE, AND PAIN, AND MADNESS? WITHOUT EVER KNOWING ... THE TOUCH OF MY CHILD'S HAND?
LARA...
WE... WE ARE TOGETHER AT LEAST, AT THE LAST.
JOR-EL ...?
FROM THE MOMENT I WAS FIRST SHOWN YOUR HOLO-IMAGE, AND TOLD YOUR SEED AND MINE WOULD BE MINGLED IN THE MATRIX, I HAVE FELT AN UNKNOWN EMOTION STIRRING IN MY HEART.
OUR WORLD HAS NOT HAD A PLACE FOR WHAT I FEEL. NOT IN A HUNDRED CENTURIES.
BUT I HAVE STUDIED WELL THE HABITS OF THE EARTHLINGS, AND I HAVE LEARNED FROM THEM AN UNDERSTANDING OF WHAT I FEEL.
AND EVEN THOUGH WE DIE, I AM CONTENT, SO LONG AS WE DIE TOGETHER.
22

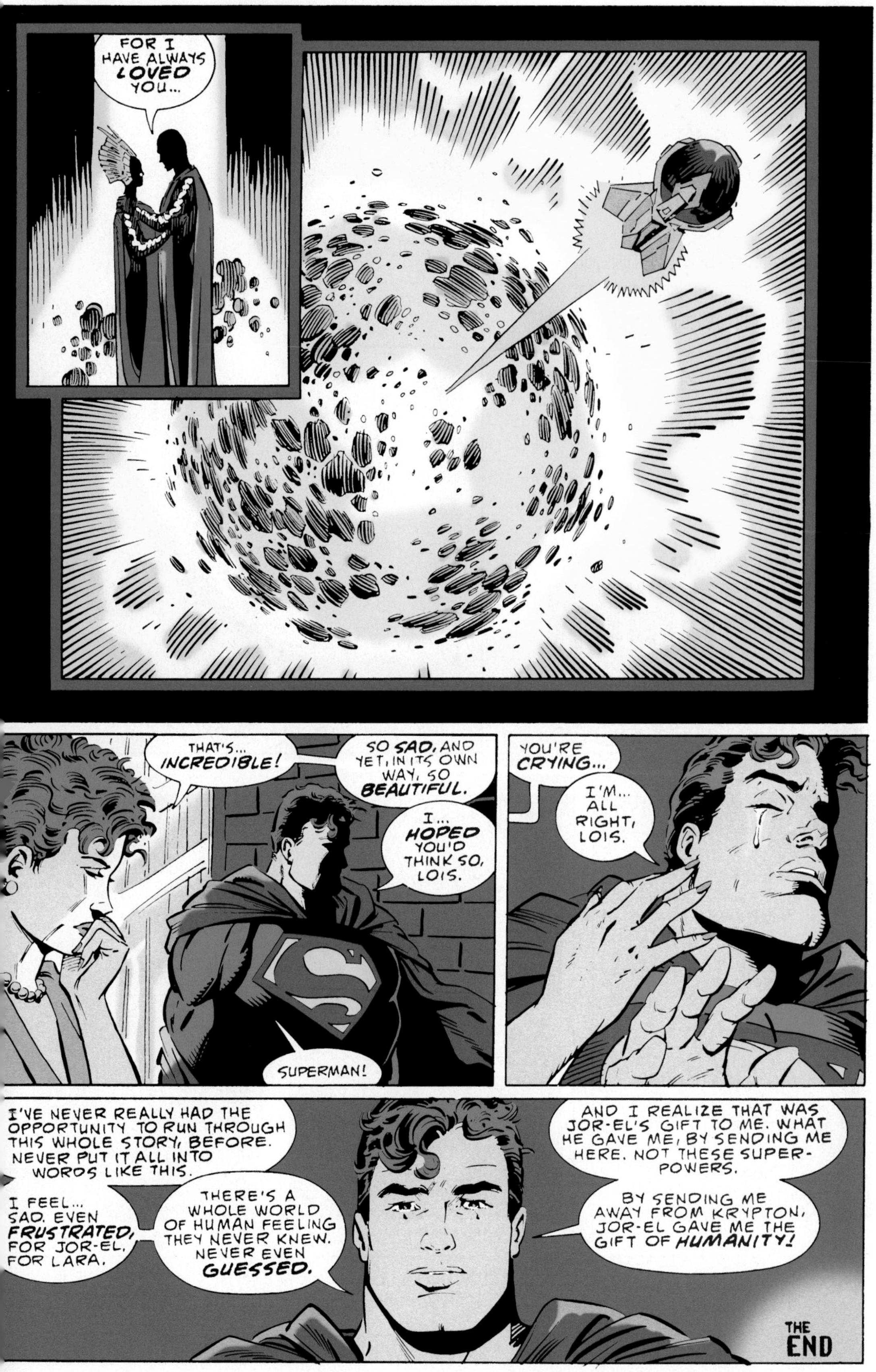
FOR I HAVE ALWAYS LOVED YOU...
THAT'S... INCREDIBLE!
SO SAD. AND YET, IN ITS OWN WAY, SO BEAUTIFUL.
I... HOPED YOU'D THINK SO, LOIS.
SUPERMAN!
YOU'RE CRYING...
I'M... ALL RIGHT, LOIS.
I'VE NEVER REALLY HAD THE OPPORTUNITY TO RUN THROUGH THIS WHOLE STORY, BEFORE. NEVER PUT IT ALL INTO WORDS LIKE THIS.
I FEEL... SAD. EVEN FRUSTRATED, FOR JOR-EL, FOR LARA.
THERE'S A WHOLE WORLD OF HUMAN FEELING THEY NEVER KNEW. NEVER EVEN GUESSED.
AND I REALIZE THAT WAS JOR-EL'S GIFT TO ME. WHAT HE GAVE ME, BY SENDING ME HERE. NOT THESE SUPER-POWERS.
BY SENDING ME AWAY FROM KRYPTON, JOR-EL GAVE ME THE GIFT OF HUMANITY!
THE END

DC UNIVERSE REBIRTH

> "That gorgeous spectacle is an undeniable part of Superman's appeal, but the family dynamics are what make it such an engaging read."
> – A.V. CLUB

> "Head and shoulders above the rest."
> – NEWSARAMA

DC UNIVERSE REBIRTH

SUPERMAN

VOL. 1: SON OF SUPERMAN

PETER J. TOMASI with PATRICK GLEASON, DOUG MAHNKE & JORGE JIMENEZ

VOL.1 SON OF SUPERMAN
PETER J.TOMASI • PATRICK GLEASON • DOUG MAHNKE • JORGE JIMENEZ • MICK GRAY

**SUPERGIRL VOL. 1:
REIGN OF THE SUPERMEN**

**ACTION COMICS VOL. 1:
PATH OF DOOM**

**BATMAN VOL. 1:
I AM GOTHAM**